The
Heritage
of American Catholicism

A TWENTY-EIGHT-VOLUME SERIES DOCUMENTING THE HISTORY
OF AMERICA'S LARGEST RELIGIOUS DENOMINATION

EDITED BY

Timothy Walch

ASSOCIATE EDITOR
U.S. Catholic Historian

A Garland Series

A Church of Many Cultures

SELECTED HISTORICAL ESSAYS ON ETHNIC AMERICAN
CATHOLICISM

EDITED WITH AN INTRODUCTION BY
DOLORES LIPTAK, R.S.M.

Garland Publishing, Inc.
New York & London
1988

LIBRARY OF CONGRESS CATALOGING-IN-PUBLICATION DATA

A Church of many cultures : selected historical essays on ethnic American Catholicism
/ edited with an introduction by Dolores Liptak.
   p. cm. -- (The Heritage of American Catholicism)
   Includes bibliographies.
   ISBN 0-8240-4081-3 (alk. paper)
   1. Catholics--United States--History. 2. Catholic Church--United States--History.
 3. United States--Ethnic relations. 4. Immigrants--United States--History. 5. United
States--Church history. 6. Ethnicity--United States. I. Liptak, Dolores Ann.
II. Series.
E184.C3C48 1988
305.6'2'073--dc19   88-24490

DESIGN BY MARY BETH BRENNAN

PRINTED ON ACID-FREE, 250-YEAR-LIFE PAPER.
MANUFACTURED IN THE UNITED STATES OF AMERICA

Contents

Acknowledgments

The editor and publisher are grateful to the following for permission to reproduce copyright material in this volume. Any further reproduction is prohibited without the permission of the copyright holder:

The Journal of Social History and Carnegie Mellon University for material in the *Journal*; Catholic Charities, U.S.A. for material in *Social Thought*; the Catholic University of America Press for material in *The Catholic Historical Review*; St. Mary's College of California for material in *An American Church*; the Center for Migration Studies of New York, Inc. for *A Lesson from History*; The American Society of Church History for material in *Church History*; William B. Eerdman's Publishing Co. for material in *Ethnic Chicago*; the University of North Carolina Press for material in *The Countryside in the Age of Capitalist Transformations*, © 1985; Temple University Press for material in *Immigrants and Religion in Urban America*; the U. S. Catholic Historical Society for material in *U. S. Catholic Historian*; Worzalla Publishing, Co. for material in *Poles in America*; the American Catholic Historical Society for material in their *Records*; Routledge & Kegan Paul for material in *Ethnic and Racial Studies*; Rev. William Wolkovich-Valkavicius; Nelson Hall, Inc for material in *Catholic Immigrants in America*; United States Catholic Conference for *Pastoral Care of Vietnamese Catholics in the United States* © 1985.

Introduction

The United States Catholic Church can only be understood in terms of its multi-ethnic heritage. Pope John Paul II specifically highlighted this characteristic as an intrinsic one in remarks to American bishops during their *ad limina* visits to Rome in 1988. The Pope's comment, made shortly after his second visit to the United States in 1987, was hardly earthshaking. The American Church's impressive multicultured ecclesial reality was generally recognized as early as the second half of the nineteenth century.

Yet, as recently as twenty years ago the significance of the Church's ethnic features went largely unrecognized by historians and other scholars. Among historians, ethnicity rarely was considered as a serious research direction. In fact, the noted ethnic historian and promoter of Jewish studies, Moses Rischin, gently chided his colleagues for their apparent lack of consideration of what he termed the "almost unique cosmopolitan sweep" of Catholic immigration. According to Rischin, the ethnic development of the Church was worthy of serious investigation as one of the most important aspects of the Catholic historical experience. To his mind, there could be no real understanding of the Catholic Church in the United States apart from attention to the ethnic factor in its development.

Rischin has been something of a prophet without honor. Church officials and scholars of the American Catholic Church have been extremely slow in acknowledging the ethnic dimensions of the U.S. Catholic Church. Few have been as convinced as Rischin that the very identity of the Church is tied to the reality of ethnic diversity.

The explanation for this somewhat myopic view is simple enough. For one thing, the immigrant struggle for full membership in the U.S. Catholic Church had produced unfavorable publicity that irritated those who were intent upon proclaiming the American features of U.S. Catholicism. Embarrassment over the behavior of the "hordes" of newcomers—especially the "ill-suited" southern and eastern European immigrants—also seemed to prevent them from seeing these later additions to the Church in a positive light.

Only recently, as the Church in the United States gained a more solidly American identity and acceptance, has the Church as a whole been able to face the ramifications of the immigrant past and acknowledge the degree to which the multicultures of its membership did shape Catholicism in the United States. Only in recent years have scholars of American Catholicism directed their attention to the Church's patchwork dimensions and suggested that the varied and rich immigrant backgrounds of American Catholics should not only be studied but also be seen as providing the special mission of the U.S. Catholic church.1

That is not to say that the immigrant nature of the Church in the United States was ever totally ignored. Who, for example, could overlook the incredible impact of immigration that, despite tenuous beginnings, made Catholicism the largest single religious denomination in the United States by 1850? Who could overlook the importance of the Catholic "immigrant" vote? A recent article in the *Washington Post* (June 7, 1988) is clear indication of the interest concerning this phenomenon. In it, "the Catholic Connection" is claimed to be essentially an ethnic connection—and, for that reason, a vital ingredient in previous and present presidential campaigns.

Still, discussions of immigrant roots in studies of American Catholicism in the 1950s were done more to explain the political or social problems that arose within the dominant American or Catholic culture than to suggest ethnicity as an essential characteristic of the ongoing identity of American Catholics. By the mid-1950s, in fact, sociologists, such as Will Herberg and Andrew Greeley, who were students of the Catholic experience, had even begun to argue that the ethnic factor of U.S. Catholicism was no longer of significance in understanding the Church in the United States. Since the majority members of the Church no longer derived their identity from their ethnic roots, these experts argued, American Catholicism should no longer be described as an "immigrant church."

Since the 1970s, however, scholars have gained a new appreciation of how ethnicity has influenced Catholic life in the United States. Today the argument that ethnicity must be studied as more than a passing phenomenon receives sympathetic response from Catholic historians. Something mysterious and holistic was at work, many have concluded, which contributed to the making of an unique local Catholic experience. In fact, multicultural development has allowed the Church in the United States to mirror the universality of the Roman Catholic Church perhaps better than the Church in any other contemporary setting. Thus, while some Catholic historians have continued their task of documenting the development of the U.S. Catholic Church structurally, numerically, or regionally and of grappling with the question of U.S. Catholic identity, a new group of specialists has emerged. To the more traditional studies depicting the Church as a highly competitive American religious institution, these scholars have added studies based on the experience of an ethnic Catholic people.

Whatever ethnic perspective chosen, however, some aspects of the history of the U.S. Catholic Church have continued to be portrayed as in the past. Thus, Irish-Americans, as the predominant ethnic group, have loomed dramatically in the forefront of every investigation. After all, the majority of the Church's leadership has historically claimed an Irish heritage. This ethnic hegemony has, in fact, been so taken for granted that both Catholics and non-Catholics have tended to use Irish-American perspectives as the measure for U.S. Catholic identity. Certain contemporary events, however, force a reevaluation of this viewpoint. The civil rights era of the 1960s—when blacks reminded all Americans of the injustice of homogenizing or prioritizing on the basis of race, ethnicity, or dominant culture—made way for a consciousness-raising that encouraged a reconsideration of Catholic identity based solely upon the dominant Irish-American culture.

At the same time, increasing numbers of historians and sociologists began to return to the notion that religion should be seen as a basic element in the understanding of the ethnic makeup of a people. Believing, instead, that religion and ethnicity are enduring and intertwining aspects of the sense of "peoplehood" that any group develops they produced studies on the history and behavior of specific immigrant groups within the Church. Their interest in the dynamic relationship which they discovered between religion and ethnicity gave rise to new explorations of the ethnic dimensions of American Catholicism.

Among the first scholars to recommend that the Catholic scholarly community attend more seriously to ethnicity within American Catholicism, especially as it affected attitudes and behavior, were the historian, Philip Gleason, and the sociologist, Harold Abramson. Two of their essays, ultimately challenging others to such studies, form the introductory section of this book. Clearly it was Gleason's own investigation of the German-American Catholic community and Abramson's interest in comparing generational patterns among different Catholic ethnic groups that had initially brought each to a greater appreciation of the need to confront the prevailing, oversimplified approach to Catholic history. Their continued research in, and promotion of, the significance of ethnicity in understanding American Catholicism has done much to redirect U.S. Catholic studies. In fact, a number of the authors whose work is included in this book have been influenced by the challenge presented by Gleason and Abramson.

Although inspired by Gleason and Abramson, those engaged in Catholic ethnic studies have, for the most part, followed the pathway blazed by Timothy L. Smith, professor of history at Johns Hopkins University, who initiated a reinterpretation of American Catholic history that incorporates ethnicity as an essential feature.2 Smith's general thesis, namely that the soul of an ethnic group is religion, finds constant reiteration throughout this book. Agreeing with this contention, these authors have indicated that the immigrants' expression of religion in the New World was a statement about ethnicity, and that, here, the inextricable and dynamic relationship that exists between religion and ethnicity both created and recreated their Catholic sense of being people. In their work, finally, one finds ample support for another of Smith's positions: that the very act of migration was a theologizing process engaged in by these covenanted or "pilgrim" people.

Each of the articles furthers Gleason's challenge and substantiates certain aspects of the Smith thesis. Generally the authors demonstrate the way that immigrants held tenaciously to the external ethnic expression of their faith within the structures of the American Catholic Church. Some indicate the manner in which the official Church—even if it seemed reluctant to do so—recognized its responsibilities to immigrants and, consequently, became the beneficiary of their special gifts. Others have based studies on specific immigrant communities; their work reveals how the shared bond of faith drew immigrants to the Catholic Church in the United States and, regardless of ethnic differences, sustained immigrants. Often these authors also show the ways in which the religion of the immigrants actually took on heightened meaning and different dimensions that allowed them to overcome the trauma of emigration and to move successfully towards adaptation to new world religious realities.

Several authors specifically investigate the "national parish," the typical juridical means used by Church authorities to establish immigrants in parishes where their adjustment to the Church could take place. By researching German national parishes begun in New York and Philadelphia, Jay P. Dolan became one of the first historians to study the consequences of this decision upon both the Church and the immigrant community. In the article reprinted here Dolan explains the defensive posture that German immigrants assumed and the "ethnic fortresses" they built to protect themselves in a strange new land. Seeing the German strategy of requesting national parishes as a way to safeguard their "faith," Dolan draws attention to the fear of losing status or Catholic faith that motivated immigrants. Because of the religious dominance of Irish-Americans and the ethnic influence of German-Protestants, Dolan has argued, German Catholics became the first immigrants to champion separate parishes that could serve to preserve both faith and culture.

Several other articles illustrate parallel experiences especially among Eastern European immigrant groups. Studies by William Wolkovich-Valkavicius on Lithuanians and June Granatir Alexander on the Slovak experience demonstrate the deliberate means employed by these groups to safeguard both faith and culture through a pattern of parish building and community organization. Wolkovich's article is biographical—pointing out the significant role played by Joseph Zebris, the outstanding immigrant pastor and founder of New England's Lithuanian Catholic community. Alexander's investigation of Slovaks concentrates instead on the community itself and the influences consequent upon the chain migration that brought Catholic Slovaks to the Pittsburgh area.

Both authors, however, see the leadership of immigrant pastors as crucial to the creating of separate ethnic enclaves and the interaction of their congregations as equally essential in sustaining the vitality of the community. Among the two minorities they studied, for example, Churches and Church-sponsored organizations became the principal means of maintaining ethnic and cultural identity for the Catholic community as a whole. In both cases, immigrants cooperated with bishops and fellow Catholics to create worlds that were both isolating and insulating. As Wolkovich and Alexander describe it, the resulting immigrant world worked despite anxiety and because of ingenuity. It was a world that, for a time at least, prevented newcomers from losing their old world culture and enabled them to build "citadels" of religious and cultural achievement in the new world setting.

Interest in the immigrant community has also led some scholars to reexamine those aspects of immigrant life about which the most documentation is available, namely, the highly publicized disputes that developed between immigrant groups and the institutional Church. The result of this research has deepened our understanding not only about the sources of immigrant dissatisfaction but also about the motivation and conduct of Church officials in their response to ethnic minorities. Articles of Anthony Kuzniewski, Gerald Fogarty, and Richard Sorrell verify the degree to which mistrust experienced by Slavic or French-Canadian immigrants dramatically interfered with the ability of these minorities to adjust to the American church. While Kuzniewski's study reviews the overall "faithful" experience of Polish-Americans, whom he describes sympathetically as "God's madmen," Fogarty documents one episode of heavy-handed treatment by Church leaders that so humiliated Ukrainian-Ruthenian Catholics of Greek-rite that it eventually led many to permanent separation from the U.S. Catholic Church. As both authors point out, for those who wished to maintain their rituals, devotional practices, and customs in the presence of disapproving or authoritarian officials, the path toward separation seemed, at the very least, tempting and, perhaps, even inevitable. In a similar way, Sorrell demonstrates how concerns over religious and cultural *survivance* under Irish-American leadership initiated vitriolic attacks and repeated protests on the part of several French-Canadian communities in New England. When discontent of this sort was sustained, moreover, celebrated "affairs" that involved such "outside" authorities as the apostolic delegate or the Pope became *de rigeur*.

Although all three authors indicate that accord was usually reached between officials of the American Church and the emerging communities, they stress the negative and long-lasting impact of such struggles. The residue of bitterness and suspicion that has continued to plague these minority groups in particular further underscores the lingering effects of presumed ethnic bias.

The attention given to the "Italian problem" has led to another series of investigations aimed at verifying the truth of the generalization that Italian immigrants were poorly treated by the Church. Articles by Mary Elizabeth Brown and James Divita address this issue specifically. Both point out that the earlier assumption that Italians could not adjust to the requirements of the Church here, or that they were neglected by Church leaders who saw them as spiritually destitute, may have been exaggerated. Both authors discovered solid evidence that some bishops and clergy were clearly concerned over the desperate physical and spiritual conditions of Italians.

They also found that Italians themselves sought constructive ways to surmount the difficult situations that befell them. Brown's study discusses the early struggles of New York Italians that were somewhat assuaged by the pastoral strategies of the archbishop of New York, Michael Corrigan, and by the assistance of several religious congregations Corrigan invited to the city. Divita's research on immigrant Italians living in the less-populated Indiana area also provides proof that, regardless of motive, there were Catholic leaders who sought means to incorporate them into the American Church. As both authors indicate, concerns that Italians could easily succumb to Protestant proselytism certainly influenced—perhaps even dictated—this official approach to Italians. But both studies also reveal the depth of Italian devotion to the Church. Although Italians seemed attracted to the various Protestant groups that promised to help them, they clung to old-world religious traditions and avoided permanently severing their ties with the U.S. Catholic Church.

Protestant evangelization of immigrants is another theme examined by several authors. Yet much of the research directed toward examining the impact of competing religions or ideologies in the American setting has verified the conclusion that competing ideologies or religions did not have serious negative consequences for Catholic immigrant congregations in general.. In fact, it is probable that such influences may even have strengthened previous religious, cultural, and political convictions as immigrants adapted to the Catholic Church here.

Some authors have viewed both the deferential manner employed by the Slovaks and the stubborn persistence of the Poles in their negotiations with Church leaders as contributory to the success of these immigrants in adjusting to status within the Church. In her research on German-American Catholic farm families in Minnesota, moreover, Kathleen Neils Conzen has shown that German-American Catholic families even continued the same manner of adapting to farm life here (a pattern which differentiated them from German Protestants abroad). The result was both strong farm families and parish communities and a kind of organizational life that clearly delineated them from other Minnesotans. Inheritance practices sustained here by German Catholic families, in particular, demonstrate not only how basic religion was to the adaptation of Germans to the American environment but also how the Catholic faith helped them to maintain their separateness even from other Germans.

The mutual embarrassment on the part of both Church and immigrant leaders over episodes of discord no longer seems to divert Church historians from studying the roots of discontent within immigrant Catholic communities. Here, too, research into the specific ways in which immigrant groups related to their Church has led to a general reevaluation of episcopal efforts to incorporate their massive numbers. In the face of new evidence, a number of ethnic historians have been required to rethink generalizations decrying unjust treatment by bishops and to eschew continued uncritical reliance upon the historic accounts of immigrant communities themselves.

Sifting through the tangled web of charges and countercharges regarding such struggles that have been preserved in diocesan archives, today's specialists have often discovered evidence of episcopal support on behalf of the immigrant and complicating circumstances that have required them to discard oversimplistic conclusions. The research of Silvano Tomasi and Dolores Liptak has indicated that the previous assumptions must be altered. Both Tomasi and Liptak supply evidence that there were some dioceses, in particular, where bishops did respond in both creative and constructive ways to immigrant demands. For these reasons they have maintained that one must look elsewhere for reasons why this criticism of Church leadership has been so widespread.

The basis for problems that beset immigrant minorities and their bishops also has been skillfully reflected by several other ethnic historians. Henry Leonard's investigation of Cleveland and its emergence as a highly efficient twentieth century Catholic diocese, for example, found ethnic tension between priests and their bishops rather than between the bishop and immigrant congregations. Leonard argues that ethnic dissension was provoked by Cleveland's Irish-American clergy who became involved in struggles that essentially pitted them against their German bishops—a situation that was summarily settled in favor of the Irish during the episcopacy of Bishop

John P. Farrelly (1909–1921).

Other studies have demonstrated how misleading allegations of episcopal ineptitude with regard to either immigrant clergy or laity could be. In his investigation of the Polish in Chicago, for example, William Galush cogently discerns an ethnic clerical strategy for preference. His suggestion, that some Polish priests sided with Irish bishops because it allowed them to retain clerical prerogatives among their congregations, underscores the complicated causality behind bruised egos that always accompanied episcopal-immigrant negotiations.

That dissension did not necessarily begin on the level of the parish over dissatisfaction with episcopal intentions in their regard has also found support in the work of other historians. Instead of pointing to ethnic priests or parishioners wronged by Irish bishops, they, too, have found evidence that immigrant priests often cooperated with their Irish bishops against members of their own ethnic group. And they cite examples of immigrant parishioners joining bishops against their own pastors or of bishops attempting either to conciliate or to make sense of intra-parish problems. The basis of complaints and charges against bishops have been so undermined by new research on immigrant groups that, albeit begrudgingly, some scholars have been led to agree with one historian's recent comment about episcopal policy. "Whatever their shortcomings," Michael Funchion suggests in his article on Irish-Americans, Church officials did, indeed, "deserve some credit. . . ."

Finally, one of the most interesting insights gained through recent studies concerning immigrants and their Church is that there were distinct ways in which immigrants—regardless of the nation of origin—showed enthusiasm about becoming American Catholics and partaking fully in the benefits of American society. Daniel O'Neill's study of St. Paul's priests illumines this particular aspect with reference to a diocese in which Irish-Americans early came to dominate the ranks of clergy. According to O'Neill, it was the "American" background of its episcopacy that led to the establishing of a diocesan seminary in 1885 and it was the Americanization of its overwhelmingly Irish-American membership that fostered interest in training native-born candidates to the priesthood. Becoming American was the decided aim of episcopal strategy in St. Paul; the continued recruitment of priests from both Ireland and Canada was clearly seen as a deterrent to the pace of Americanization in that diocese.

Aspects of this "American" mentality have always been clear to Catholic historians. The republican ideals of religious liberty were eloquently championed by the immigrant-bishop John England in the early decades of the nineteenth century and they continued to be espoused by other famed Americanists, including St. Paul's archbishop, John Ireland. Both Patrick Carey and Michael Funchion, in their studies of nineteenth century Irish-Americans, have documented these episcopal ideals and expectations as expressive of immigrants in general. Both Carey and Funchion provide examples of immigrants who valued the American concept of separation of church and state; they both depict immigrants who were easily adapted to the American way of providing political and social services. In particular, Funchion shows how Irish-Americans found political action especially compatible with both their interests and their talents. As these authors note concerning Irish immigrants, so too have ethnic historians been able to document with regard to "other immigrants."

As the contents of this book make clear, the insistence that the story of immigrants must be examined has clearly added more than content to Catholic historiography. Starting with studies mainly involving interaction between Irish- or German-Americans, such research has broadened to identify Catholics along a multicolored ethnic spectrum and opened the way for a deeper understanding of Catholic identity and peoplehood. Studies such as these have not only prompted revisions of sometimes unflattering generalizations concerning the response of immigrants but historical investigation has served the Church in solving some of the more serious challenges presently facing it. Already the analyses of previous strategies have enabled the development of new diocesan strategies regarding today's immigrants and have uncovered possibilities for the future. As conservators of their faith as well, today's immigrants and their Church continue to learn from the examples of the past as they work toward fashioning the contemporary Church.

The last section of this anthology has been devoted to articles that elucidate the way that history can help the Church meet a present challenge: the incorporation of today's newest minority Catholics. While some demographers suggest that, by the twenty-first century, Hispanic American Catholics will become the majority ethnic group within the Church, James Olson reports a story of Hispanics within the Church that repeats the pattern generally experienced by southern and eastern European immigrants. The endemic prejudice against foreigners fostered since colonial times has adversely affected Catholic response to these migrants from countries once dominated by Spain, France, or Portugal. Even Black-American Catholics, whose numbers barely reach beyond two percent of the Catholic population, continue to suffer the consequences of their painful history of segregation and discrimination.

Articles prepared by the National Catholic Conference of Bishops, as well as by James Olson and Cyprian Davis, review the plight of these minorities and indicate that recent generations are still facing some of the same struggles in finding their rightful place within both Church and society. They show how isolation and neglect have continued to force these groups to seek consolation in their own way: Hispanic devotions have been refashioned in mission churches; the rich gospel traditions of Black Catholics have been nurtured to serve present needs. As both Davis and Olson demonstrate, Hispanic and Black groups now stand in a position to point out the mistakes of the past perpetrated against them and to underscore the newly discovered lesson of history: that their style of worship—albeit dramatically different from the institution that wishes to claim them—must be at the basis of their Catholic peoplehood and parish development. They make clear that these modern pilgrim people are as eager to help establish the "New Jerusalem" as were the European immigrants of the past century. Finally, their work stands as a reminder that the Catholic Church will be far better served if yesterday's lessons are remembered.

We offer the articles included in this anthology not only as an example of new directions of historical investigation but also as a sign of hope that knowledge of the past can assist the present "immigrant" Church to understand itself. A Church, which over two centuries ago took up the challenge of the founding fathers by attempting to locate here the "City Upon a Hill," can continue to help its members search for the promised land. A Church, fully influenced by its American context yet constantly re-created by people from every nation, can provide the proper challenge for every age. This book should aid in both illuminating that Catholic church and allowing us to see how a multicultured church can richly benefit the lives of both Catholics and Americans.

Dolores Liptak, RSM
May, 1988

NOTES

1. *The Catholic Church in the United States: At the Crossroads*; Bulletin 94/3, prepared by Dolores Liptak, RSM (Belgium, Pro Mundi Vita, 1983), *passim*.

2. Timothy L. Smith, "Religion and Ethnicity in America," *American Historical Review*, Volume 83, No. 5, 1978, *passim*.

HAROLD J. ABRAMSON

ETHNIC DIVERSITY WITHIN CATHOLICISM: A COMPARATIVE ANALYSIS OF CONTEMPORARY AND HISTORICAL RELIGION

The historical and sociological fact of ethnic diversity within religion is well known. Church scholars have often incorporated the phenomenon into discourses on the social history of religion.[1] Historians of nationalism have examined the role of religion in the socio-political movements of European peoples, and have pointed out the dissonant or consonant relationships of ethnic minorities with religious institutions.[2] And sociologists have examined different kinds of social systems, in terms of ethnic heterogeneity and religious conflict.[3]

From a comparative point of view, however, the sociological and historical analysis of religion and ethnicity has been neglected. A problem for sociology is the understanding of elements which contribute to the shape of religious behavior, and the search for meaningful social and cultural patterns among the welter of historical facts.[4] The exploration of the roots of ethnic diversity within a shared religion affords such an opportunity for sociological and historical research.

HAROLD J. ABRAMSON is in the Department of Sociology at the University of Connecticut. This is a revised version of a paper read at the meetings of the Society for the Scientific Study of Religion, Boston, October 1969.

1. For example, H. Richard Niebuhr, *The Social Sources of Denominationalism* (New York, 1929); Kenneth Scott Latourette, *Christianity in a Revolutionary Age* (New York, 1958–1962), Vols. 1–5.
2. Salo W. Baron, *Modern Nationalism and Religion* (New York, 1960); Walter Kolarz, *Myths and Realities in Eastern Europe* (London, 1946); Hans Kohn, *Nationalism: Its Meaning and History* (New York, 1956).
3. Louis Wirth, "The Problem of Minority Groups," in *The Science of Man in the World Crisis*, ed. Ralph Linton (New York, 1945), 347–72; Werner J. Cahnman, "Religion and Nationality," in *Sociology and History*, ed. Werner J. Cahnman and Alvin Boskoff (New York, 1964), 271–80.
4. Yinger has raised a number of problems and ideas in this area, most of which are yet to be examined with sustained study. J. Milton Yinger, *Sociology Looks at Religion* (New York, 1963).

TABLE 1. FOREIGN-BORN CATHOLIC CHURCH ATTENDANCE AND SUPPORT OF AVAILABLE CATHOLIC ELEMENTARY SCHOOLS, BY ETHNICITY AND SOCIO-ECONOMIC STATUS BACKGROUND (Percent to Mass once a week or more, and percent children to available Catholic schools)

	Mother's church attendance		Father's church attendance		Children with some or all Catholic elementary schooling	
	Low SES (1–2)	High SES (3–10)	Low SES (1–2)	High SES (3–10)	Low SES (1–2)	High SES (3–10)
French-Canadian	97(38)*	95(19)	95(37)	78(18)	97(34)	100(15)
Irish	91(22)	100(24)	82(22)	89(282)	94(16)	96(25)
German	86(29)	78(27)	74(31)	69(29)	60(15)	72(18)
Polish	78(55)	77(26)	78(60)	66(32)	86(51)	92(24)
Italian	67(112)	76(110)	40(125)	39(127)	29(86)	43(96)
Spanish-speaking	56(62)	65(23)	41(66)	31(26)	28(39)	50(16)
TOTAL†	73(390)	79(264)	59(417)	55(297)	59(292)	64(216)

* The numbers in parentheses refer to the case bases from which the percentages are derived.

† Total refers to the sum of the total sample born-Catholics who constitute the cases in each category. It is not the sum of the groups selected in the table.

There has been enough empirical documentation of distinctive ethnic styles in religious behavior in the United States, for example, to warrant an investigation for the sociological and historical background which may help explain this diversity.[5] Table 1 offers recent data from a national sample of white Catholic Americans on ethnic heterogeneity, with regard to such measures of formal religious involvement as church attendance and the support of available Catholic parochial schools.[6]

5. For some recent evidence of ethnic heterogeneity within American Catholicism, as well as denominational diversity within American Protestantism, see Harold J. Abramson and C. Edward Noll, "Religion, Ethnicity, and Social Change," *Review of Religious Research* 8 (Fall 1966), 11–26. For a broader discussion of ethnic diversity, see Nathan Glazer and Daniel Patrick Moynihan, *Beyond the Melting Pot* (Cambridge, 1963).

6. The data used in table 1 originate from a National Opinion Research Center study of the effects of parochial school education among Catholic Americans. The universe sampled is the total noninstitutionalized white Catholic population of the United States, 23 to 57 years of age. The sample is limited to those respondents who identified themselves as Catholic, in reply to a question on current religious preference. The total sample size numbers 2,071 respondents, drawn from a standard multistage area probability sample. Questions asking for nationality background of fathers and mothers supply the data on ethnicity. For a fuller description of the survey and the final report, see Andrew M. Greeley and Peter H. Rossi, *The Education of Catholic Americans* (Chicago, 1966). For more extensive analysis of the data used in table 1, see Harold J. Abramson, "The Ethnic Factor in American Catholicism: an Analysis of Inter-Ethnic Marriage and Religious Involvement," doctoral dissertation, University of Chicago, 1969.

The rank orders of associational involvement for the different Catholic ethnic groups show the Irish and the French-Canadians to be the most consistently involved, the German and Polish Catholics at a relatively intermediate position, and the Italians and Spanish-speaking Puerto Ricans and Mexicans among the least involved in the formal requirements of their shared religion.

Only differences in ethnic background can explain such diversity. The data of the table are limited to the foreign-born parents of the survey's born-Catholics—hence excluding generational factors—and come closest to reflecting the state of formal religious involvement for the immigrants and their countries of origin. Mothers and fathers are of ethnically endogamous marriages, so that the presumed influences of intermarriage and of spouses of differing ethnic backgrounds are eliminated.

Finally, it has often been shown that social class plays a role in one's religious behavior; those of higher status tend to go to formal services more regularly and are more supportive of the religious school system.[7] Accordingly, there is a control for household socio-economic status background in table 1.[8] It is apparent that class background makes no difference in the rank order of these foreign-born ethnic groups, and that ethnicity is the stronger factor. Indeed, the most involved Irish and French-Canadians are just as likely to send their children to the available Catholic school system when they are poor, as when they are of some higher class. The relative position of the Italian and Spanish-speaking Catholics also remains; even the more affluent members of these ethnic groups are among the least supportive of the denominational school program.[9]

Given evidence of ethnic diversity within the Catholic Church, a number of questions need to be raised. What are the structural sources of the religious traditions which the different immigrant groups brought with them to America? What religious and national

7. This is as true in the United States as it is in Europe. See Gerhard Lenski, *The Religious Factor* (New York, 1961), chap. 2; also, E. R. Wickham, *Church and People in an Industrial City* (London, 1957); Emile Pin, *Pratique Religieuse et Classes Sociales dans une Paroisse Urbaine Saint-Pothin à Lyon* (Paris, 1956).
8. Social class background is measured by the Duncan scale, based on the respondent's occupation. For explanation, see O. D. Duncan, "A Socio-Economic Index for All Occupations," in *Occupations and Social Status*, ed. Albert J. Reiss, Jr. (New York, 1961).
9. It is also true that socio-economic background has some influence on Italian and Spanish-speaking Catholics. They are considerably more likely to support the parochial school system, when they are of higher status, although not to the extent of their class counterparts from other ethnic groups.

characteristics help explain these distinctive levels of ethnic involvement among the foreign-born Catholics in the United States? Considerable research has been done on individual ethnic backgrounds, and some of this is cited in subsequent sections of this paper, but what comparative analysis can be employed for all six ethnic backgrounds? These are the questions which prompt this inquiry.

Comparison is developed around a model of societal competition, based on the social and political characteristics of national Catholicism in the histories of the six ethnic groups discussed. The research is necessarily limited in a number of different ways. A good deal of religious involvement certainly is to be explained by social psychological factors, such as matters of subjective ethnic identification, cultural and religious value systems, and the nature of national character. This paper will not dwell as much on the psychological determinants of religious association as it will on the more sociological and political factors which contribute to the shape of religio-ethnicity.

Second, the emphasis is on formal religious association and involvement, and not on "religiosity" or the measure of religious experience, feeling, or piety. The distinction is between that which is public, formal, and integrated into Church requirements, as opposed to that which is private, informal, and at variance with Church norms.

A third point refers to the factor of immigration. The investigation will not probe into the meaning of the change or the persistence of ethnic behavior after immigration to the United States, but will explore the traditional sources of the old country, which are presumed to give rise to traits and values brought to America with immigration. It is assumed that an understanding of the roots of ethnicity is important and basic for subsequent study into the changes brought about by the American experience. Finally, the research is limited by reliance upon the secondary literature. Perhaps future efforts in social history and the sociology of religion and ethnicity will survey original sources in developing explanatory hypotheses for comparative ethnic behavior.

THE NATURE OF SOCIETAL COMPETITION

There may be numerous approaches for explaining the differential religious involvement of Catholic groups, but one of the more common problems is the lack of empirical data with which to make a systematic beginning. In this regard, an important contribution to the comparative study of religious behavior is Michael Fogarty's *Christian Democracy in Western Europe*, for its valuable work on socioreligious movements.[10]

Fogarty is concerned with associational involvement within Protestantism and Catholicism. "Across Western Europe, from Flanders to Venice, there lies a belt of high religious observance, where people are more likely than elsewhere not only to profess a religion but to practice it; a sort of heartland of European Christianity."[11] With due concern for the imperfect statistics of religious practice, Fogarty tentatively argues that this phenomenon might be traced, as in the frequency of Protestant religious observance in Germany, to the nature of religious competition and the proportions of different religions in the population:

One explanation might be that religion thrives on competition, since the areas of low observance tend also to be those where the proportion of Protestants in the total population is highest. Silesia, an eastern territory, but one where the balance between Catholics and Protestants was till the Second World War more equal than elsewhere, showed till then a rather high level of observance among Protestants. But if there is such a rule it should apply also to Catholics, whereas in fact the statistics show that Catholic observance is high in the mainly Catholic west and south, but falls away, like observance among Protestants, toward the mainly Protestant east and north.[12]

Thus, within Germany, the relationship between high observance and the viability of religious competition does not seem to hold for Catholics. Fogarty pursues this further, with an examination of the more specific geographical outlines of the "heartland" of practicing Christianity, both Catholic and Protestant:

High observance ... is most commonly to be found in the belt, which includes Holland, Belgium, French Flanders, Alsace-Lorraine, Westfalia, the Rhineland, most of south Germany and Austria, Switzerland (although here statistics are lacking), and parts of north Italy. There are large Protestant as well as Catholic populations in this area, and the tendency to high observance applies to both. As the case of Germany shows, competition between religions is probably not by itself enough to explain this. But it may be that competition of a more general kind is at the bottom of it; for this is a land not only of political but also of linguistic and cultural frontiers.[13]

10. Michael P. Fogarty, *Christian Democracy in Western Europe 1820–1953* (London, 1957).

11. Ibid., 7.   12. Ibid.   13. Ibid., 8.

Fogarty stops here with this particular hypothesis, but the idea of linguistic and cultural competition might well be developed as a basic dimension of the level of religious involvement. Indeed, had Fogarty considered the cases of Ireland and Quebec (which were excluded from his survey of Western Europe), the argument for the influence of cultural competition on religious observance would have assumed even stronger tones.

The concept of societal competition, whether political-linguistic or political-cultural, is a relevant one for the sociology of religio-ethnic systems. As Fogarty suggests in the case of Germany, mere religious heterogeneity within a society is not sufficient for explaining levels of religious involvement. More to the point is the proximity to and the salience of religious and cultural differences within the ethnic orientation of a people. Thus, the idea of the frontier between competing groups serves as a symbol of competition and diversity, and especially so if the frontier represents a border separating the powerful from the powerless.

The idea of societal competition then embraces at least two specific macro-sociological factors. The first would be the basic presence of religious differences, reinforced by linguistic and cultural competition. The extent of conflict which is generated by the competition may vary, but the sense of competition is the important issue. It is reasonable to suppose that the greater the conflict, the more salient the sense of religious distinctiveness and the higher the level of religious involvement, for the competitively subordinate group.

A second major factor refers to the degree of political autonomy enjoyed by the cultural groups involved. Competition between religio-ethnic systems might be present within the borders of the same geographical area, or the competition might be an expression of distinctiveness across frontiers. Political control by a different religio-ethnic group may be present within the given society (as a kind of internal colonialism), or it may extend across geographical borders (in the classic conventions of external colonialism).[14] In either event, the reality of societal competition is expected to show differences in political power and the probability of controlling behavior.

Following fairly closely from Fogarty's suggestion, the model of societal competition is based on the two dimensions: differences in

---

14. The distinction is made by Blauner in the context of black-white relations in the United States. Robert Blauner, "Internal Colonialism and Ghetto Revolt," *Social Problems* 16 (Spring 1969): 393–408.

religio-cultural systems and differences in their political power. Other points might well be taken into consideration. Religio-ethnic distinctiveness in the past has often led to nationalist movements, and the institutionalization of religio-ethnic differences under certain conditions may lead to political movements of secession and independence. These movements reinforce religious consciousness, along with other aspects of cultural identity. The converse of this relationship may also be true. Emergent nationalism may stimulate dormant religio-ethnic distinctiveness, and the new consciousness then reinforces the political movement.

Other, more micro-sociological, factors are presumably relevant in the context of societal competition. The extent of religio-communal organization, the relationship of religion to the needs of the people, and the extent to which there is conflict of class interests within the given religio-ethnic group, for example, are important questions, and they will be considered in the subsequent analysis.

It is proposed then that the condition of societal competition, with its characteristics of religio-ethnic differences, conflict, and corresponding levels of power, is a positive correlate of the degree of religio-ethnic activity and consciousness. A review of the state of Catholicity in the background histories of six American ethnic groups will document the degree of societal competition experienced by these peoples and, it is proposed, will help explain their varied levels of involvement within their common religion.[15]

THE IRISH

Perhaps the greatest difficulty which confronts the historian of the Irish is that of differentiating between the specifically Irish and specifically Catholic aspects of their lives. They had emerged into the modern world from a past in which Catholicism had played a stronger role than among any other people of Western Europe. By the end of the seventeenth century, the Irish were a conquered people, their leaders had either fled or been despoiled, and thereafter Gaelic cultural disintegration matched strides with the expansion of English authority. The peasant Irish, therefore, found their securities in the Church and their leadership in the priesthood. Hatred and fear of English Protestantism were part of their cultural heritage.[16]

---

15. The review is presented in the following order of involvement within the Church: highest, the Irish and the French-Canadians; lowest, the Southern Italians and the Spanish-speaking Mexicans and Puerto Ricans; intermediate, the German Catholics and the Polish Catholics.

16. Thomas N. Brown, *Irish-American Nationalism 1870–1890* (Philadelphia, 1966), 34–35.

The fusion of religion and nationality, inherent in the above quotation from Thomas Brown, is perhaps the most recurrent theme in the meaning of Irish ethnicity. The fusion was the consequence of centuries of societal competition with the Protestant English. For the Irish the competition meant conflict, and the conflict itself was virtually institutionalized within the structure of the society. It incorporated every aspect of life, including that of religion.

Irish Catholicism was different from the Church in France, Spain, or Italy. Religion in Ireland did not mean vested interests, the dilemmas of institutionalization, or priorities in whatever established society there happened to be, to the degree that religion on the Continent did. Far longer in history, the Church in Ireland had been poor, landless, and without power. It was more objectively and subjectively an integral part of the peasant's own poverty, and could not be held as responsible for the problems of such poverty. It shared a subordinate status, and this fact facilitated the identification which the individual Irishman made of his struggling religion with his struggling nationality.

Instead of a prevailing class of prosperous clergy to contrast with the poverty of the peasants, many Irish priests were close to and among the people. The closing of the monasteries threw the friars out to beg among the poor. O'Faolain writes of the rebellious strain among the clergy when, in the period from 1805 to 1845, the forces of O'Connellism in the presbytery were fighting and defeating the monarchists and their traditions of Gallicanism in the seminary, or even more actively and in still earlier years, when priests either died with guns in their hands during the 1798 Rebellion or were taken to be hanged after the Rising ended.[17]

Potter notes that the fusion of religion and nationality was so complete in Irish Catholic culture that it extended even to their linguistic view of the English.[18] The Irish word, Sassenach, for example, means both Protestant and Englishman. Apostasy from Catholicism was considered the greatest of crimes in the sight of the Irish peasant; the apostate was thought to be a betrayer, not only of religion, but also of

17. Sean O'Faolain, *The Irish: A Character Study* (New York, 1949). This is not to imply that all relations between clergy and laymen were close, or that divisions along ideological lines did not emerge among the Churchmen themselves. See O'Faolain for discussion of these aspects as well. Also, R. E. Burns, "Parsons, Priests, and the People: The Rise of Irish Anti-Clericalism 1785–1789," *Church History* 31 (1962): 151–63.
18. George W. Potter, *To the Golden Door: The Story of the Irish in Ireland and America* (Boston, 1960).

nationality.[19] This is an excellent example of what Fishman, in another context, has called the far-reaching syncretism of ethnic and religious values and traditions: culminating in the "sanctification" of ethnicity and the "ethnization" of religion.[20]

Thus was so much of Irish Catholicism a response to the societal conflict confronting the people. There was always England, identified with contempt and hate, trying to Anglicize Ireland and proscribe everything Irish, including the Irish religion. The persecution fostered the integration of the nationality with the religion, and contributed a great deal to the emergence of the feelings of nationalism.

Glazer has remarked how the Irish Catholic immigrants in the United States were more likely to identify themselves first as being from Ireland, rather than Galway or Cork, as opposed to the Italian Catholics, whose lack of national consciousness had them view their primary origins as Sicily or Calabria (or even villages and communes within these regions), instead of Italy.[21] The choice of local or national identification probably has much to do with the extent of religio-ethnic involvement and degree of societal competition.

The question of national identification should not be confused with the ideology of nationalism. The former sentiment, developed around anti-English themes, was probably much more pervasive than the reality of nationalism, with its complicated sets of opposing issues and directions.[22] The movement for nationalism, however, was based upon the foundation of societal competition and gathered much of its strength and logic from the argument for religio-ethnic distinctiveness.[23]

9

---

19. Ibid.
20. Vladimir C. Nahirny and Joshua A. Fishman, "Ukrainian Language Maintenance Efforts in the United States," in *Language Loyalty in the United States*, ed. Joshua A. Fishman, et al. (The Hague: 1966), 318–57.
21. Nathan Glazer, "Ethnic Groups in America," in *Freedom and Control in Modern Society*, ed. Morroe Berger, et al. (New York, 1954), 158–73.
22. On the complications in the relations between the movement for nationalism and the institutions of Church and State, see Emmet Larkin, "Church and State in Ireland in the Nineteenth Century," *Church History* 31 (1962): 294–306. For a discussion of the personification of this problem, see Emmet Larkin, *James Larkin: Irish Labour Leader 1876–1947* (Cambridge, 1965).
23. The argument for religio-ethnic distinctiveness may be clearer than the precise nature of the Irish Church or Irish Catholicism. O'Dea has pointed out that religion and nationality came to dominate the Irishman's conception of his self, partly because Catholicism in Ireland seldom assumed the posture of defensiveness. Despite the occasional clashes between religion and nationalism, as illustrated by the problems of Parnell, the norm was more likely to be the militance of the local clergy in support of the peasantry. See Thomas F. O'Dea, "The Catholic Immigrant and the American Scene,"

The history of societal competition, with its elements of religio-ethnic conflict and corresponding facts of Irish powerlessness, contributed a good deal to the shape of Irish Catholicity.[24] It was a heritage developed in Ireland and represented quite clearly by the Irish immigrants in the United States, not only in the development of the structure of the Catholic Church in America but also in their high level of association with and involvement in its religious requirements.

THE FRENCH-CANADIANS

The religious element was never absent from the second Hundred Years' War which the French and English waged against each other in America until the downfall of New France. This fact has left its mark on the French-Canadian mentality, which weds the concept of nationality to that of religion and asserts its separateness from English-speaking North America on both counts.[25]

This historical accounting of the French-Canadians by Mason Wade suggests the important similarity shared with the Irish: the interpenetration of religion and nationality in confrontation with the Protestant English-speaking Canadians. The parallels with the Irish in terms of societal competition are striking, especially for the similar end results of extremely close association with the religious and educational requirements of the Catholic Church.

Despite general similarity, the Catholic history of the French-Canadians has some uniqueness, and this has contributed a more tradition-based, parochial social organization to French-Canadian religious life. The French in Canada never experienced the degree of devastation of their society and culture which the Irish did. While party to the political conflicts and different views of the relationship

---

Thought 31 (Summer 1956): 251–70. On the other hand, Larkin argues that competition has created a specific defensiveness: "A hostile English Government in the seventeenth century, a proselytizing Protestantism in the eighteenth century, and a revolutionary Nationalism in the nineteenth century all had put the Irish Church on the defensive. The result was that the Church in Ireland reacted negatively rather than positively to the ways of the world." Emmet Larkin, "Socialism and Catholicism in Ireland," *Church History* 33 (1964): 481. The difference here may be due to confusion between national identification and ideology of nationalism. The former may have been less threatening and more of an asset than the latter.

24.   The historical pattern itself was probably one of increasing religious involvement. After the Great Famine of 1846, ironically, religious and related economic activity increased. Emmet Larkin, "Economic Growth, Capital Investment, and the Roman Catholic Church in Nineteenth-Century Ireland," *American Historical Review* 72 (April 1967): 852–75.

25.   Mason Wade, *The French-Canadian Outlook* (Toronto, 1964), 3–4.

between Church and State, the French-Canadians in Quebec had the geographical insularity and enough ultimate sovereignty for the elaborate development of a parish-dominated social organization.

The problems of conflict and powerlessness, as well as a resultant nationalism, are quite explicit in the bilingual and bicultural consciousness which characterizes contemporary Canada.[26] They are symbolized in the separatist movement in Quebec and have come to prevail in much of the analysis of French-Canadian society and culture. Quoting Marcel Rioux, Dumont offers a summary of the national character:

11

"The French-Canadian ideology has always rested on three characteristics of the French-Canadian culture—the fact that it is a minority culture, that it is Catholic, and that it is French. It is from these characteristics, first envisaged concretely but, with the passing of time, more and more as a framework, that ideology has formulated its national doctrine and has come to control the thinking of most of the educational and intellectual institutions of Quebec." As can be seen, here again the Conquest has not been forgotten.[27]

The distinctiveness of societal competition rests as much with economic disparity as it does with the question of political power. Much has been written about the conscious and unconscious confinement of French-Canadian resources.[28] The "second-class citizenship" qualities which are perceived to arise from the ethnic division of labor in Canada are not unlike some of the economic and social problems between blacks and whites in the United States.

While similar to the religio-ethnic conflicts of the Irish and the English, if not in intensity then in kind, the Church in Quebec has been able to take advantage of opportunities for its development. In his review of the place of Catholicism in French Canada, Falardeau notes that from the beginning of its settlement, Quebec society has been completely surrounded by and dominated by the influence of Catholicism. "The history of French Canada is the history of the Church in Canada and vice versa."[29]

---

26. In a recent survey, considerable ethnic differences were found in perceptions of Canadian society. See John C. Johnstone, Jean-Claude Willig, and Joseph M. Spina, *Young People's Images of Canadian Society* (Ottawa, Studies of the Royal Commission on Bilingualism and Biculturalism, 1969).
27. Fernand Dumont, "The Systematic Study of the French-Canadian Total Society," in *French-Canadian Society*, vol. 1, ed. Marcel Rioux and Yves Martin (Toronto, 1965), 392.
28. See the numerous essays in Rioux and Martin.
29. Jean-Charles Falardeau, "The Role and Importance of the Church in French Canada," in Rioux and Martin, 342.

Tied to the notions of church and society are the two central themes of language and nationalism. The French language is more than a medium of communication or a carrier of culture in Quebec. It is almost mystically regarded as the "guardian of the faith." As another instance of the "sanctification" of ethnicity, the loss of language is believed frequently to lead to the loss of Catholicism, and the depth of this conviction has led to the elaborate development of the parochial school system, not only in Quebec, but also among the American children of the French-Canadian immigrants in New England.[30]

The politico-religious philosophy of French-Canadian nationalism has also gained explicit and universal support among clergy and laymen alike. "This was the belief in French Canada's fortunate vocation based on one obvious sign—the fact that modern France, in becoming secular and atheistic, had abandoned its mission as the older daughter of the Church, while the French Canadians had remained faithful to the past and to God, and must therefore replace a France who had betrayed its trust."[31] The intensity of this feeling, as exemplified by the involvement and association of French-Canadians with their religion, is evident.

In terms of the more micro-sociological aspects of religion in the French-Canadian community, the pervasive Catholicity stands out still more sharply. In his discussion of the growth of industry and the changes in the economic and social order of French Canada, Hughes points out how the parish persists as the central aspect of the French-Canadian's life: "The parish was historically the first institution of local self-government in rural Quebec; it remains the point of active integration of religious and secular matters. The roles of parishioner and of citizen are scarcely distinguishable."[32]

The role of religion in the daily routine of rural Quebec is so predominant as to comprise in itself the meaning of communality. In his account of St. Denis, Miner observes the Mass to be so important to the social system of the parish that he devotes an entire chapter to the effect it has on village life: "Masses are public religious celebrations whether they are Sunday Masses or Masses for marriages, anniversaries of death, burial, or special supplication. They are prac-

---

30. Ibid.
31. Ibid., 350–51.
32. Everett C. Hughes, *French-Canada in Transition* (Chicago, 1943), 10.

tically the only activity in which the whole parish participates as a group."[33]

The clergy of Quebec are an essential part of this communality. Like the priests of Ireland, they share similar backgrounds and values with their parishioners. The historical pattern is important because it means that the clergy of French Canada has rarely been recruited from a single social class, let alone a dominant status, in contrast to the custom of many European countries. "One seldom finds a French-Canadian family that does not include a member or a relative who is in the clergy or in one of the orders," writes Falardeau.[34] The clergy are within and of all strata of the society.

The traditions of Quebec province were transplanted in New England by the French-Canadians who immigrated, and the transplanting was an easier task because of the proximity to Canada. They concentrated almost exclusively on the reestablishment of the parish-centered social organization.[35] On the communication between the two countries, Ducharme writes: "By visit and by letter a sort of communal life exists. Birth and marriage and death are the interest of all, and the frontier is no barrier, for it merely serves to separate the clans temporarily."[36]

In his fictional representation of French-Canadian life in New England, Ducharme conveys the importance of the religious traditions: "The Church meant a great deal to the French Canadian who had left his country. It was like the hub of a wheel to which he gravitated once a week, and which set his pace. There he could always hear his own language spoken, and there he could find solace in time of trouble. Not yet broken was the spell that the village church had for him when he was on his farm in Quebec."[37]

As with all immigrant groups, there are interests in and attempts at maintaining the traditions of the Old World.[38] The Irish and the French-Canadians each brought their own distinctive views of religion and styles of group involvement. Because of the extent of cultural and religious conflict and competition within their respective

13

---

33. Horace M. Miner, *St. Denis, a French-Canadian Parish* (Chicago, 1939), 105.
34. Farlardeau in Rioux and Martin, 355.
35. George F. Theriault, "The Franco-Americans of New England," in *Canadian Dualism,* ed. Mason Wade (Toronto, 1960), 392–411.
36. Jacques Ducharme, *The Shadows of the Trees* (New York, 1943), 14.
37. Jacques Ducharme, *The Delusson Family* (New York, 1939), 52.
38. Robert E. Park and Herbert A. Miller, *Old World Traits Transplanted* (New York, 1921).

societies, and helped by well-developed communal organizations, they brought to the United States their own intimate association with formal religion. Other Catholic groups had other kinds of historical experiences, and brought other religious traditions.

THE SOUTHERN ITALIANS

They unfurled a red-white-and-green handkerchief from the church-tower, they rang the bells in a frenzy, and they began to shout in the village square, "Hurray for Liberty!"

Like the sea in storm. The crowd foamed and swayed in front of the club of the gentry, and outside the Town Hall, and on the steps of the church— a sea of white stocking-caps, axes and sickles glittering. Then they burst into the little street.

"Your turn first, baron! You who have had folks cudgelled by your estate-keepers!"

At the head of all the people a witch, with her old hair sticking up, armed with nothing but her nails. "Your turn, priest of the devil! for you've sucked the soul out of us!"

... Then for his Reverence who used to preach Hell for anybody who stole a bit of bread. He was just coming back from saying mass, with the consecrated Host inside his fat belly. "Don't kill me, I am in mortal sin!" Neighbor Lucia being the mortal sin; Neighbor Lucia whose father had sold her to the priest when she was fourteen years old, at the time of the famine winter, and she had ever since been filling the streets and the Refuge with hungry brats. . . .[39]

The stories of Verga, as well as the novels of other Italian writers, are dramatic sources for illustrating the estrangement of the southern Italians from the Catholic Church.[40] Indeed, the quoted episode goes further than suggesting the contempt of these mob-stricken peasants for the Church; it points to the links of anticlericalism with the nationalist mood.

In stark contrast to the Catholicity of the Irish and the French-Canadians, the state of formal church-involved religiousness in Sicily and other regions of southern Italy was in a precarious condition, a legacy of the alliance between the Church and the Old Order.

---

39. Giovanni Verga, *Little Novels of Sicily* (New York, 1953), 197–198.
40. Many novels, especially those by Levi and Silone, illustrate this mood. For example, Carlo Levi, *Christ Stopped at Eboli* (New York, 1947); Ignazio Silone, *A Handful of Blackberries* (New York, 1953).

The idea and reality of societal competition—that network of conflicts between linguistic and religious differences—were nonexistent
in southern Italy. There was no identification of a populist religion or
church with powerlessness and national identity. The history of the
nineteenth century in Italy shows the Catholic Church to be, for the
most part, an established force against national consciousness and,
directly and indirectly, for maintaining the powerlessness of the poor.
In a real sense, the institutional Church itself was the alien religion—
the Catholicism of Rome, the North, the upper classes, and the status
quo.[41]

From the point of view of the educated classes of the South, the
Papacy and the State were one. This helped to produce both anti-
clericalism and widespread indifference to formal religion, just as the
interlocking of religion and nationality helped to create intense
identification with Catholicism among the Irish and the French-
Canadians. In the Italy of the nineteenth century, resistance or indifference to the social order would extend to religion.

The fact that cultural distinctions prevailed between the North and
the South of Italy did not change with political unification. Latourette notes how important geography was in the structure of the
Catholic Church in Italy.[42] It was from the regions north of Rome
where most of the active support of the Church could be found. All
of the popes of the nineteenth century were born in the North, with
the sole exception of Leo XIII.[43] Most of the new congregations had
their beginnings in the North. Little activity and even less support
could be traced to the *Mezzogiorno*. And it was from the South of
Italy that the vast majority of immigrants to the United States had
come.[44]

The writings of many scholars, both proclerical and anticlerical in
temperament, provide evidence of the popular moods toward reli-
gious involvement with formal Catholicism. The struggles between the
Church and the movement for unification left their mark, as noted in
Henry Browne's survey of the "Italian problem" within American
Catholicism: "The comments of an anti-papal Italian traveller to
America suggest that almost of necessity the political affairs of Italy,
which for years made it practically impossible for a good Catholic

15

---

41. A. C. Jemolo, *Church and State in Italy 1850–1950* (Oxford, 1960); see also Baron.
42. Latourette, vol. 1 : 415–19.
43. Even Leo XIII was a native of the region only slightly to the south of Rome, ibid.
44. Robert F. Foerster, *The Italian Emigration of Our Times* (Cambridge, 1919).

to be a good citizen of the newly united Italy, had an influence on the religious mentality of Italians even after migration."[45]

In his autobiography, Panunzio describes the memories of his boyhood in Apulia, in a home that can be said to be comfortable, if neither affluent nor impoverished:

While we all received instruction of various kinds, dealing mainly with good manners and proper conduct, our religious education was very limited, almost a negligible factor in our lives. Religion was considered primarily a woman's function, unnecessary to men, and a matter about which they continually joked. . . . We children continuously heard our male relatives speak disparagingly of religion, if religion it could be called. They would speak of the corruption of the Church.[46]

Among the poorest classes, educational and religious instruction in formal Catholicism were even less common and characteristic. Feelings against the Church were widespread, if not always vocal. Banfield describes the lack of both religious and secular influence of the two churches and their priests in Montegrano.[47] Barely more than ten percent of the 3,400 Montegranesi go to hear Mass on a Sunday, and most of these are women:

By tradition the men of Montegrano are anticlerical. The tradition goes back a century or more to a time when the church had vast holdings in Southern Italy and was callous and corrupt. Today it owns only one small farm in Montegrano, and the village priests are both known to be kindly and respectable men. Nevertheless priests in general—so many Montegranesi insist—are money-grubbers, hypocrites, and worse.[48]

The feelings had become a tradition, despite changes in the social system. And the tradition of relative indifference to and contempt for the formal Church was brought to the United States with immigration.

It is ironic that the indifference to the formal doctrines of Catholicism among the southern Italians persisted despite the fact that so many of the *contadini* were fairly isolated in their peasant villages from the currents of anticlericalism and changing political thought

45. Henry J. Browne, "The 'Italian Problem' in the Catholic Church of the United States, 1880–1900," *United States Catholic Historical Society, Historical Records and Studies* 35 (1946): 46–72.
46. Constantine M. Panunzio, *The Soul of an Immigrant* (New York, 1921), 18.
47. Montegrano is the fictitiously named commune in Southern Italy which was the location for Banfield's study of the conditions of political and communal organization. Edward C. Banfield, *The Moral Basis of a Backward Society* (New York, 1958).
48. Ibid., 17–18.

abroad throughout Italy.[49] As Vecoli points out, much of this is due to the particularistic folk-ceremonies of the local varieties of religion: "While nominally Roman Catholics, theirs was a folk religion, a fusion of Christianity and pre-Christian elements, of animism, polytheism, and sorcery with the sacraments of the Church. . . . Dominated by a sense of awe, fear, and reverence for the supernatural, the peasants were profoundly religious. However, their beliefs and practices did not conform to the doctrines and liturgy of the Church."[50] This variant of religion, of course, clashed with the more institutional ecclesiasticism of the Vatican, as it clashed after immigration with the Irish style of Catholicism predominant in America.[51] Regardless of the lack of ideological anticlericalism, the poor in southern Italy, in marked contrast to the poor in Ireland and Quebec, often showed contempt for the formal religion. For this they had the justification of their own experience. Vecoli summarizes this orientation:

17

> For the Church as an institution the South Italian peasants had little sense of reverence. Historically it had been allied with the landowning aristocracy and had shown little sympathy for the misery of the *contadini*. Although surrounded by a multitude of clergy, the people by and large were not instructed in the fundamental doctrines of the Catholic faith. Toward their village priests, whom they regarded as parasites living off their labors, the peasants often displayed attitudes of familiar contempt. Clerical immorality and greed figured largely in the folk humor of Italy.[52]

The lack of involvement in the Church in southern Italy, it is proposed, is comparatively explained by the absence of societal competition between distinct cultural and religious systems, and the attendant identification of religion, not with an emerging sense of social and political reform, but with the existing policies of the old order. The characteristics of competition as defined—the extent of religio-ethnic conflict and the salience of powerlessness—which contributed to high Church involvement and religious observance among the Irish and the French-Canadians were absent in southern Italy. Indeed the model of competition worked in reverse because it was the Church

---

49. Rudolph J. Vecoli, "Prelates and Peasants: Italian Immigrants and the Catholic Church," *Journal of Social History* 2 (Spring 1969): 217–68.
50. Ibid., 228.
51. Ibid.
52. Ibid., 229. In contrast again to the Irish, few priests wanted to accompany Italian Catholics during emigration, and few wanted to serve in Italian parishes in the United States. According to Vecoli, this was not due to the desire of Italian clergy to remain in Italy. It was more often explained by outright hostility and disrespect. Ibid., 235.

which was held responsible for social problems and not some foreign cultural system.

THE MEXICANS AND THE PUERTO RICANS

A factor all but universal in Spanish America ... was the shock brought to the Roman Catholic Church by independence and the inevitably painful adjustments. Crises arose from the disorders which were features of the wars of independence, from the Spanish birth of many of the clergy, from the historic patronage exercised by the crown, from the insistence of new governments on the transfer to them of that authority, from the unwillingness of Madrid to surrender its prerogatives, and from the political situation in Spain which made Rome hesitate to go counter to Spanish claims.[53]

Societal competition between religious and cultural systems was also lacking in Mexico and Puerto Rico, as elsewhere throughout Latin America, and some of the same problems of the history of Church and State in Italy could be seen in the history of Spanish-speaking America. Most notable, as the above quotation suggests, is the universality of Church power and control.

To varying extents, Latin American countries were considered as mission territories by the Church. This led to a number of unique factors which were subsequently seen to contribute to the lack of involvement of Latin Americans in the formal religious system of Catholicism. Both Mexico and Puerto Rico emerged from the Spanish colonial tradition, and the attachments of Mexicans and Puerto Ricans to the Church were founded not so much on the basis of instruction and conviction—both positive values of Catholicism—as on the presence of social and religious customs, artifactual medals, holy pictures, and fiestas.[54]

According to a recent study by Houtart and Pin, data on the low religious observance of Latin American Catholics form a regular pattern which is traced to and explained by the predominance of the colonial tradition itself.[55] The people of Latin America are ascribed Catholics, and subsequently religion becomes a mere social attribute. Religion then becomes nothing more than another characteristic with which one is born.

---

53. Latourette, 3 : 295.
54. Joseph P. Fitzpatrick, "Mexicans and Puerto Ricans Build a Bridge," *America* 94 (31 December 1955) : 373–75.
55. Francois Houtart and Emile Pin, *The Church and the Latin American Revolution* (New York, 1965).

The state of Catholicity in Latin America is further affected by the underdeveloped conditions of religio-communal organization, data for which will be presented below. The numbers of priests are few, relative to the size of the population in Latin America, and parishes are too large and thus inadequate for religious organization.[56] Above all, the clergy were traditionally recruited from Europe, during early years of colonization, in keeping with the missionary perspective of the areas. This only served to maintain the problem of the social and religious distance between parishioner and Church.

The distance between the clergy and the people mirrors the broader problems of Church and State. As in Italy, there was no competition with alien cultures and religions. Instead, there was conflict with the established powers of Catholicism. Mecham has pointed out how much at odds were the Church and its Spanish-born clergy with the movements for political independence.[57] In the subsequent conflicts in the different countries, the clergy were often divided. With few exceptions, the general division saw the bishops and higher clergy standing for the monarchical form of government, and the lower clergy (increasingly, as the societies grew more populous, native-born to Latin America) on the side of change.

In Mexico, the leadership in the political struggle for independence came at first from local village priests, close to the pressing social problems of the population.[58] In this, as far as the role of the local village priest was concerned, the Mexican struggle was similar to the Irish. The differences for the larger societies, however, are evident. There was less division among the clergy in Ireland, partly because of the overwhelming presence of religious and cultural differences with the English lords. In Mexico, as elsewhere in Latin America, the clergy who did take the side of independence found themselves in a position which the Church hierarchy deplored. It was a classic case of pervasive role conflict. In Spanish America, it was the religiously homogeneous society which was in competition with itself; there was no alien religio-cultural scapegoat, real or imagined.

19

---

56. Ibid. Countries such as Venezuela, Paraguay, Costa Rica, and Ecuador have concentrations of between 50 and 78 percent of their Catholic clergy in their capital cities. In Uruguay and Cuba, the percentages are even higher. See Carlos M. Rama, "Pasado Y Presente de la Religion En America Latina," *Cuadernos Americanos* 26 (July-August 1967): 25–43.
57. J. Lloyd Mecham, *Church and State in Latin America* (Chapel Hill, 1934).
58. Ibid.

In Puerto Rico too, as throughout much of Latin America, orthodoxy within Catholicism prevailed almost exclusively among the
upper classes. Despite the Church's standardized doctrines and procedures, local communities in Puerto Rico blended formal Catholicism with cults of saints, witchcraft, spiritualism, and later in the
twentieth century, even elements of Protestantism.[59] The fact of
variation from the formal religion of Catholicism is not unlike the
deviations found in the religious life of southern Italy.

Steward draws attention to a number of factors which prevented
the integration of the greater proportion of Puerto Ricans into the
institutionalized life of the Church.[60] Poverty, dispersal of the population, inadequate clergy, missionary attitudes of patronization,
and the inconsistent stands of the Church on social issues (e.g.,
slavery), all contributed to the shape of religion in Puerto Rico. As in
Mexico, there was no historical confrontation for Catholicism in
Puerto Rico, and this fact would influence not only the Church's
view of Latin Americans but also the population's view of the
Church.

After the United States became sovereign over Puerto Rico, there
came a complete separation of religion from the government. The
island was opened, for the first time, to missionary activity by
Protestant groups. Steward argues that these two events introduced
still more heterogeneity to the Catholicism of the island, and even
worked to supplant the traditional religious forms in some areas of
Puerto Rico.[61]

Studies of Mexican and Puerto Rican communities in the United
States document quite consistently the "token bond" with formal
Catholicism which characterizes the Spanish-speaking groups.[62]
Like the Italians, the Mexicans and the Puerto Ricans brought with
them to the United States their ethnic indifference to a religious
system which they, for the most part, either traditionally took for
granted or perceived to be standing in the way of change and pressing

---

59. Julian H. Steward, et al., *The People of Puerto Rico* (Champaign, 1956).
60. Ibid.
61. Ibid. If Protestantism in Puerto Rico is identified with Anglo-Saxon culture, it
would be interesting to see if higher levels of religious involvement among both Catholics and Protestants on the island result from instances of religio-cultural competition.
62. For Mexican communities, see Arthur J. Rubel, *Across the Tracks: Mexican-
Americans in a Texas City* (Austin, 1966); Ruth D. Tuck, *Not with the Fist* (New York,
1946). For Puerto Rican communities, see Glazer and Moynihan; C. Wright Mills,
Clarence Senior, and Rose K. Goldsen, *The Puerto Rican Journey* (New York, 1950);
Elena Padilla, *Up from Puerto Rico* (New York, 1958).

reform. They differ quite essentially from the Irish and the French-Canadians, for whom the fights for autonomy in matters of nationality and religion substantially reinforced each other.

THE POLISH CATHOLICS

Religion was . . . in some measure a field of national cooperation, particularly in the southeastern part of Russian Poland, Lithuania, and White Ruthenia, where religious and national interests went hand in hand. . . . But aesthetic and intellectual interests had but little influence upon the large masses of the population and . . . the role of the Catholic Church in Polish national life was limited by its international politics. The most secure and the widest ground of national cooperation lay elsewhere—in the economic domain.[63]

21

The Polish Catholics, like the German Catholics to be discussed next, show a degree of involvement not exactly like the four backgrounds already presented. The Poles are indeed well involved in their religion, and thus they are decidedly different from the Italians and the Spanish-speaking of Latin America. But given the empirical levels of religious and educational involvement, the Poles do not represent the type of intensity which characterizes the place of the Irish and the French-Canadians in historical and contemporary Catholicism. They reflect a kind of intermediacy.

It is frequently observed that the state of Catholicism in Poland has been historically similar to the religious situation of Ireland and Quebec. Baron offers Polish history as another instance of the coincidence of national interests and religious loyalties.[64] Fishman discusses the presumed consequence of ethnic and political allegiances for the individual peasant in rural Poland.[65] While there is no denial of some historical similarities, certain differences have been overlooked and the above quotation from Thomas and Znaniecki suggests that the history and the role of the Church in Poland, in its bearing on the individual Catholic, may not have been as close to that in Ireland and Quebec as commonly thought.

In terms of the concept of societal competition, cultural and religious differences were not as graphic in Poland as they were in

---

63. W. I. Thomas and Florian Znaniecki, *The Polish Peasant in Europe and America* (New York, 1927), 2:1440.
64. Baron, 96–108.
65. Fishman.

Ireland and Quebec. There was more diffuse heterogeneity within Poland, as a result of the many competing national and religious groups within constantly shifting and arbitrarily drawn boundary lines. Iwanska cites figures which put the Catholic proportion of the Polish territory between World Wars I and II as approximately 65 percent of the total. The remaining 35 percent included Jews, the Eastern Orthodox, Protestants, and Eastern Rite Catholics, all representing different national origins.[66] This kind of heterogeneity blurred the focus of religion and nationality which emerged with so much intensity in overwhelmingly Catholic Ireland and Quebec.

A second point might be made of the fact that Poland was geographically in confrontation with not one major power, but two, flanking her on both sides; in the east there was Orthodox Russia, and in the west there was Protestant Prussia. Both situations, it has been argued, served to sharpen the consciousness of Polish national identity with the Catholic Church.[67] But at the same time, this dual confrontation became a thorn in the side of political compromise. Accommodation with one power at the expense of the other continually created problems, not only for the Church, but for the cause of Polish nationalism as well.[68]

Complicating matters even more, Prussia had her own Catholic minority, and Poland of course had her religious groups. All of these factors did not lead to any measure of unqualified or predictable support by the Vatican or create the kind of symbolic competition that Catholic Ireland or Catholic Quebec experienced with the Protestant English. In both of these cases, the English were the only major problems perceived by the Catholics of Quebec and Ireland, and the energies of religious and national movement were all the more easily channeled in the one direction.

Within Poland too, the Church did not enjoy the same kind of secular support that it did in Ireland and Quebec. Its appreciation and backing by the peasants were limited fairly much to religious affairs. "Polish peasants were never very clear about how to define the role of their priest. They felt uncomfortable about the two overlapping roles of the parish priest, his secular role as the representative of the parish, and his religious role as the representative of God. The

66. Alicja Iwanska, ed. *Contemporary Poland: Society, Politics, Economy* (Chicago, Human Relations Area Files, 1955), 189.
67. Kolarz, 103.
68. Baron.

memoirs of Polish peasants of the interwar period reveal great bitterness toward their village priests."[69]

It might well be argued that memoir-writing is an avocation more often associated with the class of intellectuals than with the peasants, and that the above quotation from Iwanska is somewhat biased. But even at the level of the intellectuals and the educated classes, the differences with the view of the Church in Quebec and Ireland are apparent.

One of the reasons for this disparity is the role the Church adopted within Poland toward the forces of social change. Thomas and Znaniecki write of the breakdown of the peasant community and the lack of any vehicle for the reincorporation of Poles into a viable national community:

23

> Religion and the church organization might have been, indeed, powerful means of unifying the peasant primary groups; but they could not be used, partly because of the unwillingness of the central Catholic Church authorities to let the Polish clergy commit itself in national and social struggles, partly because of the suspicion with which the Russian and Prussian governments looked upon the activities of the Polish clergy, partly also because of the undemocratic character of the church hierarchy.[70]

In Poland, very few priests were found among the peasant leaders.[71] The Church and its representatives were based on the existing social order, and they thwarted the drives toward change, especially in the field of popular education.[72] Having little leadership among the clergy in secular affairs, the Polish Catholics did not identify their Church (in distinction to their religion) with a national identity, to the degree evident among the Irish and the French-Canadians. The nature of societal competition was not as clearly expressive to the Poles, in terms of religion and ethnic conflict, as it was to these other two nationalities.

Parish organization itself appears to have been the salient basis of the traditional way of life in Poland, but there was a strong separation in the peasant's view of the role of the Church and the role of society. They did not merge in traditional Poland. Finestone compares the value systems and peasant communities of rural Poland and southern Italy, and finds that the Church has a greater integrative

---

69. Iwanska, 196.
70. Thomas and Znaniecki, 2:1368.
71. Ibid., 1310.
72. Ibid., 1298.

function in Poland than in Italy.[73] In terms of societal competition, the integrative function of the church and society finds still more expression in the history of Ireland and Quebec.

THE GERMAN CATHOLICS

Religiously the complexion of Germany was determined by the rulers of the several states. By the principle of *cuius regio, eius religio* every prince decided which form of Christianity would prevail in his domain. Some states were Catholic, some Lutheran, and some Reformed. Throughout the nineteenth century each state had its established church and sought to control ecclesiastical affairs within its borders. These *Landeskirchen* persisted into the twentieth century. In the empire Roman Catholics were a minority. At the close of the century they constituted about 36 per cent of the population. The North was fairly solidly Protestant. The Catholic Church was strongest in the South.[74]

The sixth and last group to be discussed are the Catholics of Germany. While considered in the United States as among the most active supporters of the Catholic Church, the German Catholics share a kind of intermediacy with the Poles, in terms of the level of religious involvement.

The nature of cultural and religious competition in Germany has been a mixed phenomenon, as the above quotation suggests. On the one hand, religious affiliation tended to predominate by region within the country. On the other hand, religious groups have competed socially as a consequence of the political unification of the late nineteenth century, despite the fact that in all cases the groups are German.[75]

As Fogarty points out, and as cited above, religious observance tends to be higher only in those areas of the country which are close to the frontiers of actual cultural competition. From the societal point of view, Catholicism in Germany is one of several religious affiliations. And from the regional or subsocietal position, Catholicism in Germany is either a majority or minority religion.

---

73. Harold Finestone, "A Comparative Study of Reformation and Recidivism among Italian and Polish Criminal Offenders," doctoral dissertation, University of Chicago, 1963, chap. IV.
74. Latourette, 1:434.
75. Competition, in terms of the "adjustment of multiple loyalties," among German Catholics and German Protestants in America is discussed by Philip Gleason in *The Conservative Reformers: German-American Catholics and the Social Order* (Notre Dame, 1968), 144–71.

The latter fact poses an important qualification to the overall societal pluralism.

For comparative purposes, societal competition in Germany or with cultural systems outside of Germany has been relevant to German history, but not nearly as exclusively as the conflicts between the Catholics of Quebec and Protestant Canada, or the struggles of Catholic Ireland with Anglican England. The presence of such competition is best illustrated by the *Kulturkampf* which Bismarck's Prussia waged with German Catholicism. The conflict between the Church and the forces for nationalist unification of Germany under the leadership of Protestant Prussia led in itself to the emigration of many German Catholics to the United States, for the expressed purpose of greater freedom in religious observance.[76] Latourette associates this religious competition with the high involvement of German Catholics in the Church: "The effort to defeat Bismarck drew German Roman Catholics together and strengthened their loyalty to the Pope and their church."[77]

25

On the other hand, much of the *Kulturkampf* varied by region, and the efforts of Bismarck to achieve national unity took advantage of regional differences. Accommodations were made with religious distinctions, and national interests seemed to prevail over sectional ones.[78] The conflicts that were endemic between cultures and religions in Ireland and Quebec were not really sustained over time or pitched to the same degree of intensity in Germany.

With regard to religio-communal organization, German Catholicism achieved considerable development. According to Latourette, Roman Catholicism in Germany attained a kind of national solidarity which was in sharp contrast to the divided Catholicism of France, or the indifferent Catholicism of Italy.[79] The solidarity was helped along by the conflicts with statism, but German Catholicism was popularly based on numerous associations organized early in the nineteenth century. Associations with various institutional interests— the Center Party, the Federation of Christian Trade Unions, the religious groups such as the Society of St. Boniface, and the populistic *Volkverein* and *Gesellenverein*—all contributed to the growth and involvement of German Catholics in their religion.

---

76. Colman J. Barry, *The Catholic Church and German-Americans* (Washington, 1953).
77. Latourette, 1:292.
78. Ibid.
79. Ibid.

The twentieth century witnessed still more development. Organizational participation grew during the Weimar Republic. The most well-known Catholic associations were those of the trade unions and employers' groups for lay activity. But there were also "societies of mothers, of rural laborers, of store clerks, of school teachers, of waiters in hotels and restaurants, and to aid discharged prisoners."[80] Latourette documents the extent of activity within the Church at all levels of society. The rise of Nazism brought about the dissolution of most of these Catholic organizations, but involvement within the religion continued with a concentration of activity in the life of the parish.[81]

German Catholicism appears to have been as well developed as the religion of Ireland and Quebec, especially in terms of parish communities and religious association. But it was decidedly communal in its cast. Largely because of regionalism, German Catholicism lacked the nationalist overtones that colored the religion of the Irish and the French-Canadians.

26

OVERVIEW AND SUMMARY

Comparative data on specific developments in the religious history of each of the areas described are not easily available. By way of summary, however, some comparison may be made from recent data

TABLE 2. RATIOS OF CATHOLIC POPULATION TO NUMBER OF PARISHES, SELECTED COUNTRIES AND PROVINCES, FOR 1949, 1953, 1957, 1961

Country or Province	Parish Ratios* (Number of Catholics per Parish)			
	1949	1953	1957	1961
Quebec	2,168	2,225	2,326	2,421
Germany	2,173	2,179	2,206	2,245
Ireland	3,041	3,078	3,067	3,028
Poland	3,645	3,358	3,658	3,529
Sicily	3,744	3,757	3,640	3,499
Mexico	10,295	11,310	11,768	14,511
Puerto Rico	18,485	20,047	18,468	20,513

SOURCE: *Annuario Pontificio*, 1949, 1953, 1957, 1961. Citta del Vaticano.
* Ratios are calculated to the nearest whole number, from estimates of Catholic population and numbers of parishes, presented by sees and dioceses of each country shown.

80. Ibid., 4:185.
81. Ibid.

on the number of parishes and clergies reported for the different dioceses and sees within the Catholic Church. Tables 2 and 3 offer the ratios of Catholic population to the number of parishes and the number of clergies, respectively. The latter figures refer to the total number of diocesan priests, clergies in religious orders (males only), and seminarians.[82]

For both tables 2 and 3, the ratios are provided for four different years (arbitrarily chosen, every fourth year after the data first were available in published form) for each of the countries or provinces discussed. Table 2 provides parish ratios, or the number of Catholics per parish in the designated area. It is suggested that the fewer numbers of Catholics per parish, the more elaborate the organization of the Church for the given area. This is an indication of parish development, and serves as a clue to the distance between the Church and the religious involvement of the individual Catholics.[83]

The rank orders of these parish ratios for the four years presented in table 2 are very close, and the ratios themselves do not change considerably from one column to the next. If there is any bias in the reporting of these data, it does not seem to be erratic. The rank orders correlate fairly well with the religious behavior documented for the Catholic Americans originating from these countries, and with the state of Catholicity arising from the degree of societal competition and cultural conflict.

There is evidence of greater parish organization for Quebec, Germany, and Ireland. Poland and Sicily are next in order, and Mexico and Puerto Rico are the most underdeveloped. In view of the condition of Catholicity in Latin America, and the factors discussed above, it is not surprising to see these parish ratios for Mexico and Puerto Rico. The ratios for Sicily, however, are higher than one might expect in view of the lack of formal involvement in southern

27

---

82. The source for these data is the *Annuario Pontificio* (Vatican Yearbook) for 1949, 1953, 1957, and 1961. The problem of reliability is considerable; data are reported by the diocesan curias concerned and are not subject to any controls. Another important problem refers to the shifting boundaries within dioceses and general population movements. I made the effort to include the total populations of the same sees and dioceses for each year shown. Estimates of Catholics include all who are baptized as Catholics and who are not apostatized. A third problem is the gross comparability between these recent years and the historical decades of emigration to the United States. Unfortunately, similar figures are not available for years prior to World War II. As a result, I am leaning on the assumption that these figures represent some continuity and historical pattern, unless otherwise noted.
83. Fitzpatrick; Rama.

28

Italy. This is probably explained by the presence of the Vatican in Rome, and the existence of a formal religious structure throughout Italy which has developed despite generalized indifference.

Table 3 offers the ratios of Catholic population to clergies. Nationalities of the priests are not known, but it is assumed that with some exceptions among religious orders and the missionary groups in Mexico and Puerto Rico most of the clerics and seminarians are native to the areas shown. These ratios may serve to illustrate the extent to which clerical development varies with the different Catholic regions.

TABLE 3. RATIOS OF CATHOLIC POPULATION TO NUMBER OF CLERGIES, SELECTED COUNTRIES AND PROVINCES, 1949, 1953, 1957, 1961

Country or Province	Clergy Ratios* (Number of Catholics per Cleric)			
	1949	1953	1957	1961
Quebec	417	425	436	437
Ireland	423	410	383	356
Sicily	816	849	965	953
Germany	862	844	872	879
Poland	1,666	1,494	1,311	1,307
Mexico	3,501	3,336	3,100	3,657
Puerto Rico	6,512	6,479	5,216	4,948

SOURCE: *Annuario Pontificio*, 1949, 1953, 1957, 1961. Citta del Vaticano.

* Ratios are calculated to the nearest whole number, from estimates of Catholic population and numbers of clergy (defined as diocesan priests, clerics in religious orders, and unordained seminarians), reported by sees and dioceses of each country shown.

For the four years of table 3, the rank orders are again very approximate to each other, and the ratios are fairly constant for the years reported. Ireland and Quebec are both the lands of priests; the prevalence of clergy among the Irish and the French-Canadians confirms the past histories of these peoples.

Sicily is relatively well endowed with clergymen, comparing similarly with Germany. Again, as with the indications of parish development, the traditions of southern Italy and Sicily have produced an indifference to the Church in the face of well organized parish systems and the availability of priests.

For the remaining three areas—Poland, Mexico, and Puerto Rico —the proportions of population to religious functionaries yield ratios of well over one thousand. The ratios for Poland may reflect the newer post-World War II problems of church and state under communism. But the ratios for Mexico and Puerto Rico again confirm the expectation that there is little clerical assistance for the size of the Latin American Catholic population.

ဘဘ

The comparative analysis of the historical backgrounds of six Catholic ethnic groups in the United States has explored selective facets of the nature of religio-ethnic systems. The major goal has been an explanation of the religious involvement of these ethnic groups primarily in terms of a model of societal competition based on religious and cultural differences.

29

The highest involvement of the Irish and the French-Canadians in the Catholic Church is a function of the intense societal competition each of these groups experienced throughout history. Catholics in other countries, whose social systems were not subject to the conflicts brought about by different religio-cultural traditions, did not emerge with the same religio-ethnic identification and close association with the Church, which characterizes the Irish and French-Canadians. Correlating with this kind of societal competition is a fairly well-developed parish system and religious communal organization.

The intermediate position of the German and Polish Catholics is explained by the mixture of competition which marked their histories. Catholics in Germany and Poland were subject to qualified degrees of competition and conflict, not equal to the intense variety which prevailed in Quebec and Ireland. Modifying factors, such as regionalism in Germany and the inconsistent role of the Church on social, economic, and political problems in Poland, prevented the complete identification of ethnicity with religion that was so pervasive in Ireland and Quebec.

The low involvement of the Italian and Spanish-speaking Catholics is related to the lack of any societal competition which would have fostered the relevance of religious observance and the Church for these people. The indifference of the Latin Catholics is further traced to the factor of church-state alliances, and the identification of the Church with the established order and against the movements for nationalism, social justice, and change.

As an exploration into the relationship between religion and ethnicity, this paper has attempted to integrate sociological and historical concerns. A good deal more research is needed, not only for an appreciation of the roots of diversity in religion and ethnicity, but also for an understanding of the process of change in these areas of life. The blending of historical and sociological inquiries and styles of research should contribute to these endeavors.

30

Ethnicity, Immigration and American Catholic History   3

by Philip Gleason, Ph.D. and
David Salvaterra, A.B.D.

Ethnicity emerged rapidly and unexpectedly as a public issue
on the contemporary American scene. A few years ago, the word
itself was an exotic term which had only recently come into use
among social scientists. The substantive form, "ethnicity," does
not even appear in the 1968 *Random House Dictionary of the
English Language*, although "ethnic" and "ethnic group" are
there. Since the early 1970's, however, we have had such a blos-
soming of ethnic studies programs and discussions of the new
ethnicity that practically everyone must at least have heard the
word, although not many would be able to say precisely what it
means.

The upswing of interest in ethnicity is deserving of particular
notice by Catholics for several reasons. In the first place, Catholics
form a large proportion of the population often referred to as
white ethnics—that is, persons of southern or eastern European
background whose ancestors came from Italy, Poland, or the lands
of the old Austro-Hungarian empire. In addition, Chicanos are
overwhelmingly Catholic in religion, and they constitute a very
large ethnic group whose situation presents complicated problems (such as the question of undocumented workers), which are
still unresolved.

Then, too, Catholics figure very prominently among the leaders
of the new ethnicity. That is perhaps natural in view of the fact
that Catholics are so numerous among the ethnic population.
However that may be, Catholics have been highly visible in the
movement. Michael Novak could certainly be called a major

Philip Gleason is Professor of History at the University of Notre Dame,
where he has taught since 1959. He has published widely in the field of
American Catholic history and is a former President of the American
Catholic Historical Society. David Salvaterra, who received his undergraduate degree from Pennsylvania State University, is presently a doctoral candidate in American Catholic History at Notre Dame.

Social Thought, Summer 1978
© 1978 *National Conference of Catholic Charities*
Washington, D.C.

prophet and publicist of the new ethnicity. His *Rise of the Unmeltable Ethnics* (1971) is still the outstanding manifesto, and Novak remains actively engaged in the movement, speaking and writing widely.

Two priests, Andrew Greeley and Geno Baroni, cover the areas of social scientific research and practical organizational work. Greeley, who is a prolific writer and vigorous controversialist as well as being an established authority in the field of national-survey research, has contributed immensely to putting the discussion of ethnicity on firmer ground, both conceptually and in terms of empirical evidence. His *Why Can't They Be Like Us?* (1971) and *Ethnicity in the United States* (1974) are influential works, and as long as Greeley is around no one is going to exclude the Irish from the ranks of the ethnics (although he suggests in *That Most Distressful Nation* (1972) that they tried hard to put themselves out of business as an ethnic group).

Geno Baroni, the son of an Italian immigrant miner in Pennsylvania, is now Assistant Secretary for Neighborhoods, Voluntary Associations, and Consumer Protection in the U.S. Department of Housing and Urban Development. He won this high post by a record of unmatched effectiveness as an organizer of community development programs in ethnic neighborhoods in a number of American cities. Another Italian-American priest, Silvano Tomasi, plays an on-going role in ethnic affairs as director of the Center for Migration Studies in New York, and as editor of the Center's *International Migration Review*. Three years ago, Tomasi also published *Piety and Power*, an important historical study of Italian Catholics in the New York area in the late nineteenth and early twentieth centuries.

Although one would have to introduce a number of qualifications even to do justice to the individuals just named, it is a fair generalization that spokesmen for the new ethnicity are highly critical of the way America treats its ethnics. This means that they also present a generally unfavorable picture of the history of immigration and ethnic affairs in the past. A negative portrayal is built into their approach. After all, the past shaped the present; if the present is bad, the past must be what made it that way. This kind of logic naturally operates when Catholics committed to the ethnic cause look at the Catholic past, as well as when they look at more general matters like national policy on immigration, nativism, and so on. Even without special animus on their part, the perspective from which they undertake the inquiry pretty well predetermines the kind of historical evidence that seems more relevant and the sort of interpretation that best explains the events of the past. In other words, they are apt to go looking for negative evidence without consciously intending to do any such thing. And those predisposed to find negative evidence in history are rarely disappointed.

This kind of process has tended to create a vague impression that, historically, the Catholic record on ethnicity is somewhere between embarrassing and disgraceful. The picture of the past, as it emerges from the writings of new ethnic spokesmen, is dominated by an intolerant Irish-American hierarchy, at best indifferent to the material needs and cultural values of non-English-speaking Catholics, and periodically aroused to campaigns of chauvinistic Americanization. While there is evidence that can be interpreted this way, and while the interpretation is sometimes justified, we are convinced that this very negative picture is a gross distortion of the past. Moreover, to the degree that it prevails, it hampers current efforts to deal constructively with the ethnic problems of our own day.

This brief essay cannot pretend to give anything approaching an adequate review of the history of millions of Catholic immigrants from dozens of different ethnic groups. Thus, it is not our intention to try to tell the complex story of the Mexican-Americans—or that of the Germans, Poles, Italians, or any other group. Neither do we intend to "answer" the new ethnic critics of the Catholic record, although we willingly affirm that our overall judgment is more positive in evaluating the way in which Church leaders dealt with these matters. Rather, what we wish to do here is to highlight some of the most important general features of the history of immigration and ethnicity in American Catholicism. We begin with some observations about the Catholic Church as an institution in a society initially quite hostile to Catholicism. Then we shall examine some of the recurring features in the development of Catholic immigrant groups. (Incidentally, we shall speak mainly of immigrants, rather than ethnics, for that was the terminology used by Catholics at the time.)

The Catholic Church as an Institutional Immigrant

All churches except the few (such as the Mormons) that originated in the United States are institutional immigrants in the sense that they were transplanted from abroad and had to adjust to a novel environment in this country. But as H. Richard Niebuhr pointed out fifty years ago in his *Social Sources of Denominationalism* (1929), these problems of adjustment were ag-

6

gravated for what he called the "Churches of the Immigrants." And among such immigrant churches, the difficulties of the Catholic Church were easily the most extreme, since what it had to adjust itself to was a society whose most influential founders had defined themselves "over against" Catholicism. For what was it that the Puritans wished to purify out of the Church of England but the vestiges of Catholicism? Throughout the colonial period and into the nineteenth century, innumerable earnest and well-meaning American Protestants believed the Pope was literally the Antichrist spoken of in the Book of Revelations. The organization over which the Pope presided was in no sense to be thought of as a branch of the Christian Church. His followers could never become good Americans because, in the minds of these Protestants, one of the things that defined Americanism was rejection of the Pope of Rome.

This apocalyptic view of Catholicism blended, in the era of the War for Independence, with the millenial republicanism of the revolutionary generation. The Papacy and Catholicism were identified with the depraved political order of Europe toward which America had decisively turned her back. Thus John Adams (who is not usually classed among the most enthusiastic visionaries of the age) attacked the politico-religious system of Europe in his *Dissertation on the Canon and the Federal Law* (1765)—a work which the modern scholar, Ernest Tuveson, identified a few years ago as an important document in the tradition of American millenialism.[1] Thomas Jefferson differed with his New England friend on many matters, but he was in full accord with Adams's negative view of the Catholic Middle Ages, and he regarded all ecclesiastical institutions as hindrances to true religion. He and other representatives of the enlightened intelligentsia looked upon Catholicism as part of a benighted and vicious system, wholly at odds with republicanism, tolerable only because it was rapidly passing off the scene in Europe and because it could never prosper in the free air of America.

The virulence of these views ebbed with the passing of revolutionary and revivalistic millenialism, but the conviction remained among many Americans—liberals as well as evangelical Protestants—that Catholicism was intrinsically irreconcilable with Americanism on the level of principle. This conviction constituted a special problem for those responsible for the Catholic Church in America, notably the bishops, and it helps explain why they were always so sensitive to the need to vindicate the compatibility of Catholicism and Americanism. It likewise makes more understandable the desire of some churchmen to eliminate whatever stood in the way of appropriate Americanization of the Catholic religion.

Institutional Americanization

Some forms of Americanization were bound to occur anyhow, because the Church had to adjust itself to the new environment just as an individual immigrant did. One such adjustment was the development of the Catholic school system. Other factors were also involved, but the basic reason a system extending from kindergarten through graduate school developed here and not elsewhere in the Catholic world was that here the Church found itself in a society that placed a higher value on universal education than any other in human history, and that established free public educational institutions on an unprecedented scale. If they did not want to see their young people absorbed by a system that was definitely hostile to Catholicism in its formative years, and that consistently regarded the "proper" socialization of children as a primary responsibility, there was little that Catholic churchmen could do but encourage the establishment of schools where Catholic children could be socialized in their own tradition, and where they would not be subject to overt or covert proselytization.

Considered as a positive accommodation to the needs and challenges of the American social environment, Catholic schools clearly illustrate a kind of Americanization. Moreover, they continued to be Americanized in the sense that their development was molded by the evolving forces of the American educational environment. The requirements for certification worked out by state departments of education and by independent accrediting agencies, for example, were highly concrete manifestations of the Americanizing influence of the surrounding social milieu. But if the Catholic schools cooperated with this kind of Americanization, they did not always do so with much enthusiasm, and, viewed in another light, the whole Catholic educational enterprise was animated by a desire to resist Americanization. This was, of course, most obvious at the beginning when Americanization was virtually indistinguishable from Protestantization in the minds of many public school educators.[2] But even in the mid-twentieth century there were those who argued that Catholic schools were un-American because they were "divisive," and Catholics have continued to resist Americanization if it is understood to require their giving up their schools.

8 Americanization, with all its ambiguities and contradictory meanings, extended far beyond the question of educational relations between Catholics and the larger society. It was also an intra-Catholic problem. Here, too, the schools were involved, but so was a whole range of other issues over which Catholics disagreed with one another—matters extending from the question of ethnic representation on the hierarchy to temperance, which some Catholics supported as a way of making the Church more acceptable to Americans but which others scorned as an offshoot of Puritan nativism. In all such controversies about Americanization, the fundamental difference of opinion among Catholics arose over what was the *right kind* of adjustment to make to American society. There was obviously no single, universally applicable, "correct" answer to this question. On the contrary, there was wide leeway for legitimate difference of opinion.

Controversy over Americanization

Controversy over these matters was most intense in the 1880's and 1890's.[3] Those who became known as Americanists, or Americanizers—notably Archbishop John Ireland of St. Paul, Bishop John J. Keane of the Catholic University of America, Denis O'Connell of the North American College in Rome, and, in a less partisan way, Cardinal James Gibbons of Baltimore—took what was thought of at the time and later as the liberal position. That is, they admired the open, equalitarian American system; they thought the Church would flourish better here in a free republican society than she had in the tradition-bound states of Europe; and they therefore favored as much accommodation to the prevailing American ways as was compatible with essential Catholic doctrine. Their conservative opponents, led by Archbishop Michael Corrigan of New York, were unpersuaded on these points. They were convinced that maintenance of the traditional forms of Catholic life and thought was the surest way to preserve the faith of the immigrants and their children. They were skeptical of the rosy future painted by the liberals; they feared that flexibility might become laxity, and that adjustment to a new environment could lead to capitulation to the enemy.

Ethnicity was involved in these controversies in ways too tangled to unravel here. It was most explicit in the battle over the role of German Catholics in the Church, a controversy often labelled "Cahenslyism" after Peter Paul Cahensly, a German Catholic layman who played a prominent role in the dispute. It was also referred to as the "nationality question," and that term gets to the heart of the matter but is misleading in suggesting that this was the *only* nationality question — in fact, there were similar, but less publicized, battles over Irish, French-Canadian, Polish, and other nationalities at various times.

The fundamental issue in all these nationality disputes was whether Catholic immigrants and their descendants should be encouraged to adapt to American ways, or should be encouraged to resist adaptation and to preserve as long as possible their inherited patterns of culture and conduct. In keeping with their generally positive attitude toward the American future, the liberals pushed adaptation and were adamantly opposed to any systematic efforts to perpetuate "foreign" languages and cultural forms beyond the not-very-long period which they thought of as appropriate for the transition to Americanism. For this reason, they looked askance at Catholic schools where foreign-language instruction functioned to preserve a transplanted language and culture beyond the span of time in which it would otherwise tend to disappear. They also opposed efforts to bind the American-born offspring of immigrants to national parishes if these young people were of age, could understand English, and wished to transfer out of the national parish.

The leaders of the German Catholics, on the other hand, insisted that systematic efforts to preserve language and culture were absolutely essential. Their arguments — which were, *mutatis mutandis*, the same as those of other Catholic ethnic groups — stressed the point that language saves faith, that if the children of the immigrants gave up their mother tongue they would also very likely give up their religion. One may doubt, however, that they valued language *solely* as a means of preserving faith. Rather, language, religion, and culture interpenetrated each other so thoroughly that it was impossible to think of them separately.[4] They made up an undifferentiated unity, and it was hard to conceive of this unity's being sundered, with language and culture withering away while religion adapted itself to a different cultural matrix in the alien soul of American society.

Being thus passionately committed to a radically conservative position in the nationality question, the German Catholics were naturally disposed to a conservative stance on other disputed issues of the 1880's and 1890's, such as whether Catholics could join secret societies like the Odd Fellows, whether they could take part in inter-faith gatherings, and so on. In the heat of battle, both sides were driven to extreme positions and could be found uttering sentiments which, if taken out of context, appear rigid, doc-

10

trinaire, or even abhorrent. Yet, enough has surely been said to make clear that both sides had legitimate arguments, and that to treat "Americanization" as an ugly term associated with nothing but narrow chauvinism distorts the historical situation beyond recognition. For Americanization was also a strategy for adapting the Church to certain features of American life that we take for granted today, but which were not part of the nineteenth-century European Catholic tradition—such things as the acceptance of republican government, social equalitarianism, separation of church and state, religious freedom, and willingness to cooperate with other religionists in social and civic undertakings. The Americanists were sometimes insensitive to the values of immigrants, but their conservative antagonists were slow to appreciate the positive American values that the liberals espoused.

Recurring Patterns in Catholic Immigrant Experience

While it is useful for analytical purposes to distinguish between the Church considered as an institutional immigrant and the immigrant peoples who comprised the Catholic population, the two dimensions merge together in practical life. Having considered the matter first on the rather abstract level of institutional policy, let us look now at the experience of the actual immigrants who made up the great mass of the Catholic faithful. Because of the great number and variety of Catholic immigrant groups, all we can do here is touch lightly on certain patterns that recur with most of them.

Uprootedness and Instability

First, all the immigrants experienced to a greater or lesser extent what Oscar Handlin taught us to call "uprootedness."[5] Moving to a strange land, and often continuing to move about during their first few years in America, the immigrants were jarred loose from their social and psychic moorings. A common result was disorientation for the individual and instability for the group. A German priest working in Wisconsin touched on the heart of the matter in an 1855 letter to a mission-support society headquartered in Vienna. "All the resolutions made in Europe dissolve as soon as one feels the breezes of the American coastline," he wrote, and "every tie, including the one with God, must be retied here and must undergo the American '*probatum est*' before it can be said that it is secure."[6]

The adaptation of old habits and institutions and the creation of stable new relationships that this astute observer had in mind were not easily achieved for most Catholic immigrant groups. In religious behavior, the symptoms of unsettledness might either be apathy or chronic intra-group bickering. It was not unheard of for such quarrels to reach the stage of physical violence. In rural northern Ohio, for example, Catholic immigrants from different parts of Germany fell out over whose traditional hymns would be sung at Mass, and the quarrel grew so embittered that one faction burned down the church.[7]

An important factor in such instability was the characteristic shortage of priests in the earlier phases of the immigration of nearly all groups—and which continued as a more or less permanent shortage with the Italians. Without priests of their own, the religious situation of Catholic immigrants was inherently unstable. In cases where there was no other Catholic church near enough to attend, the immigrants were left utterly without the Mass and the sacraments which were essential to Catholic worship, and around which the religious and social life of the group could have formed itself. Even where there was an existing church nearby, it was never fully satisfactory if dominated by another group, for that usually meant differences in language and in devotional practices. Immigrants could not feel at home, religiously, in such circumstances; and if they were numerous enough to draw much attention to themselves, one fears that they were apt to be treated as intruders by the original Catholic congregation.

Hence it is understandable that Poles, for example, who often started out in German parishes, or Lithuanians, who started out in Polish parishes, hived off as soon as they could to establish their own churches. The characteristic method was to form a church-building society to collect funds, acquire real estate, and purchase or build a structure to serve as a house of worship.[8] Once possessed of a building, Catholic immigrants were all the more determined to get their own priest, if they did not already have one. They importuned bishops and were resentful when no priest was assigned, even though the bishop who failed to comply ordinarily did so simply because he had no priest. The immigrants might also try to attract a priest from the homeland, or from elsewhere in the U.S. where their countrymen were settled. Unfortunately, not all priests who made themselves available to serve immigrant congregations were of the best quality, and bishops as far back as John Carroll complained bitterly of the problems created by the kind of vagrant clergymen whom Carroll once characterized as "missionary adventurers."[9] The fault, of course, was not always on the side of the priests; and from their point of view the real problem was episcopal despotism. But however one distributes the blame, dissensions were chronic in the formative years of many,

12

perhaps most, immigrant congregations, as pastors came and went with dizzying rapidity. One student of Lithuanian immigration, for example, tells of a parish in Mount Carmel, Pennsylvania that had seventeen pastors in twenty years.[10]

Trusteeism in Immigrant Congregations

In the early nineteenth century, the term "trusteeism" was associated with troubles of this sort.[11] The term was derived from the legal arrangement widely prevailing in those days whereby ownership of local church property was vested in the hands of congregational trustees, nearly all of whom were laymen. Since they controlled the church property and the revenues accruing to it, the trustees were in a strong position to defy the bishop if he told them to accept as pastor a priest whom they disliked, or to dismiss one they did like, or if some other grievance arose between bishop and congregation. When such troubles developed, the congregation often split internally, so that trusteeism usually involved a struggle within the local group as well as between the local group and the bishop.

Disputes of this sort continued throughout the period of immigration.[12] Irish and German congregations were affected earliest because they were first on the scene; later in the nineteenth century, the French-Canadians, the Poles, the Italians, and other Catholic immigrant groups all went through the same thing. Trusteeism was a more serious matter in the early days, simply because the organizational structure of the Church was so fragile at the time, and because the groups involved came closer to including the whole of the Catholic population then. But the phenomenon itself recurred as each new group passed through the period of instability characteristic of its formative years.

Trustee controversies usually healed with time, but in some cases permanent or long-standing schisms occurred. In the case of Eastern rite groups like the Ruthenians (also known as Rusins and sometimes Ukrainians), disaffected congregations often switched over to the Orthodox Church.[13] Three examples among Roman Catholic groups illustrate the continuity of the issues. The Hogan Schism (named after the rebellious Irish priest, William Hogan) grew out of trustee problems in Philadelphia in the 1820's and lasted a number of years.[14] Similar difficulties among Polish immigrants in Scranton in the 1890's ultimately led to the creation of the schismatic Polish National Catholic Church. The leader here was the Reverend Francis Hodur, a Polish immigrant priest who was consecrated a bishop by an Old Catholic prelate in Europe in

40

1907.[15] And within the past year, a congregation of Vietnamese refugees in Port Arthur, Texas went into schism after a quarrel with their bishop that had all the classic elements of trusteeism. The bishop refused to appoint as pastor of the refugees the priest who came with them until the group turned over to him the deed to the building they had purchased as a place of worship. This the congregation was unwilling to do. They gave the bishop a deadline to meet their demands, and when he did not, they linked up with Archbishop Marcel Lefebvre's traditionalist Society of St. Pius X, where their desire to keep the Latin Mass (which is their mother tongue in religious matters) will not be the problem it might have been had they remained in the Roman Catholic Church.[16]

The determination of the Vietnamese in Texas to remain together and to reconstruct as much as possible of the religious life of their homeland is also a classic pattern among immigrants. This brings us to the "national parish," a characteristic feature of the Catholic immigrant scene, and the device that made it possible for many groups to achieve what the Vietnamese had in mind.

The National Parish

According to the provisions of the Council of Trent, all Catholics residing in a given area were supposed to belong to the territorial parish established for that locality. But in America, immigrants using different languages were settled heterogeneously in the same area, and it was obviously desirable for them to attend churches where they could hear the word of God preached in a language they understood. Hence, the national parish was one in which membership was defined according to language or nationality, rather than by place of residence. One or more national parishes might be established in a locality already served by a territorial parish, with each of the former serving its own specific ethnic clientele.

Theoretically, or officially, language rather than nationality itself furnished the pastoral justification for departure from the norm set up by Trent. But for the immigrants, there was more to it than language. Since language, culture, and religion were all bound up in an undifferentiated unity, the desire of immigrants to have "their own" churches went deeper than the mere question of being able to understand the sermon or go to confession conveniently in the mother tongue. For that reason, it was not enough to have one sermon a week in the mother tongue, or even to use the basement of the territorial church on a regular basis. Rather, as

Silvano Tomasi has shown for the Italians of New York, these were but the stages that preceded a successful group's establishment of its own autonomous parish.[17]

Not all ethnic parishes were national parishes. For if a certain nationality was first on the scene, and dominant in an area, they simply set up a church which became the territorial church of the locality. Thus, in some rural areas of the Midwest, the local church was "German" even though it was not a national parish. Similarly, a "Polish church" might be the territorial church for a neighborhood in Chicago. Indeed, Jay Dolan goes so far as to say that in New York City before the Civil War the coincidence of ethnic settlement and neighborhood made the distinction between national and territorial parishes "more fiction than fact."[18]

Topping off these complications, there were the Irish. They were certainly an ethnic group like other immigrant Catholics; yet they spoke English, and therefore their parishes were normally territorial rather than national parishes. Their situation was ambiguous and their feelings were correspondingly ambivalent.[19] They wanted "their own" churches just as the others did. And while they could accommodate the presence of a small number of outsiders in their midst, they were put off when the Germans, or Franco-Americans, or Italians, or whoever it might be, became numerous enough to be visible as a corporate body and assertive enough to demand special attention to their needs. But although they were as possessive as other groups about their parishes, the Irish also felt that, since they spoke the language of the country, they constituted the American Catholic norm and that it was up to the others to assimilate themselves to the language, mentality, and outlook of the Irish.

Given all these complications, plus the fact that the same parish might change its ethnic composition entirely as a result of continuing immigration and population shifts, it is entirely understandable that controversy often swirled around the national parish. It was so from the beginning. The first national parish was Holy Trinity in Philadelphia, formed in the 1780's by a group of Germans who split off from St. Mary's, which had previously served all of the Catholics of the city, both English- and German-speaking. In its first decade of existence, Holy Trinity went through the pattern that became all too familiar—a dispute with the bishop over who was to be the first pastor, subsequent disenchantment on the part of the trustees with their first choice, his dismissal and replacement, the appearance of still another attractive candidate for pastor, internal divisions in the congregation, a more serious dispute with the bishop, and then into schism for several years.[20]

Since national parishes and trustee-type upheavals so often went together, bishops had good reason to regard them warily. But the arrangement was so obviously necessary to meet the overwhelming pressure for pastoral care of the immigrants that the bishops had no real choice but to employ it. Hence, the national parish appeared everywhere that non-English-speaking immigrants were present in any numbers in the nineteenth century. Contrary to the impression sometimes given, the national parish did not have to be forced down the throats of the Americanizing bishops in the 1880's and 1890's.[21] Cardinal Gibbons and his episcopal allies recognized as well as anyone else that the national parish performed an indispensable function. The point on which they would differ from the spokesmen for the Germans at the time of the nationality controversy was *how long* the national parish would be needed to perform this function.

If there was active opposition to the formation of national parishes, it was more apt to come from the pastors of territorial parishes who were reluctant to see a portion of "their" congregations spin off to establish churches that would compete with the territorial churches for support from the surrounding Catholic population. Pastors of national parishes, for their part, often leveled a charge against the territorial churches that amounted to poaching—that is, they claimed that territorial pastors received into their churches persons who really belonged to the national church, even though they might live within the geographic confines of the territorial parish.[22]

The poaching charge obviously raised the question of how permanently people were bound to the national parish. Must an immigrant always belong to a national parish even if he understood English and found it more convenient to attend the regular territorial church? And what about the American-born children of the national parish, who were ordinarily more adept in English than in the ancestral tongue, except in cases where the ethnic group was unusually isolated? Were they still obligated to attend and support the national church they grew up in?

Here, we are back at a question already identified as one of the real issues dividing the Americanizers from those whom we can call ethnic loyalists. And while the desire of the latter to bind the second generation firmly to the national parish is perfectly understandable, still it seems to us that the Americanizers were correct in insisting that it should be a matter of free choice with the second generation whether they stayed in the national parish or joined an English-speaking territorial parish. So far as we know, Archbishop George Mundelein of Chicago was the first Americanizing prelate who has been shown to have followed a deliberate policy of holding back on the erection of new national parishes, and even he had to bend on this matter, especially with the Poles.[23] He pushed this policy most vigorously in the 1920's, which was a particularly sensitive time with respect to the Catholic un-Americanism charge; and, by that date, Mundelein could argue plausibly that the increasing numbers of the second generation made the need for new national parishes less pressing.

Generational Transition, the Language Question, and Immigrant Institutions

Generational transition—perhaps the most profound and poignant theme in immigration history—affected the other institutions besides the national parish.[24] We shall look briefly at how it interacted with three very important immigrant institutions, viz., the schools, the press, and the network of associations created by each ethnic group.

But first another word about the Irish. Their situation was anomalous among Catholic immigrant groups because they spoke English. Like all the others, the Irish established schools, newspapers, and various kinds of associations. But the fact that they used English affected the development of these institutions in two significant and inter-related ways. First, it meant that they were spared the "language question," the anguishing conflict over the dropping of the mother tongue and the shift to English that normally marked the transition of generations in non-English-speaking groups. Without the language shift, which was a conspicuous barometer of the overall change in foreign-language groups, generational transition among Irish Catholics was both less traumatic and less visible.

Secondly, the fact that Irish Catholic schools, newspapers, and societies used the language of the country made them more generically American and less particularistically Irish. This served to make the transition from Irish Catholicism to American Catholicism both easier and more elusive—elusive in the sense that it is difficult to get a grip on the process and trace its evolution. The linguistic situation of the Irish was thus a significant factor—together with their vast numbers, their early arrival, and their unusually high production of priestly vocations—in making the Irish the dominant group in shaping the Catholic Church in the

United States and in predisposing their leaders toward an Americanizing position.

Conversely, the need to resist linguistic assimilation predisposed the leaders of non-English-speaking groups toward an anti-Americanizing position. For though Americanization might be a murky matter in some respects, language was not one of them. Here the meaning of Americanization was brutally clear: it meant loss of the mother tongue with all its precious associations. Hence, the language question looms large in the story of the schools, press, and societies of foreign-speaking groups, and the transition of generations was tangled with the inflammatory issue of language transition.

In the case of the schools, preservation of the mother tongue was one of the primary goals of the institution itself. Bound up as it was with religion and culture, language was an integral part of the heritage which German, Franco-American, Polish, and other Catholic immigrants wished to hand on to their children through education. The Italians were a notable exception in failing to exhibit enthusiasm for the establishment of their own Catholic schools.[25] More typical were the Germans who claimed special credit for being more sensitive to the need for parochial schools than the Irish were. Since the aim was to socialize young children into the religiolinguistic culture of the ethnic group, the main effort was characteristically centered on elementary-level schools, but various groups also set up their own colleges and seminaries. It was more difficult to maintain foreign-language institutions of higher education, however, simply because the potential clientele was much smaller than in the case of primary schools.[26]

But besides wanting the schools to bind the young to their inherited culture, the immigrants also wanted them to prepare their children to advance in the new society in which they had been born. That these two goals were in tension with each other became unmistakable at the secondary and collegiate levels. On the one hand, it was clearly desirable from the viewpoint of ethnic group interests that promising young people receive higher education in order to prepare a leadership elite. But on the other hand it was even clearer that higher education often had the effect of moving the young people who received it "up and out" of the ethnic group. Here generational transition was coupled with upward social mobility and both were keyed to higher education.[27]

The dilemma worsened in the twentieth century as educational opportunities were extended to wider segments of the population, first on the secondary level and then on the collegiate. Although different groups responded in somewhat different ways, the overwhelming trend in the last half-century has been for second- and third-generation immigrant Catholics to pursue the available educational opportunities as far as they could.[28] In doing so, they became very much de-ethnicized in comparison with the immigrant generation. This came about, not because of any systematic program of Americanization carried out by the schools, but simply because these generations were born and lived in a different world from that of their parents and grandparents—a world made different to some extent by the widened horizons produced by increased educational opportunities.

Unlike the schools, which were developed with the needs of the second generation in mind, the other major immigrant institutions (the press and societies) evolved to meet the needs of the first generation. Among foreign language groups, newspapers in the mother tongue were an obvious necessity for persons who immigrated as adults knowing no English. Hardly any group was too small to support its own newspapers and magazines, and the larger Catholic groups boasted scores of such publications. The German Catholics, for example, founded some sixty-four daily, weekly, and monthly publications between 1837 and 1937.[29]

The real problems of the foreign-language press came with the maturing of the second generation, for the American-born did not depend on materials published in the ancestral language as their parents did. The second-generation problem was masked, however, so long as immigration continued in heavy volume, since losses among American-born readers were made good by newcomers from abroad. But when immigration from the old country dropped off, a steady decline soon set in. Again, the Germans furnish an apt illustration. Immigration fell off sharply in the 1890's and the next decade saw the beginnings of an irreversible deterioration. The oldest German Catholic paper in the country, the *Wahrheits-Freund* of Cincinnati, founded in 1837, complained in 1900 that the young people would have nothing to do with the "Dutch language," and seven years later it gave up the struggle and closed its doors forever.[30]

The linguistic-generational transition is also observable among immigrant societies. As in the case of the press, it produced here a good deal of bitterness and recrimination on the part of the older generation who regarded their American-born offspring as betraying their heritage. Although understandable, this reaction was somewhat unfair since the second generation included many who wished to remain loyal to their heritage. The more perceptive of these younger ethnic loyalists were aware, however, that modifications would have to be made in order to retain a hold on those for whom America was the mother country. Thus they could argue with good justification that, far from being a betrayal, the shift to English was the only thing that could preserve the cultural identity of the group and prevent its institutions from dying out with the passing of the first generation. The bilingual phase—the use of both English and the mother tongue in the meetings and publications of an ethnic association—was a sure sign that the linguistic-generational transition was well advanced.[31]

The Role of Immigrant Societies and Associations

Besides the generational problem, another thing that the associational life of Catholic immigrant groups had in common was the basic role played by benevolent, or mutual-aid, societies. Generally rooted in the ethnic parish, either territorial or national, the mutual-aid society provided a rudimentary form of economic protection from loss of income due to illness or injury. More comprehensive insurance schemes developed when the local societies joined together to form large national associations such as the German Catholic Central Verein (1855), the Irish Catholic Benevolence Union (1869), the Polish Roman Catholic Union (1874), or the First Catholic Slovak Union (1890).

More important than their insurance function, however, was the role played by the national federation as the representative organization of the ethnic group. All matters of interest to the group—such as immigrant aid work, the situation of the homeland, school matters, etc.—were discussed in the annual conventions, which were sometimes associated with open mass meetings featuring special speakers, musical presentations, and so on. In this manner, the national ethnic federation became a focus of the immigrant Catholic's loyalties and a kind of symbol of the group itself. For the German Catholic to belong to the Central Verein, let us say, or even to read about its doings in the paper, gave him a better sense of who he was and what it meant to be a German-American Catholic. Indeed, Victor Greene, who has done important work on the subject, argues that the origins of Polish ethnic consciousness in America are to be sought in the competing claims put forward by the two leading Polish societies, the Polish National Alliance (PNA) and the Polish Roman Catholic Union (PRCU). Confronted with these two versions of Polishness represented by the PNA and the PRCU, the Polish immigrant had to decide for himself what it meant to be a Pole.[32]

The split between the PNA and the PRCU was between "nationalists" and "clericalists." For the former, the political dimension of ethnicity was uppermost, and the true Pole was one who threw himself into the cause of the oppressed fatherland (which had ceased to exist politically in the 1790's after being dismembered by Russia, Prussia, and Austria). The leaders of the PNA recognized a close connection between Catholicity and Polishness, but they did not regard religion as an indispensable element in their national identity. They welcomed all Poles to their ranks, including liberals or nonbelievers, and they refused to be bound by clerical direction in their struggle for Polish liberation. The PRCU, on the other hand, held that one who was not a Catholic could not be a true Pole. It was founded by a priest and tightly controlled by clerics who were deeply suspicious of the irreligious tendencies of the lay nationalist PNA. The appeal of Poland's national cause for the immigrant rank and file eventually led the PRCU to a closer approximation of the nationalism of the competing organization.

The nationalist/clericalist split played a more prominent role among the Poles than with most other groups, but it was present in one form or another with a number of others. Clerical leaders were alert to prevent their people from being led astray by secular nationalists, and the First Catholic Slovak Union is not the only example of a national federation that was organized primarily to head off such a threat.[33] But this did not mean that clerical leaders were not nationalists themselves. A great many of them were strongly nationalistic. Where they differed from the secular political nationalists was in their understanding of nationality. From their viewpoint, nationality could not be divorced from religion, and neither could movements mobilizing the spiritual allegiance of a people be safely entrusted to any but religious authorities.

Since the clergy assumed so great a leadership role among Catholic immigrants, it is not surprising that another kind of ethnic society found among many groups was the priests' society. And since the priests were quite self-conscious about their leadership function, it was likewise natural that such clerical associations often took a highly militant line in championing the cause of whatever group was involved, asserting its rights, and so on. Thanks to the research of Colman J. Barry, O.S.B., we know more about the German Catholic Priester Verein[34] than about other priests' societies, but similar associations existed among the Belgians and Dutch,[35] the Poles,[36] and the Slovaks.[37] Even the Irish[38] formed such a society in Wisconsin, one of the few places they felt themselves to be the wronged minority. And a Lithuanian priests' society that was formed early in the twentieth century is still actively engaged in championing the ethnic cause: its vice-president demanded at the NCCB's "Ethnicity and Race" hearing in Newark in 1975 "That the American ethnic cultural parish be considered as being of permanent status because of its contributions religiously and culturally."[39] PADRES, organized by Mexican-American priests in 1969, is merely the most recent of such ethnic clerical associations which are dedicated to furthering the "religious, educational, and social rights" of the groups they represent. The very name PADRES declares this purpose, for it is an acronym for "Padres Asociado para Derechos Religiosos, Educativos y Sociales."

Conclusion

Mention of PADRES brings us to the present. Although much more could be said, we will conclude with a few observations suggested by consideration of the new ethnicity against the background of Catholic immigrant history.

In the first place, the fact that PADRES was founded less than a decade ago highlights the point that the Catholic population is not only diverse in background, but also that its constituent parts stand at different stages in their historical evolution. Despite having deep roots in the southwestern United States, the Mexican-Americans (and other Hispanics to an even greater degree) are the most recent immigrants among American Catholic ethnic groups. A heavy influx from Mexico continued after immigration from Europe was largely cut off. That fact, besides other factors contributing to their social isolation, kept the Mexican-American population at what might be called a first-generation stage of development long after second- and third-generation Mexican-Americans became numerically predominant.[40] The relative importance of the Spanish language among Mexican-Americans, as compared, say, to that of Polish among Polish-Americans today, confirms that the former group is only beginning to emerge from the first-generation stage of its evolution.

Comparing the Mexican-Americans with the Poles, to say nothing of the Irish or Germans, makes clear that the content of a group's ethnicity does not remain the same over a period of time. Rather, the history of a group—what happens to it over a period of time—is intrinsic to its ethnic identity at different points in its development. The history of the group is shaped by a multiplicity of factors that can be classed in two broad categories: those that are internal to the group, and those that impinge upon it from the surrounding culture. These factors interact with each other and with the biological constant of generational transition.

Examples of what we would call internal factors are such things as the size of the group, whether its settlement pattern was scattered or compact, the class and educational status of its members, and for Catholic groups, whether religion was closely associated with a people's struggle for national identity (as with Franco-Americans and Poles, for example) or whether the Church was only remotely connected with the self-identity of the group. A very important external factor would be the structure of economic and educational opportunity in American society when an ethnic group arrived, or when its second generation reached maturity. Thus, it was fortunate for the Irish that, having few skills, they arrived at a time when there was a great demand for unskilled workers in a country that was in the midst of such fabulous expansion that even unskilled labor constituted a promising launching point. And that coming of age of many second-generation Irish at the turn of the century meant that they were in a position to take advantage of new opportunities in such white-collar careers as schoolteaching.

Another kind of external factor, and one very pertinent today, is the prevailing American attitude toward immigration and assimilation. Contrast, for example, the coming of age of a second-generation German-American during World War I or the nativistic 1920's with the coming of age of a second-generation Mexican-American in the 1970's. In the former case, the weight of societal pressure would surely reinforce whatever tendency the individual felt toward affirmation of an "American" identity. But today one would certainly expect the young Chicano to be more assertive about his "ethnic identity." In fact, "Chicano" seems a good deal more attractive a designation than "Anglo," a term used in the southwest for non-Hispanic Americans which is working its way into general usage, and which carries with it the negative connotations it bears in its place of origin. And WASP, as John Higham has pointed out, is the only ethnic slur still permissible among right-thinking persons.[41]

Indeed, it almost seems today that, for the first time in our national history, it is more honorific to claim an "ethnic" identity than simply to affirm that one is an American. Or, if one does make such an affirmation, he invites the retort that there is no such thing as an American identity as such—there are only WASPS and other less unattractive ethnics. While this simply removes Americanness as an available option, it is not the worst that has happened to the linguistic symbols of national identity, for "Americanization" has been turned into a term of abuse. The same is true of the closely associated terms "assimilation" and "Melting Pot."

It strikes us as a symptom of profound national self-loathing that such a rhetorical situation could have developed in the discussion of ethnic affairs. For what this kind of language implies is that the nation no longer represents values deserving to be held up as ideals for immigrants to accept, identify themselves with, and defend. Considering the background of Vietnam, Watergate, and the domestic traumas associated with the Black Revolution, campus upheavals, the counter-culture, and womens' liberation, it would not be difficult to explain how this discrediting of traditional national symbols came about. But leaving all this aside, one can still say that the situation is an unnatural and unhealthy one. It is unnatural and unhealthy because a people that does not believe in itself is in trouble, and the continued association of terms like "Americanism" and "Americanization" with what are portrayed as being reprehensible policies inevitably tends to erode belief in the values that have given the nation a sense of what it stands for.

In respect to American Catholic immigrant history, the prevailing rhetoric has tended to create stereotyped attitudes and expectations—prejudices, in other words—as mistaken and misleading as any they have replaced. Few commentators today, for example, would hesitate to brand as naive and simplistic the view that the nationalism of the Americanizers was always legitimate, and that they always acted justly in dealing with obstreperous ethnic groups. But would not one whose views were shaped by the current discussion be very likely to assume that every expression of ethnic nationalism was legitimate in the controversies of the past, and that justice was always on the side of the immigrant groups who claimed to be resisting oppression by an intolerant hierarchy? Would that stereotyped expectation also be recognized as naive and simplistic?

We believe both sets of stereotyped expectations—both prejudices—are crippling to efforts to understand the Catholic ethnic situation, either in the past or at present. There were real conflicts of value between different groups representing different policy options in the past, and there are also real conflicts in the 1970's. We have to take seriously the claims of both sides. Today that means refusing to be made to feel guilty about Americanization as much as it ever meant refusing to feel guilty about resisting Americanization in the past.

Footnotes

[1] Ernest L. Tuveson. *Redeemer Nation: The Idea of America's Millenial Role* (Chicago: University of Chicago Press, 1968). The standard work on attitudes toward Catholics in early America is Mary Augustina Ray, *American Opinion of Roman Catholicism in the Eighteenth Century* (New York: Columbia University Press, 1936). See also David B. Davis, "Some Themes of Countersubversion: An Analysis of Anti-Masonic, Anti-Catholic, and Anti-Mormon Literature," *Mississippi Valley Historical Review*, 47 (September, 1960), 205–224; and Clifford S. Griffin, "Converting the Catholics: American Benevolent Societies and the Ante-Bellum Crusade Against the Church," *Catholic Historical Review*, 47 (October, 1961), 325–41.

[2] Timothy L. Smith. "Protestant Schooling and American Nationality, 1800–1850," *Journal of American History* 53 (March 1967), pp. 679–695. The most recent general survey of American Catholic educational efforts is Harold A. Buetow *Of Singular Benefit: The Story of U.S. Catholic Education* (New York: Macmillan, 1970); see Vincent P. Lannie, *Public Money and Parochial Education: Bishop Hughes, Governor Seward and the New York School Controversy* (Cleveland: Press of Case Western Reserve University, 1968) for a good case study of a particular educational controversy.

[3] Thomas T. McAvoy, C.S.C.. *The Great Crisis in American Catholic History 1895–1900* (Chicago: Henry Regnery, 1957) has coverage of the controversy in detail. Other aspects of it are dealt with in Robert D. Cross, *The Emergence of Liberal Catholicism in America* (Cambridge: Harvard University Press, 1958) and John Tracy Ellis, *The Life of James Cardinal Gibbons, Archbishop of Baltimore, 1834–1921*, 2 vols. (Milwaukee: Bruce Publishing Co., 1952), especially vol. II, chap. 16. Philip Gleason, "Coming to Terms with American Catholic History," *Societas* 3 (Autumn, 1973), 283–312, contains a review of the pertinent literature.

[4] G. F. Theriault. "The Franco-Americans in a New England Community: An Experiment in Survival," unpubl. Ph.D. Diss. Harvard University, 1951 contains the best discussion of language and religion, p. 538ff.

[5] Oscar Handlin. *The Uprooted: The Epic Story of The Great Migrations that Made the American People* (Boston: Little, Brown, 1951). For a critique of Handlin's view see Rudolph J. Vecoli, "The Contadini in Chicago: A Critique of *The Uprooted*," *Journal of American History* 51 (December 1964), pp. 404–417.

[6] Philip Gleason. *The Conservative Reformers German-American Catholics and the Social Order* (Notre Dame, Indiana, University of Notre Dame Press 1968), p. 21.

[7] Ibid., p. 21.

[8] Victor Greene. *For God and Country The Rise of Polish and Lithuanian Consciousness in America 1860–1910* (Madison, Wisconsin: State Historical Society of Wisconsin Press 1975), chs. 2 and 3 contain information on the propensity of immigrants to acquire property. See also Timothy L. Smith. "Lay Initiative in the Religious Life of American Immigrants, 1880–1950," in Tamara K. Hareven (ed.) *Anonymous Americans Explorations in Nineteenth Century Social History* (Englewood Cliffs, New Jersey: Prentice Hall, 1971), pp. 214–249.

[9] Thomas O'Brien Hanley (ed.). *The John Carroll Papers*, 3 vols., (Notre Dame, Indiana: Univ. of Notre Dame Press, 1976), I, pp. 292, 389, 431.

[10] Sr. M. Timothy Audyaitis. "Catholic Action of the Lithuanians in the United States: A History of the American Lithuanian Roman Catholic

Federation, 1906–1956," unpub. M.A. Thesis, Loyola University (Chicago), 1958, p. 26. Daniel Buczek, *Immigrant Pastor* (Waterbury, Conn.: Heminway Corp., 1974), is a superb history of a Polish parish and biography of a Polish-American priest, Msgr. Lucyan Bójnowski, which illuminates many of the themes mentioned in this article.

[11]Among the older works on trusteeism are: Patrick J. Dignan. *A History of the Legal Incorporation of Church Property in the United States, 1784–1932* (Washington, D.C.: Cath. Univ. of Amer. Press, 1933); Peter Guilday *The Catholic Church in Virginia 1815–1822* (New York: U.S. Catholic Historical Soc., 1924); Guilday *The Life and Times of John England, First Bishop of Charleston (1786–1842),* 2 vols., (New York: America Press, 1927), I, chs. VI–XIV; Guilday "Trusteeism," *Historical Records and Studies,* 18 (1928), p. 7–73; Robert F. McNamara "Trusteeism in the Atlantic States, 1785–1863," *Catholic Historical Review* 30 (July 1944), pp. 135–154; Albert G. Stritch "Trusteeism in the Old Northwest, 1800–1850," ibid., pp. 155–164. Two more recent treatments are: Jo Ann Manfra "The Catholic Episcopacy in America, 1789–1852," unpubl. Ph.D. Diss., University of Iowa, 1975, ch. V; and Patrick W. Carey "John England and Irish American Catholicism 1815–1842; A Study of Conflict," unpubl. Ph.D. Diss., Fordham University, 1975, chs. III–IV. Carey is now at work on a badly needed general study of the subject.

[12]For examples of trustee-type problems among later arrivals, see Henry B. Leonard, "Ethnic Conflict and Episcopal Power: the Diocese of Cleveland, 1847–1870," *Catholic Historical Review* 62 (July 1976) pp. 388–407; Greene *For God and Country,* esp. chs. 4–6; and Richard S. Sorrell "The Sentinelle Affair (1924–1929) and *Militant Survivance:* The Franco-American Experience in Woonsocket, Rhode Island," unpubl. Ph.D. Diss., State University of New York at Buffalo, 1975, esp. ch. 4. Immigrants from foreign countries were not the only ones affected. See Sr. Ramona Mattingly, *The Catholic Church on the Kentucky Frontier (1785–1812)* (Washington, D.C.: Cath. U. of America Press, 1936), pp. 93–4, 139 for reference to a "republican" or "presbyterian" constitution for a parish in Kentucky in 1807.

[13]Gerald P. Fogarty, S. J. "The American Hierarchy and Oriental Rite Catholics 1890–1907," *Records of the American Catholic Historical Society of Philadelphia* 85 (March–June 1974), pp. 17–28. Cf. also, Bohdan P. Procko, "The Establishment of the Ruthenian Church in the United States, 1884–1907," *Pennsylvania History,* 42 (April, 1975) 137–54; and Procko, "Sotor Ortynsky, First Ruthenian Bishop in the United States, 1907–1916," *Catholic Historical Review,* 58 (Jan., 1973), 513–33.

[14]Hugh J. Nolan. *The Most Reverend Francis Patrick Kenrick, Third Bishop of Philadelphia, 1830–1851* (Philadelphia: American Catholic Historical Society, 1948) contains a good account of the Hogan Schism. For a longer account see Francis E. Tourscher, *The Hogan Schism and Trustee Troubles in St. Mary's Church, Philadelphia, 1820–1829* (Philadelphia: Peter Reilly Co., 1930).

[15]Warren C. Platt. "The Polish National Catholic Church: An Inquiry Into Its Origins," *Church History* 46 (December 1977), pp. 474–489; William Galush, "The Polish National Catholic Church: A Survey of its Origins, Development and Missions," *Records of the American Catholic Historical Society of Philadelphia* 83 (September–December 1972), pp. 131–149. Cf also Buczek, *Immigrant Pastor, passim.*

[16]"Vietnamese Join Traditionalists." *National Catholic Reporter,* 13 January 1978, p. 5.

[17]Silvano M. Tomasi. *Piety and Power: The Role of The Italian Parishes.*

26

in the *New York Metropolitan Area, 1880–1930* (Staten Island, New York: Center for Migration Studies, 1975), p. 62, 76 ff.

[18]Jay P. Dolan. *The Immigrant Church: New York's Irish and German Catholics, 1815–1865* (Baltimore: Johns Hopkins University Press, 1975), p. 21.

[19]This notion is similar to that found in Milton L. Barron, "Intermediacy: Conceptualization of Irish Status in America," *Social Forces* 27 (March 1949), pp. 256–263. Carl Wittke. *The Irish in America* (Baton Rouge: Louisiana State Univ. Press, 1956), ch. 9, is an informative, brief discussion of "The Irish and the Catholic Church."

[20]Francis Hertkorn. *A Retrospect of Holy Trinity Parish* (Philadelphia: Press of F. McManus, Jr. and Co., 1914); Vincent J. Fecher, S.V.D. *A Study of the Movement for German National Parishes in Philadelphia and Baltimore (1787–1802)* (Rome: Apud Aedes Universitatis Gregorianae 1955).

[21]A recent student of Franco-Americans in New England, who were among the bitterest resisters of Americanization, has this to say: "Finally the militant Franco-American claim of unrelenting persecution by the Irish Church hierarchy is false. It is true that the Church was often more assimilationist than civil authorities in America, something which was hard for French-Canadian immigrants to realize since in Quebec Catholicism was the bulwark of *survivance*. However, outward harrassment by Irish bishops was the exception. Most of the New England bishops from 1870 until the 1920's, including those of the Rhode Island diocese, were willing to allow the formation of Franco-American national parishes and the continuation of the French language, as long as bilingualism was provided for. Between 1865 and 1890 there was only one attempt (Fall River) to prevent the establishment of a Franco-American parish. But the assimilationist atmosphere was pervasive, and its veiled and sometimes insidious nature made Franco-Americans quick to seize upon any evident harrassment." Sorrell, "The Sentinelle Affair" p. 137.

[22]For resistance on the part of territorial pastors see Tomasi, *Piety and Power*, p. 80. An example of the problems sometimes created is given by James W. Sanders, *The Education of an Urban Minority: Catholics in Chicago, 1833–1965* (New York: Oxford Univ. Press, 1977), p. 49 in describing the situation of a German church becoming Polish. "The crisis between St. Boniface and the encircling Polish strongholds produced a comedy of ethnic errors. First, the strongly nationalistic German pastor tried 'every promising means' to 'keep his own people clustered around the church.' The efforts included successful lobbying for newly paved streets, sewer installation, and even the 10-acre Eckert Park. Meanwhile, he spoke publicly against the Poles, snubbed them in the streets, and made them generally unwelcome in parish and school. But to no avail. The Germans departed anyway, and the parish income no longer met expenses, nor could it even pay interest on the debt. Finally, in 1916, the Archbishop appointed a new, more realistic German pastor who welcomed the Poles and laboriously learned their language. For his efforts he earned the bitter accusations of neighboring Polish pastors for enticing their parishioners into the German church." p. 49.

[23]Sanders. *Education of an Urban Minority*, ch. 7; Andrew Greeley "Catholicism in America: 200 Years and Counting," *The Critic* 34 (Summer 1976), p. 32. For another view see Charles H. Shanabruch, "The Catholic Church's Role in the Americanization of Chicago's Immigrants, 1833–1928," unpubl. Ph.D. Diss., University of Chicago, 1975, ch. 9.

[24]Gleason. *Conservative Reformers* is a detailed treatment of this theme in regard to German-American Catholics.

[25]Sanders. *Education of an Urban Minority*, pp. 67–71.

[26]When the American founder of Benedictine monasticism, Boniface Wimmer, O.S.B., came to the U.S. in 1846, he planned to serve German Catholics exclusively and to provide schools for them up through the seminary level. Within a year of his arrival, however, Wimmer had to advise his sponsors in Bavaria that this plan was impracticable because the Germans were too mixed together with Americans and Irish. Hence Wimmer shifted to a plan for educating a bilingual clergy, according to which he would admit English-speaking as well as German students. "Henceforth, he proposed to educate English boys for the Germans and German boys for the English. Moreover, he stated that by accepting English students he would avoid conflicts with Irish bishops and at the same time contribute towards the amalgamation of the two Catholic elements in America which had continued to oppose each other to the detriment of both." Henry A. Szarnicki, "The Episcopate of Michael O'Connor, First Bishop of Pittsburgh, 1843–1860" unpubl. Ph.D. Diss. Catholic University of America, 1971, pp. 179–80.

[27]Philip Gleason, "American Catholic Higher Education: A Historical Perspective," in *The Shape of Catholic Higher Education*, ed. by Robert Hassenger (Chicago: Univ. of Chicago Press, 1967), p. 23.

[28]Andrew M. Greeley. *Religion and Career* (New York: Sheed and Ward, 1963); Greeley, *The Education of Catholic Americans* (Chicago: Aldine Pub. Co., 1966); Greeley, *From Backwater to Mainstream* (New York: McGraw-Hill, 1969); and Stephen Steinberg, *The Academic Melting Pot* (New York: McGraw-Hill, 1974).

[29]Gleason, *Conservative Reformers* p. 48.

[30]Ibid.

[31]Ibid., ch. III and passim.

[32]Greene, *For God and Country* and for a shorter version see his article "For God and Country" *Church History* 35 (December 1966), pp. 446–460.

[33]Cf. Sr. M. Martina Tybor, S.S.C.M., "Slovak American Catholics," *Jednota Annual Furdek* 16 (January 1977), p. 60.

[34]Colman J. Barry, O.S.B. *The Catholic Church and German Americans* (Milwaukee: Bruce Pub. Co., 1953), p. 98 ff.

[35]Gerald F. De Jong, *The Dutch in America 1609–1974* (Boston: Twayne Publishers, 1975), pp. 200–1.

[36]Greene, *For God and Country*, p. 169.

[37]Tybor, "Slovak American Catholics," p. 61.

[38]Barry, *The Catholic Church and German Americans* p. 125.

[39]*Liberty and Justice for All*. Newark Hearing (Washington: National Conference of Catholic Bishops, 1975), p. 20.

[40]As Celia Heller notes, "What typically took place in immigrant groups in the second generation is now occurring among third- and fourth-generation Mexican Americans. . . . Also, these third- and fourth-generation Americans are facing the problems of marginality and assimilation which other ethnic groups met in the second generation." Celia S. Heller, *New Converts to the American Dream? Mobility Aspirations of Young Mexican Americans* (New Haven: College and University Press, 1971), p. 14.

[41]John Higham, *Send These To Me* (New York: Atheneum, 1975), p. 13. Higham adds in a footnote that he can only trace WASP back to 1964, but

28 that when it was picked up by writers like Peter Schrag and Michael Novak it "became synonymous with a dessicated, life-denying culture." See also Irving Lewis Allen, "WASP—From Sociological Concept to Epithet," *Ethnicity*, 2 (1975), 153–62.

THE NATIONAL PARISH: CONCEPT AND CONSEQUENCES FOR THE DIOCESE OF HARTFORD, 1890-1930

BY

DOLORES ANN LIPTAK, R.S.M.[*]

The precise meaning of the term "national parish" apparently presents difficulties even for those quite knowledgeable about the Catholic Church in the United States. For some, it connotes beleaguered minority groups valiantly—or even deviously—attempting to preserve their ethnic or cultural rights in the face of unco-operative and insensitive bishops. For others, more familiar with the ethnic experience within the Church, it simply signifies a distinct status of parochial existence in certain dioceses for Catholics whose membership in the Church somehow differed from the perceived ecclesiastical norm. In either case, the national parish has been viewed as the exception to the rule, a variant of the primary organizational unit within the Church.[1]

Confusion about the national parish in the United States has been compounded by the fact that the American Church functioned as a mission from its organization in 1790 until 1908. While the American Church remained a missionary Church, its hierarchy did not possess all the same canonical prerogatives as European diocesan bishops; thus, they were not empowered to establish parishes, in the strict canonical sense of the term. In fact, it was not until the revision of canon law was further clarified in 1922 that all parishes in the United States were finally raised to the level of canonical parishes. Thus, an investigation of the national parish, especially its development as an American Catholic phenomenon, can only help to

---

*Sister Dolores Ann is a historical and archival consultant and the historian of the Archdiocese of Hartford.

[1] Although historians of various Catholic ethnic minority groups have written the history of particular parishes or dioceses within the American Catholic experience, only one unpublished doctoral dissertation has specifically addressed itself to the "national parish" *per se* (see following footnote). Until the 1960's, furthermore, Catholic historians have fallen back upon arguments first developed by Colman J. Barry, O.S.B., in his *The Catholic Church and German Americans* (Milwaukee, 1953), which concentrates upon the negative impact of the development of national parishes. As Moses Rischin remarked in "The New American Catholic History," *Church History*, XLI (June, 1972), 227: "It seems apparent that American Catholic historians have not yet settled upon stratagems to incorporate the newer ethnics into their story so as to portray the almost unique cosmopolitan sweep of American Catholicism."

illumine questions concerning the origin and character of American parochial organization, as well as provide insights into the specific purpose and value of the national parish.[2]

What is the essence of the national parish? How and why did the national parish originate and develop in the United States and, more specifically, in certain American dioceses? Finally, why has the national parish so often been viewed as an exceptional (deviant) form of parochial organization—so much so, in fact, that misunderstandings, even controversies over its composition and role, have persisted to the present day?[3]

According to Joseph E. Ciesluk, whose 1944 doctoral dissertation, "National Parishes in the United States," provided much of the informational background regarding canonical aspects of the American parochial system for this paper, the national parish has been an integral part of Church jurisdiction for centuries. Described under the category "non-territorial" or "personal," it has long been used by bishops when they believed that the simpler, more popular "territorial principle" of organization did not adequately address the needs of the Catholic people entrusted to their care. First recognized in the Fourth Lateran Council and in the thirteenth-century decretals of Gregory IX, and later acknowledged by the Council of Trent in the sixteenth century, the "non-territorial" principle of formation meant that parishes were organized not on the basis of numbers and locations but according to the particular character of the people or families requiring service. Whenever the common ties that bound a particular group of people together became the primary reason for the formation of a separate parish, bishops had the power to establish non-territorial, or personal, parishes.[4]

In the United States, the national parish became a particular American version of the non-territorial parish. Utilized by bishops to deal with large immigrant communities whose language and nationality set them apart from other Catholics, the national parish made its appearance during the

[2] Joseph E. Ciesluk, *National Parishes in the United States* ("The Catholic University of America, Canon Law Studies," No. 190 [Washington, D.C., 1944]). Ciesluk has written the definitive monograph on the development of the national parish from the medieval European experiences to its American metamorphosis.

[3] According to Thomas T. McAvoy, C.S.C., an eminent Catholic historian, the origin of the use of national parishes in the United States stems from the controversy aroused by the Reverend Peter Abbelen in 1886. In that year, permission was obtained from Rome for bishops to erect national parishes in the United States. See Thomas T. McAvoy, *The History of the Catholic Church in the United States* (Notre Dame, Indiana, 1969), p. 274.

[4] Ciesluk, *op. cit.*, pp. 17-25.

episcopate of the first ordinary of the United States, John Carroll, the first
Bishop of Baltimore. As early as 1791, moreover, specific legislation to
provide for non-English-speaking Catholics was incorporated within the
original code of laws issued by the American Catholic clergy. With the
revision of the Code of Canon Law in 1918, the twin elements that, for
more than a century, had been used to distinguish national parishes in the
United States—language and nationality—continued as the basic reason
for the creation of national rather than territorial parishes.[5]

The record of national parish formation in the United States, however,
clearly indicates that the decisions involving the establishment of national
parishes differed from diocese to diocese, and often met with mixed results.
From the start, of course, the motivating force behind the formation of
national parishes had been practical: providing for the spiritual welfare of
an ever-expanding, non-English-speaking Catholic population. Thus,
from the middle of the nineteenth century, bishops not only had authorized the establishment of numerous German and French parishes, but then
had also begun to organize parishes for Slavic and Italian immigrants as
well. By the 1870's, a dozen or more national parishes had already been
established in each of the growing metropolises of New York and Chicago,
while half that number served varied immigrant communities in Pittsburgh, Cleveland, and several other industrializing communities.[6] Moreover, in the years that bridged 1900, as many more thousands of new
immigrants from southern and eastern Europe began to crowd the nation's
cities, some bishops reacted to the constant barrage of new immigrant
requests by founding a mosaic of national parishes, especially in the large
urban areas of the mid-Atlantic and Midwestern states. However, a review
of the dioceses that developed within these areas reveals that in relatively
few does there seem to have been any comprehensive plan for the incorporation of new immigrants. The evidence also suggests that, even in dioceses sensitive to the needs of newcomers, efforts expended to assist
immigrants tended to meet so much opposition as to render them only
moderately successful.[7]

59

---

[5] There were, however, dioceses that avoided the creation of national parishes. Thus,
according to *The Catholic Directory* (1909), the Dioceses of Springfield (Massachusetts),
Manchester (New Hampshire), and Portland (Maine) did not even list national parishes,
despite the presence of ethnic minorities previously cited as members of certain parishes.

[6] *Catholic Directory*, 1875.

[7] For this variety of experiences, see Richard M. Linkh, *American Catholicism and European Immigrants, 1900-1924* (New York, 1975). Also see Charles Shanabruch, *Chicago's
Catholics: The Evolution of an American Identity* (Notre Dame, Indiana, 1981).

The Diocese of Hartford, now the Archdiocese of Hartford with two suffragan sees, Bridgeport and Norwich, is an interesting example. Of all the dioceses of New England, it was the only one that responded effectively and consistently to immigrant requests, eventually establishing a remarkably diverse network of national parishes. So committed were its bishops to finding priests and developing procedures to incorporate immigrants that, by 1930, almost thirty percent of the parishes of the diocese were specifically national parishes, while almost twenty percent of the clergy derived from "new immigrant" background. A policy of parochial development first set into motion under its turn-of-the-century bishops, Lawrence S. McMahon (1879-1893) and Michael Tierney (1894-1908), this concerted effort to provide appropriate personnel and to establish parishes for immigrants can today be viewed as one of the most outstanding achievements of the diocese. Yet, the value of these efforts remains to this day a controversial subject. For that reason, it seems useful to investigate the specific phenomenon of national parish formation as it occurred within the Diocese of Hartford.[8]

Bishop McMahon was the first of Connecticut's early bishops to formulate a clear policy with respect to immigrants' requests for parishes. In matter-of-fact tones, he answered a letter written in 1889 by an Irish lawyer acting on behalf of a group that referred to itself as "Slovanians." "If they act like other Catholics," the bishop advised, "I will help them all I can."[9] McMahon was suggesting, in effect, that he would co-operate fully with immigrant Catholics if they met the same criteria as the diocese used with respect to other requesting groups, namely, that there was a sufficiently large number petitioning for the new parish, and that there were funds not only to establish but also to maintain it. In the case presented here, the bishop's advice was accepted; by 1891 St. John Nepomucene—perhaps the first ethnic-Slovak parish in the United States—had been founded.[10] By the end of his administration in 1893,

[8]See Dolores Ann Liptak, "European Immigrants and the Catholic Church in Connecticut" (Ph.D. dissertation, University of Connecticut, 1979; to be published by the Center for Migration Studies), Chapter II, "The Formation and Consolidation of the Multi-Ethnic Diocese of Hartford," pp. 80-163.

[9]Bishop Lawrence McMahon to S. Loewith, April 9, 1889, Episcopal Papers, Archives of the Archdiocese of Hartford (cited hereafter as Episcopal Papers, *AAH*). For biographical data on Bishop McMahon, see James H. O'Donnell, *History of the Diocese of Hartford* (Boston, 1900), pp. 166-178.

[10]According to some Slovak historians, the first Slovak parishes were in Streator, Illinois, and Hazelton, Pennsylvania. Yet Hoffmanns' *Catholic Directory* for both 1889—the year before the Bridgeport petition—and 1892—the year after the Bridgeport parish was

moreover, McMahon had followed the same procedures, entailing the same criteria, in establishing eleven national parishes, three of these specifically organized to serve new immigrant Slovak, Polish, and Italian congregations. At the time of his death, he was also considering the establishment of what would later become the first Lithuanian parish in New England.[11]

What Bishop McMahon inaugurated would come to full fruition during the administration of his successor, Michael Tierney. During the latter's productive term of office, one of the most creative and ambitious programs for immigrants devised by any American Catholic bishop was developed. Only one month after he was consecrated sixth ordinary of Hartford, Tierney initiated his involvement with immigrant groups by granting the pending request of Waterbury's Lithuanian community to establish their own parish. His respect for the uniqueness of each immigrant constituency and readiness to assist them was apparent. Thus he was able to witness the dedications of both a Lithuanian and a Polish parish in New Britain during the same year, 1896, while in Bridgeport he took note of the sensitivity of a small Hungarian community, allowing them to establish a parish separate from the one already established by their fellow Austro-Hungarians, the "ethnic-Slovaks" of St. John's. In fact, to every request or demand for incorporation within the diocese submitted by immigrant groups, Tierney gave a constructive, pastoral response. By the end of his administration in 1908, twenty-eight national parishes had been organized; eleven of these were for Polish Catholics; seven, for Italians; four, for Lithuanians; and two apiece for French-Canadians, Hungarians, and Slovaks.[12]

61

---

formed—does not support this contention since, for both years, they are referred to as Hungarian parishes. In the same directory, the Bridgeport church is referred to as "Slavonian." In our opinion, this distinction is significant because it indicates the way the ethnic people involved viewed themselves at that time and how they were seen by their church officials. Bridgeport's Slovak church is acknowledged as "Mother parish of Slovaks" with regard to New England at least. See *Bridgeport Sunday Post*, May 18, 1941 and February 6, 1963.

[11] The national parishes were St. John Nepomucene (Slovak), Bridgeport; St. Stanislaus (Polish), Meriden; and St. Michael (Italian), New Haven. The Lithuanian parish, incorporated soon after the consecration of his successor, was St. Joseph, Waterbury.

[12] For details of Tierney's treatment of ethnic minorities, see Liptak, *op. cit.*, pp. 112-128, and Appendix, "Parishes for Ethnic Minorities Established During the Administration of Bishop Michael Tierney (1894-1908)," pp. 424-425. His sensitivity to immigrant needs was the chief characteristic noted at the time of his death by both Catholic and secular newspapers; see *The Catholic Transcript*, October 8, 1908; also *Hartford Times* and *Hartford Courant*, October 8, 1908.

The cities of the diocese were the most affected by Bishop Tierney's liberal policy of establishing national parishes. Eight of Bridgeport's thirteen parishes, four of New Britain's five, and almost half of the parishes serving the state's other major cities (Hartford, New Haven, and Waterbury) were organized to serve the newest immigrants. No other New England diocese—regardless of its ethnic makeup or numbers—could claim such a number and such a variety of national parishes. By contrast, the bustling immigrant entrepôt of Boston could list only nine national parishes among its fifty-seven parishes. Elsewhere in the Northeast, only the Dioceses of Newark, Brooklyn, and New York could approximate Hartford's record.[13]

The legacy of Bishops McMahon and Tierney, especially with regard to the needs of southern and eastern Europeans, also informed the course of action undertaken by John Nilan, Bishop of Hartford from 1910 to 1934. Almost a third of the parishes founded during his twenty-four-year tenure would be for the "new immigrants" of the diocese. But Nilan had one advantage over earlier bishops: He could place in charge of many of the national parishes Connecticut-born, second-generation American priests, themselves the products of the very national parishes that had been founded by his predecessors.[14]

What, then, accounts for the widely credited assumption that the attempts of Catholic Church leaders in the United States to establish national parishes and attend to immigrants' needs were undistinguished, even unsuccessful? Why does the argument persist that most attempts made by bishops to establish parishes can be explained more by the bishops' desire to control groups that might threaten their power than by any appropriate concern to provide properly for all Catholics committed to their care?[15]

[13] *The Catholic Directory*, 1909; see also Liptak, *op. cit.*, "Urban Parishes Founded by End of Bishop Tierney's Administration (1908)," Appendix A, pp. 427-428.

[14] For listing of national parishes founded by Nilan, see Liptak, *op. cit.*, Appendix, pp. 426, and pp. 128-137. Thus, it would be Bishop Nilan who would place Paul Piechocki, the first Polish-American to attend the minor seminary founded by Bishop Tierney, in charge of a Polish congregation in Union City, Connecticut.

[15] Besides Linkh, *American Catholicism and European Immigrants*, there are other historical and sociological works which consistently argue this negative perspective. See Rudolph J. Vecoli, "Prelates and Peasants: Italian Immigrants and the Catholic Church," *Journal of Social History*, II (Spring, 1969), 217-268; Michael Novak, *The Rise of the Unmeltable Ethnics* (New York, 1972), or Daniel S. Buczek, *Immigrant Pastor: The Life of the Right Reverend Lucyan Bójnowski of New Britain, Connecticut* (Waterbury, Connecticut, 1974). The viewpoint seems particularly strong in writings by authors who belong to the same ethnic constituency about which they are writing.

To my mind, the principal reason for these critical conclusions derives primarily from highly publicized stories of controversy and struggle that did, indeed, bedevil the initial stages of almost every national parish, and that, therefore, could be used to suggest that official Church policy was mainly self-serving. A review of some of the problems encountered during the episcopates of Bishops McMahon, Tierney, and Nilan in pursuit of their goal of national parish-building in the Diocese of Hartford should help to illustrate how easily such an erroneous position could gain credence.

Mark, for example, the disappointment expressed in McMahon's reply to the Congregation de Propaganda Fide in 1888 when questioned about an Italian priest whom he had appointed pastor of an immigrant congregation in New Haven:

> . . . After a little time it was evident that (   ) had more zeal for his own interests than for the salvation of souls. The principal object of his exhortations was the obligation on the part of the people to give money to the priests. He claimed injuries against his Italian compatriots . . . . He made no secret in public of his contempt for the poor and unhappy people . . . . He has served the Italians . . . for seven or eight months . . . and has received . . . 750 *lire* besides his board and lodging. He has received more than these works have merited according to justice and more than he would have received if he had been fully Rector.[16]

It was because the priest had ". . . shown himself altogether devoid of apostolic zeal, tact, and prudence in caring for the people, and as he was perfectly useless for the ministry in spite of several repeated warnings," the bishop further explained, that he had informed the priest "that his time of testing was past and there was no further need of him."[17]

His first attempt to provide for the spiritual welfare of the Italian immigrants having failed so drastically, Bishop McMahon sought another way to achieve his goal. Within a year of the priest's departure, the bishop had managed to acquire the services of a newly organized religious community, the Society of St. Charles Borromeo, whose headquarters were in Piacenza, Italy. Later referred to as the "Scalabrinians," the community not only brought order to St. Michael Parish, taking charge of it in 1889, but was soon involved in the formation of two additional New Haven parishes.[18] Their assistance notwithstanding, dissension continued to disturb

63

---

[16]Bishop Lawrence Stephen McMahon to Cardinal Simeoni, Rome (translated by the Reverend E. O'Hara), February 10, 1888, Episcopal Papers, AAH.

[17]*Ibid.*

[18]Giovanni Schiavo, *Italian-American History*, Vol. II: *The Italian Contribution to the Catholic Church in America* (New York, 1949), p. 570.

the Italian immigrant community. In 1904, for example, McMahon's successor, Michael Tierney, wrote to Bishop Scalabrini in Italy that he needed "two priests of strong character" to reassert discipline in New Haven. He added this stern warning:

> Recently, I explained to Father Novati, superior of the congregation of St. Charles in this country, that if the Fathers found it impossible to maintain discipline in the parish, I could put diocesan priests in charge, as there are 20 of the diocesan clergy who speak Italian . . . .[19]

Over the next several years, the struggle for harmony and discipline hung in the balance more than once, even while the numbers of Italian national parishes increased. Despite the fact that, by the 1920's, five Italian parishes had been organized to serve New Haven Italians alone—three more Italian parishes had been founded in the Greater New Haven area—the legacy of dissension lingered on, obscuring what otherwise might have been considered an impressive story of Italian national parish development.[20]

Episodes in early Polish immigrant communities of the diocese indicate that the phenomenon of internal discord that divided parishioners and drove out clergy was by no means unique to newly migrated Italians.[21] Indeed, open conflict greatly disturbed the formative years of almost every Polish national parish of the diocese. For example, the first reports of St. Stanislaus, Meriden, the oldest Polish national parish in the diocese, paint the same dismal picture of intramural dissension. According to its first pastor, "designing people" were, in fact, working to destroy his credibility for their own selfish ends. Once he asked Bishop McMahon how he was to clear his own reputation when accused of "thievishness and other crimes." How was he, moreover, to prevent "faithless men from convoking meetings, taking up Sunday collections, electing their own slate of trustees?" What should he do about parishioners whom he described as "conspirators" and "some sort of unduly americanized old Polish patriots" who "day and night in their Jewish-Polish saloons harassed the Polish people against me, telling them to expel the Priest and paid no heed to the Incorporation-act published solemnly at the church by the Reverend Rector."[22] After this

<hr>

[19] Bishop Michael Tierney to Diomede Falconio, Apostolic Delegate, Washington, D.C., December 21, 1904, Episcopal Papers, AAH.

[20] Liptak, op. cit., pp. 230-236; Appendix, pp. 424-428.

[21] This is well documented in Buczek, op. cit., passim.

[22] The infighting in this parish is chronicled in a series of parish reports and letters appended to the first financial statements sent by the parish to Bishop McMahon and contained in the Parish Annual Reports, 1893, AAH.

distraught priest's early resignation—he would later re-emerge in the role
of pastor for a Polish National Catholic (schismatic) Church in Chicago—
the administration of St. Stanislaus changed hands five times as Polish
pastors continued to experience degrees of discontent. Then under the
administration of the Reverend John Ceppa, who became pastor in 1906
and remained until his death forty-two years later, parish unity was finally
forged.[23]

In parish after parish among the early Polish settlers in Connecticut
episodes involving name-calling, protest, and riot told of a people torn
between competing factions involving clerical and lay leadership within
their own communities, and ultimately uniting only when one leader
gained the respect of all. In every case, there was little the bishop could do
beyond searching for acceptable candidates to replace those rejected by the
congregation. As with the Italian community, most of the drama had to be
played out within the confines of the parish, and some kind of compromise
would ultimately relax the tensions. Even in the peaceful aftermath,
however, bitter memories lingered. They cast a shadow over the efforts of
diocesan leaders, of course, but, unfortunately, they harmed the image of
the national parish even more.[24]

For the most part, then, dissension involving Catholic communities
remained intramural. But from time to time, even in a diocese where
bishops worked to implement a policy of accommodation, internal discord
in a parish would smolder for a period and then erupt with a violence that
convulsed the whole local community. The furor that burst out in 1916 at
SS. Cyril and Methodius, Bridgeport, probably had its beginnings years
earlier, when parishioners of the historic St. John Nepomucene (Slovak)
Church asked Bishop Tierney for permission to organize a new parish to be
established just a few blocks from St. John's. The correspondence that this
petition set in motion reveals a growing difference of opinion between the
pastor and parishioners of St. John's, and demonstrates that there was no
way that the bishop could have avoided the issue.

---

[23]The Reverend A. Klawiter left Meriden in 1893. According to the Reverend M. J. Madaj,
archivist of the Archdiocese of Chicago (oral interview, 1978), Father Klawiter subsequently
went to Chicago, where he became a priest in the schismatic Polish National Church. For
history of parish, see "St. Stanislaus Roman Catholic Church, 1891-1976," published privately
for the 85th Anniversary Celebration, Parish Histories, AAH.

[24]Seldom does a parish history reveal the many internecine debates. One exception is
"Golden Jubilee, St. Michael Parish, Derby, Connecticut, 1905-1955" (Derby, 1955), *Parish
Files*, St. Thomas Seminary Library.

At first, Bishop Tierney attempted to point out that establishing a second Slovak parish in close proximity to the first would be counter-productive, and suggested instead that the Slovaks build on the other side of the city. To this the petitioners responded in resounding tones: "It is impossible for us to build a church in the West End as we are all residing in the East Side.... We have enough for a new Church... and you are asking us too many questions which keep us back...."[25] At one point the voice of Father Joseph Kossalko, pastor of St. John's, was added to the debate. Humiliated because his parishioners had initiated a petition for a new parish without his knowledge or consent, he complained to the bishop of his treatment at the hands of his ungrateful flock:

> There are in my Congregation, as there are everywhere in our parishes of immigrants—some troublesome and turbulent men, who without any visible, or reasonable cause, are discontent with the incumbent priests, and avail themselves of every opportunity to mortify, to torment, and to worry out their priest, and to foment the discord among the parishioners.[26]

In turn, the petitioners became more specific in their arguments for a parish:

> We also cannot stay in this small church and with only one old deaf priest. We hear that his assistant is going to leave him. You see yourself that no priest will stay with him. If he remains himself again he cannot supply our needs as he stays on the farm all week and comes in the city on Saturday to unite marriages and on Sunday to say mass.[27]

Moreover, Bishop Tierney had also been informed by the Apostolic Delegate that the "old deaf priest" of St. John's was creating other problems among members of a national Slovak organization.[28] In the hope that a division of the parish might be a step toward making some sense of a difficult situation, the bishop agreed to the petitioners' plan and worked closely with them in order to find an acceptable pastor for the new church. Despite this co-operation, trouble would continue to plague the Slovak community, and the divisiveness that had forced the creation of the second parish, SS. Cyril and Methodius, would resurface even more dramatically nine years after its establishment.

[25] Michael Quaka and others to Bishop Tierney, August 12, 1907, Episcopal Papers, AAH.

[26] Joseph Kossalko, rector, St. John Nepomucene, to Bishop Tierney, June 18, 1907, Episcopal Papers, AAH.

[27] Michael Quaka and others to Bishop Tierney, September 14, 1907, Episcopal Papers, AAH.

[28] In 1906, Kossalko had written a circular letter to the American Bishops critical of the Church's work on behalf of Slovaks in general. Kossalko had also publicized his intention to boycott a Slavic Congress approved by the American hierarchy; see Diomede Falconio, Apostolic Delegate, to Michael Tierney, November 29, 1907, Episcopal Papers, AAH.

In 1916, the unexpected illness and death of the Reverend Matthew Jankola, pastor of SS. Cyril and Methodius, set off perhaps the most bizarre episode of parochial conflict in the diocese's history. Despite the prompt appointment of the Reverend Gaspar Panik, a qualified and highly respected young Slovak priest chosen to succeed Jankola, the parishioners of the new parish remained deeply agitated. Within two weeks after Panik took up his responsibilities at the parish, an incident widely reported in the Bridgeport newspapers rocked the immigrant community.[29]

Alleging that the new pastor was guilty of a number of improprieties, a group of women "armed with eggs ... bricks, and stones" and supported by hundreds of onlookers stormed the rectory, refusing to leave until they could directly confront the priest. The arrest of thirteen women did not end the affair. Prompted, for some reason, to sustain the confrontation, the women refused bail. According to newspaper accounts, they spent the night in jail, "singing, laughing, telling humorous stories, . . . nursing babies ... and partaking of the food brought in by families and friends." To eyewitnesses, a "sort of carnival spirit" prevailed.[30]

Even during the crisis, observers attempted to discover the reasons for such an outburst. The readiest alleged explanation, to be sure, involved episcopal insensitivity with regard to the appointment of Father Panik. But the harassed pastor's immediate reaction, as reported on the front pages of the Bridgeport papers, suggested that there was much more to the situation than an administrative error. To reporters, Panik commented:

> One of the chief causes of this morning's outbreak ... is my sincere regard for Father Kamora [sic], pastor of St. John's in this city. The deceased priest of SS. Cyril and Methodius was not on friendly terms with Father Kamora and it is my belief that the congregation became imbued with the attitude of their pastor toward him.[31]

Was not Father Panik suggesting that the new Slovak community feared that the co-operation between both pastors might undo their efforts at separation executed only a few years previously? Komara, pastor of St. John's, also felt that the complaints of the women had no foundation. But he was at a loss to explain such an irrational display. Thus, he attributed the riot to outside "fanatical agitators craving excitement and novelties."

[29] *Bridgeport Telegram*, May 25, 26, and 29, 1916. See also *Torrington Register*, which reported the event because the newly appointed pastor had been transferred from Torrington.

[30] *Bridgeport Telegram*, May 25, 1916.

[31] *Ibid.*

"They do not represent the majority of Slavic Roman Catholics," he confidently added. "Slavonian [*sic*] Catholics are known for their respect for the lawfully constituted ecclesiastic [*sic*] authorities."[32]

What the two priests seemed to be arguing was that the charges by the women really pointed to beneath-the-surface issues that had probably been festering since the time of the division of St. John's, and that the action of the bishop in appointing the new pastor had merely brought to the surface the pent-up animosity within the ethnic community itself. The passage of time was to lend support to both priests' assessments. For, if the conflict had been provoked by the faults of church authorities, another set of questions emerges. Why, for example, were the charges against the priest not pursued after this emotional scene? Why was the pastor not re-assigned, as was so often done when similar troubles occurred? The fact is that the very opposite situation developed. Every trace of accusation and insinuation vanished—even from the folklore of the parish—and Father Panik stayed on at SS. Cyril and Methodius, acquiring such an excellent reputation among his own people and the Bridgeport citizenry in general that to this day he is remembered as one of the city's most distinguished residents.[33] Undoubtedly, other factors than those alleged by the women lent support to the widespread notion that the national parish was an inadequate answer to the needs of immigrant Catholics.

Episodes such as these help to explain why even the most enlightened policies of bishops could be rendered relatively ineffectual in countering any general argument concerning the failure of the Church in dealing with the "immigrant problem." Moreover, the waste of energy during the all-too-many years of internal struggle as Italian, Slavic, Hungarian, and Lithuanian parishes gradually found stability took its toll upon the diocese as a whole, reinforcing the assumption that little was done to reach out to the new immigrants. Thus, bishops were often called to task, sometimes by civil authorities, sometimes by the Apostolic Delegate's office in Washington or by the Congregation for the Propagation of the Faith in Rome, sometimes by their fellow bishops and even by priests and laity of the diocese itself—all of whom did not hesitate to reprove the bishops for their deficiencies with regard to the immigrant.[34]

[32]*Ibid.*

[33]*Bridgeport Times-Star,* January 28, 1933. Oral interviews, Dr. Michael Simko, Edward Behuncik, Bridgeport, 1975.

[34]The Poles and French-Canadians were particularly adept at this. See Liptak, *op. cit.,* Chapter V, "Episodes of Discord in Polish and French-Canadian Catholic Churches," pp. 249-308.

In the long run, however, those most hurt by the episodes of discord were the pastors of the national parishes and their congregations. A sense of isolation developed around the national parish, the pastor's effectiveness in uniting the parish being so essential that, in actuality, his very success prevented him from integration with the diocesan officialdom. As a consequence, although a number of immigrant pastors actually earned national reputations among their ethnic peers and won applause of diocesan leaders, they often remained within the confines of one parish throughout their entire priestly careers. An unforeseen and unintended outcome of diocesan planning on behalf of immigrants, this separate treatment may, indeed, have been the most tragic consequence of all, and a basic cause of the misunderstanding that still lingers about national parishes.

69

This is not to suggest, in conclusion, that the performance of the Catholic Church should not come under scrutiny and be examined as to its particular role with respect to immigrant groups. Nor is it to deny that faults can be discovered in the methods used by the Church in the United States to confront the problems of integrating immigrants within its structure. However, when one reviews the lengths to which the bishops of Hartford, in particular, went in order to help immigrant groups to establish themselves in the diocese, one must at least concede that factors external to church administration should also be considered when seeking to understand why controversies over the nature and value of the national parish still continue to confront the Church.

ST. PAUL'S PRIESTS, 1850 - 1930: RECRUITMENT, ETHNICITY AND AMERICANIZATION

Daniel P. O'Neill

Friendly, hostile, and neutral observers have assumed that the Catholic church had some impact on the adjustment of the millions of Catholic immigrants in the United States. Whether the church helped or hindered their adjustment is an important but not fully explored question. Most studies that touch on this question have focused on the pronouncements of the hierarchy. Yet in the eyes of most Catholics, the bishops were aloof and far away; for most parishioners the church was synonymous with the parish priests, the nuns and the brothers. Most historical studies, however, have paid scant attention to these men and women and their role in the acculturation of the immigrants.

Who were they? How were they recruited? What types of careers did they have within the institutional church? Did they persist in their religious vocations? Where were they trained? What was their national or ethnic identity? From what social classes were they drawn?

Answers to these questions may be found by looking at the history of individual dioceses and religious orders over time. In other words, the case study approach. This paper concentrates on the diocesan clergy of the St. Paul diocese between 1850 and 1930. It is part of a larger study which is a collective biography of the 855 men who functioned as diocesan priests in the parishes and institutions of the diocese during that period. Based upon both quantitative and traditional methods, the larger study examines patterns of recruitment and types of clerical careers. More specifically, it investigates the social origins of the clergy, mobility into the hierarchy, and the emergence of a native-born clergy. The data base for this study contains the following information on each individual: name, birth date and place, ordination date and place, diocese or order ordained for, death date and place, date began and ended ministry in St. Paul diocese, theology, philosophy and classics schools attended, ethnic group, relatives in priesthood, residence on matriculating for the St. Paul clergy, number of assignments, first assignment, second assignmnent, and where applicable, assignment in 1860, 1870, 1880, 1890, 1900, 1910, 1920 and 1930. This data was gathered from individual census cards in the St. Paul chancery office, educational survey of priests in the diocese in 1938, student registers of St. Paul Seminary 1894-1930, obituaries, city directories, Catholic directories, death certificates, and the 1949 historical survey of the parishes in the diocese.[1] This data was transcribed, coded, keypunched and then analyzed using the Statistical Package for the Social Sciences, a program widely used for research in social history.

This paper will examine two issues: the ethnic identity and the entry status of priests who were recruited into the St. Paul diocese between 1840 and 1930. The term entry status is used to differentiate those who came into the diocese as priests or seminarians from natives of the diocese who were recruited into the priesthood.

I have selected the diocese of St. Paul for a number of reasons: size, ethnic diversity, mixture of cities, towns and rural areas, the numerical predominance of secular priests, its transition from a frontier to a settled community in the period under study, the prominence of John Ireland, the ordinary between 1884 and 1918 in the americanizing party within the hierarchy and, last but not least, because I live and teach in Minnesota.

After the Sioux treaties of 1851 transferred control of millions of acres to the federal government, a mass movement of white settlers into Minnesota began. The rapidity of settlement is evident from the following population figures:

71

Table 1 - Population of Minnesota

Year of census	Population in thousands
1850	6
1855	40
1860	172
1870	439
1880	780

Source: Theodore Blegen, *Minnesota* (Minneapolis, 1975)
(Unless otherwise noted, the source for the subsequent tables is the data base.)

In anticipation of this settlement, the diocese of St. Paul had been established in 1850. At that time there were three French-speaking priests in the Minnesota and Dakota territories, the original jurisdiction of the diocese. To meet the religious needs of the expanding number of Catholic settlers, priests, seminarians, and lay candidates for the priesthood were recruited in Europe, Canada, and the eastern part of the United States. A sense of the scale of recruitment can be obtained by looking at the number of priests who began their ministry in the diocese in the various decades covered by this study:

Table 2 - Recruitment of priests by decade

Decade	Number who began ministry in St. Paul diocese
1841-1850	4
1851-1860	27
1861-1870	47
1871-1880	88
1881-1890	147
1891-1900	125
1901-1910	167
1911-1920	119
1921-1930	130

It is important to realize that these are composite figures covering all types of recruitment. Later this paper will examine specific types of recruitment in more detail. In a very rough way, these figures also suggest the growth of the diocesan clergy over time as well as that of the Catholic population that they served. The following table provides evidence concerning the growth:

Table 3 · Diocesan statistics

Year	Diocesan priests	Catholic population in thousands
1861	19	50
1870	47	85
1880	90	118
1890	110	?
1900	184	215
1910	263	260
1920	293	265
1930	362	281

Source: *Catholic Directories, 1861-1930*

In examining recruitment the national identity of the candidates, American or foreign, is a very important dimension. During the nineteenth century, articles in clerical journals argued that the Catholic church in the United States would not be a viable institution if it continued to depend on foreign missionaries to staff its institutions. The decline of the church in China, where European missionaries had failed to develop a native clergy, was often cited as a warning. Ideally, some writers contended, the church in the United States should be staffed by American born and trained priests. Many bishops accepted the validity of these arguments. It was seventy years, however, before this policy began to be realized in a significant way in the St. Paul diocese.2

In the following discussion individuals who immigrated to the United States as children are considered American. Between 1841 and 1880, 90% of the clerical recruits were European or Canadian in origin; between 1881 and 1910, 66%. In the decade after 1911 the foreign component dropped to 38% and in the 1920s to 23%.

Examining these figures in another way, before 1880 10% of the priests who served in the diocese were of American stock; between then and 1910, the American percentage increased to 33%. It was only in the decade after 1911 that Americans made up more than half of the new recruits. By the 1920s, the American component increased to almost 80%. The turning point in the ethnic composition of the clergy began with the ordination class of 1906, that is the graduating class of the St. Paul Seminary in that year; from that point on, with two close exceptions, half of every ordination class was American born. These figures on national identity are a rough index of the relatively slow process of "Americanizing" the diocesan clergy of St. Paul.

Obviously more specific information on national identity can be provided than the breakdown given above. The 855 priests in this study can be identified as follows: American born or raised 40%, European 53%, Canadian 5%, unknown 2%. Of the 46 Canadians, 25 were French; the rest were mainly of Irish stock.

The European group can be broken down as follows: Irish 35%, German speaking 21%, French speaking 16%, Bohemian 3% and miscellaneous 22%.

A more useful way to handle identity would be to focus on the larger groups and to combine both the European and American members of an ethnic group into one category as in the following table:

Table 4 - Composite ethnic groups combining
European and American members

Group	Percentage
French	10
German	22
Irish	45
Bohemian	5
Polish	5
Other foreign	7
American unspecified	4
Unknown	2

73

In this compilation French-speaking priests from Europe and Canada are included under the heading French; German-speaking priests from the German states, Austria-Hungary and Luxembourg as well as German-Americans are listed as German; Irish natives, Irish-Canadians and Irish-Americans are identified as Irish.

Now let us see how these composite ethnic groups were distributed over time. The founding role played by the French and the French-Canadian missionaries is reflected in the proportion that this composite group contributed to the clergy in the early decades of the diocese: in the 1840s 100%; in the 1850s 46%. In the former period, Lucien Galtier, Augustine Ravoux and George Belcourt, the literal founders of the church in the region, began their work; in the latter, Joseph Cretin, the first bishop, and his band of missionaries from Ain and neighboring departments in western France arrived. The French predominance in the diocese proved to be short-lived, however, Although their contribution from 1850 to 1910 was consistently in the range of 8 to 15 each decade, their proportion of each decade's entering class declined dramatically with the arrival of German-speaking and Irish priests in increasingly large numbers. In the 1860s, for instance, 49% of the new arrivals were German, 26% Irish and 18% French.

The 1870s entering class was notably cosmopolitan in its origins: 36% Irish, 20% German, 17% French, 8% Polish, 7% Bohemian and 8% miscellaneous foreign. This rank ordering generally held true until 1910 when the French dropped to the end of the list. The French share of recruit classes declined mainly because few Minnesotans of French origin entered the diocesan priesthood in the period under study. In this respect they differed from other major contributing groups which drew 40% to 50% of their candidates from the United States.

Table 5 · Origin of composite ethnic groups

Group	Foreign-born	American-born or raised
Bohemians	23	23
Polish	20	23
German	119	72
Irish	201	183
French	81	2
Dutch	12	0
Belgian	11	0
Italian	8	0

74

As can be seen from Table 5 the French production of American vocations was similar to that of the smaller ethnic groups on the list. Two explanations might be offered to explain the French group's low productivity of native vocations: first, many of the French clerics might have been "wandering priests" who spent only a short period in the diocese; second, the French, and maybe some of the other low producers as well, were missionaries in the strictest sense, that is they set out to convert or to minister to peoples who were not of the same ethnic group as themselves.

The German and Irish predominance among the clergy began in the 1860s; in that decade the former contributed 49% and the latter 26%. In the following decade, positions were reversed with the Irish share 36% and the German 21%; this ranking would remain the pattern in subsequent decades. From 1880 to 1930, the Irish and Germans on the average accounted for 70% of each decade's entering class; the former's share of each class ranged from 42% to 54%, the latter's 18% to 26%.

So FAR WE HAVE LOOKED AT recruitment in terms of numbers, foreign or native identity and ethnicity. Obviously there were different paths of entry into the St. Paul clergy: some came as priests, others as seminarians, yet others were drawn to study for the priesthood as young boys living in the diocese itself. Of our total group, 335 entered the diocese as priests having been ordained elsewhere for service in other dioceses or religious orders; these account for 39% of the total. 296 volunteered for service while still students in the seminary in Europe, Canada or elsewhere in the United States; these account for 35%. The third source was candidates recruited from within the diocese itself; this source provided 222 priests, 26% of the recruits. The men in the first two groups, 74% of the total, were already in or on the road to the priesthood when they volunteered for St. Paul. Their affiliation with St. Paul was strictly speaking a matter of transferring to another diocese. The third group, on the other hand, represents recruitment at its most basic level, the actual cultivation or fostering of vocations in young men who had not already made career choices. Of this group, 164 were natives of Minnesota, 47 entered as children, 8 as youths and 3 as adults. Table 6 shows how entry status changed over time.

Table 6 - Status on affiliating with diocese

Decade	Priests %	Seminarians %	Native candidates %
1841-1850	100	0	0
1851-1860	52	48	0
1861-1870	36	60	4
1871-1880	62	30	8
1881-1890	45	40	14
1891-1900	38	47	15
1901-1910	47	30	22
1911-1920	24	24	52
1921-1930	19	24	57

The most striking thing about these figures is the duration of the "missionary era" in the St. Paul diocese. As late as the decade ending in 1910, nearly 80% of the new priests were drawn from outside of the diocese. These men were recruited as priests or seminary students from Europe, Canada, and the eastern part of the United States. The rank ordering of priests and seminarians in each decadal class until 1910 varied but not in any discernable pattern. After 1911, however, the "outsiders" share declined to less than half.

From another perspective, these figures chart the emergence of a native clergy in St. Paul. As noted before, the native category includes individuals who came into the state as children as well as literal natives. The first Minnesotans to enter the priesthood, John Ireland and Thomas O'Gorman, are examples of the former. Both came to the territory as boys in 1855 and were ordained in the 1860s. Before 1880, the native proportion of recruit classes was very small. Between 1881 and 1900, however, it increased to about 15%. An important factor contributing to this increase was the establishment of a seminary in St. Paul in 1885. Before this time, most candidates were educated in Europe, Canada, or the east. A better sense of the increase in the native group can be seen by looking at actual numbers rather than percentages as the total size of decadal classes fluctuated erratically.

Table 7 - Native candidates

Decade	Number
1861-1870	2
1871-1880	7
1881-1890	21
1891-1900	19
1901-1910	37
1911-1920	62
1921-1930	74

In the 1880s there were three times as many natives as there had been in the previous decade. The 1901-1910 group, on the other hand, had twice as many natives as there had been in the 1890s.

Returning to the total class composition, the native component reached 50% between 1911-1920 and almost 60% between 1921-1930. From a long range perspective, a native clergy began to emerge in the diocese in 1911, 70 years after the establishment of the institutional church in Minnesota. Assuming ordination at 26, this means that Minnesotans constituting the native majority in classes after 1911 were born from 1885 on. Obviously in that period, there were Minnesota Catholic families that had the resources and the values which would cause them to encourage or to accept a vocation to the priesthood for one of their sons. Subsequent research hopefully will allow us to describe these families more concretely and see if they were representative of the larger population.

76 So far this paper has examined patterns of recruitment. It would be worthwhile also to look at the process of recruitment at various levels. From an institutional perspective, the bishops were concerned with providing priests for new and expanding parishes. They were looking for candidates with the appropriate moral, personal, and professional qualifications, however, these were defined. In the early days, it was a matter of providing a French, Sioux, English, or German-speaking priest, or even better, one who spoke two or more of these languages. As the ethnic composition of the state changed there were demands for Bohemian, Polish, and Italian-speaking priests as well. But finding priests with the appropriate spiritual qualities, pastoral ability, and language skills did not complete the bishop's agenda as there were other needs. These depended, in part, on the bishop's priorities and the resources of the diocese at a given time. Thus, priests were needed to teach in the seminary, to organize ethnic settlements on railroad lands, to edit a newspaper, to work full time in the temperance movement, to superintend the Catholic schools, and to direct Catholic charities. Priests trained for conventional parish work might not be prepared for these more specialized apostolates.

On another level, individual priests often paved the way for the entry of friends or acquaintances into the diocesan clergy. Sometimes this was a matter of encouraging friends from the home province or seminary to emigrate to Minnesota. Sometimes the ties were of blood as well as language or culture. Three McGolrick brothers from County Tipperary were ordained for St. Paul in 1867, 1874 and 1881. This family also gave two daughters to the local community of the Sisters of St. Joseph in St. Paul. Two Hughes brothers from Prince Edward Island and two Dolphin brothers from Massachusetts also came to the diocese. And from France came Jean and Gabriel Andre, uncle and nephew. There are other cases of kinship which can be documented as well. Probably more common, however, were networks of recruitment established in some provinces and seminaries. Francis X. Pirec, an early Indian missionary from Austrian Carniola, established that province's tradition of sending missionaries to Minnesota. On trips home, this nineteenth century clerical "Pied Piper" recruited 31 priests and seminarians. Among them were Joseph Buy, a prominent missionary in northeastern Minnesota, and James Trobec and John Stariha, both of whom were named bishop. All Hallows, the Irish seminary for foreign missions, sent 33 of its graduates to St. Paul.

In Minnesota itself the most basic form of recruitment went on, attracting talented boys and young men to begin studies for the priesthood. Among the parishes contributing a high number of vocations to the diocesan priesthood were: St. Agnes 5, St. Mark 6, St. Francis 7, all in St. Paul; Ascension

9, Immaculate Conception (later called Basilica) 16, both in Minneapolis; and New Prague's St. Wenceslaus 9. These six parishes produced almost a quarter of the 222 native vocations. In 1900, there were 125 parishes staffed by diocesan priests. The figures suggest that for some priests cultivating vocations held a high priority. A good example is Francis Tichy, who was pastor at New Prague and Silver Lake. He was credited with fostering the vocations of nine priests who were ordained for St. Paul.[3]

I T WOULD BE APPROPRIATE to place the findings on American and foreign identity in some perspective. One way of doing this is to compare the priests with their parishioners. Were the proportion of foreign and native in each group similar? Admittedly there are problems in comparing an unmarried subgroup with a total population but it is worth doing nonetheless. In the 1890 census, 36% of the population of Minnesota was foreign born; on the other hand, 65% of the clergy who came into the diocese in the previous decade were also foreign born. In the 1910 census, the foreign born component had declined to 26%; among the clergy, it had risen slightly to 67%. As the Irish and the Germans, the largest Catholic ethnic groups, had come into Minnesota mainly before 1880, while Protestant Scandinavians were coming in increasing numbers after then, it is likely that the Catholic population at these enumerations was more native born than that of the state as a whole. If this is so it further accentuates the foreign character of the pastors as compared to the increasingly native character of the parishioners.

77

The findings show some significant changes in the personnel of the institutional church: 1) the Americanization of the St. Paul clergy; after 1911, 62% of the new recruits were American born or raised; 2) the nativization of the clergy; after 1921, 57% of the clergy recruits were natives of the diocese.

The Americanization of the Catholic community in the St. Paul diocese happened at different times. From 1859, all of the bishops of the diocese were American; by 1890 more than 66% of the lay population was American born; after 1911, the clergy began to attract more American than foreign recruits. Thus, the church was Americanized at the top first, the rank and file next and the middle last. From another perspective, all of these changes might be described as phases in the de-missionization of the Catholic church in the St. Paul diocese.

Footnotes

1   James Reardon, *The Catholic Church in the Diocese of St.Paul* (St. Paul, 1952), the only published study of the diocese, is more accurately described as a chronicle than a history. My main sources for this paper have been: St. Paul Chancery office files, student registers of the St. Paul Seminary, *Northwestern Chronicle* 1866-1893, *Catholic Bulletin* 1911-1975, both published in St. Paul.

2   For a discussion of the nativity of bishops and priests see Thomas McAvoy, *A History of the Catholic Church in the United States* (Notre Dame, 1969) and John T. Ellis, "The Formation of the American Priest," John T. Ellis, ed., *The Catholic Priest in the United States: Historical Investigations* (Collegeville, 1971), 3-110

3   *Catholic Bulletin*, April 19, 1913, July 18, 1925.

A LESSON FROM HISTORY:
THE INTEGRATION OF IMMIGRANTS IN THE PASTORAL PRACTICE OF THE CHURCH IN THE UNITED STATES

79

Silvano M. Tomasi, c.s.

1987

Center for Migration Studies

New York

The Center for Migration Studies is an educational non-profit institute founded in New York in 1964, committed to encourage and facilitate the study of sociodemographic, economic, political, historical, legislative and pastoral aspects of human migration and refugee movements. The opinions expressed in this work are those of the author.

This paper was originally presented at the International Conference on "Religious and the Pastoral Care of People on the Move", Rome, December 4-6, 1986, sponsored by the Pontifical Commission on Migration and Itinerant Peoples.

80

A LESSON FROM HISTORY: THE INTEGRATION OF IMMIGRANTS IN THE PASTORAL PRACTICE OF THE CHURCH IN THE UNITED STATES

Pastoral Series: Occasional Paper #7

The Center for Migration Studies
of New York, Inc.

209 Flagg Place
Staten Island, New York 10304-1148

ISBN 0-934733-22-8

A LESSON FROM HISTORY: THE INTEGRATION OF IMMIGRANTS IN THE PASTORAL PRACTICE OF THE CHURCH IN THE UNITED STATES

1. On July 4, 1986 an exhuberant national celebration marked the centennial anniversary of the Statue of Liberty, a popular symbol of the self-image of the United States as a refuge for the oppressed of the world. The United States is not the only nation of immigrants in modern history. Australia, Canada and Argentina, for example, can also claim the same designation. The variety of sources, the volume, and persistance of immigration, however, make the United States a kaleidoscope of changing ethnic groups. The American experiment in bringing such a variety of people to live together socially, politically and economically, is still in progress. In 1985, 570,000 immigrants arrived into the country legally: 264,691 from Asia, 63,043 from Europe, 83,281 from the Caribbean, 65,360 from Central and South America. With the net addition of 200,000 illegal migrants, a conservative figure used by the Census Bureau for its intercensal estimates, one-third (33 percent) of the U.S. population growth is due to net migration. "The U.S., with 5 percent of the world's population, takes about 50 percent of its international migrants, not counting refugees"(1). This changing face of America affects the Church as well in always new ways. The National Conference of Catholic Bishops has just issued a pastoral statement: Together, a New People, which starts by saying: "The loving concern of the Church for immigrants and refugees is a thread that ties together more than three centuries of its history in the United States. The growth and crises, the achievements and occasional failures of the Church are linked to its struggle to include in

1

one community of faith peoples from a hundred diverse cultures and then lead this new People of God toward a creative service in a pluralistic society"(2). The historian that analyzes the process of inclusion in society and in the church of people who come from all over the world is challenged by complex questions stemming from the background of the immigrants, the historical moment of their arrival , the attitudes of the receiving society, the nature of the relationship between religion and ethnicity. The maintenance of ethnic and religious identities is indeed a question raised by social analysts, especially since these variables defy expected patterns of assimilation(3). A 1980 examination of data on the religious composition of the American population showed that about 64 percent of the people surveyed were Protestants, 25 percent Catholics, 2 percent were Jews, over 1 percent belonged to other religions, and 7 percent had no church ties. Ethnic and social backgrounds and religion were strongly related and linked to historical patterns of immigration (Table 1).

TABLE 1

Religious Composition of America's Largest Ethnic Groups, 1977, 1978, 1980

National origin	Protestant	Catholic	Jewish	No Religion	Other
Africa	89.6	3.9	0.0	5.2	1.3
England, Scotland, Wales	82.7	8.0	0.3	7.7	1.3
Germany	70.1	20.7	1.0	7.7	0.5
Ireland	54.7	37.4	0.5	7.2	0.2
Italy	9.6	80.3	0.5	7.1	2.5
Poland	12.1	71.8	12.1	4.0	0.0
Scandanavia	85.3	10.4	0.0	4.3	0.0

Source: General Social Survey Cumulative File, 1972-1980, NORC. Data extraction and computations done by Thomas J. Archdeacon.

2

One hundred years after the start of southern and eastern European immigration, the religious affiliation of Poles and Italians, for example, was slightly changed since 72 percent and 80 percent of them respectively are Catholic today. The transition from immigrant to ethnic groups took place along a continuum that moves from marginality to participation, even in the church community, through a process of conflict and adaptation. An attempt is made in this paper to identify pastoral policies and strategies adopted by United States dioceses for the incorporation of new immigrants. The specific angle of analysis is that of pastoral care understood primarily as the preservation of the faith and the support of religious practice during the educational and cultural evolution of the immigrant groups within the host society. The development of pastoral policies came about either because of episcopal initiative or because of tolerance of the immigrants' own action to find a response to spiritual needs(4).

2.   The bishops of the United States in dealing with arriving immigrants have not followed uniform strategies. The diversity of regional traditions, the composition of a diocese population, the availability of church personnel within the immigrant communities and the local church, ideological stands of individual bishops on the Church's role in America, are all elements that determined local responses to newcomers(5). Church historigraphy is now looking at all these variables at work in specific dioceses. Together with a multiplicity of approaches, it discovered that ethnicity is a dynamic force that keeps the church in constant flux and that contributes to its constant creativity. Widely accepted conclusions have already been reached in the scholarly community: the interplay between religion and

culture within every immigrant group and between these groups and the receiving chuch; the link between class and devotional expressions; the persistence of diversity beyond the first generation; the movement with the passing of time toward integration in a multi-cultural church and into the mainstream of society. All these themes are evident even in selected cases of particular dioceses and language groups when a review is made of the critical initial stage of integration into the local church.

3.   In 1820 there was in the United States an estimated population of 195,000 Catholics. It passed the three million mark in 1860 and reached 18 million by 1920. Immigration explains the extraordinary growth of the Church and the fact that no massive loss of faith took place among immigrants. "Surely there was almost no apostasy among the German immigrants, and the survey data show very little among the Italian and the Eastern European immigrants and their descendants"(6). The Catholic Church in the United States had to manage an incredible diversity of groups speaking twenty-eight languages in the early part of the twentieth century. The dialectical process between unity and cultural pluralism became the trade mark of Catholicism in the United States and it continues to the present(7). A common faith and allegiance to a common church and country gave a basic unity that was strengthened by the similarity of the integration experience the many immigrant groups were facing throughout the United States. On the other hand, each ethnic group had its own style of devotional life, parish organization, old country traditions that gave the identity it needed while looking for its place in the structure of the new society. Irish immigrants were the first to create a typical new world strategy for the preservation of their faith in

4

combination with social advancement. "Their strategy lay in creating for the Irish, and any other Catholics, an insulated niche within the society, served by 2 series of church sponsored institutions that duplicated those of the larger community. Within these alternative structures, all Catholics would be able to prepare themselves to compete for the nation's material goods, to avoid discrimination, to mature and live without danger to their faith, and to demonstrate in time moral and intellectual superiority. The church sponsored colleges, hospitals, newspapers, and orphanages, but parochial elementary schools were the linchpin of the program"(8). The model introduced by Irish immigrants became the standard for all European immigrants and historians agree now that the parish was the focal point, in its social and religious function, in immigrant Catholic life: it was the key to the survival of religion. In the Protestant American context, then, a standard landmark in the Irish neighborhood was the parish as symbol and critical expression of nationality and religion. For Germans, Italians, Polish and other immigrants, language was an additional necessary reason for their own parishes. In this way, language or national parishes became the most important and successful strategy for the preservation of the faith and the human promotion of the immigrants, especially when the Catholic school was attached to the parish. The historian Jay Dolan observes about the national parish: "One institution that remained in the neighborhood and helped to give it a special identity was the immigrant parish. Most often founded by the people, the church was the most enduring and important cultural institution in the neighborhood. As a social organization that brought people together through a network of societies and clubs, it helped to establish a sense of community. As an educational organization, it taught both young and old the meaning of America, its language as well as its culture; as a religious organization, it brought the presence of God to the neighborhood, nurturing and sustaining the presence of the holy through worship, devotional services, and neighborhood processions. Important as this religious dimension was, the immigrant parish was more than just a religious institution in which people could satisfy their spiritual needs and desires. This was the manifest purpose of the parish, but it also was a key social institution. Indeed in most Catholic neighborhoods it was the cement that bound the people together, enabling them to establish some semblance of a community life. Families were indeed the building blocks of every immigrant community, but the church was the mortar that sought to bind them together"(9). The experience of each immigrant group could be studied from the point of view of the pastoral strategies used. The dioceses of Boston, Hartford, Providence, New York, Newark, Chicago, Detroit, for example, had an active policy of responding to the immigrants' arrival by establishing for them parishes of their language. Thus, in the New York metropolitan area, by 1918 there were 101 Italian churches and 26 Italian chapels and 25 of these churches and 7 chapels were staffed by 77 religious priests. These churches maintained the faith of these immigrants and effectively blocked proselytizing inroads. In 1917 the combined membership of the most active Protestant denominations at work among Italians had only 13,700 church members and 13,900 church school pupils in an estimated Italian population of well over three million(10). Another obvious case where the parish and its related institutions preserved the immigrants' faith is American Polonia that developed an extensive network of Polish parishes, schools,

6

theological seminaries, religious congregations, publications and church organizations. In 1958, on the occasion of Poland's Millenium, a tentative list of Polish Roman Catholic parishes in the United States was compiled from various diocesan and archdiocesan histories, parochial anniversary books, the Official Catholic Directory of the United States, questionnaires sent to priests. By then, a number of parishes established by Polish Americans had undergone a change of character, becoming either mixed or territorial, while some had entirely ceased to exist. The statistical summary of Polish parishes in American archdioceses and dioceses gave the figure of 769 with the largest concentration in the geographical areas of heaviest Polish immigration: 57 in Chicago, 43 in Buffalo, 42 in Scranton, 36 in Detroit, 30 in Philadelphia(11). Immigrants were predominantly working-class people. The financial investment in the building and support of parishes and schools as it was demanding so it was a sign of commitment to a way of life where religion has a central place, In 1918, for example, the then thirty-eight Polish parishes of the archdiocese of Chicago had a combined phenomenal value of church property of $10,393,000.00 of the time. "These parishes also maintained elementary schools and contributed to the support of five Polish high schools and one college. They also pooled their resources to sustain several orphanages, welfare agencies, a hospital, several newspapers, various cultural centers and libraries, the national offices of the major fraternals and even a cemetery"(12). In this period of unparalleled expansion within the Church in the United States, diocesan bishops turned to religious congregations. For the Poles in Chicago, the Congregation of the Resurrection was entrusted at first with their pastoral care by Bishop Thomas Foley in 1870 and the Resurrectionists spearheaded the establishment of many parishes in the Mid-West as well as their organizational model(13). A similar role was played for Italian immigrants by the Congregation of the Missionaries of St. Charles (Scalabrinians) in several dioceses(14). Practically all religious orders were engaged in some way with immigrants and their children. Franciscans and Jesuits, Benedictines and Salesians, Redemptorists and Pallotines, just to mention a few(15). The extensive pioneer activities of these priests and religious men and women recorded in the languages of the ethnic groups they ministered to, are slowly finding their way into the standard histories of the Church in America. It can be stated of religious communities what Daniel Buczek said of Catholic laity and diocesan priest leaders that "unknown thus far even to specialists of American ethnic studies, performed near-herculean feats" in their efforts to help immigrants in American society achieve a viable community within the larger American community (16). Often inseparable from the parish, the Catholic elementary schools had been successfully used by the immigrant missionary and bishop of Philadelphia, St. John Newman, C.SS.R., for German immigrants(17). They proved an invaluable strategy for Christian education and they provided the immigrants with the language and cultural knowledge they needed to participate fully into American life. In fact, in Catholic schools immigrant children found in many instances a cultural continuity of values and traditions that made adaptation to America less traumatic and less disruptive than in public schools and their impact on the formation of a Catholic identity can be illustrated again in American Polonia. For example, in 1912, in the city of Buffalo, there were 6,071 children in the public schools and 5,729 in Catholic schools. Once the period of building of national Polish parishes was concluded in

8

the Buffalo diocese, during the 1923-24 school year, 225 Felician sisters were staffing thirty out of the thirty-three Polish parochial schools and teaching 16,000 children. Another 1,200 Polish children were taught in the remaining Polish Catholic schools(18). Although the Buffalo case is exceptional that the majority of children of an ethnic group were in Catholic schools, it shows the commitmenht to hand on the faith according to their own cultural traditions. In 1920, some 400,000 Polish students were in Catholic schools so that they might "preserve the faith, the language, the spirit of the family and national customs of Poland." A survey of the contribution of Polish-American sisters in the united States conducted in 1957-58 found that 17 congregations of Polish origin with 10,162 sisters were caring for an extraordinary network of educational and social institutions(19). As Table 2 shows, these institutions included 690 elementary schools, 85 high schools, 518 catechetical instruction centers, 18 orphanages and 19 houses for the aged and 51 hospitals. With a varied degree of commitment, other European immigrants supported Catholic schools. By 1909, fifty-five thousand children were attending 133 French-Canadian parochial schools in New England. About one-third of Italian children attended parochial schools in the early twentieth century(20). Language parishes and schools were the mainstay of pastoral outreach to European immigrants and their service has proven successful. Lay and clergy Catholic immigrant associations, however, Catholic newspapers and other publications in the language of the immigrants, missions, Catholic social assistance agencies for arriving immigrants, for their orphan children or their sick and elderly were all part of an institutional arrangement that completed the pastoral plan for the continuity of the faith in the new environment of the United States.

Table 2

POLISH AMERICAN SISTERS IN THE UNITED STATES
1957–1958

| *Total Number of Sisterhoods* .... 17 |
| *Total Number of Sisters* .... 10,162 |

APOSTOLATE	Number of Institutions	Persons Served during the Year
Teaching :		
Elementary Schools...................	690	250.255
High Schools	85	21.429
Colleges for Members	9	510
Senior Colleges for Lay and Religious ..	2	431
Schools of Nursing	11	682
Kindergartens	170	8.760
Special Educational Programs	14	1.132
Catechetical Schools	24	7.261
Catechetical Instruction Centers........	518	63.250
Publication and Printing Centers.......	1	—
Care of the Sick :		
Hospitals............................	51	388.665
Clinics (not connected with hospitals) ..	2	92
Convalescent and Rest Homes.........	9	611
Homes for Mentally Deficient Children .	1	54
Home Nursing Centers................	1	778
Miscellaneous :		
Orphanages	18	2.082
Homes for the Aged.................	19	1.694
Day Nurseries	10	667
Sunday Infant Nurseries	2	152
Boarding Homes for Student Girls	9	365
Residences for Women................	7	496
Children's Summer Camps.............	4	1.126
Lay Retreat Centers	17	7.514
Social Work Centers	2	1.137
Liturgical Vestment Workshops........	4	—
Diocesan and Parish Census Taking	7	—
Care of Altars and Sacristies	558	—
Domestic Departments at Seminaries ...	7	1.194

The lines were often blurred between the concern for language and national identity maintenance and for the preservation of the faith: ethnicity and religion were the expression of one identity(21). Episcopal policy accepted the limited institutional diversity introduced and developed by the immigrants' initiative, but in the end it chose the way of Americanization. In concluding his careful study of Polish Catholic in Chicago, Parot rightly points out that in the frequent and bitter conflicts in the period of mass immigration ethnocentrism and assimilationist Americanization were exaggerated positions(22). The hierarchy calling for a Catholic identity as all important for the future vitality of the Church pushed a form of Americanization that failed to take into account the historically slow process of cultural change and the possibility of cultural pluralism. The immigrants advocating the preservation of the faith that they saw inextricably linked to their language and traditions, pushed for the preservation also of national cultural forms inevitably destined to disappear in the new country. On the other hand, in the organizational structures and defense of national culture of the immigrants were the premises for an acceptance of pluralism in the Church that would become episcopal policy in the post-Vatican II period when the language of the immigrants would be used in the liturgy, bishops from specific ethnic and racial groups would be recommended and appointed, multiculturalism in catechesis and inculturation of the faith would become the way of evangelization(23). A lesson that emerges from the experience of the Church with European immigrants is that the pastoral institutional structures they developed separately became in time the successful strategies for inclusion in the catholic community at large. Further evidence is found in the case of non Latin-rite newcomers. When the culture of the immigrants was embodied in a different rite, the issues of separation, equality and communion in the same Church were brought to a new level of debate. The preservation of faith and ecclesial unity was achieved through the creation of separate dioceses for immigrants of Eastern rites in the territory of Latin rite dioceses. In 1985 there were in the United States nine Byzantine-Ruthenian Rite and Byantine-Ukrainian Rite dioceses and one each for the Armenian, Maronite, Chaldean and Melkite Rite Catholics(24).

The relationship between the Catholic Church and American society has changed in the post Vatican II era: its insularity and defensiveness have largely been left behind and the Church has become in a sense a critical conscience for the nation. The newest immigrants, however, are still confronted by old difficulties. Mexicans don't see themselves as worshipping like other U.S. Catholics and popular religiosity does not fit well in a middle class American parish. Bishop Placido Rodriguez of Chicago observes: "Frequently, (Hispanics) do not feel welcome in many United States Catholic parishes, therefore many of them stay home or switch to Protestant churches. Although mass attendance is the major U.S. yardstick of what it means to be a Catholic, Hispanics have a different cultural and religious perspective—one more rooted in the very structure of society, faith and life...For the Hispanic person, faith, culture and language are all woven out of the same cloth"(25). Can the pastoral strategies of the past apply in the new circumstances? How effective are present pastoral policies? Current history reflects the past at least to the extent that there is no uniform answer, even though national coordination has increased due to the post-conciliar role of Catholic Conferences(26). Among the 800,000 refugees

11

arrived in the United States from Southeast Asia since 1975, two thirds are Vietnamese. It is estimated that over 150,000 Vietnamese are Catholics, who came with their priests and sisters who reach now over 240 and 300 respectively. In a decade, the Vietnamese developed an articulate network of successful Catholic communities, movements, publications and associations because of the committed leadership of their religious personnel. "Over 130 Vietnamese Catholic communities and Catholic Vietnamese Unions are actively functioning in 28 dioceses throughout the United States. Among these, ten ethnic and personal parishes have been decreed and established by the Bishops in various states from Virginia to Nebraska"(27). The outcome of the Vietnamese Catholic organization is an outreach to non-Christian Vietnamese to join the Church and the failure among their group of fundamentalist proselytizing. Recent immigrants are also the Haitians, whose arrival started in the 1960's and now reach 800,000, mostly along the East Coast of the United States. The lack of clergy and organized Catholic communities is problematic. The vast majority of the Haitians are baptized Catholics, but in the uprootedness of the immigration experience and without adequate assistance, a significant change of religious affiliation or indifference take place. For example, the Southern Baptist Convention had 80 Haitian Churches affiliated in 1985(28). Thus the journey continues, with drama and success and a renewed challenge for the Church to create other pastoral strategies for today's conditions. In fact, immigration and birth-rate trends remain a powerful source of change, that affects the future of the Catholic community. If current patterns hold, slightly more than half of all Americans will be Hispanics, Asians and blacks by the year 2080 and how the church will fare among them depends on how it acts now with these newcomers.

4.   The leadership of immigrant pastors, the service of religious women, the
      ultimate sense of catholicity of bishops and the hope in their American
      future of the immigrant families, converged in substantially incorporating
      the European and Middle East immigrants into one Church. Tragic
      misunderstandings, however, were not absent and they illustrate how
      troublesome immigrant priests, cultural clashes and inability to allow
      participation in church government led to open schism. All Catholic
      immigrant groups have been embroiled in some forms of conflict with
      diocesan bishops and in most cases a resolution was found. German
      immigrants rebelled against the first American bishop John Carroll in
      1787 and settled their quarrel once a German-language parish was
      established for them(29).   More than a century later some Italian
      immigrants attempted to establish in the 1930's an independent Roman
      Catholic Apostolic National Italian Church, a very minor incident in their
      protest against perceived abuses from Irish American clergy(30). Two
      major breaks with the American bishops had a lasting effect in the history
      of Polish and Ukrainian immigrants. After a stormy encounter between
      the archbishop of Minneapolis John Ireland and Father Alexis Toth in
      1889, immigrant Ukrainian priests and people whose style of worship,
      language and ancient customs, like that of married clergy, were not
      accepted, rather than become Latinized, left the Catholic church. The
      conflict was brought to Rome and Propaganda Fide replied at first that
      for the time being married priests could exercise the ministry, even if
      monks should be used as much as possible. The American archbishops,
      however, insisted in 1893 on celibacy, saying about the presence of

94

13

married priests of the Greek rite: "the sooner this point of discipline is abolished. . ., the better for religion, because the possible loss of a few souls of the Greek rite bears no proportion to the blessings resulting from uniformity of discipline." Competing political loyalties, ethnic issues, church customs and other causes of conflict led from one third to one-half of the Ruthenians into schism, i.e., the loss of 225,000 Carpatho-Russian and Galician Uniates to the Orthodox Church(31). During the 1890's schismatic independent churches emerged also in the Polish communities of Chicago, Buffalo, Scranton and other cities and after 1904 became the Polish National Catholic church. In the turmoil of the immigration years, the sources of conflict were many even within the same ethnic group: control over parish property, maintenance of language and religious rituals, personality and ideological contrasts among the immigrant priests or with the diocesan bishop, the desire for pastors and bishops of the same ethnic group. For the Poles, the Lithuanians, the French Canadians as for the Germans before and the Vietnamese after them, the pattern of parish conflict was simply part of the immigrant condition and destined to explode when "there was some abuse at the local or diocesan level that moved a segment of irrepressible immigrants to seek an alternative vehicle for their religious life" (32) or when "different traditions, various concepts of the Roman Catholic Church in American circumstances" and different expectations from the same religious institutions come into clash without room for adaptation and compromise(33). In 1962, the Polish Catholic National Church had in the United States a membership close to 300,000 faithful with 162 churches and 151 priests(34).

95

14

5.   In the perpective of history, even a cursory review of the interplay of religion and immigration shows a complex process of transition of the various immigrant groups into the same church. In the journey toward integration, the social and cultural strategies adopted were normally anchored on the language parish and developed in response to its needs. They were parochial schools, immigrant associations, social agencies, ethnic seminaries, among others. When ethnic priests were not recruited, the cultural identity of the immigrants ignored, their request of community in the form of national parishes denied or political factions and partisan groups of immigrant priests became emotionally uncompromising, conflict inevitably arose even to the point of schism. A percentage of immigrants, varied for each ethnic group, fell away from the Church. In the overall picture, however, of the immigrant experience, beyond the tragic and sometimes colorful fights, an accommodation took place that allowed inclusion and participation in one multicultural ecclesial community. Diocesan and religious priests and women religious, the tactful and zealous concern of many bishops, through their open welcome and cultural affinity, served as "a bridge for millions of Catholic immigrants on the move from a peasant to an urban religiosity"(35). Projected of necessity and by choice into the future, the immigrants and their priests and sisters used the continuity with the past as a base on which to stand and chart their road into a dynamic and fast-changing New World.

1. U.S. Immigration and naturalization Service (INS), <u>Statistical Yearbook of the Immigration and Naturalization Service, 1985.</u> Daniel Heath, Ed. <u>America in Persepctive:</u> Major Trends in the United States through the 1990's. Boston: Houghton Mifflin Company, 1986, P.20

2. National Conference of Catholic Bishops, Administrative Committee. <u>Together, A New People: Pastoral Statement on Migrants and Refugees.</u> Washington, D.C.: 1980.

3. For a discussion of the relationship between religion and immigrants, see: Philip Gleason, "Ethnicity, Immigration and American Catholic History," <u>Social Thought,</u> 4 (Summer, 1978),3-28; Moses Rischin, "The New American Catholic History," <u>Church History,</u> 41 (June, 1972), 228f. Timothy L. Smith, "Religion and Ethnicity in America," <u>The American Historical Review,</u> 83 (December 1978), 1155-1185; Harold J. Abramson, "Religion," in Stephen Thernstrom, ed. <u>Harvard Encyclopedia of American Ethnic Groups.</u> Cambridge, MA: Harvard University Press, 1980. Pp.869-75.

4. Jay P. Dolan. <u>The American Catholic Experience.</u> A History from Colonial Times to the Present. Garden City, N.Y.: Doubleday, 1985-In ch.VI, discussing the role of the parish, Dolan points out the different type of initiative of the various immigrant goups. For cases of episcopal intervention in response to the immigrants' presence, see: Dolores A. Liptak, R.S.M., "The National Parish: Concept and Consequences for the Diocese of Hartford, 1890-1930," <u>The Catholic Historical Review,</u> 71 (January, 1985), 52-64; Stephen M. Di Giovanni, "Michael Augustine Corrigan and the Italian Immigrants: The Relationship Between the Church and the Italians in the Archdiocese of New York, 1885-1902." Unpublished Ph.D. Dissertation, Pontifical Gregorian University, Rome, 1983.

5. For the opposing views of American Bishops on the "German question" in the United States, see: Gerald P. Fogarty. <u>The Vatican and the Americanist Crisis:</u> Denis J. O'Connell, American Agent in Rome, 1885-1903. Rome: Gregorian University, 1974. Pp. 121-153. For a case of German-Polish confrontation, cf. Anthony J. Kwzniewski. <u>Faith and Fatherland.</u> The Polish Church War in Wisconsin, 1896-1918. Notre Dame: University of Notre Dame Press, 1980.

6. Andrew M. Greeley. <u>The American Catholic.</u> A Social Portrait. New York: Basic Books, Inc. 1977, p.37. For an extensive discussion on losses of European immigrants, cf. Gerald Shaughnessy. <u>Has the Immigrant Kept the Faith?</u> New York: Arno Press, 1969 (a 1925 reprint).

7. In the November 1986 General Meeting of the National Conference of Catholic Bishops, the "National Pastoral Plan for Hispanic Ministry" was presented. It states: "The plan has its origins in our Pastoral Letter. . .It takes into account the socio-cultural reality of our Hispanic people and suggests a style of pastoral ministry and model of Church in harmony with their faith and culture. For this reason it requires an affirmation of the concept of cultural pluralism in our Church within a fundamental unity of doctrine as expressed so many times by our magisterium."

97

16

8. Thomas J. Archdeacon. Becoming American. An Ethnic History. New York: The Free Press, 1983. p.101.

9. Jay P. Dolan, op. cit. p.204.

10. Silvano M. Tomasi. Piety and Power. The Role of Italian Parishes in the New York Metropolitan Area, 1880-1930. New York: Center for Migration Studies, 1975. Pp.101 and 146-156.

11. Z. Peszkowski, "List of Polish Roman Catholic Parishes in the United States," Sacrum Poloniae Millenium, VI (Rzym 1959), 255-369.

12. Joseph F. Parot. Polish Catholics in Chicago, 1984-1920. A Religious History. DeKalb, II: Northern Illinois University Press, 1981. Pp. 226

13. John Iwicki. The First One Hundred Years. A Study of the Apostolate of the Congregation of Resurrection in the United States, 1866-1966. Rome, 1966. Also, Joseph J. Parot, op. cit. pp.46-58.

14. Mario Francesconi. Storia della Congregazione Scalabriniana Rome: Centro Studi Emigrazione, 1974. Voll. 1-1V

15. For an overview, cf. C.E. McGuire, ed. Catholic Builders of the Nation. Boston: Continental Press, Inc. 1923. 5 Vols. For the Franciscans' work among Italian and Croatian immigrants, for example, see: Leonard F. Bacigalupo. The Franciscans and Italian Immigration in America. Hicksville, New York: Exposition Press, 1977; Vladimir Stankovic, "The Catholic Church and the Croatians in Foreign Lands." Mimeo. Zagreb, 1985.For the work of Frances X. Cabrini and her first sisters, see Mary Louise Sullivan, "Mother Cabrini: Italian Immigrant of the Century." Unpublished Ph.D. Dissertation, Bryn Mawr College, 1984.

16. Daniel S. Buczek. Immigrant Pastor. The Life of the Right Reverend Monsignor Lucyan Bojnowski of New Britain, Connecticut. Waterbury, CT: Heminway, 1974.

17. Michael J. Curley. Bishop John Neumann, C.SS.R., Fourth Bishop of Philadelphia. Phildelphia, PA: Bishop Newmann Center, 1952.

18. Ellen Marie Kuznicki, CSSF, "The Polish American Parochial Schools," in Frank Mocha, ed., Poles in America. Bicentennial Essays. Steven Point, WI: Wozzalla, 1978. Pp 435-60. See also Kuznicki's paper: "The Role of the Felician Sisters in the Shaping of American Polonia." Mimeo, 1986.

19. Mary Tullia Doman, CSSF, "Polish American Sisterhoods and Their Contributions to the Catholic Church in the U.S.A.," Sacrum Poloniae Millenium, VI (Rzym, 1959), 371-608

20. Jay Dolan, op. cit., pp. 278-82

21. For a recent case study of the social and religious role of the churches of the immigrants in an industrial city, see: Raymond A. Mohl and Neil Betten. Steel City: Urban and Ethnic Patterns in Gary, Indiana, 1906-1950. New York: Holmes and Meier, 1986. Pp. 161-218

22.   Joseph J. Parot, op. cit., p. 229

23.   National Conference of Catholic Bishops. <u>Pastoral Letters of the United States Bishops, 1792-1983</u>. Vol. IV. "Cultural Pluralism in the United States." (April 15, 1980), pp. 364-376. Washington, D.C., 1984. Ibid. <u>The Hispanic Presence: Challenge and Commitment</u>. A Pastoral Letter on Hispanic Ministry. Washington, D.C., 1983.

24.   <u>The Official Catholic Directory, 1985</u>. Wilmette, IL: P.J. Kenedy & Sons, 1985.

25.   "Hispanic Catholics: How Culture Shock Can Charge Up a Parish. The editors interview Bishop Placido Rodriguez, C.M.F.," <u>U.S. Catholic</u>, 51 (December, 1986), 33-39.

26.   The NCCB "National Pastoral Plan for Hispanic Ministry" (1986) is to be coordinated by the Secretariat for Hispanic Affairs of the United States Catholic Conference of Bishops - For coordination of pastoral care of some Asian groups, see: NCCB Bishops' Committee on Migration, Office of Pastoral Care of Migrants and Refugees. <u>Welcome into the Community of Faith</u>. Washington, D.C.:1986.

27.   NCCB Committee on Migration. Office of Pastoral Care of Migrants and Refugees, "Pastoral Care of Vietnamese Catholics in the United States. A Preliminary Report." (Unpublished). Washington, D.C.:1985.

28.   cf. <u>Houston '85: Let Ethnic America Hear His Voice</u>. Arcadia, CA.: National Convocation on Evangelizing Ethnic America, 1985. Also, John Dart, "Immigrants called 'Ripe Harvest Field' for Churches," <u>Los Angeles Times</u>, Part II, April 20, 1985, p.6.

29.   V.J. Fecher, S.V.D. <u>A Study of the Movement for German National Parishes in Philadelphia and Baltimore (1787-1802)</u>. Analecta Gregoriana, Vol. LXXVII. Rome: Gregorian University, 1955.

30.   Silvano M. Tomasi, op. cit., p. 149f. Jonathan Trela, "The Italian National Catholic Church: An Experiment that Failed," <u>PNCC Studies</u> 2, (1981), 31-41. Joseph W. Wieczerzak, "The Multi-ethnic Activities of an Ethnic Church: Outreaches of the Polish National Catholic Church During the Hodur Era," <u>PNCC Studies</u> 2 (1981), 1-30.

31.   Gerald P. Fogarty. <u>The Vatican and the American Hierarchy from 1870 to 1965</u>. Stuttgart: Anton Hiersemann, 1982. Pp. 62-64. Keith P. Dyrud, "The Establishment of the Greek Catholic Rite in America as a Competitor to Orthodoxy," in <u>The Other Catholic</u>. New York: Arno Press, 1978. Pp. 190-226.

32.   William Wolkovich-Valkavicius, "Origins of the Polish National Catholic Church in the Roman Catholic Archdiocese of Boston," <u>PNCC Studies</u> 6 (1985), p.51.

33.   Hieronim Kubiak. <u>The Polish National Catholic Church in the United States of America from 1897 to 1980</u>. Its Social Conditioning and Social Functions. Warszawa-Krakow: Nakladem Universytetu Jagiellonskiego,

99

1982. Pp. 89-93. For the bishop-immigrant conflict in an ethnic church among today's immigrant Vietnamese, cf. Human Rights or Church Rights/Nhan Quyen hay Giao Quyen. San Jose, CA: Vietnamese Catholic Council, Our Lady Queen of Martyrs' Mission, 1986.

34.   Hieronim Kubiak, op, cit., p. 121.

35.   Silvano M. Tomasi, "L'assistenza religiosa agli Italiani in USA e il Prelato per l'emigrazione italiana: 1920-1949." Studi Emigrazione, 19 (June, 1982), 167-189.

Voluntaryism: An Irish Catholic Tradition

Patrick Carey

Oscar Handlin noted some years ago that most immigrants to the United States found the voluntary practices of American religious institutions "unfamilar and disturbing."[1] This was not the case with the Irish Catholic immigrants in this country. They had little difficulty adjusting to these practices in America since they had developed them in Ireland before coming to the United States. Thus, many American Irish Catholics viewed voluntaryism not as a uniquely Protestant or American experience; they saw it as part of their Irish Catholic tradition.

This tradition is clearly evident in early nineteenth-century Irish Catholicism, even though its roots can be found in earlier Post-Reformation Catholicism in Ireland. This study focuses upon the transition of the tradition from Ireland to the United States, and concentrates upon the efforts of John England (1786-1842), a nineteenth-century Irish priest (1808-1820) and Bishop of Charleston, South Carolina (1820-1842), to articulate and defend that tradition in Ireland and the United States. Before analyzing England's advocacy of the practices and principles, however, the paper outlines the historical context of the tradition.

The Irish Catholic Church since the Protestant Reformation, and more particularly since the death of the Pretender Stuart James III in 1766, was a voluntary association; that is, membership in the church rested upon the individual's free, uncoerced consent. Likewise, it was a voluntary institution in the sense that the ministry and other ecclesiastical institutions were supported primarily by the free-will offerings of the laity.

The voluntary status of the Irish Church was a result of political circumstances. Except for a few brief interludes during the sixteenth and seventeenth centuries, Irish Catholics enjoyed a practical separation of their church from the state (i.e., their church was not a legally established state church), even though they did not enjoy the full civil and religious liberties that are usually associated with that separation in the United States. The experience of the union of the Anglican Church and state was historically inimical to the Irish Catholics' civil and religious welfare. That alliance produced the penal laws against Catholicism and kept many Catholics

---

1. Oscar Handlin, *The Uprooted: The Epic Story of the Great Migration that made the American People* (Boston, 1951), p. 126.

Mr. Carey is assistant professor of theology in Marquette University, Milwaukee, Wisconsin.

impoverished, poorly educated, and politically inactive. It also made the Catholic Church, however, a free church by forcing it to rely primarily upon the laity's voluntary contributions.

The situation of the Catholic Church in England differed. There the church depended upon the financial support of the Catholic landed families. As a result of this dependence, many of the English Catholics who lived in the neighborhood of the gentry's manor left the Catholic Church when the gentry conformed to the Established Church. The organization of the parish church in England depended to a large extent on the manors of the gentry. The "big house" became the place for the celebration of religious services and a religious refuge for neighboring Catholic families. When the landed families converted to the Protestant Church, therefore, the parish structure was immediately destroyed.[2] This was not the case in Ireland. There the Catholics paid tithes to the Protestant Churches while continuing to support, as much as they could with money, corn and other supplies, their pastors and parish chapels.

Even though the Catholic Church was separated from the English government, still it was somewhat influenced by the Pretender Stuarts until the death of James III in 1766. Before James' death, the Stuarts exercised their influence over the Catholic Church by participating in the nomination of bishops to Irish Sees. After his death, however, the papacy no longer acknowledged the Stuarts as the rightful rulers of England and Ireland, and the pope omitted the name of the Stuarts in the appointments of Irish bishops. Thus, after 1766, the Irish Catholic Church experienced no direct control or influence from any political power and had more freedom in its own internal operations (especially in the selection of the clergy) than the Catholic Church had in many of the countries of Europe where Catholicism was the state religion, and where Catholic rulers constantly intervened in church appointments and in church policy.[3] During the later half of the eighteenth and throughout the nineteenth centuries, therefore, the Irish Catholic Church persevered as a voluntary communion.

The Irish Catholic experience of voluntaryism produced two different effects. On the one hand, it created bonds of intimacy between the local parish priests and their parishioners. In many places, because they were forced to live on the voluntary offerings of their poor peasants or take to farming and cattle raising for their support, the Irish Catholic clergy became identified with their parishioners' poverty and persecution. On the other hand, the practice of voluntaryism occasioned numerous clerical abuses. Because the Irish were poor, their voluntary contributions to their pastors

2. Maureen Wall, *The Penal Laws, 1691–1760: Church and State from the Treaty of Limerick to the Accession of George III* (Dundalk, 1961), p. 35. I would like to thank Professor Maurice O'Connell of Fordham University for drawing my attention to this work.
3. Ibid., p. 69.

were meagre. To supplement the clerical income, therefore, it was customary to take up collections for the priest at weddings and funerals.[4] Some priests, however, corrupted this tradition by extorting fees for the administration of all sacraments and sacramentals, especially baptisms, confessions, marriages, visits to the sick, and funerals. As a result of these simoniacal means, the peasants at times rose up in rebellion against their "greedy" pastors[5] and the bishops periodically legislated against such clerical avarice.[6] In 1808, for example, the bishops of the province of Cashel forcefully condemned clerical simony as "injurious to religion, unbecoming to the sacred ministry, and disgraceful to their character." They judged that some priests were

> *justly* [*sic*] charged with odious extortion, or even with a rigorous exaction of their established dues; they cannot but consider it, with us, indispensably incumbent on them, never to bargin mercenarily for their dues; nor even to withhold from their people the sacrament of marriage, or any other sacrament, upon the pretext of not being paid by them.[7]

Thus, the historical effects of the vountary experience in Ireland not only created intimate bonds between the clergy and the laity, but also caused episcopal censures and "the bond [between clergy and laity] to chafe at times."[8]

Irish Catholic voluntaryism, like that in the United States, evolved initially as a response to cultural and political factors, and it was voluntary primarily in the sense that there was little political coercion. It was not, however, completely voluntary. Family custom, hatred of the British, and other cultural and sociological factors influenced the Irish Catholic's identification with the Catholic Church. The system of free-will support, moreover, was voluntary in the sense that it had no legal basis of compulsion as had the tithe system; nevertheless, custom, necessity and community pressure ensured that it had a real sanction in fact.[9] Because of this some might interpret Irish Catholic voluntaryism as cultural Catholicism, an element of political necessity, and there is no doubt some truth to the charge. The Irish Catholic experience, however, was not purely cultural, nor simply a matter of expediency.

What was in the beginning an historical necessity, developed into a religious ideal. The historical experience, regardless of its original source,

---

4. Ibid., p. 58.
5. See Robert E. Burns, "Parson, Priests and the People: The Rise of Irish Anti-Clericalism, 1785-89," *Church History* 31 (1962):151-163.
6. See the eighth decree of the 1817 Provincial Council of Tuam, *Acta et Decreta Sacrorum Conciliorum Recentiorum Collectio Lacensis*, 8 vols. (Friburg, 1875), 3:763.
7. *Statuta Synodalia Pro Unitis Dioecesibus Cassel et Imelac . . . 1810* (Dublin, 1813), p. 123.
8. John A. Murphy, "Priests and People in Modern Irish History," *Christus Rex* 23 (October 1969):245.
9. John A. Murphy, "The Support of the Catholic Clergy in Ireland, 1750-1850," *Historical Studies* 5 (1965):104.

became the basis of an articulate Irish Catholic intellectual tradition. During the early nineteenth century, in particular, Irish Catholic leaders of public opinion perceived the voluntary experience not as a necessity forced upon them by the English government, but as a religious ideal. The historical experience of voluntaryism and the persecution of the tithing system taught many Irish Catholics on the one hand to abhor the union of church and state, and, on the other, to value the principles of religious liberty, separation of church and state, and voluntaryism. It is not unusual, therefore, to find early nineteenth-century Irish Catholic bishops, priests, and political leaders who advocated these values from an ideological as well as a pragmatic point of view.

104

Irish Catholic leaders propagated voluntaryism as a religious principle most forcefully during the veto crisis, between 1808 and 1816. At various times during these years, English and Irish politicians presented bills in the House of Commons for state payment of the Catholic clergy and full emancipation for Catholics. In exchange for these provisions, the bill asked the Catholic Church to grant the English government the right to veto nominations of bishops to Irish Sees. Daniel O'Connell (1775-1847), Father John England, the national Irish episcopacy, and a host of clerical and lay committees throughout Ireland rejected the bills and led a national campaign against the veto. They objected to the legislation on the grounds that it would unite the church and state; they wanted to maintain the separation of the Irish Catholic Church from the state in order to preserve the freedom of both. They also felt that the church could remain free when it relied only on the liberal contributions of the laity.

Daniel O'Connell led the fight against the veto bill and state aid to the clergy. He believed that government pensions would only enslave Irish Catholics more than they had been in the past. He praised the Irish Catholic episcopacy's rejection of the measures on the ground that they were preserving the independence of the church.

> The prelates, if they had given their countenance and support to this bill, might have consulted and advanced their worldly interests. But the sacred calls of duty made them reject both considerations with contempt. . . . the corrupt influence of the government is not to be extended to your Church . . . there remains, and will remain in Ireland, one spot free from ministerial pollution.[10]

According to O'Connell and the anti-vetoists, the Catholic Church would only be made "the hireling of the [British] Ministry"[11] if it accepted clerical pensions from the government. If the veto and state aid were granted "men would be selected [bishops] who could sacrifice their consciences to the

10. John O'Connell (ed.), *The Select Speeches of Daniel O'Connell, M.P.*, 2 vols. (Dublin, 1867), 1:165, 169.
11. Ibid., 1:321.

interest of their patrons."[12] State payment was to be rejected on the grounds of two principles.

> Let us also advocate our cause on the two great principles—first, that of the eternal separation in spirituals between our church and the state; secondly, that of the eternal right to freedom of conscience.[13]

The Irish Catholic episcopacy, induced by O'Connell and other anti-vetoists, also refused to accept state pensions. From 1808 to 1816, they published yearly pastorals against the measure. On September 15, 1808, they issued their first condemnation of the proposal saying it was "inexpedient to introduce any alteration in the Canonical mode hitherto observed in the nomination to Irish Roman Catholic Bishops."[14] In 1810, they reaffirmed their 1808 resolution against the bill and assured the Irish Catholic clergy and laity that they neither sought nor desired any "earthly considerations" (a reference to state aid) from the government in exchange for general Catholic emancipation; they sought and desired only what the laity "may from a sense of religion and duty, voluntarily afford us."[15] With increasingly more forceful statements after 1810, the bishops continued to oppose the veto bill and supported the Irish Catholic tradition of voluntaryism.[16] During these years, from 1813 to 1816 in particular, numerous lay and clerical conferences throughout Ireland encouraged and commended the bishops in their attempt to preserve the Irish custom and maintain the liberty of the church.[17]

105

While most the liberal Irish Catholic lay and clerical leaders were unalterably opposed to state aid, some anti-vetoists, like O'Connell and Bishop James Warren Doyle (1786-1837),[18] were not absolutely nor consistently opposed. In 1825, for example, O'Connell agreed to the measure

12. Ibid., 1:420.
13. Ibid., 2:16. On O'Connell's position on separation and religious liberty see the excellent study by Sister Helen Coldrick, "Daniel O'Connell and Religious Freedom," (Ph.D. dissertation, Fordham University, 1974).
14. Quoted in [John England], *The Religious Repertory* (Cork, 1814), p. 35. Peter Guilday, *The Life and Times of John England*, 2 vols. (New York, 1927), 1:119-120, indicated that he could not uncover any documentary evidence of England's direct role in the veto controversy. Specially, he was unable to discover any copies of the *Repertory* (see ibid. 1:83) or any of the *Cork Mercantile Chronicle* which England edited (see ibid. 1:111). In 1974, I uncovered three volumes of the *Repertory* and numerous issues of the *Chronicle* (1808-1818) in the National Library in Dublin, Ireland, St. Patrick's College, Maynooth, and St. Patrick's College, Carlow. These documents throw new light on England's early clerical career in Ireland and upon his early intellectual development.
15. Ibid., pp. 40-41.
16. The bishops' statements for 1813 and 1814 can be found in England, *Repertory*, pp. 41-44.
17. On the resolutions from these conferences, see ibid., pp. 53-64; 70; 137; 201-207; 345-350; cf. also *Cork Mercantile Chronicle*, May 18, 20, 27, 1814.
18. On Doyle, see William Fitzpatrick, *The Life, Times, and Correspondence of the Right Rev. Dr. Doyle*, 2 vols. (Boston, 1862).

in order to achieve emancipation; he later changed his mind and withdrew his support when he discovered that it was rejected by a majority of the liberal Irish spokesmen.[19] After 1825, he remained inexorably opposed to state aid. Doctor Doyle, the foremost clerical leader in the movement for Irish emancipation after 1823, felt that pensioning the clergy should not be considered a means for emancipation,[20] but his opposition was not absolute. He believed that

> if the Catholics were emancipated a provision could be made for the Catholic clergy unconnected with, and totally independent of court favour, and which would not add probably a single shilling to the burthens of the country.[21]

106

Unlike O'Connell and Doyle, Father John England, a priest from Cork who edited the *Cork Mercantile Chronicle,* a radical anti-veto paper during the height of the veto controversy, represented an uncompromising liberal position on the principle of voluntaryism. His position deserves a more extended consideration in this essay not only because he represented the uncompromising Irish Catholic tradition but also because he illustrated the ease with which the Irish Catholic immigrant accepted the American principle and practice of voluntaryism. In 1820 he immigrated to the United States after being consecrated Bishop of Charleston, South Carolina. During his ministry in Ireland and throughout his episcopacy in the United States, he consistently and unequivocally rejected all proposals for state support of religion as inconsistent with the Irish Catholic experience and as contrary to the ideals of religious liberty and separation of church and state.[22]

As a priest-editor, England led a political campaign against state payment of the clergy because he felt that the Irish Catholic clergy had existed in the past on the liberality of their people and they did not want nor would they consent to any change in that custom which had created bonds of intimate friendship and "fellow feeling" between the priests and the people.[23] Likewise, the clergy desired no state pensions because they wanted no conflicts between their duties to religion and their obligations to the state. When those who advocated state aid objected to England's position saying "rely on your own integrity," England replied: "We will not put ourselves in the way of temptation."[24] He believed the vetoists had underestimated the weakness of human nature and the power of the state; also, they had not

19. See Coldrick, "Daniel O'Connell," pp. 207-237 and Ignatius A. Reynolds (ed.), *The Works of the Right Reverend John England,* 5 vols. (Baltimore, 1849), 3:511.
20. James W. Doyle, *A Defense of His Vindication of the Religious and Civil Principles of the Irish Catholics* (Dublin, 1824), p. 41.
21. James W. Doyle, *Letters on the State of Ireland* (Dublin, 1825), p. 291.
22. On England's position on religious liberty, see Patrick Carey, "John England and Irish American Catholicism 1815-1842: A Study of Conflict," (Ph.D. dissertation, Fordham University, 1975), pp. 79-110; see also Richard Rousseau, "Bishop John England and American Church-State Theory," (Ph.D. dissertation, Saint Paul University, 1969).
23. *Cork Mercantile Chronicle,* May 10, 1813.
24. Ibid., June 6, 1814.

perceived the historical evils that resulted from state payment of the clergy. Under state pensions, the clergy of the Established Church and even the Presbyterian ministers had bartered and forfeited the rights of the Irish people in exchange for a life of material comfort and ease.[25]

State payment of the clergy or any other financial aid to the church, according to England, not only made the clergy appendages of the state, it also contradicted the spirit of the Christian religion. When Protestant societies established the "London Society for Converting the Jews to Christianity" in the city of Cork in 1814, England viciously attacked their methods of conversion.

> Accustomed to traffic in everything, they [English Protestants] made religion a trade, and call it a conversion, when by the granting of a privilege, or the giving of a sum of money, they get a person to say that he is of their religion. If the belief in the utility of money, and of power, be the fundamental articles of their creed, it is indeed sufficiently universal to be catholic—but it is not the religion of that Redeemer, who only promised persecution, and recommended poverty to his followers, and who said, that his kingdom was not of this world, but of the next.[26]

107

England maintained that the Irish Catholic clergy preferred the poverty and oppression of the religion of Jesus to the comfort and ease of a state-supported church. During the peak of the veto debate, he drew up a petition, signed by the Catholic priests of Cork, which condemned state aid and declared:

> The clergy ask for no riches, no power, no advantages,—all they want is, that the faith preserved by their predecessors amidst every oppression and penalty, shall be protected from ministerial or political influence at present.[27]

Neither England nor his fellow anti-veto agitators acknowledged the corruptions of the practice of voluntaryism. They were interested in preserving what they considered the ideal of voluntaryism.

The Irish Catholic support for voluntaryism, articulated by England and others, attracted some attention on the Continent. In the 1830s, Félicité de Lamennais called upon the French Catholics to imitate Irish Catholics by resisting state payment of the clergy and creating a voluntary system of church support. For him, the Irish Catholics had protected the liberty of the church by preserving their tradition of voluntaryism.

> At all times, we ought to declare, and loudly declare, that, there is no possible liberty for the church but under a condition, which without doubt, will suppress the annual salary given by the state to the clergy. Whoever is paid depends on those who pay him. This kind of servitude has been rightly judged by the

25. England, like many of the Irish Catholic liberals, overestimated the financial importance of the *regium donum* to the Presbyterians. On this, see James C. Beckett, *Protestant Dissent in Ireland 1687-1780*, Vol. 2 of *Studies In Irish History*, ed. T. W. Moody, R. Dudley Edwards and David B. Quinn (London, 1948), pp. 106-115.
26. England, *Repertory*, p. 181.
27. *Cork Mercantile Chronicle*, June 6, 1814.

Catholics of Ireland, who have withstood and repelled the various attempts of
English imposition. As long as we cease to imitate their example, catholicity will
have but a precarious and feeble existence among us. . . . Among the Catholics of
Europe, there are none more indigent than the catholics of Ireland, and there is
not any place where religion is better supported; for this support is given by the
poor.[28]

For John England, as for Lamennais and many of the Irish Catholic
liberals, the Catholic Church should be supported by the laity rather than
the state because only in this way could the church be independent.
Moreover, the church, founded by Jesus Christ, was grounded on the basis of
a free act of faith; it could use, therefore, no other means but spiritual
persuasion to sustain or increase membership. Jesus "taught truth, and
gained converts by persuasion."[29] For Arthur O'Leary, one of England's
intellectual progenitors, Jesus furnished Christians "with no other means of
making proselytes to his religion but persuasion, prayer and good example. . . . the Kingdom of God is not of this world."[30]

The Irish Catholic anti-vetoists believed that the church should follow
Jesus' example in using only spiritual means to promote and maintain the
faith. If a minister, for instance, should find anyone in error, he should
follow the "Divine Master's" example and "endeavour to reclaim him by
argument and by persuasion."[31] Likewise, neither the church nor any other
institution should subject a man to covert and subtle offers of temporal
privileges and advantages in exchange for a change in his religious opinions
and beliefs.[32] The church was a free association of believers, and this
communion could only be legitimately maintained and increased by personal
conviction. Experience and the Christian heritage worked together in
building up an Irish Catholic enthusiasm for the principle of volun-
tarism.

When Irish Catholics came to the United States they carried their
tradition of voluntaryism with them. This was clearly evident in their
continued financial support of their parish priests. In 1836, John Dubois,
Bishop of New York, acknowledged this tradition when he compared the
Irish practices to those of other Catholic immigrants. In a report to the
Archbishop of Vienna, Dubois outlined the different voluntary practices
among the various immigrants in his diocese.

The missions have only voluntary incomes which are small and uncertain; or in
the cities where there are churches, an income is derived from the pew rents. The
contributions of the French often amount to nothing. German and European

28. *Journal des Debats*, October 19, 1830 quoted in *United States Catholic Miscellany*,
    December 11, 1830, p. 190.
29. *Cork Mercantile Chronicle*, September 5, 1814.
30. Arthur O'Leary, *Miscellaneous Tracts*, 2nd ed. (Dublin, 1781), p. 345.
31. *Cork Mercantile Chronicle*, September 5, 1814.
32. Ibid., December 8, 1815.

immigrants coming from Catholic countries, who are accustomed to assist at Church services without payment, refuse all contributions, even conditional. It should be noted that they are very poor. However, as there are very many of them, they prevent all progress of the mission in places where they are numerous in as much as they throw the entire burden upon the small number of Americans and Irish who are unable to bear the load. The Irish immigrants act very differently. Accustomed as they are at home to support their pastors and pay for the building and maintenance of their churches, they show their willingness here also. Unfortunately they are so scattered, that it is impossible to bring them together in sufficient numbers to provide for the parishes. Their efforts, moreover, are apt to be thwarted by being mingled with other nationalities.[33]

John England found similar experiences in South Carolina in 1820 when he came to Charleston as bishop of that diocese. He believed that Irish religious practices more closely approximated those in the United States than did those of any other immigrant group.[34] Thus, in promoting the practice of voluntaryism, he held up the Irish Catholic tradition as an example for the American Catholic Church. He maintained that the Irish Catholic priests, like the clergy of the primitive church, had lived in poverty as a result of the generous, but meagre, gifts of the laity. These clergy, however, believed that "their kingdom was not of this world."[35] This faith kept the church free and independent.

Throughout his ministry in the United States, England advocated the principle of voluntaryism on two different fronts. On the one, he fought against those who sought state aid for religious purposes; on the other, he rejected exclusive lay trustee control of voluntary contributions. For him, the principle meant that the church, and the clergy in particular, had to be free from lay as well as governmental dominance in the care of ecclesiastical institutions.

Periodically from 1820 to 1842, Bishop England rejected proposals to use state funds for religion. He opposed, for example, those in South Carolina who suggested that additional taxes be imposed on whiskey for the purpose of giving the added tax revenue to religious missionaries.[36] He believed that whenever the state supported the church, the church lived in a degree of wealth and comfort, but this almost always distracted the clergy from their proper religious vocations and sometimes made them pawns of the state.[37] He preferred, therefore, "infinitely more, church liberty and poverty to this subjugation accompanied by the most splendid endowments."[38] Voluntary

33. "Bishop Dubois on New York in 1836," *United States Catholic Historical Society Historical Records and Studies* 10 (January 1917):126.
34. England to Dr. Michael O'Connor, February 25, 1835, in Guilday, 1:481–482.
35. Reynolds, *Works*, 3:505; cf. also "Papers Relating to the Church in America from the Port-folios of the Irish College in Rome," *Records of the American Catholic Historical Society* 8 (1897):305-308.
36. Reynolds, *Works*, 4:49.
37. Ibid., 1:438; cf. also 3:512.
38. "Papers Relating," pp. 303, 306.

support was the principal means of preserving the liberty of the church.[39]

In the 1840s, when Bishop John Hughes and Father John Power requested financial aid for Catholic schools from the New York City Council and the Common School Fund, England told his readers in the *United States Catholic Miscellany* that he was "not disappointed by the result of the application." He did not consider the city council's refusal just; but, it was unjust, he thought, because it was based upon prejudice against Catholics. He did not raise the issue of state aid to religion in this case but simply maintained that Catholics had the responsibility to assert their rights in a free society. He was more interested in defending the Catholic struggle to overcome "hatred, bigotry and oppression" than he was in demanding state aid for the schools.[40] He never supported, however, Catholic attempts to obtain state aid for their schools.

England also rejected exclusive lay trustee control of church finances. During the first years of his episcopal administration in South Carolina, at the height of the Philadelphia trustee conflicts (1820-1829), he criticized the American Catholic trustee system because he believed the exclusive trustee control of ecclesiastical temporalities had endangered clerical liberty and the freedom of the gospel within the church. The trustee system, he wrote, produced "the curse of an oligarchical tyranny of the worst description."[41] He felt that whoever controlled the purse controlled the pastor—and the trustees controlled the purse. The trustees' particular system required "from the clergyman concessions incompatible with his duty, and reduced him to the alternative of betraying his conscience, or forfeiting the means of his support."[42] England, therefore, opposed such a system with as much vigor as he had the veto and the union of church and state in Ireland.

The trustee system of church financing, according to England, also conflicted with the true purpose of the church. The trustees had rented out the pews of the churches in order to support the church and the pastors. England criticized the manner of collecting support because

> By their means a very painful and galling distinction is created between the rich and poor which causes pride and conceit in the one, and mortification and shame in the other, where both ought to be on a footing of equality before their common maker.[43]

In order to secure the liberty of the church and preserve its communal nature, England reformed the trustee system in his diocese. The system was not inherently evil; however, it did need a few limitations. When he dedicated

---

39. *United States Catholic Miscellany,* January 15, 1831, pp. 230-231; January 31, 1832, p. 236.
40. Ibid., February 27, 1841; cf. also Reynolds, *Works,* 4:114-115.
41. "Papers Relating," p. 312.
42. "Diurnal of the Right Rev. John England, First Bishop of Charleston, South Carolina, 1820-1823," *Records of the American Catholic Historical Society* 6 (1895):204.
43. Ibid., p. 202.

the first new church in Charleston, therefore, he eliminated the pew rent system of church support and indicated that everyone in the Catholic Church, regardless of the amount of his church support, should have equal approach to the advantages of religion and that neither privilege nor financial prominence should be acknowledged within the ecclesiastical community.

> There are no pews nor private seats in the church which has been erected, nor is it intended there should be, for it is conceived by its superintendents that the house of God should be open to all, and that the benefits of religion should not be confined to a few purchasers and sold like the goods of this world; but that the poor should have equal opportunities of being instructed as the rich—there are convenient benches which are equally free to persons of all persuasions—no member of the congregation having a right of precedence to any other well conducted person who may be present.[44]

In order to procure further the values of voluntary religion for all the members of the diocese and to avoid the abuses of the trustee system, England created a legal constitution for the government of the diocese.[45] Modelled after the federal constitution, his diocesan constitution established controls upon the trustees in the area of the collection and distribution of voluntary offerings so that the clergy's evangelical freedom would be upheld and the laity's right to an effective voice through their contributions would also be maintained. Neither the clergy nor the laity were to dominate the church through the management of voluntary offerings. England felt that only through voluntary support, regulated by specific laws, could a balanced relationship be realized between the clergy and the people; through his system of church government, the clergy were still dependent upon the laity's voluntary contributions for their sustenance, but they were not controlled by them in the exercise of their clerical functions. He held that the relationship between the pastor and his people should be one of friendship and that the voluntary system of support could "cement this affection."

> A pastor who feels himself to a certain extent dependent upon the good will of his flock, will be frequently urged to reflect upon the best mode of securing their affection, for it is his interest. He is not the slave of any individual nor of any faction, though he must endeavor to conciliate all.[46]

The principle of voluntaryism implied more than the free-will support of the church. It also meant that there was freedom within the church. England's diocesan constitution recognized and accepted the fact that in the United States religious associations could not be "legally held without their voluntary acceptance."[47] England found this legal circumstance particularly valuable for the government of the Catholic Church in that it allowed the

---

44. *United States Catholic Miscellany,* June 5, 1822, p. 5.
45. Reynolds, *Works,* 5:91–105.
46. "Papers Relating," p. 307.
47. Ibid., p. 317.

church a maximum amount of freedom in establishing its own constitutional basis for church government. In 1836, he pointed out this benefit of the American law when he reported to the Society for the Propagation of the Faith in France:

> In a word, they [Catholics] can voluntarily bind themselves by special acts to maintain and observe the whole doctrine and discipline of their church, and can regulate that no person shall be admitted a member of their association without his undertaking this obligation, or shall continue a member if he violates his contract for such observance.[48]

As the American laws recognized the perfect freedom of all individuals to join their own voluntary corporations, so his constitution acknowledged the liberty of all Catholics to accept or reject the provisions of the diocesan constitution. No parish, priest or layman had to accept the document. If Catholics did not choose willingly to approve it, they were not to be cut off from Catholic communion. In fact, "they shall have our good wishes, our friendly offices and our religious intercourse" even if they did not accept the constitution.[49]

For England, the Catholics of the diocese were not only free to accept or reject the constitution, they were also at liberty to express themselves openly at the annual diocesan conventions provided for by the constitution. Periodically, he asked the convention delegates to suggest useful modifications in the government of the diocese in order to bring more effective administration into the diocese.[50] Only if there were free expression and voluntary acceptance could there be an enthusiastic support for any system of government in the church. For England, Christian liberty could be properly exercised within the Catholic Church if the rights and duties of all were concisely defined and limited by ecclesiastical constitutions. His own constitution served as a remarkable instrument for implementing the exercise of Christian freedom within the diocesan church.

The high priority Americans put on freedom influenced England not only in the construction of this constitution, but also in his frequent attempts to explain the nature of liberty within the Catholic Church. In opposition to the American Protestants who denied that there was any freedom within the Catholic Church, England maintained that it was a general practice among prelates in the Catholic Church to seek the advice and opinions of the clergy and laity on matters which related to their welfare. At times the clergy and laity disagreed with their bishops; but, there "is ample scope for differences of opinion" in the church as long as the differences do not deny or contradict the defined doctrines of the church. In the area of church discipline,

> we are at liberty respectfully to give our opinion regarding the expediency or

48. Reynolds, *Works*, 3:241-242.
49. Ibid., 5:421.
50. Ibid., 4:334.

inexpediency of the law, the utility or the inaptitude of the discipline. We have therefore all that liberty which is consistent with good sense, good order, and the general good. We have just as much as any citizen has in any well organized state. It is true that we believe the Constitution of the Church cannot be changed; because it emanates from God and not from man; . . . but the legislation of the church is so far liable to change, as that it may by proper tribunals be accommodated to the circumstances of time and place not only to preserve order but to promote the purity and the prosperity of the body of the faithful.[51]

In view of the position he took in Ireland, his American emphasis cannot be considered expediency.

The church was also free to entertain a variety of religious opinions. Where God did not teach, Christians were at perfect liberty to form their own opinions.[52] Having said this, however, England reminded Catholics that religion was not simply a matter of opinion, but fact; freedom was allowed for inquiry where the fact of revelation had not been decided.[53] Where the church had not defined the meaning of revelation, there was room for a great diversity of speculation.[54] Even in church councils, where matters of doctrine were to be defined, bishops had the maximum amount of freedom to investigate the evidence and to express their own opinions. Truth could be reached only through such free investigation and expression of opinion in the church.[55]

The Irish Catholic tradition of voluntaryism, articulated by John England and others, prepared the Irish for their experiences in America. For them, voluntaryism in practice and principle was not necessarily a Protestant, nor even an exclusively American phenomenon; it was a continuation and extension of the Irish Catholic heritage. Like the native Americans, the American Irish Catholics freely supported their church and saw this as a means of preserving the freedom of their church. Like their American neighbors, moreover, they advocated religious liberty and separation of church and state as the religious principles upon which voluntaryism was based. Furthermore, they saw faith, freedom, participation, discussion, persuasion, and cooperation between the clergy and laity within the church itself as implications of voluntaryism. Unlike some of their Protestant neighbors, however, they saw dangers inherent within the American practice of voluntaryism. That practice, which had in many instances given the laity complete control of ecclesiastical temporalities, tended to enslave the clergy to the cultural values of the congregations. Even though many Catholic clergy, like those in Protestantism, did not rise above the cultural values, nevertheless many Catholic ecclesiastics saw the necessity of structuring the church in

113

51. Ibid., 1:435–436. England's ideas on freedom within the church were realized in his diocese, but not in many other dioceses at the time.
52. Ibid., 2:81; 1:166, 249.
53. *United States Catholic Miscellany*, February 4, 1824, p. 66.
54. Reynolds, *Works*, 3:454.
55. Ibid., 2:82.

such a way as to provide for evangelical freedom of the clergy within the church.

Throughout the middle and later half of the nineteenth century, American Catholics continued to profess their adherence to the principle of voluntaryism; but they also began to depart from the implications of the principle. Their almost exclusive emphasis upon the clergy's freedom within the church tended to reduce the laity's freedoms and to relegate their participation to financial contributions and a passive obedience to the clergy. By seeking state aid for their struggling schools, moreover, American Catholics (and Irish immigrants among the leaders) diminished the clarity of the earlier Irish Catholic advocacy of voluntaryism. By gradually withdrawing itself from the implications of voluntaryism, the American Catholic Church gave Protestants reason to criticize the church's lack of freedom. Present Catholic interest in co-responsibility and democracy within the church seems to be a reflection of the implications of the earlier Irish Catholic tradition. Likewise, however, present attempts to obtain state aid for Catholic schools reveal the tensions inherent in American Catholic approaches to voluntaryism.

Chapter I

MICHAEL F. FUNCHION

Irish Chicago:
Church, Homeland, Politics, and Class—The Shaping of an Ethnic Group, 1870-1900

> *The country has survived the Irish emigration—*
> *the worst with which any other country was ever*
> *afflicted. The Irish fill our prisons, our reform*
> *schools, our hospitals. . . . Scratch a convict or*
> *a pauper and the chances are that you tickle the*
> *skin of an Irish Catholic . . . made a criminal or*
> *a pauper by the priest and politician who have*
> *deceived him and kept him in ignorance, in a*
> *word, a savage, as he was born.*
> *—Chicago Evening Post, 1868*

> *We are a distinctive historic people, and we have*
> *done the Americans a great deal of good by com-*
> *ing to this country.*
> —John Fitzgibbon, *Chicago Irish Businessman*

$\mathbf{T}$HE IRISH FIRST CAME TO THE CHI-
cago region in large numbers in 1836, one year before the incorporation
of the city.[1] Lured by promises of good wages and steady employment,
scores of Irishmen—some with experience on eastern canals, others
fresh off the boat—came to build the Illinois and Michigan Canal, an
ambitious project designed to link Lake Michigan with the Illinois
River. By the time the canal was completed in 1848, thousands of Irish
laborers had left their picks and shovels and had moved to Chicago or
to Bridgeport, the northeastern terminus of the canal which at that time
was a village separate from Chicago. There, along with other Irish
immigrants, they worked mainly as unskilled laborers in meat-packing
plants, brickyards, and the like. By 1850, 6,096, or about 20 percent, of
Chicago's inhabitants were Irish immigrants. During the next twenty
years, as Chicago grew by leaps and bounds and emerged as the transportation, manufacturing, and commercial mecca of the Midwest, thousands more Irish arrived in the city seeking jobs and a better life than
they had had back home. By 1870, almost 40,000 Irish natives were
living in the city.[2]

During the last three decades of the nineteenth century, the Irish-
born population continued to grow, although far more slowly than before. Between 1870 and 1900, the number of Irish immigrants in the
city rose from 39,988 to 73,912, or by some 85 percent (see Table I), a
substantial increase but not nearly so dramatic as the jump of 556 per-

TABLE I
IRISH-BORN IN CHICAGO, 1870–1900

	Number of Irish-born	Percent of Foreign-born Population	Percent of Total Population
1870	39,988	27.66%	13.37%
1880	44,411	21.68%	8.83%
1890	70,028	15.54%	6.37%
1900	73,912	12.59%	4.35%

Source: U.S., *Ninth Census, 1870*, Vol. I, "Population," pp. 386–391; *Tenth Census, 1880*, "Population," pp. 538–541; *Eleventh Census, 1890*, "Population," Part I, pp. 670–673; *Twelfth Census, 1900*, Vol. I, "Population," Part I, pp. 796–799.

cent that had occurred in the twenty years prior to 1870. The Irishborn, of course, were not the only Irish in Chicago. During the three decades after the Great Fire of 1871, the American-born Irish population expanded rapidly. By 1890, the first year in which the federal census listed the number of Chicagoans of foreign parentage, the Irish population, first and second generations included, totaled 183,844 (see Table II).[3] Of these, only 38 percent were immigrants, and ten years later the Irish-born represented even fewer—31 percent of the 237,478 Irish in the city. Among the adult population, it appears that until sometime during the 1890s, Irish immigrants outnumbered their American-born kinsmen.[4]

117

TABLE II
FIRST- AND SECOND-GENERATION IRISH IN CHICAGO, 1890-1900

	Number	Percent of Total Population
1890	183,844	16.72%
1900	237,478	13.98%

Source: U.S., *Eleventh Census, 1890*, "Population," Part I, pp. 708, 714, 720, 726, 728; *Twelfth Census, 1900*, Vol. 1, "Population," Part I, pp. 874–875, 882–883, 890–891, 898–899, 902–903.

Nonetheless, from the 1870s on, when a number of them began to reach maturity, the American-born children of immigrants played a significant role in the institutional life of Irish Chicago. Indeed, one of the factors that distinguishes the last three decades of the century from the previous period was the emergence of the second-generation Irish.[5] No statistics are available for the third generation; but considering the years of Irish immigration to the United States, it appears that up until 1900 the overwhelming majority were children. After that date, as a number of these children reached adulthood, Irish Chicago became a community dominated by three instead of two generations.

Compared to that of other cities, the Irish population of Chicago was impressive in size. In 1890, for example, only three American cities—New York, Philadelphia, and Brooklyn—had more Irish than did Chicago.[6] Yet within Chicago the Irish were a minority, and one that was declining relative to the total population (see Tables I and II). Both Germans and Americans of native parentage outnumbered the Irish; toward the end of the century the ratio of Germans to Irish was more than two to one in Chicago. And while other groups—Scandinavians, Poles, Bohemians, and Italians—were less numerous than the Irish, they were increasing at a faster rate.[7]

A minority in the city as a whole, the Irish were also a minority in most of the neighborhoods where they lived. In the decades after the Great Fire, most Irish lived on the South and West sides; except for a small area on the near North Side, they were only sparsely settled in the northern sections of the city. But despite their concentration on the South and West sides, relatively few Irish lived in real ethnic ghettos. The school census of 1884, for example, reveals that out of 303 census canvass districts in the city, the Irish formed a majority of the population in only eleven. Since these eleven districts contained only about 14 percent of the city's Irish, it meant that 86 percent of them lived in areas where they were in a minority.[8] Similarly, a study of the school census of 1898 shows that the Irish were the most dispersed of ten ethnic groups studied.[9] The historian, of course, must be careful not to exaggerate the significance of such dispersal. Geographical proximity to other groups, for example, did not necessarily lead to social interaction with them. This was particularly true when neighboring groups spoke different languages and attended different churches and schools. In fact, one could argue that proximity had the opposite effect: rubbing shoulders with a people of a different national background could often lead to increased resentment.

Though few lived in real ethnic ghettos, the late nineteenth-century Chicago Irish nonetheless formed a highly visible and relatively cohesive ethnic community. Like other immigrants, the Irish derived their sense of unity from a common religious and ethnic heritage, a heritage they preserved through certain key institutions. And like other immigrants, their basic cohesiveness was further strengthened by certain forces and conditions they encountered in Chicago.

Most important in maintaining a separate Irish identity was their Catholicism, which, like the Polish variety, was inextricably intertwined with their national consciousness. Ever since the Protestant Reformation, the ancient Anglo-Irish struggle had been religious as well as national. Even though recent research has shown that the pre-Famine Irish did not practice their religion as devoutly as we have commonly assumed,[10] centuries of religious persecution had ingrained in them a deep attachment to the Church of Rome, an attachment that usually remained strong after their arrival in America. And since the United States was an overwhelmingly Protestant nation, Catholicism was one of the chief factors that distinguished the Irish from other Americans.

Although the first Catholics in the frontier town of Chicago were mainly of French and French-Indian origin, these were overwhelmed in the late 1830s and 1840s by the large influx of Irish as well as Ger-

118

man immigrants. Until the 1870s, the Catholic Church remained a predominantly Irish and German institution, with the Irish outnumbering
the Germans.[11] Toward the end of the century, as the "new immigrants"
arrived from southern and eastern Europe, the church became increasingly multiethnic, though as late as 1900 the Irish still formed the
largest bloc of Catholics.

Because of their numerical superiority, and because the American
hierarchy looked favorably on English-speaking prelates, the Irish
dominated the ecclesiastical administration in Chicago throughout the
nineteenth century. From the appointment of the first bishop, William
Quarter, in 1844 until the death of Archbishop James Quigley in 1915,
all the bishops of Chicago were either Irish-born or of Irish parentage,
with the one exception of Bishop James Van De Velde, a Belgian who
briefly presided over the diocese from 1849 to 1854. The Germans, the
French, and later immigrants naturally resented this Irish domination.
They demanded a greater voice in the administration of the diocese,
and at times they even demanded the creation of separate dioceses for
the various foreign-language groups. And yet, except for a schism among
the Poles, the various immigrant groups remained within the Irish fold
of Roman Catholicism.

For this the Irish bishops, whatever their shortcomings, deserve
some credit. They did much to quell ethnic tensions in the church by
permitting the establishment of separate or national parishes for the
Germans and other non-English-speaking immigrants. Begun in the
1840s by Bishop Quarter, a native of County Offaly, this practice of
creating national parishes was faithfully followed by his successors. By
1870, Chicago had nine national parishes besides the sixteen territorial
ones which served English-speaking Catholics. And during the next
thirty-odd years, when Bishop Thomas Foley (1870–1879) and Archbishop Patrick Feehan (1880–1902) presided over the diocese, sixty-
three national churches, in addition to forty-seven territorial churches,
were established. Feehan, an Irish immigrant from County Tipperary
and the former bishop of Nashville, strongly emphasized the need for
national parishes, believing that they were one of the best means of
protecting the faith of non-English-speaking immigrants. The Germans
and others obviously agreed with Feehan and praised him for his sensitivity to their needs.[12] One German Catholic editor remarked that
"he has proven himself a truly Catholic prelate, guided by principle
and zeal, regardless of national consideration."[13] And when he died in
1902, the *Chicago Tribune* lauded him for his "diplomatic handling of
the Irish, German, Polish, Bohemian, French and Italian elements in
the diocese."[14]

The system of national parishes not only helped to diffuse the po-

119

Bishop William J. Quarter, the first bishop of the Chicago Diocese. Beginning with Quarter in 1844 until the death of Archbishop James E. Quigley in 1915, all of the bishops (with one exception) were either Irish born or of Irish parentage. *Courtesy of the Chicago* CATHOLIC.

tential ethnic powderkeg in the church; it also effectively separated the Irish from other Catholics. Although in theory territorial parishes were not necessarily Irish, in practice they were, since virtually all English-speaking Catholics in Chicago were Irish. An Irishman attending mass or a parish function might occasionally meet a non-Irish Catholic, perhaps a convert, but by and large the only people he saw were fellow Irishmen. Thus membership in a universal church did little—at least at this time—to undermine Irish ethnic solidarity.

Just as in Ireland, the local parish played a central role in the lives of the people. Not only did it serve their religious needs, but it also provided a host of other services. Most pastors took a vital interest in the lives of their parishioners. For example, Father Maurice Dorney, pastor of the St. Gabriel parish in the Stockyards District from its es-

121

Archbishop James E. Quigley and his Irish-American predecessors had eased ethnic tensions in the church by permitting the establishment of separate — or national — parishes for non-English-speaking immigrants. Theoretically, this should have resulted in non-ethnic territorial parishes, but in reality they were predominantly Irish, since virtually all English-speaking Catholics in nineteenth-century Chicago were Irish. *Courtesy of the Chicago* CATHOLIC.

tablishment in 1880 until his death in 1914, was an extremely active figure in his community. He often provided food and fuel to the needy, found jobs for the unemployed, and at times served as an arbitrator in settling strikes and other labor disputes at the stockyards. Keenly aware of the particular evils of alcohol among his Irish flock, he campaigned against its abuse and was, in fact, successful in getting saloons removed from a small area of the Stockyards District.[15] Other priests might not have been as well known or as flamboyant as Dorney, but most shared with him a concern for the material as well as the spiritual welfare of their parishioners.

Affiliated with each parish was a variety of societies designed to meet the spiritual, social, and material needs of the parishioners. Some of these were linked with similar groups in other parishes through central organizations. Among the more common organizations were the St. Vincent de Paul Society, which tried to put the teachings of Christian charity into practice by helping the poor; the Catholic Total Abstinence Union of America, whose members completely abstained from alcohol; and the Catholic Order of Foresters, a mutual aid fraternity which provided assistance to its members in time of need.[16] Most parishes also had various sodalities, youth clubs, and the like; and, of course, there were the inevitable christenings, weddings, and funerals, where old friends could reminisce about the past or gossip about the present. All of these organizations and events helped to lighten the burdens of urban life and to bring the Irish into closer contact with one another.

Of all the institutions attached to a parish, probably the most important was the parochial school. Traditionally, the Catholic Church taught that religious instruction should be an integral part of a general education. To prepare a child for this life and forget about the next was, from the Catholic point of view, morally undesirable, to say the least. Throughout the nineteenth century the Catholic hierarchy in the United States had emphasized the need for Catholic schools. At the Third Plenary Council in Baltimore in 1884, for example, the bishops directed that every Catholic parish have a parochial school and that parents send their children to it.[17]

Yet Catholic educational philosophy was not the only reason behind the decision to build a parochial school system in Chicago. During the decades before 1870 the public schools in Chicago were not simply secular institutions; they were in fact quasi-Protestant schools. Practically all members of the Board of Education were Protestants; Protestants held a virtual monopoly on teaching positions; and the King James Bible was read in the classroom.[18] One Catholic newspaper no doubt typified the view of many Irish parents when it complained that Catholic children "are taught to feel ashamed of the creed of their forefathers."[19]

In the decades after 1870 this situation improved somewhat. Despite a storm of protest, Catholics, liberal Protestants, and others succeeded in getting the King James Bible banned from the classroom in 1875, and by the 1890s more and more Catholics were teaching in the public schools. Yet the schools continued to have a Protestant flavor. Protestants still dominated the Board of Education, and textbooks and other aspects of the curriculum seemed at times to present Catholicism in an unfavorable light.[20]

For these reasons the Irish developed their own parochial school system. By the late nineteenth century most Irish parishes had their own schools, which were attended probably by at least half of the Irish school-age children.[21] Staffed mainly by nuns and—to a lesser extent— brothers of Irish origin, these schools gave their students the standard elementary education, an understanding of the Catholic faith, and perhaps some appreciation for their Irish cultural heritage; and they instilled in them a loyalty toward the United States.

Clearly, the local parish, with its school and various societies, was the most important institution in Irish Chicago. It touched the lives of more Irishmen than did any other institution in the Irish community, for the overwhelming majority of Irish remained practicing Catholics. And while support for the church was an expression of a sincere religious commitment, it was also a manifestation of Irish ethnic identity. Finally, the point bears repeating that while devotion to the church was a legacy of their Irish heritage, it in turn did much to preserve that very heritage; paradoxically, the universal church brought the Irish closer together, by separating them not only from Protestant Chicagoans but from other Catholics as well.

Besides Catholicism, the second major force in the lives of the late nineteenth-century Chicago Irish was Irish nationalism. Like those in other parts of the United States, the Chicago Irish showed a deep and abiding interest in the political future of their homeland. As early as 1842, Chicago had a branch of Daniel O'Connell's Repeal Association, which sought to undo the union between Great Britain and Ireland through nonviolent agitation. After this movement collapsed, the Chicago Irish turned to various revolutionary groups. Of these, the most popular during the years before the Great Fire was the Fenian Brotherhood. Founded in New York in 1858, the Fenians sent money, arms, and men across the sea to the Irish Republican Brotherhood in an effort to help them overthrow British rule in Ireland. Although an uprising did take place in 1867, it ended in a dismal failure. Meanwhile, in

123

America the Fenians had split into two factions: one group wished to concentrate on military activity in Ireland, while the other advocated an invasion of Canada. The latter faction, known as the "Senate Wing," hoped a Canadian invasion would cause an Anglo-American war, which might possibly lead to the liberation of Ireland. Most Chicago Fenians supported the "Senate Wing," and a number of them, in fact, participated in a series of quixotic raids on Canada. These, like the uprising in Ireland, were total fiascos, and they brought public ridicule upon Chicago's Irish.[22]

Rent by factionalism and failure, Fenian membership quickly dwindled in Chicago, as it did elsewhere. But if as an organization the Fenian Brotherhood was gasping its last breath, its spirit was very much alive. In 1867 a group of disgruntled New York Fenians established the Clan-na-Gael, a secret, oath-bound society which, like the Fenians, was dedicated to "the attainment of the complete and absolute independence of Ireland by the overthrow of English domination" by means of physical force.[23] Irish nationalists in Chicago quickly flocked to this new revolutionary society. In 1869, Chicago's first Clan-na-Gael "camp," as local branches were known, was established in the Bridgeport area.[24] Others soon followed, and for the rest of the century—and indeed beyond it—the Clan was to serve as the nucleus of Irish nationalist activity in Chicago. Led for much of the period by Alexander Sullivan, a crafty lawyer with a rather seamy past, the Clan numbered among its ranks some of the most influential Irishmen in the city. These included, among others: John M. Smyth, a prominent Republican politician and large furniture dealer; Daniel Corkery, a wealthy coal merchant and Democratic leader; John F. Finerty, a one-term congressman and publisher of the *Citizen*, an Irish weekly; and John P. Hopkins, first Irish Catholic mayor of Chicago, from 1893 to 1895.[25]

Although the Clan was never large in numbers, its doctrine of revolutionary republicanism seemed to permeate the Irish community; and it exerted considerable influence over other larger Irish nationalist organizations. Clansmen or individuals sympathetic to their aims dominated the leadership of the Ancient Order of Hibernians and the local branches of the Irish National Land League, the Irish National League, and the Irish National Federation.[26] As affiliates of the Irish Parliamentary party, these latter three groups were ostensibly dedicated to achieving Irish self-government through nonviolent means alone.[27] In practice, however, their members followed the Clan's policy. Although willing to lend moral and monetary support to the Irish Parliamentary party's peaceful efforts on behalf of home rule, they were more than eager, should the opportunity arise, to back a full-scale rebellion to secure an independent Irish Republic.

The Clan also managed to spread its message of revolutionary nationalism to the Irish community at large. Each week Finerty's *Citizen* informed its readers of the latest English misdeeds in Ireland and reminded them of the need for militant action. Furthermore, thousands of Irish Chicagoans, many of whom were probably not members of any nationalist group, attended rallies either sponsored or cosponsored by the Clan-na-Gael. In addition to St. Patrick's Day, major Irish gatherings were held on March 4th, the anniversary of the execution of the patriot Robert Emmet; on August 15th, the Feast of the Assumption; and on November 22, the date three Fenians, known as the Manchester Martyrs, were executed by the British in 1867. Orators at these rallies rekindled the embers of Irish nationalism—if indeed they needed rekindling—among their audiences, recounting the long history of English misrule in Ireland. Though they had kind words for English leaders who were sympathetic to Irish grievances, they often harped on the theme that words alone would never change the hearts of most Englishmen. English deafness to Irish problems, they argued, could only be cured by the bullet and the bomb.[28]

However, if many Irish Chicagoans seemed to support the Clan's revolutionary philosophy, the organization was not without its problems. During the last fifteen years of the century the Clan was plagued by the old Irish nemesis of factionalism. During the mid-1880s a relatively small group of Chicago Clansmen broke with the parent organization run by Sullivan, claiming that he was a thief who used the Irish cause for his own selfish ends. Though small in numbers, the dissidents carried on a vigorous campaign against Sullivan and his cronies. This campaign became intensely bitter after 1889, when one of the dissident leaders, Dr. Patrick Henry Cronin, was murdered by a few of Sullivan's henchmen, an event that brought shock and disgrace to the city's Irish.

While these events undermined some of its popularity, Irish nationalism remained a viable movement in Chicago simply because its underlying causes continued to survive. Concern for the political future of Ireland was a way of reaffirming one's Irishness, a way of keeping in touch with one's roots. Yet there was more behind Irish-American nationalism than the simple need to reinforce a common ethnic bond. Irish-American nationalism was characterized by an intense hatred of England to a much greater degree than was the movement in Ireland itself. After all, the majority of the late nineteenth-century Chicago Irish had either emigrated from Ireland during or in the decade immediately following the Great Famine, or they were the children of such emigrants. Since few returned for any length of time, their memories of Ireland were frozen at a time when British rule was, or at least

126

Dr. Patrick H. Cronin, a critic of the financial irregularities of Chicago's Clan-na-Gael, was the victim of a ghastly and sensational murder in 1889. The Clan used both violence and non-violence in its efforts to win independence for Ireland, and was an important force in the lives of Chicago's Irish. *Courtesy of the Chicago Historical Society.*

seemed to be, at its worst. They neither could nor would forget the hunger, the evictions, and the poverty, and they took up the cause of Irish nationalism not only in the hope of seeing an independent Ireland but also as an expression of vengeance on England. Indeed, sheer hatred of England does much to explain phenomena like the reckless and futile dynamite campaign that the Clan launched against Britain in the early 1880s. Although it did nothing to bring the dream of an independent Ireland any closer to reality, it served at least to give "Mother England" a few sleepless nights.[29]

Furthermore, as Thomas N. Brown has argued, the fires of Irish-American nationalism were fueled by a need for respect. Coming from a land ruled by authorities who had shown little but contempt for their way of life, and coming to a nation where—at least in the beginning—they had been scorned for their poverty, religion, and culture, the

American Irish had developed a collective sense of inferiority. Perhaps nothing intensified these feelings so much as the fact that their homeland was still in the hands of a foreign power.[30] John Finerty probably typified the sentiments of many Irish Chicagoans when he claimed (forgetting the Jews) that "all other foreign elements in this country, with, perhaps, the exception of the Poles, have strong governments behind them, and they are held in more respect than the Irish who have no government of their own to boast of."[31] Thus, for Ireland to gain self-government would lead to a greater respect for the American Irish.

Finally, Irish-American nationalism helped to meet some of the social and economic needs of the community. Nationalist organizations and rallies provided excellent opportunities for Irish-Americans to mingle with fellow Irishmen. The August 15 picnic in particular was a major social occasion attended by thousands of men, women, and children from various parts of the city. Furthermore, membership in nationalist groups like the Clan-na-Gael often led to economic rewards in the form of jobs. And nationalist connections were particularly useful for advancement in local politics.

The forces sustaining Irish nationalism were much the same in Chicago as elsewhere in Irish-America. Yet Irish nationalist activity in Chicago differed in one respect, and that was in the complete absence of any true constitutional nationalist movement. Chicago did have branches of constitutional organizations like the Irish National League, but behind these there always lurked the shadow of the gunman. In several other cities, however, mainly those in New England and the state of New York, constitutional groups were often what they claimed to be, and a number of their leaders were quick to denounce the revolutionary brand of Irish nationalism.

The differences between the Irish nationalism of Chicago and of the cities in New York and New England can be largely explained, I believe, by the respective attitudes of the church toward nationalism in these areas. The bishops and clergy in New York and New England were for the most part strongly opposed to secret revolutionary organizations. They agreed with traditional Catholic teaching that membership in such groups was sinful because their required oaths conflicted with one's religious and civic obligations and because their revolutionary aims violated the conditions for a just war.[32] As a result, they encouraged their flocks to turn away from revolutionary societies and to support instead the nonviolent nationalism espoused by the Irish Parliamentary party. In fact, a number of priests, such as Father Thomas Conaty of Worcester, Massachusetts and Father Lawrence Walsh of

127

Waterbury, Connecticut, provided some of the leadership for constitutional Irish-American nationalism during the 1880s and 1890s.[33]

Of all the clerical opponents of revolutionary Irish nationalism,
none was so bitter as Archbishop Michael Corrigan of New York and
Bishop Bernard McQuaid of Rochester. During the latter eighties and
early nineties they did their utmost to have the Clan-na-Gael officially
condemned by the Committee of Archbishops, which had ecclesiastical
responsibility for such matters. That action, however, was continually
blocked by three "liberal" archbishops—James Gibbons of Baltimore,
John Ireland of St. Paul, and Feehan of Chicago. These prelates believed it was best to interfere as little as possible in the political activities of the laity, for to do so might needlessly alienate otherwise loyal
Catholics.[34] Feehan, who had grown up in one of the more nationalist
areas of Ireland, went even further than that.[35] Though never publicly
condoning violent methods, he freely associated with Clansmen and
was particularly friendly with Alexander Sullivan and his wife, Margaret, a journalist active in Irish affairs. He also contributed to the
Clan's nonviolent projects, such as its burial plot at Mount Olivet Cemetery. Obviously, Feehan believed that one could be a good Catholic
and still belong to the Clan-na-Gael.[36]

Considering the archbishop's friendly attitude toward the Clan, it
is not surprising that most Irish priests in Chicago felt and acted similarly. Father Dorney, the Stockyards priest, was active in the inner
circles of the Clan. Other priests often attended Clan demonstrations
as honored guests and permitted the Clan as an organization to attend
special masses or other church services. While some priests chose sides
after the Clan-na-Gael split into factions, criticizing the opposing faction, I have found no Chicago priests who condemned revolutionary
activities as such.[37]

The amicable relationship between cleric and Clansman was clearly
the major reason Chicago lacked a constitutional nationalist movement.
There was no encouragement from the Chicago pulpit to leave the
Clan and support nonviolent Irish nationalism as there was in New
York and Rochester. There were a few constitutional nationalists like
W. P. Rend, a wealthy coal dealer, and William Onahan, a long-time
Democratic politican; but without the church pushing people in their
direction, they were voices crying in the wilderness. Although Irish
Chicago suffered from a certain degree of factionalism, no split ever
developed between the church and the Clan, nor did the nationalist
movement ever divide along constitutional-extremist lines. In this respect, at least, the Irish in Chicago manifested a level of solidarity
absent in cities in New York and New England.

128

Unlike Catholicism and Irish nationalism, which had their origins in the Irish past, the third important force in Irish Chicago—the local political system—was primarily an American institution. Perhaps because of its rapid growth rate, or perhaps because of a confusing set of overlapping city, county, and township jurisdictions, late nineteenth-century Chicago had a fragmented system of politics. Neither the Republicans, who dominated the city council, nor the Democrats, who occupied the mayor's office more often than the GOP did, were controlled by a centralized political machine like New York's Tammany Hall. Instead, each party was divided into a motley array of factions, or "mini-machines," which were continually involved in making deals with one another. In fact, on the local level at least, deals frequently occurred across party lines: the spoils of office took precedence over party loyalty. Unlike the relatively small group of mainly middle-class Protestant Reformers, who emphasized honest and efficient government, most Chicago politicians looked upon politics as a business designed to bring power and financial rewards to its practitioners. "Boodle" aldermen voted to give contracts and franchises to businessmen willing to pay handsome kickbacks. Local precinct captains and policemen took bribes from owners of gambling and prostitution establishments and in return protected them from the law. But the system also had its positive aspects: machine politicians provided jobs and other needed services to their constituents.[38]

Although their influence was not as extensive as some contemporary newspapers and journals would have us believe, there is little doubt that the Irish played a significant role in Chicago politics. In 1890, for example, when they made up just 17 percent of the city's population, the Irish held at least twenty-three of the sixty-eight seats on the city council. Of these twenty-three councilmen, nineteen were Democrats.[39] The Chicago Irish, like those in other cities, gave the bulk of their support to the Democratic party because it had been traditionally more sympathetic to their needs than had the Republicans. Not only were most Irishmen Democrats, but most Democrats were Irish. In 1885, for instance, the Irish occupied fourteen of the eighteen seats on the Democratic City Central Committee,[40] and in 1890 they accounted for about two-thirds of the Democratic aldermen. Furthermore, most of the major Democratic bosses during the period were Irishmen: Dan O'Hara in the seventies; Mike McDonald and "Chesterfield" Joe Mackin in the eighties; and John Powers, "Bathhouse" John Coughlin, and "Hinky Dink" Kenna in the nineties.[41] A handful of Irishmen, of course, became Republicans, either for practical political reasons or because they felt the national Democratic party had not properly rewarded the Irish for their loyalty. Two of the more promi-

129

nent of these were John M. Smyth, the furniture dealer, and Martin B. Madden, owner of a large stone company. Smyth and Madden, who both served as aldermen for a time, wielded considerable power in local Republican affairs.[42]

But whether Republicans or Democrats, Irish politicians generally played the game of machine politics. Like others on the city council, most Irish aldermen sold their votes to entrepreneurs seeking municipal franchises and contracts. Irish politicians also successfully mastered the art of election fraud. Several owned saloons where they supplied the party faithful with ample refreshments on election days, encouraging them to vote early and often. Itinerants, illegally naturalized citizens, and even the dead were often duly registered as voters. Frequently, party toughs would pound the heads of opposition voters, or friendly policemen would jail them. And if all else failed, the ballots of a rival faction occasionally landed in the Chicago River.[43]

There is no doubt that the Irish were successful practitioners of urban politics. But why? For one thing, their past experience in Ireland preconditioned them to participate in a political milieu that flaunted the law. The English legal system as practiced in Ireland was anything but just. It often discriminated against Catholics and favored the mighty landlord over the lowly tenant farmer. As a result, the Irish immigrant had developed little respect for the law; instead, he tried to evade it as much as possible and was thus more easily able to adapt himself to a political system that skirted legal refinements.[44] Secondly, the Irish were culturally far more Anglo-Saxon than they liked to admit. An ability to speak English gave them an edge over foreign-speaking immigrants like the Germans, while a familiarity with British election procedures provided them with a better understanding of the workings of American politics. From the 1790s to the 1820s they had watched the landlords organize tenant farmers into effective voting blocs, and in the 1820s they had participated in O'Connell's successful drive to weld the Irish masses into a well-disciplined political force to win Catholic emancipation. The Irish clearly came to the United States well schooled in political organization and electioneering tactics.[45]

If their past experiences in Ireland prepared the Chicago Irish to operate effectively in the political arena, employment opportunities provided the immediate incentive that drew them into it in such large numbers. Several leading Irish politicians, who were also lawyers and businessmen, used their political connections to increase their incomes. Lawyers sometimes served as judges or represented companies with municipal franchises, while building contractors made handsome profits from city contracts. And for many of the party faithful who had neither the education nor financial resources to launch professional or business careers, political patronage jobs on the police force, in the water department, and the like provided them with their only source of livelihood. The federal census of 1900, for example, reported that 43 percent of "watchmen, policemen, firemen, etc." were either Irish immigrants or their children, even though they represented only 14 percent of the city's male labor force.[46] Besides municipal employment, the Irish also held what might be termed indirect patronage jobs, that is, jobs in companies holding city franchises and contracts. In 1900, 58 percent of all gas works employees were first- or second-generation Irish-Americans.[47] And employment was not the only economic service Irish politicians rendered to their constituents; they occasionally helped widows, the unemployed, and the destitute, providing them with modest handouts of food, fuel, and other services.

131

It was largely for economic reasons that the Clan-na-Gael participated in Chicago politics from the 1870s onward. Though most Irish politicians were probably not Clansmen, virtually all Clansmen—except for the relatively small group of dissidents—were deeply entrenched in machine politics. In fact, with a decentralized political system, the Clan had a golden opportunity to operate as a "minimachine," wheeling and dealing with various Democratic and Republican factions. Several Clansmen held influential political positions (mainly in the Democratic party) and were able to supply the rank and file with countless patronage jobs. For example, Daniel Corkery was a Democratic leader in Bridgeport during much of the period; Frank Agnew, a building contractor from the near North Side, served for a time as Chairman of the Cook County Democratic Central Committee; and Michael McInerney, owner of a large undertaking establishment, was the Democratic boss of the Stockyards District during the 1880s and 1890s. Besides getting jobs through its own members, the Clan also made deals with other politicians. In the early 1880s, Alexander Sullivan backed Mayor Carter Harrison I for mayor and in return was permitted to name several Clansmen to the police department. He also obtained positions for Clansmen in other city and county offices, so that the Clan-na-Gael could be found everywhere from lofty judicial chambers to the city sewer system.[48]

Politics, then, played an important role in the lives of many Irish Chicagoans.* While the church and Irish nationalism primarily filled their spiritual and emotional needs as Irish Catholics, politics helped to satisfy their practical needs as urban Americans by providing them with jobs and other economic benefits. Since in one way or another these jobs and services were obtained through Irish connections, the

---

*For a detailed, revisionist treatment of Irish politics in Chicago, see Chapter 12, *below*, by Paul Michael Green.

32

Chicago's police department, symbolized here by the Haymarket Riot statue, was predom-inately Irish by the 1890s. The policeman, the priest, and the politician formed the trinity of occupations dominated by the Irish in many cities such as Chicago. *Courtesy of the Chicago Police Department.*

political system helped to reinforce rather than lessen their sense of Irishness and thus helped to strengthen community cohesiveness. Un-doubtedly, the politician, with jobs and other favors at his disposal, was a leading figure in Irish Chicago. Along with the priest and patriot, he formed part of an important trinity that gave direction and stability to the community.

If the church, Irish nationalism, and politics served to strengthen community ties, so did the fact that most Irish Chicagoans were mem-bers of the same general socio-economic class. As Table III shows, from

1870 to 1890 the overwhelming majority of Irish immigrants were manual workers, probably over 85 percent, since it is more than likely that most of those in unclassifiable and unlisted occupations also held blue-collar jobs. (Indeed, in the case of the Irish female labor force in 1890, where over 96 percent could be classified, 88 percent were manual laborers.) Of these blue-collar workers, about half of the men were unskilled laborers, while about three-fourths of the women were domestic servants.[49] In contrast to this, the number of Irish immigrants in the professions or in big business was minuscule.

TABLE III

OCCUPATIONAL DISTRIBUTION OF IRISH-BORN CHICAGOANS, BY PERCENTAGE, 1870–1890

133

	1870 (Male & Female) (N=22,337)	1880 (Male & Female) (N=23,918)	1890 (Male) (N=32,482)	1890 (Female) (N=8,552)
Professional	0.52	0.97	1.60	0.93
Owners and Officials of Large Businesses	—	—	1.11	—
Owners of Small Businesses	3.98	4.21	1.83	2.89
Other White-Collar Workers	3.67	4.56	7.48	4.71
Manual Workers	76.76	74.08	75.41	88.06
Unclassifiable	8.90	9.48	4.09	1.22
Unlisted	6.17	6.70	8.47	2.19

Source: U.S., *Ninth Census, 1870,* Vol. I, "Population," p. 782; *Tenth Census, 1880,* "Population," p. 870; *Eleventh Census, 1890,* "Population," Part II, pp. 650–651.

The statistics for 1900 (see Table IV), unlike those for 1870 through 1890, include the second-generation Irish; unfortunately, they lump them together with the Irish-born, thus precluding any exact comparison between the two. Yet it seems clear that the American-born Irish had more white-collar workers among their ranks than did the immigrants, because the percentage of nonmanual workers, which had hovered around 10 percent from 1870 to 1890, jumped rather substantially in the 1900 census, when the second generation was included. In 1900, over 25 percent of Irish men and about 60 percent of Irish women were business proprietors, professionals, or in other white-collar jobs. It would seem that, had the second generation been included in the labor statistics prior to 1890, one would have seen a gradual increase in the

number of Irish white-collar workers from 1870 onward, as the children
of Irish immigrants entered the work force.

TABLE IV
OCCUPATIONAL DISTRIBUTION OF FIRST- AND SECOND-
GENERATION IRISH CHICAGOANS, BY PERCENTAGE, 1900

	Male (N=75,695)	Female (N=25,016)
Professional	4.01	8.51
Owners and Officials of Large Businesses	2.19	0.10
Owners of Small Businesses	4.80	3.35
Other White-Collar Workers	16.58	25.19
Manual Workers	69.78	59.90
Unlisted	2.64	2.95

Source: U.S., *Twelfth Census, 1900*, "Special Reports: Occupations," pp. 516–523.

134

Nonetheless, even at the turn of the century most Irish Chicagoans
were still manual workers. Furthermore, one would suspect that the
gulf between them and white-collar workers was not too great, since
the latter had grown up mainly in working-class environments and
probably still had one or more members of their families among the
blue-collar ranks. For example, biographical sketches of the leading
Irishmen in Chicago in 1897 show that virtually all had come from
rather humble backgrounds and that a number had worked as manual
laborers before achieving success in business, politics, or the professions. Some, particularly the politicians, continued to live in working-
class neighborhoods; and though others were members of the elite
Columbus Club, many were also active in religious and nationalist
societies made up of individuals from all classes. Relatively few joined
the select groups dominated by upper- and upper-middle-class Protestant Americans.[50] Although there were some signs of class differences, particularly during the 1890s, late nineteenth-century Irish
Chicago had a predominantly working-class flavor.[51]

In this respect, of course, the Irish were not unique. During the
late nineteenth century, blue-collar workers dominated Chicago's work
force as a whole. Until the 1890s, when the "new immigration" began
to change the composition of the city's labor force, the Irish were on
the lower rung of the occupational ladder. As Table V shows, they had
a greater percentage of blue-collar workers than did either Americans
of native parentage or the British-born; and although they had roughly
the same percentage of manual workers as the German-born did and

TABLE V
PERCENTAGE OF MANUAL WORKERS OF SELECTED
GROUPS IN THE LABOR FORCE, CHICAGO, 1890*

	Male	Female
Native White of Native Parentage	53.56	55.59
British-born	72.40	71.73
German-born	85.85	90.48
Irish-born	86.24	91.17
Swedish- and Norwegian-born	90.39	95.10
Danish-born	86.02	91.44

*These percentages are based on the total labor force *less* the number in unlisted and unclassifiable occupations. (Compare percentages of Irish manual workers in this table with those in Table III.) The percentage of workers in unlisted and unclassifiable occupations ranged from a high of 19.50 percent for native white males of native parentage to a low of 2.25 percent for Swedish- and Norwegian-born females.

Source: U.S., *Eleventh Census, 1890,* "Population," Part II, pp. 650–651.

a somewhat smaller percentage than the Scandinavian-born did, they had a greater percentage of unskilled workers than did either of these two groups.[52] In the last decade of the century, however, the Irish began to move up the economic ladder (see Table VI). Definitely better off than the "new immigrants," such as the Poles and Italians, they were slightly ahead of the Scandinavians and had narrowed the gap between themselves and the Germans. They still trailed Americans of native parentage and the British.[53]

The economic position of the Irish relative to these last two groups no doubt helped to reinforce their sense of inferiority, for it mirrored the long-standing economic disparity between the Saxon and the Celt. Group inferiority complexes are difficult to quantify, and it is quite conceivable that many Irish, particularly the uneducated and unskilled laborers, never gave the matter much thought. But it certainly bothered the educated middle-class Irish who sought respectability and who often rubbed shoulders with Anglo-Saxons in the workaday world. Much as they liked to talk about the lack of materialism among Celts, they measured success in terms of economic and social mobility; and when they looked at their fellow countrymen, they saw that they fell short of the mark. John Finerty probably expressed the feelings of many of these "respectable" Irish when he advised prospective immigrants to remain in Ireland, claiming that in America the Irishman "is nothing but a poor emigrant, who is left to paddle his own canoe as best he may, and who, however, delicately nurtured at home, must take, at last, to the pick and shovel, perhaps to the recruiting office, or become a

TABLE VI
PERCENTAGE OF MANUAL WORKERS OF SELECTED
GROUPS IN THE LABOR FORCE, CHICAGO, 1900. (Statistics for
ethnic groups include immigrants and their children)*

	Male	Female
Native White of Native Parentage	43.16	39.18
British	56.07	45.53
Germans	69.03	70.03
Irish	71.67	61.72
Scandinavian	78.02	80.54
Poles	90.67	87.66
Italians	83.99	80.03

*These percentages are based on the total labor force *less* the number in unlisted occupations. (Compare percentages of Irish manual workers in this table with those in Table IV.) Unlike the 1890 census all listed occupations could be classified and the percentage of unlisted occupations was less than 5 percent for most groups.
Source: U.S., *Twelfth Census, 1900,* "Special Reports: Occupations," pp. 516-523.

charge upon the country."[54] Such sentiments did not die easily; they lingered on well into the twentieth century, albeit in more subtle ways.

In addition to feeling inferior to Anglo-Americans, the Irish also felt the sting of the anti-Catholic and anti-Irish attitudes of some. Such prejudice was not simply a source of irritation to the Irish, but it also played an important role in reinforcing their sense of group consciousness, for it reminded them that they were a people somewhat apart from the mainstream of American life.

As an infant city, where all groups—native and foreign—were relative newcomers facing the common problems of a semifrontier environment, Chicago did not experience the more rampant anti-Catholic nativism that plagued several eastern cities during the two or three decades before the Civil War. Nonetheless, anti-Irish and, to a lesser extent, anti-German sentiment did exist. Some Americans resented the Irish for their political power, for their support of liberal drinking laws, for their sometimes squalid living conditions, and most of all for their Catholicism, which they felt posed a threat to the very fabric of American life. They often viewed Irish attempts to get public monies for their schools or to ban the King James Bible in the common schools as part of a concerted Roman attack on free American institutions. Only once during the decades before the Civil War, however, did nativism score a major triumph in Chicago. This occurred in 1855, when, after capturing the city council and the mayor's office, the nativist and xenophobic Know-Nothing party passed legislation requiring all applicants for municipal jobs to be native-born Americans. They also increased the cost of beer licenses, which led to the Lager Beer Riots, in which the Germans and Irish teamed up together to battle the nativist authorities. But the Know-Nothing victory, caused as much by a disruption in the two-party system over the slavery issue as by anti-Catholicism, proved to be short-lived. The following year the Know-Nothings were defeated, and their legislation was promptly repealed.[55]

Although the xenophobic occurrences of 1855 were never repeated again, anti-Catholicism continued to survive in Chicago. In the years after the Civil War, certain Protestant ministers repeatedly warned their congregations that the "demon of Romanism" was prowling about, seeking to undermine the democratic institutions of America.[56] Several Protestant newspaper editors and political reformers attacked the Irish for polluting municipal politics. Although most were sincere reformers and not really bigots in the true sense of the word, they often seemed to be more concerned about the number of Irish politicians than about the actual corruption they were responsible for.[57]

During the late 1880s anti-Catholicism, which had been relatively low-keyed and somewhat sporadic since the Know-Nothing period, became more blatant and organized. This new wave of nativism was, of course, a national as well as a local phenomenon. Partially caused by the steady increase in Irish political power—city after city seemed to be electing Irish Catholic mayors—and by the tremendous growth of the Catholic Church and its parochial school system, it also arose from the increasing alienation of middle Americans, or "in-betweeners," as John Higham has described them. Made up mainly of white-collar workers, small businessmen, and non-unionized workers, the "in-betweeners" felt lost in an increasingly industrialized and urbanized America, where giant corporations, labor unions, and political machines rather than individuals seemed to be controlling the nation's destiny. Wishing to return to an earlier and less complex America, they lashed out at the foreign element, which in one way or another seemed to be connected with these new forces.[58] When speaking of the foreign element, they really meant Catholics, not Protestant immigrants. In fact, in many areas foreign-born Protestants actively participated in nativist groups; and in Chicago a number of British and Protestant Irish newcomers were in the forefront of the anti-Catholic crusade.[59]

Of the various anti-Catholic groups active in Chicago during the late 1880s and early 1890s, the most prominent were the United Order of Deputies, founded there in 1886, and the American Protective As-

137

sociation, which opened its first branch in the city in 1888 and eventually made its national headquarters there. Among other demands, these groups advocated immigration restriction, encouraged employers to fire Catholics, campaigned to defeat Catholic political candidates, and supported school laws like the Edwards Law (passed in 1889), which gave local public school boards some control over parochial schools.[60] Besides anti-Catholic organizations, Chicago also had a few short-lived nativist newspapers, including the *Weekly Native Citizen* and *America*, whose editor, Slason Thompson, claimed that "the civilization of Ireland [was] a hissing and a reproach in the ears of history for the past 300 years."[61]

138

One must be careful not to overemphasize the extent of anti-Irish bigotry in late nineteenth-century Chicago. The more virulent form lasted only a decade, roughly from 1886 to 1896, after which nativists began to ease up on their anti-Irish and anti-German attacks and concentrate their opposition more fully on the large numbers of Catholic and Jewish immigrants arriving from eastern and southern Europe. Even at the height of its popularity, the power of anti-Irish prejudice was far from unlimited, a fact perhaps most forcibly demonstrated by the election of John P. Hopkins as Chicago's first Irish Catholic mayor in 1893. After all, outright bigots formed only a small minority of the city's population. In fact, several Protestant leaders, including a number of ministers, spoke out in defense of the Irish and other Catholics.[62] Nonetheless, anti-Irish sentiment was a fact of life for the Irish in Chicago: it constantly forced them to defend their own traditions, as well as their loyalty to the United States, and, in the process, reinforce their ethnic identity.

In the eyes of anti-Catholic bigots not only, but of most non-Irish Chicagoans, Irish-Americans were a monolithic group. And yet, although they certainly formed a relatively cohesive community, the Chicago Irish were by no means a homogeneous lot. Like any other ethnic group, they exhibited a degree of diversity and disunity. First of all, despite a common Irish Catholic heritage, their geographical backgrounds were far from identical. The most obvious difference, of course, existed between those born in Ireland and those born in America. The former had grown up in a predominantly Catholic, rural, and old-world environment, the latter largely in one that was Protestant, urban, and industrialized. There is no doubt that this resulted in a great many different experiences in their formative years. Since the American-born Irish ranked higher than the immigrants on the occupational ladder, there may also have been certain class differences between the two. Yet the gap between the immigrant and his American-born cousin must not have been as great among the Irish as it was among the non-English-speaking ethnic groups; for both the Irish immigrant and the "narrowback" (a term used for an American-born Irishman) had been exposed to Anglo-Saxon influences in their youth, and both spoke the same language with equal fluency, albeit with different accents. Although there probably was a tendency for immigrants to associate more with other immigrants, and American-born with American-born, I have found that relations between the two were harmonious for the most part. Immigrants and "narrowbacks," for example, seemed to mingle quite well in organizations like the Clan-na-Gael and the Ancient Order of Hibernians.[63] The only major dispute between the two groups occurred in the church, when, at the turn of the century, a band of Irish-born priests tried to block the appointment of the American-born Father Peter Muldoon as an auxiliary bishop of Chicago, claiming that he was prejudiced against native Irish priests. But even this was not a simple generational conflict. The dissident priests had other reasons for opposing Muldoon, and support for and opposition to Muldoon align imperfectly between the two groups: it is noteworthy that the Irish-born Feehan had nominated Muldoon, and that—for a time at least—the disgruntled priests received the support of the American-born bishop of Peoria, John Lancaster Spalding.[64]

139

If those born in Ireland and the United States came from somewhat different backgrounds but generally got along well together, the same can be said for groups within these two major categories. The native Irish population in Chicago was made up of individuals from every Irish county, though most of them seem to have come from counties in the western provinces of Munster and Connacht. While it is true that in the early days of Chicago, brawls frequently occurred among men from different parts of Ireland, such rampant factionalism had declined by 1870.[65] Immigrants arriving in the years after 1870 came from an Ireland where better communications and a more fully developed national system of education had significantly reduced provincialism. Still, the Chicago Irish were quite aware of county differences. Good-natured rivalries prevailed among men from different counties, and there probably was a tendency for those from the same localities to fraternize more with one another than with other Irishmen.[66]

Far less noticeable than the differences among those of Irish birth were the diverse origins of the American-born Irish. Although the published censuses do not break down the second-generation Irish by state, county, or city of birth, it is apparent that a considerable number of them had spent their formative years in places other than Chicago. Of the 126 American-born Irish Catholics listed in Charles Ffrench's *Biographical History of the American Irish in Chicago*, 69 were born outside the city, and of these the majority arrived there as adults. Most came from the Midwest and the East, some from large and middle-sized cities, others from small towns and farms.[67] It is difficult to know exactly how these individuals differed from the native Chicago Irish, but it seems likely that they tended to blur the distinction between immigrant and "narrowback." They held a sort of intermediary position between those reared in Chicago and those in Ireland, sharing with the former an American upbringing and with the latter the experiences of adjusting to an unfamiliar city.

Chicago's Irish, therefore, came from diverse origins, although it must be emphasized that this diversity rarely led to any serious dissension. Similarly, the class distinctions we have already mentioned never posed any major barriers to community solidarity. However, more research is needed before one can fully grasp the nuances of Irish life in Chicago. Of course, some of the necessary research material is unavailable. No sociological surveys on the Irish of this period exist; virtually all of those who might have been interviewed are dead; and the records of many organizations have been lost forever. Yet an intensive study of the census manuscripts, parish records, and the like may yield some additional insights; interviews with the children of the late nineteenth-century Irish, many of whom are still alive, would also be valuable.

In any event, the sources that are available indicate that differences in background and class caused relatively little friction among the Chicago Irish. The community experienced discord from other quarters. Machine politics, for example, was a perpetual source of trouble. Although Irish "boodle" politicians usually cooperated with one another, no election seemed to pass without dissension on the part of one faction or another. Since political power and patronage jobs were at stake, the struggles were usually bitter and at times led to violence.[68] If Irish machine politicians sometimes fought among themselves, they also had to contend with opposition from a small group of reform-minded Irish. These individuals came from a variety of backgrounds but shared a common feeling that the existing political system was demeaning to the Irish. Rarely successful, they did manage to score a few upsets, most notably in 1882, when the then Independent Democrat John Finerty defeated Henry F. Sheridan, the regular Democratic candidate, in the Second Congressional District race.[69]

The most visible split in Irish Chicago occurred among the ranks of the Irish nationalists. The trouble started shortly after Alexander Sullivan was elected chairman of the national executive committee of the Clan-na-Gael in August 1881. Sullivan and two other members of the committee, who were collectively known as "the Triangle," pursued some rather questionable practices and policies that disgusted a number of Clansmen. They ran the organization in a high-handed and dictatorial manner, launched a futile two-year dynamite campaign in England against the express wishes of the Irish Republican Brotherhood, their affiliate in Ireland and Britain, and apparently pilfered nationalist funds for their own use.

As a result of this, during the winter of 1884-1885 a group of New York Clansmen, led by the former Fenian John Devoy, began a national campaign to oust Sullivan and his cronies from the Clan. Devoy picked up support in Chicago from a small but vocal band of Clansmen, including Patrick Dunne (the father of a future Chicago mayor and governor of Illinois, Edward F. Dunne), who as early as 1882 had publicly complained that Sullivan was using nationalist monies to speculate on the Chicago Board of Trade; William J. Hynes, a local Democratic politician and former congressman from Arkansas; and the ill-fated Dr. Patrick Cronin, who had recently arrived in Chicago from St. Louis.

141

For fifteen years, up until 1900, when the Clan was finally reunited, the Devoyites waged a relentless crusade against Sullivan and his followers, a crusade that took a tragic turn in May 1889, when a group of Sullivan's followers assassinated Dr. Cronin in a lonely Lake View cottage. Setting up their own Clan-na-Gael and joining the Ancient Order of Hibernians, Board of Erin, which was separate from the Sullivanite-dominated A.O.H., the Devoyites held rival demonstrations on all the major Irish holidays, where they denounced Sullivan and his gang as phony patriots who were using the Irish cause to further their own selfish political ambitions. Since Finerty, a Sullivan supporter since 1885, generally denied them access to the columns of the *Citizen*, they used the pages of the daily press to inform the public about the seamier activities of their enemies. They also joined forces with political reformers in an attempt to undermine Sullivan and the political system in which he was so intimately involved. Yet, as Devoy himself admitted, the anti-Sullivan forces gained the allegiance of only a small minority of Chicago's Irish nationalists. The majority remained loyal to the Sullivanites, for not only did the latter cater to their nationalist aspirations as Irishmen but, by playing the game of machine politics, they also met their economic needs as Chicagoans. If they wondered at times about Sullivan's more dubious activities, the Irish were willing to give him the benefit of the doubt; for he was one of them, one of their own kind, and he had enough detractors in Protestant America. Besides, they probably reasoned, could a man who was the friend of so many priests and of Archbishop Feehan be all that bad?[70]

If the anti-Sullivanites received the support of only a minority of Chicago's Irish, their presence nonetheless points to the fact that the

Irish community had its fissures and cracks. Although such factionalism—whether among nationalists, clerics, or politicians—failed to destroy the essential unity of Irish Chicago, it at least tended to weaken it, and it certainly belied any claims that the Irish were a monolithic people. Furthermore, if not a monolith, neither was Irish Chicago cut off from the rest of the city: every day, in varying ways, the Irish came into contact with the larger urban community.

One of the major ways the Irish encountered other peoples was through their jobs. Whether working on construction projects, in the stockyards, or on street railways, most Irish labored alongside other Chicagoans. And labor unions like the Knights of Labor had a good mixture of Irish and non-Irish members.[71] Of particular importance in bringing the Irish into contact with the outside world were the large numbers of Irish women who worked as domestic servants in the homes of upper- and upper-middle-class Americans. No doubt they were influenced to some degree by the manners and customs of their employers, and since many of them later married, their families were also probably affected by their experiences, although in what way and to what extent is a matter of speculation.

If contacts made at work helped to break down some of the isolation between the Irish immigrants and the wider society, so did the fact that virtually all Irish Chicagoans spoke the English language. Having English as a mother tongue undoubtedly made their adjustment to American life much less complicated than it would have been had they still spoken Irish, the common language of much of Ireland until the early nineteenth century.[72] English helped to make them feel more American, more a part of the city and nation in which they lived. And while it did not put them on the higher rungs of the economic ladder, knowledge of English gave them an advantage in certain areas, such as politics. Furthermore, it meant that the ethnic newspaper was far less important to the Irish than to non-English-speaking immigrants. Unlike these groups, the Irish never had a daily newspaper of their own, and their one successful weekly, the *Citizen*, did not begin publication until 1882. Like the Americans and the British, the Irish kept up on the world around them by reading the regular daily newspapers, most of which, incidentally, gave rather detailed coverage of Irish events on both sides of the Atlantic. Reading the English-language dailies, of course, brought the Irish into more direct contact with the Anglo-American world, but it did not necessarily lead to better relations with it, for the local press could often be quite hostile to the Irish, particularly to Irish politicians.

Jobs and a knowledge of the English language were not the only factors that promoted interaction between the Irish and non-Irish. Each

142

of the three main institutions in Irish Chicago—the church, the Irish nationalist movement, and the local political system—helped to link the Irish with other Chicagoans in varying degrees. Most important was politics, in which the Irish constantly had to deal with native Americans, Germans, and Scandinavians, and later on with immigrants from southern and eastern Europe. True, political factions often divided along ethnic lines, but there was also a good deal of interethnic cooperation. In the early 1870s, Irish politicians teamed up with Germans and machine-minded Americans to form the People's party, a coalition of Democrats and Republicans which defeated the reformist Fire Proof Ticket in 1873.[73] Throughout the 1880s and 1890s, Irish politicians had to deal with American politicians like Mayor Carter Harrison I and Alfred Trude, and with Germans like Washington Hessing and John Peter Altgeld. And although the "new immigrants" had few influential political leaders during this period, the Irish had to cater to their needs, since they supplied an ever-increasing bloc of votes. Alderman Johnny Powers, for example, kept a hold on the Nineteenth Ward long after most Irish had left, by providing jobs and other favors to the Italians who moved in.[74] Powers was typical of most Irish bosses in Chicago. With a relatively small proportion of the city's population, the Irish knew that cooperation with other groups was essential to their political survival. Friction often occurred when other ethnics saw the Irish take more than their fair share of the prizes. But the Irish usually allowed their non-Irish political allies enough of the patronage to keep their allegiance. As a result, they managed to exercise a degree of political power out of all proportion to their numbers. If in the present century Chicago politics, to use John Allswang's words, indeed became "a house for all peoples,"[75] it was one in which the Irish generally seemed to occupy the best rooms.

143

Although it failed to bring the Irish into contact with the larger community to the same extent that politics did, the church served as a catalyst in linking the Irish with other Catholics in the city. This is not to deny what was said above: the Irish were indeed separated from other Catholics by language, customs, and the system of national parishes. Yet running through the motley fabric of Chicago Catholicism was the single thread of a common faith. A shared religious belief probably gave the Irish a better understanding of other Catholic groups than they might otherwise have had. And there is a great deal of truth in the claim that a common religious background was one of the reasons Irish politicians were able to deal more effectively with the "new immigrants" than were their American counterparts. While ethnic rivalries often overshadowed the universality of the church, there was a degree of Catholic solidarity that could become formidable in periods of anti-Catholic nativism. In the early 1890s, for instance, the Irish supported German Catholics in their campaign to repeal the Edwards Law, which threatened to undermine their parochial schools.[76] Of course, in time, as the non-English-speaking groups lost their native languages and became more Americanized, ethnic differences among Catholics would decrease significantly.

At first glance it may seem that Irish nationalism would have only served to isolate Chicago's Irish from the larger urban community. Yet in certain respects the opposite is true: it tended to make them more tolerant and broad-minded in some matters. Since Irish nationalists played down the Catholic element in Irish identity and emphasized that all Irishmen, be they Catholics, Anglicans, or Presbyterians, were true sons of Erin, and since some of the more notable nationalist leaders like Charles Stewart Parnell were Protestants, the creed of Irish nationalism tended to dilute Irish Catholic prejudice against Protestants. Of course, more often than not, Irish Protestants were the objects of Catholic scorn, since most of them supported the British connection; but it must be emphasized that Catholics generally disliked their Protestant fellow countrymen because they were pro-British, and not because of their religion. Let any Irish Protestant wave the green flag, and he immediately became a hero to Irish Catholics. Arthur Dixon, an Ulster-born Protestant and long-time Republican alderman who supported Irish Home Rule, was revered by Irish nationalists in the city.[77] Two of the most popular out-of-state speakers at Irish meetings in Chicago were George Betts and George Pepper, the former an Episcopalian clergyman from St. Louis, the latter a Methodist minister from Ohio. A correspondent writing to the *Citizen* after hearing Pepper speak at an August 15 rally expressed the feelings of many Irish Catholic Chicagoans when he declared: "It was indeed a happy sight to observe the Rev. Dr. Pepper, a Methodist minister, and the Rev. Father Hayes, a Catholic priest, standing on the same platform. Such a scene augurs well for the future of Ireland."[78]

Secondly, the nationalist tradition helped to give at least some Chicago Irish a sense of empathy for the problems of other peoples. *Citizen* editor Finerty, for example, championed Cuban independence, defended the "new immigration," advocated the teaching of German and other foreign languages in the public schools, and condemned anti-Semitism in the United States and Great Britain.[79] Similarly, Alexander Sullivan professed concern for the plight of American blacks. Though many Irish opposed the antislavery movement, after the death of the New England abolitionist Wendell Phillips, Sullivan recalled that he "was one of the first men whose utterances aroused in my blood hatred of human slavery, and gave my tongue some of its little power to denounce bondage even before I reached manhood."[80] The Irish nationalist experience clearly failed to wipe out Irish prejudice toward other groups, but it probably helped to diminish it. Anyone who spent time condemning English misrule in Ireland must have had some pangs of guilt when he acted in a bigoted manner toward others. Certainly, the frustration of seeing a foreign power control their homeland helps to explain why bishops like Foley and Feehan were willing to grant a certain degree of autonomy in the form of national parishes to the various Catholic ethnic groups.

Finally, and perhaps most important, the Irish were linked to other Chicagoans by a common loyalty to and faith in the United States. Most Irish immigrants came to America to stay, and of these the overwhelming majority became citizens.[81] They were no doubt only too anxious to renounce their legal allegiance to the British crown; but they became citizens more importantly out of a commitment to their adopted country, the country that was to be their home and the home of their children and grandchildren. On meeting with economic hardships or anti-Catholic prejudice they might grow despondent; but by and large they looked on America as a good land, a land that certainly offered them a better future than Ireland had.

145

Indeed, the Irish identified very closely with the United States. As one Chicago Irishman said some years after the turn of the century, "They're none of them foreigners when they come here, for their hearts and love were in America long before they thought of sailin' for America."[82] Irish-American apologists continually emphasized that the Irish had made significant contributions to the United States. Counting up the number of Irish troops in the Revolutionary War, they claimed that the Irish had played a major role in America's struggle for independence, though they failed to mention that most of these troops were of Ulster Protestant origins. Far more justifiably, they noted the numbers of Irish soldiers who had fought to preserve the Union during the Civil War. Similarly, they recalled that several Irish policemen were wounded (one fatally) in the Haymarket Square Riot of 1886 as they were trying to preserve the American system from the alleged anarchists. And to charges that their commitment to Irish nationalism proved they were Irish first and Americans second, the Irish answered that their concern for Ireland in no way diminished their love for America. After all, they argued, in fighting to overthrow British rule in Ireland, were they not following the example set by America a century before?

Nineteenth-century Irish Chicago, then, was not an isolated enclave cut off from the rest of the city. While they formed a highly self-conscious and relatively cohesive ethnic community, the Irish also came into contact with other Chicagoans. In the present century, of course, the Irish became more totally integrated into the larger urban society. Much of their cohesiveness vanished as the factors that had sustained it changed. The ties that bound third-, fourth-, and fifth-generation Irish-Americans to Ireland were naturally weaker than those that bound the immigrants and their children. The creation of the Irish Free State in 1922 did much to undermine the raison d'être of Irish-American nationalism, though, of course, some Irish Chicagoans continued to show an interest in ousting the British from Northern Ireland. Increased social and economic mobility tended to fragment what had once been a predominantly working-class community. Intermarriage with other ethnic groups (mainly Catholic), the decline of anti-Irish prejudice, and an increasing solidarity with other white groups against a growing black population tied the Irish more closely to other Chicagoans of a European background.

146

Yet it would be premature to sound the death knell for Irish Chicago. Today there is still a small nucleus of highly ethnic-conscious Irish Chicagoans who support various Irish cultural, athletic, and nationalist organizations in the city. Besides these there are countless others who are aware of their Irish heritage in varying degrees. Indeed, during the past decade or so, in view of the new emphasis on ethnicity, a number of once-marginal Irish have begun to rediscover their Irish past. Young men and women whose grandparents or great-grandparents came from Ireland study Irish history and literature at colleges and universities which once spurned these subjects as too parochial for an institution of higher learning. In recent years increasing numbers of Irish-Americans have visited Ireland, thanks to the fast and relatively cheap transatlantic travel available in this jet age. On the whole, it is probably easier for these Irish-Americans to get back to their roots than it is for the descendants of non-English-speaking immigrants. Unlike them, Irish-Americans speak the language of their immigrant ancestors and the language of present-day Ireland. Ironically, for this, of course, the English are responsible.

KATHLEEN NEILS CONZEN

9. Peasant Pioneers

GENERATIONAL SUCCESSION AMONG GERMAN

FARMERS IN FRONTIER MINNESOTA

Over the course of the nineteenth century, hundreds of thousands of Euro- *147*
pean peasants transplanted themselves, their families, and their farming
operations to the fields and plains of America.* By the end of the century,
they and their children made up more than one-quarter of all those who
earned a living from agriculture in the United States.[1] The peasant world
that so many of the immigrant farmers had left behind revolved around the
central relationship between the family and its land. The land nourished the
peasant family, determined its status in the community, indeed shaped its
very structure. Recent scholarship has illuminated the ways in which family
strategies to insure sufficient labor to work the land and to pass it on to the
next generation influenced every aspect of the peasant family, from its size,
composition, residential patterns, and life cycle to its internal relationships
and its external links to the wider world.[2] For many peasants, it was the
final realization that this traditional symbiosis was no longer viable in the
changing homeland that led to emigration.[3]

What then was the fate of traditional patterns of peasant family life as the
family reestablished itself amid the very different conditions of America?
Historians of rural America, obsessed with questions of farming technology
and the income and status of farmers, have paid little attention to the
"family" component in nineteenth-century "family farming." Conventional
wisdom postulated loose family ties among American farmers, early dispersal of family members, and lack of sentiment surrounding family land and
its inheritance.[4] Until recently, Turnerian notions of frontier individual-

*I wish gratefully to acknowledge the support of the American Council of Learned
Societies and the Charles Warren Center for Studies in American History of Har-
vard University for the larger project of which this is a part. I am also grateful to
Carolyn Walker and Andrew Yox for their research assistance; to the Zapp Abstract
Co. of St. Cloud, Minnesota, for making available to me its abstracts of land trans-
actions within St. Martin township; and to William L. Cofell of St. John's University,
Collegeville, Minn., for sharing with me his special insight into twentieth-century
St. Martin.

ism, combined with later perceptions that older American rural family strategies were simply incompatible with market agriculture, served to discourage reexamination of how families functioned in the context of husbandry. Impressed by the readiness with which immigrant farmers adopted American settlement forms, crops, and methods of cultivation, historians tended to find peasant cultural baggage of little relevance to nineteenth-century American farming.[5]

148

But the question remains open, if only because work in other contexts has repeatedly demonstrated that the family was a fundamental carrier of traditional values. Immigration historians, for example, have demonstrated the extent to which traditional family strategies and goals influenced the accommodation of European peasants to American cities.[6] A study of the adaptability of traditional peasant family patterns to the American farming frontier provides an opportunity both to assess the utility of customary family strategies in mediating adjustment to American life and to delineate one possible relationship between family and farm under conditions of nineteenth-century frontier agriculture. The detail necessary to illuminate that relationship can be achieved only at the local level. Accordingly, this essay investigates the strategies toward land and family adopted by German immigrant farmers in a central Minnesota community, from the establishment of the community in the late 1850s through the second generation's coming of age in the early twentieth century.

I

The area examined here is the 36-square-mile federal survey township of St. Martin, Minnesota, located in the heart of Stearns County some 70 miles northwest of Minneapolis on the Sauk River, an unnavigable tributary of the Mississippi (see Map 9.1). The township functioned as the basic unit of local government and was, for most of the period, virtually coterminous with the Catholic parish from which it took its name. Except for several sections of excellent prairie, most of the land was rolling to hilly, of moderately good soil quality and initially covered by a mixture of hardwood forest and scrub. At the time of initial settlement in the late 1850s, St. Martin lay on a branch of the territory's major route, the legendary ox-cart trail linking the fur-rich Red River Valley with St. Paul and the Mississippi River system. Its first railroad shipping point was established in 1872 about 6 miles beyond the township's boundaries. In the southeastern corner lay St. Martin's only nucleated settlement, a small village of the same name that grew up around the church, the general store, and several other small businesses serving the surrounding rural area. St. Martin's pioneer farmers participated in the wheat boom of the Minnesota frontier, but were beginning a

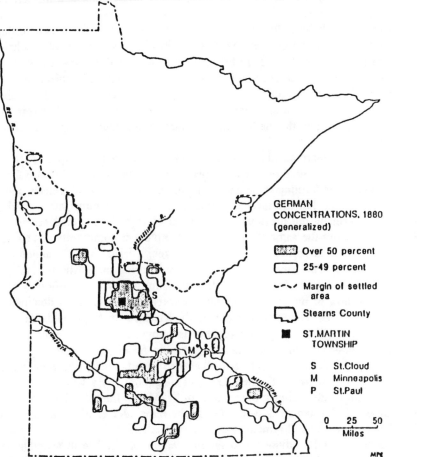

9.1. *Location of St. Martin Township and Stearns County, in the context of German set-tlement concentrations in Minnesota, 1880 (derived from Map 8.3, "Germans in Minnesota Rural Areas, 1880,"* in They Chose Minnesota: A Survey of the State's Ethnic Groups, *ed. June Drenning Holmquist, St. Paul: Minnesota Historical Society Press, 1981, p. 156.)*

transition to dairying as the pioneer generation ended its farming career. It was in 1897 that the first local cooperative creamery was established.[7]

By 1851, when the area of Stearns County was opened for settlement, Germans were becoming the nation's single largest immigrant group and were moving rapidly into agriculture. German farmers had already staked out large settlement areas in Missouri, Texas, Wisconsin, and elsewhere in the Midwest; they now turned their attention to the new Minnesota frontier.[8] The enthusiastic letters of a missionary priest published in German Catholic newspapers in the United States and Europe attracted the first German Catholic settlers to Stearns County. When a German Benedictine monastery was founded within the county in 1856, its German and Catholic future was assured. By 1870 twenty of the county's thirty-seven townships were at least 60 percent German and largely Catholic; nine of them were over 80 percent German. The county's 3,053 German-born residents constituted 21.5 percent of its total population and 58.5 percent of its foreign-born population; the native-born population included many children of German parents.[9]

150   The first German pioneers arrived in St. Martin township in 1856 or 1857. They included four families that had migrated westward from a German Catholic farming settlement in Fond du Lac County, Wisconsin, and a fifth that had initially located elsewhere in Stearns County after arriving from Germany the previous year. Several New Yorkers settled across the river at about the same time. By 1860, the pioneer community of 116 was multiethnic, harboring 12 German, 9 Yankee, 4 Irish, and 2 Scandinavian households. The pace of settlement slowed during the Civil War and the Sioux Uprising of 1862, so that the population in 1870 was still only 267, but the flow of new settlement soon quickened, and German domination intensified. By 1880, 76 percent of St. Martin's 86 households were of German stock; by 1905, 86 percent of 118 households were German. Most of the non-Germans were German-speaking Alsatians, Luxemburgers, or Dutch, with the exception of a small core of Irish families, who were beginning to intermarry with their German neighbors.[10] As late as the mid-twentieth century, almost nine-tenths of St. Martin household heads would still be of German stock, with most of the remainder at least half German. The community still remained exclusively Catholic.[11]

    The cultural traditions and familial values of St. Martin's immigrant generation of German farmers were nurtured primarily in Prussia's Rhine Province, in the isolated, backward villages of the rugged Eifel uplands and in the bordering Rhine and Moselle valleys (see Map 9.2). Because St. Martin was not the product of group colonization and subsequent chain migration from a circumscribed German locality, the precise origins of its settlers are difficult to trace. Local tradition insists that St. Martin's immigrant farmers were "Germans from the banks of the Rhine and the Mosel," and indeed they named their church and their community for one of that region's most venerated saints.[12] But specific information on place of origin is available for only fourteen St. Martin families, eleven of which came from the Eifel or neighboring areas. Migration chains certainly continued to link the township with the Eifelers who had originally settled the Fond du Lac County, Wisconsin, community from which St. Martin's pioneers had set out, and undoubtedly also with the Rhine Province itself. Federal and state

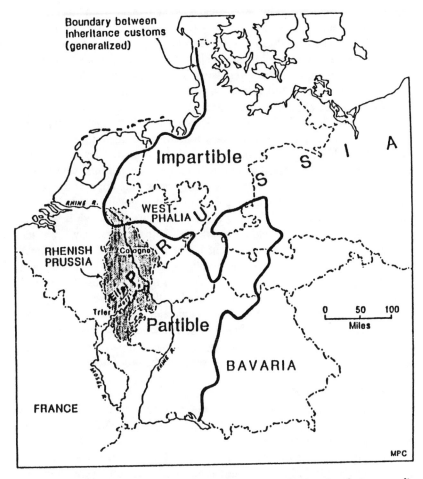

9.2. *Location of the German States of Origin of St. Martin Settlers, in relation to traditional areas of partible and impartible inheritance customs in Germany (derived from map in Lutz K. Berkner, "Inheritance, Land Tenure and Peasant Family Structure: A German Regional Comparison," in* Family and Inheritance: Rural Society in Western Europe, 1200–1800, *eds. Jack Goody, Joan Thirsk, and E. P. Thompson, Cambridge, Eng.: Cambridge University Press, 1976, p. 75.)*

censuses, however, tell us only that the great majority of St. Martin's Germans were Prussians, with Bavarians temporarily forming a small secondary group in the 1880s.[13]

In the mid-nineteenth century, the Rhine Province south of the Cologne–Aachen line was still an area of traditional village agriculture, where marginal soil and poor accessibility everywhere except in the wine-growing regions along the major rivers confined most peasants to little more than subsistence agriculture. The three-field system remained dominant, with each farmer owning widely scattered parcels in the open fields that lay around the village, as well as rights in the village's meadow, pasture, wasteland, and forest commons. The small size of individual parcels meant that communal decisions necessarily regulated farming operations, but the years of French occupation during the Napoleonic era had left most of the Rhineland an area of small peasant freeholders.[14]

The imposition of the Code Napoléon during those same years confirmed the partible inheritance customs traditional throughout most of this part of the Rhine Province. Sons and daughters inherited equally. Estates were frequently distributed during the lifetimes of the parents, whose support in retirement by one or more of the heirs constituted part of the settlement agreement. Each individual parcel of land might be divided, or the parcels could be distributed among the various heirs. Although it was unusual for sibling groups to hold and work their land cooperatively, it was not uncommon for one heir to sell or rent his or her land to another, thereby creating larger, more viable economic units. Marriage meant the pooling of two inheritances as well as creating the basis of the workforce. The system encouraged neolocal residence and nuclear families; it tied succeeding generations to the village, though it clearly could not link family identity over time with any particular piece of land. The residence, however, the visible symbol of the family in the community, could pass only to a single heir, in return for extra compensation to the parents or the other heirs.[15]

By the mid-nineteenth century these inheritance customs had created a "dwarf economy" of tiny marginal holdings in much of this part of the Rhine Province. Only widespread opportunities for supplementary earnings in small-scale mining, metal working, textile production, and similar activities permitted the system to function. In the 1840s, when poor harvests coincided with the collapse of the region's traditional cottage industries in the face of outside industrial competition, many peasants were forced to consider emigration. Between 1840 and 1871, the nine administrative districts of the Eifel alone registered 24,333 emigrants. Two-thirds to four-fifths of the emigrants were peasants, the remainder mainly artisans sharing the values of the peasants among whom they lived. Probably an equal number emigrated illegally. America was the goal for the majority.[16]

Even those St. Martinites who came from areas of Germany where impartible inheritance prevailed—Bavaria, for instance, or Westphalia—would have shared many of the familial expectations of the Rhinelanders. Partible inheritance was associated with open-field agriculture; impartible inheritance prevailed in areas of larger, unified holdings where peasants lived on their own farms. Impartible inheritance encouraged the creation of stem families in which the parental couple and the single heir and his family shared a common residence, either before or after the heir took over legal possession of the estate. It encouraged large farming units and considerable geographic mobility among nonheirs or those not marrying heirs.[17] But, at least in principle, nonheirs received compensation from the estate in forms other than land. The heir's wife's dowry provided needed cash for the settlements, and premortem division followed by support during retirement was common. Moreover, inheritance that was effectively partible could still occur in times of economic prosperity, when additional land might be purchased for other children.[18]

Both systems thus rested upon essentially similar conceptions of what has been termed the "perennial family." Under this general pattern, joint inheritances of the parental couple and the joint labor of parents and youngsters provided a stake in life for the children in the earlier phases of the family cycle. In the later phases, it facilitated the retirement of parents, which in turn provided the means and incentive for children to remain on the land, insuring that the bond of land, family, and village would endure for another generation.[19]

Emigrants from the Rhineland undoubtedly took it for granted that such traditional family strategies would continue to guide their actions in the New World. A government official in Trier reported in 1847 that one of the main reasons for the unprecedented emigration from this part of the Rhine Province the previous year was the uncertain future that peasants perceived for their children in their home villages. "By contrast," he went on to note, "America opens up to them the seductive prospect of being able to acquire with a small capital a considerable property and to leave to their children and their children's children a farm capable of providing them with an abundant livelihood."[20]

Many achieved the security they dreamed of, but it is less clear whether the immigrant farmers were equally successful in transplanting the familial patterns which that security was meant to support. Research, much of it designed to test Frederick Jackson Turner's hypothesis of rapid Americanization in frontier settings, has tended to stress the extent to which immigrant farming operations paralleled those of nonimmigrant neighbors. In place of communal villages and open fields, immigrants settled on dispersed farmsteads set in the midst of their own acres; production of staple crops for market replaced mixed subsistence farming and cottage industry; traditional house and barn types yielded to American-style farmsteads. The physical and economic context of farming was so different, the impact of American example so strong, that historians examining numerous groups in a variety of different settings have found few major differences attributable to ethnicity in farming practices, tenure, or persistence and success rates, except in isolated instances in which homogeneous groups of religiously motivated emigrants established their own colonies. "The old ways proved ineffective under new conditions and the new life quite different from the old," Oscar Handlin has argued. The differences "were not only in the surface appearance of things; they penetrated his whole life as a farmer."[21]

Yet, where such studies *have* found distinctive ethnic patterns, particularly among German immigrant farmers, they are precisely in those areas where one could expect traditional familial strategies to reveal themselves. Nineteenth-century German-Americans cherished what they saw as a stereotypical contrast between Yankee and German farmers. The Yankee farmer, according to this image, lacked any kind of sentimental attachment to his land. Ever ready to sell out for a profit and move further west, he planted the same crop year after year, paying little attention to the fertility of his soil, the well-being of his livestock, or the condition of his tools and machinery, and he plowed too much of his profit back into an elegant dwelling and a genteel life for his womenfolk. By contrast, the German farmer was stereotyped as deeply rooted in an intimate, permanent relationship with his land. His farm was an object of care and piety rather than of speculation. His deepest desire was to leave it debtfree to succeeding generations. He placed the comfort of his stock over that of his family. He carefully manured his land, chose his crops rationally to suit the soil, and let "painful order" rule in field and farmyard. His wife and children worked alongside him in the fields as the family slowly built up the capital to expand operations and to support a more comfortable existence.[22]

Central to this imagery is the German's view of the land as a family trust in traditional terms; this conception has been supported by scholarly findings of greater geographical stability, emphasis on ownership, soil conservation practices, and both intensity and productivity of farming practices. All of these characteristics can be traced to a perception of the farm as a long-term "home place" and vocation for the family over generations, rather than as a short-term investment.[23]

It seems clear, for example, that family strategies devised with that end in view would have placed little obstacle in the way of new farming practices or farmstead layouts if such innovations helped to achieve the economic security the immigrant family sought. The economic deficiencies of open-field village agriculture were likewise sufficiently evident that even newcomers accustomed to that pattern must have greeted the prospect of owning and residing on their own farms with relief and enthusiasm. So too, American customs of equal inheritance for all offspring were compatible with the assumptions underlying either German inheritance system.

It is equally clear, however, that the strategies adopted to achieve traditional familial goals must have undergone sometimes significant modification. Could those who made the transition from open-field to farm-based agriculture, for example, expect to continue traditional practices of land parcelization, or would they have to find new incentives to insure their

154

children's continued presence on the farm and in the community? Families were, of course, more likely to replant old values when supported by their new communities. Where a settlement was sufficiently large and ethnically homogeneous, it could presumably achieve the degree of cultural autonomy necessary to insulate its children from values at odds with those of the peasant family. And where the community also possessed a strong religious focus, both the autonomy and the commitment to traditional familial values would be further reinforced. To the extent that such values insured the continuing presence of the founding families in the community, they were fundamental to the survival of the ethnically distinctive character of the community itself.

155

St. Martin, with its ethnic homogeneity, religious solidarity, and institutional self-sufficiency, offered a relatively favorable environment for old values to put down new roots. Did St. Martin's German farmers attempt to maintain an approximation of the peasant bond linking families, land, and community? If so, what strategies did they adopt to achieve that bond under the conditions of the Midwestern frontier and postfrontier farming? Answers to these questions can be sought in the ways in which they resolved the basic problems of first retaining their children as a family labor force, and then of guaranteeing the transmission of the farm to the next generation.

II

A letter to the editor published in Stearns County's German newspaper, some twenty years after St. Martin was first settled, suggests some of the obstacles immigrant farmers faced in transplanting customary family patterns. A young farmer's son pointed out that if local farmers wished to keep their sons working on their farms, they would have to realize that young men desire amusement as well as work, that sons had to be given interesting tasks, responsibility, praise, some money of their own ("don't say it will all come to him in ten or fifteen years anyway, most would rather have a dollar now than ten dollars in ten or fifteen years"), and some land to manage for themselves.[24]

Another article printed in the same paper that year makes clear that many families were successfully adapting traditional patterns of behavior to combat the lure of life away from the farm. This second article, entitled "A Stearns County Wooing," embedded a local genre piece within a vignette advertising Stearns County businesses. The story begins one morning just after Christmas, as Heinrich, a young man of twenty-three, was addressed by his father:

"I'm getting old. I don't want to and can't really work the way I used to, and God be thanked, I've set enough aside so that I can spend the rest of my days with the old one there"—and here he grinned at his wife who was sitting behind the stove—"without such tiring work. And so I thought," he continued, glancing at his wife as if he expected her agreement, "that you should take over the farm, which you've been running anyway for several years now." "Yes," interjected the old woman, "as far as taking over goes, it's like this: I don't want to spend the whole day, and the evening too, on my feet any more. I'd have absolutely no rest. No, no, it doesn't matter, if he'll take over the farm—I have no objections, I'll be happy—but he should get married first."

Heinrich blushed, and it soon became clear that he was favorably inclined toward a certain Katie, the daughter of another Stearns County German farmer, though he had said nothing to her. Heinrich's father assured him that if he could get married within the month, he could take over the farm in the spring, and that once Heinrich had won Katie's hand, the two fathers could get together to make the necessary arrangements. Heinrich immediately hitched the horses to the buggy and set out with a friend to visit Katie, stopping, it seemed, at nearly every tavern along the route for courage. Katie, his friend had told him on hearing of the impending courtship, "is really a fine young lady, and I think she'll make a good housewife too." The two young men finally arrived at Katie's father's farm, bearing presents for Katie and her family. "As the two arrivals came into the house, the girls put aside their work and shook hands with the young men. Heinrich, who was inching his chair ever closer to Katie, made his offer in a few words, and Katie answered happily, yes. Then he went into the next room, where her parents were sitting, and soon walked out beaming with joy." The following Monday found the engaged couple on a shopping spree in the county seat buying clothing, furniture, a stove, and other iron and tinware for their new home.[25]

Laid out in this vignette are many of the elements of traditional family strategy seemingly intact on the Minnesota frontier—the retirement of the parents, the transfer of the farm to the son who had been working it, the dependence of the transfer on his marriage, his reluctance to go wooing until he was assured of farm ownership, the importance given to the housewifely attainments of his intended, the hint of dowry arrangements, the businesslike nature of the whole romance. It is necessary to turn to the complex record of intrafamilial land transactions, however, to document the prevalence of such strategies in St. Martin, the means by which they were realized, and some of their consequences for farm, family, and community.[26]

The relative cultural homogeneity necessary to support a communitywide set of norms regarding farm and family was achieved as non-German families moved away or died, new German families replaced them, and earlier German families expanded their holdings and persisted (Table 9.1). Such dominance came only gradually. Through 1880 the German community grew absolutely, owing to the arrival of newcomers and the expansion of the number of farms under cultivation; it grew relatively owing to the failure of groups other than the Germans and Irish to maintain themselves. After 1880 the number of farms in the township stabilized and the proportion of newcomers declined in the face of cumulative persistence and the increasing pace of takeover of farms by the second generation.

157

Nearly all farmers after the initial period were landowners. From 1880 onward, the proportion of persons listed as farmers in the census whose local land holdings could be documented in deeds records remained at 94–95 percent. Such high levels of landownership by farm operators are one indication that retired St. Martin farmers preferred to alienate the land they were no longer farming rather than rent it out. The figures also help account for the high levels of farm family persistence, particularly among those who arrived early in St. Martin. Some 73 percent of the 1860 initial census cohort of German farm families were still farming in the township after twenty years, and 54 percent of the second cohort after twenty-five years, though only 38 percent of the third cohort persisted for a similar interval. In 1880, 55 percent of all landowners had been in the township less than a decade. By 1895, 37 percent of the landowners had arrived sometime during the previous fifteen years. Ten years later, only 15 percent of the landowners had arrived during the previous decade.[27]

Such figures begin to suggest that St. Martin farmers were indeed able to convert homesteads into enduring "home places." By 1895, 24 percent of all German-stock farm owners in St. Martin were members of the second generation to farm in the township; a decade later, the offspring of local farmers made up 38 percent of the German-stock farm owners. Comparable figures for the much smaller Irish community were even higher: 33 percent and 46 percent, respectively. Among the new farm owners of the 1895–1905 decade, there were 2.5 members of the second generation for every outsider who had purchased township land. By 1905, almost half of the pioneer German families of the late 1850s and 1860s had successfully established one or more children on local farms, while another sixth were still farming themselves (Table 9.2). Two-thirds of the Irish families had similar success in setting up their children on local farms. None of the original Yankee settlers was succeeded by his children, however, including the four who continued to hold their township land until retirement or death.

As in the old country, direct family aid played a crucial role in guarantee-

9.1. *Arrival and Survival Cohorts of St. Martin Farmer-Owners by Generation*

| | | | Farmer-Owners Who | | | |
| | | | 1860 | | 1870 | |
Census Year	Total Farmers (Census)	Farmer-Owners (Deeds)	1st Gen.	2d Gen.	1st Gen.	2d Gen.
1860						
Germans	23	15	14	1		
Irish	6	6	6	—		
Yankees	11	8	8	—		
Other	2	2	2	—		
1870						
Germans	31	26	10	1	15	—
Irish	7	6	3	—	3	—
Yankees	4	4	2	—	2	—
Other	5	5	—	—	5	—
1880						
Germans	57	53	10	1	11	2
Irish	15	15	3	—	4	—
Yankees	2	2	1	—	—	—
Other	5	5	—	—	2	—
1895						
Germans	81	76	6	7	8	6
Irish	13	12	2	1	1	—
Yankees	1	1	—	—	—	—
Other	—	—	—	—	—	—
1905						
Germans	83	78	1	8	2	12
Irish	13	13	1	3	1	1
Yankees	—	—	—	—	—	—
Other	—	—	—	—	—	—

Source: Manuscript population schedules of the federal census (microfilm, National Archives, Washington, D.C.) and the Minnesota state census (microfilm, Minnesota Historical Society, St. Paul, Minn.); Deed Record, Register of Deeds, Stearns County Courthouse, St. Cloud, Minn.; abstracts, Zapp Abstract Co., St. Cloud, Minn.; manuscript agricultural schedules of the federal census (Minnesota State Archives, St. Paul, Minn.).

| Family First Appeared in Census in: | | | | | |
| 1880 | | 1895 | | 1905 | |
1st *Gen.*	*2d* *Gen.*	*1st* *Gen.*	*2d* *Gen.*	*1st* *Gen.*	*2d* *Gen.*
29	—				
8	—				
1	—				
3	—				
18	3	26	2		
3	2	2	1		
1	—	—	—		
—	—	—	—		
12	8	21	2	12	—
3	2	1	—	1	—
—	—	—	—	—	—
—	—	—	—	—	—

159

ing that the next generation would continue to farm in the township. It is possible to trace some of the means by which farms were obtained for twenty-six of the thirty second-generation farm owners in 1905.[28] Deeds records indicate that twenty-one of these twenty-six young farmers had acquired at least some of their land directly from other family members. Only one of those twenty-one had acquired all of his land from his family through inheritance alone. Fifteen acquired their land solely from family members, five from both family and nonfamily members, and two by that combination plus inheritance. The average age at which the first parcel of land was acquired was 28.5. Birth order played little clear role in determining which sons remained as farm owners in the community.

160

III

The minimal role played by inheritance in land acquisition among the second generation and the relatively early age at which sons became landowners indicate the extent to which St. Martin's immigrant farmers succeeded in maintaining traditional customs of lifetime transmission of land to their children. At the same time, however, American conditions apparently made it unnecessary to tie such land transmission to a single distribution among all heirs at the time of the farmer's retirement. It remained possible, of course, to deed over the land at the time of retirement in return for a support agreement of the kind familiar in Germany. Such agreements were common in other areas of German settlement in the Midwest and appear with some frequency in Stearns County deeds records, but were used only twice in family transactions in St. Martin. In a third instance, a childless couple deeded their land to a neighbor in return for an essentially similar support agreement.[29] Far more common was a gradual process of land transfer to one or more sons (and occasionally sons-in-law) as they matured, culminating in the father's retirement and the final distribution of the remaining land. This process of land distribution was generally preceded or accompanied by a period of additional land acquisition by the father. The terms of transfer were not recorded with any consistency, but it seems clear that in most instances sons were not simply given land, but purchased it from the father, who frequently financed the purchase.

Several examples illustrate the strategies used. One extreme instance is represented by a thirty-eight-year-old farmer who settled on 160 acres of mortgaged land in 1869. His wife would bear him ten children, five of them sons. When his eldest boy was twenty and his second fifteen, the farmer took out another mortgage to acquire an additional 160 acres, and four years later added a third quarter-section, also mortgaged. The following year, he sold one of the quarter-sections to his eldest son (then twenty-five

9.2. *Patterns of Land Transfer among Arrival Cohorts in St. Martin*

	Germans		Irish		Yankees		Other	
	No.	%	No.	%	No.	%	No.	%
Farmer-Owners in 1860 Who:								
a) completed the sale of all holdings to nonfamily members during the interval ending:								
1870	2	13	1	17	3	43	2	100
1880	—	—	—	—	—	—	—	—
1890	1	7	—	—	3	43	—	—
1905	3	20	—	—	1	14	—	—
b) still held land in 1905 and had transferred none to the second generation	2	13	—	—	—	—	—	—
c) were in the process of or had completed transferring land to the second generation by 1905	7	47	5	83	—	—	—	—
New Farmer-Owners in 1870 Who:[a]								
a) 1880	3	19	—	—	1	50	3	60
1890	1	6	—	—	—	—	2	40
1905	2	13	1	33	1	50	—	—
b)	3	19	1	33	—	—	—	—
c)	7	44	1	33	—	—	—	—
New Farmer-Owners in 1880 Who:[a]								
a) 1890	8	27	3	38	—	—	2	66
1905	6	20	1	12	—	—	1	33
b)	11	37	2	25	—	—	—	—
c)	5	17	2	25	—	—	—	—
New Farmer-Owners in 1895 Who:[a]								
a) 1905	4	16	—	—	—	—	—	—
b)	15	60	—	—	—	—	—	—
c)	6	24	1	100	—	—	—	—

[a]Headings are the same as those for 1860.

Source: Manuscript population schedules of the federal census (microfilm, National Archives, Washington, D.C.) and the Minnesota state census (microfilm, Minnesota Historical Society, St. Paul, Minn.); Deed Record, Register of Deeds, Stearns County Courthouse, St. Cloud, Minn.; abstracts, Zapp Abstract Co., St. Cloud, Minn.; manuscript agricultural schedules of the federal census (Minnesota State Archives, St. Paul, Minn.).

years of age and either recently married or about to marry). Three years later his second son, now twenty-four, was also ready for marriage and purchased one of the two remaining quarter-sections from his father.

The next two sons were at that point eighteen and sixteen, respectively. The father, reduced to his original homestead, again entered the rapidly constricting local land market. The 40 acres he was able to purchase outright in 1892 were insufficient when his third son reached twenty-five and was ready for marriage, so the father sold him the original homestead. The farmer was now sixty-five years old, with one daughter and two sons, aged twenty-two and eighteen, still at home. As the depression years of the 1890s began to wane, and as his fourth son's twenty-fifth birthday approached, the farmer returned once more to the land market, laboriously putting together a farm from small lots as they became available, picking up 20 acres here, 48 acres there, 30 acres from another seller. By 1898 he had 138 acres to transfer. By 1903 the widowed father, now seventy-two, could finally settle down to well-earned retirement with the family of one of his daughters. Only the youngest son's fate was still unclear.

The financial arrangements between this father and his sons are as interesting as the pace of land acquisition and transfer. Clearly, the father was pooling his labor and that of his growing sons, along with his established credit, to finance the initial purchases of land. Then, as each son withdrew from the family "pool," the money with which the son purchased land from the father helped finance further land acquisition and, ultimately, the father's retirement. The first son paid his father using a mortgage obtained from a Massachusetts bank. The second son (who would later sell out and leave the township in 1905) evidently paid with cash or with an unsecured note. The father accepted his third son's mortgage note himself. The arrangement apparently encountered problems, however, as this son was forced to resell the land to his father in 1898, using a bond for deed to gain final title by 1903. Perhaps for this reason, when the fourth son purchased his land in 1898, he too signed a deed contract, whereby he would receive title only when the $3,700 purchase price had been repaid at 7 percent annual interest. He was able to pay his father and gain title in 1903, using a $2,700 mortgage from an outside lender. It was only then, when the third and fourth sons finally paid their father, that the farmer's retirement became possible.

This saga represents one father's heroic attempts to provide equally for all of his sons as they came of age. More typical in its mixed success was the case of another farmer, who purchased 280 acres in the township in 1884. He was already fifty-two years old at the time, with five children, including three sons over age twenty. The eldest son seems to have quickly struck out on his own, and the second son purchased a local quarter-section without recorded involvement of his father. Four years later, however, the father sold 160 acres to his youngest son, retaining 120 acres for himself and his wife, which he still held at the time of his death. His widow then sold these in equal shares to the two sons still in the township, undoubtedly to provide for her own old age.

Other German farmers attempted to follow essentially similar strategies in establishing their sons locally, but without success. Take, for example, the case of a Civil War veteran, thirty years old when he first took up a quarter-section homestead in 1869. His family would include five sons and seven daughters. In 1890, as his children were growing up, he used a mortgage to purchase an additional 120 acres, but sold the new farm outside the family two years later. His oldest son had married and left town in 1889 at the age of twenty-four; the second and fourth sons would follow, one to join a religious order. The third married in 1898 and evidently continued to farm the home place with his father and youngest brother. Then the youngest left home, and when the sixty-five-year-old father was ready to retire in 1904, he gave the third son a deed contract for the homestead. This son, however, was either unwilling or unable to make a go of farming on his own to fulfill the contract. After trying and failing to assist at least one and possibly more of his children to farm ownership and community permanence, the farmer was forced to finance his retirement in 1906 by sale of the homestead to a nonfamily member.

163

As these examples suggest, St. Martin's German pioneers developed a complex set of strategies, all based upon the expanding resources of the family as maturing sons joined their father in working family land, and all aimed at assisting the sons to establish themselves as independent farmers at an early age, retaining the home place within the family, and making possible the parents' retirement. Fathers could not simply give the land to their sons, because they had to consider the claims of other children and the desirability of maintaining parental independence in old age. One alternative, of course, would have been to rent out the family land (either to children or outsiders), use the rental income to support retirement, and distribute the land to the children as an inheritance after death. Data from ownership records and the census, however, suggest that extended rental was relatively uncommon in St. Martin's German families. Without the security of ownership, a son would have little incentive to invest heavily in the farm; indeed, without ownership, evidently few married sons were willing to remain in town.

With parental help, a son could acquire a farm much sooner than would otherwise be possible, and would be more likely to remain in the township. With children safely settled in the area, parents, in turn, could rest assured that what they had created in America would remain an enduring "home place" for the family, and that children would be available to comfort (and if necessary, support) their old age. As a farmer of German descent in a neighboring township would later recall, "Dad said, 'I am getting old and I cannot work the farm anymore.' That's how I was hooked with it; I couldn't say no and leave them sit there. I could have gotten a job somewhere, gone away. But I couldn't do that to my parents."[30] German parents could not preserve their children from knowledge of opportunities elsewhere, but they did create a local culture that offered both positive inducements and internalized norms to keep some at least of the next generation on the farm and in the community.

164   I V

As in the last example cited, many in the first two pioneer cohorts who farmed for at least a decade in the township—long enough to be regarded as permanent settlers—but who failed to establish their children, probably also shared the familial values of those who were more successful. Another example of a family with fourteen children, none of whom continued to farm in the township, indicates the possibility of alternative values. In this household, the only offspring to remain in St. Martin was a storekeeper who had received a normal school education. Two other "unsuccessful" farmers in these two pioneer cohorts were childless, a third lost his land through foreclosure in 1894, and a fourth lost two sons to out-migration but could at least rejoice that his eldest son was well-established on a prosperous father-in-law's property in a neighboring township. In the latter case, the farmer—an Alsatian, not a Prussian, as it happens—retained his land until his death after his eightieth birthday. By that time all of his thirteen children had departed. None was apparently willing to return and take up farming on the family land; the children gradually sold their inheritance to neighbors.

Closer examination of those cases in St. Martin in which land transfer was delayed until after a father's death suggests that the transfer frequently involved similar risks for farm and family. Sixty-one conveyances of real estate at death occurred in St. Martin between 1859 and 1915, forty-four of which involved the estates of persons of German birth or stock. Of those forty-four persons, 43 percent died intestate. The wills of an additional 9 percent effectively used standard intestacy provisions, whereas in two instances wills were set aside in favor of the more liberal widow's rights under Minnesota's intestacy statutes.[31] Ten of the remaining twenty-one testators used their wills to make more favorable provision for their spouses; one left his property to a woman in Fond du Lac County, Wisconsin; the remaining ten made more complex arrangements for the division of their property within the family.

In general, intestacy characterized farmers who either died very young, had few or no children or had little land to dispose of, or who died at a ripe old age having already made some provision for their children. In cases in which the estate was complex, the children numerous, and the farmer not caught by early death, there was usually a will. In one case in which the husband died intestate at age seventy-five, after having transferred land to his elder but not to his younger son, we can see some of the complications that wills were often designed to avert: His widow, oldest son, and two daughters had to enter into a complicated series of arrangements to insure that the youngest son could purchase from the other heirs the land clearly meant for him after a three-year rental period intended to permit him time to accumulate the needed funds.

165

Often the continuity of intrafamily land transfer already under way was secured by leaving the land to the widow. In other instances, however, the will spelled out more detailed procedures. One father who died as his son was approaching twenty-one, for example, left everything to his wife, with the proviso that should she choose to sell, she was to give $1,000 to each of their two daughters and $1,200 to the son, assuming that he had reached twenty-one; she in fact soon sold the land to the son. In another example, a mother's will made explicit the relationship between previous help given by parents to children, aid from children to parents, and inheritance, by leaving an extra $400 to the daughter who had remained at home to care for her widowed mother, and by making no provision for two sons who "have received their full share during my lifetime." The same connection was made evident in another instance in the terms of a sale of land from father to son: The son purchased his father's land for $1,100 down, $100 a year for the next four years, and $3,000 at 5 percent interest to be paid to the estate one year after the death of the last parent—obviously to provide for the other children. The proviso was added that if the son sold the land in the meantime (i.e., alienated it from family ownership), "then the balance will be at six per cent interest."

Where intestacy provisions applied, by law daughters received shares in the estate equal to those of their brothers. Most wills likewise treated daughters simply as "children" who participated equally in the division of the estate. Their shares, however, were generally converted to cash rather than taken as land. Two instances in which wills attempted to provide monetary settlements for daughters and land for sons make such norms explicit, but such expectations are equally evident in the complex intrafamily arrangements that frequently followed upon the "undivided" transmission of estates to all heirs in cases of intestacy. Here the usual pattern was for female heirs to sell their interests to one or more brothers, unless the estate was sold out of the family altogether. Undoubtedly, daughters also received premortem assistance as did their brothers, but in the form of dowry or other kinds of payments rather than in land.

V

The effective functioning of such a system among the pioneer generation was a product of the relatively slow pace of settlement within the township and of generous federal land laws that encouraged rapid accumulations of acreage far larger than the family was initially able to farm. About half of the township land was alienated from the federal government by the early 1860s, most of the remainder by 1870, leaving only a few scattered pockets (as well as the two state sections of school land) for later sale.[32] About half of the land in the township was acquired under the provisions of the Homestead Act, mainly by Germans. The fifteen German landowners present in 1860 were able to acquire an average of 264 acres each before 1880 or their first sale of land, with no accumulations smaller than a quarter-section and one as large as 400 acres. Such large initial claims could be divided into farms and brought into production as family needs and labor supply dictated; as late as 1880, St. Martin's ratio of improved to unimproved land was only one to two.

Early speculator activity within the township provided a further land bank upon which German farmers could draw as more acreage was needed. Of the ten quarter-sections still held by three Yankee speculators in 1880, for example, four were sold to German newcomers by 1900 and the other six provided additional land for already established German families. The state land of sections 16 and 36 performed a similar function as it was sold on credit during the 1880s and 1890s, approximately half to established families and half to German newcomers. Another section or so of land had been broken up early into numerous parcels, some as small as 10 acres, and sold as woodlots to settlers on the treeless prairie of the neighboring town. This land, too, found its way into the hands of members of three established and one new St. Martin German family once it had been stripped of its timber. Finally, as Yankees and other early settlers moved on or died, Germans took their places. One German pioneer of 1860 was able to add two Yankee farms to his holdings, two other Yankee farmsteads passed into the hands of two second-generation German brothers, and German newcomers moved onto other parcels. The only land still in Yankee ownership by 1905 was held in litigation by the heirs of its original patentee.

St. Martin's land, of course, was ultimately as finite as that of any European village. By the late 1880s further stocks of available land for German expansion within the township were becoming increasingly rare, and St. Martin itself was surrounded by other German-settled townships with similarly expanding populations. In this situation, however, St. Martin farmers did not resort to the parcelization of land characteristic of much of the Eifel and neighboring areas in Germany. Mean size of individual holdings remained relatively constant. Indeed, the proportion of farmers with holdings

166

over 200 acres increased from 4 percent in 1860 to 16 percent in 1880 and 32 percent by 1905, as the number of farms first rose from thirty-seven in 1870 to ninety by 1895, and then ten years later dropped to eighty-two. One early will of 1870 attempted to break up a farm into three 40-acre parcels for distribution to each of three sons, but such a strategy found few imitators. During the pioneer decades farmers were able to expand their holdings to provide land for their sons; when that possibility receded, they proved reluctant to revert to a practice of subdivision below local norms of viable farm size. By the turn of the century, no more than 20 percent of the farms were smaller than a quarter-section.

Nor did St. Martin farmers effectively reduce the size of their families as they began to exhaust the abundance of the frontier period. There was a slight decline in the fertility ratio from the extreme peaks of the early frontier period, but traditional values continued to encourage exceptionally large families.[33] The mean number of children residing in homes of mothers in their forties—a rough estimate of completed family size—remained stable at 4.7 between 1880 and 1905. As late as 1940 St. Martin would have a fertility ratio higher than that exhibited in 1875 by a comparable Yankee-dominated Minnesota township.[34]

167

Moreover, the nuclear family remained the dominant context of both residence and farm labor. Despite the frequency with which a son took over the family farm upon his father's retirement, there is little evidence of a tendency toward the stem family form often associated with farm-based agriculture in Germany. In 1880, 70 percent of all households contained only a nuclear family, extended neither by other relatives nor by hired hands. By 1905, when the variety of kin relationships within the community was much greater than twenty-five years earlier, 69 percent of all households still contained only a nuclear family. Only about 5 percent of all households in either census year contained a second-generation married couple, and fewer than 8 percent had one or more grandparents sharing the dwelling. Parental households could expand temporarily to take in a married child and family, as occurred at one point during the family cycle in four of the pioneer 1860 cohort of German families. A second-generation household might expand to harbor a widowed parent (two of the pioneers found themselves in such a situation) or to house a single sibling of the head (as occurred twice for this pioneer cohort). But the norm was for married children to establish separate households quickly, even if on the same farmstead, and for aging parents likewise to maintain their own households, either on the farm or in the village, until the death of one spouse brought the likelihood of residence with a married child for the surviving partner. The nuclear family was flexible in its willingness to take in other relatives at various phases in the family cycle, but extended coresidence of an heir and his family with his parents, or of a retired parental couple with the family of the child who had taken over the farm, was never the norm.[35]

The combination of large families, separate and usually nuclear households, stable size of holdings, and limited availability of land inevitably meant that over time increasing numbers of children would have to leave the community at maturity (Table 9.3). By 1885, 37 percent of the males who had resided in the township in 1875 were no longer present, a proportion that increased to 50 percent for the 1895–1905 period. Future outmigrants were 57 percent of males between the ages of ten and nineteen in 1875, 70 percent by 1895. By the late 1890s more than two-thirds of the maturing generation of young men were leaving their community in their teens and early twenties. About one-sixth of these could be traced to other Stearns County townships in 1900 and 1905; the remainder sought their fortunes further afield.[36]

For those who remained in St. Martin, however, the result was a familial system strong enough to endure long after the pioneer period—indeed, well into the twentieth century, as William Cofell documented in a 1950 study of St. Martin families. Only 7 percent of the farm owners at that time had inherited their farms, whereas 88 percent had acquired them by purchase (no information was available on the remaining 5 percent). Of the purchasers, however, 85 percent had acquired their farms from relatives, usually parents. Then as during the pioneer period, fathers aimed at purchasing additional land as sons began to reach maturity. Father and sons worked the farm together, all income accruing to the father to help repay his initial investment. When a son decided to marry, the father rented him the land for a year or two and, if he proved successful, the father sold him the farm for significantly less than the initial purchase price. Sons were also often furnished with machinery and livestock; daughters who married farmers received gifts of money, household articles, and perhaps livestock. The advantages of such strategies, as Cofell pointed out, were that the father could expand his operation while his family laborforce was growing, decrease it as his sons left home, avoid a cash outlay as each son married, yet still provide as much aid as possible. As one interviewee put it, "while we're waiting for the son to get married his farm is paying for itself." At an appropriate time, the home farm itself would then be sold to one of the children, and the parents would retire.[37]

V I

Frontier Minnesota conditions permitted German immigrant farmers and their children to maintain and revitalize traditional familial values through adaptations of old-country strategies. They continued to place central em-

9.3. Out-Migration and Persistence of St. Martin Males by Age, 1875–1905

Out-Migration

Age Group	1875 Males No Longer Present in 1885, by Age in 1875		1895 Males No Longer Present in 1905, by Age in 1895	
	No.	% of Age Group	No.	► % of Age Group
0–9	77	21	127	45
10–19	51	57	74	70
20–29	21	52	103	41
30–39	18	33	41	51
40–49	20	35	23	39
50–59	17	41	17	47
60–69	7	29	20	50
70–79	—	—	14	86
80 +	—	—	—	—
Total	211	37	419	50

Persistence

Age Group	1885 Males Present Since 1875, by Age in 1885		1905 Males Present Since 1895, by Age in 1905	
	No.	% of Age Group	No.	% of Age Group
10–19	85	72	102	75
20–29	52	42	59	53
30–39	23	43	41	51
40–49	20	60	33	70
50–59	24	54	25	76
60–69	24	63	12	75
70–79	4	100	8	100
80 +	2	100	5	80
Total	235	59	285	67

Source: Manuscript population schedules of the Minnesota state census, 1875–1905 (microfilm, Minnesota Historical Society, St. Paul, Minn.).

phasis upon the assistance of their children toward an early start in farming. They retained the principle of treating all children equally. They continued to stress early retirement from both farming and landownership in order to provide incentives for children to remain as farmers on the family land and to preserve the family name in the community.

The means by which these traditional goals were achieved underwent modifications, of course. The early commercialization of local agriculture made it far easier to convert joint interests in the family enterprise into cash or credit than it had been in the old country, and the expanding national economy offered ample opportunities elsewhere, both agricultural and nonagricultural. One result was that the inefficient subdivision of land that had characterized the Rhineland system of partible inheritance could be abandoned even while maintaining the *principle* of partible division. The home place was frequently transmitted to only one child, as under the German system of impartible inheritance, but this did not create disadvantages for other children, who could be assisted toward other land purchases or careers, initially within the township itself. The practice of joint households, sometimes characteristic of German areas in which a single son took over the family land, was never necessary in St. Martin. The perennial cycle of the family farm maintained itself, from intergenerational cooperation to retirement, generational succession, and renewed father–son cooperation. But it could proceed more gradually, without the single climactic act of a succession agreement, and it could be embodied now in commercial conveyances that replaced old in-kind payments with cash installment or interest payments.

The successful transplantation of elements of peasant family goals rested in large part on the "window of opportunity" that frontier conditions offered the immigrant generation. This is not to dismiss the back-breaking toil and adversity faced by these pioneers, or the significant number who failed. Nevertheless, their traditional familial orientation served St. Martinites well in the task of frontier farm making. The labor of the entire family, more willingly invested when all perceived an equal stake in the outcome, replaced the capital the family lacked; large families meant that the increasing needs of the family were matched by the growing productivity of both the maturing workforce and the virgin acreage that it gradually brought into production. The initial abundance of land held out the promise of the traditional manner of provision for all children, which American law with its emphasis upon equal inheritance only confirmed.

Community support, however, was equally fundamental to the maintenance of traditional family values. The willingness of parents to forgo the psychological dividends of landlord status and parental power in their later years, the willingness of at least some children to resist the siren call of other ways of life, the ability to close the local land market to outside purchasers—all this required a value consensus that the ethnic and religious homogeneity and relative isolation of St. Martin were able to provide. In turn, the continuity of families on the land and expansion onto neighboring territory insured the survival and extension of the ethnic culture.[38]

In this respect at least, St. Martin farmers fit the old stereotype of the German farmer in America. Their counterparts in other areas of rural German-American concentration may have been equally successful in transplanting the basic bond of farm and family. The tendency for many initial clusters of German immigrants to expand through the acquisition of land previously owned by non-Germans is well documented, and rural sociologists earlier in the twentieth century often found farmers in such areas generally more successful in keeping the farm in the family than were most other Midwestern farmers. Family strategies similar to those of the St. Martinites were often the reasons.[39]

But German peasants from other parts of Germany brought different customs with them to America, and encountered varying circumstances where they chose to settle. American farming communities, even when solidly German, frequently included persons of German origins sufficiently different to necessitate a kind of cultural syncretism even in the absence of much contact with American customs.[40] Variations among areas of rural German settlement were probably as significant as the commonalities. By the late nineteenth century, for example, some Wisconsin German settlers had reportedly begun to honor old-country customs of family land subdivision. Similar subdivision characterized a central Illinois community of low German-speaking Lutheran East Frisians, where it combined with reduced levels of fertility to allow the survival of the ethnic community but not its expansion.[41] Further research is needed to document the differences and similarities in family strategies and their consequences for farm and family in rural German settlement clusters.

Such research is also necessary, of course, to clarify the strategies of other Midwestern farmers, and of Germans living outside their ethnic clusters. There is evidence to suggest, for example, that a different pattern developed in some Midwestern areas settled by native-stock farmers in the mid-nineteenth century, a pattern that accords more closely with the notorious restlessness of the American farmer and the speculative nature of the frontier. Although familial behavior fairly close to German patterns seems to have characterized many Yankee farmers in older settled areas, studies by rural sociologists and land economists in the early decades of the twentieth century found that many native-stock Midwestern farmers preferred to retain their land until death before bequeathing it equally to all children. Retirement for them usually involved a gradual withdrawal from farming and the leasing rather than the sale of the land. Sons often worked their fathers' land, but usually as tenants. If a tenant son desired to take over the farm after his father's death, he would reach an accord with his coheirs to buy out their interests or he would take a chance at the inevitable public auction, even though he would have had little chance to build up equity or credit. By the 1930s, scholars were coming to realize the extent to which increasing levels of tenancy resulted from the normal life cycle when combined with a set of values that encouraged transmission primarily through inheritance and multigeniture. Rather than the establishment of generations of stable families of owner-operators as in St. Martin, the results were more often high levels of tenancy and turnover, difficult prospects of ultimate ownership for the next generation, and low community cohesiveness.[42]

How widespread this latter pattern was and what factors were associated with its emergence require historical documentation. Ethnicity is clearly only one of many factors influencing processes of generational succession among farm families, and both the nature and the success of specific strategies could vary, not only from group to group and area to area but even from family to family, as St. Martin patterns suggest. Nevertheless, it is clear that the few Yankees who settled in St. Martin failed to follow the German course. There were six native-stock families (four farming families and two speculators) who held land within the township for a significant length of time. One farmer sold out and left town when he was seventy-six. The heirs of the other three husbandmen, as well as those of one of the speculators, first leased and then sold their inheritances after a period of joint ownership, while the legacy of the other speculator was still being contested at the end of the period. Although the German character of St. Martin obviously gave Yankee heirs little incentive to remain, it may be significant that most Yankee farmers waited until death to deal with the disposal of their land.[43]

St. Martin's Irish, unlike the Yankees, succeeded in establishing very stable intergenerational farms, but did not expand their holdings in the manner of the Germans. Although their numbers are too small to permit much generalization, there are indications of a tendency among Irish farmers to retain their land until extreme old age or death, to assist only one son directly (or at least to differentiate treatment among sons), and to reside in old age with the child who would ultimately inherit the land. In the case of one extensive Irish clan, the pattern more closely approached a process traditional in Ireland and also evident among the central Illinois Irish studied by Sonya Salamon, than it did either the practices of their Yankee neighbors or the American adaptation worked out by their German fellow Catholics.[44]

Other groups may have exhibited still other variations. Robert Ostergren, in a significant study of several mostly Swedish communities in Isanti County, Minnesota, found patterns resembling those of St. Martin among communities settled by farmers drawn from a relatively isolated area of Sweden. Farmers from more commercialized areas of Sweden, and those who settled outside the Swedish communities, exhibited the same Yankee tendency to prefer post- to predeath settlements and similarly low rates of interfamily farm transmission. Emphasis on educating children for nonfarm occupations rather than preserving the family farm may have had similar consequences, as other studies of Scandinavian-American farming communities suggest.[45]

Stearns County's Germans were able to develop and preserve a distinctive ethnic culture firmly based on the triad of farm, family, and community, which has to a significant degree endured to the present. Neither the content of that culture nor its survival can be understood without taking into account the extent to which pioneers were able to transplant traditional values supporting family continuity on the land. To look only at farming practices in the strictest sense is to miss, as Ostergren has pointed out, the critical familial nexus that linked the economic sphere, where the immigrant readily assimilated, to the cultural and social sphere, where traditional values usually retained their force.[46] To overlook the family is, in fact, to overlook the medium in which those values were nurtured. Agricultural commercialization in America proved consonant with a variety of different family strategies and goals, whose contours remain to be explored by historians. Attention to patterns of inter vivos land transmission as well as to inheritance, as demonstrated in this essay, should be combined with examination of the widely varying ethnic heritages of those who settled the Midwestern heartland and the differing ideals by which they defined "success" on the farming frontier. For many a Yankee, such accomplishment may well have meant expansive acreage and money at interest. But for most St. Martinites, at least, and for others like them, it was the successful transplanting of the perennial bond between family, land, and community.

173

NOTES

1. U.S. Senate, *Abstracts of Reports of the Immigration Commission*, document no. 747, 61st Cong., 3d sess., 1911, 799. There were 2,105,766 first- and second-generation German farmers and farm laborers in the country in 1900.

2. Michael Mitterauer and Reinhard Sieder, *The European Family: Patriarchy to Partnership from the Middle Ages to the Present* (Chicago, 1982); Heidi Rosenbaum, *Formen der Familie: Untersuchungen zum Zusammenhang von Familienverhältnissen, Sozialstruktur und sozialem Wandel in der deutschen Gesellschaft des 19. Jahrhunderts* (Frankfurt am Main, 1982), 47–120; Tamara K. Hareven, "The Family as Process: The Historical Study of the Family Cycle," *Journal of Social History* 7 (1974):322–29; H. J. Habakkuk, "Family Structure and Economic Change in Nineteenth-Century Europe," *Journal of Economic History* 15 (1955):1–12; Lutz K. Berkner, "Rural Family Organization in Europe: A Problem in Comparative History," *Peasant Studies Newsletter* 1 (1972):145–56; Lutz K. Berkner, "Inheritance, Land Tenure and Peasant Family Structure: A German Regional Comparison," in Jack Goody, Joan Thirsk, and E. P. Thompson, eds., *Family and Inheritance: Rural Society in Western Europe, 1200–1800* (Cambridge, Eng., 1976), 71–95; David Sabean, "Aspects of Kinship Behavior and Property in Rural Western Europe before 1800," in Goody,

Thirsk, and Thompson, eds., *Family and Inheritance*, 96–111. The extensive debate on the exact definition of peasant society is not critical for present purposes: "Peasant" here refers to primarily, although not exclusively, subsistence farmers with vested rights in their land who exist within a larger political and social system. See Walter Goldschmidt and Evalyn Jacobson Kunkel, "The Structure of the Peasant Family," *American Anthropologist* 73 (1971):1058–76; Teodor Shanin, "Peasantry: Delineation of a Sociological Concept and a Field of Study," *Peasant Studies Newsletter* 2 (1973):1–11. For present purposes, immigrants of "sub-peasant" status without full rights in land can be presumed to have shared the familial norms of their peasant neighbors.

3. For a classic statement of this theme, see Marcus Lee Hansen, *The Atlantic Migration, 1607–1860* (Cambridge, Mass., 1940).

4. Arthur W. Calhoun, *A Social History of the American Family*, repr. (New York, 1973), 9–77, 131–48. Richard Easterlin and his associates have suggested that declining rural fertility rates were related to the desire of American farmers to provide their children with land in their vicinity, but cite little evidence on land transmission patterns to support their suggestion; see Richard A. Easterlin, "Factors in the Decline of Farm Family Fertility in the United States: Some Preliminary Research Results," *Journal of American History* 63 (1976):600–614; Richard A. Easterlin, George Alter, and Gretchen A. Condran, "Farms and Farm Families in Old and New Areas: The Northern States in 1860," in Tamara K. Hareven and Maris A. Vinovskis, eds., *Family and Population in Nineteenth-Century America* (Princeton, N.J., 1978), 22–84.

5. For a discussion of this literature, see Kathleen Neils Conzen, "Historical Approaches to the Study of Rural Ethnic Communities," in Frederick C. Luebke, ed., *Ethnicity on the Great Plains* (Lincoln, Neb., 1980), 1–18.

6. For example, see Josef J. Barton, *Peasants and Strangers: Italians, Rumanians, and Slovaks in an American City, 1890–1950* (Cambridge, Mass., 1975); Virginia Yans-McLaughlin, *Family and Community: Italian Immigrants in Buffalo, 1830–1930* (Ithaca, N.Y., 1977); Tamara K. Hareven, "Family Time and Industrial Time," *Journal of Urban History* 1 (1975):365–89; John Bodnar, "Immigration and Modernization: The Case of Slavic Peasants in Industrial America," *Journal of Social History* 10 (1976):44–71.

7. Minnesota Historical Records Survey Project, Works Projects Administration, *Inventory of the County Archives of Minnesota: No. 73, Stearns County* (St. Paul, 1940), 4–23; Cyril Ortmann, *Saint Martin: A Century of Catholic Parish and Community Life* (St. Martin, Minn., 1958), 19–20, 62–64; Surveyor's Field Notes, Township 124 N, Range 32 W (1856), Minnesota State Archives, St. Paul; Merrill E. Jarchow, *The Earth Brought Forth: A History of Minnesota Agriculture to 1885* (St. Paul, 1949), 165–222. Stearns County's reported wheat output expanded from about 56,000 bushels in 1860 and 370,000 in 1870 to about 1.1 million in 1880, 2 million in 1890, and 3 million in 1900, while its fluid milk production climbed from 108 gallons in 1870 to about 43,000 gallons by 1880, over 3.9 million gallons in 1890, and 7.7 million gallons in 1900; *Eighth Census* (Washington, D.C., 1860), Agriculture, 80–81; *Ninth Census* (Washington, D.C., 1870), Wealth and Industry, 180–83; *Tenth Census* (Washington, D.C., 1880), Agriculture, 194, 159; *Eleventh Census* (Washington,

D.C., 1890), Agriculture, 372, 293; *Twelfth Census* (Washington, D.C., 1900), Agriculture, Part I, 170, 607.

8. Max Hannemann, "Das Deutschtum in den Vereinigten Staaten: seine Verbreitung und Entwicklung seit der Mitte des 19. Jahrhunderts," Ergänzungsheft Nr. 225, *Petermann's Mitteilungen* (1936); Hildegard Binder Johnson, "The Location of German Immigrants in the Middle West," *Annals of the Association of American Geographers* 41 (1951):1–41.

9. Ingolf Vogeler, "The Roman Catholic Culture Region of Central Minnesota," *Pioneer America* 8 (1976): 71–83; U.S. Census, *Population* (Washington, D.C., 1880), 515. By 1890, 68.1 percent of the native-born population of the county was of foreign parentage.

10. St. Martin's population was 516 in 1880, 692 in 1890, 623 in 1900, 601 in 1910, and 752 in 1920. The community included thirteen Irish households in both 1880 and 1905, as well as three Yankee and five other nationality households in 1880, which declined to one and two, respectively, by 1905, according to manuscript federal (microfilm, National Archives, Washington, D.C.) and state (microfilm, Minnesota Historical Society, St. Paul, Minn.) census schedules.

11. William L. Cofell, "An Analysis of the Formation of Community Attitudes Toward Secondary Education in St. Martin," M.S. Thesis, University of Minnesota, 1958.

12. Ortmann, *Saint Martin*, 21; Adam Wrede, *Eifeler Volkskunde* (Bonn, 1960), 175, 329. In attempting to link St. Martin families to their German villages of origin and to places of earlier settlement in the United States, I have drawn upon materials in the collections of the Stearns County Historical Society, St. Cloud, Minn., including oral histories; obituary files and other newspaper clippings; and interviews conducted by the Works Progress Administration. I have also consulted Civil War veterans pension records in the National Archives, Washington, D.C.; biographical compilations in William Bell Mitchell, *History of Stearns County, Minnesota*, 2 vols. (Chicago, 1915), in Western Historical Company, *The History of Fond du Lac County, Wisconsin* (Chicago, 1880), and in Maurice McKenna, ed., *Fond du Lac County, Wisconsin: Past and Present* (Chicago, 1912); and two Wisconsin parish histories: P. Corbinian Vieracker, *Geschichte von Mount Calvary, Fond du Lac County, Wis.: Ein Festgabe zum Goldenen Jubilaeum der ersten Ordensniederlassung der Kapuzinerväter in Nordamerika, 25 Juni 1907* (Milwaukee, n.d.) and B. J. Blied, *St. John the Baptist Congregation, Johnsburg, Wisconsin* (Johnsburg, Wis., 1957). Minnesota naturalization papers for this period (deposited in the Minnesota State Archives, St. Paul, Minn.) do not record village or province of origin.

13. In 1870, 86 percent of St. Martin's German household heads were born in Prussia, 72 percent in 1880, and 91 percent in 1895. Bavarians comprised 5 percent, 26 percent, and 3 percent of the St. Martin population, respectively, in each of the census years; manuscript population schedules of the federal census, 1870 and 1880 (microfilm, National Archives, Washington, D.C.); manuscript population schedules of the Minnesota state census, 1895 (microfilm, Minnesota Historical Society, St. Paul, Minn.).

14. Richard Graafen, *Die Aus- und Abwanderung aus der Eifel in den Jahren 1815 bis 1955. Forschungen zur deutschen Landeskunde*, 127 (Bad Godesberg, 1961); Josef

175

Mergen, *Die Amerika-Auswanderung aus dem Stadtkreis Trier im 19. Jahrhundert* (Trier, 1962); Max Sering, "Das Moselland in der Vergangenheit und Gegenwart," in Max Sering, ed., *Das Moselland* (Leipzig, 1910), 1–34; Franz Brümmer, "Der Notstand in der Eifel, seine Ursachen und die Massnahmen der Staatsregierung zu seiner Behabung," in Sering, ed., *Das Moselland*, 157–74.

15. Karl Rogge, "Gegenwartsfragen der Freiteilung des ländlichen Grundbesitzes in Westdeutschland," in Max Sering and Constantin von Dietze, eds., *Die Vererbung des ländlichen Grundbesitzes in der Nachkriegszeit* (München and Leipzig, 1930), 331–84; Brümmer, "Notstand in der Eifel"; Max Sering, ed., *Die Vererbung des ländlichen Grundbesitzes im Königreich Preussen*, 3 vols. (Berlin, 1899), 1:1–154.

16. Graafen, *Aus- und Abwanderung*, 43–52; figures cited on 50–51.

17. Berkner, "Inheritance, Land Tenure and Peasant Family Structure," and Lutz K. Berkner, "The Stem Family and the Developmental Cycle of the Peasant Household: An Eighteenth-Century Austrian Example," *American Historical Review* 77 (1972):398–418; Michael Mitterauer and Reinhard Sieder, "The Developmental Process of Domestic Groups: Problems of Reconstruction and Possibilities of Interpretation," *Journal of Family History* 4 (1979): 257–84; Michel Verdon, "The Stem Family: Toward a General Theory," *Journal of Interdisciplinary History* 10 (1979):87–105. The technical terms for the two inheritance systems are *Realteilung* (partible) and *Anerbenrecht* (impartible); there is a considerable literature relating to the relationship between the two systems and the incidence of emigration; see Walter D. Kamphoefner, "Transplanted Westfalians: Persistence and Transformation of Socioeconomic and Cultural Patterns in the Northwest German Migration to Missouri," Diss., University of Missouri, Columbia, 1978, 28–72.

18. Helmut Röhm, *Die Vererbung des landwirtschaftlichen Grundeigentums in Baden-Württemberg* (Remagen/Rh., 1957); Peter Brugger, *Das Anerbe und das Schicksal seiner Geschwister in mehreren Oberämter des Württ. Oberlandes. Berichte über Landwirtschaft* 21 (1936), Sonderheft; Ulrich Planck, "Hofstellenchronik von Bölgental 1650–1966: Strukturwandlungen in einem fränkischen Weiler," in Heinz Haushofer and Willi A. Boelcke, eds., *Wege und Forschungen der Agrargeschichte* (Frankfurt am Main, 1967):242–66; Joseph Baumgartner, "Die Vererbung des landwirtschaftlichen Grundbesitzes in Bayern rechts des Rheins," in Sering and von Dietze, eds., *Vererbung*, 397–405.

19. Mitterauer and Sieder, *European Family*, 152; see also Ulrich Planck, *Der Bäuerliche Familienbetrieb: Zwischen Patriarchat und Partnerschaft* (Stuttgart, 1964).

20. Quoted in Mergen, *Amerika-Auswanderung*, 45.

21. Oscar Handlin, *The Uprooted* (New York, 1951), 83, 86. See Joseph Schafer, *The Social History of American Agriculture* (New York, 1936), 209–16; Merle Curti et al., *The Making of an American Community: A Case Study of Democracy in a Frontier County* (Stanford, Calif., 1959); Allan G. Bogue, *From Prairie to Corn Belt: Farming on the Illinois and Iowa Prairies in the Nineteenth Century* (Chicago, 1963); Michael P. Conzen, *Frontier Farming in an Urban Shadow* (Madison, Wisc., 1971); Seddie Cogswell, Jr., *Tenure, Nativity, and Age as Factors in Iowa Agriculture, 1850–1880* (Ames, Ia., 1975); D. Aidan McQuillan, "Adaptation of Three Immigrant Groups to Farming in Central Kansas, 1875–1925," Diss., University of Wisconsin, Madison, 1975; Donald L. Winters, *Farmers Without Farms: Agricultural Tenancy in Nineteenth-*

Century Iowa (Westport, Conn., 1978); see also Robert P. Swierenga, "Ethnicity and American Agriculture," *Ohio History* 89 (1980):323–44, for a summary of this work.

22. For a representative rendering of the stereotype, see Wilhelm Hense-Jensen, *Wisconsins Deutsch-Amerikaner*, 2 vols. (Milwaukee, 1900), 1:282–85.

23. Terry G. Jordan, *German Seed in Texas Soil: Immigrant Farmers in Nineteenth-Century Texas* (Austin, 1966); Russel L. Gerlach, *Immigrants in the Ozarks: A Study in Ethnic Geography* (Columbia, Mo., 1976); Arthur B. Cozzens, "Conservation in German Settlements of the Missouri Ozarks," *Geographical Review* 33 (1943):286–98.

24. *Der Nordstern* (St. Cloud, Minn.), 12 July 1876.

25. Ibid., 28 December 1876.

26. The following discussion rests upon linked analyses of the manuscript population schedules of the federal censuses of 1860 through 1880 and 1900 (microfilm, National Archives, Washington, D.C.); manuscript population schedules of the State of Minnesota decennial censuses of 1865 through 1905 (microfilm, Minnesota Historical Society, St. Paul, Minn.); the manuscript agricultural schedules of the federal censuses of 1860 through 1880 (Minnesota State Archives, St. Paul, Minn.); the St. Martin parish marriage register (St. Martin rectory, St. Martin, Minn.); the Assessment Books for St. Martin township (Stearns County, Auditor, Stearns County Courthouse, St. Cloud, Minn.), sampled at five-year intervals 1860–1905; and a complete reconstruction of all land transactions within the township from its founding through 1915. (Because of the necessity of linking ownership to residence within the township, the present discussion is confined largely to ownership patterns through 1905 only.) The files of the Zapp Abstract Co., St. Cloud, Minn., which are arranged by section within the township and by parcels within each section, made it a relatively straightforward process to compile basic data on individual land transactions by parcel for the entire township; it was then possible, where necessary, to compile further information on individual transactions from the Deed Record, the Mortgage Record, the Mortgage Satisfaction Record, and the other miscellaneous records of the Register of Deeds, Stearns County Courthouse, St. Cloud, Minn. The chaotic alphabetizing within the grantor-grantee indexes of the Register of Deeds made it far more difficult to trace purchases by St. Martinites of land outside the township. Because this discussion cannot take into account land held outside the township, its estimates of landownership and intrafamily assistance must be regarded as *minimums* only.

27. Scholars generally have found a positive correlation between landownership and persistence in farming communities; see the summary discussion in Conzen, *Frontier Farming*. Because retired landless farmers are not classified by the census as farm operators, they do not affect the percentages relating to landownership among farmers. "Cohort" as used here refers to all farmers who were listed in the same census for the first time, that is, who had arrived during the preceding decade.

28. A variety of possible types of assistance went unrecorded, and cannot be included in this discussion; they could range from monetary gifts, unsecured loans, and advantageous rental agreements to dowries, gifts of livestock and machinery, and labor assistance. Thus the *minimal* nature of these estimates of intrafamily arrangements must be emphasized again.

29. H. W. Spiegel, "The Altenteil: German Farmers' Old Age Security," *Rural*

Sociology 4 (1939):203–17; Carl F. Wehrwein, "Bonds of Maintenance as Aids in Acquiring Farm Ownership," *Journal of Land and Public Utility Economics* 8 (1932): 396–403. The provisions of one such St. Martin agreement (Book H, p. 614, Deed Record, Register of Deeds, Stearns County Courthouse, St. Cloud, Minn.) specify that "in consideration of the sale by the first parties unto the second party of the lands described. . . . The said party of the second part hereby contracts and agrees to furnish unto first parties, or either of them, during their remaining years of life . . . the sum of $100 in cash annually any day within the year due, 100 lbs. pork and 25 lbs. beef each year in the customary season, 200 lbs. best wheat flour, delivered as needed 1 lb. butter weekly, also 1 doz. eggs each week, potatoes as much as needed from time to time, besides ready made fuel necessary for comfortable use, also free lodging, either with family in the same house, or, if preferred, erect necessary comfortable abode separate from family home, same preferred by said first parties to be located upon the lands above described."

30. Quoted in *Stones and Hills: Reflections—St. John the Baptist Parish: 1875–1975* (Collegeville, Minn., 1975), 67.

31. Minnesota law in 1878 abolished the traditional right of dower, giving the surviving spouse a life interest in the homestead (not to exceed 80 acres) and an undivided one-third of all other land in fee simple in cases of intestacy; children were also to receive equal and undivided shares of the remaining land, as well as of the homestead after the death of the surviving spouse; *Minnesota Statutes Annotated* (1975), sect. 525.16, 510.02, 525.145. This discussion is based on analyses of the wills of St. Martin landowners recorded in the Wills Book, Register of Deeds, Stearns County Courthouse, St. Cloud, Minn.; the recording of probate judgments in the Deed Record, and the subsequent ownership histories of the estates involved as reconstructed for this project from the Deed Record and the abstract files of the Zapp Abstract Co.

32. The following statements are based upon data extracted from federal and state land entry records, Minnesota Historical Society, St. Paul.

33. The fertility ratio (defined as the ratio of children under the age of five to women aged twenty to forty-four multiplied by 1,000) was 1,490 in 1875, 1,380 in 1884, 1,280 in 1895, and 1,100 in 1905.

34. Douglas C. Marshall, "The Decline in Farm Family Fertility and Its Relationship to Nationality and Religious Background," *Rural Sociology* 15 (1950):42–49.

35. Cross-sectional analysis of life cycle stages for 1860, 1880, and 1905 suggests that at no point in the middle years of the life cycle did more than one-quarter of the households have parents residing with them. One-third and one-half of the households headed by parents in their sixties had married children resident in 1880 and 1905, respectively, but this involved only six households in the first census year, four in the second. In 1880, twelve of the seventy-four married women in St. Martin between the ages of eighteen and twenty-nine were living with their husbands' parents, and one married man in the same age group was living with his wife's family; this was characteristic of no other age group. There were no sons-in-law and only four daughters-in-law resident in parental households in 1905. Cf. Goldschmidt and Kunkel, "Structure of the Peasant Family": "It is our impression that when a rural community becomes highly monetized, the heirs tend to translate their

rights into cash rather than to entangle themselves in joint family economic enterprises" (1069).

36. It is impossible to determine at this stage in the research the extent to which they also benefited from parental assistance; they certainly shared equally in the distribution of estates after the deaths of their parents.

37. Cofell, "Community Attitudes," 19–20.

38. For the character and continuity of St. Martin's distinctive culture well into the twentieth century, see Cofell, "Community Attitudes"; Ronald G. Kleitsch, "The Religious Social System of the German-Catholics of the Sauk," M.A. Thesis, University of Minnesota, 1958; Marian MacNeil Deininger, "Some Differential Characteristics of Minnesota's Major Ethnic Groups in Selected Rural Townships," Diss., University of Minnesota, 1958; Douglas G. Marshall and Milo Peterson, "Factors Associated with Variations in School Attendance of Minnesota Farm Boys," *Minnesota Agricultural Experiment Station Paper* no. 635, Miscellaneous Journal Series (July 1948); Marshall, "Decline in Farm Fertility"; Samuel Lubell, *The Future of American Politics* (New York, 1952); Paul Folsum, "Rural Ministry: A Response to Change," Doctorate of Ministry Pastoral Project, Aquinas Institute of Theology (Dubuque, Ia., 1976); Roberta Walburn, "Stearns Syndrome Only Hurts If You Don't Laugh," *Minneapolis Tribune*, 2 January 1979.

179

39. For an area with customs very similar to those of St. Martin, see Oscar F. Hoffman, "Culture of the Centerville-Mosel Germans in Manitowoc and Sheboygan Counties, Wisconsin," Diss., University of North Carolina, 1942; see also Joseph Schafer, *The Winnebago-Horicon Basin: A Type Study in Western History* (Madison, Wisc., 1937), 162–66, 239–40; Walter L. Slocum, "Ethnic Stocks as Cultural Types in Rural Wisconsin," Diss., University of Wisconsin, 1940; Kenneth H. Parsons and Eliot O. Waples, "Keeping the Farm in the Family: A Study of Ownership Processes in a Low Tenancy Area of Eastern Wisconsin," *Wisconsin Agricultural Experiment Station Research Bulletin* no. 157 (1945); George S. Wehrwein, "The Problem of Inheritance in American Land Tenure," *Journal of Farm Economics* 9 (1927): 163–75; A. B. Hollingshead, "Changes in Land Ownership as an Index of Succession in Rural Communities," *American Journal of Sociology* 43 (1937):764–77; Marlan Deininger and Douglas Marshall, "A Study of Land Ownership by Ethnic Groups from Frontier Times to the Present in a Marginal Farming Area of Minnesota," *Land Economics* (1955): 351–60; Cozzens, "Conservation in German Settlements"; Jordan, *German Seed in Texas Soil*; Gerlach, *Immigrants in the Ozarks*.

40. Cf. Ns. Gonner, *Die Luxemburger in der neuen Welt* (Dubuque, Ia., 1889), 184–88, for an excellent contemporary discussion of such syncretism in German regional dialects in American settlements.

41. Ibid., 164; Sonya Salamon, "Ethnic Differences in Farm Family Land Transfer," *Rural Sociology* 45 (1980): 290–308.

42. The literature from which this model is derived includes Don Kanel, "The Land Tenure Process in American Agriculture: The Competitive Status of Family Farms and their Adjustment to the Life Cycle of Farm Families," Diss., University of Wisconsin, 1953; Robert Diller, *Farm Ownership, Tenancy, and Land Use in a Nebraska Community* (Chicago, 1941); Richard Ely and Charles J. Galpin, "Tenancy in an Ideal System of Landownership," *American Economic Review* 9 (1919 suppl.):

196–211; Kenneth H. Parsons, "Research in the Succession of Farms: A Comment on Methodology," Land Economics 24 (1948):293–302; Sidney Henderson, "A Plan for Transfering the Farm from Father to Son," Land Economics 34 (1948):82–85; Harold A. Pederson, "A Cultural Evaluation of the Family Farm Concept," Land Economics 26 (1950):52–64; James D. Tarver, "Intra-Family Farm Succession Practices," Rural Sociology 17 (1952): 266–71; W. A. Anderson, "The Transmission of Farming as an Occupation," Rural Sociology 4 (1939):433–48; W. J. Spillman, "The Agricultural Ladder," American Economic Review 9 (1919 suppl.):170–79; Erven J. Long, "The Agricultural Ladder: Its Adequacy as a Model for Farm Tenure Research," Land Economics 26 (1950):268–73. For earlier American patterns, see, for example, Philip J. Greven, Four Generations: Population, Land, and Family in Colonial Andover, Massachusetts (Ithaca, N.Y., 1970); James A. Henretta, "Families and Farms: Mentalité in Pre-Industrial America," William and Mary Quarterly 3d ser. 35 (1978):3–32; Mary P. Ryan, Cradle of the Middle Class: The Family in Oneida County, New York, 1790–1865 (New York, 1981), 18–59.

43. Mark Friedberger's recent study of inheritance practices in several Iowa and Illinois townships, though not directly addressing the question of ethnic differences, does provide data that support an argument for the general dominance of transfer through inheritance rather than inter vivos transmission, and for distinctive differences among German Catholics; see his "The Farm Family and the Inheritance Process: Evidence from the Corn Belt, 1870–1950," Agricultural History 57 (1983): 1–13.

44. Conrad Arensberg and Solon T. Kimball, Family and Community in Ireland (New York, 1940); Salamon, "Ethnic Differences." The only St. Martin farmer to partially disinherit one son for "dissolute" behavior was a member of the pioneer generation of Irish farmers.

45. Robert C. Ostergren, "Land and Family in Rural Immigrant Communities," Annals of the Association of American Geographers 71 (1981):400–411; Peter A. Munch, "Social Adjustment among Wisconsin Norwegians," American Sociological Review 14 (1949):780–87; Deininger, "Differential Characteristics of Minnesota's Major Ethnic Groups"; Robert Harold Brown, "The Upsala, Minnesota Community: A Study in Rural Dynamics," Annals of the Association of American Geographers 57 (1967):267–300.

46. Ostergren, "Land and Family."

180

Chapter 4

Philadelphia and the German Catholic Community

Jay P. Dolan

The history of German-American Catholicism began more than two hundred years ago. Long before the Revolution of 1776 the Gospel was preached to German Catholics in their mother tongue, especially in Pennsylvania, where two-thirds of the Catholic population in 1757 was German. However, the number of Catholics in colonial America was small, so meager in fact that John Adams observed that in his home town a Catholic was about as "rare as a comet or an earthquake." But if you wanted to find a Catholic in colonial America, and in particular a German-speaking Catholic, a good place to look was Philadelphia.[1]

German-speaking and English-speaking Catholics had worshiped together in St. Joseph's Church and later at St. Mary's Church before the Revolution. Yet the small band of German Catholics was already showing a sense of distinctive group consciousness in the eighteenth century. In 1768 they purchased their own burial ground, and it was evident that the separation of Catholics along lines of nationality was beginning to develop. In 1787 Germans organized the German Catholic Society and informed John Carroll, then Prefect Apostolic of the United States, that in order "to keep up their respective nation and Language" they were "fully determined to build and erect another new place of divine worship for the better convenience and accommodation of Catholics of all nations particularly the Germans under whose direction the building was to be constructed."[2] Two years later, the new church, Holy Trinity, was opened for service. In organizing their own church the Philadelphia Germans gained the distinction of founding the first national parish in the United States; the subsequent history of Holy Trinity illustrates how difficult and contentious such a development would be. From the very beginning German Catholics had to do battle with Church authorities who desired both an American church that knew no national distinctions and an hierarchically structured church that recognized no lay authority in ecclesiastical affairs. The hierarchy lost the battle against the national parish, but they ultimately won the war by gaining control of the system of lay trusteeism.

182

Throughout the nineteenth century the German American Catholic community increased numerically in both Philadelphia and the nation, principally through large waves of immigration in the 1850s and the 1880s. In 1840 one of every ten Catholics in the United States was German (70,592 of 663,000). In the next thirty years, the German Catholic population increased fourteen times, and by 1870 about one of four Catholics was of German stock (1,044,711 of 4,504,000). The Catholic Church had become the single largest denomination in the country, and German Catholics were fast becoming the largest subgroup of church Germans. After the heavy immigration of the 1880s, the number of German Catholics increased to approximately two million by 1890, a 100 percent increase in twenty years.[3] Thereafter, a decline set in as immigration from German-speaking countries ebbed, and the descendents of earlier immigrants became less distinctively German. In 1916 only one of ten Catholics (1,672,670 of 15,721, 815) worshiped in a church that used the German language.[4] Despite the decrease in the German Catholic presence, they had the distinction of being the largest subgroup of church Germans, numbering "slightly less than the total membership of several German Protestant denominations."[5] Within the Catholic Church they were still the largest foreign-language group.

The dominance that German Catholics enjoyed in Philadelphia in the colonial period did not persist into the nineteenth century. By 1842, German Catholics had increased to approximately 12,000, or 20 to 25 percent of Philadelphia's Catholics (about 50,000). Proportionately this was a significant decline from the days when three out of five Catholics in Philadelphia were Germans. By the sheer force of numbers the Irish had gained control of the Church and the Germans had slipped back into second place. In the next fifty years the increase in the German Catholic community was slight. In 1869 they numbered 21,000; by 1892 a rough estimate would put their population at 35,000, or approximately 17 percent of Philadelphia's Catholic population.[6] More significantly, the German Catholic population represented only 3 percent of the city's population in 1890; the entire foreign-born German community equaled only 7 percent of the city's population.[7] What had happened is obvious from the hindsight of history. Like other Germans, Catholic Germans had bypassed Philadelphia in the nineteenth century and chose to settle elsewhere, principally in the Midwestern triangle bounded by the cities of Cincinnati, Milwaukee, and St. Louis. The story of German-American Catholicism, which began in Philadelphia in the eighteenth century, had shifted west following the flow of German immigrants.

183

In the nineteenth century German-American Catholics had become a minority population in Philadelphia. As Catholics they were outsiders in the larger Protestant culture of the city. As Germans they were a minority both in the city and the Church. To preserve their religion in an alien society and to preserve their ethnicity in an Irish church, they followed the patterns set by their colonial ancestors. They formed their own national parishes which, in the mind of one German priest, were "the best means to protect the Catholic immigrants against the loss of their faith, to safeguard them against the inducements and seductions of our adversaries, and to enable them to preserve incorrupt the sacred treasures of religion and to transmit it to their children."[8]

The national parish was the institutionalized attempt of an immigrant group to preserve the religious life of the old country. Among German Catholics it became a distinctive trademark in the nineteenth century. The heart of the issue was language. German Catholic immigrants came from many different countries in Western Europe, but they shared two common traits—language and religion. The two were inextricably joined together. "Language saves faith" was the slogan of German-American Catholics.

Reflecting this mentality, an immigrant guidebook advised

newly arrived Germans not to "settle in districts and places where there are no German priests, churches and schools."[9] To settle in an English-speaking parish was "the greatest of all dangers" since "experience teaches that even in places where there are English Catholic churches but no German-speaking priests, German Catholics will become indifferent to the Church within a short time and in due course will be even worse than Protestants and pagans."[10] To this author the English-speaking parish was as great a threat to the faith as a Methodist church. Loss of language meant loss of faith, and it did not matter how you lost the mother tongue, the outcome was inevitably the same. This heightened sense of ethnicity caused one observer to remark that the Germans wanted "everything in German and if they are ever obliged to have Irish or American priests, they complain loudly about this insult."[11]

This fear of the loss of faith, as extreme as it was, appeared to be justified. In Philadelphia, "that irreligious and immoral city," the vitality of religion in the German community was directly connected with the availability of German-speaking parishes. In 1840 the "greater number" of the German community lived in the upper part of the city, where rent was cheaper because of its "distance from the center of the city and because of the poverty of those sections." But the only German parish, Holy Trinity, was located in the lower part of the city. Even under the best of circumstances it could not serve the needs of Philadelphia's 12,000 German Catholics. Thus, many Germans appeared to have "fallen away from the Faith." In 1843 the church of St. Peter's was organized for the German Catholics who lived north of Vine Street in the upper part of the city. From the very beginning the parish began to attract German Catholics from this part of the city as well as from the suburbs of Kensington and North Liberty. According to one writer, the establishment of St. Peter's Church prompted "very many" German Catholics to return to "the one saving faith of their fathers which they had given up either in part or completely."[12] St. Peter's eventually became the showcase of German Catholicism in Philadelphia. By 1848 the congregation numbered 3,000; fifteen years later it was the largest German parish in the city with 10,000 people.[13] The same pattern occurred in the founding of St. Alphonsus Church. Because of trustee trou-

184

bles, Holy Trinity parish was placed under an interdict and the church was closed. As a result, the Germans of South Philadelphia were without a church, and this caused a "great falling away from the Church."[14] To remedy the situation, the new parish of St. Alphonsus was organized in 1853.

The loss of faith among German immigrants was a serious problem. The most obvious index of this was participation in church services. Only 40 to 60 percent of the Catholic immigrants regularly attended church on Sunday, and many German Catholic immigrants received the sacraments every twenty, thirty, or even forty years. Another less tangible indicator was the decline, or even the absence, of religion itself among the immigrants. German observers noted that their countrymen were not only lax in practicing their religion, but were becoming indifferent as well—"religious only in appearance," as they described it. Others commented that "many had given up the Catholic faith; others were Catholic in name only." The lack of priests and churches deprived them of the support needed to keep the religion of the old country alive. "What else can be expected under such conditions," wrote a German priest, "than that the priceless heritage these people brought from the Fatherland gradually disappears."[14] Church authorities were very concerned about the low level of religious practice and the decline of religious fervor among the immigrants. One means they chose to remedy the situation was the national parish. No one knows how extensive the loss of faith was among German immigrants, but one thing is certain: it would have been considerably greater without the ethnic parish.

Another reason for the establishment of the national parish was the tendency of immigrants to settle in a distinct city neighborhood. By the end of the nineteenth century the majority of German-Americans lived in the city, and this pattern of settlement "put an unmistakably urban stamp upon German-American Catholicism."[16] In Philadelphia "the mid-nineteenth century was *par excellence* the era of the urban parish church."[17] It was a time when Philadelphians were creating their own island communities in a city that was slowly becoming segregated along ethnic, social, and residential lines. Philadelphia Germans were no different from their neighbors. They tended to gather together in dis-

185

tinctively German neighborhoods and to form their own clubs, lodges, and benefit associations. For Catholic Germans the institution that outranked all others in importance was the parish. It was not only the center of both their religious and social lives, but it also was an ethnic fortress which enabled the immigrants to resist the onslaught of the surrounding Protestant culture on their faith and tradition.

For the fifty-three years prior to 1842 there was only one German Catholic parish in Philadelphia. In the next half-century twelve more German parishes were organized.[18] As in other foreign-language groups, the laity played a prominent role in the organization of the parish. Generally they would form a society, raise the necessary money, and purchase the land for their church. They would then petition the bishop for approval of their action and request the assistance of a German-speaking priest. This pattern especially characterized the early years of development, but even in the late nineteenth century German Catholics had to take matters into their own hands if they wanted a new German parish. German Catholics accepted membership in an English-speaking parish reluctantly and only as a temporary arrangement. The Germans, like the Italians and later the Poles, were not satisfied until they had their own church. For them it was as much a cultural institution as it was a center of religion. As Catholics they desired the bishop's blessing on their work, but as Germans they would not wait for him to act. When they finished their work, the bishop had little alternative but to approve their decision.

As a link with the old country, the ethnic parish was the place where Philadelphia Germans recreated the familiar religious customs of the fatherland. According to the theologian, Catholicism was a transnational religion that knew no national distinctions. The Mass, celebrated in Latin in Irish and German parishes, was identical. The devotional life of nineteenth-century Catholicism was also strikingly similar, with special attention rendered to Jesus Christ and Mary. But the Germans, like other ethnic groups, put their own stamp on Catholic piety. They loved pageantry and pomp. They took obvious pride in elaborate ceremonies which they enthusiastically commented on in the German press. A common religion naturally exhibits similarities of

186

expression regardless of nationality, but in those customs "not essential to Catholic faith and life" German Catholics evidenced a style of their own.[19]

Most striking was the German love of music. The parish choir was an accepted organization in any German parish, and to encourage this development Philadelphia Germans organized a city-wide Caecilien Verein in 1882.[20] Every Mass on Sunday, unlike other Catholic parishes, featured music; at the Solemn Sunday Mass an orchestra together with the choir often performed. Parish financial reports indicated that when it came to church music, money was no problem; it was generally the most costly item in the church budget.

Germans loved a parade both in and outside of church. Parish societies, outfitted in their colorful regalia and each displaying its own banner, paraded along the streets of North Philadelphia on special feast days. It was inconceivable for German Catholics to celebrate a religious festival without a colorful procession.

Spiritual confraternities were also common among German Catholics. In addition to these societies, the parish fostered the growth of mutual benefit societies. The majority of Philadelphia parishes had such *Unterstützung–Vereine*. Philadelphia Germans also belonged to the national Central Verein and in 1876 organized this society on a city-wide basis.[21] The rationale behind these benefit societies "which are found in almost every German parish" was not hard to discover.[22] They provided financial assistance in case of sickness or death; they also were a Catholic alternative to similar societies sponsored by the non-Catholic German community. The Church frowned on Catholics joining such non-Catholic vereins since they were a risk to one's "faith and eternal salvation." But a German Catholic newspaper editor argued that Catholic vereins "contribute to one's spiritual end and the good of the church."[23] Such a separatist mentality encouraged the multiplication of a panoply of parish societies for every age group. In the process it reinforced the sense of community in the parish by separating Catholics from their non-Catholic countrymen.

In addition to benefit societies, Philadelphia Germans also organized their own hospital, St. Mary's, and an orphan asylum, St. Vincent's.[24] Both institutions served the city-wide German com-

187

munity. Philadelphia Catholics had other hospitals and orphanages, but here too the Germans felt the need to establish
their own institutions. This was especially clear in the organization of St. Vincent's orphanage. Philadelphia had three orphan
asylums for young Catholic children when John Nepomucene
Neumann became bishop of the diocese in 1852, but these
asylums catered to the Irish and the French. Neumann saw the
need for another orphanage to care for the increasing number of
homeless German children. Benevolent institutions organized
along lines of nationality were a common feature of mid-
nineteenth-century urban Catholicism. The acute sense of
ethnicity, reinforced by the language barrier, demanded it. But
another major motivation was to save the children from
Protestantism. As Neumann put it, "asylums for our German
children are most important and most necessary. These must be
regarded as the best and only means of wresting them from the
grasp of error, of infidelity and even godlessness."[25] St.
Vincent's opened in 1855 in Tacony and eventually became a
center of German Catholicism in Northeast Philadelphia.

The fear of children losing the faith also encouraged the founding of parish schools. "By all means," urged a German guidebook, "keep your children away from the public schools which
properly ought to be called pagan schools or even worse."[26]
Equally essential was the necessity to foster the mother tongue
among the children and thus help them preserve the religious
heritage of the old country. A dilemma arose, however, because
parents also wanted their children to learn English. As a result
many parents did not heed the counsel of the clergy and sent their
children to public schools. In an attempt to counteract this
tendency German parochial schools began to use both English
and German in classroom instruction. This bilingual approach became the norm in German schools in the nineteenth century.

In Philadelphia every German parish listed in the German-
American Catholic Directory of 1892 had a school. St. Peter's,
described as "one of the most progressive city parochial
schools," was the largest German school, numbering 1,145
students; the Christian Brothers taught the boys and the School
Sisters of Notre Dame instructed the girls.[27] As was true in other
cities, however, the parochial school could never serve the

188

educational needs of all German children of school age. As Bishop James Wood observed in reference to the parish of St. Boniface, it was obvious "that many do not send their children to the Catholic school."[28] Given this limitation, Philadelphia Germans in particular and German Catholics in general manifested an intense commitment to parochial education. Thus, it is not surprising to discover that in 1914 over 95 percent of the German parishes in the United States had a parochial school.[29]

In building up their ethnic fortress German Catholics set themselves off from other German-Americans. In their desire to preserve their own sense of identity they "displayed fierce antagonisms against any group that infringed upon their rights."[30] Protestant Germans were a frequent object of attack. This hostile attitude was transplanted from Europe, where Protestant and Catholic Germans had been doing battle since the Reformation. "Martin Luther and his latter day followers," noted one historian, "were always the worst of heretics. In 1883, the four-hundredth anniversary of Luther's birth, the Catholic *Volkszeitung* of Baltimore, an arch-conservative paper with a national circulation, noted the occasion with a series of more than sixty articles ripping Luther, the Reformation, and Protestantism to shreds."[31] Club Germans were also objects of Catholic prejudice. Priests warned their parishioners under pain of excommunication to avoid joining such secret societies as the Freemasons, the Red Men, and the Odd Fellows, as well as the popular Turnverein.

German Catholics were also inclined to do battle among themselves. One German priest wrote that "for no other intention is there more need for prayer than for unity among the Germans—not only in the German fatherland, but also here in America."[32] The history of Holy Trinity parish, as stormy as it was, was not untypical. Factions often developed among the people causing a schism in the parish. This would result in the founding of a new parish only a few blocks away from the mother church. This was the case in Philadelphia when conflict in Holy Trinity gave birth to St. Alphonsus parish.[33] As John Hughes, the Archbishop of New York observed, German Catholics were indeed "exceedingly prone to division among themselves."[34]

The most celebrated conflict that German Catholics entered

189

was the struggle against the Irish-American hierarchy during the 1880s and 1890s. This was an intensely heated debate that principally involved the German communities of the Midwest triangle. The Germans of Philadelphia and Baltimore did not appear to be caught up in the issue, though this did not mean that they were unsympathetic to the cause of their Midwestern countrymen.

At the heart of the issue was the German insistence on equal rights in the American Catholic Church. This demand focused on the rights of German Catholics to have their own independent national parish where they could foster the religious heritage of the fatherland. Catholic Germans did not want to be "kept in a position inferior to that of the Irish," wrote Father Peter Abbelen of Milwaukee. "By granting the equal position which we ask," he continued," no right of the Irish would be impaired, while an injustice and a disgrace would be removed from the Germans."[35] The demand for equality for German parishes was simple enough and not a serious problem, but the hidden agenda advocated a move toward a German church independent of the Irish-American hierarchy. The Germans asked Rome to intervene on their behalf. However, the Vatican's inclination to favor the German petition and the Roman proposal to appoint a cardinal protector for German Catholics in the United States aroused the wrath of the more liberal American wing of the hierarchy. The issue was momentarily resolved in 1887, when Rome spoke out in favor of the national parish, but refused to grant further privileges to German-American Catholics.

Three years later the Lucerne Memorial rekindled the debate. The memorial was a document drawn up in Lucerne, Switzerland, in 1890 by the international representatives of the St. Raphael Verein, an immigrant aid society. The document was sent to Pope Leo XIII asking for definite rights for Catholic immigrants. In the United States it was interpreted "as another movement for German particularism." This time the demands were more comprehensive and more explicit. The goal was not just national parishes, but the development of a national clergy, national schools, and "most important of all, proportional representation in the hierarchy for each nationality."[36] The Lucerne Memorial attracted national attention in the United States. It was denounced in the Senate, and President Benjamin Harrison

190

viewed it with concern. To both the politician and the churchman the issue was the same—the interference of foreigners in American affairs. In the 1880s and 1890s the introduction of foreign nationalism in the Catholic Church chiefly meant German nationalism, which was riding high both in the fatherland and in the United States. The reply of Rome once again favored the Americanist position, by stating that the proposals of the Lucerne Memorial were neither opportune nor necessary.

Despite the continued denial of discrimination against the Germans, they did have a legitimate complaint. Germans were not well represented in the hierarchy. In 1869 only 11 percent of the bishops were German (6 of 56). In 1900 after more than a decade of debate on the issue the proportion had increased to only 14 percent (13 of 90). The Irish had gained control of the hierarchy, and by 1900 one out of two bishops was Irish.[37] Bishops were also slow to recognize the demands of the Germans. In Philadelphia one historian observed that Bishop Wood evidenced "an unfriendly attitude toward the Germans."[38] In other cities controlled by the Irish, people complained that Church authorities "almost ignored the existence of" the Germans.[39] But it is worth noting that when the Germans gained control of the Church, as they did in Wisconsin, they began to act like the Irish in their relations with the recently arrived Polish Catholics. Fearing a German *Kulturkampf* in the Church, the Poles pushed for the same demands that Germans had fought for twenty years earlier. What was one man's cultural pluralism in the 1880s had become another person's nativism in the 1900s.[40]

What happened in Wisconsin reflected the acculturation of German-American Catholics in the years before World War I. The German language was dying out, American habits were being adopted, and the United States was becoming the fatherland for most German-Americans. Immigration of German Catholics had decreased rapidly after 1900, and the use of the German-language newspaper was also on the decline. Only three new publications appeared between 1900 and 1918.[41] In Pennsylvania the same decline was evident, and as early as 1890 "no person who taught elementary subjects in the German language was available in Pennsylvania."[42] In 1911 state law designated English as the only language of the classroom. In the parochial school the last vestige

191

of a commitment to the mother tongue was the use of the German-language catechism.

The national parish was another victim of the gradual Americanization of German Catholics. In 1869 the German Catholic Directory counted 705 churches in which German was the only language used. By 1906 the number had declined to 500; ten years later it decreased to 206. More symptomatic of the times in 1916 was the existence of 1,684 parishes in which both English and German were used.[43]

St. Boniface parish in Philadelphia illustrated the change that was taking place in urban America. Founded as a German parish in 1866, it reached a population of some 1,600 families in the 1890s. In the first decade of the century the parish population declined slightly. In the next decade, according to one observer, "many of the German people began to move north, and to the south and west the colored people came in. At the same time, it became clear that the younger generation did not understand German well enough to derive any real benefit from sermons and instructions in that language."[44]

Germans were becoming Americanized, and the old nineteenth-century settlement was breaking up as the residential patterns of twentieth-century cities shifted. Germans remained concentrated in North Philadelphia, but the patterns of future change were already emerging. The mother tongue was becoming obsolete, and the nineteenth-century German parish was steadily losing its ethnic constituency as the population of the neighborhood changed. By the end of the 1920s, writes Frederick Luebke, "most German Catholics agreed that the goals of the church could not be served by the preservation of German language and culture."[45] Obviously the anti-German hysteria of World War I hastened the process of Americanization. German-American Catholics were disappearing as a distinctive subculture. The rise of Adolf Hitler and the onslaught of World War II intensified the tendency of German-Americans to bury their ethnicity. Even though 25.5 million Americans identified themselves as individuals of German descent as recently as 1972, the group consciousness of Germans had disintegrated. Only the faintest traces of German ethnic life remained.

In the Catholic community, people of German descent number

more than eight million, but the national parish has vanished.[46] No one clamors anymore for German bishops. The Irish are no longer the enemy. In fact, the opposite appears to be the case. If a German Catholic marries outside his group, he will most likely marry into an Irish family.[47] "If you cannot beat them, marry them" seems to be the current strategy of German-Americans.

In the nineteenth century German Catholics struggled to maintain their ethnic identity in the American Catholic Church. To a great extent they succeeded. But history was not on their side as the passage of years weakened the link with the fatherland and encouraged new allegiances to America. In 1900 the issue at stake was the persistence of German-American Catholicism. Today the question no longer is what does it mean to be a German-American Catholic, rather what does it mean to be a Catholic in America?

193

Notes

1. Francis J. Herktorn, *A Retrospect of Holy Trinity Parish* (Philadelphia, 1914), pp. 6–7.

2. Ibid., p. 22.

3. These figures were calculated by Gerald Shaughnessy, *Has the Immigrant Kept the Faith?* (New York, 1925), pp.237–238, 251; and also Ernst A. Reiter, *Schematismus der katholischen deutschen Geistlichkeit* (New York, 1869), p. 232.

4. Bureau of the Census, *Religious Bodies 1916*, 2 (Washington, D.C., 1919), 654.

5. Frederick C. Luebke, *Bonds of Loyalty: German Americans and World War I* (DeKalb, Ill., 1974), p. 35.

6. Joseph Salzbacher, *Meine Reise nach Nord-Amerika im Jahre 1842* (Vienna, 1845), p. 112; Reiter, *Schematismus*, pp. 15–17; the 1892 figures are my own estimates based on data in J. N. Enzlberger, *Schematismus der katholischen Geistlichkeit deutscher Zunge in den Ver. Staaten Amerikas* (Milwaukee, 1892), pp. 232–235; *Report on Statistics of Churches in the U.S. at 11th Census 1890* (Washington, D.C., 1894), p. 245; and *Historical Sketches of the Catholic Churches and Institutions of Philadelphia* (Philadelphia, 1895), p. 18.

7. Caroline Golab, "The Immigrant and the City: Poles, Italians and Jews in Philadelphia, 1870–1920," in *The Peoples of Philadelphia*, eds. Allen F. Davis and Mark H. Haller (Philadelphia, 1973), p. 205.

8. *Berichte der Leopoldinen Stiftung*, Oct. 12, 1844, quoted by Joseph White in "German Catholics in the Diocese of Vincennes in the Nine-

teenth Century" (unpub. seminar paper, Dept. of History, University of Notre Dame, Spring 1975).

9. "Historical Studies and Notes: A Guide for Catholic German Immigrants 1869," *Social Justice Review*, 52 (July–Aug. 1959), 135.

10. John M. Lenhart, O.F.M., "Historical Studies and Notes: Statistical Accounts of Membership of German Catholics in America," *Social Justice Review*, 51 (Jan. 1959), 312.

11. Jay P. Dolan, *The Immigrant Church: New York's Irish and German Catholics, 1815–1865* (Baltimore, 1975), p. 71.

12. John M. Lenhart, O.F.M., "Historical Studies and Notes: German Catholics in the Diocese of Philadelphia in 1846," *Central-Blatt and Social Justice*, 26 (July–Aug. 1933), 131.

13. *Historical Sketches of the Catholic Churches*, p. 73.

14. Michael J. Curley, C.SS.R., *Venerable John Neumann* (New York, 1952), pp. 222–223.

15. Quoted in Dolan, *Immigrant Church*, pp. 84–85.

16. Luebke, *Bonds of Loyalty*, p. 36.

17. Sam Bass Warner Jr., *The Private City* (Philadelphia, 1971), p. 61.

18. Enzlberger, *Schematismus*, pp. 232–235.

19. Dolan, *The Immigrant Church*, pp. 79–80.

20. Enzlberger, *Schematismus*, p. 325.

21. Ibid., p. 324; these parish societies are listed in *Historical Sketches of the Catholic Churches*, pp. lvii–lviii.

22. "Historical Studies and Notes: A Guide," p. 166.

23. Ibid.; *Katholische Kirchenzeitung*, Sept. 2, 1858.

24. Enzlberger, *Schematismus*, p. 181.

25. Curley, *Venerable John Neumann*, pp. 260–261; see also Francis X. Roth, *History of St. Vincent's Orphan Asylum, Tacony, Philadelphia* (Philadelphia, 1934). On the German Catholics' unhappy experience in public hospitals which led to the establishment of German hospitals see Archives of the Archdiocese of New York, Claims of the Fathers and the Congregation of the Church of the Most Holy Redeemer, New York, to St. Francis Hospital, Fifth Street, New York, July 20, 1868.

26. "Historical Studies and Notes: A Guide," p. 167.

27. Enzlberger, *Schematismus*, pp. 232–235; Thomas J. Donaghy, *Philadelphia's Finest: A History of Education in the Catholic Archdiocese 1692–1970* (Philadelphia, 1972), p. 88.

28. John F. Byrne, C.SS.R., *The Redemptorist Centenaries* (Philadelphia, 1932), p. 193.

29. Richard M. Linkh, *American Catholicism and European Immigrants* (Staten Island, N.Y., 1975), p. 110.

30. Luebke, *Bonds of Loyalty*, p. 36.

31. Ibid., p. 37.

32. Quoted by Sister M. Mileta Ludwig, F.S.P.A., "Sources for the Biography of Michael Heiss, Bishop of LaCrosse, 1868–1880 and Archbishop of Milwaukee, 1881–1890," *Records of the American Catholic Historical Society of Philadelphia*, 79 (Dec. 1968), 210.

33. Curley, *Venerable John Neumann*, pp. 222–224.

34. Archives of the University of Notre Dame, *Scritture Riferite nei Congressi; American Centrale*, vol. 18, letter 1417, John Hughes to Prefect of Propaganda Fide, Mar. 23, 1858, f. 511.

35. Colman J. Barry, *The Catholic Church and German Americans* (Milwaukee, 1953), p. 291.

36. Colman J. Barry, "The German Catholic Immigrant," in *Roman Catholicism and the American Way of Life*, ed., Thomas T. McAvoy (Notre Dame, 1960), p. 199.

37. These figures were calculated from Reiter, *Schematismus*, p. 232 and p. 234; the list of German clergy compiled in Enzlberger, *Schematismus*, pp. 352–381; Bernard J. Code, *Dictionary of the American Hierarchy* (New York, 1940); and the *U.S. Catholic Directory 1900*.

38. Michael J. Curley, C.SS.R., *The Provincial Story* (New York, 1963), p. 161.

39. Dolan, *Immigrant Church*, p. 72.

40. Anthony J. Kuzniewski Jr., "Faith and Fatherland: An Intellectual History of the Polish Immigrant Community in Wisconsin, 1838–1918" (unpub. doctoral dissertation, Harvard University, 1973).

41. Philip Gleason, *The Conservative Reformers* (Notre Dame, 1968), p. 48.

42. Homer Tope Rosenberger, *The Pennsylvania Germans 1891–1965* (Lancaster, 1966), pp. 70–71.

43. Reiter, *Schematismus*, p. 232; Linkh, *American Catholicism*, pp. 108–110.

44. Byrne, *The Redemptorist Centenaries*, p. 188.

45. Luebke, *Bonds of Loyalty*, p. 317.

46. Harold J. Abramson, *Ethnic Diversity in Catholic America* (New York, 1973), p. 19.

47. Ibid., pp. 51–67.

ETHNIC TENSIONS, EPISCOPAL LEADERSHIP, AND THE EMERGENCE OF THE TWENTIETH-CENTURY AMERICAN CATHOLIC CHURCH: THE CLEVELAND EXPERIENCE

BY

HENRY B. LEONARD*

In his official report to Rome for the year 1909, his first as Bishop of Cleveland, John P. Farrelly noted, "The zeal for factions, with which the diocese has been troubled now for about thirty years . . . has almost completely disappeared. Most of the troublemakers are dead, others have departed from the diocese, the rest, who still remain in the diocese, either labor under extreme old age or have no authority."[1] Although the factionalism had in fact existed for considerably longer and although he was overly optimistic in saying that it had virtually disappeared, Farrelly's assessment of diocesan history was generally accurate. From almost the year of its foundation as a diocese in 1847, Cleveland was beset by two factions, one composed of ethnically self-conscious Irish clerics and laymen and the other of Germans, whose ethnic jealousies found expression in a multitude of issues and controversies. The two factions attempted in particular to control the diocese by ensuring that as many representatives of their own ethnic group as possible should fill important positions. They were especially anxious that the bishop be of their own nationality, both because of the great power he exercised and because of the ethnic recognition his position automatically conferred. Irish-German infighting was especially rife, therefore, whenever a new bishop was to be selected, as was the case in 1870-1872, 1891, and 1908-1909. Although one cannot say that either faction clearly controlled the diocese, the Germans were generally more successful in gaining important positions of power and in exerting influence over bishops, even over those who were not of German stock.

*Mr. Leonard is an associate professor of history in Kent State University (Ohio).
[1]Report of Bishop John P. Farrelly to Rome for the year ending December 31, 1909, Archives of the Diocese of Cleveland, Chancery Building, Cleveland, Ohio (hereafter cited ADC).

Farrelly's tenure in Cleveland (1909-1921) marked a distinct break with the past. Of Irish stock, he removed many Germans from power and replaced them with priests of Irish background. Never again were German clerics to exercise such a powerful influence in the diocese, and the long-standing and divisive German-Irish antagonism became less important in diocesan affairs. But to focus exclusively on the nationalities involved, to see Farrelly's actions as only the last stage of a decades-long ethnic struggle is to miss a more important point — Farrelly and those closely associated with him in Cleveland personified a new style of episcopal leadership which came to dominate many American sees in the early twentieth century. Predominantly but not exclusively of Irish stock, usually Roman-trained and intensely loyal to the Vatican, they were as much administrators as pastors. They were determined to create an efficient, modern bureaucracy, to bring system and order to their rapidly growing but often haphazardly controlled dioceses.

197

In Cleveland, as elsewhere, divisive ethnic bickering had flourished not only because of the strength of the emotions involved but also because of the lack, in a youthful church, of systems of discipline and bureaucratic control. As Farrelly himself recognized, he was able to mute, if not entirely end, intense German-Irish bickering, in part because of the advanced age of some of the principals involved, especially the German leaders. But more to the point is that Farrelly, operating out of a model of leadership and administrative control more fully developed than that of his predecessors, believed that ethnic power struggles not only were unpleasant and un-Christian but also had no place in the modern, twentieth-century American Church which should be run with order, discipline, and efficiency. And he moved quickly to see that his blueprint of a properly run diocese became a reality. Bishop Farrelly, as well as bishops of a similar persuasion, also have a significance for the broad course of American history in the early twentieth century, for they represented in the Catholic Church similar forces of professionalism, bureaucracy, and order that affected all areas of American life in the early 1900's, from business to government, from social work to the armed forces.[2]

Ethnic conflict in nineteenth-century Cleveland, as in other dioceses growing rapidly as a result of European Catholic immigration, was partly a consequence of the newcomers' desires for separate ethnic parishes and parochial schools, staffed by priests of their own nationality, to care for

---

[2]For these broad trends in American life at the turn of the century, see Robert Wiebe's provocative *The Search for Order: 1877-1920* (New York, 1967).

both their religious and social needs. Immigrant groups vied with one another for control of parishes, and with bishops who, for a variety of reasons, were often reluctant to grant their requests for separate facilities.[3] Strife was particularly severe in the Diocese of Cleveland, where the first bishop was Louis Amadeus Rappe, a combative, authoritarian Frenchman. A successful missionary in northwestern Ohio before his elevation to the new see of Cleveland, he presided over dramatic growth in his diocese. Between 1847 and 1870, when he resigned as bishop, the number of Catholics under his care swelled to about 100,000, the clergy from sixteen to 117 priests, and churches and chapels from thirty-three to 160. Despite this healthy expansion, however, Rappe's tenure in Cleveland was a troubled one. Although a European immigrant himself, he was determined to purge the Church in his diocese of ethnic nationalism, not only because he believed it divided the Church but also, and equally important, because it was ethnic groups, galvanized by national pride and ethnic sensitivity, which most frequently challenged his decisions. And above all else, Rappe was determined to maintain his authority. At first, he adamantly refused to establish national parishes or to permit parochial schools where foreign languages were taught. This policy first angered the German Catholics who complained to Rome so bitterly that Rappe was forced to alter course, but he did so only reluctantly. By 1865, he had gained the grudging tolerance of the Germans, but by then his relations were stormy with the Irish who charged that he mistreated Irish priests as well as Irish students in the diocesan seminary.[4]

By the late 1860's, the Cleveland diocese was in a state of turmoil. As bishop, Rappe was supposed to be a force for unity in the diocese. In fact, he was just the opposite. He not only stepped on sensitive ethnic toes; he also attempted to play the Germans and the Irish off against each other in order to keep them off balance and thus to preserve his own authority, the exercise of which his increasingly numerous critics charged was despotic. The majority of the laity and clergy had little respect for or confidence in Rappe who, convinced that he was surrounded on every side by rebellious

---

[3]An excellent study of nationality tensions in the Catholic Church is Jay P. Dolan's *The Immigrant Church: New York's Irish and German Catholics, 1815-1865* (Baltimore and London, 1975).

[4]For a discussion of Bishop Rappe's troubles with immigrants and ethnicity in Cleveland, see Henry B. Leonard, "Ethnic Conflict and Episcopal Power: The Diocese of Cleveland, 1847-1870," *Catholic Historical Review*, LXII (July, 1976), 388-407.

cabals, trusted and respected few of them.[5] The result was a state of such deep demoralization in Cleveland that ethnic divisions and guerrilla warfare saturated the diocese and virtually overwhelmed the unity of faith. Alarmed by conditions in Cleveland and impatient with Rappe's constant evasion in responding to questions as well as his tardiness in following instructions, Roman officials decided to question the prelate when he was in Rome in 1870 for the First Vatican Council. Also in Rome was Father Eugene M. O'Callaghan, a diocesan priest, who had come to present personally his grievances of having been mistreated by Rappe. He also brought "grave charges against his [Rappe's] own life and morals," meaning undoubtedly solicitation in the confessional. Convinced that Rappe's continued presence in Cleveland was incompatible with the good of religion, Rome pressed the bishop for his resignation, which he tendered in July, 1870.[6]

199

Far from ending the turmoil in Cleveland, however, Bishop Rappe's resignation only exacerbated it. In fact, by providing the material out of which was fashioned a portrait of a saintly bishop having been unfairly destroyed by Irish Catholic partisans who would stop at nothing to achieve their goals, the circumstances of Rappe's removal immeasurably strengthened ethnic factionalism and affected the diocese for the next forty years. For several months after his resignation, Rappe tried to clear his own name, basing his defense on the claim that he had been the victim of Irish conspirators who, duping gullible and insensitive Roman officials in the process, secured his removal. As he wrote Archbishop Martin John Spalding of Baltimore, his opponents, mostly Irish, had tried to force his resignation by exciting "feelings of Nationalism" over his policies regarding clerical appointments and the seminary but that, having failed, they formed a "secret society" which, under the leadership of O'Callaghan, extracted accusations against his character from unwary women "by lie, by

[5]Michael O. Brown, "The Catholic Priest in Northern Ohio: Life-styles, 1860-1885," *Resonance*, VII, #1 (1972), 90-92.

[6]O'Callaghan to Propaganda, May 10, 1870, Archives of the Sacred Congregation de Propaganda Fide, *Scritture Riferite nei Congressi: America centrale dal Canadá all'istmo di Panama* (hereafter cited *Congressi*), Vol. 23, fols. 327-338. Microfilm copies of the American material for this period are deposited in the Archives of the University of Notre Dame. For events in 1870 and some of the controversy surrounding them, see Leonard, *op. cit.*, pp. 405-406 and especially footnote 68. For a different view of the Rappe administration see W. A. Jurgens, "Bishop Rappe and His Diocese" (unpublished manuscript, 1965); Paul J. Hallinan, "Richard Gilmour, Second Bishop of Cleveland, 1872-1891" (unpublished Ph.D. dissertation, Western Reserve University, 1963), pp. 100-107, and the various histories of the diocese by George F. Houck, cited in footnote 19 below.

terror" and by using "the confessional as a tribunal of inquisition."[7] Rappe's charges of an Irish cabal were quickly echoed by some of his supporters who, using pen names, wrote a series of vitriolic letters to the editor which were published in the Cleveland *Leader* between September, 1870, and September, 1871. Their appearance, of course, prompted ripostes from the other side. In one such exchange in the fall of 1871, "P.K.W." claimed that the Irish, far from leading a conspiracy, were justifiably angered at Rappe because his advisors played loose with diocesan funds and "it was Irish earnings they were pillaging." "Star" laughingly replied that there were no Irish earnings for churchmen to pillage since most of their wages were "appropriated for whiskey."[8]

It was in the midst of this highly charged atmosphere that the German and Irish factions in the diocese, their ethnic sensitivities piqued by Rappe's policies and the newspaper war, sought to ensure the appointment of a bishop to their liking—hopefully, one of their own. So compelling was the ethnic issue, in fact, that few gave any thought to what should be a prime quality in a bishop—the ability to be a unifying force in his diocese. Within days of Rappe's departure from the city, some German priests held a strategy meeting, and at the end of the year several of them petitioned Rome for a bishop who could speak German and who would respect their nationality.[9] The Irish also quickly sought to protect their own interests. Claiming that at least one-half of the Catholics in Cleveland were Irish or Irish-American, Father Robert Sidley of Sandusky argued for the selection of an English-speaking candidate. He hoped for someone of Irish stock, but if that were impossible, he sought at least to avoid a German. As he complained to Archbishop John Baptist Purcell of Cincinnati, "It makes me disgusted to see Americans become Germans without necessity."[10]

Hoping that the tumult in the diocese would die down, the bishops of the Province of Cincinnati, who would select three names to place before Rome for the vacant see, waited until the fall of 1871 to consider candidates. Archbishop Purcell let it be known in the meantime that he

[7] Rappe to Spalding, Fall (?), 1870, Spalding Mss., Archives of the Archdiocese of Baltimore, Chancery Building, Baltimore, Maryland.

[8] Cleveland *Leader*, September 4 and 5, 1871.

[9] Edward Hannin to Archbishop John B. Purcell, Purcell Mss., Archives of the University of Notre Dame, Notre Dame, Indiana; petition of December 14, 1870, Archives of the Sacred Congregation de Propaganda Fide, *Congressi*, Vol. 23, fols. 614-615.

[10] Sidley to Purcell, September 3, 1870, Purcell Mss., Archives of the Archdiocese of Cincinnati, Mt. St. Mary's Seminary of the West, Cincinnati (Mt. Washington), Ohio (hereafter cited AACin).

would "not think of proposing, under the present circumstances, a German, a Frenchman, nor Irishman for that See."[11] He got his wish. In February, 1872, Father Richard Gilmour, of St. Joseph's Church in Dayton and a converted Scotch Presbyterian, was appointed bishop.

Although the new bishop wrote Father O'Callaghan that "no good can come from stirring up the history of the past," both Gilmour and the diocese were deeply affected by the Rappe controversy.[12] Gilmour visited Rappe in Vermont in 1872, a meeting which the former bishop characterized as "very satisfactory."[13] And although Gilmour did not return parroting Rappe's views of his troubles, he was nevertheless deeply impressed by what he had heard in Vermont. In fact, as Gilmour's own troubles with his clergy, especially the Irish, and with Rome mounted, he became increasingly convinced not only that Rappe had been correct in his assessment of conspiring Irish priests and an unreliable Rome but that he himself was being similarly victimized.

Like Rappe, he came to believe that Father O'Callaghan was the leader of the Irish forces arrayed against him. Gilmour frequently tangled with O'Callaghan who challenged several of the bishop's decisions and policies and who, in general, protested what he saw as Gilmour's arbitrary use of episcopal power, just as he had protested Rappe's. Also reminiscent of the past, Rome decided to investigate the Gilmour administration in 1889 as the turmoil in Cleveland mounted.[14] Upon hearing of Rome's intention and also of its decision against him in a case involving a priest who had brought a grievance against him, Gilmour exploded to the Archbishop of Cincinnati, William Henry Elder:

> Now we will see what we will see and Rome will be well off if she has not another of the scandals on her hands of which she has been the fruitful source. Rome has done all the outrage she can do to me and as far as the bishop is concerned has destroyed him in Cleveland now as she did with Bishop Rappe. However, Amadeus Rappe lives and will live in spite of the outrage done him

[11] Purcell to Spalding, March 31, 1871, Purcell Mss., Archives of the University of Notre Dame.

[12] Quoted in Hallinan, op. cit., p. 109.

[13] Rappe to Sylvester Hogan, July 1, 1872, copy in the possession of the Reverend Nelson J. Callahan, Diocese of Cleveland.

[14] Nelson J. Callahan, A Case for Due Process in the Church: Father Eugene O'Callaghan, American Pioneer of Dissent (Staten Island, 1971), pp. 47-71; Brown, op. cit., pp. 67-68; Cardinal Giovanni Simeoni to ?, August 3, 1889, ADC; Gerald P. Fogarty, S.J., The Vatican and the Americanist Crisis: Denis J. O'Connell, American Agent in Rome, 1885-1903 (Rome, 1974), p. 130, footnote 30.

as bishop and Richard Gilmour will live—bishop or no bishop, Rome or no Rome.[15]

Significantly, it was the German priests who helped Gilmour defend his administration of the diocese before Roman officials.[16] In fact, as Gilmour became convinced of the existence of a powerful Irish clique opposed both to himself and to his predecessor, clerics of German extraction gained increasing power in the diocese. Gilmour and the Germans generally got on well despite the fact that he was one of several prelates, including Cardinal James Gibbons of Baltimore, Archbishop John Ireland of St. Paul, and Bishop John Lancaster Spalding of Peoria, who were convinced in the 1880's and 1890's that Germans were attempting to dominate the American Church and who worked assiduously to prevent it.[17] In his own diocese, Germans were irritated by Gilmour's frequently expressed hope that German, and, indeed, all foreign languages would speedily be replaced by English in church services and parochial schools. But the bishop's Americanizing bark was usually worse than his bite.

The result was that Gilmour, more suspicious of the Irish than of the Germans in his diocese, appointed Germans to powerful positions. Among them were the Reverend Fathers Nicholas Pfeil, Casimir Reichlin, pastor of St. Stephen's, and Francis Westerholt, pastor of St. Peter's, both German parishes in Cleveland. Especially important were the Reverend Seraphim Bauer and George F. Houck. Born in France but of a German father and reared and educated primarily in Germany, Bauer in 1854 emigrated to Cleveland, where he was ordained by Bishop Rappe. During Rappe's tenure, Bauer pictured himself as a Frenchman, perhaps to please his superior. But after the bishop's resignation, Bauer's true loyalties quickly emerged. He was among the German priests who in December, 1870, complained that Rappe had harmed German Catholics by disdaining their language and culture and who asked for a new bishop who would respect their nationality. Pastor of St. Joseph's Church in Fremont since 1862, Bauer was made an irremovable rector in 1889 by Gilmour, who at the same time appointed him *procurator fiscalis* for the investigation and prosecution of criminal and disciplinary cases involving the clergy.[18]

[15]Gilmour to Elder, December 5, 1889, AACin.

[16]Draft of a letter from Gilmour to Propaganda, 1889, marked "never sent," ADC.

[17]For the "German problem" in the Church, see Colman J. Barry, O.S.B., *The Catholic Church and German Americans* (Milwaukee, 1953), and Fogarty, *op. cit.*, pp. 121-153.

[18]Petition of December 14, 1870, Archives of the Sacred Congregation de Propaganda Fide; Michael W. Carr, *A History of Catholicity in Northern Ohio and in the Diocese of Cleveland — Biographical* (Cleveland, 1903), II, 52-58.

Houck was born of German parents, was ordained in Cleveland in 1875, and in 1877 was appointed both Gilmour's secretary and chancellor of the diocese. And it was Father Houck who wrote several histories of the diocese which some Irish clerics found so biased and insulting that they protested their publication. They were particularly angered by Houck's historical treatment of Rappe, whose career and moral reputation, he wrote, had been ruined by a foul Irish conspiracy.[19] Like the Republican Party's "waving the bloody shirt," Houck's history was frequently hauled out by the Germans in order to unify their ranks and to blacken the reputation of their Irish brethren.

At Gilmour's death in April, 1891, the Irish and Germans once more battled over the succession. That the ethnic issue was again paramount was to a considerable degree a result of Gilmour's style of leadership. Not only had he played the ethnic game himself by rewarding the Germans and punishing the Irish. He had also stifled the growth of any sense of clerical brotherhood, which might in time have overcome national animosities, by discouraging priests from visiting one another and meeting among themselves. Such gatherings, he was convinced, were plots to circumvent his authority. He also encouraged his priests to inform on one another. The result was a clergy suspicious of each other and still deeply divided along ethnic lines.[20]

The election of Gilmour's successor, in fact, took on national significance since Cardinal Gibbons and Archbishops Ireland and Elder, among other Americanizing prelates, were determined to prevent a German from being appointed to another important American see. When the diocesan consultors and irremovable rectors met in May, however, the German element, including Fathers Bauer, Reichlin, and Westerholt, was in the majority, a situation which Gilmour himself had created by appointing so

203

[19] *Ibid.*, pp. 206-208; George F. Houck, *A History of Catholicity in Northern Ohio and in the Diocese of Cleveland from 1749 to December 31, 1900* (Cleveland, 1903), I, 89-92; F. Doherty to Bishop Ignatius Horstmann, June 10, 1900, ADC. For a discussion of Houck's various histories of the diocese, see W. A. Jurgens, *A History of the Diocese of Cleveland: The Prehistory of the Diocese to its Establishment in 1847* (Cleveland, 1980), I, 17-19. After reading Houck's accusations of the role of the Irish clergy in Rappe's resignation, which appeared in Houck's *A Memoir of the Right Reverend Amadeus Rappe, First Bishop of Cleveland* (Cleveland, 1888), Bauer wrote approvingly, "Those terrible pages will act like concentrated nitric acid on the rough nails of the roughboard coffin into which ... ghoulish undertakers have undertaken to pull down and bury out-of-sight the name and fame of the saintly bishop. The acid will eat out the nails, burn the wood, and also *blister the fingers of those that might attempt to stay its action!*" Bauer to Houck, December 18, 1888, ADC.

[20] Brown, *op. cit.*, pp. 91-93.

many to important positions. All three names, in order of preference, on the terna drawn up at the May meeting were Germans who were already bishops elsewhere.[21]

Negative reaction to the terna by non-Germans was immediate. The Reverend James Molony, the irremovable rector of St. Malachy's in Cleveland who was present at the May meeting, wrote Archbishop Elder that some Irish candidates had received a few votes but that "The German priests as you saw voted as one—I earnestly hope they will not succeed."[22] Cardinal Gibbons was so upset by the result that he wrote Elder from "a sick room, but I regard the subject . . . of such importance that I have no hesitation in giving my views . . . at the risk of overtaxing my strength . . . An American bishop . . . should be a man possessed of a deep love not only for his church but also for this country, and a thorough acquaintance and sympathy with our political institutions."[23] At their meeting on June 9, the bishops of the province rejected the entire diocesan terna and placed at the head of their own list an Irish candidate, Father Thomas Byrne of Cincinnati, followed by Ignatius Horstmann of Philadelphia and John Schoenhoft of Cincinnati, both Germans.[24] The decision now rested in Rome's hands.

In the meantime, rumors circulated in Cleveland that Rome would select Horstmann. Seeking to derail his appointment, an Irish-led group of clergymen, which also included one Hungarian and one German priest, sent a circular letter on September 12 to all priests in the diocese, asking them to vote for three of their own number to be placed on a list which would be sent directly to Rome for its consideration.[25] Four days later, Fathers Westerholt, Moes, Reichlin, and Bauer sent out their own letter, written in German, to most but not all of the diocese's German priests. Asserting that the diocesan terna was "an excellent one in every respect," and warning that the September 12 circular letter was "a private action which could easily be injurious," they asked the recipients to trust the consultors and to "endorse the choice made by them."[26] At the end of the

[21] Joseph H. Lackner, S.M., "Bishop Ignatius F. Horstmann and the Americanization of the Roman Catholic Church in the United States" (unpublished Ph.D. dissertation, St. Louis University, 1977), p. 34.

[22] Molony to Elder, May 15, 1891, AACin.

[23] Gibbons to Elder, June 3, 1891, copy, Archives of the Archdiocese of Baltimore.

[24] Lackner, op. cit., pp. 39-40.

[25] Mears, Molony, Furdek, and Klute to 'Rev. Dear Father,' September 12, 1891, ADC.

[26] Westerholt, Moes, Reichlin, and Bauer to 'Rev. and very esteemed brother,' ADC.

204

month, the Irish group (interestingly, the German priest had by now withdrawn) reported the results of their canvass, noting that "all the nationalities of the diocese" had received votes. The writers took the opportunity to compare the "openness and fairness" of their letter to that of their opponents, written "in the *German* language ... sent ... to the *German speaking* priests alone and *not* to *all* of them ... [it was] sent to a class of priests only."[27]

By late September, the clerical politics had found its way into the Cleveland newspapers. "An American" (in fact, Alexander R. Sidley, pastor of Cleveland's Immaculate Conception Church) charged that "partisan" Germans, acting in a manner "neither Catholic or American," were engaged in "arrogant and insolent ... scheming" to control both the diocese and the province of Cincinnati. "An American but not from Ireland" soon replied, arguing that the Irish, as usual, claimed that Irish and American were synonymous terms and that, under the colors of Americanism, they were themselves attempting to dominate the Church. Charging that the Irish had persecuted Bishops Rappe and Gilmour, the writer vowed that "All non-Irish Catholic Americans are tired of Irish tyranny and will refuse to bear it any longer."[28]

Rome's choice, announced in December, 1891, was Ignatius Horstmann. Both Cleveland's Irish and Archbishop Ireland and his allies were not pleased. As Ireland wrote, Horstmann's Americanism "rests on a very thick German foundation. ..."[29] The new bishop's administration was more peaceful than those of his predecessors, partly because he had a less combative personality and thus he generally got on better with the laity and the clergy. Consequently, there were fewer complaints carried to Rome, and in any case Horstmann himself rarely questioned Vatican decisions, unlike Rappe and Gilmour.

But German-Irish antagonism was still a powerful force. And German clerics were still very powerful in diocesan affairs. Houck, in fact, was Horstmann's secretary and continued as chancellor. And although the bishop was by no means their prisoner, he tended to see the diocese and its history through their eyes and, consequently, he was suspicious of the Irish. As he wrote Cardinal Satolli, "In this Diocese of Cleveland there has been and is a body of Irish or Irish-American priests who constitute a clique that is determined to rule." They disgraced Rappe and opposed Gilmour, he

[27] Molony, Mears, and Furdek to 'Rev. dear Father,' September 30, 1891, ADC.
[28] Cleveland *Press*, September 28, October 3, October 7, and October 10, 1891.
[29] Quoted in Lackner, *op. cit.*, p. 39.

continued. "I thought that I had broken it up but I find that it is as strong as ever."[30] The Irish were equally suspicious of Horstmann and, convinced that he was the tool of Bauer and Houck, saw him as the personification of German power in the diocese.

These traditional ethnic animosities were especially noticeable during the bishop's four-year-long effort to have Father Joseph M. Koudelka appointed his auxiliary bishop, with special responsibility for Cleveland's Slavic Catholics. Born in Bohemia, Koudelka was of inestimable service to Horstmann, securing much-needed priests in Europe and settling disputes which frequently broke out in Slavic, especially Polish, parishes. It seemed only natural to Horstmann, therefore, when he was visiting Rome in 1904, to ask for Koudelka's appointment as auxiliary, a step which Horstmann assumed would cause no difficulty. He was wrong. In 1906, the appointment had still not been made, much to Horstmann's anger. Although there was no incontrovertible evidence to support his suspicion, the bishop was nonetheless convinced that powerful Irish priests in Cleveland were responsible for the delay.[31] And, indeed, the Irish saw Koudelka as more German than Bohemian because he had been pastor of Cleveland's important German-language St. Michael's Parish since 1883 and was a close friend of Fathers Bauer, Houck, and Reichlin. In fact, many Slavs saw him as a German and therefore distrusted him as well.

After further lobbying in Rome on Horstmann's part, Koudelka was finally appointed auxiliary in late 1907. The public announcement of Koudelka's appointment in early January, 1908, released a storm of Irish indignation. Writing in the very same issue of the *Catholic Universe*, the official diocesan paper, in which the announcement was made, the Reverend William McMahon, its editor, commented, "No doubt most of our people were very much surprised to learn" of Koudelka's new position. McMahon also reprimanded various German groups which had praised Koudelka's elevation as an honor to German Catholics. "We are of the opinion," the editor wrote, "that individuals and societies who emphasize their nationality very much emphasize their Catholicity very little."[32] The city's Central Verein, an organization of German Catholic laymen, passed resolutions condemning the *Universe's* anti-German sentiments. The Cleveland *Wachter und Anzeiger*, in fact, called McMahon and his

[30]Horstmann to Cardinal Francesco Satolli, March 7, 1900, ADC.

[31]Horstmann to Satolli, April 18, 1906, ADC. For a detailed analysis of the controversy, see Lackner, *op. cit.*, pp. 154-184.

[32]*Catholic Universe*, January 10, 1908.

associates a "clique of local Irish Catholics," a charge which McMahon labelled "gross libel . . . a great outrage and a grave injustice against our name, our character and our standing."[33] Outraged by McMahon's comments and by the Irish opposition to Koudelka's appointment, Horstmann was equally angered by the refusal of most Irish priests to participate in Koudelka's consecration ceremony. The bishop wrote Archbishop Henry Moeller of Cincinnati:

> Not one of the English-speaking priests of Irish extraction of the city of Cleveland and Toledo was present at the consecration or banquet. I had invited Drs. Farrell and O'Reilly to act as Masters of Ceremony. Dr. Farrell was unwell and asked to be excused from the banquet. Dr. O'Reilly flatly refused to be present. The country priests would not sign their names as present saying that if they did so they would be "marked."[34]

207

On May 13, 1908, Bishop Horstmann suddenly died. Even his funeral deepened animosities. Father Houck angered the Irish by appointing as officers at the ceremonies nearly all Germans. At the Month's Mind for the late bishop, the administrator of the diocese, Father Felix Boff, who was no friend of the Germans, discarded them in favor of the Irish, one of whom was Father Francis T. Moran of St. Patrick's in Cleveland, who had opposed the Koudelka appointment. Moran's selection to preach so upset the German priests that twenty-eight of them, including Father Reichlin, protested to Archbishop Moeller, claiming that Moran had insulted Horstmann shortly before his death and that his selection was an insult both to the dead bishop and to all German Catholics. Moran, in turn, demanded an official investigation of the charges, which Moeller avoided by persuading the Germans to drop the issue.[35]

In the midst of this turmoil, the diocesan consultors and irremovable rectors met in early June to draw up the terna for Horstmann's successor. As it turned out, this particular struggle marked the end of an era, both in terms of the warring cast of characters and the kind of bishop ultimately appointed. Although they did not hold a clear majority, the Germans, including Koudelka, Houck, Reichlin, Pfeil, and Bauer, were able to draw up a list generally to their liking, in order of preference—Koudelka, Houck, and Dr. Thomas Mahar of Akron, an Irish-American.

[33]*Ibid.,* January 31, 1908.

[34]Horstmann to Moeller, March 3, 1908, AACin.

[35]Boff to 'Dear Father,' July 13, 1908; Moeller to Boff, July 17, 1908; German priests to Moeller, July 22, 1908; Moeller to Rev. Anthony Eilert, July 26, 1908; Moran to Moeller, August 14, 1908; and Moeller to Eilert, August 17, 1908, AACin. Boff to Moeller, July 27, 1908, ADC.

The Irish members on the selection committee, Fathers William McMahon and Edward Mears, refused to accept the result without a fight and challenged the votes of Koudelka, Bauer, Houck, and Aloysius Hoeffel, another German-American. They claimed that since Koudelka and Houck were vicars general, they could not also be diocesan consultors and thus had no right to vote. Since Bauer had been declared mentally incompetent as a result of morphine addiction, they urged that his vote should be disregarded. Hoeffel could not attend the meeting in person because he was ill, and in their opinion, he should not have been permitted to vote by proxy. Relying on Father Louis J. Nau, the German-American procurator of the Archdiocese of Cincinnati and friend of Houck, to investigate the dispute, Archbishop Moeller, himself a friend of the German party, rejected the charges of McMahon and Mears and upheld the validity of the election.[36] Some Germans were so determined to secure the selection of Koudelka that they lobbied through influential friends at the Vatican, and Fathers Pfeil and Reichlin themselves traveled to Rome in the summer of 1908, apparently for the same purpose.[37]

But it was all to no avail. In March, 1909, Rome announced the appointment to Cleveland of John P. Farrelly, a priest of Irish stock whose name was not on the lists prepared either by the diocesan electors or the bishops of the province, although he received a few votes at both meetings.[38] Since 1887, he had lived in Rome where he was secretary to the rector of the North American College, Denis J. O'Connell, and, since 1894, had been spiritual director of the institution. Dismayed at an Irish-American and a distinct outsider as bishop, the Germans, led by Fathers Pfeil and Reichlin, quickly sought to limit the potential damage. Reichlin wrote Farrelly in late April, solicitously offering to explain to a "stranger" in Cleveland the history and present condition of the diocese. Rappe, Gilmour, and Horstmann had been persecuted, he carefully but naively explained, by a clique of Irish priests. The Irish, in fact, could not be trusted; they were disloyal to their bishops and frequently neglected their parochial schools. The Germans, on the other hand, were just the opposite: "as a body there are no more law-abiding and hard-working priests in the diocese." Claiming that he sought no preferment for himself but only to

[36]Election of Nominees for Cleveland file; Nau to Cardinal Diomede Falconio, June 23, 1908, ADC. Moeller to Rev. J. A. TePas, June 6, 1908; Moeller to Falconio, June 23, 1908; Moeller to Nicholas Pfeil, July 11, 1908, AACin. Cleveland *Press*, July 13, 1908.

[37]Rev. J. Bernard Dolbing to Pfeil, June 19, 1908, and January 12, 1909, Cleveland Mss., University of Notre Dame. Cleveland *Press*, July 14, 1908.

[38]*Catholic Universe*, March 19, 1909.

tell "the truth as I see it," he ended his letter by strongly urging the reappointment of Houck as chancellor and Koudelka as auxiliary, both of whom the Germans revered, he explained. He also issued a veiled threat— "You may rest assured that you will have no trouble with the Germans as long as you treat them with fairness and justice."[39]

Fathers Reichlin and Pfeil had seriously misjudged their man. Farrelly was not just angered by their advice. He flatly rejected most of it and, soon after his consecration, sought to destroy German power in the diocese. Despite Houck's efforts to keep his position and Reichlin's and Pfeil's petition campaign to save their ally and friend, Houck was not reappointed chancellor. Houck's appeals to the Apostolic Delegate were unavailing, and, after he refused to accept the irremovable rectorate at Delphos, Ohio, he spent the remainder of his life as chaplain at St. Augustine's Convent in Lakewood, where he died in 1916.[40] Farrelly also broke with Koudelka. Asserting that he did not need an auxiliary, the bishop did not renew Koudelka's appointment. Angry and feeling snubbed, Koudelka, doing, in his own words, "my filial duty," coldly sent Farrelly and "our poor diocese" his best wishes of the season in late December, 1909. He wrote pointedly, "Although Your Lordship seems to ignore me entirely . . . I shall never ignore and forget my duties to my Superior Bishop. May the Divine Babe grant me grace to carry patiently the cross, which He in his infinite mercy has laid upon me through Your Lordship and your advisers."[41] Relations between the two improved not at all during the next two years, and in September, 1911, Koudelka was appointed auxiliary bishop in Milwaukee, prompting his friends to charge bitterly that Farrelly had forced him out. As for Fathers Pfeil and Reichlin, Farrelly tried, with some success, to keep them on a short leash, although as late as 1918 he was complaining to Rome about their continuing interference in matters outside their own parishes.[42] Seraphim Bauer retired to a rest home in Indiana, where he died in 1911.

209

[39] Reichlin to Farrelly, April 24, 1909, ADC.

[40] Houck to Archbishop P. J. Ryan, April 12, 1909; Pfeil to Farrelly, June 30, 1909; Houck to Falconio, July 26, 1910; Farrelly to Falconio, December 17, 1910; and Farrelly to Cardinal Gaetano DeLai, September 5, 1911, ADC.

[41] Koudelka to Farrelly, December 23, 1909, ADC. I am grateful to Father Ladislas Örsy, S.J., of the Catholic University of America, for explaining that an auxiliary bishop was given *personae episcopi*, not *sedi*, unless the bull of appointment stated the attachment differently. Hence, an auxiliary bishop's office (in this case Koudelka's) expired whenever the bishop's office expired, in this instance through the death of Bishop Horstmann.

[42] Farrelly to Propaganda (?), Apostolic Delegate file, 1917-1918, ADC.

In replacing Germans in positions of power in the diocese, Farrelly was careful to appoint representatives of many nationalities. But the fact remains that the new officials were predominantly of Irish-American stock. As chancellor, he selected the Reverend Thomas C. O'Reilly, who later became vicar general; as his secretary he chose the Reverend William A. Scullen, who subsequently became chancellor. He had known both in Rome, where Scullen had in fact been his secretary. The first director of the Board of Charities was Father Hubert LeBlond, who was part-Irish. Priests of Irish background, including O'Reilly and George F. Murphy, were added to the bishop's Council.[43]

210

In a sense, the Irish in Cleveland had thus won their struggle for dominance in the diocese. However, to focus exclusively on the ethnic aspect of Farrelly's accession to and appointment policies in Cleveland is to miss a more important point. Farrelly was not simply an Irish-American bishop, born in the nineteenth century, who settled nineteenth-century ethnic scores in the early twentieth. In dismissing old German leaders, he symbolically jettisoned the past and brought his diocese into the modern era. He represented the emergence in the early twentieth-century American Church of modern, administratively-minded bishops, as well as other officials, of all nationalities, although Irish-Americans clearly predominated. They were pastors of their flocks, but they were equally interested in developing and rationalizing the operations of their dioceses. Like their predecessors, they built churches, but they also created bureaucracies to run charities, schools, and other services efficiently. They sought to consolidate power in the central diocesan administration, thereby limiting the autonomy of parishes and parish priests. Whereas their predecessors had devoutly hoped for obedience from the laity and clergy, they insisted on it. In addition, unlike many of their nineteenth-century forebears, they willingly looked to Rome for direction.

Farrelly clearly fitted this new mold of American episcopal leadership. Though born in Memphis, Tennessee, he was European and, indeed, Roman by training and residence. After some time at Georgetown College, he completed his preparatory courses in Belgium. In 1875 he enrolled in the North American College in Rome and studied philosophy and theology at the Urban College of the Propaganda, which awarded him a doctorate. Between his ordination in Rome in 1880 and his arrival in Cleveland in 1909, he lived in the United States in his diocese, Nashville, for only about

[43]Farrelly to DeLai, September 5, 1911, ADC; Hynes, *History of the Diocese of Cleveland: Origin and Growth, 1847-1952* (Cleveland, 1953), pp. 278, 301.

five years, in the middle 1880's. Otherwise, he lived in Rome where he was close to important centers of power. He was an advisor to the Propaganda as well as the confidential agent in Rome for several American bishops. Well acquainted with high Vatican officials, he was also a friend of the conservative Pope Pius X, who was elected in 1903.[44] Farrelly was also highly knowledgeable about conditions in the American Church. But the fact remains that he was extremely deferential to Rome and Roman authority, an attachment which one diocesan historian has called "almost passionate."[45] As a result, his administration avoided the almost constant tension with Vatican officials that had marked the tenures of Bishops Rappe and Gilmour. Farrelly's generally harmonious relationship with Rome was perhaps also a consequence of the fact that, in 1908, the American Church, achieving recognition of its maturity, was removed from the control of the Congregation of the Propaganda and thus released from its missionary status. American bishops were no longer under the supervision of a single congregation of the Roman Curia, the Propaganda, a situation which, by focusing lines of authority, had been the source of frequent friction in Cleveland and elsewhere. Bishops could now deal on a regular basis with the several congregations of the Curia, which in turn normalized relations with Rome and diffused the potential for conflict.

211

Within his own diocese, Farrelly was a strict disciplinarian who did not tolerate opposition. He emphasized efficient administration, especially in financial matters. Far more than his predecessors, he kept a close watch on priests to ensure that they paid their parish bills on time, presented accurate and thorough financial reports to the diocese, and did not borrow more money than authorized. Woe betide the priest who could not pass muster. To the pastor of St. Barbara's Polish Parish in Cleveland, he wrote in his characteristically blunt manner that either he pay his bills or he would be relieved of his position. "It has been one constant repetition of troubles with you and your congregation . . . and it must stop or I shall have to provide a pastor for St. Barbara's in whose competency to care for it I shall have more confidence than your administration is calculated to inspire."[46]

Farrelly was also determined to bring structure and organization to his rapidly growing diocese. Although previous bishops had started the pro-

[44]*Ibid.*, pp. 266-268, 297; Cleveland *Press*, March 16, 1909; *Universe Bulletin*, March 19, 1909. For a brief sketch of Farrelly's life, see Thomas J. Stritch, "Three Catholic Bishops from Tennessee," *Tennessee Historical Quarterly*, XXXVII (Spring, 1978), 3-35.

[45]Hynes, *op. cit.*, p. 296.

[46]Farrelly to Sierzputowski, November 23, 1909, ADC.

cess, Farrelly took it up with gusto. Reflecting his years at the Vatican, he was attempting to create in his own diocese a miniature Roman Curia. The matrimonial court and other episcopal agencies were established. The building commission was given control of all new construction in the diocese. The board of charities, established in 1911, was replaced in 1919 by the Catholic Charities Corporation, which collected larger sums of money more efficiently. Farrelly took the first effective steps toward the unification and standardization of the parochial schools and toward uniformity of teacher training on a diocesan scale.[47]

212

Farrelly's deference toward Rome, his authoritarianism, and his interest in bringing order, centralization, and efficiency to his diocese also describe other American prelates appointed in the early twentieth century. George W. Mundelein, named Archbishop of Chicago in 1915, saw the Church as an army in which the laymen were footsoldiers, and the priests and bishops were officers. He ran his archdiocese like a general and demanded absolute loyalty. In addition, as an historian of the Chicago scene writes, "The era of parochial autonomy ... ended with the arrival of Mundelein. In the fashion of the new generation of businessmen, he systematized and centralized all operations in the name of efficiency and order."[48] Mundelein was of German stock. William Henry O'Connell, who became Bishop of Portland in 1901 and Archbishop of Boston in 1907, was of Irish descent. Nationality was of less importance than loyalty to Rome and administrative style in defining the new generation of American bishops. An outsider in both Portland and Boston and closely connected with high Vatican officials, especially the conservatives, O'Connell brought to his work in New England the principles of organization, order, and control which he had learned at the North American College in Rome. In Boston, "stress was now focused on projecting a massive ecclesiastical presence, resting upon sound administration and equal to the power and wealth of government and business institutions."[49]

[47] Hynes, op. cit., pp. 279, 283, 299-300.

[48] Charles Shanabruch, Chicago's Catholics: The Evolution of an American Identity (Notre Dame, Indiana, 1981), p. 164. See also Edward R. Kantowicz, "Cardinal Mundelein of Chicago and the Shaping of Twentieth-Century American Catholicism," Journal of American History. LXVIII (June, 1981), 52-68, and Kantowicz, Corporation Sole: Cardinal Mundelein and Chicago Catholicism (Notre Dame, Indiana, 1983).

[49] James Gaffey, "The Changing of the Guard: The Rise of Cardinal O'Connell of Boston," Catholic Historical Review, LIX (July, 1973), 243-244.

In the perspective of the history of American Catholicism, the emergence of men like Farrelly, Mundelein, and O'Connell marks a striking break with the past, the end of one era and the start of another. Men like John Ireland, John Lancaster Spalding, and even Richard Gilmour had sought to Americanize the Catholic Church, to bring it into harmony with American institutions. They consciously sought to develop in the United States a brand of enlightened Catholicism, free from what they saw as the outmoded ideas and even decadence of the European Church. The Church in America was to be distinctive, though still Roman and Catholic.[50] They recognized that achieving these goals would undoubtedly provoke a confrontation with Rome, and, in fact, it was some of these very same men who vehemently opposed the appointment of a permanent papal representative in the United States, fearing that he would severely limit American episcopal autonomy.[51] They lost. The Apostolic Delegation was established in 1893. In 1899, Leo XIII, in his encyclical *Testem Benevolentiae,* condemned the heresy of "Americanism." In retrospect, these two events marked the precipitate decline in the fortunes of liberals and Americanizers in the Church in the United States and the rise of conservatives and Roman loyalists.[52]

213

Paradoxically, new men like Farrelly, Mundelein, and O'Connell in fact "Americanized" the Church, by emphasizing its massive presence as a power to be reckoned with and by institutionalizing it in conformity with emerging bureaucratic patterns in business and government. But this was certainly not the vision or perspective of late nineteenth-century Americanizers, and it lacked the sense of creative distinctiveness and independence of the American Church which they had cherished. Farrelly was part of what an historian of the Boston Catholic experience calls "an emerging colonial officialdom with first loyalties to Rome" who worked for and within a "Pax Romana."[53] It was almost as if the Church in the United

---

[50]Of the many scholarly studies of the drive to Americanize the Church, see Fogarty, *op. cit.,* Robert D. Cross, *The Emergence of Liberal Catholicism in America* (Chicago, 1968), and, for the conservative point of view, Robert Emmett Curran, S.J., *Michael Augustine Corrigan and the Shaping of Conservative Catholicism in America, 1878-1902* (New York, 1978). On changing relationships between Rome and American bishops, see Gerald P. Fogarty, S.J., *The Vatican and the American Hierarchy from 1870 to 1965* (Stuttgart, 1982).

[51]Fogarty, *The Vatican and the Americanist Crisis,* pp. 219-250.

[52]Donna Merwick, *Boston Priests, 1848-1910. A Study of Social and Intellectual Change* (Cambridge, Massachusetts, 1973), pp. 150-151.

[53]*Ibid.,* p. 147. See also Gaffey, *op. cit.,* p. 226.

States were released from the supervision of the Propaganda only after Rome had assured herself of her ability to control the American Church through the Apostolic Delegation and the appointment of bishops whose loyalty was unquestioned.

Bishop Farrelly, therefore, personified a significant change in the character of Catholic Church leadership in the United States. In Cleveland, nineteenth-century men, nineteenth-century ethnic hostilities, nineteenth-century patterns of diocesan flexibility were subsumed in an increasingly effective march toward order and efficiency. The freewheeling, often chaotic growth of an earlier era was being replaced by consolidation and, inexorably, by the bureaucracy that accompanied it. In this environment, in Cleveland at least, divisive nineteenth-century German-Irish bickering had no place.

214

THE MAKING OF ITALIAN-AMERICAN CATHOLICS: JESUIT WORK ON THE LOWER EAST SIDE, NEW YORK, 1890's-1950's

BY

Mary Elizabeth Brown*

Historians have been aware of the challenge presented to American Catholicism by the Italian immigration of 1880-1924. An important chapter in the history of the Archdiocese of New York during that period is the effort of a largely Irish-American institution to minister to a minority group. One well-documented example of the mission to the Italians is the work of the Jesuits on the Lower East Side of Manhattan from 1891 to the early 1950's. The story of Our Lady of Loreto mission and Nativity parish shows the importance of neighborhood and parish history, and also the different concepts of the Italian apostolate among the people involved: archbishops, secular clergy, religious, Italians, and non-Italians.[1]

215

Siciliani and *calabresi* began filling in the Jersey Street tenements behind Saint Patrick's Cathedral on Mott Street in the early 1870's, just before the parish lost its cathedral status in 1879. Pastor John F. Kearney, who had been baptized at Saint Patrick's in 1839 and who had been away from the parish only to study for ordination,[2] got an Italian curate to help with the new parishioners.[3] In 1882, an Italian sub-congregation was

---

*Miss Brown teaches American history at Pace University and at Marymount Manhattan College
[1]Helpful works on this subject are Henry J. Browne, "The 'Italian Problem' in the Catholic Church in the United States, 1880-1900," United States Catholic Historical Society *Records and Studies*, XXXV (1946), 46-72; Rudolph J. Vecoli, "Prelates and Peasants: Italian Immigrants and the Catholic Church," *Journal of Social History*, II (Spring, 1967), 217-268; Silvano M. Tomasi, C.S., *Piety and Power: The Role of the Italian Parishes in the New York Metropolitan Area, 1880-1930* (New York, 1975); and Stephen M. DiGiovanni, "Michael Augustine Corrigan and the Italian Immigrants: The Relationship Between the Church and the Italians in the Archdiocese of New York, 1885-1902" (unpublished doctoral dissertation, Gregorian University, 1983).
[2]New York *Times*, April 12, 1923, p. 19, col. 5.
[3]Saint Patrick's Old Cathedral, New York, New York, Baptismal Register, 1879-1901. Access to these documents provided by the Reverend James Flannagan and Ms. Connie Sciarra.

created and the basement of Saint Patrick's turned over to it. A lay committee supervised the basement. Two Italian priests, members of the regular
parish staff, handled Italian baptisms, marriages, and sick calls. The priests
said three Masses on Sundays and holydays, and sang Mass on Italian
feastdays. During Lent and Advent and prior to the feast of Saint Anthony
of Padua the Italians said their rosaries and made their Stations of the
Cross and their novenas in their own tongue. Only the children mixed
with the non-Italian congregation, in the parochial and Sunday schools.[4]

According to John Talbot Smith, the contemporary archdiocesan historian, "when custom had paved the way," Kearney "abolished the distinction of races, and made Italians and natives join in the same services."[5]
According to Nicholas Russo, S.J., another contemporary, "[t]he results
were far from encouraging," and "after several years' trial, the parish priest
was disgusted, asked the archbishop to make other provisions for them,
and the basement of the church was consequently closed to the Italians."[6]
Given the history of Italian-American churches in the neighborhood after
the 1890's, the experiment must have ended unsatisfactorily.

One problem with the sub-congregation arrangement was the availability of Italian secular priests to act as curates. Italian priests did not emigrate in sufficient numbers; some of those who did emigrate were unsuitable; and those few made bishops and priests suspicious of the rest.[7] One
of Saint Patrick's neighboring churches, Transfiguration, Mott Street, used
Franciscan priests from Saint Anthony of Padua as chaplains of its sub-congregation, but treating the Italians as a distinct congregation and using
religious order priests created problems of authority and jurisdiction.[8]

Kearney left nothing to indicate his thoughts on the problems with
sub-congregations, but a certain amount may be inferred from what his
parishioners and his *confrères* on the Lower East Side wrote. The nostalgia for the good old days that marks Saint Patrick's 1909 centenary book
was not just the spirit of the occasion. The neighborhood of Saint Pa-

216

[4][Stephen I. Hannigan], *Souvenir of the Centennial Celebration of Saint Patrick's Old
Cathedral, New York, 1809-1909* (New York, 1909).

[5]John Talbot Smith, *The Catholic Church in New York: A History of the New York Diocese
from its Establishment in 1808 to the Present Time* (New York, 1905), p. 471.

[6]Nicholas Russo, S.J., "The Origin and Progress of our Italian Mission in New York,"
Woodstock Letters, XXV (1896), 135-136.

[7]DiGiovanni, *op. cit.,* pp. 171-186.

[8]Thomas P. McLaughlin to Michael A. Corrigan, November 10, 1898; xerox copy in the
Archives of the Archdiocese of New York at the Center for Migration Studies, Staten Island,
New York; Italian-Americans and Religion, Series I, Box 1, Transfiguration folder. Hereafter
cited as "CMS: IAR:I:1."

trick's Old Cathedral had changed since the increase of non-residential buildings in the 1880's had started the area's Irish looking for better housing elsewhere. The parish was losing population, income, and position in the community before the Italians became a significant factor.[9]

The Lower East Side pastors could not move uptown with their former parishioners, and their new Italian congregations seemed unattractive. One journalist, writing about the Italian sub-congregation at Transfiguration, castigated the Italians for their ignorance of the faith, dismissed their *feste* for the Madonna and village patron saints as "the luxuries of religion without its substantials," and criticized the low standard of living of Italian slum dwellers as thriftiness directed to long-term material gain that sacrificed the spiritual welfare of the children.[10] Pastor after pastor complained that Italians seldom came to church, received the sacraments, contributed to the collection, or assimilated with the "American" portion of the congregation. The characterization was biased and did not take into account the Italians' circumstances in Italy or in their new home, but it was true that the Italians kept their distance from the established parishes, and this affected the established pastors, cutting into their income and making them less useful in their communities.[11]

Michael Augustine Corrigan, Archbishop of New York from 1885 to 1902 (and coadjutor, 1880-1885), saw the Italians in the light of the long-term goal of making the Catholic Church an accepted institution in a predominantly Protestant country with a bias against foreign influence. To do that Catholicism would have to be made to appear acceptably American. "[O]ne of the greatest drawbacks to the progress of our holy faith," Corrigan wrote to immigrant benefactor Peter Paul Cahensly,

> is the taunt continually cast up to us that we are *aliens*, and the Catholic Church is a *foreign institution*. The prejudice is unjust; but nevertheless it has a most real existence, and we are continually obliged to show that we Catholics are not opposed to the institutions of this country; that we are not

[9]Hannigan, *op. cit.*

[10]Bernard Lynch, "The Italian in New York," *Catholic World*, XLVII (1888), 67-73. The quote is on p. 70.

[11]Two neighboring parishes with similar situations were Transfiguration, Mott Street, and Saint Brigid's, Tompkins Square. Transfiguration records are gathered in CMS:IAR:I:1, Transfiguration folder. Saint Brigid's records are in the Archives of the Archdiocese of New York, parish files, Saint Brigid's folder. (Hereafter cited as "AANY.") For Saint Brigid's, see also Patrick D. O'Flaherty, "The History of St. Brigid's Parish in the City of New York under the Administration of the Rev. Patrick F. McSweeney, 1877-1907" (unpublished M.A. thesis, Fordham University, New York, 1952), and Deborah Beatrice Honig, "The Church of Mary, Help of Christians, New York City: The National Parish as a Solution to the 'Italian Problem'" (unpublished M.A. thesis, Columbia University, New York, 1966).

subjects of a foreign potentate; and are sincerely attached to the land of our birth and adoption.[12]

A church in which new immigrants, old immigrants, and native Americans shared the same pews, the same pious customs, and the same charitable institutions would create a different impression.

This America-first ideology was one reason why Corrigan opposed naming bishops to reflect the multi-national origins of the Catholics in the United States. The American hierarchy could not afford the appearance of too many foreign ties and influences among its legislators and policy-makers.[13]

218

Corrigan adhered to different standards on the pastoral level. From the point of view of demonstrating the compatibility of Catholicism and Americanism, immigrants who lost their faith in the United States would be no more useful than practicing immigrants who never assimilated. Corrigan was open to assigning Italian curates to parishes, where they would minister to their compatriots under the supervision of non-Italian pastors. When this arrangement foundered on the unavailability of curates and the lack of co-operation among pastors, and when it became apparent that there were too many Italians and the assimilation process was too slow to entrust to temporary sub-congregations, Corrigan followed his predecessor in soliciting Italian-based religious orders. The Franciscans had been at Saint Anthony of Padua since 1866; in 1894 they took Most Precious Blood, Baxter Street. In 1884, the Pallottines opened Our Lady of Mount Carmel in East Harlem. The Scalabrinians arrived in 1888 to open parishes on the Lower East Side and to serve as chaplains and agents for the Saint Rafael Society for Italian Immigrants. They were followed in 1889 by the Missionary Sisters of the Sacred Heart. This left a gap in the neighborhood of Saint Patrick's, and Corrigan turned to another religious order, the Jesuits. The provincial, Thomas Campbell, assigned Father Nicholas Russo to the job.[14]

This was Russo's second career. He was born in Ascoli Satriano, eighteen miles south of Foggia (in southeastern Italy), in 1845. He came to the United States in 1875, and after his ordination in 1877 he spent eleven years at Boston College, teaching logic and philosophy, serving as vice-rector, and publishing two theological works. In 1888 he became procurator at Saint Francis Xavier, New York, and also moderator of cases of conscience for the archdiocese. Russo spent 1889 as professor

[12]Corrigan to Peter Paul Cahensly, July 22, 1891, CMS:IAR:I:1, Misc. Corresp. St. Raphaels-verein folder.
[13]*Ibid.*
[14]DiGiovanni, *op. cit.*, p. 344.

of philosophy at Georgetown University, where he published his third book. In 1890 he returned to New York, to Saint Ignatius Loyola.[15] By then, Corrigan was relying on him to draft speeches and papers.[16]

The academician first visited Saint Patrick's to preach an Advent mission in 1889. It was a bad experience. He and his *confrère* were refused the use of the upper church for the occasion, "for reasons which a priest should feel ashamed to give."[17] When Russo first interested himself in the immigrant apostolate, he placed "their own indifference" high on the list of the immigrants' problems in practicing the faith in their new home, ahead of "want of means" and "want of zeal on the part of those charged by the ordinary to look after [their] spiritual welfare."[18] After five years of experience in this ministry, Russo revised his list:

> . . . I cannot help believing that things would not be in so bad a shape now, if more care had been bestowed upon them, and if they had been taken in hand in due time, when the evil was recent and more easily remedied. Look back to the first years of Italian immigration. Who was there to smoothe their first difficulties, to warn them of the danger, to sympathize with their distressed condition, to turn their mind to heaven, and to remind them of their immortal soul?[19]

Russo and Aloysius Romano, S.J., rented a barroom on Elizabeth Street, converted it to a chapel, and named it in honor of Our Lady of Loreto. Knowing the Mass-going habits of the Italians, particularly the men, Russo chose Sunday, August 16, 1891, the feast of San Rocco, as opening day. He invited the local San Rocco Society to participate, which they did, in full regalia and with a police escort. "The opening was pronounced a success but I could not help looking with dread to the following Sunday." The chapel filled rapidly, and by May, 1891, Russo bought two adjoining tenements across Elizabeth Street to accommodate his congregation.[20]

Russo's sympathy and sense of proportion stood him in good stead in establishing himself among his neighbors. When he bought the Elizabeth Street tenements, the previous owner ordered all the tenants out by May 3, and started eviction proceedings against those who did not comply.

[15]"Father Nicholas Russo," *Woodstock Letters,* XXXI (1902), 281-282.
[16]Russo to Corrigan, n.d. (early 1891?), AANY microfilm reel #14, letter beginning "I thought I would send you the enclosed before Christmas but was unable to do so."
[17]Russo to Corrigan, October 24, 1891, AANY microfilm reel #14.
[18]Russo to Corrigan, n.d. (July, 1891?), AANY microfilm reel #14, letter beginning with reference to word from Cardinal Mazzella regarding pope's letter.
[19]Russo, "Origin and Progress," p. 138.
[20]*Ibid.,* pp. 137-138.

The tenants avenged themselves by demolishing the interiors of the buildings before their departure. Russo thought his refusal to press vandalism charges gained him much in the eyes of the people.[21]

The goodwill of Russo's colleagues was not so easily won. A few months after coming to Elizabeth Street, Russo wrote Corrigan to complain of Father Kearney's attitude. Russo had suspected that Kearney thought of him as an intruder, and he tried to smooth relations by encouraging Kearney to continue to minister to the Italians if he wished, and to receive the children in his parochial schools. However, Kearney continued to administer almost all the sacraments, and in the process, "[h]e is taking the very bread from us," getting stipends Russo needed to pay the rent. Russo carefully denied that he thought Kearney was after stipends alone: "I feel he is not prompted to act for the sake of money. Such an idea did not even come to my mind. There is probably something else at the bottom of all that, which *will have to come out* to light sooner or later."[22]

The stipends could not have been worth the fight. Russo wrote of his adult parishioners: "We were oftentimes received with the coldest indifference: not seldom avoided, at times we were greeted with insulting remarks."[23] The only entry to some families was through their children, and the staff of Our Lady of Loreto devoted their best efforts to this most malleable sector of the population.

Contemporaries criticized Italians for not sending their children to parochial school, but Russo attracted two hundred children to the six-room school in Loreto's basement. Not many stayed, "as much was said against our keeping the children in dark rooms without ventilation, using only gaslight, *etc.*"[24] When two houses adjoining Loreto were offered for sale, Russo bought them for a school, which opened in October, 1895. In 1898, a rear building was reconstructed and the school divided into girls' and boys' departments.[25]

Nineteenth- and early twentieth-century American parishes met the spiritual-social needs of their congregations by encouraging men, women, and children to attend sodalities appropriate to their age and sex. Our Lady of Loreto sponsored a Holy Rosary Society for men, a Holy

---

[21]*Ibid.*, p. 140.

[22]Russo to Corrigan, October 24, 1891, AANY microfilm reel #14.

[23]Russo, "Origin and Progress," p. 139.

[24]*Ibid.*, p. 141.

[25]*A Short History of the Mission of Our Lady of Loretto* [sic], *303 Elizabeth Street, New York, for Italians of the Lower East Side, by Some of the Boys: Souvenir of the Silver Jubilee, 1916* (New York, 1916), p. 4.

Rosary and a Saint Fortunata Society for women, and a Sodality of the Sacred Heart, a popular Jesuit devotion. A Saint Aloysius Club was established for the boys. When the club, and some of the boys, got too big, a separate Loreto Club was organized for the young men. Russo took particular interest in the little boys, meeting with them Saturdays from ten to noon for crafts, games, and dramatics.[26]

While Our Lady of Loreto developed into an American parish, albeit Italian-speaking, Jesuit-run, and with national rather than territorial boundaries, Saint Patrick's suffered a population crisis. In 1891, the parish had 996 baptisms: 271 in non-Italian families, 721 in Italian families, and 4 of persons whose family background is unclear. The next year, the first full year of operation for Loreto, the figures were 234 total, 182 non-Italians, 47 Italians, and 5 unknown. Non-Italians continued to move out of the area; by 1897 the baptismal figures were 97 total, 63 non-Italians, and 34 Italians.[27] Early in 1898, Kearney took steps to continue Saint Patrick's ministry in its community. He revived the Italian apostolate.[28]

221

Russo wrote Corrigan twice about this question of justice. The Italians were removed from Kearney's jurisdiction at Kearney's request and given to the Jesuits, whose commitment could be measured not only in work, but in the $60,000 invested so far in the church and school. The mission still was not self-supporting; Russo had had to borrow $2,000 in January, 1898, to meet current expenses. Now he was threatened by the fine church, convenient location, flourishing parochial schools, and debt-free condition of Saint Patrick's. Despite Russo's protests, the Italians remained welcome at Saint Patrick's. When Kearney died in his rectory in 1923, three of his four curates and most of his parishioners were Italian-American.[29]

Russo died April 1, 1902. According to a recent historian, Stephen DiGiovanni, the Jesuits intended to send a Neapolitan Jesuit, then working in the Rocky Mountains, to succeed him, but had to divert the Neapolitan to another mission. Instead, in July, 1903, forty-eight-year-old, New York-born William H. Walsh, S.J., came to Loreto. Walsh maintained that he was appointed shortly after Russo died, but his duties at Saint Andrew-on-Hudson kept him from immediately assuming the post.[30]

---

[26]"Father Nicholas Russo," p. 284.

[27]Saint Patrick's Old Cathedral, New York, Baptismal Register, 1879-1901.

[28]Russo to Corrigan, February 22 and 24, 1898, CMS:IAR:I:1, Loreto folder.

[29]New York *Times*, April 12, 1923, p. 19, col. 5.

[30]DiGiovanni, *op. cit*, pp. 352-353; William H. Walsh, S.J., to Father Provincial, March 17, 1942, Archives of the New York Province of the Society of Jesus, Nativity, 1933-1947, folder.

After Walsh had established himself at Loreto, a report came from the mission that characterized the adult Italians as "unresponsive to religious influences, distrustful of the church, and careless about the great obligations, Mass, Easter Communion, Friday abstinence," and the children as ignorant of basic prayers.[31] This was harsher language than Russo would have used. If the situation was viewed as more troublesome, the solution was applied more vigorously. Russo had been interested in the neighborhood boys; under Walsh, Loreto's ministry to Italians became a ministry to youth.

222

Walsh appointed Miss Louise Rossi, a Frenchwoman, principal of the boys' department of the parochial school in 1905. Miss Rossi also directed the boys' choir, which sang at all church functions and at annual entertainments for the mission's "American friends." Male Loreto graduates went to the Jesuit Saint Francis Xavier High School on West 16th Street to prepare for Fordham University. Walsh provided a study hall for the high school (or "college") boys, and play space for the grammar school. All the boys joined him in evening prayers. During the summer, Walsh moved to Monroe, New York, where groups of parochial and Sunday school boys came for two weeks of fresh air. Such attention encouraged at least ten young men in their Jesuit vocations.[32]

The devotional life of these young Italian-Americans did not focus on the traditional Italian saints. Walsh was the promoter of a devotion to the Boy Savior, the young manhood of Jesus. After he left the Italian mission he worked full time to popularize this devotion in Jesuit schools.[33]

The girls' department of the parochial school was given to the Sisters of Jesus and Mary. Walsh directed that children of both sexes should not be withdrawn from parochial school after First Communion, but should complete the academic course, and the teaching staff of the girls' school

Hereafter cited as "NYSJ." Access to these archives was provided by Brother Eugene Dowling, S.J., and the Reverend Louis Mounteer, S.J.

[31]"Our Church for the Italians," *Woodstock Letters*, XXXIV (1905), 449.

[32]*Short History*, pp. 6-8; William H. Walsh, S.J., "A Rambling Bit of History about the Jesuit Italian Mission and the Barat Settlement" (unpublished ms., 1942), n.p., NYSJ: Nativity, 1933-1947.

[33]Walsh to Father Provincial, March 17, 1942, *ibid.* Most Jesuits addressed their superior simply as "Father Provincial" in their letters, and this has been retained in the footnotes. However, the Fathers Provincial were: Joseph H. Rockwell (July 31, 1918-June 23, 1922), Laurence J. Kelly (June 23, 1922-September 12, 1928), Edward C. Phillips (September 12, 1928-August 28, 1935), Joseph A. Murphy (August 28, 1935-October 7, 1939), James P. Sweeney (October 7, 1939-October 30, 1945), Francis A. McQuade (October 30, 1945-March 4, 1948), and John J. McMahon (March 4, 1948-June 25, 1954).

increased accordingly. Miss Magdalen Bernan supervised a sodality for public school girls. The Children of Mary of Manhattanville, alumnae of the Mesdames of the Sacred Heart Academy, conducted a sewing school on East Houston Street, and invited the girls to their country houses for day trips in the summer.[34] In 1912 the house which the Children of Mary had been renting was sold. Walsh used donations to the Jesuits to purchase a house on Chrystie Street, east of the Bowery, which he rented to the women for a new, larger project: the Barat Settlement House and Day Nursery.[35]

Walsh himself spent more time east of the Bowery after 1906, catechizing youths in a former barber shop on Stanton Street.[36] Saint Patrick's, once it committed itself to the Italians, had the resources to conduct a mission among them. Nativity, one block east of the Bowery on Second Avenue, did not. The Christian Brothers ran LaSalle Academy next door to its rectory, but Nativity had no parochial school. It depended on entertainments and fund-raisers to meet its current expenses. A pastor who had been a near-invalid for many years had been succeeded by one whose shyness had the same effect on parish leadership.[37] The parish did attempt to comply with Archbishop Farley's request that it minister to the Italians in the area; nevertheless there was a void and Walsh filled it. As the situation west of the Bowery grew more stable and the need to the east more pressing, Walsh asked the archdiocese for facilities east of the Bowery from which to conduct his work. In May, 1917, he found himself with Nativity. Although what Farley had done was to give the Jesuits Nativity in exchange for Loreto, a diocesan priest was not assigned to Loreto for another two years. During that time Walsh was in charge of the mission and the parish, the parochial school at Loreto, and the summer camp at Monroe.[38]

Walsh collapsed suddenly in July, 1919. Although he recovered and lived to be ninety, he did not return to Nativity. Instead, Daniel Quinn, S.J., a fifty-four-year-old New Yorker who had been in charge of Loreto boys' school between Russo's and Walsh's pastorates, came down from Saint Ignatius Loyola on Park Avenue to Nativity.

[34]"Our Church for the Italians," p. 449.
[35]"Report of Father Zwinge" (provincial procurator), typescript, January 22, 1913, NYSJ: Loretto [sic]-Nativity.
[36]"Our Church for the Italians," loc. cit.
[37]Dominic Cirigliano, S.J., "Jottings on the History of Nativity Church in Preparation for the Centenary Celebration of 1942," NYSJ: History of Nativity Parish, 1842-1917; Bernard J. Reilly to Walsh, January 20, 1926, NYSJ: Nativity, 1922-1932.
[38]Correspondence from Walsh during January and February, 1917, in NYSJ: Loreto-Nativity, might suggest Walsh engineered the exchange. However, as early as 1893, Corrigan was

Quinn was appalled by the situation in his new parish. Two of his Italian assistants left soon after he came; the remaining two were elderly and ailing. The school was unfit for occupation and was closed September, 1919. The financial records were in disarray, the only certainties being mortgages on the Barat Settlement and on the summer camp at Monroe, and a debt for the newly renovated Nativity rectory. A secular priest finally came to Loreto in November, 1919, but it took another year to finalize the exchange. The few Irish left at Nativity resented the Jesuits and their Italian apostolate.[39]

Although he had admired Walsh's work from afar, Quinn the pastor thought the boys' ministry had been allowed to dominate and distort parish life. Fresh-air camps were expensive; Monroe was particularly extravagant. After Walsh's departure, Miss Rossi ran the summer camp "without a single reference to me," Quinn complained to his superior. Along with the practicality and propriety, Quinn questioned the philosophy: "All the uplift schemes now so popular are protestantizing and pauperizing in their effects. Better to teach our people ... that the 'way of the Cross' leads to glory."[40]

If Quinn doubted the wisdom of a special program for youth, he doubted the feasibility of an Italian ministry even more. "[N]othing short of a miracle of grace will bring them [Italians] to the Church they hate and curse."[41] Quinn was afraid that the Italians would never contribute enough to keep Nativity solvent, especially since archdiocesan officials had informed him that Nativity was a regular territorial parish and was expected to be self-supporting.[42] Although he went to some trouble to secure a young and energetic Italian-American assistant, Dominic Cirigliano, and although he thought that "Father Ciri" was an excellent curate,[43] Quinn doubted he would make a good pastor for Nativity; he was too concerned to "italianize" the parish. For Quinn, the solution lay not in any special program devoted to the Italians, but in organizing the parish as all other parishes were organized: "The only results we get are

---

looking for a territorial parish to give the Jesuits for their Italian work: Thomas Campbell to Corrigan, November 6, 1893, AANY microfilm reel #5.

[39]Daniel A. Quinn, S.J., to Father Provincial, August 21, October 1, 20, and 29, November 1, and December 1, 1919, NYSJ: Loretto-Nativity; Joseph H. Fargis to Joseph H. Rockwell, S.J., September 20, 1920. Quinn was not the first to complain of Walsh's record-keeping style; see "Report of Father Zwinge," typescripts dated January 22, 1913, and May, 1914, and Zwinge to Rockwell, November 10, 1918, *ibid.*

[40]Quinn to Father Provincial, October 13, 1920, *ibid.*

[41]*Ibid.*

[42]Quinn to Father Provincial, October 29, 1919, *ibid.*

[43]Quinn to Father Provincial, September 22, 1920, *ibid.*

obtained by a quiet and faithful attention to ordinary parish duties—solidifying and unifying the congregation, preaching the gospel, and administering the sacraments.[44]

Judged by the standards of his letters, Quinn was a conscientious pastor. The parish had its Irish nights and its spaghetti dinners, but Quinn was more concerned with scheduling regular Italian and English recitations of the rosary, Holy Hours, First Fridays, and Benedictions. The Holy Name Society survived from pre-Jesuit days, but Quinn organized new sodalities for women and young people, including a new club for young men. Although he never contemplated opening a school, Quinn attended to Christian education: the children displaced by the closing of Loreto were admitted to Saint Patrick's, and the Barat Settlement, which stayed at Christie Street rent-free because Quinn could not discern from the financial records why the women should pay, continued to catechize the public school children. Gradually the parish, as Quinn described it, "solidified."[45]

Transfers for 1922 sent Quinn to Philadelphia and brought fifty-six-year-old Patrick F. Quinnan to Nativity for five years. Quinnan's one extended comment on his parishioners came twenty years after his pastorate, but nostalgia alone does not account for his remembrance of them as "lovable, kind-hearted, and deeply appreciative of our interest in them," and at least as generous as their co-religionists in neighboring parishes.[46]

One reason for Quinnan's sanguine characterization of his parishioners lay in his own relaxed personality. Quinnan was more amenable to the Italians' suggestions for special devotions than Quinn had been, and less insistent that they observe Irish-American standards in matters such as times for baptism, marriage, and confession. Dominic Cirigliano, curate to both men, wrote that while Quinn neglected the Italians in favor of the English-speaking congregation, Quinnan favored the Italians and neglected the English.[47]

225

---

[44]Quinn to Father Provincial, October 13, 1920, *ibid.* It is only fair to point out that this is the only letter in which Quinn was really critical of his parishioners, and he sent a great many letters to his Father Provincial in his three years at Nativity.

[45]Quinn to Father Provincial, August 21, 1919, October 29, 1919, March 3 and 19, 1920, September 10, 1920, and October 13, 1920, *ibid.*; William H. Walsh, "Some Remarks on the Ownership of the Chrystie Street Property," July 22, 1922 (typescript), *ibid.*

[46]Patrick F. Quinnan, S.J., to Father Provincial, December 19, 1947, NYSJ: Nativity, 1933-1947.

[47]Dominic Cirigliano, S.J., to Father Provincial, January 4, 1924, NYSJ: Nativity, 1922-1932.

Secondly, Quinnan's congregation was more stable than those of his predecessors. Quotas restricted the influx of Italians. Without new arrivals to accommodate, the parish could concentrate on those who had been in the country long enough to acclimate themselves to American pious customs. For example, one of Quinnan's biggest projects was to organize a multi-parish procession, not for an Italian patron saint and not composed of Italian mutual benefit societies, but for Holy Name Sunday, and composed of the Italian Holy Name Societies.[48]

Finally, the people of Nativity were somewhat more prosperous in the 1920's than they had been in the era of mass migration before World War I, and Quinnan could treat them as having middle-class standards and expectations for themselves and their children. Quinnan's youth ministry supplies some examples of this attitude in action.

Unlike Quinn, Quinnan regarded summer camps as a necessity, especially in the face of similar, Protestant-run, efforts. He reopened Monroe the same summer he took over Nativity. However, the most important institution for the Americanization of children, and of the parish, was a parochial school. Quinnan's first chance to acquire a school came in 1923, when the Christian Brothers suggested they might close LaSalle Academy. Quinnan was ready to buy, even to assume a mortgage: "[The parishioners] can pay for this building and I think it would make them better Catholics, strengthen them in their faith and get into their hearts a greater devotion to the church if they felt they were bound in conscience to make this sacrifice for the Christian education of their children."[49] The Christian Brothers did not sell, and Quinnan, unable to get a school, turned to trying to get an alternative.

Nativity had use of Public School 63 for its Bellarmine Boys Clubs, the 1920's incarnation of the boys' work done by Quinn, Walsh, and Russo. In September, 1925, Quinnan received permission to use P.S. 91 for girls' work, and began searching for a community of sisters to do the work, and a place to house the sisters. (Nativity already had several Immaculate Heart of Mary sisters serving as catechists, office help, sacristans, and choristers, but the rules of their order did not allow full-time social and recreation work.) Quinnan bought a tenement on Forsythe Street, five blocks from Nativity, late in 1925 or early in 1926. Late in 1926 he opened negotiations with the Mission Helpers of the Sacred Heart, but not until October, 1927, did the sisters begin their work in the parish.[50]

[48]Thomas J. Reilly, S.J., to Father Provincial, April 26, 1925, *ibid.*
[49]Quinnan to Father Provincial, June 9, 1923, *ibid.*
[50]Quinnan to Cardinal Hayes, July 6, 1925, *ibid.*; Quinnan to Father Provincial, September 15, 1925, February 10, October 2, and December 14, 1926, *ibid.*; Cirigliano to Father Provincial, October 8, 1927, and March 26, 1928, *ibid.*

The Barat Settlement had long been providing Nativity with the same services as Quinnan sought from the Mission Helpers. Shortly after Quinnan took office, the Barat Settlement, Inc., prodded the Jesuits to try to determine whether the Society or Nativity actually owned the Chrystie Street property. Barat hoped to buy the two tenements it was then using and to get Catholic Charities funds to remodel, expand, and update their recreational facilities. They also wanted to abandon their day nursery in favor of more catechetical work. The Jesuit provincial superior encouraged the Barat women in their project, but Quinnan had a different perspective on settlement work: "Settlement houses do some good in a parish but it [sic] . . . . cannot take the place of a parochial school, where devoted religious women are with children day after day." The Barat women, he wrote,

227

> . . . took up this work in a missionary spirit and principally among neglected children. The parishioners in general in Nativity took good care of their children and desired and expected more from the Church than that which a settlement house could give.[51]

Between 1912 and the 1920's the Jesuits' Italian mission had become a parish, and a parish was expected to provide its own parochial school, or at least Sunday school, and not to rely on volunteer, extra-parochial help.[52]

Quinnan was transferred in 1927. From then until 1952 Nativity was in the hands of Italian-American men raised in contact with the Jesuits at Loreto or Nativity. Dominic Cirigliano (pastor 1927-1933, 1937-1940) had been born in Potenza but brought up around Nicholas Russo at Loreto; he had been curate to all Jesuit pastors at Nativity. Sante Catalano (1933-1937) was another Loreto alumnus and had been curate to Cirigliano. Anthony DeMaria (1940-1946) was the first Nativity-born Jesuit pastor, and had been curate during Cirigliano's second term. Francis Doino (1946-1952) had grown up in Nativity but had served in the Philippines prior to becoming pastor.[53]

During this period the *italianità* of Nativity was a little more apparent. A local mutual benefit society dedicated to San Gondolfo asked, for the first time, to celebrate its *festa* at Nativity, so as to have a curate there, who had written a life of the saint, deliver the panegyric.[54] The assistants requested Italian newspapers to sharpen their language skills,[55] and it was still important that everyone assigned to the parish have at least a

[51]Quinnan to Father Provincial, December 19, 1947, NYSJ: Nativity, 1933-1947.
[52]*Ibid.*
[53]*Church of the Nativity, New York City* (South Hackensack, New Jersey, 1971), pp. 6-7.
[54]Sante Catalano, S.J., to Father Provincial, August 17, 1933, NYSJ: Nativity, 1933-1947.
[55]Anthony Russo-Alesi, S.J., to Father Provincial, January 20, 1943, *ibid.*

Berlitz-course understanding of Italian.[56] After World War II Nativity hosted Italian priests touring the United States on behalf of charities in the homeland.[57]

The Italianisms still evident at Nativity, however, were not conscious preservations of a heritage but a *mélange* of customs suited to a particular local situation. For example, when one Italian-American curate accused the Italian-American pastor of insensitivity to the Italian custom of getting married late Saturday afternoon, the other Italian-American curate described the same matter without using the word "Italian": couples wanted to get married late in the day in order to go immediately to a local hall for an evening reception, but the pastor thought Saturday afternoon a better time to schedule confessions.[58]

Parish life at Nativity in the 1930's and 1940's was lively, and not particularly Italian. Despite the revival of efforts to schedule sacraments, confessions, baptisms, and weddings took place at all hours.[59] Holy Hours twice a week, once in Italian and once in English, gave way to Miraculous Medal novenas thrice weekly, twice in English and once in Italian.[60] After 1949 a new devotion, to Mary, Mediatrix of All Graces, was introduced.[61] The preacher for the San Gondolfo *festa* continued William Walsh's work as promoter of the Boy Savior devotion.[62] When Nativity church was redecorated, the pastor added not statues of Italian saints, but statues of Jesuit saints, the Sacred Heart, and the patrons of youth.[63]

At the rectory choirs rehearsed, committees met, and sodalities gathered. The young boys had a Scout troop and a Catholic Youth Organization, the adolescents a Barat Catholic Club and Catholic Action Club, the family men their Holy Name Society, and the women their Sodality of Our Lady.[64] Co-education entered the parish through weekly cate-

228

[56]Francis A. McQuade, S.J., to Anthony DeMaria, S.J., December 2, 1945, *ibid*.

[57]Francis Doino, S.J., to Father Provincial, July 9, 1947, *ibid*.

[58]Russo-Alesi to Father Provincial, March 15, 1944, *ibid.*; George P. Barbera, S.J., to Father Provincial, May 12, 1944, *ibid.*; DeMaria to Father Provincial, September 21, 1944, *ibid*.

[59]DeMaria to Father Provincial, February 20, 1940, *ibid*.

[60]DeMaria to Father Provincial, August 1, 1938, *ibid*.

[61]Doino to John J. McMahon, November 25, 1949, NYSJ: Nativity, 1948-1959.

[62]Doino to Father Provincial, September 4, 1947, NYSJ: Nativity, 1933-1947.

[63]Cirigliano to Father Provincial, May 16, 1938, *ibid.* Unfortunately, the church is no longer standing. In 1963 it was discovered that a 1912 fire had caused such structural damage as to preclude major renovations; the building was torn down and replaced instead. Descriptions and photographs of the original church are on file at New York City Landmarks Commission, Church of the Nativity folder.

[64]Gabriel Zema, S.J., to Father Provincial, June 16, 1934, NYSJ: Nativity, 1933-1947; DeMaria to Father Provincial, August 1, 1938, *ibid*.

chetical-social evenings, in addition to Sunday school for the youngsters. Adolescents met each other at the rectory and beggars came to the door, much to the consternation of those Jesuits (and their superiors) who tried to make time and room for community life.[65]

Parish social life included dances, raffles, movies,[66] and the summer camp at Monroe, which by 1938 accepted girls as well as boys.[67] Perhaps the Jesuits had expanded their concept of their ministry to youth; it is also true that in the early years the parents still followed the Italian custom of carefully supervising their daughters and keeping them close to home.

One of its priests described Nativity as "poor" but "financially stable."[68] Dominic Cirigliano and Anthony DeMaria renovated the sanctuary during their pastorates, and DeMaria made improvements in the rectory in 1944; yet whatever debts may have been contracted for repairs were cancelled by 1946.[69] Although Nativity never did open a parochial school in this era, another attempt was made in 1947, a sign that the pastor, at least, thought the parish could stand a major new expense.[70]

Nativity's own finances are not an adequate clue to the declining fortunes of the Bowery in the 1940's. One could measure the decreasing income of the neighborhood by the increasing number of panhandlers at the rectory door, or one could count the abandoned buildings, including the Barat Settlement. Most obvious was the depopulation. The First Communion class of 1942 was "the smallest so far."[71] Attendance at Mass and devotions dropped. The priests blamed their own community for not bringing in the congregation as of old, but also realized that many parishioners had moved to Corona, Astoria, or Coney Island.[72]

Other parishes have retained their Italian identity, partly because they are in the remnants of New York's Little Italies, and partly because the priests and laity have made attempts to maintain their heritage through *feste* or by being the American shrine of an Italian saint. The Jesuits of Loreto and Nativity had other goals. Even Nicholas Russo had

[65]Visitation Memorial, March 31, 1939, *ibid.*
[66]DeMaria to Father Provincial, February 16, 1939, *ibid.*
[67]DeMaria to Father Provincial, August 1, 1939, *ibid.*
[68]Barbera to Father Provincial, August 25, 1947, *ibid.*
[69]Cirigliano to Father Provincial, May 16, 1938, *ibid.*; James P. Sweeney to DeMaria, January 2, 1944, *ibid.*
[70]"Statement of Financial Condition, December 31, 1946," and attached papers, *ibid.*
[71]Barbera to Father Provincial, July 21, 1943, *ibid.*
[72]Barbera to Father Provincial, January 27, 1943, *ibid.*

not planned to preserve Italian culture. His charge that the Italians had been neglected in this country referred not to the appreciation of their style of Catholicism, but to the lack of priests who had the language skills and sympathy necessary to try to capture the Italians' affections for the Church in this country. Russo concentrated on winning the loyalties of the children, and he used American methods, such as parochial schools.

Walsh and Quinn did not have Russo's sympathies, but they shared his goals. Walsh attempted to bind the affections of the young to the Church. Quinn was more concerned to create a well-regulated, self-supporting parish. Quinnan, while less critical of the Italians, measured the health of their parish by its ability to buy a parochial school or, barring that, to pay its sister-catechists. All three pastors used non-Italian means: Jesuit saints, parochial schools, and an insistence on regularity, order, and community support of the parish.

Cirigliano, Catalano, DeMaria, and Doino were the success stories of the Loreto-Nativity mission. Their pastorates showed how well they had absorbed their elders' assumptions and methods. Their goal was to bind the people to the larger Church through the local parish. Proof of this binding was the disciplined congregation that acted according to accepted standards: attending to sacraments and services, contributing to the church, and raising the children in the faith. The ties that bound were the sacraments, devotions, sodalities, and a bit of social life. For the children, the ties included catechesis, a social-recreational program that protected them from unwholesome influences, and, ideally, a school.

The Italian-American Jesuits learned their lessons so well that they applied them to the new ethnic minority replacing the Italians east of the Bowery. In February, 1952, Francis Doino called his superiors' attention to the many Puerto Ricans in the area and to the dangers of failing to bring them into the parish:

> In our endeavor to get interracial justice we cannot afford to neglect or by-pass this very large portion of our own Catholic vineyard. If we lose these already baptized Catholics to the Church our enemies will surely welcome their immense numbers.[73]

The latter part of this statement is reminiscent of earlier Loreto and Nativity priests worrying about Protestant missionaries (which were probably Doino's concern, too). The reference to "interracial justice" is new, and indicates new trends of thought that would guide Nativity's subsequent Hispanic mission.

[73]Doino to McMahon, February 7, 1952, NYSJ: Nativity, 1948-1959.

The Indiana Churches and the Italian Immigrant, 1890–1935

by James J. Divita

The Italian Catholic of the late nineteenth and early twentieth centuries found it difficult to reconcile love of God and country. Unlike the Irishman and Pole who identified Church membership with patriotism, the Italian perceived an antagonism between religious commitment and national loyalty. The head of the Church was one of several princes in the peninsula who ordinarily opposed the major goal of nationalism: the political unification of Italy. When the Sardinian government unified the country and ended papal temporal sovereignty (1859–1870), the popes decreed that no Catholic in good standing could participate in Italian political life. Consequently, in a country which according to the 1901 census was 97.1% Catholic, the national government was anti-clerical and hostile to religion.

Italians were attracted to Indiana to work in its coal mines and gas fields, in its produce markets, on its railroads, and in its stone quarries, mills, and factories. In 1890, 468 Italians resided in the state; in 1930 the federal census reported 16,536 Hoosiers of Italian background, primarily residing in Lake, Marion, Vermillion, St. Joseph, and Elkhart counties. Between 1899 and 1914, almost 3,500 northern Italians and over 5,000 southern Italians entered the United States with Indiana their announced destination.[1] The northerner, living longer under anti-clerical government

---

1. For population statistics, see U.S. Secretary of the Interior, *The Statistics of the Population of the United States, Ninth Census* (Washington, 1872), I, 341; and U.S. Department of Commerce, Bureau of the Census, *Fifteenth Census of the United States: 1930* (Washington, 1932–33), II, 273, and III, 720–723. For immigration figures, see U.S. Bureau of Immigration and Naturalization, *Annual Report of the Commissioner-General of Immigration* (Washington), 1899–1914 editions.

or foreign domination than his southern brother, brought a religious indifference easily fanned into violent anti-clericalism. The southerner
brought with him his town's patron saint whose public veneration, called
festa in Italian, was a unique combination of secular carnival, familial
loyalty, and religious excess. Although others strongly criticized the *festa,*
southerners viewed it as indispensable for obtaining spiritual favors through
the saint's intercession.

The clergy did not play a major role in the Italian's spiritual cosmos.
The priest celebrated Mass preceding the procession of the sacred statue
or picture through the streets, but the organizational and financial responsibilities for the *festa* were always in the hands of the independent lay
committee. When Italian Inspector of Foreign Emigration G. E. Di
Palma-Castiglione reported on the situation in Clinton, Indiana, and other
midwestern towns in 1915, he concluded that the priest enjoyed little
status among his countrymen.[2] Generally Italians feared the priest more
than they respected him, for he could withhold his spiritual services at the
three important moments in the life cycle—baptism, marriage, and burial.
Observing this attitude, a Logansport pastor born in Mishawaka termed it
the "hatch, match, and dispatch" syndrome. Immigrants, moreover, were
quick to charge the clergy with greed, hypocrisy, or sexual peccadillos.[3]
Yet Italian clerics in Indianapolis, Gary, and East Chicago were influential, but this influence seems to have resulted more from the priest's personality and leadership qualities than because of his office.

Italians ordinarily had little regard for theology and were uninterested
in the Church's life. Neither attending Mass nor giving financial support
was a personal concern. In northern Italy the government nationalized
church property after 1850 and the Church survived; in southern Italy the
landowner maintained the church and supported the priest, who was
viewed as the landowner's man. Italians believed that the Church had
always existed and ordinary people were not obliged to support it.

With these notions on Church, saints, clergy, finances, and personal
practice long nurtured in their homeland, Italian immigrants found the
Catholic Church in Indiana strange indeed. Clergy of Irish and German
origin demanded regular Mass attendance and reception of sacraments,

---

2. G. E. Di Palma-Castiglione, "Vari Centri Italiani negli Stati di Indiana, Ohio, Michigan, Minnesota e Wisconsin," in Italy Ministero degli Affari esteri, Commissariato dell'Emigrazione, *Bollet-
tino dell'Emigrazione,* 15 June 1915, 36.

3. Interview with Reverend Fred Schroeder of St. Joseph's parish, Logansport, 15 October 1982.
Italian interviewees frequently relate stories about the sexual misconduct of an Italian priest in East
Chicago and another in Elkhart. No diocesan archival documentation has been located even to raise
suspicion about these two priests.

James J. Divita

financial contributions, and respect for clergy as signs of religious commitment. Some priests refused to baptize babies if they knew that the parents did not practice their religion.[4] Pastors in Clinton, Diamond, Bedford, and Elkhart all complained to their bishops that Italians did not perform ordinary religious duties. When the pastor of St. Vincent's parish in Elkhart announced that he would not baptize an infant if its parents did not enroll their older children in the Catholic school, Italian parents sometimes circumvented his policy by boarding a train for Chicago to present the newborn child at an Italian church there.[5]

The bishops of the two Indiana dioceses at the time were Francis Silas Chatard of Indianapolis (1878–1918) and Herman Joseph Alerding of Fort Wayne (1900–1924). For twenty years resident in Rome first as a student and ultimately as rector of North American College, Chatard spoke Italian and sometimes arranged baptisms for Italians at St. John's

---

4. Bishop H. J. Alerding of Fort Wayne to Reverend F. Thos. Jansen of Gary, 26 May 1910, advised pastor to baptize the child in return for parents receiving sacraments. Letter in Fort Wayne Diocesan Archives (hereafter cited as FtWDA).

5. In Alerding to Reverend F. J. Jansen of Elkhart, 6 October 1910, the bishop reported the response of Archbishop James E. Quigley of Chicago to the pastor's charge that Italian clergy and laity in Chicago were lax. FtWDA. For Jansen's account of how he forced Italian children to attend his school, see his memoirs entitled *Souvenir of the Golden Sacerdotal Jubilee of the Right Reverend Monsignor F. J. Jansen,* published at Hammond in 1948,11–12. Also see parish reports for Clinton (1899, 1901, 1903), Diamond (during pastorate of Reverend Michael Seter, 1904–10), and Bedford (1909) in the Indianapolis Archdiocesan Archives (hereafter cited as IAA).

Francis S. Chatard, Bishop of Indianapolis, 1878–1918, a former rector of the North American College in Rome, was particularly concerned about the fate of Italian-Americans.

in downtown Indianapolis.[6] Yet at the Third Plenary Baltimore Council he favored the substitution of a general statement on immigrants for one which specifically addressed the religious needs of Italian immigrants.[7] He was devoted to Rome and always loyal to papal temporal pretensions. Eight years before arriving in Indiana, Chatard had written Pope Pius IX offering to arm his seminarians to fight Italians intent on unification.[8] In 1892 he complained to the Archbishop of New York that "Liberal Italians, and infidels" had participated in Indianapolis' Columbus Day parade.[9] Even his cathedral symbolized his loyalty. Built in Roman basilica style, he dedicated it to the great patronal saints of Rome, Peter and Paul, in 1906. Alerding considered immigrants settling in northern Lake

---

6. For example, Chatard signed the baptismal entry of Matilda Teresa Solimano on 30 March 1879.

7. Henry J. Browne, "The 'Italian Problem' in the Catholic Church of the United States, 1880–1900," in U.S. Catholic Historical Society, *Historical Records and Studies*, XXXV (1946): 57–58.

8. Robert F. McNamara, *The American College in Rome, 1855–1955* (Rochester, N.Y., 1956), 187–188.

9. Chatard to Michael Corrigan, 8 November 1892. Notre Dame Archives.

County a troublesome financial burden for his diocese.[10] Elkhart's pastor, a close personal friend of Alerding, once declared that he had found the antidote for Italian religious indifference. "Oh? What is it?" the bishop inquired. "Machine gun all the older people," the astonished bishop was told, "and put the kids in Catholic orphanages."[11] Burdened by the Protestant notion that Catholicism was a foreign institution, the bishops considered submersion of the immigrant in the broader community and his Americanization most desirable goals. Chatard wrote: Nothing could be better for the Italian emigrant, physically, socially, and morally, introducing him gradually into the ways of American life. . . .[12] Although German-born, Alerding was identified as American, his biography in *The Catholic Encyclopedia* reporting his birthplace as the Diocese of Covington, Kentucky, where he was raised.[13] He wrote Judge Elbert H. Gary, board chairman of United States Steel Corporation, that these foreigners "cling each stubbornly to their national traditions and customs. Of course all this will be different when once they have imbibed the American spirit."[14]

235

Although they were well aware of the value of ethnically oriented parishes (German national parishes already existed in many Hoosier towns), the two bishops believed that the small number of Italian immigrants did not call for a special effort to provide for their spiritual welfare. At St. Patrick's parish in Indianapolis, within whose boundaries lived Indiana's largest single permanent concentration of Italians, three assistants who knew Italian were not encouraged to develop a special ministry to these newcomers.[15] At neighboring St. Mary's, a German national parish, where the assistant learned enough Italian to teach catechism, Italian children who attended the parish school were expected to learn German. In Logansport, after complaining to Alerding that St. Vincent's pastor was uninterested in them, some Italians attended the more distant St. Joseph's

10. Alerding's pastoral letter, 8 December 1913, and Alerding to Reverend Riccardo Fantozzi, C.PP.S., 9 April 1919. FtWDA.

11. Interview with Reverend Fred J. Cardinali, first American-born priest of Italian origin among the diocesan clergy of Fort Wayne-South Bend and long-time assistant to Msgr. Francis J. Jansen, the Elkhart pastor quoted here, 16 August 1982.

12. Chatard to Milwaukee *Catholic Citizen,* reprinted in *The Catholic Record* (3 February 1898):1.

13. See 1922 supplement, XVII, 317. Also Charles Blanchard, *The History of the Catholic Church in Indiana* (Logansport, 1898), II, 33.

14. Alerding to E. H. Gary, 10 March 1913. FtWDA.

15. They were Reverend William Maher (1896–1900), later pastor of Sacred Heart, Clinton, who built the permanent church there in 1909; Reverend Raymond Noll (1905–1910) and Reverend William Keefe (1909–1911), both North American College graduates. Keefe was Clinton pastor from 1911 to 1924.

Church and school.[16] In 1912 South Bend Italians complained to Rome that they had no priest to preach or hear confessions in their own language.[17] The bishops simply ignored Italian religious culture and recent history by expecting Italians to join local parishes and conform to existing religious norms.

Then came the Protestants. Between 1908 and 1917, four Protestant missions were established to serve Italians in Indiana. The Methodist Episcopal Church set up an Indianapolis mission, the Presbyterian Church in the USA organized one in Gary and another in Clinton, and the Protestant Episcopal Church established one in Gary. They also wished to Americanize the immigrants, for, as Bishop William Burt, head of the Methodist Church's Italian Mission, informed the 1916 General conference:

> These Italians are all about us, three millions of them, and nearly all accessible to our Christian influence. Their children are to be our future citizens. How can we expect to save our country, our Christian ideals or ourselves and not save them?[18]

Reverend Nicolò Accomando, founder of the Methodist mission in Indianapolis, was a native of Palermo and had probably been a Catholic seminarian. He entered the United States in 1906 and soon threafter undertook Methodist work in Paterson, New Jersey, before arriving in the Hoosier capital. The mission was located near Fletcher Place Methodist Church at the intersection of South Street, Virginia Avenue, and East Street, close to where Sicilian fruit vendors and Calabrian laborers had settled. The Indianapolis work was under the auspices of the "Italian Mission," a special national effort to evangelize Italian immigrants authorized by the Church's General Conference in 1908. The mission stressed Sunday School and sponsored night classes in English.

---

16. Alerding to Messrs. G. Caruso and Company, 16 March 1911. FtWDA. The Italian mutual aid society was founded on 5 March 1910 and named St. Joseph. The pastor of St. Joseph's, a German national parish, blessed the society's banners. *Logansport Pharos-Tribune*, 21 October 1975. On 26 September 1911 Giuseppe Caruso and others incorporated the society with the St. Joseph name, leading to the conclusion that peace between St. Vincent's pastor and the Italians was not forthcoming.

17. Cardinal Gaetano de Lai transmitted this complaint to Alerding in a letter dated 23 December 1912. Alerding responded to de Lai on 21 March 1913 after receiving a report from South Bend that priests of a particular language are always provided when need arises. FtWDA.

18. Edwin Locke, ed., *Journal of the Twenty-seventh Delegated General Conference of the Methodist Episcopal Church Held in Saratoga Springs, New York, May 1–May 29, 1916* (New York, n.d.), 920. Burt was born in England.

237

Italian-Americans were exceptionally loyal and patriotic. Pictured is an Italian-American class at the turn of the century.

Neighborhood House, founded in 1909, was the first Christian settlement house in Gary. Its staff set up a day nursery, provided bathing facilities, conducted classes in sewing, English, and cooking, and sponsored an Italian band. This Presbyterian mission moved to larger quarters at 17th Avenue and Adams Street in 1912. Four years later, Neighborhood House was enlarged to provide space for a chapel, called the Church of Our Savior, where services for Italians and other immigrants were conducted. By 1925, it was estimated that this $75,000 facility was subject to 100,000 visits annually.[19]

Hill Crest Community Center, an Italian mission at 8th and Oak Streets, Clinton, originated in 1910, the brainchild of J. W. Robb, elder in the First Presbyterian Church. Prominent in the business community since 1882, Robb was an officer of the building and loan association, manager of the local paving brick manufacturing plant (second largest in the state), and

---

19. *The Indiana Presbyterian,* December 1925:2.

officer and manager of the local electric power company. Hill Crest's founding minister was Calogero Benedetto Papa, New York lawyer and graduate of the German Theological School in Bloomfield, New Jersey. He founded a fraternal association for men, the Giordano Bruno Society, named after the sixteenth century Neapolitan free thinker. Papa's work was highly regarded:

He dedicates all his intelligence, education, and energy to profit the Italians. . . . He struggles for the progress and the uprightness of his co-nationals, on whom he lavishes help and advice. He is respected by the Americans and is useful to the Italians.[20]

238

Hill Crest would sponsor sewing, woodcraft, and citizenship classes, build the largest church-owned gymnasium in town, and become an extremely popular gathering place for neighborhood youth.

The St. Antonio Episcopal Mission, located at 19th Avenue and Adams Street in Gary, was founded in 1917 by Nicolò Accomando, now an Episcopal priest. He was especially active in Italian club and community affairs and published a newspaper-magazine called *Il Corriere del Popolo Italo-Americano,* renamed *Americans All* in 1924. His magazine published in Italian and English the text of the United States Constitution as well as the questions a judge would ask a candidate for citizenship.[21]

The establishment of these four missions resulted in denominational interaction and called the attention of the Catholic hierarchy to Italian spiritual needs.

Already in summer 1908, Methodist volunteers conducted Bible lessons for Italians settled on Indianapolis's southeast side. Yet when Italian-born Reverend Marino Priori arrived in the diocese in June 1908, Bishop Chatard gave him charge of the Italian limestone quarry workers in Bedford. Then in November the Methodist Home Mission Board formalized the Church's work among Italians by appropriating $700 for an Indianapolis mission[22] and arranging for Accomando to move there. Chatard immediately transferred Priori to Indianapolis and in January 1909 purchased property in the Italian neighborhood.[23] In early May Priori dedicated a frame chapel to Our Lady of the Most Holy Rosary and soon

---

20. *La Fiaccola,* 24 October 1912:4.

21. *Americans All,* November-December 1925:33–35; and December 1925–January 1926:15. The title "Americans All" may have come from the inscription on a very popular 1919 Liberty Loan poster by Howard Chandler Christy.

22. The total appropriation for Italian work that year was $18,490. See Joseph B. Hingeley, ed., *Journal of the Twenty-sixth General Conference of the Methodist Episcopal Church held in Minneapolis, Minnesota, May 1–May 29, 1912* (New York, n.d.), 1555–1556.

23. Deed and abstract in "Holy Rosary Indianapolis" folder, Indianapolis Archdiocesan Business Office.

developed plans for a brick church. "We always informed him," reported one elderly Italian man, retired from the produce business, "that if he demanded too much money from us we'd go join the Methodists." In fact, Methodist statistics revealed that the Indianapolis mission peaked with 72 members and 25 Sunday School students in 1911, the same year that Priori began building his permanent church and launched his fund-raising campaign.[24] Observing this situation, Priori decided to claim Italian youth by organizing a grade school. In early 1912, he roofed over the basement of his church and, to raise funds for his school and to publicize his work, began in 1913 to publish a Catholic paper called *Eternal Light,* its name and cover similar to the name and masthead of the Methodist newspaper *La Fiaccola* (The Torch). Meanwhile, Accomando was succeeded at the Methodist mission by Reverend Luigi Lops, former Catholic priest from Youngstown, Ohio.[25] Lops decided that ritual-ceremony and greater structure would help him preserve his congregation. He filed with the Indiana Secretary of State on 16 November 1912 articles of incorporation for an Old Catholic diocese to be seated in Indianapolis. Lops would be bishop and four Italian signatories would be his counsellors.[26] A desire for familiarity appeared in the new church's official name (American Orthodox Apostolic Old Roman Catholic Church) and in the fact that the inscription on its seal would be in Latin. But Lops's move was stillborn, for by 1914 his congregation dwindled to 32 members and 15 Sunday School students.[27] Lops left Indianapolis and the Methodist ministry for the Episcopal Church, his proposed Old Catholic Diocese an historical curiosity.

In Clinton the Catholic pastor built a permanent church modeled after the cathedral in Thurles, Ireland, his birthplace. Although the church was located some distance away from the Italian neighborhood, he changed the parish name from St. Patrick to an ethnically neutral Sacred Heart in

239

---

24. Interview with Tudie P. Miceli, 5 March 1984. Statistics in *Minutes of the Annual Conferences of the Methodist Episcopal Church* (New York, 1911), 936.

25. Lops was a Pugliese appointed assistant to the ailing pastor of St. Anthony Italian Parish in Youngstown in 1906. When the pastor died, parishioners wanted Lops to succeed him. When the bishop appointed another priest pastor, Lops and his supporters formed St. Rocco's Independent Catholic Church nearby. After a short marriage to a teenage parishioner, Lops lost lay support and joined the Erie Conference of the Methodist Episcopal Church. Facts from James Conrady of Amherst, Ohio, who has done graduate research on the St. Anthony schism. For mention of Lops in the New York area, see Joseph Lackner's essay "Problems with clergy . . ." in this publication, and see Silvano M. Tomasi, *Piety and Power: The Role of the Italian Parishes in the New York Metropolitan Area, 1880–1930* (Staten Island, N.Y., 1975), 151.

26. Original articles of incorporation signed by Lops, Antonio Sciarra (chancellor and secretary), Frank Montesano (treasurer), and Emil D'Erminio, Joseph and Sebastiano Modafferi (counsellors) in Indiana State Archives.

27. *Minutes of the Annual Conferences of the Methodist Episcopal Church* (New York, 1914), 276.

240

Not all Italians were Catholic. The Reverend Nicolo Accomando, born in Palermo, was a Methodist minister engaged in the Italian American missions.

summer 1909 to attract the town's northern Italian coal miners. When he insisted that they attend Mass and contribute regularly to reduce the debt on the new church before he would provide spiritual services, five men attempted to destroy the church with almost a hundred sticks of dynamite in November 1909.[28] Noting this disaffection, Elder Robb proposed at a session meeting in January 1910 the establishment of a Presbyterian mission in the North End, the heart of the Italian neighborhood.[29] He obtained the approval of the Crawfordsville Presbytery for this venture the following July.[30] Then four months later, Sacred Heart's new pastor and Priori from Indianapolis conducted a census of Clinton's Italian population, Priori promising to build a chapel in early spring 1911. The effectiveness of Robb and Papa was evident when it was reported that Priori was

somewhat chagrined to find that his plans were interfered with by an outside religious effort that was entirely uncalled for. However, he sincerely hopes that brotherly love will still continue to guide the efforts of his colaborers in the vineyard of the Lord.[31]

---

28. *The Weekly Clintonian,* 19 November 1909:1.

29. First Presbyterian Church (Clinton), "Minutes of Sessions and Trustees, Register of Communicants, Baptisms, Marriages, and Deaths 1909–35," session meeting of 21 January 1910, p. 8. Clinton United Presbyterian Church archives. The session is the official governing body of a local Presbyterian church.

30. *Clintonian,* 29 July 1910:8.

31. *Ibid.,* 22 November 1910:3. Reverend James Bolin (1909–1911), Maher's successor at Clinton, tried to conciliate Italians and make the parish school attractive to them.

The immediate outcome of this competition was that no Catholic chapel was built in the North End; on 29 October 1911, Presbyterians dedicated their chapel there.

In early 1913, Mother Maria Teresa Tauscher, foundress of the Carmelite Sisters of the Divine Heart of Jesus, requested Bishop Alerding's permission to establish a house in East Chicago.[32] Her community was interested in working with spiritually lukewarm immigrants and in establishing day nurseries. In June the bishop assented to its ministry among the thousands of foreign mill and factory workers in Lake County.[33] These Carmelites had worked with Italians in Germany and Switzerland and maintained their motherhouse at Rocca di Papa, southeast of Rome. They soon strove to counteract religious apathy among East Chicago's southern Italians and to care for the motherless children of working fathers. Then in December Reverend Frederick H. Wright, superintendent of the Methodist Italian Mission, visited East Chicago. "From what we saw we were convinced that a good opportunity is afforded for an Italian Mission in that vicinity."[34] He raised $1,200 from local and national sources. Fearful that Catholic children would be sent to the nearby Methodist home, the Carmelites enlarged their facilities in 1914.[35] Stepping up their spiritual services, they brought the first Italian priest to East Chicago. He lived in the heart of the Italian district and earned his keep by serving as their chaplain. The Sisters engendered such religious enthusiasm that forty-five Italians signed a petition asking Alerding for their own church and promised that they would support the priest financially if he stayed in East Chicago.[36] After he resigned for health reasons in summer 1915, the Carmelites welcomed Riccardo Fantozzi, C.PP.S., and Ottavio Zavatta (Ciavatta), C.PP.S., recently expelled from the Mexican missions. The Italian Precious Blood Fathers staffed Sacred Heart Mission for their compatriots in a storefront building near 148th Street and Tod Avenue.

East Chicago Italians were stunned when Zavatta announced in 1927 his decision to close the mission and return to Italy. In the past few years he had spent much time organizing the Mexican parish in Indiana Harbor

241

---

32. Alerding to Mother Maria Teresa, 28 April 1913, informed her that a final decision on permission to establish a house had to await the diocesan consultor's meeting in June. FtWDA.

33. Alerding to Mother Maria Teresa, 7 June 1913. FtWDA.

34. Superintendent's notes in *La Fiaccola*, 25 December 1913:1

35. Mother Mary Teresa of St. Joseph, *An Autobiography* (Wauwatosa, Wisconsin, 1953), 199–200.

36. The priest was Reverend Giulio Boffa, on leave from the Archdiocese of Conza outside Naples. His credentials as well as this petition in FtWDA.

(now part of East Chicago), but no one predicted that the Precious Blood Fathers would completely abandon East Chicago.[37] For the next six years Italians either heard Mass at nearby Irish and Polish parishes or became spiritually apathetic again. Since national parishes served other ethnic groups and their community pride suffered without their own church, East Chicago Italian leaders traveled to distant Fort Wayne to petition Bishop John F. Noll (Alerding's successor) to send them a priest.[38] Italian-born Reverend Michael A. Campagna, a canon lawyer who had just completed his Rome studies, admitted that Noll sent him to East Chicago in 1933 to fulfill his promise to the leaders, fully expecting that the founding of an Italian parish during the Depression was financially impossible.[39] But Campagna's personal magnetism and consequent high church attendance persuaded Noll to appoint Campagna founding pastor of Immaculate Conception parish.[40] Salvaging bricks from city streets and an abandoned brick yard and utilizing the labor of unemployed masons and parishioners, Campagna completed the church and hall in 1935. Together with Holy Rosary parish in Indianapolis, Immaculate Conception remains today one of the two Italian national parishes in Indiana.

242

Neighboring Gary, founded by the United States Steel Corporation in 1906, attracted Italians to its mill and railroad jobs. Alerding appointed Italian-born Reverend John Baptist de Ville to Gary in 1911 at the time of the expansion of Neighborhood House, but in the following year he was transferred to Huntington to serve as assistant editor of the new *Our Sunday Visitor*. After his departure Mother Maria Teresa rented a store at 15th Avenue and Madison Street and recruited Italian priests to minister there.[41] When informed that none of them was successful in raising funds for a permanent church, Alerding called Italians "not the better class" and concluded that God would give a greater reward to those who ministered to Italians because their efforts "are done without any appreciation on the part of these people."[42] The bishop then encouraged the use of threat to induce generosity.

---

37. Zavatta found a Mexican priest to succeed him in Indiana Harbor and possibly viewed his Italian work in East Chicago as without promise. Within a year after returning to Italy, he was appointed provincial and then elected vice moderator general of the Congregation of the Most Precious Blood. Biographical data from Reverend Andrew J. Pollack, archivist at the Precious Blood Generalate in Rome. Probably Zavatta's departure from East Chicago related to his own personal ambitions and to the financial condition of his religious community.

38. Michael A. Campagna, *A Little Love* (n.p., 1972), 31.

39. *Ibid.*, 32.

40. *Ibid.*, 35.

41. Alerding to Reverend F. Thos. Jansen, 19 November 1914, and Alerding to Mother Maria Teresa, same date. FtWDA.

42. Alerding to Mother Maria Teresa, 2 January 1915. FtWDA.

It almost surpasses belief that these Italian Catholics are so indifferent that they do not seem to care whether their priest remains or leaves them, all for the lack of a little generosity on their part to support him. I can only suggest [the priest tell them] that they must supply him with what is absolutely needed or he will have to leave them. It is a fair test and it can hardly be expected that one should help those who are unwilling to help themselves.[43]

These demands for operating funds undoubtedly confirmed the Italian view that the clergy were greedy. Three months later, in July 1915, the priest departed and Alerding left the Italian post vacant.[44]

The impression that Gary Italians were "hard of heart" is mitigated, however, when we note that on 24 May 1916, ten months after the departure of their Catholic priest, seventy-six Italians petitioned Bishop John Hazen White of the Episcopal Diocese of Northern Indiana to provide them a spiritual home. "They feel that when and so soon as they have a Church and a minister large numbers of Italians from the whole Calumet region will come to them."[45] Since Bishop White advocated the inclusion of ethnic minorities in the Episcopal Church (he had recently welcomed a South Bend Hungarian congregation into his diocese), he and the diocesan missionary committee approved the Italian petition. In February 1917 White confirmed former Methodist minister Accomando and placed him in charge of the new St. Antonio Mission.[46] Here he confirmed over three hundred Italians and Hispanics between 1917 and 1923. Meanwhile, Alerding, assessing the new situation in Gary, concluded, "The place is a hot-bed of proselytism and something should be done to counteract its venomous influence."[47] In 1919 the indefatigable Father de Ville returned to Gary.

In Elkhart, Protestant activity among Italians did not exist to counterbalance the formidable presence of the city's German-born Catholic pas-

243

---

43. Alerding to F. Thos. Jansen, 14 April 1915. FtWDA. He asked Jansen to suggest this approach to Reverend Serafino Matesi, who had asked Alerding for Mass stipends to survive financially.

44. Alerding to Serafino Matesi, 20 July 1915. FtWDA. Reverend Joseph Monaco ministered there briefly in 1914–1915; and Reverend Francis Molino, in mid-1916. However, the position is vacant in the 1916 *Official Catholic Directory* and unlisted in the 1917 and 1918 editions.

45. White, writing in the *Diocesan Journal*, quoted in Christ Church *Parish Messenger*, IX. 3 (April 1927):4. Also see account in James E. Foster, *Christ Church, Gary, Indiana: a Sketch Book of Parish History, 1907–1940* ([Gary, 1940]), 18.

46. Christ Church (Episcopal), Gary, *Service Record Book 1917–43*, notation for 4 February 1917. Calumet Regional Archives (hereafter cited as CRA). Also see Foster, p. 18.

47. Alerding to Reverend J. E. Burke, Catholic Welfare Council chairman, 14 March 1920. FtWDA. Raymond A. Mohl and Neil Betten in *Steel City: Urban and Ethnic Patterns in Gary, Indiana, 1906–1950* (New York, 1986) generalize that "all of Gary's immigrant Catholic parishes were lay-founded" (p. 163). Religious and clergy worked to initiate an Italian parish. The authors conclude that because of their "hostility for the institutional church, Gary Italians had little incentive to establish an ethnic parish" (p. 167). Southern Italian apathy, not hostility, interrupted Catholic efforts. Then laymen petitioned another institutional church to establish an Episcopal mission.

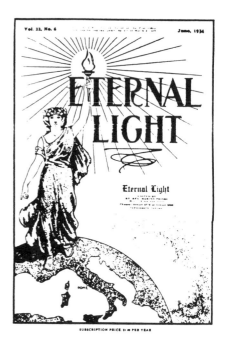

The Eternal Light *was a Catholic*
publication founded in 1913 to
appeal to the Italian Catholics of
Indianapolis to remain loyal
to the Church.

tor. When in 1913 a priest accompanied railroad workers from their home
town in Italy, Alerding encouraged him to raise funds for a mission in the
Italian neighborhood. The pastor, however, discouraged any such project
and was even unwilling to pay the Italian an assistant pastor's salary.[48] In
1916, frustrated by his pastor and apparent Italian indifference, the priest
returned home.[49] In place of the mission rose the Italian-American Club
on Harrison Street, since then a major center of Elkhart's Italian life.

Lack of Protestant competition also affected the course of events in
Fort Wayne. Italians who heard Mass attended Immaculate Conception
Cathedral or St. Mary's, but at St. Mary's they were relegated to the
balcony. The religious inspiration among the city's Italian shopkeepers,
railroaders, and factory workers was the educated Neapolitan Loreto J.
Starace, pious lawyer, translator, and journalist. At first he used to leave
Catholic religious tracts in public places. Then he assembled Italians at
Library Hall adjoining the Cathedral to sing hymns and pray together, and

---

48. Alerding to F. J. Jansen, 21 April 1914. FtWDA. Also see the Golden Jubilee history of St.
Vincent's published in 1918, p. 23, for Jansen's attitude toward Reverend Vincent Dellesite.

49. Alerding was very sympathetic when Dellesite decided to leave Elkhart and provided him with
a favorable reference. Alerding to Dellesite, 3 September 1915. FtWDA.

organized the Pio Decimo (Pius X) Society.[50] Alerding always rejected the constant stream of requests from Italian clergy for posts in his diocese; but when Starace wrote him requesting an Italian priest to save the faith of the Italians, the bishop was moved to permit the layman to seek out an acceptable candidate.[51]

Reverend Anthony Petrilli founded St. Joseph's Mission for Italians in a two-story house on Bass Street near Fairfield Avenue in late 1913. St. Joseph's, however, was handicapped when the devout Starace returned to Italy upon the outbreak of World War I in summer 1914. Killed at the front near Trieste the following year, Lieutenant Starace's reputation for holiness led to his being investigated for possible beatification in the 1930s.[52] Back in Fort Wayne, the Irish-American pastor of St. Patrick's parish, within whose territory the Bass Street site lay, successfully opposed St. Joseph's permanent location there. Alerding decided to make St. Joseph's a territorial parish west of St. Mary's River, in an area popularly called "Nebraska" because it was so far away from the heart of the city. Here Petrilli built a frame church in 1916 and opened a school in 1918. Removed from its Italian neighborhood, the parish's attractiveness to Italians slowly declined.[53] Discouraged by this situation and his lack of acceptance by diocesan clergy, Petrilli returned to his native Montefalcone Valfortore, Benevento province, in 1919. His non-Italian successor, who disliked St. Joseph's Italian and American parishioners, persuaded Alerding in 1921 to suppress the parish for financial reasons, the only closing of an urban parish in this state before World War II.

In scarcely a decade Italians had become the object of special Catholic, Methodist, Presbyterian, and Episcopal solicitude. A financial commitment from the denomination was always necessary because Italians remained tightfisted contributors. Not only did they not have a tradition of church support in the old country, but they also had emigrated to earn money and save, not to be generous. All four denominations were concerned with what today we would call "cost effectiveness."

When Father Riccardo Fantozzi asked Alerding for a $7,000 loan to build an Italian church in Gary, the bishop's response was hardly ambiguous.

245

---

50. Articles of incorporation for the Italian Benevolent Society Pio Decimo, notarized on 31 October 1913, were witnessed by Starace, Girolamo Amato, Davide Cardinali, and Antimo Vastano. Indiana State Archives.

51. Alerding to Starace, Alerding to Reverend J. R. Quinlan, 24 August 1913. FtWDA.

52. C. M. Starace, "Loreto Starace—a Lay Apostle," *America*, 2 February 1935:394–395.

53. John F. Noll, *The Diocese of Fort Wayne: Fragments of History* (n.p., 1941), II, 188–189.

246

Herman J. Alerding, Bishop of Fort Wayne, 1900–1924, considered the immigrants moving into his diocese to be a troublesome financial burden.

In order that there may be no misunderstanding on this point, I wish you to understand distinctly that I take upon myself no responsibility of a financial character in providing a church for the Italian Catholics of Gary or anywhere else.[54]

When Papa at Clinton Hill Crest asked for a raise in April 1915, the home missions committee granted him $100 over the next six months and any Sabbath offerings he collected (probably very little). It also went on record encouraging a change of workers at the end of the six-month period.[55] To save his job, Papa then presented a petition containing twenty-five signatures calling for the formal establishment of an Italian Presbyterian church in Clinton, a move supported by the minister of the existing First Presbyterian Church.[56] In response, the committee only agreed to organize and finance a catechetical class at Clinton and authorized Papa to work outside of the presbytery.[57] Within a month the Italian minister departed for Pennsylvania and became a Methodist.[58]

When Accomando's St. Antonio Mission began to face financial problems in 1920, the vestry of Christ Church, Gary's richest Episcopal congregation, viewed them as not its, but a diocesan, responsibility; other-

54. Alerding to Fantozzi, 9 April 1919. FtWDA.

55. Crawfordsville Presbytery, *Minutes* for 21 April 1913:X, 109.

56. *Ibid.,* 15 September 1913:135.

57. *Ibid.,* 14 October 1913:152–153.

58. *La Fiaccola,* 23 October 1913:3; 6 November 1913:3; 14 May 1914:1.

wise, it recommended that the mission be closed.[59] When the mission faced foreclosure in 1922, the rector of Christ Church reported that the national Triennial Convention had received Accomando's request for support and had listed St. Antonio thirty-ninth on its priority list of forty worthy projects.[60] Christ Church offered no support despite the $40,000 it received from United States Steel in 1925,[61] and St. Antonio closed two years later.

Between 1908 and 1916 Methodists probably spent $50,000 annually to evangelize Italians east of the Mississippi River, but they abandoned their special effort after jurisdictional disputes arose between the Italian Mission and the various conferences.[62] When the Methodist yearbook misidentified Bishop Burt in 1915, he wrote its editor:

247

Why did you not give me "Italian Mission" as part of my Area? It is generally treated with discourtesy, but I did not think that you would leave it out in the cold![63]

Reverend Wright, superintendent of the Italian Mission, had twice urged the Indiana Conference to accept the Indianapolis mission as its special project;[64] but within a few years of the demise of the national effort and the end of its subsidies, the Indianapolis mission closed and the Italian minister departed for Pennsylvania.

---

59. "Report of the Vestry Committee for St. Antonio's Mission," Christ Church Vestry, *Minutes,* 2 December 1920, 59. CRA. Gary Neighborhood House governing committee members also questioned the value of religious instruction for foreigners, comments which drew a sharp defense from Reverend Ralph Cummins, Neighborhood House superintendent. Gary Neighborhood House, *Minutes,* 5 June 1922, 99. CRA.

60. *Parish Messenger,* IV, 7 (October 1922).

61. *Ibid.,* VII, 7 (November 1925).

62. See Hingeley, *General Conference 1912,* 571–572, 696. In spring 1916 the ministers of the Italian Mission voted to continue their organization despite challenges. *La Fiaccola,* 12 April 1916:1. For the resolution they passed, see Locke, *General Conference 1916,* 528–529, 645. Yet in summer the Board of Home Missions and Church Extension recommended discontinuance of the Italian Mission, effective 1 October 1916. Notice published without comment in *La Fiaccola,* 27 July 1916:1.

63. Frederick De Land Leete, *Methodist Bishops: Personal Notes and Bibliography* (Nashville. 1948), 293.

64. Superintendent's Report, *La Fiaccola,* 17 June 1915:1; also *ibid.,* 27 January 1916:3; and Missione Italiana della Chiesa Metodista Episcopale, *Verbali per l'Anno 1916* (New York: La Fiaccola, n.d.), 13. For Catholic criticism of Methodist fund-raising for the Indianapolis mission, see editorial in *Indiana Catholic and Record,* 8 December 1916:4. Its minister was Reverend Ugo Crivelli (1913–1920), described as "an eloquent, inspiring, uncompromising preacher" in Erie Conference of the Methodist Church, *Official Journal and Year Book 1961,* 596. Wright also visited Hartford City where he found 200 Italians "and not a thing being done for them religiously." *La Fiaccola,* 3 December 1914:1. He cajoled the local congregation into being concerned about Italians. but no evidence of results from his visit there appeared in *La Fiaccola.*

After the pastor of St. Joseph's, Fort Wayne, startled his parishioners with the unexpected announcement one Sunday that the parish would close down immediately because of its $20,000 debt, angry non-Italian parishioners communicated with the Italian-born Apostolic Delegate in Washington and sent anonymous notes to the bishop and Cathedral clergy. They used the Italian origin of the parish and the few Italians still members to accuse Alerding of being anti-Italian, unfair to the poor, and money-oriented. After three years the bishop reconstituted St. Joseph's as a territorial parish.[65]

248

In Indianapolis, Holy Rosary's fine brick church, school, and convent were completed in 1925, the most extravagant Italian religious plant in the state. Always pressed for money although several banana kings were among his parishioners, Priori soon earned a reputation for unethical fundraising. His $200,000 parish debt so alarmed Bishop Joseph E. Ritter in 1934 that he replaced Priori with non-Italian clergy and charged them with reducing the debt—a twelve-year process which necessitated mammoth weekly bingo games, crowded annual street festivals, popular monthly spaghetti dinners, a profitable parish-owned gas station, and a mandatory seat offering at late Mass on Sundays![66] The ordinary Sunday collection was still predominately nickles and dimes.

From the financial viewpoint, the Presbyterian missions at Gary and Clinton appear to have been the most successful, long-lived Protestant efforts among Italians. Neighborhod House did not minister to them after 1925, however, since they generally attended St. Anthony's Catholic Chapel or had moved from the Central District to outlying areas by that date, their places taken by Mexicans and Blacks.[67] Although Neighborhood House operated until 1973, after 1936 it was supported primarily by the Community Chest rather than by Presbyterian contributions. Clinton Hill Crest, which merged with the First Presbyterian Church of Clinton in 1962, was never self-supporting. It was financed by Elder Robb's bequest in 1928 and by appropriations from the National Missions Committee of the Synod of Indiana. The committee caused Hill Crest to close/merge

65. Open letter of St. Joseph's Church Association Publicity Committee (E. J. Girard, Harry Boxberger, and D. Landolfi), 15 June 1921, sent to Archbishop John Bonzano; Bonzano to Alerding, 20 June 1921; and Alerding to Bonzano, 24 June 1921. Anonymous notes also in FtWDA. Although the bishop defended his action, in mid-January 1922 he had a real estate title abstract prepared on lots less than two blocks from the earlier church and obtained title to them two months later. St. Joseph's reopened at this new site in 1924.

66. Ritter to Priori, 20 June 1934. IAA. Also see James J. Divita, The Italians of Indianapolis: The Story of Holy Rosary Catholic Parish 1909–1984 (Indianapolis, 1984), 44–45.

67. "National Mission Report," Minutes of the 104th Meeting of the Synod of Indiana of the Presbyterian Church in the U.S.A. (1929), 18.

249

The Reverend Nicolo Accomando, an Episcopal priest, established this mission in Gary in 1917. He used newspaper advertisements to attract Catholics to his church.

when it dropped Hill Crest as a project so that it could concentrate its efforts on building suburban churches and developing university campus religious centers.[68]

To judge cost effectiveness, moreover, we also need to consider the number of adherents attracted to a religious institution. Indiana Protestant missions, with the exception of Clinton Hill Crest, failed to attract or retain Italian membership. The Protestants taught the Word of God and offered Christian morality, but not the comfortable cosmos of patron saints and outdoor processions. Traditionally Italian religion was ostentatious, so churches without statues and candles were viewed as sterile. Also, stress on total abstinence among a people who drank wine as their everyday beverage made Protestantism hard to accept. Protestant missioners found it difficult to form a community sense, for so many Italians viewed their American stay as temporary and returned to the old country, or

---

68. See "National Mission Report" in *1958 Synod Minutes,* 54–57, and *1963 Synod Minutes,* 101–102.

moved to another district or city and did not affiliate with the same denomination.[69]

The Indianapolis Methodist Mission reported ten full members (four of whom lived elsewhere) at the time the national Italian Mission subsidy ended.[70] Neighborhood House employed three clerics to minister to Italians in the Church of Our Savior. Each stayed about one year. The third of them, born in Calabria, betrayed his frustration when he appeared before the governing committee: "He told of the difficulty in reaching adults, most of whom are Sicilians, ignorant and prejudiced."[71] When the vestry of Christ Church in Gary inquired of the superintendent of Neighborhood House and active members of St. Antonio Mission how successful was work among Italians,

250

The reports agreed that work among the Italian people was very difficult, that our work had not been successful, and that there was considerable doubt as to whether it ever would be as it is at present carried on.[72]

Italian Protestant missions were also hard pressed when Catholics launched a campaign to regain "lost souls." In 1917, in answer to St. Antonio Episcopal Mission, Precious Blood Father Fantozzi organized a struggling St. Joseph's Parish for Italians at 17th Avenue and Washington Street in Gary. When Father de Ville, a man of broad experience and great vitality,[73] succeeded Fantozzi, he appropriated the Episcopal mission's name, changing St. Joseph's to St. Anthony's. He organized the Catholic Instruction League of religious and lay women who by 1923 taught catechism to over two thousand students through the released-time program of the Gary public school system. He began to organize a Catholic settlement house (first projected in 1917) and proposed that it be

---

69. For a national perspective on Italian immigrant religion in a Catholic-Protestant context, see Rudolph J. Vecoli, "Prelates and Peasants, Italian Immigrants and the Catholic Church," *Journal of Social History* (Spring 1969); Antonio Mangano, *Sons of Italy: A Social and Religious Study of the Italians in America* (New York, 1917); F. Aurelio Palmieri, "Italian Protestantism in the United States," *Catholic World* (May 1918); and Howard V. Yergin, "Italian Evangelization in New York City," unpublished study, Board of National Missions of the Presbyterian Church in the U.S.A., 1912.

70. *Minutes of the 85th Session, Indiana Annual Conference of the Methodist Episcopal Church* (Spring 1916), 416.

71. Reverend Vincent Sproviero in Gary Neighborhood House, *Minutes*, 1 April 1919, 66. CRA. Preceding him were Reverend Aurelio Sofia (1916–17) and Reverend Francesco Paolo Patrono (1917–18). Sofia was a McCormick Seminary student. Patrono served in Washington, Pennsylvania, for many years after leaving Gary.

72. "Report of the Vestry Committee for St. Antonio's Mission," Christ Church Vestry, *Minutes*, 2 December 1920, 59. CRA.

73. For his refugee work during World War I, see Father Jean B. De Ville, *Back from Belgium: A Secret History of Three Years Within the German Lines* (New York, 1918).

251

*Holding the children to Catholicism was a major concern of Italian
American pastors. Depicted is a first Communion class.*

linked to a real church home for Italians and Mexicans. Alerding was
overwhelmed with all this sudden activity. In summer 1920 he wrote de
Ville: "I thank God for having sent you to Gary. May He still further
bless and prosper you!"[74]

And so He did. The Italian priest overcame the financial handicap of
ministering to Italians by publicly refuting criticism of United States Steel
Corporation and developing a strong Americanization program. Then he
approached United States Steel's board chairman Elbert H. Gary for
support to neutralize foreign socialism.[75] Soon United States Steel sent

74. Alerding to de Ville, 18 July 1920. FtWDA.

75. Alerding to Elbert H. Gary, 14 March 1920; Alerding to de Ville, 16 February 1921. FtWDA.
Ruth Hutchinson Crocker, "Sympathy and Silence: the Settlement Movement in Gary and Indianapolis" (unpublished doctoral thesis, Purdue University, 1982), 392–410, discusses de Ville and
United States Steel. She views de Ville as a conservative supporter of capitalism, while I view him as
pragmatic, not doctrinaire. To serve downtrodden and unchurched, he had to appeal for company
financial support since immigrants had not developed a monied class.

Alerding $100,000 for Gary parishes and donated $130,000 to de Ville for his special projects. In 1922 de Ville broke ground for the Judge Gary-Bishop Alerding Settlement House, named for his two benefactors, and dedicated it on 18 May 1924. This 40-room center housed a gymnasium, auditorium, pool room, two-lane bowling alley, medical center, and craft rooms. Following the same successful approach as Clinton Hill Crest, de Ville made Gary-Alerding a community and religious center offering attractive athletic and practical programs. However, he did not forget the "lost souls." He established St. Anthony Chapel for Latins at Gary-Alerding and directed both until 1930, when he retired for health reasons to Italy. By that time, his chapel at 15th and Van Buren, only a few blocks from both Neighborhood House and St. Antonio Mission, served as a magnet for Latin Presbyterians and Episcopalians. "A new attitude on the part of the Catholics was noted" by the Neighborhood House governing committee already in 1922.[76] When St. Antonio Mission closed in 1927, the rector of Christ Church tersely explained: "The Roman Church extended itself to reclaim those whom it called its children."[77]

The one bright spot in the darkness of Protestant failure among Italians was Clinton Hill Crest. Operating for forty years after other Protestant missions disappeared, in 1956 it reported 173 members and 251 Sunday School students.[78] It succeeded because it provided necessary community services, was conveniently located, and because Catholic pastors after 1911 evidently did not attempt to reclaim members. They may well have feared reproducing the situation preceding the 1909 church explosion. During a recent interview, several ladies of northern Italian background were asked why they were Presbyterian. All answered that early ministers or settlement workers were interested in them as individuals and that they and their families responded to this personal concern. Not one mentioned an attractive Protestant theology, but all related horror stories about the Catholic clergy in Italy. A retired elementary school principal reported that her father was indifferent to religion, but her mother was a devout Catholic, niece of a bishop in the old country. Every Sunday she attended 8 A.M. Mass with Mama, then went to 10 A.M. service and 2 P.M. Sunday School at Hill Crest because she wanted to belong to its Girl Scout troop. When the Catholic priest warned him about Hill Crest, her father responded that God could be found even in a synagogue. When the Presbyterian minister was a house guest and spotted a wine barrel, she

---

76. Gary Neighborhood House, *Minutes,* 5 June 1922, 100. CRA.

77. Foster, 18, and *Parish Messenger,* IX, 3 (April 1927):4–5.

78. *Minutes of the General Assembly of the Presbyterian Church in the United States of America, 1956* (Philadelphia, 1957), III, 111.

reported that he had the good sense not to say anything about it. A 40-year-old part-time librarian reported that her father always responded "Hill Crest" whenever anyone asked to which church he belonged, but he did not attend services there for years.[79] What was clear after interviewing these Italian Presbyterians is that they reflected the traditional Italian religious orientation more closely than Italian Catholics educated in parochial schools, where church membership is identified with practice.

By the 1930s interdenominational rivalry over Italians had diminished. The National Origins Act, passed by Congress in 1924, established a quota system and severely restricted Italian immigration to the United States. Then in 1929, the signing of the Lateran Pacts normalized church-state relations in Italy and reduced the traditional antagonism between religious commitment and patriotism. In this new situation, the Catholic hierarchy in Indiana consciously utilized its "Italian resources" to work with the immigrants and their families. The Bishop of Fort Wayne incardinated two Italian-born priests (de Ville and Campagna) and the Bishop of Indianapolis incardinated one (Priori). The first Indiana-born priest of Italian ancestry was appointed assistant at Holy Rosary, Indianapolis, in 1929 and returned as pastor in 1951. The first Fort Wayne priest of Italian ancestry was appointed to St. Anthony's, Gary, immediately after ordination. He retired as pastor of St. Vincent's, Elkhart.[80] As late as 1949 the Archbishop of Indianapolis sent to Bedford a priest of Italian ancestry born in Seymour, Indiana,

253

with the hope that you will give special attention to the good people of Oolitic, quite a number of whom are of Italian extraction . . . Perhaps one as yourself, bearing an Italian name, will be more obediently received by them . . .[81]

Ordinarily graduates of Rome's North American College, because they had some fluency in Italian, served on the pastoral staffs of Italian-populated parishes. This policy resulted in the best educated, and reputedly the cream, of diocesan clergy ministering to Italians. The first such appointment was to the pastorate of Sacred Heart parish, Clinton, in 1911. Several North American alumni were also appointed to St. Anthony's, Gary, St. Vincent's, Elkhart, and to Holy Rosary, Indianapolis, where they served almost continuously from 1939 to 1972.

---

79. Interviews with Irma Pesavento and Margo Fenoglio, 7 March 1983.

80. They are Reverend Augustine J. Sansone of Indianapolis and Reverend Fred J. Cardinali of Fort Wayne.

81. Archbishop Paul C. Schulte to Reverend John N. Sciarra, 31 October 1949, original in latter's possession.

254

Father John B. deVille worked among the Italians of Gary, Indiana.

This utilization of Italian resources by the Catholic bishops in Indiana and the resultant increase in religious commitment among Italian immigrants and their descendants contrast strongly with the late nineteenth/ early twentieth century situation. The immigrants' religious education was minimal and their commitment to the Church clouded by traditional apathy and political antagonism. Some Catholics viewed Italians as Catholic primarily because they were not members of other churches. When they first arrived on the Hoosier scene with their anti-clericalism and *festa* mentality, Catholic authorities ignored their peculiar spiritual needs on the ground that their small numbers would facilitate assimilation and produce an Italian who conformed to American Catholic norms. This simple, unrealistic solution became inoperative when three mainline Protestant denominations concluded that many Italians were not practicing Catholics, but were unchurched. Their efforts to evangelize Italians failed because immigrant cultural values differed from theirs, because they could not develop a sense of fellowship on account of Italian workers' mobility, and because the wider American Protestant community lacked interest in and did not sufficiently fund evangelization of Italians. The Protestant effort among Italians, however, awakened the Catholic hierarchy to the Italian presence. To blunt the Protestant challenge on what they now considered their own turf, Catholic bishops employed clergy who were Italian-born, Italian-speaking, or of Italian heritage to minister to these immigrants. "You can't make a good Scotch-Irish Presbyterian out of an Italian or Pole," the Synod of Indiana was once told, "but you can help them to be good, strong Christians."[82] Indeed, without yesterday's interdenominational rivalry, Christ might never have been made real for many Italian immigrant families.

255

---

82. "National Mission Report" in *1938 Synod Minutes,* 40.

BOTH POLISH AND CATHOLIC:
IMMIGRANT CLERGY IN THE AMERICAN CHURCH

BY

WILLIAM GALUSH*

In 1902 Father Stanislaus Nawrocki wrote of his peers in America: "In addition to their heavy clerical obligations, [they] must function as collectors, builders, contractors, bankers, judges, teachers, accountants, organizers, etc. . . . "[1] Busy men in burgeoning parishes, they found America as novel as did their lay countrymen. Dwelling in ethnic enclaves lacking the accustomed secular leadership provided at home by the nobility and intelligentsia, immigrant clergy went beyond their spiritual role to assist the largely peasant newcomers in other aspects of existence.[2] Persons of high status in the old country observed this process with some regret, seeing it as giving a clerical cast to the Polish-American community.[3] The slow growth of a better-educated and more assertive lay elite, including some articulate anticlericals, came to offer alternative

---

*Mr. Galush is an assistant professor of history in Loyola University of Chicago.

[1] *Naród Polski* [*Polish Nation*, Chicago], April 30, 1902, p. 1; see also January 20, 1904, p. 2.

[2] The clergy always figure in any broad study of Poles in America, as well as works focused on religion among these immigrants. There is a common perception of the centrality of the priests in the homeland village and in the new land, often including examples of enlarged roles here. The tendency has been to examine individuals, or clergy acting together on specific issues, rather than their efforts at organizational formation and the mechanisms to attain it. This essay is an effort to initiate such an investigation.

For representative comments on clerical roles, see Daniel Buczek, *Immigrant Pastor: The Life of the Right Reverend Monsignor Lucyan Bójnowski of New Britain, Connecticut* (Waterbury, Connecticut, 1974), pp. i, 141; Victor Greene, *For God and Country: The Rise of Polish and Lithuanian Ethnic Consciousness in America, 1860-1910* (Madison, 1975), pp. 26-27; Edward Kantowicz, *Polish-American Politics in Chicago, 1888-1940* (Chicago, 1975), pp. 30-31; and Anthony Kuzniewski, S.J., *Faith and Fatherland: The Polish Church War in Wisconsin, 1896-1918* (Notre Dame, Indiana, 1980), p. 13.

[3] *Przegląd Emigracyjny* [*Emigration Review*, Lwów], July 1, 1982, pp. 3-4. Cf. Charles Morley (ed.), *Portrait of America: Letters of Henry Sienkiewicz* (New York, 1959), pp. 272, 282 and passim for similar observations in the late 1870's.

sources of information and leadership to the masses. Simultaneously the priests had to deal with unfamiliar non-Polish religious superiors whose concerns were indifferent or even hostile to ethnicity.[4] Challenges from different sides, as well as a natural inclination for companionship and support from persons of similar calling, prompted the scattered missionaries to form clerical associations, which in turn formulated and promoted common goals. Inevitably this process included conflict as well as co-operation.[5] But the priests successfully combined loyalty to Roman Catholicism in the new land with a strong retention of Polishness (*Polskość*) to pursue religious and ethnic goals. Before World War I they pragmatically allied with either bishops or laity as specific issues dictated, in the process developing greater group consciousness and organizational solidarity.

257

The background of the immigrant clergy conditioned their interaction with American Catholicism. As Oscar Handlin has observed, Roman Catholicism is "... universal rather than national in organization, and catholic in essential dogma, [yet] it nevertheless partook of the quality of men who professed it...."[6] Poles accepted Latin Christianity near the beginning of their national existence, and after the partitions of the late eighteenth century the Church was the only institution transcending the borders of the conquering powers. The Polish clergy nurtured a rudimentary national consciousness through persistent use of their native tongue for preaching and teaching. In the Russian and German partitions official efforts to stifle Polishness prompted many clergymen to defend their cultural and national as well as religious heritage.[7] Austria-Hungary, a Catholic power, combined Josephinist state control and demands for dynastic loyalty with increasing toleration of nationalistic activity by the late nineteenth century. Some

[4]See Richard Linkh, *American Catholicism and European Immigrants, 1900-1924* (New York, 1975), pp. 4-8, 22-28, 44; James Moynihan, *The Life of Archbishop John Ireland* (New York, 1953), pp. 54-78.

[5]Conflict need not be viewed solely as a negative phenomenon. Lewis Coser argues persuasively that some conflict can aid the formation and persistence of groups, with struggle for a supra-individual cause conferring a respectability of acting in a representative role rather than simply promoting self-interest. In the end conflict might modify or create new rules of behavior, form new structures, or at least make the participants conscious of rules dormant before the conflict. These observations have relevance to such issues as trusteeism and the quest for a Polish-American bishop. See Lewis Coser, *The Functions of Social Conflict* (New York, 1964), pp. 31, 114-115, 121-128.

[6]Oscar Handlin, *Boston's Immigrants* (New York, 1968), p. 128.

[7]Aleksander Gieysztor, *History of Poland* (Warsaw, 1968), pp. 533-540; Norman Davies, *God's Playground: A History of Poland* (New York, 1982), II, 209-217.

priests here felt their Galician brethren were seduced into support for the Hapsburgs by subsidy and permissiveness.[8] With some variation the priesthood was an object of official pressure in all the Polish lands.

In addition to the state, there were three other sources of influence upon the priest. A declining but long-standing one was the patron, often a noble, whose familial generosity had purchased certain privileges in the endowed parish.[9] Another factor was the general laity, traditionally passive and ill-organized, but occasionally aroused and clamorous.[10] Finally there was the religious superior, usually a bishop and in any case a Polish-speaker.[11] This pattern of pressures changed significantly in the American environment, the locale for increasing numbers of clerics after the Civil War.

258

Movement of Poles to the United States in numbers sufficient to hinder rapid assimilation began in the 1850's but reached the scale of thousands per year only in the 1870's.[12] The newcomers were overwhelmingly peasants, whose lives took meaning from the soil, family, and faith. Seeking familiarity amidst strangeness, they clustered in colonies, first rural but increasingly in urban settings. The first settlement was Panna

[8]*Ibid.*, p. 209; *Polak w Ameryce* [*The Pole in America*, Buffalo], March 1, 1897, p. 1; March 4, 1897, p. 1.

[9]Patronage *(patronat)* in Poland was a traditional and canonically sanctioned arrangement, as elsewhere in Catholic Europe, but subject to varying state regulation in the partition period. See "Poland," *Catholic Encyclopedia* (New York, 1913), XII, 187-192; "Patronage," *ibid.*, XI, 560-562; "Patronat w Polsce" ["Patronage in Poland"], *Encyklopedja Kościelna* [Church Encyclopedia] (Warsaw, 1892), XVIII, 380-399. Patrons could still exercise the right of presentation of candidates in Galicia at the turn of the century, but the government could reject the nominee. See *Polak w Ameryce*, March 4, 1897, p. 1. By the eve of the war the authorities were allegedly considering widening the right of presentation to include the generality of parishioners. *Kuryer Polski* [*The Polish Courier*, Milwaukee], September 26, 1913, p. 4.

[10]William I. Thomas and Florian Znaniecki, *The Polish Peasant in Europe and America* (New York, 1958), I, 143 and 275.

[11]The religious authority structure in Poland was more elaborate than in the contemporary United States. In addition to bishops, secular clergy were subordinate to active "deans," priests with limited supervisory power over others in their vicinity. Moreover, the proportionately greater number of clergy meant that more were assistants, unlike America where the shortage of Polish priests meant a rapid rise to a pastorate. For comparative comments, see *Naród Polski* [*The Polish Nation*, Chicago], May 14, 1902, p. 1.

[12]Victor Greene," Pre-World War I Polish Emigration to the United States: Motives and Statistics," *Polish Review*, VI (Summer, 1961), 46-47; Jerzy Zubrycki, "Emigration from Poland in the Nineteenth and Twentieth Centuries," *Population Studies*, VI (March, 1953), 248-272.

Maria in Texas, led by Father Leopold Moczygemba. Beginning in 1854, he drew entire families from Silesia into a very different rural environment. The unsuccessful uprising of 1863, the *Kulturkampf* of the next decade in German Poland, and poverty in general drove swelling thousands to seek a new life in America, where most settled in the industrializing northeast quarter of the nation.[13] With them came a few men in black: Polish priests going to the missions across the sea.

The United States offered several novelties of particular interest to these immigrant clerics. Here the state stood aloof from religion, protecting a *laissez-faire* competition which seemed to foster denominational anarchy but gave a greater boon—no government control. A necessary consequence was less easily assimilated: solicitation of voluntary contributions from the laity. Priests accustomed to endowments and government subsidies were unfamiliar with stimulating many small donations. In the course of years they developed the necessary skills and instilled the appropriate habits in their parishioners. Prior to World War I, however, there was an annual assessment or pew rental which constituted the largest single source of income in many parishes. While in Chicago and perhaps elsewhere the collector was a priest, laymen often performed this function.[14] They easily equated this with collection of dues for fraternal insurance societies, and the aid from laity with basic business experience fostered the proliferation of parish committees. Assistance in parochial administration implied to some laymen that they might have rights as well as obligations.

In terms of the schema noted above, the sources of pressure on the clergy were halved. Bishops and laity alone remained. Yet there was novelty here as well. Intellectually the priests had realized that their new superiors would be non-Poles, but the actual experience too often was unhappy. They found some bishops of German extraction, whose background was familiar if not beloved. New were the ubiquitous Irish-Americans, whose intense Catholicism became less attractive as closer contact revealed many to be assimilationists. Multi-lingual Polish priests found them insular, and difficulties of communication fostered some mistrust on both sides. The

259

---

[13]Caroline Golab offers a useful discussion of the settlement patterns of Poles and other European immigrants in *Immigrant Destinations* (Philadelphia, 1977).

[14]For Chicago, the largest Polish-American center, see Edward Kantowicz, *Corporation Sole: Cardinal Mundelein and Chicago Catholicism* (Notre Dame, Indiana, 1983), p. 69; for the lay role in several cities, see William Galush, "Forming Polonia: A Study of Four Polish-American Communities, 1890-1940" (unpublished Ph.D. dissertation, University of Minnesota, 1975), pp. 95-97, 156-158; *Zgoda*, January 19, 1905, p. 2.

outcome, while not inevitable, was ethnic segregation in a Church reluctant to acknowledge its pluralism, with a tiny fraction passing into outright rebellion.[15]

The Polish-American laity was surprising as well. They were mainly ex-peasants, with the rustic manners and speech of their relatives at home; yet they were different. They had removed themselves from the stultifying grip of village society, with its conservatism and fatalism. Though they participated in America overwhelmingly at its lower levels, they were absorbing new values of optimism, activism, and individualism.[16] They joined these to the thrift and fortitude of their ancestral culture to begin a slow but steady improvement of their material condition.[17] These immigrants formed a more familiar environment through residential concentration, and within these urban villages they wove a dense web of supportive institutions. The most widespread form of voluntary association was the fraternal insurance society, probably patterned after similar bodies seen among neighboring older ethnic groups. Most newcomers retained their Catholicism, but worship among Irish, Germans, or even Bohemians was less comforting than the ways of home. They sought the familiar forms of Polish Catholicism, and for that they needed a Polish priest. An immigrant cleric found a warm welcome in a developing colony.

Central to the enclave was a Polish parish. Congregational formation was common here, a striking difference from the homeland where parishioners worshiped in a church whose existence seemed to transcend time. Most often concerned laymen democratically chose a committee to collect funds, buy land, and construct an edifice. At the inception, or sometimes later, a Polish priest entered the process, and ultimately the bishop had to designate a pastor and dedicate the church.[18] The participation in the foundation, and usually in subsequent administration, inflated lay aspirations regarding control of the parish.

[15]Anthony Kuzniewski offers a suggestive interpretation of the alternatives for Poles and the American Catholic Church in "Wenceslaus Kruszka and the Fight for a Polish Bishop," Working Paper — Notre Dame Seminar, 1977; also *Faith and Fatherland*, pp. 124-128 and passim.

[16]Thomas and Znaniecki, *op. cit.*, I, 89-97 on Poland, pp. 98-104 on attitudinal changes in the United States; Father Anthony Gorski also noted the greater independence of Poles here. See *Naród Polski*, May 14, 1902, p. 1.

[17]Galush, *op. cit.*, pp. 106-136 and 267-280 for occupational and other mobility.

[18]*Ibid.*, pp. 82-105; see also John Gallagher, *A Century of History: The Diocese of Scranton, 1868-1968* (Scranton, 1968), pp. 156-171 for occasionally more extreme examples of lay assertiveness in the anthracite region, and the representative contemporary account of a New York parish in *Naród Polski*, January 20, 1904, p. 2.

The parish was the largest and most important local institution, but it was just that — local. Immigrant clergy saw themselves as nurturing Polishness, but the formulation and promotion of ethnicity could be more efficiently sponsored at a level above the congregation. Since the diocese was indisputably in non-Polish hands, clerical patriots sought a vehicle which could foster religion and ethnicity while remaining under Polish control. They chose the fraternal aid federation. In so choosing, they created a means for exceptional priests to exercise influence far beyond their parochial borders.

The process began in the 1870's, when Poles were yet relatively few in number and uninclined to make demands on the American episcopate, The concrete expression of this desire for supra-parochial organization was the Polish Roman Catholic Union (Zjednoczenie Polskie Rzymsko-Katolickie), initiated by Father Theodore Gieryk, a secular priest, in 1873. He was soon joined by the Resurrectionist Vincent Barzynski and his lay brother John, editor of *Pielgrzym (The Pilgrim)*, who ardently supported the project in his newspaper. The involvement of the energetic and assertive Father Barzynski significantly altered the membership philosophy of the proposed federation. While Gieryk wanted the Union open to all who felt themselves Polish, Barzynski successfully pressed for a narrower basis: Poles who professed the Roman Catholic faith. The Resurrectionist triumphed and the PRCU emerged under the slogan "Bóg i Ojczyzna" (God and Fatherland).[19]

The constitution of the Union called for the maintenance of the holy faith, mutual aid, and cultural improvement.[20] Article III required members to revere their priests and obey their bishops, among other items on religion and discipline. Article XI enjoined commemoration of two nationalistic holidays. Religion and patriotism went hand in hand, and prior to 1880 several priests served as presidents, while Barzynski cast his shadow over PRCU headquarters from his immense parish a few blocks away.[21]

Despite the clerical presence, the PRCU was mainly lay in leadership and overwhelmingly so in membership, and as a democratic organization necessarily catered to its major constituency. Clerical contacts had

---

[19]Mieczysław Haiman, *Zjednoczenie Polskie Rzymsko-Katolickie w Ameryce, 1873-1948 [The Polish Roman Catholic Union of America]* (Chicago, 1948), pp. 23-42.
[20]*Gazeta Polska Katolicka [The Polish Catholic Gazette, Chicago]*, May 20, 1875, p. 3.
[21]Haiman, *op. cit.*, pp. 54-55; Greene, *For God and Country*, pp. 75-77, 85-89.

increased through the formation of the Union, and with it the perception that their distinctive status would be best served by an exclusive society. In 1875, under the leadership of Father Barzynski, some priests in Illinois and states east formed the Association of Polish Roman Catholic Priests in the United States (Tow. Księży Rzymsko-Katolickich Polskich w Stanach Zjednoczonych). Its stated goals were the fostering of clerical unity, assisting American bishops, avoiding giving scandal to the faithful, and guiding the laity.[22] The aims indicated both difficulties and aspirations. Scattered widely and as yet few in number, these clerical immigrants consciously sought to promote discipline and concord amidst strangeness and heavy burdens. The passage of years brought increasing confidence and other aims, though the original goals proved difficult to meet. By 1887 the group numbered thirty, and Barzynski brought it into the Polish Roman Catholic Union as a member lodge, symbolic of priestly approval of the federation.[23]

Barzynski might well have felt the need to strengthen the Union, for the 1880's opened with a challenge to the clerical definition of ethnicity.[24] A well-publicized plea from the noted patriot in Swiss exile, Agaton Giller, catalyzed discontent with the PRCU and led several prominent laymen to form the Polish National Alliance (Związek Narodowy Polski) in 1880. This new fraternal federation took in all who declared themselves Poles, regardless of religion. Non-believers and Jews thus could join, though the vast majority of members were Roman Catholics. The Alliance was exclusively lay-led, but despite Catholic criticism its alleged anticlericalism was occasional rather than consistent, varying largely by the personal inclinations of national officers. It soon attracted some priests, notably Fathers Dominic Majer of St. Paul and Constantine Domagalski of Cincinnati, with most from Minnesota and Wisconsin. Perhaps more significantly, all were diocesan clergy, unlike the mixture of seculars and

[22]John Iwicki, C.R., *The First Hundred Years: A Study of the Apostolate of the Congregation of the Resurrection in the United States, 1866-1966* (Rome, 1966), p. 239. For regional origins, see Haiman, *op. cit.*, pp. 83-84.

[23]Iwicki, *op. cit.*, p. 240. The clerical association's constitution also called for support of Polish parochial education and the encouragement of a Polish Catholic press. The former was so generally accepted by the laity that it never became an issue before 1914, while the latter was vague and in practice was left almost entirely to lay initiative.

[24]For perceptive comments on the role of the ethnic elite in formulating group goals, see Philip Gleason, "The Crisis of Americanization" in Gleason (ed.) *Contemporary Catholicism in the United States* (Notre Dame, Indiana, 1969), pp. 3-32.

Resurrectionists in the PRCU lodge.[25] They were more sympathetic to the Jagiellonian spirit of the PNA, hearkening back to a Polish state of many nations and creeds. Soon Father Barzynski led what came to be termed the "Union" priests in denunciations of the so-called "Alliance" clergy.[26] In March of 1887 the Alliance priests were driven to a collective affirmation:

... we, the undersigned, all have Alliance groups in our parishes, and they are truly ornaments of our parishes, and the same as church brotherhoods. They are practicing Catholics ....
... We see the Polish National Alliance as a very noble institution for our nationality and our people.[27]

263

The pro-Catholic editor of Zgoda (Harmony), the PNA organ, supported the Alliance priests through articles affirming the federation's essential Catholicism and cited approval by various bishops.[28] Not only did this avail nothing with the Unionist critics, but the clerics in the Alliance were conditional in their support. Their commitment was contingent on a continuing perception of the PNA as basically Catholic.

The national Alliance convention of 1889 shattered clerical confidence. In an atmosphere of episcopal fears of secret societies and radicalism, the priests had successfully demanded the expulsion of a socialist-inclined lodge the year before. Now Fathers Majer and Domagalski led an effort to oust socialists and other undesirables throughout the federation. The attempt failed in a stormy confrontation, and the clergy and some laymen quit the PNA, opening the way for the election of anticlerical officers and editor.[29] Rivalries of personality more than principle disinclined the

[25]The PNA-affiliated priests called themselves the Society of Polish Priests (Stowarzyszenie Księży Polskich) and their membership included no regulars. See Zgoda [Harmony, Chicago], March 2, 1887, p. 2. The Resurrectionists then and later were portrayed by their lay and clerical critics as aggressive, intriguing, or at least pursuing interests specific to their order. These perceptions, coupled with other factors operating after 1890, led to a decline in their influence among the clergy. Cf. Zgoda, February 9, 1887, p. 4; February 20, 1889, p. 1, August 6, 1896, p. 4; Wiarus [The Veteran, Winona, Minnesota], September 3, 1896, p. 1; Wenceslaus Kruszka, Historja Polska w Ameryce od czasów najdawnejszych aż do najnowszych [A History of Poles in America from the Earliest to the Most Recent Times] (Milwaukee, 1937), I, 720-722, 767-769.

[26]Wiarus, December 30, 1886, p. 1; Zgoda, February 9, 1887, p. 1; Haiman, op. cit., pp. 79-84.

[27]Zgoda, March 2, 1887, p. 4.

[28]Ibid., January 19, 1887, p. 4; February 20, 1889, p. 1; April 18, 1889, p. 1.

[29]Ibid., September 18, 1889, p. 1; Wiarus, September 19, 1889, p. 1; see also Stanisław Osada, Historia Związku Narodowego Polskiego [A History of the Polish National Alliance] (Chicago, 1957), I, 285-296; Haiman, op. cit., pp. 93-99.

former Alliance clergy from joining Barzynski's association, and after Father Majer established a new fraternal federation, the Polish Union of America (Unja Polska w Ameryce), most joined it in a clerical lodge.[30]

The 1890's saw a continuation of clerical division, much lamented by priests of the day.[31] In reality, they did come together for particular purposes, such as the Polish Emigration Society (Polskie Towarzysztwo Emigracyjny) to aid new immigrants or to organize the first Polish Catholic Congress in 1896.[32] Clergymen such as John Pitass of Buffalo, Vincent Barzynski of Chicago, and Jacob Pacholski of Minnesota might be in competing clerical societies, but they could co-operate in and even lead such special projects.[33] Yet being elected to a post in a Polish society did not have the same significance as priestly participation in their primary institutional affiliation: the Roman Catholic Church. As the Church was an authoritarian organization, with its major leaders being bishops consecrated in the apostolic succession, no elective office could equal the episcopate. This conception of rank gives added meaning to the quest for and subsequent role of Polish-American bishops.

264

[30] *Wiarus*, September 5, 1889, p. 7; *Naród Polski*, July 27, 1904, p. 5.

[31] E.g., Father Stanisław Radziejewski in *Kuryer Polski*, June 16, 1894, p. 3; "Father Marek" (pseud.) in *Gazeta Katolicka* [*The Catholic Gazette*, Chicago], February 2, 1899, p. 1.

[32] "Z Ameryki" ["In America"], *Niedziela* [*Sunday*, Detroit], January 23, 1896, pp. 61-62; "Sprawozdanie z przedkongresowej konferencyi odbytej dnia 11 czerwca b. r. w Detroit, Mich., w plebanii wielebnego ks. P. Gutowskiego" ["Report of the Pre-Congress Conference of June 11 in Detroit, Mich., in the Rectory of Father P. Gutowski"], *ibid.*, June 18, 1896, pp. 399-400.

[33] The first example refers to the effort to establish an immigrant home in New York City, and reasonably enough all priests save one were from seaboard states. While five were present or past members of the "Alliance" priests or its successor organization in the Polish Union of America, the affiliation status of the others is uncertain. It may be that the Alliance-Union conflict was seen by eastern priests as having a regional character in which they felt no need to choose sides.

The pre-congress conference is more significant since it involved issues of concern to all clergy. Excluding the few laymen, the fourteen clerics were evenly divided between seaboard and inland states, indicating an effort at regional balance. More importantly, at least four, including the chairman, John Pitass, and Dominic Majer, were of "Alliance" background while at least three, among them Vincent Barzynski, had "Union" roots.

For members of various clerical organizations, see Haiman, *op. cit.*, p. 83 ("Union"); *Zgoda*, March 2, 1887, p. 4 ("Alliance"); "Z Ameryki," *Niedziela*, September 24, 1893, p. 623 (Polish Union of America). While a suspicion among the Resurrectionists among many secular clergy may have given a vague ideological content to affiliation, I believe that most priests were moved by such factors as personal acquaintance, perceptions of relative status of competing societies or other idiosyncratic factors in choosing (or not choosing) to join.

The best example of lay-clerical alliance was the drive for representation in the American episcopate. In this instance religious desires for a proper leader were interwoven with ethnic concerns for recognition, but lay-oriented publicity was largely in the latter terms. The general (but not universal) desire of the clerics for bishops was the most important factor in consolidating them in a single dominant association.

Ironically in view of later developments, Father Barzynski seems to have been the first to write of the need for a Polish bishop. In 1870 he envisioned a Slavic Vicariate Apostolic whose bishop would be able to "speak, write, listen, and judge in Polish" and complained bitterly of neglect of these new immigrants.[34] Such concerns remained within clerical ranks for many years, but their saliency grew with the tide of Polish newcomers. In April of 1886 Father Ignatius Barszcz, a diocesan priest from New Jersey, brought it to the attention of the hierarchy in a letter to Bishop Richard Gilmour of Cleveland. He urged the desirability of a national leader of the Poles, though he ingenuously asserted that such a man would be a suffragan to Gilmour. Already suspicious of German-American Catholic efforts to alter their ecclesiastical status, the bishop was not sympathetic.[35] Submission of the Abbelen Memorial later that year and the subsequent Cahenslyist movement for ethnic hierarchies drew some Polish support. But the hostile reaction of the American bishops gave them pause, and Polish priests largely recast their hopes in terms of auxiliary bishops for existing dioceses. They also realized that priestly pressure was insufficient and began to enlist lay support.

265

The priests made adroit use of the ethnic press and techniques of organization honed as leaders of young and growing parishes. In 1888 Father Barszcz was able to advocate the creation of a separate diocese of SS. Cyril and Methodius in the secularist weekly *Gazeta Polska (The Polish Gazette)*, alerting the laity to the matter.[36] In 1891 Father John Machinowski sent a petition allegedly signed by 100,000 Poles to the Holy See advocating Polish-American bishops.[37] The public movement for

---

[34]Kruszka, *op. cit.*, I, 516.

[35]Father Ignatius Barszcz to Bishop Richard Gilmour, April 8, 1886, Archives of the Diocese of Cleveland; see also Colman J. Barry, O.S.B., *The Catholic Church and German-Americans* (Milwaukee, 1953), pp. 56-68.

[36]*Gazeta Polska [The Polish Gazette,* Chicago], March 1, 1888, p. 2.

[37]Joseph Swastek, "The Formative Years of the Polish Seminary in the United States," in *The Contribution of the Poles to the Growth of Catholicism in the United States,* edd. F. Domanski *et al. (Sacrum Poloniae Millennium,* Vol. VI [Rome, 1959]), p. 130.

bishops was promoted under the catchword "equality" *(równouprawnienie),* a much more evocative term than possible alternatives such as "representation" *(representacja).* Poles proud of their ethnicity but acutely conscious of their inferior status in the multi-national American Church found demands for parity rather than tokenism satisfying.

Priests leading the movement for an episcopal presence used the device of mixed lay-clerical conventions to publicize and co-ordinate the effort. The upsurge of independentism, embodied in several small but noisy "Polish Catholic" denominations, led loyal clergy to link equality with the fight against schism from about 1895.[38] The first Polish Catholic Congress was held in Buffalo in 1896, the stronghold of the redoubtable Father John Pitass. Reflecting clerical intent to involve the laity, topics included education and workers' concerns, but the main item was equality. Barzynski, reversing his position of 1870, moved for requesting a Polish advisor to the Apostolic Delegate.[39] As the second congress was to show more clearly, the clerics were dividing. The Resurrectionists were losing their enthusiasm for Polish-American bishops, while Pitass and other seculars, both "Union" and "Alliance," became increasingly supportive. Non-participants in the 1896 congress criticized it as unrepresentative and a vehicle for the ambitions of Pitass and Barzynski.[40] The lack of a mechanism to implement convention resolutions meant there was little concrete effect, but equality received much publicity in the ethnic press.

The next Polish Catholic Congress convened in a different environment. Father Vincent Barzynski had died in 1899, and with him passed much of the Resurrectionists' influence. Father Pitass, even more active than before, promoted Buffalo as the site and functioned as president of the congress. As an Ohio priest noted, planning and representation this time included the local PNA as well as Catholic fraternal lodges and parishes, with a wide range of topics for discussion.[41] Clerics chaired all seven

---

[38]Daniel Buczek, "Polish-Americans and the Roman Catholic Church," *Polish Review,* XXI, esp. 50-52; also *Naród Polski,* April 30, 1902, p. 1; for a general history of independentism, see Hieronim Kubiak, *The Polish National Catholic Church in the United States of America from 1897 to 1980* (Cracow, 1982).

[39]*Niedziela,* March 26, 1896, p. 208.

[40]As Joseph Parot notes, the congress movement has not yet been adequately studied, but he and others have information on it in works which have sections on the quest for bishops. See Joseph Parot, *Polish Catholics in Chicago, 1850-1920* (Dekalb, Illinois, 1981), pp. 133-160; Greene, *For God and Country,* pp. 122-142; Buczek, "Polish-Americans," pp. 50-54.

[41]*Dziennik Chicagoski [Chicago Daily News,* Chicago], April 21, 1901, p. 2. See also *ibid.,* September 30, 1901, p. 2.

committees save that on business.[42] Equality headed the agenda, but while laymen proved highly supportive, the clergy were divided. The "Union" priests were split since the Resurrectionists now openly opposed pressing for bishops. In an interview shortly before the congress convened, their Superior General, Paul Smolikowski, termed equality a challenge to the American hierarchy which would produce polemical ammunition for antireligious persons to set diocesan clergy against regulars and then against the bishops. He then went on to accuse Pitass of conniving to keep the Resurrectionists out of the congress.[43] Whatever the validity of the Resurrectionist's remarks, they were out of step with the desires of most priests and laity, and clerical societies thereafter were under secular domination. *Naród Polski,* organ of the PRCU, contended that the order was cool to equality since they already had a bishop in their general, and the congress went on to strongly urge the appointment of Polish-American bishops.[44] An executive committee was set up to implement convention resolutions and the congress voted to send a delegation to the Vatican to lobby for the cause.[45] In this context the leading promoter of the episcopal cause became Father Wenceslaus Kruszka of Wisconsin, a prolific author and independent and original thinker. After considerable difficulty, he went to Rome and pressed the pope on the matter, returning in 1904 in a mood of high optimism, which in the event proved premature.[46]

267

Improved clerical organization accompanied efforts for equality. In addition to the cleric-dominated executive committee, the diocesan clergy established the Secular Priests Society (Tow. Księży Świeckich) in 1902 in "defense of Polish clerical interests" and pointedly excluded the Resurrectionists.[47] Pleas to bishops for support for Polish episcopal

---

[42]*Ibid.,* April 23, 1901, p. 2.; Wenceslaus Kruszka, *Siedem siedmioleci czyli pół wieku życia [Forty-nine Years or a Half-Century of Life]* (Milwaukee, 1924), I, 423-424.

[43]*Dziennik Chicagoski,* September 30, 1901, p. 2. So distressed was the editor of the paper, Resurrectionist in origin, that he appended a long statement asserting his independence from the congregation. Congress coverage was in fact extensive and reasonably objective.

[44]*Naród Polski,* May 7, 1902, p. 4.

[45]*Dziennik Chicagoski,* September 30, 1901, p. 2; October 1, 1901, p. 2; *Naród Polski,* January 8, 1902, p. 1.

[46]The career of this fascinating and maverick cleric has been best studied by A. Kuzniewski for the period of this essay. Kuzniewski rightly stresses the theological basis of Kruszka's call for polyglot bishops over Greene's more secular interpretation. See Kuzniewski, *Faith and Fatherland,* esp. pp. 45-46; Greene, *For God and Country,* esp. pp. 133-134.

[47]*Dziennik Chicagoski,* February 7, 1902, p. 2; Greene, *For God and Country,* p. 132.

representation aroused little interest or ineffective agreement prior to the last congress in 1904.[48]

The third and last Polish Catholic Congress was held in 1904 and imitated its predecessor. It originated through the secular clergy and convened in Pittsburgh to discuss a wide variety of topics. Father Kruszka, having recently returned from Rome, gave an optimistic report on prospects for at least one bishop.[49] Press coverage was again generous, and clerics and supportive laymen looked with hope to the future, but action did not soon follow words. The arrival of a papal investigator, Archbishop Albin Symon, in mid-1905 aroused expectations once more. This was an ethnic event of the first magnitude, as the head of the third convention's executive committee, Father Casimir Truszynski, led Symon on a tour orchestrated by the Secular Priests Society.[50] Symon made his sympathy plain and once again hopes rose, only to subside with no concrete result.[51] Finally, in 1907 Archbishop James F. Quigley of Chicago, convinced of the necessity for a Polish auxiliary in the ethnic capital, applied successfully to Rome. He further earned the gratitude of his Chicago Polish priests by requesting them to nominate a candidate from their own ranks. They chose Paul Rhode, soft-spoken but determined and in accord with their view of the role of a Polish bishop in America.[52]

Rhode proved to be an excellent choice for the post. While maintaining good relations with his superior, he traveled widely and established himself in the long-awaited role of "moral guide to Poles in America."[53] If one bishop was hardly "equality," the immense publicity surrounding his installation and his subsequent active leadership satisfied most Poles. The clergy had successfully interested the religionist and even many secularist laity in an issue remote to them by framing the matter largely in ethnic terms. The long-divided priests had a more immediate interest in a leader of their own ancestry from a mixture of religious and ethnic motives. The

[48]*Naród Polski*, January 22, 1902, p. 1; May 22, 1902, p. 1.

[49]*Ibid.*, April 20, 1904, p. 2; April 27, 1904, p. 2 on clerical initiatives for a third congress; October 12, 1904, p. 4 for topics; Greene, *For God and Country*, pp. 136-138; Parot, *op. cit.*, pp. 152-153.

[50]*Naród Polski*, June 7, 1905, p. 1; June 14, 1905, p. 1.

[51]*Ibid.*, June 28, 1905, p. 5; July 12, 1905, p. 4.

[52]Greene, *For God and Country*, pp. 141-142; Parot, *op. cit.*, p. 158.

[53]Buczek, *Immigrant Pastor*, p. 72 for this description of Rhode in the 1920's. Numerous earlier references by clerics and Catholic laymen exist in the religionist Polish press. E.g., *Polak w Ameryce*, April 6, 1894, p. 1; *Dziennik Chicagoski*, September 13, 1901, p. 2; *Naród Polski*, September 10, 1902, p. 1.

incomparable status of the episcopal office conferred an authority
unmatched by secular elections and brought with it the hope of unity and
order long sought but hitherto unattainable. Recalling Rhode's installation,
Edward Kozlowski, himself the second Polish auxiliary (1914-1915), put
this perception of the new bishop's leadership role clearly:

> And I whispered to my colleagues seated around me: 'At long last we have a
> leader — we are assigned to him as a staff and officer corps and we owe him
> military obedience — and he will lead American Polonia to victory.'[54]

For the priests, and indirectly the laity, his national leadership took
concrete shape with the formation of the Union of Polish Priests
(Zjednoczenie Kapłanów Polskich) about 1911. Bishop Rhode became
president by acclamation, and this was the largest of clerical societies, with
some three hundred members spread across the nation.[55] It served as a
forum to discuss issues of ethnic and religious importance and to frame
common policy under Rhode's direction. While it depended on moral
suasion rather than the force of canon law, it was the framework for a
quasi-denomination for Poles in America.[56]

    The quest for bishops coincided with a less dramatic effort to undergird
an ethnic Catholicism: establishment and maintenance of a Polish

269

[54]Bishop Edward Kozlowski, "Postulaty naszego społczeństwa pod względem zachowania
wiary św. naszego ludu" ["Postulates of our Society with Regard to the Preservation of the
Holy Faith among our People"], *Przegląd Kościelny* [*The Church Review*, Chicago], II
(May-June, 1915), 150.

[55]*Ibid.*, p. 151 for membership. The article is a very suggestive survey of the quest for
leadership and the nature of clerical and episcopal authority for the Polish clergy and for the
generality of Poles in America.

[56]Kantowicz insightfully discusses the role of various ethnic "quasi-denominations" in his
recent work, *Corporation Sole*, esp. pp. 71-72. See also Timothy Smith, "Religious
Denominations as Ethnic Communities: A Regional Case Study," *Church History*, XXXV
(June, 1966), 217-222 for such among Slovenes.

    Listings of officials of the U.P.P. c. 1914 show how Rhode sought inclusivity for the new
society. The sixteen directors were all seculars and evenly split between seaboard and inland
states. While the officers were mainly from inland states, two of the six were Resurrectionists,
including Joseph Weber of Chicago, who was named honorary president. Weber was titular
Archbishop of Darnis and high in a society mistrusted by many secular priests. Already in his
sixties, he arrived in Chicago only months before Rhode's selection as episcopal candidate, all
of which seems to have prevented his assuming the role of national Polish religious leader.
Given Parot's suggestion of Resurrectionist efforts to block Kruszka's mission, Weber's
inclusion in the high council of the U.P.P. is a tribute to Rhode's diplomacy. See Parot, *op. cit.*,
pp. 154-155; "Zarząd Glowny Zjednoczenia Kaplanów Polskich w Ameryce Północnej"
["Central Board of the Union of Polish Priests in North America"], *Przegląd Kościelny*, II
(January-February, 1915), 1.

seminary. This lacked the glamor of mitres, but many priests saw such an institution as essential for fostering Polish Catholicism here. In the face of episcopal apathy or hostility, and occasionally divided clerical ranks, concerned clergy mobilized the support of their colleagues and laity for the project.

The idea of an ethnic seminary was broached in 1869 by Father Joseph Dąbrowski (Dombrowski), a Polish missionary, who urged the Resurrectionists to undertake its foundation. Not only did they not do so, but Dąbrowski himself promoted it and became its first rector when it opened in 1886 as SS. Cyril and Methodius Seminary.[57] He and other advocates of the institution made a significant choice. They forsook the establishment of Polish programs at existing diocesan seminaries, an option open and even practiced occasionally in the eighties and nineties, to tread the path of separate development.[58] The ethnic advantage lay in greater control, and the promoters wanted a religionist institution — both Polish and Catholic. Bishop Caspar Borgess of Detroit was hospitable to the idea and the seminary was begun there.[59]

The seminary's early experience reflected the stresses of contemporary Polish-American society. Hardly was it founded when Union and Alliance priests contended for clerical and lay support, while Father Dąbrowski sought to maintain neutrality and to keep all sources of income open for the struggling institution.[60] For some years the secularist Polish National Alliance proved more willing to donate funds and scholarships than the religionist Polish Roman Catholic Union, and even after the 1889 PNA convention, money flowed to what Dąbrowski successfully portrayed as an ethnic as well as religious institution.[61] While the first Polish Catholic Congress included the seminary on its agenda, the school as an issue lacked

---

[57]Swastek, op. cit., pp. 48-59, 72. His is the best work on the school.

[58]For examples of Polish student groups or special courses at diocesan seminaries, see ibid., p. 95; Wiarus, November 9, 1906, p. 4. Clubs had irregular existence while courses depended on permission of local ordinaries.

[59]Swastek, op. cit., pp. 59-60.

[60]Ibid., pp. 88-89.

[61]Ibid., pp. 95-99. Dąbrowski publicly thanked the Alliance for its support in Zgoda, February 22, 1893, p. 1. For general comments in 1911 in an official Alliance publication, see "Pamiętnik wzniesienia i odsłonięcia pomników Tadeusza Kościuski i Kazimierza Pułaskiego tudzież połączonego z tą uroczystocią pierwszego Kongresu Narodowego Polskiego" ["Memorial Book of the Erection and Unveiling of the Thaddeus Kosciuszko and Casimir Pulaski Monuments as well as the Occasion of the First Polish National Congress"] (Chicago, 1911), p. 22.

the breadth of clerical constituency enjoyed by equality, and its continuation was due to the persistence of a small number of concerned clergy.[62]

To improve its financial position and to enlarge the student body, there were curriculum innovations unthinkable in Poland: extensive business courses along with the theological program. In 1905 a skeptical Archbishop Symon criticized the seminary as "half-secular," but the faculty realized that it broadened its constituency.[63] Moreover, the lack of homeland support lent a carping tone to Symon's comments. Seminary advocates wanted to ensure a domestic supply of clergy educated in their vision of group identity and were flexible about means.

One other departure from homeland practice stood out. About 1900 Erazm Jerzmanowski, reputedly the first Polish-American millionaire, offered to endow the institution. This gesture, in the classic tradition of the old country patron, presented a painful choice to the perennially underfunded school. After some debate, the trustees refused. The clergy would not dilute their independence. The seminary continued to rely on fees, donations from sympathetic persons or organizations, and profits from its print shop.[64] By publicly portraying the school as a bastion of Polishness, its clerical supporters ensured its existence and in effect provided the quasi-denomination headed by Bishop Rhode with its own training center.

Thus far we have shown priests pursuing "Polish" concerns through coalitions with the laity. But on some important issues the clergy had to stress their "Catholicism." Here the pattern of alliance was reversed: they sought support from their religious superiors against assertive laymen.

The outstanding example of clerical-episcopal co-operation was the common stance on parish polity. Disputes with laymen occurred over parochial title, administration, and priestly tenure. Conflict over one usually led to arguments about all, and the legal structure of American Catholicism meant episcopal involvement. The intensity of these struggles drew from sources beyond the points at issue. Timothy Smith has described

---

[62]Buczek, "Polish-Americans," p. 51n. Priests associated with the Polish Union, for example, voted $1000 for the seminary in 1893, but such support was irregular. See "Z Ameryki," *Niedziela*, December 24, 1893, p. 831.

[63]*Polonia w Ameryce* [*Polonia in America*, Cleveland], November 23, 1905, p. 1. For a similar combination of theological and business training in the new land among Finns, see Smith, "Religious Denominations as Ethnic Communities," pp. 212-214.

[64]Swastek, *op. cit.*, pp. 84-85, 96, 120 and passim.

271

migration as a theologizing experience" in which religious concerns took on heightened meaning in the new land.[65] Here a characteristically devout laity developed intense interest in the congregations which they were instrumental in establishing. On their part, priests here even more than at home saw themselves as the true guides of the "helpless immigrants" and thus could interpret lay initiative and demands as undermining their proper paternalistic role.[66]

As canonical issues, these had been settled long before the postbellum influx of Poles. In the early republic Irish or German congregations occasionally had incorporated themselves, administered affairs through elected parish committees, and even hired or discharged priests.[67] Stern papal and episcopal action presumably squelched such pretensions. In 1829 the First Provincial Council of Baltimore decreed that title was "to be assigned by a written document to the bishop in whose diocese it [the parish] was to be erected." Regarding tenure, the council affirmed that "... a right of appointing or dismissing pastors assumed by laymen is entirely repugnant to the doctrine and discipline of the church."[68] Subsequent councils elaborated on episcopal and clerical power in the Amercian Church but did nothing to weaken the earlier assertion of authority.[69]

Poles more than most post-Civil War Catholic immigrants reopened the issue of parish governance. Their background combined with their American experience inclined some laymen to challenge established Catholic practice here. At home they were acquainted with the concept, if

[65]Timothy L. Smith, "Religion and Ethnicity in America," *American Historical Review*, LXXXIII (December, 1978), esp. 1174-1179. This rich article summarizes his extensive research and reflection on these themes.

[66]This common clerical theme was strongly stressed at the first Union of Polish Priests convention. See Lucjan Redmer, "Wiec Księży Polskich w Ameryce Północnej" ["Convention of the Polish Clergy of North America"], *Przegląd Polsko-Amerykański* [*Polish-American Review*, Chicago], II (January-March, 1912), 3-5. Lay religionist papers echoed such views. Cf. *Naród Polski*, January 13, 1904, p. 1; April 13, 1904, p. 2 for examples.

[67]Patrick Carey, "A National Church: Catholic Search for Identity, 1820-1829" (Notre Dame - Working Paper Series, 1977); Jay P. Dolan, *The Immigrant Church: New York's Irish and German Catholics, 1815-1865* (Baltimore, 1975); Thomas T. McAvoy, C.S.C., *A History of the Catholic Church in the United States* (Notre Dame, Indiana, 1969), pp. 92-122.

[68]Patrick J. Dignan, *A History of the Legal Incorporation of Catholic Church Property in the United States, 1784-1932* (Washington, D.C., 1933), pp. 145-146.

[69]Kuzniewski, *op. cit.*, pp. 7-8.

not the practice, of patronage, which was occasionally collective.[70] In the United States conditions not only encouraged lay initiative, but frequently required it. Bishops were inclined to wait for organized lay requests, and promoters of a new congregation customarily drew upon experience gained as leaders of fraternal societies. These were democratic structures led by men of ambition, persuasiveness, and ability, and in turn they admired American representative government.[71]

Parochial conflicts tended to follow a pattern. The dissatisfied members necessarily took the initiative, criticizing the pastor for "tyranny" and occasionally for immorality as well. Upon refusal of the pastor to mend his ways, the dissenters went to the bishop or even to the Apostolic Delegate, list of grievances in hand.[72] The quarrel received publicity, both positive and negative, as both sides sought to express their positions through sympathetic newspapers. On the eve of World War I advocacy of "lay rights" achieved institutional form in the Milwaukee-based Federation of Polish Catholic Laymen (Federacja Świeckich Polaków Katolików w Ameryce), sponsored by Michael Kruszka's *Kuryer Polski* in 1911. The following editorial drew upon traditional acquaintance with patronage:

> In the old country the founders and benefactors [of a parish — the patron(s)] had a voice not only in the running of church affairs, but in the selection of the pastor. Here in America, the founders and benefactors of the Polish churches, the Polish people, should certainly have the same rights and privileges.[73]

The Federation imitated the popular fraternal society structure with local lodges, pressing for a more democratic polity while trying for a time to distinguish its goals from the schismatic Polish National Catholic

273

---

[70]A "collegium" of patrons was an accepted variant of patronage. See "Patronat" ["Patronage"], *Encykopedja Kościelna*, XVIII, 378-379. In a random selection of ten Galician parishes, at least three had multiple patrons, usually delegates of villages within the parish. See Józef P. Chodkiewicz, *Kościół katolicki na ziemiach polskich przed wojną europejską* [*The Catholic Church on Polish Soil Before the European War*] (Pulaski, Wisconisn, 1914).

[71]See Galush, *op. cit.*, pp. 82-100 for examples of lay activity in the formation of four congregations.

[72]Examples of parish conflict may be found *ibid.*, pp. 217-241; Gallagher, *op. cit.*, pp. 210-223; Greene, *For God and Country*, pp. 70-78 and passim.

[73]*Kuryer Polski*, January 25, 1912, p. 4; also August 17, 1912, p. 4.

Church.[74] The untenability of this limited form of rebellion led some to use the movement as a transition to independency, and the Federation itself evolved into another fraternal insurance organization.[75]

The Polish-American clergy saw such agitation, whether home-grown or Federation-assisted, as a challenge to their legitimate authority, and implicitly to their paternalistic role. In their adversity they appealed to their bishops, who supported clerical prerogatives even when they transferred or disciplined priests for improprieties.[76] Both bishops and priests shared common perceptions of authority in parish affairs, and so there was usually no difficulty in obtaining episcopal assistance.

Lay attacks were also an occasion for manifesting clerical solidarity, and beleaguered priests received moral support from fellow members of clerical associations.[77] The religionist press was encouraged to condemn rebellion.

The very real possibility of schism resulting from parish conflict offers a more complex example of clerical concern for their Catholicity. More than other Roman Catholics, Poles were inclined to set up independent denominations claiming to be Catholic, which by 1907 consolidated into the Polish National Catholic Church. The leader was Father Francis Hodur, a dissenting priest whose episcopal consecration by the Old Catholic Archbishop of Utrecht testified both to his regard for the apostolic succession and to his feeling that Polishness could only be preserved outside the Roman obedience.[78] Though ardent evangelists, the "independents" (niezależnicy) attracted less than five percent of Polish-

[74]Ibid., September 6, 1912, p. 4. The Federation established chapters in Wisconsin, Minnesota, Indiana, Ohio, and elsewhere, utilizing the services of an itinerant organizer as well as local initiative stimulated through the Kuryer. Many of these branches were probably short-lived. See Kuryer Polski, January 29, 1912, p. 2; March 4, 1912, p. 2; August 13, 1912, p. 4 and passim.

[75]The Federation began offering insurance about a year after its founding and then changed its name to the less provocative "Federation of Poles in America" (Federacja Polaków w Ameryce) in late 1913.

[76]E.g., Kubiak, op. cit., pp. 102-106; Galush, op. cit., pp. 221-222, 236-237; idem, "The Polish National Catholic Church: A Survey of Its Origins, Development and Missions," Records of the American Catholic Historical Society of Philadelphia, LXXXIII (September-December, 1972), 135-136.

[77]Wiarus, August 13, 1914, p. 4 for an example of a clerical society meeting at the rectory of a church during a bitter parish controversy.

[78]"Po drodze życia w 25-ta rocznice powstania Polskiego Narodowego Kościoła" ["On the Road of Life — The 25th Anniversary of the Birth of the Polish National Catholic Church"] (Scranton, 1922), p. 135.

Americans, who overwhelmingly maintained their loyalty to the ancestral faith.[79] The challenge of independency provided an opportunity for loyal clerics to pursue two disparate goals under the banner of Roman Catholicism.

Their first and more overt aim was to identify "lay rights" with schism or heresy. Since Hodur and similar dissenters advocated the holding of title by the congregation, lay administration in non-spiritual affairs, and a popular voice in selection of pastors, such demands from any source were anti-Roman Catholic. This identification was both strategic and realistic. It tarnished lay-rights demands with disloyalty and reflected the fact that association with such groups as the FPCL was often a stage on the road to the Polish National Catholic Church.[80] Prelates such as Sebastian Messmer, Archbishop of Milwaukee, co-operated in issuing condemnations of the Federation "since the aim of this association is to encourage confusion and even schism...."[81] Clerics also sought to mobilize lay opinion by discussing the dangers of independency at the Polish Catholic Congresses.[82] Uncompromising rejection of lay demands and incessant attack on the PNCC testified to the loyalty of Polish priests to the Roman Catholic Church.

275

A second aspect of this stalwart defense of Roman Catholicism was that loyalty should be rewarded. The priests linked the fight against independency with their pleas for Polish bishops, who would be unifiers and defenders of the faith.[83] Less dramatically, ordinaries could publicly demonstrate their regard for faithful Polish-American clergy by naming them as diocesan consultors or permanent rectors, and in fact promotion

---

[79]Kubiak (*op. cit.*, p. 121) notes about 15,000 members in 1906 and only about 20,000 by 1916, a tiny fraction of the over two million Poles in the United States by then. For causes of parish quarrels, *ibid.*, pp. 91-93.

[80]This can be seen in at least two instances — Minneapolis and Cleveland in 1914. As the Federation became less concerned with parochial reform, this relationship probably disappeared. See Galush, "Forming Polonia," pp. 217-241.

[81]*Wiarus*, February 22, 1912, p. 4.

[82]Parot, *op. cit.*, pp. 144-147; *Naród Polski*, October 12, 1904, p. 4.

[83]*Ibid.*, p. 146.

increased significantly from 1895 to 1910.[84] While a tie between public marks of favor and the fight against the PNCC can only be inferred, bishops were aware of Polish loyalist difficulties and the favorable publicity surrounding such appointments.

The collective story of the Polish clergy was thus a struggle for cohesion and status in a novel and challenging environment. Their inclination to form clerical societies was stimulated by several factors. They saw themselves as distinct from lay immigrants both in their paternalistic role and in having interests specific to their calling. Yet their non-Polish clerical brethren monopolized the episcopate and were apathetic or hostile to Polish ethnic concerns. Holding to a more pluralistic vision of Catholicism, but unable to promote it effectively within the larger American Church, the ethnic clergy segregated themselves in Polish parishes and various societies. Fortunately for them, lay-run ethnic organizations were usually more pragmatic than ideological, which allowed them to mobilize the immigrant masses and leaders in causes the clerics advocated. They facilitated this by portraying their concerns to the laity mainly in ethnic terms, making support of such causes a proof of Polishness. Yet they also liked the enhanced authority of the pastor in American Catholicism and co-operated with the non-Polish bishops in defense of their prerogatives and legitimate polity.

The result of this successful effort to appear both Polish and Catholic made them the most influential group of their size in Polish America and won them increasing recognition from the bishops. They were well placed to play a major role in the great testing time of World War I.

[84] The representation of Poles in diocesan posts of honor where the ethnic group was numerically strong increased significantly, but not in proportion to their numbers. Figures are taken from the *Official Catholic Directory* for 1895 and 1910.

DIOCESE	1895				1910			
	DC	PR	VG	BP	DC	PR	VG	BP
Buffalo		(na)			1	1		
Chicago		(na)			1	2	1	1
Cleveland		(na)						
Detroit					1			
Milwaukee	1	(na)			1	(na)		
New York		(na)				(na)		

DC - diocesan consultor/council; PR - permanent rector; VG - vicar general; BP - bishop; (na) - not available.

7

Anthony J. Kuzniewski, S. J.

THE CATHOLIC CHURCH
IN THE LIFE OF THE
POLISH-AMERICANS

"It has never been easy to be Polish," said a sympathetic observer.[1] Her statement is generally true, not only for the Gomułka régime in People's Poland which she had studied, but for Poles of other times and in other places. For the vagaries of history have engendered within the Polish heart a determination to survive; and the desire to preserve the notion of Polish independence, particularly during the century and a half of political suppression, most often rested upon a bittersweet combination of political loyalty and Roman Catholicism. To attend to either priority would have been difficult enough. But to nurture both, as Poles were sometimes called to do during the nineteenth century, created a special national character and an all but blind attachment to its two singular components. Faith and fatherland—bright imperatives spurring the intellectuals to lives of passionate commitment, and dimmer awarenesses in the confused understanding of the peasant majority—these allegiances were the most important part of the spiritual legacy which immigrants from Poland brought to the New World.

Between the Civil War and World War I they came to America for bread. For the most part they ate their fill, but the cost of this unaccustomed abundance was high. Religious prejudice periodically challenged their Catholicism. Racism denigrated the Slavic background. Their language sounded strange and even comic to the Americans. Under the circumstances, Christian Poles gathered together in urban ghettoes, centering their common life and hopes in large measure around the leaders and structures of the Catholic Church. But even here, in the bosom of an institution they regarded as a special mother, the burden of their past and the complica-

tions of American circumstances frequently made it difficult to be
Polish.

Being Polish at the end of the nineteenth century most often meant
to be Catholic, agricultural, and poor.[2] The ethnic and religious diversity of the Polish areas of central Europe notwithstanding, only
Roman Catholics were fully accepted as Poles. Jews, the most numerous group after the Catholics, generally lived at peace with their
neighbors, but the force of tradition supported an anti-Semitism
which excluded Jews from full membership in the village communes.
Catholicism, still reflecting some of the superstitious elements of the
peasantry, permeated all phases of life. The Church mediated the
individual's relationship to God and to his fellows, providing dignity
for even the humblest soul. "Praised be Jesus Christ!" was the commonest greeting, to which the answer was invariably given: "Forever
and ever. Amen." The priest had a special role in this society. As
a special representative of God he was constrained to be conscientious
in representing the community to the Almighty. Often the only person in the village to have been formally educated, the priest served
as counsellor in the secular as well as the spiritual realm.[3]

The religious and economic elements in the life of the peasantry
coincided most closely in the production of food. Władysław Reymont
speaks of the harvest as "a Divine Service of hard and ceaseless and
most fruitful work," in which all participated: children, the elderly
and invalids; even the dogs frisked about in the fields.[4] This mindset
stressed the importance of land as the key to the wealth which harvests produced and as an indication of the importance of the individual who possessed it. But in Poland, as elsewhere in Europe, the
land ultimately proved insufficient to sustain the lives of the rapidly
growing population. The number of people in the Russian Partition
tripled in the course of the nineteenth century; in Galicia, where the
subdivided parcels of land were too small to be recorded on official
charts, 50,000 people were starving each year in the late 1880's.[5]
The necessity to stay alive and the lack of urban industries to employ
the landless peasantry led to the great emigration. At first the Poles
came mostly from Poznania and other areas controlled by the Germans. But by 1890 German industrialization all but stopped the
outflow. After the turn of the century, Polish immigrants arrived
almost exclusively from the Russian and Austrian sectors. By the
time of the assassination at Sarajevo, 2.2 million Poles had embarked
for the United States.[6]

The chart by decades tells the story. In the decade before the Civil
War only about a thousand came each year. In the 1860's the num-

278

ber rose to 5000 per year. In the 1870's, the annual average increased to 12,000, and in the 1880's to 34,000. After a dip during the 1890's, the figures climbed dramatically: the years between 1901 and 1914 brought an average of 100,000 Polish immigrants each year.[7] Generally they settled north of the Ohio River and east of the Mississippi. Important agricultural settlements were established in Texas, Wisconsin, and New England, but for the most part the Poles settled in the cities. Chicago became the capital of these new plantations with 250,000 Polish residents in 1905 and 400,000 by 1920. New York City was the home of 200,000 Polish-Americans by the latter date; Pittsburgh had 125,000; and Buffalo, Milwaukee, and Detroit each had 100,000. Other large concentrations appeared in Cleveland, Toledo, Philadelphia, Baltimore, and Boston.[8] In 1920 the community of Polish-Americans numbered at least three million, and a half century later, mostly because of natural increase, the size had approximately doubled.[9]

279

The religious life of these millions took on unusual importance because the forms and content of the faith were one of their few sources of continuity and stability. Although there had been a few Polish priests in the United States early in the nineteenth century,[10] their number was insufficient after the Civil War. Frantic American bishops and overburdened Polish-American pastors criss-crossed Europe in the search for priests and pleaded at the offices of religious orders and congregations in Rome. "I [am] asking you for the love of God and of the Faith of our Polish people here to take charge of our Polish congregations. . . ." wrote a bishop from Kansas. "Please have the kindness to send us a Polish priest who would help us build our church and become our pastor. . . . we have no one to turn to," implored laymen from Chicago.[11] Józef Dąbrowski, pioneer pastor in central Wisconsin, found the religious conditions of the Polish colonies "in every way . . . deplorable":

> Our Polish people are living without the Mass, confession, Sunday sermons, and adequate education. Some have settled in the large cities and because of the lack of priests and the preaching of the Word of God, do not attend church services. Without any religious formation, they will surely be lost to the Church.[12]

Such pleas evoked a generous response. In a short time, newly arrived religious men and women began to assume prominent roles in the lives of the Poles in America.

Building a church was usually the first priority. Some immigrants planned ahead. Those who left Poland for Panna Maria, Texas at the end of 1854 packed a large crucifix and church bells into their

carts along with the household goods and agricultural implements.
Under the leadership of the Polish Franciscan who had invited them
to America, they formed the first Polish-American parish, opening
their church in the autumn of 1856.[13] In places where a priest was
not waiting to receive them, laymen often took the initiative. Joining a non-Polish parish, they would form a mutual aid society for
their countrymen. Eventually, under a board of trustees who were
the rising leaders of the new group, funds were collected for a
church structure. When the group had attained sufficient size and
financial strength to sustain a parish, they would petition the local
bishop for permission to build a church and for a priest.[14]

280

After the arrival of the priest, but sometimes even before, the
parish church was built. Often there was a stark contrast between
the poverty of the people and splendor of the churches. In Chicago's
St. Stanislaus Kostka Parish, for example, crowding at the turn of
the century was comparable to that of Calcutta or Tokyo. One small
block held over 1600 people; another was home for 1300 children.
The numerous basement apartments were likely to become foul-
smelling swamps during rainy weather.[15] Nevertheless, the worth
of the parish properties in 1899 was placed at $500,000.[16] Part of the
reason for the magnificence of the churches was the encouragement
of the pastors. When Wenceslaus Kruszka became the founding pastor of the Polish parish in Ripon, Wisconsin, he told his parishioners:
"The house of God must be beautiful if it is to be for the praise
of God."[17] Such exhortations do not in themselves account for the
lavishness with which the Poles constructed their churches. Built
for the glory of God, the structures satisfied deeply human needs.
They were symbols of the community's solidarity in the service of
God. They also reflected the aesthetic longings of the newcomers and
provided suitable settings for celebration and blessing of significant
human milestones.[18] Sometimes unrealistically grand designs and
financial mismanagement led to unjustified expense. The construction
of a domed basilica left St. Josaphat's Congregation in Milwaukee
with a crushing debt. Members who had loaned money to the parish,
some by mortgaging their houses, received only partial repayment.
Yet even in Milwaukee the enthusiasm for splendid churches was
not diminished. In its 1923 report to the Vatican, the Chancery Office there included four Polish churches among the seven singled
out as exceptional in construction and furnishing.[19]

From the largest to the smallest, the churches were tangible signs
of the quasi-reconstructed village life of the Old Country which centered on the parish. In the larger settlements where there were a

number of parishes, each took on a life of its own. Congregations lent their names to the districts, and individuals thought of themselves as living in St. Stan's or St. Hedwig's rather than in Polish Downtown or on the North Side. Thomas and Znaniecki, authors of the classic *The Polish Peasant in Europe and America,* concluded that the parish helped to break down the anonymity of life in America and provided a center for the unification and organization of the community. The societies and brotherhoods grouped around each congregation helped to fill a human need by giving public recognition to the members. A normal parishioner, belonging to several such groups, could in the course of his life hold a number of offices, thereby experiencing a sense of personal dignity and affirmation not available in the other public areas of his life.[20]

The parishes were as widely scattered and as varied in size as the Polish communities themselves. At the turn of the century Wenceslaus Kruszka identified 810 Polish settlements, located in almost every state. Including mission stations, there were 517 Polish churches. One congregation, St. Stanislaus Kostka in Chicago, had 45,000 members and was believed by many to be the largest Roman Catholic parish in the world. Thirteen Catholic dioceses and archdioceses had at least 50,000 Polish members.[21] This growth won wide recognition. By 1910, when the number of Polish parishes was set at 530, the *Catholic Encyclopedia* credited the Poles in America with having a greater number of churchgoing men than any other nationality. They were also characterized as builders, generous and prompt in sharing their resources.[22]

Central in the life of each parish was the Polish clergyman. Habitual Old World attitudes as well as the need for strong leadership at the beginning of immigrant life emphasized the priest's role. In his religious and social functions, the cleric became a man who "embodied religion, language, and national culture in his own person."[23] Scarcity accented the importance of the few priests who were present. In 1900, the ratio of clergy to lay people was 1:4000 for Polish-Americans, compared with a figure of 1:1000 for the American Church as a whole.[24] Access to power gave the priests the opportunity to do great good or harm. The churchmen themselves admitted their power,[25] and generally attempted to exercise it in a constructive manner. But the clergy were fettered to some extent by their own backgrounds and experience and defensive in their actions for their people. Resurrectionists in Chicago, for instance, generally favored anti-reform and anti-Progressive local politicians, preferring to work with the Democratic bosses who could give tangible benefits to the

281

Poles.[26] In New Britain, Lucjan Bójnowski influenced local politics for years, in addition to his role as moral teacher and minister of the sacraments.[27] His experience in this regard was not unusual, particularly in the early years.

The reaction of the Polish-Americans to their pastors was generally positive. Grateful for the unselfish dedication he had witnessed, one writer rhapsodized about the qualities of Polonia's priests:

> To our forgotten, unknown settlements in America came the priest-countryman. He came like a missionary and taught us how to pray, how to read in Polish; he told us what a Pole is and who the Polish people are—what their feelings and needs are. These priests, together with the people, founded our parishes, raised up our temples, built schools, orphanages, and hospitals, founded brotherhoods and other associations, introduced the idea of harmony and unity, organized mutual aid—in a word, created a community out of a disorderly multitude.[28]

282

From the start, there were Poles who disagreed. Henryk Sienkiewicz thought Chicago's Polonia resembled a society of the Middle Ages, with excessive clerical control in the secular areas of life.[29] In the long run, whatever problems might have arisen among the Polish clergy were largely mitigated by the group's own diversity. A variety of approaches, constructive mutual criticism, and, in time, intergenerational tensions helped almost all to avoid the worst temptations to abuse their personal power.

The awesome responsibilities carried by these men emphasized their personalities and sometimes led to dramatic confrontations. Particularly in the formative years, untoward incidents interrupted the peaceful development of the young communities. At Polonia, Wisconsin, parishioners angered by the pastor's insistence on moving the church from a crossroads made raucous by the presence of several saloons, sabotaged the rectory by placing in its woodpile stove-length sticks of wood which had been hollowed out, filled with gunpowder, and sealed with wax. Fortunately, Father Dąbrowski left the room just after throwing one of the sticks into his stove.[30] In Chicago, the first Polish pastor alienated some who thought his salary too high and that he spent too much time with a female cousin. Six masked gunmen broke into his rectory and beat him with rubber rods after throwing him to the ground and covering him with a sheet.[31] Such episodes, repeated with disturbing frequency before 1900, suggest the sensitivity of the pastor's office and the difficulty in finding priests with the right combination of personal qualities to enforce stability.

One solution was for the local ordinary to ask an order of religious men for assistance. Bishop Thomas Foley of Chicago chose this option in inviting the Congregation of the Resurrection (Resurrectionists) to Chicago in 1870. The group, which had had a few members serving Polish settlements in Texas, quickly built up a network of parishes and influence in this largest Polish-American community. Nine of the fifteen parishes established in Chicago between 1872 and 1899 had Resurrectionist founders. Monetary loans and other assistance extended Resurrectionist influence to several others.[32] Operating from this base, the congregation eventually opened two high schools and engaged in a journalistic apostolate through the daily *Dziennik Chicagoski* (begun in 1889) and about a dozen other publications. From the pulpit and in the pages of the *Dziennik*, whose circulation reached 42,000 in 1918, the Resurrectionists advocated a policy of close allegiance to the hierarchy and careful cooperation with them. The chief priority in Polish-American life was interpreted as commitment to the Church.[33]

283

Undoubtedly the greatest individual to emerge during the first generation of Resurrectionist service in Chicago was Vincent Barzynski, pastor of St. Stanislaus Kostka Congregation from 1874 to his death in 1899. Barzynski came to Texas in 1866 after having been imprisoned for his participation in the January Insurrection of 1863. Reassigned to St. Stanislaus in 1874, he supervised the parish as it grew from 2500 to 40,000 members. He invited the Sisters of the Holy Family of Nazareth to begin their American apostolate, built an orphanage, and pursued an active journalistic career. He organized nearly forty societies at the parish and opened a parish bank where members earned interest on deposits which were frequently loaned to new congregations for building a church. He founded the first Polish high school in Chicago and was the dominant influence and guiding spirit of the Polish Roman Catholic Union during his term as national chaplain, 1874-1891. Because of his forceful presence, his policies and principles largely determined the subsequent development of the Polish community in Chicago and beyond.[34]

In New England, the founding father of Polish Catholic life was Lucjan Bójnowski, pastor in New Britain from 1895 to 1957. A builder like Barzynski, Bójnowski constructed a large parish church, founded and built an orphanage, organized a religious congregation of teaching sisters, published a weekly newspaper, erected a home for the aged, and was involved in an immigrant home and a home for working women in New York City. His concern for cradle-to-grave care within a relatively autonomous Polish Catholic community even led him to put Turkish baths and a swimming pool in the school basement to facilitate cleanliness in the days before the bathtub was a common convenience. A proponent of ethnic and religious separateness, he elucidated ten principles for Polish life in the United States. "Marriages should be only between Polish men and Polish women," read one. Another warned: "Whoever is not with the Church is against the Church and the Fatherland." In time, younger generations grew critical of his positions and uneasy with his authoritarianism: the first generation could not easily advise the third. But even the most restive never questioned the importance of what he accomplished.[35]

284

While pastoring a congregation of "greenhorns" was the commonest occupation of Polish America's first priests, several rose to prominence in other occupations. Among them was Józef Dąbrowski. Fleeing Poland after participating in the January Insurrection, he studied theology in Rome, where he was ordained in 1869. Bishop Joseph Melcher of Green Bay offered him a German parish in Wisconsin, but Dąbrowski agreed to come only on the condition of being assigned to a Polish congregation. In 1870, the young priest assumed responsibilities at the remote town of Polonia. While there, he brought the Sisters of St. Felix (Felicians) to teach at the school and wrote a number of textbooks for use by the school children. Two disastrous fires left him undaunted, and he had rebuilt everything when health forced him to relocate to Detroit in 1880. There, he designed and helped to build an American motherhouse and novitiate for the Felicians. Later, with the permission of Bishop Borgess, he built a seminary for the training of Polish-American priests. The institution, Sts. Cyril and Methodius Seminary, was opened in Detroit in 1886. By the turn of the century, it counted thirty alumni, including Lucjan Bójnowski.[36]

Dąbrowski's work as priest-educator was paralleled in importance by Wenceslaus Kruszka's efforts as historian and national crusader. An immigrant from the German partition, Kruszka served parishes in Ripon and Milwaukee after his ordination in 1895. In his spare time, he prepared the first comprehensive history of the Poles in America, a work which appeared in thirteen small volumes between 1905 and 1908. Dedicated to the Polish cause, Kruszka worked unstintingly for the appointment of Polish bishops in the United States. In this work, he differentiated himself somewhat from Barzynski, Bójnowski, and Dąbrowski. For Kruszka, the national idea and pluralistic Catholicism were supreme concepts, and he spent his life trying to expand the actively Polish presence within the Catholic Church in the United States.[37] A few other priests supported his ideas and his work, most notably Casimir Sztuczko, C.S.C., pastor of Holy Trinity Parish in Chicago.[38] Men like Kruszka exercised a role which was at times more prophetic than priestly, and their work should be evaluated with respect for that distinction.

The necessity of service to the Church was never a debatable question for the Polish clergy, but the issue of leadership was. After the turn of the century, the leadership question increasingly focused on the effort to obtain Polish bishops. At the beginning of their stay in the United States, Poles assumed that bishops of their own ethnic background would be appointed more or less in proportion to the numerical importance of the Polish element within the Catholic Church.[39] But the struggles over Cahenslyism and Americanism during the 1890's created an atmosphere in which the national origins of each new bishop were an extremely sensitive matter.[40] Anti-Catholic nativism complicated the issue, with the result that Polish priests were not elevated to bishoprics, even after the Polish Catholic community in America had grown to several million. The relatively rapid rise of the independent churches after 1900, partly on the issue of a Polish bishop, spurred some of the Polish Roman Catholics to action.

The most articulate of this group was Wenceslaus Kruszka, who, in 1901, published an article in New York's *Freeman's Journal* to argue that bishops should know the principal languages used by Catholics in their dioceses; otherwise, the prelates would be unable to fulfill their responsibilities to the faithful.[41] This article and the extensive knowledge resulting from his research on the Polish-American history assured Kruszka of a prominent position at the Polish Catholic Convention which met in Buffalo in 1901 to debate the bishop issue and other problems. "The schismatics have the popular side of the affair," members of the congress warned the American bishops in their memorial. "They have so-called Polish bishops, whereas they accuse the Polish Roman Catholic clergy of treason to their nation when holding allegiance to Irish and German bishops, as they say."[42] Kruszka and Rev. John Pitass of Buffalo were delegated to petition the Pope directly if the memorial to the American bishops failed to achieve the desired result. Shortly after the congress, Archbishop Frederick Katzer of Milwaukee agreed to ask Leo XIII for a Polish auxiliary, but his request was refused.[43] In 1903-04, therefore, Kruszka himself travelled to Rome to petition the newly elected Pius X, who promised to resolve the impasse "according to your wishes."[44]

To the exasperation of Kruszka and an increasingly large number of Polish-American Catholics, the process moved slowly. In 1905, a papal observer visited the Polish settlements on a fact-finding mis-

285

sion from the Vatican. Even Theodore Roosevelt expressed his willingness to have a Pole in the Catholic hierarchy. Finally in 1907, Archbishop James Quigley of Chicago received permission to name a Polish auxiliary and, calling the Polish priests of his diocese together, asked them to elect one of their number. The choice fell to Paul Rhode, who was consecrated in 1908. He was later named ordinary in Green Bay, where he remained until his death in 1945.[45] Rhode's unique position as the only Polish bishop in the country won for him *de facto* recognition as a special bishop for all the Poles in the United States. Confirmations, building dedications, and other religious events brought him invitations from many places, despite his technical status as auxiliary to the Archbishop of Chicago.[46] Rhode has been followed by about fifteen additional Polish-American bishops, including Cardinal John Krol, Archbishop of Philadelphia, who has served as head of the National Conference of Catholic Bishops.

Despite the fact that American priests of Polish descent have periodically been named as bishops, protests about the lack of "equality" of Polish-American Catholics have been a continuing phenomenon. Circumstances sometimes lent weight to the allegations. When a Polish-speaking Czech was named auxiliary bishop in Milwaukee in 1911, the Polish priests of the diocese termed the appointment an insult to their nationality. The unfortunate man was soon given his own diocese, with a Pole appointed to the vacancy in Milwaukee.[47] But it was fifteen years before another Polish-American was chosen to be bishop in the United States. George Mundelein, who served as Cardinal Archbishop of Chicago between the two world wars, expressed his opposition to having a Polish auxiliary even though his diocese contained several hundred thousand Catholics of Polish descent.[48] The seeming reluctance of the American bishops to yield to the Polish claims has led Andrew Greeley to praise Archbishop Quigley and Wenceslaus Kruszka for far-sightedness which preserved the unity of the Church in the face of the ethnic issue: "The Milwaukee Polish priest-journalist and the Chicago Irish archbishop were a strange coalition, but they were many decades ahead of their time in grasping the issues and the answers for a pluralistic Catholicism."[49] Eugene Kusielewicz expressed a similar view while serving as vice-president to the Kosciuszko Foundation. He claimed that the status of Poles in the American Catholic Church has led young priests and sisters to consider their ethnic identity a liability in an institution he called "One, Holy, Irish, and Apostolic." He proposed the appointment of more Polish bishops as one suitable remedy.[50]

While most Polish Catholics have agreed on the desirability of having more of their number appointed bishops, fundamental disagreements have arisen over the best manner of achieving that goal. The Resurrectionists, for instance, have generally cautioned that attacks upon the American bishops as being anti-Polish would be counterproductive.[51] Bishop Rhode took much the same position after his consecration in 1908. And the Association of Polish Priests, meeting in Detroit in 1912, expelled Wenceslaus Kruszka from the convention for his refusal to condemn newspapers critical of the American hierarchy.[52] Thus, the bishop issue has divided the Polish Catholic community. Supporters of the cooperative approach have regarded the activists as demagogues and national chauvinists who threaten the unity of the Church. The equality crusaders, on the other hand, charge their Polish-American antagonists with apathy and a scandalous disregard of the best religious interests of the group.

287

Several explanations have been offered for the sensitivity of Polish-Americans to their status within the Church. Traditional historians have regarded the American Catholic authorities as hostile to the aspirations of the Poles. Such resistance to legitimate Polish claims, they have maintained, have forced Polish Catholics into a highly emotional campaign to secure even a fraction of the recognition which is their due.[53] But more recently Victor Greene has suggested that the fight for equality had its roots in a fundamental disagreement among the Polish leaders in America over the ordering of their religious and national priorities. The outcome was the arousal of ethnic awareness within the entire Polish community, thereby conferring major importance on an issue which had been previously nonexistent for many people.[54] Whatever its sources, the fight has added a dramatic dimension to the story of the Poles in the United States, and the elevation of a Polish-American priest to the episcopal dignity is still enough of a rarity that careful counts are kept.

By way of contrast, the least controversial element in the lives of America's Catholic Poles has probably been concern for the children. Working with a constituency whose relatively high illiteracy rate and economic insecurity frequently made them unaware of the advantages of formal schooling, the Polish priests devoted what was often the lion's share of the congregation's resources to the educational ministry. What saved the situation and made the immigrants cooperative and generous in this regard was the clear opportunity the school presented to inculcate in the next generation traditional values, beliefs, and a sense of Polish history. At its root, the school served a dual purpose: it taught the rudiments of Catholicism, and it strengthened the possibility that the Polish identity would be preserved in the midst of non-Polish America.[55] The initial difference between the Poles and the Yankees made schools especially crucial. In their study of, American Catholic education, Andrew Greeley and Peter Rossi noted that, because of their importance in preserving cultural traditions, parochial schools were stronger in Polish than in Irish areas, where the ethnic ways were closer to the dominant American pattern. Poles have maintained a high rate of attending Catholic schools even in the third and subsequent generations.[56]

288

Desiring a school and establishing one are two different matters. Finding money, teachers, buildings and equipment were a perennial problem in the years before World War I. Rapid expansion of the school system placed a heavy demand on the slender resources of the community, particularly in obtaining qualified teachers. The first formal Polish school opened at St. Stanislaus Parish in Milwaukee in 1868. In 1887, there were already fifty schools with 14,000 children attending. And by 1914, Polish Catholic schools numbered almost 400, with 128,540 students. St. Stanislaus Kostka School in Chicago reached an enrollment of over 3800 by the latter date.[57]

Necessity often dictated that the first location of the school would be makeshift, although some parishes built a school before a church. Frequently, old, poorly ventilated wooden churches were used for classrooms. A parish in Pittsburgh temporarily instructed 120 children in a room in the basement of the rectory. The lack of educational aids led to inventiveness. At one school, children wrote with chalk on stove lids instead of slate tablets. Old maps and a lack of adequate textbooks complicated the situation; and classes of 80 to 140 were not uncommon.[58] Unlike the little red schoolhouse remembered so nostalgically by many, Polish Americans tended to remember the early days of the parish schools with a sense of relief that they had ended. A parishioner at Holy Trinity Parish in Chicago described early classes in the rectory:

So many of our young people were suffocating in cramped, poorly ventilated classrooms. It was a pity to see them, packed like herrings in a barrel during the hours of instruction, poring over their books.[59]

Given these conditions, the economic circumstances which forced children to work at an early age were not an unmitigated disaster. Within the parochial system, there were not enough places to keep very many children in school for more than a few years.[60] And because of ideological hostility to the immigrants and the lack of facilities for the children of the newcomers, the public schools offered no acceptable alternative.[61]

The strongest brake on the expansion and upgrading of the system was the lack of qualified teachers. In many places, the first to teach the Three R's was the organist, frequently a man who knew no English, with the pastor supplying catechetical instructions. In 1868, Polish members of the School Sisters of Notre Dame began to teach in Milwaukee,[62] and six years later Józef Dąbrowski brought the first Polish sisters from Europe.[63] This group, the Sisters of St. Felix (Felicians), were inundated with requests to accept schools. By 1883, they had eight schools in their care; and by 1909 they had undertaken the responsibility for 98 parochial schools with a total enrollment of 36,000! Other religious sisterhoods demonstrated the same pattern. In 1909, the Sisters of the Holy Family of Nazareth, who had come to the United States just 24 years earlier, were teaching 16,000 students at 25 schools. In the same year, Sisters of St. Joseph of the Third Order of St. Francis, established in the Green Bay Diocese just after the turn of the century, were staffing 22 schools with 8500 pupils. Groups like the Bernardines, Resurrectionists, Franciscans, and School Sisters of Notre Dame also assumed heavy educational burdens. By 1914, there were 2180 teaching sisters at work in the Polish parochial school system.[64]

289

Overwhelmed with the need to staff schools which were multiplying helter-skelter, the congregations of religious women were able to provide only a minimum of training to their members. Often poorly educated before entering the convent, women were given brief but intensive instructions in the spirituality of their founders and in the subject matter which they would be teaching. Then they were rushed to the classroom. For Felicians in the early years, the training period lasted only three years. In addition to preparation for religious life, they learned English and Polish grammar and the history of Poland and of the United States. Arithmetic, singing and some handicraft instructions rounded out the course, with Józef Dąbrowski himself giving pointers on teaching methods. As circumstances permitted, teacher training was upgraded; by 1921 the Felicians received state certification for their course of preparation.[65]

Subject matter in the Polish schools reflected the training of the teachers. At the turn of the century, when most students attended school only to the time of First Communion, the course generally consisted of bible history, reading, and grammar in Polish, as well as the history and literature of Poland. In English the students learned arithmetic, American history, geography, English grammar, and penmanship.[66] Although relatively narrow, this range of subjects probably prepared the students sufficiently for the life of hard work which awaited most of them. In 1912, the Association of Polish Priests recommended reform and diversification, with the introduction of instructions in hygiene, civics, natural history, first aid, and gymnastics. Summer school programs for teachers were also urged.[67] In time, such suggestions were put into effect and Polish schools progressed accordingly.

Polish high schools, reflecting the national pattern, developed slowly. The first of them was attached to Sts. Cyril and Methodius Seminary in Detroit and was similar to a European five-year classical gymnasium. Although the school was primarily for aspiring priests, many studied there for secular occupations, particularly medicine and the law. After 1909, these institutions were moved to the more pleasant surroundings of Orchard Lake, Michigan. Other early high schools included three in Chicago: Holy Family Academy (Sisters of Nazareth, 1887), St. Stanislaus Kostka—later Weber—High School (Resurrectionists, 1890), and Holy Trinity High School (Holy Cross Fathers, 1910). St. John Kanty High School opened in Erie in 1914, promising to train young men to "stand faithfully . . . with their countrymen under the motto 'God and Country'." There were about 500 students in Polish Catholic high schools in 1914.[68]

The *sine qua non* of Polish educational efforts in the United States[69] has been the women religious who staffed them. Their dedication and perseverance under the most trying circumstances marked many of them as models of heroism and sanctity. The first Sisters of Nazareth, for instance, came to Chicago with their founder, Mother Mary Siedliska. Signifying the group's commitment to the American apostolate, Siedliska herself accepted American citizenship in 1897.[70] Always the spiritual guide of her sisters, Mother Mary urged her followers to consider their vocation a gift of God and their lives a loving response of service in God's kingdom. The inspiration of the group's unselfish work was found in ". . . the hidden life of the Holy Family, a life . . . which required the self-discipline of humility and detachment, the shedding of affectation, conceit and smugness, the fostering of universality of charity in the bond of unity of the children of God."[71] History attests that the spiritual foundations of the Sisters of Nazareth and of the others have remained a firm basis for a demanding way of life.

The role of lay people in the early development of the Catholic life of the Polish immigrants is more difficult to relate. The reasons for this are clear. Large families and slender economic resources left the lay people with little time in which to undertake larger corporate responsibilities. Furthermore, the Catholic Church in the years before Vatican II consistently worked to prevent notions of popular government from affecting ecclesiastical structures. A handbook prepared for Catholics of the Milwaukee Archdiocese in 1907 warned explicitly: ". . . the Church is not a republic or democracy, but a monarchy; . . . all her authority is from above and rests in her Hierarchy; . . . while the faithful of the laity have divinely given rights to receive all the blessed ministrations of the Church, they have absolutely no right whatever to rule and govern."[72] With authority remaining a carefully guarded prerogative of the hierarchy, the major means for lay persons to participate in Catholic life were in their financial support and through the various organizations grouped around the parish, region, and nation.

291

For Polish Catholic laymen, the foremost of these societies was the Polish Roman Catholic Union, formed in 1873 to be a mutual aid organization for all Poles regardless of religion. Very quickly, however, the PRCU fell under the influence of Vincent Barzynski and a stricter Catholic orientation resulted. The principal goals of the group were to uphold the religious and national spirit of the immigrants by guarding against the loss of Catholicism and Polishness and to prevent the denationalization of the younger generation by supporting the parochial schools. Two feasts were celebrated annually: May Third (Constitution Day), and a feast of the November Insurrection, which was a memorial day for the patriots of the uprisings against Partitions.[73] In time, the more liberal element within the Polish community formed the Polish National Alliance which, while respecting the Catholic affiliation of the majority of Poles, admitted non-Catholics to membership. The PNA was the chief proponent in the United States of the concept of the Fourth Partition —the idea that America's Poles constituted a new and free partition of Poland and were obliged to continue working for the liberation of the homeland. Although the relations between the two organizations were occasionally bitter, both were in broad agreement about the goals. The major difference was in emphasis, with the PNA consistently attracting more members.[74]

Polish lay women also organized to aid the community, although social constraints on the activities of women limited their role more than that of the men. The largest national organization was the Polish Women's Alliance of America, organized in Chicago in 1898 by Stefania Chmielinska. The group's purpose was to foster patriotism among its members and to aid the oppressed in Poland. Since its inception, the group has aided children, the elderly, and the sick in the United States and in Poland.[75] Typical of a more strictly Catholic organization was the Association of Polish Women, formed at St. Stanislaus Kostka Parish in Chicago in 1900. The members pledged to uphold the Roman Catholic faith and the Polish traditions. Charitable efforts were their hallmark. "The Association," said one jubilee book, "dries the tears of orphans, obliges itself to nurse and to assist the sick, and to spread the Catholic principles, the commands of love of God and our neighbor." Cultural evenings and periodic reception of the sacraments rounded out the group's activities.[76]

292

Apart from the lay organizations, a number of individuals rose to prominence during the early years of Polish life in America. Because of the nature of their occupations, writers and politicians tended to receive the most publicity. Anthony A. Paryski was an example of the former. An immigrant of 1888, he worked on papers in Detroit, Chicago, and Winona before establishing the immensely popular *Ameryka-Echo* at Toledo in 1902. He published and reprinted five million books at his presses during his lifetime. Prominent in the Catholic press was Jerome Derdowski, who established the arch-Catholic weekly, *Wiarus*, at Winona in 1888. Michael Kruszka, publisher of Milwaukee's *Kuryer Polski*, used journalism as a springboard to political activity. Elected to the Wisconsin Assembly in 1890, he helped repeal legislation which had severely restricted the state's immigrant and parochial schools. In Chicago, Peter Kiolbasa was a founding father *par excellence* of the Polish community. An organizer of the first Polish parish, he was elected to various local offices, including City Treasurer. His integrity in an era of municipal graft earned him the title "Honest Pete."[77]

No list of outstanding Polish immigrants who served the religious and civic interests of the community would be complete without including the gifted scholar and historian, Mieczysław Haiman. Arriving in the United States in 1913, Haiman worked in the editorial offices of Polish newspapers in Boston, Buffalo, and Chicago. The preparation of feature articles turned his interest increasingly to historical research. In 1935, when the Polish Roman Catholic Union decided to establish an archive and museum at its offices in Chicago, Haiman was named curator. In that position he published a series of *Annals* which examined Polish-American life in the colonial era, and early Polish participation in the history of California. He also wrote an excellent account of Polish-American life before 1865 and a biography of Tadeusz Kościuszko. Drawing upon the financial and moral backing of the PRCU and the good will of the Polish community generally, Haiman and his collaborator, Alphonse Wolanin, were successful·in accumulating a large research library. Concerned that the scholarship he had begun would be continued in later generations, Haiman helped to organize the Polish American Historical Association in 1948. His final effort, a lengthy history of the PRCU, was completed just before his death in 1949.[78]

After the national laws of 1921 and 1924 reduced the level of immigration, a new phase opened in the history of the Polish-American Catholics. And, because the massive infusion of fresh immigrants and traditional ideas from the Old Country had all but ended, the new era belonged increasingly to the second and third generations, people who had never seen Poland and people who, increasingly, could not speak the Polish language. Statistics told the story of an ethnic community which continued to grow and whose increasing prosperity[79] gave lie to the restrictionists' accusations of inferiority. But the statistics told little about the changing quality of life in Polish America.

293

Schools were the area of greatest growth after the First World War. By 1921, they numbered 511, with an enrollment of 220,000 students —about 2/3 of all the Polish-American children attending school that year. The Depression slowed the rise in enrollment. In 1932, the number of students was placed at 250,000. The falling birth rate of the 1930's was reflected in lower enrollments during the 1940's. By 1946, there were approximately 155,000 studying in Polish Catholic schools, a figure which rose again in the following decade, reaching 214,000 in 1957.[80] That increase, however, was only temporary. The decline in the Catholic educational network affected the Polish parishes like the others. By 1971, the total number of Polish Catholic schools had fallen to 310.[81]

Americanization efforts and the Red Scare contributed to the decline in the use of Polish in these schools. The Diocese of Buffalo mandated English-only instructions in 1923, and in Chicago Cardinal Mundelein attempted to eradicate Polish instructions in the parish schools, to minimize the use of Polish in worship services, and even to liquidate the seminary at Orchard Lake.[82] But in most places, the teaching of Polish and teaching in Polish were allowed to follow the language preferences of the broader community in a gradual transition to using English exclusively. By 1971, only three Polish schools in the United States still offered half-day instructions in Polish; fewer than 15% offered Polish language instructions as part of the curriculum.[83]

The brightest part of the Polish educational picture after the end of the great migration was the rise in the number of high schools. Reflecting the national pattern, Polish-Americans began to attend high school in larger numbers after 1920. In 1921, there were eleven Polish high schools in the United States with about 1900 students. By 1930, the number of schools had risen to 40, and student enrollment to 4000. By 1947, the figures had risen substantially: 90 Polish high schools existed in the United States with an enrollment of 15,608. The schools at Orchard Lake continued to attract a small but slowly rising group of students. Between 1930 and 1962, the numbers of students at the high school increased from 194 to 266. The seminary, by the later date, had graduated well over 2000 priests.[84]

294

During the peak years of the educational effort in the immigrant Church, teaching sisterhoods attracted large numbers of Polish women. There were about 5500 religious women teaching in Polish schools during the 1920's and 1930's. A survey of 1943 showed that there were over 9300 Polish sisters, of whom nearly 5400 were teachers. The largest groups of Polish religious women continued to be the Felicians, Sisters of Nazareth, Sisters of St. Joseph, Bernardines, Franciscan Sisters of St. Joseph, and the School Sisters of Notre Dame, each of which had over 500 Polish-American members.[85] In more recent times, these sisterhoods have expanded their activities to Spanish-speaking ministries and to participation in such government programs for the disadvantaged as Head Start.[86]

The years after Vatican II were transforming ones for Polish Catholics in America. For, in addition to the spirit of change and renewal which spread through the Church, responsibilities for Polish and Catholic life were again being passed to a new set of individuals. The younger leaders of the third generation and beyond were people who took the American way of life for granted and for whom the emotional attachment to Poland and the Polish language was tenuous.[87] In numerical terms, the first and second generations accounted for only 52% of the Polish Catholics in America in 1976.[88] Old Polish neighborhoods began to disintegrate as their occupants passed on or moved on to the ethnically mixed neighborhoods in the suburbs. Straws in the wind suggested rapid decline.

But "decline" is an elusive concept. In terms of the cultural life of the turn-of-the-century communities, there was, of course, a decline. Nevertheless, indomitable vitality contradicted the predictions of doom. The community continued to evolve, not consciously rejecting the past or living in an idealized projection of the future, but reflecting the process by which the grandchildren of the immigrants, Americans now by whatever measurement one applied, retained a set of habits, attitudes, and values which marked them as products of the Polish-American experience. Researchers at Chicago's National Opinion Research Center, for instance, have recently discovered that Polish involvement within the Catholic Church has actually increased in the course of several generations. Church attendance and support for the parochial school system have risen. The Americanization of the Polish immigrant has evidently tied him even more closely to the institutional structures of Catholic America.[89] Further evidence of constructive adaptation has appeared in Detroit where, in 1968, the Archdiocesan Conference of Polish Priests pledged itself to support the movement for equal rights in America. By 1969, meetings between Polish and Black leaders there led to the formation of the Black-Polish Conference whose goal was to "bridge the gap" in a society which often forced the two groups to live in economic competition.[90]

295

*   *   *

It has never been easy to be Polish. The record of the Poles in America and of their participation in the growth of Roman Catholicism is filled with examples. By turns defensive, aggressive, generous, and exclusive, America's Poles have always been difficult to understand and dangerous to ignore. They have contended with one another, often bitterly, over the relationship of religion to nationality. They have waged a long campaign to achieve greater recognition within the ranks of the hierarchy—an effort which has shown them at their best and at their worst. And they have responded heroically to the demands of building churches and schools, mortgaging their homes, when necessary, for the sake of the parish, only to see the inevitable transformation of the traditional ways which those structures were supposed to support.

"We Poles have no higher ambition, we boast, than to be a Christian nation. That has been not only our fault but our foolishness."[91] So lamented a Polish doctor in Pittsburgh during the mid-thirties. His critique had a point. The Catholicism of America's Poles sometimes rested on a definition of "Christian" which was naive. Blind faith in religious leaders who were only human did as much harm as the equally unrealistic attacks sometimes mounted against them. A too-strict insistence that only Roman Catholics could be Poles bred a narrowness which now hurts the individuals who are excluded from human fellowship as much as it deprives those who try to maintain thereby an un-Christian and self-righteous purity. But the doctor's comment had its limits. He was too harsh. He missed the point of the old saying: "The Poles are God's madmen, and so He takes great care to protect them."[92] For the Polish-American Catholic has been a believer. He has experienced the holy madness and divine protection from the start. Whoever doubts it has only to look around.

NOTES

[1] Eva Fournier, *Poland*, trans. by Alisa Jaffa (London: Vista Books, 1964), p. 185.

[2] See especially Stefan Kieniewicz, *The Emancipation of the Polish Peasantry* (Chicago: University of Chicago Press, 1969); and Marian Kukiel, *Dzieje Polski Porozbiorowe, 1795-1921* (London: B. Swiderski, 1961), pp. 374-506.

[3] William I. Thomas and Florian Znaniecki, *The Polish Peasant in Europe and America* (2d ed.: New York: Octagon Books, 1974), 1:205-284. See also Anthony J. Kuzniewski, Jr., "Faith and Fatherland: An Intellectual History of the Polish Immigrant Community in Wisconsin, 1838-1918" (unpublished Ph.D. dissertation, Harvard University, 1973), pp. 7-11.

[4] Ladislas Reymont, *The Peasants*, trans. by Michael Dziewicki (4 vols.; New York: Alfred A. Knopf, 1937), 4:283-84.

[5] Kuzniewski, "Faith and Fatherland," pp. 7, 20-32.

[6] Mieczyslaw Szawleski, *Wychodźstwo Polskie w Stanach Zjednoczonych Ameryki* (Lwów, 1924), p. 17.

[7] *Ibid.*

[8] Victor R. Greene, *For God and Country: The Rise of Polish and Lithuanian Ethnic Consciousness in America, 1860-1910* (Madison: The State Historical Society of Wisconsin, 1975), p. 45.

[9] Hieronim Kubiak, *Polski Narodowy Kościół Katolicki w Stanach Zjednoczonych Ameryki w Latach 1897-1965* (Wroclaw: Wydawnictwo Polskiej Akademii Nauk, 1970), p. 39, estimates a figure of six million Polish-Americans for the mid-1960's. His statistic seems reasonable, given that the size of the original migration was about 2.2 million.

[10] Mieczyslaw Haiman, *Polish Past in America, 1608-1865* (2d printing; Chicago: Polish Museum of America, 1974), pp. 65-67. One of the early priests, Francis Dzierozynski, served as provincial of the American Province of the Jesuits, 1840-43.

[11] These and other requests received by the Congregation of the Resurrection in Rome and preserved in its archives there are reprinted in John Iwicki, *The First One Hundred Years: A Study of the Apostolate of the Congregation of the Resurrection in the United States, 1866-1966* (Rome: Gregorian University Press, 1966), pp. 11-13, 49.

[12] Joseph Dąbrowski to Peter Semenenko, C.R., March 16, 1870, *ibid.*, p. 53.

[13] Joseph Swastek, *Priest and Pioneer: Rev. Leopold Moczygemba* (Detroit: The Conventual Press, 1951), pp. 3-12; [Adolf Bakanowski,] *Polish Circuit Rider: The Texas Memoirs of Adolf Bakanowski*, trans. and annotated by Marion Moore Coleman (Cheshire, Connecticut: Cherry Hill Books, 1971), pp. 15-16; Theresita Polzin, *The Polish Americans: Whence and Whither* (Pulaski, Wisconsin: Franciscan Publishers, 1973), pp. 41-43.

[14] *Ibid.*, pp. 84-85.

[15] Andrew M. Greeley, "Catholicism in America: Two Hundred Years and Counting," in *The Critic*, 34 (Summer, 1976), 35.

[16] Greene, *God and Country*, pp. 76-77.

[17] Wacław Kruszka, *Historya Polska w Ameryce* (13 vols.; Milwaukee: Drukiem Spółki Wydawniczej Kuryera, 1905-08), 8:55.

[18] Thomas and Znaniecki, *Polish Peasant*, 1:276-77.

[19] Kuzniewski, "Faith and Fatherland," pp. 116, 202-06, 316-21.

[20] Thomas and Znaniecki, *Polish Peasant*, 2:1521-41; Edward R. Kantowicz, *Polish-American Politics in Chicago, 1888-1940* (Chicago: University of Chicago Press, 1975), pp. 26-27; Oscar Handlin, *The Uprooted* (2d ed.; Boston: Little,

Brown and Co., 1973), pp. 105-28.

²¹ Kruszka, *Historya Polska*, 1:90-139, 2:6-10; Kantowicz, *Polish-American Politics*, pp. 31-32.

²² Richard M. Linkh, *American Catholicism and European Immigrants, 1900-1924* (Staten Island: Center for Migration Studies, 1975), pp. 44-45; Polzin, *Polish-Americans*, p. 89.

²³ Kantowicz, *Polish-American Politics*, pp. 30-31.

²⁴ Kubiak, *Polski Narodowy Kościół*, p. 79 n.; Kruszka, *Historya Polska*, 2:14.

²⁵ See, for example, the comments of a Polish-American priest on the role he and his associates assumed in the public life of Milwaukee: Boleslaus A. Góral, "The Poles in Milwaukee," in *Memoirs of Milwaukee County*, edited by Jerome A. Watrous (3 vols.; Madison: Western Historical Association, 1909), 1:616, 626.

²⁶ Kantowicz, *Polish-American Politics*, pp. 88-89.

²⁷ Daniel S. Buczek, *Immigrant Pastor: The Life of the Right Reverend Monsignor Lucyan Bójnowski of New Britain, Connecticut* (Waterbury: Heminway Corporation, 1974), pp. 115-16.

²⁸ Karol Wachtl, *Polonja w Ameryce* (Philadelphia: Nakładem autora, 1944), pp. 77-78.

²⁹ Józef Miąso, *Dzieje oświaty polonijnej w Stanach Zjednoczonych* (Warszawa: Państwowe Wydawnictwo Naukowe, 1970), p. 47.

³⁰ Kuzniewski, "Faith and Fatherland," pp. 130-33.

³¹ Greene, *God and Country*, pp. 71-72.

³² *Ibid.*, pp. 62-63; Kruszka, *Historya Polska*, 8:117-10:163 passim; Iwicki, *First Hundred Years*, pp. 48-108.

³³ *Ibid.*, pp. 196-220; Greene, *God and Country*, pp. 67-77.

³⁴ *Ibid.*, pp. 75-78, 87-88; see also Edward T. Janas, *Dictionary of American Resurrectionists* (Rome, 1967), pp. 6-10.

³⁵ Buczek, *Immigrant Pastor*, pp. 12, 42-44, 55-56, 62, 73, 141; John W. Michalowski, personal interview, Chestnut Hill, Massachusetts, July 1, 1976.

³⁶ Aleksander Syski, *Ks. Józef Dąbrowski: Monografia Historyczna* (Orchard Lake: Ss. Cyril and Methodius Seminary, 1942), pp. 54-185, 220-29.

³⁷ Kuzniewski, "Faith and Fatherland," pp. 160-413.

³⁸ Greene, *God and Country*, pp. 81-82.

³⁹ W. Kruszka discusses some early efforts to obtain Polish-speaking bishops in the United States in *Historya Polska*, 2:60-63. Before 1900 Poles in America were generally optimistic about the appointment of one of their number to episcopal office. Periodic rumors centered on one or another of the more prominent Polish priests. The appointment of Cardinal Mieczyslaw Ledóchowski to head the Congregation for the Propagation of the Faith encouraged the optimism. Even Cardinal Gibbons, visiting Milwaukee in 1891, made the tantalizing statement that the Poles had not been sufficiently recognized before then but that the situation would change. Kuzniewski, "Faith and Fatherland," pp. 169-73.

⁴⁰ The standard source is Thomas T. McAvoy, *The Great Crisis in American Catholic History, 1895-1900* (Chicago: Henry Regnery Co., 1957).

⁴¹ "I do affirm with certainty," Kruszka wrote, ". . . that nowadays in the United States, whosoever (a candidate) dares to assume the duties of a bishop in a polyglot diocese, without being a polyglot himself, takes duties upon himself which he knows he is unable to perform, and therefore commits a mortal sin." Kuzniewski. "Faith and Fatherland," pp. 216-219.

⁴² Wenceslaus Kruszka, *Siedm Siedmioleci czyli Pół Wieku Życia* (2 vols.; Poznań: Czcionkami Drukarni Sw. Wojciecha, 1924), 1:443.

⁴³ Kuzniewski, "Faith and Fatherland," pp. 222-25.

⁴⁴ *Ibid.*, p. 242.

⁴⁵ *Ibid.*, pp. 248-56, 307-10, 452-55.

297

[46] Greene, *God and Country*, pp. 141-42, 169-70.

[47] Kuzniewski, "Faith and Fatherland." pp. 337-42, 395-97.

[48] Wachtl, *Polonja w Ameryce*, pp. 101-11.

[49] Greeley, *The Critic*, 34:17-18.

[50] Eugene Kusielewicz, *Reflections on the Cultural Condition of the Polish American Community* (New York: Czas Publishing Co., 1969), pp. 11-13.

[51] Iwicki, *First Hundred Years*, p. 107 n.

[52] Kuzniewski, "Faith and Fatherland," pp. 356-58.

[53] Wachtl, *Polonja w Ameryce*, pp. 103-07; Kruszka, *Historya Polska*, 2:56-59.

[54] Greene, *God and Country*, pp. 5-11, 67, 162-76.

[55] Thomas and Znaniecki, *Polish Peasant*, 2:1532-33; Miąso, *Dzieje oświaty*, p. 43.

[56] Andrew M. Greeley and Peter H. Rossi, *The Education of Catholic Americans* (New York: Doubleday Anchor Books, 1968), pp. 3-4, 36-41.

[57] Miąso, *Dzieje oświaty*, pp. 110-13, 116-19, 121.

[58] *Ibid.*, pp. 110-13, 131.

[59] *Pamiętnik parafii św. Trójcy w Chicago, 1893-1918* (Chicago, 1918), p. 19, in Miąso, *Dzieje oświaty*, p. 112.

[60] *Ibid.*, pp. 114-15, 125-26.

[61] Anthony J. Kuzniewski, "Boot Straps and Book Learning: Reflections on the Education of Polish Americans," in *Polish American Studies*, 32 (Autumn, 1975), 14-23.

[62] Sister M. Nobilis, "The First Polish School in the United States," in *Polish American Studies*, 4 (January-June, 1947), 1-5.

[63] Syski, *Dąbrowski*, pp. 83-84.

[64] Miąso, *Dzieje oświaty*, pp. 119-22.

[65] *Ibid.*, p. 119.

[66] *Ibid.*, pp. 114-15, 125-26.

[67] *Ibid.*, pp. 167-68.

[68] *Ibid.*, pp. 178-83, 196-97.

[69] The concentration on the educational efforts of the Polish sisters in this article is not intended to minimize their record of service in such other apostolates as the care of the elderly and the administration of hospitals and orphanages. For a reasonably comprehensive survey of their non-educational works in 1943 see Stanislaw Targosz, *Polonia Katolicka w Stanach Zjednoczonych w Przekroju* (Detroit: Czcionkami Drukarni Kooperatywnej Barc Bros., 1943), pp. 46-73. See also Wachtl, *Polonja w Ameryce*, pp. 177-81.

[70] Sister M. DeChantal, *Out of Nazareth* (New York: Exposition Press, 1974), pp. 62, 112.

[71] *Ibid.*, p. 38.

[72] *Handbook for Parishioners of the Archdiocese of Milwaukee* (Milwaukee, 1907), pp. 23-24.

[73] Iwicki, *First Hundred Years*, pp. 229-39; Wachtl, *Polonja w Ameryce*, pp. 164-65.

[74] Joseph A. Wytrwal, *America's Polish Heritage* (Detroit: Endurance Press, 1961), pp. 172-76, 227-35.

[75] *Ibid.*, pp. 184-86.

[76] Cited in Frank Renkiewicz, editor and compiler, *The Poles in America, 1608-1972*, The Ethnic Chronology Series, Number 9 (Dobbs Ferry, New York: Oceana Publications, Inc., 1973), pp. 62-63.

[77] For information on these and other community leaders, see Francis Bolek, ed., *Who's Who in Polish America* (3d ed.; New York: Harbinger House, 1943). Thumbnail biographies of the individuals named in this paragraph may also be found in Wachtl, *Polonja w Ameryce*, pp. 227 (Paryski), 242 (Derdowski), 225-26 (M. Kruszka), and 166 (Kiolbasa). Additional information on Kiolbasa's role in

Chicago's political life is in Kantowicz, *Polish-American Politics*, pp. 45-48, 53-56, 60-61.

[78] LeRoy H. Fischer, "Mieczyslaw Haiman, Historian of Polish America," introduction to Haiman, *Polish Past*, pp. 1-u.

[79] Andrew Greeley claims spectacular success for the Poles, placing them fifth among all groups in America outside the South for average family income. Andrew Greeley with T. George Harris, "Catholics Prosper While the Church Crumbles," *Psychology Today*, June, 1976, p. 44. Michael Novak disagrees in *The Rise of the Unmeltable Ethnics* (New York: The Macmillan Co., 1971), p. 22. Evidently, more research is needed to assess the true economic status of Polish-Americans. It is clear, however, that the standard of living for the Polish-Americans has risen substantially in the course of three generations, paralleling the general developments in the nation.

[80] Miąso *Dzieje oświaty*, pp. 230-32, 266.

[81] Polzin, *Polish-Americans*, p. 148.

[82] Miąso, *Dzieje oświaty*, p. 230.

[83] Polzin, *Polish-Americans*, p. 148.

[84] Miąso, *Dzieje oświaty*, pp. 243-45, 268-71.

[85] Wachtl, *Polonja w Ameryce*, pp. 123-33; Targosz, *Polonia Katolicka*, chart facing p. 46.

[86] DeChantal, *Out of Nazareth*, pp. 253, 301-02.

[87] For an interesting discussion of the evolution of the Polish Catholic community in the Chicago Archdiocese, see M. J. Madaj, "Chicago: Polish Capital of U.S.," in *The New World* (Chicago), April 9, 1971. It should be noted that Masses in Polish, permissible since the reforms of Vatican II, have been promoted through liturgists at Orchard Lake and introduced at a number of Polish-American parishes in dioceses where the ordinary allows it.

[88] Greeley, *The Critic*, 34:18.

[89] Harold J. Abramson, *Ethnic Diversity in Catholic America* (New York: John Wiley and Sons, 1973), pp. 176-77. Applying Hansen's Law to the religious life of the descendants of immigrants, Will Herberg argued in 1955 that religious identity was strengthened by the third generation's search for ethnic roots. The point evidently has some validity for the Poles. *Protestant, Catholic, Jew* (rev. ed.; Garden City: Anchor Books, 1960), pp. 254-59.

[90] Renkiewicz, *Poles in America*, pp. 36-37. See also the "Statement of Purpose" of Detroit's' Black-Polish Conference, *ibid.*, p. 109.

[91] A. S. Małłek, "My a język polski," in *The Polish Student Bulletin*, 1 (1934), cited in Miąso, *Dzieje oświaty*, p. 257.

[92] Fournier, *Poland*, p. 116.

ADDITIONAL SOURCES

Books (including those not readily noticeable in the "Notes" above)

[Bakanowski, Adolf.] *Polish Circuit Rider: The Texas Memoirs of Adolf Bakanowski*. Translated and annotated by Marion Moore Coleman. Cheshire, Connecticut: Cherry Hill Books, 1971.

Handlin, Oscar. *The Uprooted*. 2d ed. Boston: Little, Brown and Co., 1973.

Herberg, Will. *Protestant, Catholic, Jew*. Rev. ed. Garden City: Doubleday Anchor Books, 1960.

Iwicki, John. *The First One Hundred Years: A Study of the Apostolate of the Congregation of the Resurrection in the United States, 1866-1966*. Rome: Gregorian University Press, 1966.

Jañas, Edward R. *Dictionary of American Resurrectionists, 1865-1965*. Rome, 1967.

299

Kantowicz, Edward R. *Polish-American Politics in Chicago, 1888-1940*. Chicago: University of Chicago Press, 1975.

Kukiel, Marian. *Dzieje Polski Porozbiorowe, 1795-1921*. London: B. Świderski, 1961.

McAvoy, Thomas T. *The Great Crisis in American Catholic History, 1895-1900*. Chicago: Henry Regnery Co., 1957.

Novak, Michael. *The Rise of the Unmeltable Ethnics*. New York: Macmillan Co., 1971.

Polzin, Theresita. *The Polish Americans: Whence and Whither*. Pulaski, Wisconsin: Franciscan Publishers, 1973.

Targosz, Stanisław. *Polonia Katolicka w Stanach Zjednoczonych w Przekroju*. Detroit: Nakładem autora, 1943.

Articles

Doman, Sister M. Tullia. "Polish American Sisterhoods and their Contributions to the Catholic Church in the U.S." *Sacrum Poloniae Millenium*, VI. Rome: 1959.

Fischer, LeRoy H. "Mieczysław Haiman, Historian of Polish America," introduction to Mieczysław Haiman, *Polish Past in America, 1608-1865*. Chicago: Polish Museum of America, 1974. Pp. i-u.

Góral, Boleslaus A. "The Poles of Milwaukee," in Jerome A. Watrous, ed., *Memoirs of Milwaukee County*. 3 vols. Madison: Western Historical Association, 1909. 1:612-633.

Greeley, Andrew, with Harris, T. George. "Catholics Prosper While the Church Crumbles." *Psychology Today*, June, 1976, pp. 44, 47, 49, 51, 82.

Madaj, M. J. "Chicago: Polish Capital of U.S." *The New World* (Chicago), April 9, 1971.

Unpublished Sources

Kuzniewski, Anthony J. "Faith and Fatherland: An Intellectual History of the Polish Immigrant Community in Wisconsin, 1838-1918." Unpublished Ph.D. dissertation, Harvard University. 1973.

Michalowski, John W. Personal interview, Chestnut Hill, Massachusetts, July 1, 1976.

The Laity in the Church: Slovaks and the Catholic Church in pre-World War I Pittsburgh

June Granatir Alexander

In April 1895, the *Pittsburgh Catholic*, the official diocesan newspaper, proudly reported: the "progress" of Catholicism "is conspicuously marked in this diocese by the steady increase of churches to accom[m]odate the faithful."[1] This glowing assessment was prompted by news that the city's first Slovak Catholic church, Saint Elizabeth's, had been organized. Saint Elizabeth's came into existence because Slovak lay Catholics had taken it upon themselves to found a national church. If the diocese defined "progress" as an increase in the number of churches, Pittsburgh's Slovak immigrants certainly contributed to that progress during the next decade. By 1909, lay-initiated movements had led to the formation of three more Slovak Catholic churches in Pittsburgh.[2]

The development of Slovak national churches in pre-World War I Pittsburgh provides useful material for a case study that helps clarify two important points of historical analysis. In the recent past, historians analyzing the impact of aggressive immigrant laities on the Catholic church in the United States have demonstrated that relations between some immigrant laities and church officials were less harmonious than traditional histories of the American Catholic church have suggested. It has been demonstrated, for example, that at times church officials actually had to battle assertive parishioners determined to gain control of local churches.[3] And American clergymen often disdained premigration folk traditions that

A slightly different version of this essay was presented at the annual meeting of the Organization of American Historians, held in Philadelphia in April 1982. I wish to thank Randall M. Miller and John Bodnar for their comments. Research for this essay was funded in part by a grant from the International Research and Exchanges Board.

1. 11 April 1895.
2. Because Allegheny City was annexed by Pittsburgh in 1907, Slovaks residing in that area will be considered here as part of Pittsburgh's pre-World War I Slovak population.
3. See Victor Greene, *For God and Country: The Rise of Polish and Lithuanian Ethnic Consciousness in America, 1860-1910* (Madison, 1975); Anthony J. Kuzniewski, *Faith and Fatherland: The Polish Church War in Wisconsin, 1896-1918* (Notre Dame, 1980); Joseph John Parot, *Polish Catholics in Chicago, 1850-1920* (DeKalb, IL, 1981); William J. Galush, "Faith and Fatherland: Dimensions of Polish-American Ethnoreligion, 1875-1975" in *Immigrants and Religion in Urban America* Randall M. Miller and Thomas D. Marzik, eds., (Philadelphia, 1977), pp. 84-102; M. Mark Stolarik, "Lay Initiative in

Ms. Alexander is instructor of history in the Ohio State University, Columbus, Ohio.

immigrants had incorporated into their religious practices.[4] The historians who have studied such open conflict have, in general, provided a much needed corrective view of the history of the Catholic church in the United States. But, in 1916, there were more than 2,230 Roman Catholic immigrants' congregations and another 3,846 used both English and a foreign language in services.[5] The majority of these national parishes had not experienced serious problems or engaged in heated, open conflict with their respective bishops. The Slovak parishes of pre-World War I Pittsburgh fall into this category.

This analysis offers a case study of relatively quiescent church-immigrant relations and addresses the questions: did the lack of conflict indicate that these immigrant laities were not aggressive in their dealings with their prelates; did laypersons docily accept the bishop's authority within their dioceses; how was conflict avoided? By blending the findings of those who have analyzed conflict with the results of studies of churches where there was little or no apparent conflict between immigrants and Catholic church officials, we can reach a more balanced picture of relations between immigrant laities and the American church hierarchy at the turn of the twentieth century.

An examination of the interaction of Slovak immigrants and the Catholic church hierarchy in Pittsburgh also offers an opportunity to test generalizations advanced by some historians that lay participation in parish affairs was a continuation of the laities' expanding role in their premigration churches.[6] In the case of Pittsburgh Slovaks, lay involvement did not represent such a continuation. The role of the Slovak laity underwent important changes as these Catholic immigrants interacted with and adapted to Pittsburgh's established Catholic church structure.

In the pre-World War I era, Pittsburgh's bishops welcomed the lay activism that spurred immigrants to found and take an active interest in their local churches. However, as the following discussion shows, Pittsburgh's Catholic hierarchy also feared these immigrant laities who were deferential yet assertive in their dealings with church leaders. By examining the relations

American-Slovak Parishes, 1880-1930," *Records of the American Catholic Historical Society of Philadelphia* 83 (September-December, 1972): 151-158; Rudolph J. Vecoli, "Prelates and Peasants: Italian Immigrants and the Catholic Church," *Journal of Social History* 2 (1969): 217-268.

4. Rudolph J. Vecoli, "Cult and Occult in Italian-American Culture: The Persistence of a Religious Heritage," in Miller and Marzik, *Immigrants and Religion*, pp. 25-47; Vecoli, "Prelates and Peasants," pp. 227-235.

5. U.S. Department of Commerce, Bureau of the Census, *Religious Bodies 1916*, Pt. 1, *Summary and General Tables*, p. 83.

6. See Timothy L. Smith, "Lay Initiative in the Religious Life of American Immigrants, 1880-1950" in *Anonymous Americans: Explorations in Nineteenth-Century Social History*, ed. Tamara K. Hareven (Englewood Cliffs, NJ, 1971), pp. 214-249. See also Stolarik, "Lay Initiative," p. 151; Galush, "Faith and Fatherland," pp. 85-86. On premigration voluntaryism among Irish Catholics, see Patrick Carey, "Voluntaryism: An Irish Catholic Tradition," *Church History* 48 (1979): 49-62.

between church officials and the Slovak laity and assessing the changing role of Slovak laypersons, we can further understand the mutual impact that immigrants and the Catholic church in the United States had on each other.

Founding churches was a new experience for Slovak immigrants. In northern Hungary, Slovaks worshipped in churches that were centuries old by the time immigration to the United States began in the 1870s.[7] In America, if Slovaks wanted separate churches, they would have to establish them. In Pittsburgh, Saint Elizabeth's was founded through a city-wide lay effort initiated by a Slovak fraternal organization. In February 1894, members of a branch of the First Catholic Slovak Union decided enough Slovaks lived in the Pittsburgh area so that "it would be good if there were a Slovak church" in the city.[8] These fraternal members invited other Pittsburgh branches of the First Catholic Slovak Union to attend a meeting in April to discuss plans for a church. At this general meeting, a Church Committee was chosen to supervise the effort; other committees were selected to collect money and to look for a church site. Not until May was a committee appointed to seek the bishop's permission to found a Slovak church. Once consulted, Bishop Richard Phelan immediately approved.[9]

In founding this first church, Pittsburgh's Slovak Catholics demonstrated a deference to the bishop's authority over Catholics in his diocese; but, it was an assertive deference. Slovaks sought the bishop's permission only after taking active steps toward organizing a church. Still, they recognized the bishop's legitmate authority in the diocese. Futhermore, church organizers apparently believed they had to assure their countrypeople that they had the bishop's approval for the endeavor. Saint Elizabeth's Church Committee used the bishop's sanction to encourage Slovaks to contribute money: in public appeals for donations, the committee explained that the collectors were soliciting funds "with the bishop's permission."[10] The founders of three additional Slovak Catholic Churches in Pittsburgh followed a pattern similar to that of Saint Elizabeth's organizers. Except in one case, Slovak Catholics sought the bishop's permission for a church only after lay plans were well underway. While these Slovaks did act deferentially, their deference was accompanied by

7. Spolok Sv. Vojtech, *Katolícke Slovensko* (Catholic Slovakia) (Trnava, Czechoslovakia, 1933), pp. 17–152. Not every Slovak village had a church; sometimes several neighboring villages shared a church.

8. Branch 2 (First Catholic Slovak Union), Pojednávania Schôdzi Sp. Sv. Michael Aug. 1891 do April 1900 (Minutes of the meetings of the Society of Saint Michael, August 1891 to April 1900), meeting of 14 February 1894, Branch 2 Collection, Jednota Archives and Museum, Middletown, PA.

9. Ibid., meeting of 24 April 1894; Jozef A. Kushner, *Slováci Katolíci Pittsburghského Biskupstva* (Slovak Catholics of the Pittsburgh Diocese) (Passaic, NJ, 1946), pp. 94–95; Saint Elizabeth Roman Catholic Church, *Pamätník Zlatého Jubilea to jest Pät'desiat Ročnej Slavnosti Slovenskej Rimsko-Katolíckej Osady 1894–1944* (Souvenir of the Golden Jubilee of Saint Elizabeth Roman Catholic Church) (n.p., 1944), pp. 11–15.

10. *Amerikánsko-Slovenské Noviny*, 12 December 1894, 8 January 1895.

the assumption that the bishop would simply comply with their requests. Even when the bishop hesitated to grant permission for a church, Slovak laypersons seemed convinced and determined that his approval would be forthcoming. This determination was evident in the founding of Saint Gabriel Church.

In 1902, Slovaks who lived in Woods Run approached the prelate with plans for a church. Bishop Phelan denied the request and even refused to permit a census of the Woods Run area to determine if enough Slovaks lived in the neighborhood to warrant a church. Unhappy with the bishop's decision, Slovaks visited him several times to plead their case.[11] Bishop Phelan finally agreed to allow a census but stipulated that unless one hundred Slovak Catholic families were found living in Woods Run, he would not grant permission for a Slovak church. Slovak lay persons assisted the priest charged with conducting the canvass which got underway in July 1902.[12]

While the census was being taken, and before the results were known, church organizers proceeded with plans for a dance to raise funds for the new church.[13] The organizers were not defying the bishop; indeed, they had shown deference to him. But, clearly these Slovaks optimistically assumed that the census takers would find the required number of families and that Phelan would approve their plans. The July census did not, however, reveal the requisite one hundred families, and the bishop withheld his permission. Still unhappy, but accepting the bishop's decision, laypersons persisted in the effort to find one hundred Slovak families so a church could be established. By the fall of 1902, the necessary number was obtained. The bishop yielded to lay wishes and approved the project.[14] These lay Catholics then went ahead with plans—plans they had refused to abandon—to organize a Slovak parish. By 1903, the Pittsburgh area contained another Slovak parish because lay determination superseded lay deference.

Bishop Phelan, however, rejected the name Woods Run Slovaks had given their proposed church. They wanted to name the church after Saint Michael the Archangel and had even used that name in advertising plans for the

11. Saint Gabriel Slovak Roman Catholic Church, *Pamätník Zlatého Jubilea Slovenskej Rímsko Katolíckej Osady Sv. Gabriela, N.S.* (Souvenir of the Golden Jubilee of Saint Gabriel Slovak Roman Catholic Church, North Side) (n.p., 1953).
12. Ibid., *Amerikánsko-Slovenské Noviny*, 24 July 1902.
13. *Amerikánsko-Slovenské Noviny*, 24 July and 6 August 1902.
14. According to Saint Gabriel's church history (Pamätník), the initial small count was due to interference by Saint Elizabeth's trustees who reportedly urged Wood Run Slovaks to stay members of Saint Elizabeth's. Also, some Slovaks apparently were afraid to register in a census. The Saint Gabriel parish files that were available to me contained no information explaining the bishop's actions. The papers of Bishop Richard Phelan available to me held no information concerning the bishop's decisions regarding individual parishes. The papers available were primarily official documents, minutes of general Catholic conferences, and published materials of the diocese. (The Richard Phelan papers are housed in the Archives of the Diocese of Pittsburgh, Pittsburgh, PA).

church. Stating there were already too many churches in the diocese by that name, the bishop offered three other suggestions. Slovaks accepted the bishop's rejection but none of his alternatives. They offered instead Saint Gabriel. This time, the bishop approved the choice.[15] Again, laypersons had refused to comply docily with the bishop's wishes and in this small way asserted themselves.

The establishment of Saint Elizabeth's and especially of Saint Gabriel Church shows the power the laity could wield when dealing with Pittsburgh's diocesan hierarchy. The founders of Saint Gabriel's exerted subtle pressure on the bishop by persisting in their request to establish a church. Confronted with determined, aggressive lay Catholics whose plans were already in progress, the bishop, who wanted immigrants to remain actively faithful to the Catholic church, had little alternative but to comply. Conflict was avoided because the bishop acceded to the desires of the city's Slovaks who wanted to organize parishes. Also, Bishop Richard Phelan and his successor, Regis Canevin, reflected the view of those bishops labeled "conservative." This group viewed national parishes as integral to the preservation of faith among Catholic immigrants.[16] Bishop Phelan signaled his approval of foreign language churches in 1904 when he ruled that Catholics who "habitually" frequented churches "where religious instruction is . . . in a language they do not understand" committed a grievous sin.[17] Given this attitude, Phelan apparently welcomed the lay activism that led to the formation of national churches.

The lay effort to organize Saint Joachim's in Frankstown, located in southeastern Pittsburgh, followed a somewhat different course. Frankstown Slovaks were initially less aggressive than those who had founded churches elsewhere in the city. Yet, the Frankstown effort offers an example both of assertive deference by Slovaks and the pressure these lay Catholics could have on bishops.

Frankstown Slovaks had not begun searching for a possible site nor had they raised money for the endeavor when, in 1907, they petitioned for diocesan permission to organize a Slovak parish in their neighborhood.[18] For unexplained reasons, these Slovaks seemed determined to obtain the bishop's approval before taking additional steps to found a church. At first, Bishop Canevin ignored their petition. He apparently was influenced by the pastor

305

15. Kushner, *Slováci Katolíci*, p. 102; Saint Gabriel Church, *Pamätník; Amerikánsko-Slovenské Noviny*, 24 July and 6 August 1902.
16. See Richard M. Linkh, *American Catholicism and European Immigrants, 1900-1924* (New York, 1975).
17. *Pittsburgh Catholic*, 10 November 1904. As early as 1890, Pittsburgh's Catholic church officials declared themselves in opposition to some of the positions of those who have been termed "liberal" bishops led by Archbishop John Ireland of Saint Paul. *Pittsburgh Catholic*, 17 July 1890; see also ibid., 24 August 1893.
18. *Jednota*, 3 July 1907, 16 November 1910.

of Saint Elizabeth Church, Father Gasparik, who opposed another Slovak church in Pittsburgh that would further drain his parish of members.[19]

By 1909, Slovaks in Frankstown clearly were impatient with Bishop Canevin's procrastination. In October one layman, Frank Benkovsky, conveyed this impatience to the prelate.[20] He wrote to Canevin and reminded him that two months earlier, Slovak Catholics had sent a list of persons "willing to organize a Slovak parish in Frankstown." He complained that he and his fellow countrypeople had "acted as you directed and have done everything you desire, but to this date we do not have any answer from you or [the] Chancellor ...." "Our people," Benkovsky bluntly asserted, are "very dissatisfied with this delay and in the name of Slovaks living in the vicinity of Frankstown I ask you to answer our letter." Expressing the hope that Canevin would "attend to this [matter] immediately," Benkovsky even thanked the bishop "in advance" for his cooperation. Although he adopted a properly deferential tone by closing the letter with "your obedient servant," the message was clear. While Benkovsky and the Frankstown Slovaks may have been obedient Catholics, they were growing impatient and angry. Because they accepted the bishop's authority, Frankstown Slovaks sought his permission to establish a church; however, these laypersons demanded that he act in accordance with their wishes.

Bishop Canevin feared the action these assertive Catholics might take if he continued to ignore them. Specifically, he feared they might revolt and establish an independent church. And, in 1909, the threat of a independent Slovak church loomed large in the minds of Pittsburgh's Catholic church hierarchy. A few months earlier, Slovak Catholics in Homestead had formed an independent parish.[21] Whether justified or not, diocesan officials viewed the Frankstown Slovak community with eyes focused on nearby Homestead. Within three days of receiving Benkovsky's letter, Canevin informed Father Gasparik that the diocesan office had received a "number of communications" from Slovaks in the Frankstown vicinity that indicated they were willing to support a church. He also revealed why he had decided to accede to their wishes: "I feel that the urgent demand of these people cannot be put off

306

19. This procrastination was not due to a change in diocesan policy regarding national churches when Canevin replaced Phelan. To the contrary, so many new churches were founded during Canevin's episcopacy (1904–1920) that he later was referred to in the Pittsburgh diocese's history as "preeminently a builder." Catholic Historical Society of Western Pennsylvania, ed., *Catholic Pittsburgh's One Hundred Years* (Chicago, 1943), pp. 68–69, with quotation at p. 68. Father Gasparik could have influenced the bishop since he was a member of the Diocesan Building Committee.
20. Frank Benkovsky to Rt. Rev. J. F. Regis Canevin, 20 October 1909, Saint Joachim Church, Erection and Boundaries File, Office of the Vicar-General Chancellor (hereafter referred to as OVGC), Pittsburgh, PA.
21. *Jednota*, 3 November 1909; Kushner, *Slováci Katolíci*, p. 61; interview with Margaret Kuzma, Homestead, PA, 20 November 1978. Mrs. Kuzma, as a child, was a member of the Homestead independent church.

any longer, and steps must be taken to establish a mission or parish in that locality; otherwise we may have another independent on our hands such as we now have in Homestead."[22] On the same day he wrote to Gasparik, the bishop informed Benkovsky that "we are now looking about for a priest to undertake the work of forming a mission or parish" in Frankstown.[23] Canevin wasted no time in finding a pastor to oversee the new parish; three days later, he appointed a priest to serve Frankstown Slovaks.[24] In Frankstown, assertive deference and fear combined to defuse open conflict between Slovaks and their bishop.

In the case of the Frankstown Slovak Catholics, Bishop Canevin agreed to lay demands because he feared that the aggressive lay initiative which had been responsible for the "progress" of Catholicism and the "steady increase" in the number of churches in Pittsburgh might be channeled toward organizing an independent parish. These Slovaks had not threatened to take such action and had, indeed, demonstrated considerable deference toward the bishop's authority. But when Slovak lay requests assumed a more demanding tone, the prelate interpreted them as a threat. In this instance, the bishop preferred to have one too many churches under his wing than possibly to have an independent church outside the flock.

For Pittsburgh Slovaks, founding churches represented only one aspect of their new and extended participation in church affairs. As Pittsburgh's Slovak Catholics proceeded from organizing churches to maintaining them, their role continued to change from the one they had known in their homeland. It was this increased lay involvement that helped make Pittsburgh's Slovak churches not merely transplanted but, rather, hybrid institutions.

In the Hungary from which the Slovaks had come, ordinary parishioners were not involved in the administrative or financial affairs of their local churches. The state paid clerical salaries; the other financial responsibilities for churches rested with local gentry, known as church patrons. At times, individual villagers did contribute food and other goods to their pastors or made needed repairs on the church and parish house.[25] In some areas a parish

22. Letter to Rev. C. Gasparik, 23 October 1909, Saint Joachim Church, Erections and Boundaries File, OVGC. This letter is an unsigned carbon but the contents indicate that the bishop wrote it.
23. Letter to Frank Benkovsky, 23 October 1909, Saint Joachim Church, Erections and Boundaries File, OVGC.
24. Kushner, Slováci Katolíci, p. 109; Priests' Biographies, 1906-1912, entry for Father Joseph Vrhunec, Diocesan Archives of Pittsburgh.
25. This description of lay involvement in Slovak churches in Hungary was derived from: Jednota, 20 July 1904; "Tie Kňazské dôchodky, bohatstvá" (Priest's income, wealth), Jednota Katolícky Kalendár, 1911, p. 54; Stefan Furdek, "Vel'konočné Spoved" (Easter Confession) Jednota Katolícky Kalendár, 1913, pp. 105-107; The Catholic Encyclopedia, 1913, s. v. "Hungary," by A. Aldasy; interviews with Ferdinand Dvorsky, 12 April 1977 and 28 November 1978, John Ciganik, 17 May 1977 and 30 November 1978, Andrew Holovanisin, 30 November 1978 (all held in Pittsburgh). These men came from three

priest or municipal officials occasionally petitioned the county government for financial aid for a church or for permission to institute a temporary collection for a church that had burned down or needed repairs. Such collections were conducted among villages in the region of the church requiring aid. Still, when village churches needed financial assistance, ordinary laypersons did not initiate requests for the aid, nor were parishioners the regular financial backers of individual village or town churches.[26]

In Pittsburgh, maintaining churches became a feature of Slovak parish life. The individual congregations were responsible for raising all their operating funds, and the parishes were permitted to choose the methods they wanted to garner money for the church. All of the city's Slovak parishes established a collection system whereby designated lay members visited parishioners' homes to collect monthly assessments. Some church ceremonies also served the dual function of religious services and money-raising events. In addition, religious organizations sponsored social festivities to raise funds. As a result of these various events, obtaining money for churches combined lay responsibilities with social activities among parishioners.[27]

---

different counties in northern Hungary and their descriptions of lay involvement and financial obligations reveal there was definitely a uniformity in the laity's restrictive role in local churches throughout Upper Hungary.

26. This is a composite derived from documents contained in the records of several county governments housed in three regional and one district archives in eastern Czechoslovakia. Citations for the following representative documents include collection titles and the call number of the specific documents; the numbers which follow slashes are the date (year) of the documents. Documents in the county records indicate that the practice of instituting temporary collections for churches among neighboring villages differed among the counties. Requests for collections were more common in Spiš County (State Regional Archives, Levoča, Hlavný Župan (Chief County Administrator), 601/1887, 309/1891, 318/1891, 140/1898, 498/1899; Podžupan (Assistant County Administrator), 826/1894; and in the Bratislava district (Bratislava Regional Archives, Bratislava, Zápisnice municipalného výboru, 1867-1918 (Minutes of the municipal council), 1634/455-1868, 281/43-1868, 75/42-1869, 116/78-1869, 116/19-1869. I could find petitions for only two collections in the Prešov region (State Regional Archives, Prešov, Župan, 169/1894, 208-271/1898). In the Košiče region I found no recorded petitions for collections. Documents pertaining to government involvement in the administration or financial affairs of churches include: State Regional Archives, Levoča, Podžupan, 103-118/1873; State Regional Archives, Prešov, Podžupan, 18/1873; Bratislava Regional Archives, Bratislava, Zápisnice municipalného výboru, 1867-1918, 174/53-1868, 1070/325-1869, 75/42-1869, 478/233-1869. There is some evidence that Slovaks became so accustomed to receiving support for churches that in the early years of immigration to the United States, some priests may have requested help from bishops in northern Hungary. In 1899, a Slovak pastor in McKeesport, Pennsylvania asked the Bishop of Košiče for money to buy an organ for the McKeesport Slovak Church. Letter to the Bishop of Košiče, 29 March 1899, Diocesan Archives, Košiče.

27. This is a composite description based on several sources. Saint Matthew Church, Cash books (1903-1911, 1911-1912), passim. Fraternal- and church-sponsored events were advertised in Slovak newspapers; see, for example, Amerikánsko-Slovenské Noviny, 28 February 1895, 7 and 17 November 1895, 30 January and 21 May 1896, 31 October 1901, 20 February and 6 August 1902; Jednota, 21 September 1904, 25 October 1905, 6 March 1907, 24 February 1909; interviews with Ferdinand Dvorsky, 12 April 1977 and 28 November 1978. Branch 50 (First Catholic Slovak Union), Zápisnica (minutes), 1891-1907, 1907-1933, passim, Branch 50 Collection, Jednota Archives and Museum.

Assessments and lay-sponsored social events provided only part of the moneys Slovak churches needed. Slovak parishes also relied on loans from individual parishioners. These loans were usually contracted at an interest rate of three to four percent.[28] Between 1904 and 1909, one Pittsburgh Slovak parish received loans ranging from $50 to $1,000; and in 1909, this church owed its parishioners $10,000.[29] Although they received interest, it seems that a few Slovak immigrants were willing to invest part of their savings in order to aid their church. And making such loans to churches represented a drastic departure from lay involvement in northern Hungary.

Some of Pittsburgh's Slovaks apparently balked at accepting their new lay obligations. They did not equate regular money contributions with assessments of food, labor, or small monetary contributions to their village churches. Moreover, adverse economic times prevented even regularly generous parishioners from paying their church assessments. At times, concerned laypersons took it upon themselves to remind lax members of their obligations. When some of Saint Gabriel's members decreased their church support in the depression year of 1907, one layman scolded fellow parishioners for shirking their duty. He recognized, however, that bad economic times alone did not explain why some Slovaks were neglecting their church. Their neglect, the parishioner implied, stemmed from lay obligations that were different in Pittsburgh than in Hungary. "America is not the old country," he wrote; "here the church does not have its own patron" to pay its costs.[30] In short, Slovak immigrants had to adjust to new conditions, accept extended responsibilities as parishioners, and pay for their churches out of their own pockets.[31]

In the Pittsburgh diocese, the new financial obligation was accompanied by yet another change: authorized lay participation in local parish affairs that was formalized in a parish trustee system. The establishment of a trustee system in the Pittsburgh diocese reflected an emerging change in attitude by some American Catholic church officials toward lay participation in parish

309

28. Saint Matthew Church, Financial ledger, "Pôžičky" (loans), maintained at Saint Matthew rectory, Pittsburgh, PA. This ledger reveals that at least fifty-one parishioners lent Saint Matthew's money between 1904-1907. Branch 50, Zápisnica, meetings of 20 March, 17 April and 18 December 1904. Saint Gabriel Church, Pamätnik; Kushner, Slováci Katolíci, p. 95. There are no records to indicate whether Saint Joachim's borrowed money from parishioners.
29. Computed from Saint Matthew Church, Cash book (1903-1911).
30. Jednota, 2 January 1907. A member of Saint Matthew's voiced similar complaints; see ibid. 23 October 1907. The observations suggest that Slovaks who founded churches did not equate themselves with nobles who had acted as church patrons in Hungary. For an interpretation that advances the premise that Slovaks did view themselves as similar to patrons, see Stolarik "Lay Initiative," p. 151.
31. The problem of convincing some Slovaks to accept this new responsibility was not unique to Pittsburgh; other Slovak parishes in America experienced similar problems. Jednota, 20 July 1904, 3 January 1906. Information on Pittsburgh Slovaks was also derived from an interview with Ferdinand Dvorsky, 12 April 1977.

matters. For Slovaks, as well as for other Catholics in the Pittsburgh diocese, these church-sponsored changes helped alter lay involvement in local parishes.

Although the early nineteenth-century battles over trusteeism had left America's Catholic church hierarchy wary of lay trustee systems, by the 1880s some church officials were inclined to support an expanded lay involvement in parish matters.[32] In 1884, the Third Plenary Council of Baltimore recommended that American bishops establish trustee systems in their respective dioceses.[33] In 1893, the Pittsburgh Synod, the general meeting of the diocese's Catholic clergymen, finally accepted the Council's recommendations and devised a lay trustee plan for the Pittsburgh diocese.[34] Under this administrative system, males over twenty-one years of age who had fulfilled specific religious and financial obligations could both vote and run for a trustee position in their respective churches.[35]

Pittsburgh's Catholic church officials moved cautiously into the sphere of lay trusteeism. At the outset, the diocesan statutes stressed the restrictions on parish trustees and nebulously defined their precise powers and duties. During the next decade, however, the diocesan hierarchy further clarified the duties and powers as well as restrictions on these parish officers. By 1905, Pittsburgh's lay trustees were specifically required to assume the responsibility for raising money to meet parish expenses. Moreover, besides easing the pastor's burden to allow him "to devote himself chiefly to the spiritual care of his flock," the Church Committee, comprised of trustees, was to oversee the

---

32. For a discussion of the problems stemming from "trusteeism" in the earlier part of the nineteenth century, see Thomas T. McAvoy, *A History of the Catholic Church in the United States* (Notre Dame, 1969), pp. 92–122. On changing attitudes toward the laity, see Robert D. Cross, *The Emergence of Liberal Catholicism in America* (Cambridge, MA, 1958), pp. 162–172, 181.

33. *Pittsburgh Catholic*, 25 January 1894. Perhaps because of a concern with the dramatic early nineteenth-century battles between trustees and bishops, historians, in general, have not carefully analyzed the Third Plenary Council's call for the introduction of trustee systems and the subsequent response by American bishops to this call. The issue of a renewed interest in lay trusteeism in the late nineteenth century and the responses to it in individual dioceses merits further study. Robert Cross, *Liberal Catholicism*, pp. 162–172, briefly discusses the differences between "liberal" and "conservative" bishops on the issue of a more active laity.

34. *Pittsburgh Catholic*, 24 August 1893, 25 January 1894. An analysis of the specific reasons why the Pittsburgh Catholic hierarchy responded favorably to lay trusteeism is beyond the scope of this essay. However, the Third Plenary Council's recommendation was specifically cited as the reason and justification for instituting the system in the Pittsburgh diocese (ibid., 25 January 1894, 10 November 1904.) The "conservative" position of Pittsburgh's bishops on national parishes and their "liberal" position regarding lay trusteeism suggest that the tendency in historical literature to categorize bishops in the late nineteenth and early twentieth centuries as either "liberal" or "conservative" overlooks the complexity of some bishops' positions on the varied issues that the American Catholic church encountered at the turn of the century.

35. *Statutes of the Diocese of Pittsburgh, 1893*, pp. 68–69.

pastor's handling of parish financial affairs and to submit annual reports to the bishop.[36]

The fact that the Pittsburgh diocese established this trustee system raises questions concerning claims that the development of trusteeism and lay involvement among Slovaks were outgrowths of the patron system in their homeland. The trustee system was instituted in Pittsburgh before Slovaks began founding churches. Slovak immigrants did not create the trustee system in their churches; Pittsburgh's Catholic church hierarchy did.[37]

The diocese was careful to insure that the trustee system did not undermine the pastor's authority in parishes. The pastor made all nominations for Church Committee positions; he served as ex-officio president of the Church Committee; he also hired all persons employed by the parish. Moreover, the laity could not appoint or dismiss pastors; that power rested with the bishop alone.[38]

Although the Slovak laity remained subordinate to their pastors, Pittsburgh's trustee system clearly altered traditional relations between Slovak parishioners and their pastors. In Hungary, Slovak priests may have been accustomed to meddling by governmental officials or church patrons, but clergymen had not been subject to oversight by ordinary parishioners. In Pittsburgh, they were. In the early decades of the twentieth century, Slovak participation in church matters at times could create problems for pastors as well as for parishioners. In squabbles between parishioners and pastors, Pittsburgh Slovaks viewed the bishop as the guardian of lay rights and at times forced him to intervene to defend their rights. But, anxious as the bishops were to avoid conflict, there were limits to how much the laity could count on the bishop's help.

The conflict that developed in Saint Matthew Church between the trustees and the pastor over loans the trustees made to the church shows the complex interaction that could develop from lay involvement in the maintenance and management of their church. Problems regarding parishioners' loans to Saint Matthew's surfaced in December 1909 when three trustees engaged a lawyer

311

36. Ibid.; *Statutes of the Diocese of Pittsburgh, 1905,* pp. 82–85 (with quotation at p. 83); *Pittsburgh Catholic,* 27 December 1899.

37. For analyses that claim the patron system as the antecedent of the emergence of lay involvement in American national parishes, see Stolarik, "Lay Initiative" (pp. 151–157), which focuses on Slovaks, and Galush, "Faith and Fatherland" (pp. 85–86), which focuses on Polish Catholics. See also Smith, "Lay Initiative."

38. *Statutes of the Diocese of Pittsburgh, 1905,* pp. 82–84; *Pittsburgh Catholic,* 25 September 1902. Diocesan officials also carefully insured that the trustee system did not give the laity total administrative control of churches. Deeds to church properties were held in the name of the congregations with the bishop as trustee. Decisions regarding the erection of structures or spending more than $500 had to be approved by the bishop or the appropriate diocesan committee. Pittsburgh's Slovak parishes complied with these regulations. Saint Matthew Church, Saint Elizabeth Church, Saint Gabriel Church, Saint Joachim Church, Finance and Building Files (separate file for each church), OVGC.

to sue the church for failing to repay loans they had made to the church.
When the bishop learned of these actions, he ordered the pastor to provide
him with an explanation of the terms of the loans.[39] The issue seemed to
subside, but it went unresolved. In January 1911, Saint Matthew's Church
Committee refused to sign the yearly financial reports required by the
diocese. They took this action because the pastor had not paid the interest on
loans due to two trustees. This action forced a diocesan audit of parish
records. The two trustees who wanted their money did not stop there. Later
that year, the pastor complained to Bishop Canevin that they allegedly had
approached another Slovak priest and requested his assistance in obtaining
their money. Worse yet, they reportedly also urged parishioners to stop
donating money to the church.[40] The aggressiveness of these trustees thus
created a potentially explosive situation that forced the bishop to take decisive
action.

312

Bishop Canevin intervened in this altercation on behalf of the pastor. One
of the trustees involved in the confrontation had already resigned; the bishop
dismissed the other. The discharged trustee was informed that the prelate was
taking this drastic action so "that affairs of Saint Matthew Congregation can
be conducted with less trouble to you and to the pastor."[41]

This controversy demonstrated the limitations on trustee power. Saint
Matthew's trustees could oversee the parish's financial affairs and force an
audit of church records, but they could not control the treasury even to get
money due them. When their attempts to obtain money created dissension in
the parish, the bishop stepped in to keep peace. He simply removed the
trustee causing trouble. Canevin was not prepared to allow individual
parishioners, especially trustees, blatantly to shirk their duty and simultaneously to defy diocesan regulations by urging church members to ignore
their lay obligations. It is significant that the trustees and the parish
recognized the bishop's authority to settle this parish matter. Once the bishop
issued his order, the parish accepted the decision.[42]

Not all pastors could depend on the bishop's support in a confrontation

39. The bishop learned of the proposed trustees' suit through a letter from the trustees' lawyer.
(The lawyer's letter to the bishop could not be located, but the prelate's answer has been
preserved.) Letter (unsigned carbon) to John Kulamer, 28 December 1909. Letter
(unsigned carbon) to Rev. J. Uhlyarik, 23 December 1909. Both documents are contained in
Saint Matthew Church, Finance and Building File, OVGC.
40. Assistant Chancellor to Rev. John Uhlyarik, 3 February 1911; Father J. Uhlyarik to Bishop
Canevin, undated (April 1911 (?)) (original in Latin). Asst. Chancellor to Rev. John
Uhlyarik, 21 April 1911. All documents contained in Saint Matthew Church, Finance and
Building File, OVGC; *Jednota*, 24 January 1912.
41. Assistant Chancellor to trustee, 29 July 1977, Saint Matthew Church, Church Committee
File, OVGC.
42. Both trustees remained members of Saint Matthew's. There was no serious decline in the
membership of Saint Matthew's; indeed, the number of individuals increased from 1130 in
1911 to 1385 in 1912; the number of families decreased from 214 to 203. Diocese of
Pittsburgh, Church Reports, City of Pittsburgh, entry for Saint Matthew Church, OVGC.

with laypersons. In January 1915, Father Gasparik outraged parishioners when he arbitrarily reappointed Saint Elizabeth's incumbent 1913–1914 Church Committee. They petitioned the bishop to force Gasparik to hold elections and referred specifically to diocesan statutes to support their case.[43] The petitioners seemed determined to insure that established lay rights not be violated, and they expected the bishop to protect those rights.

Even though 150 persons signed the petition, the bishop initially ignored the parishioners' complaints. Canevin's apparent indifference did not deter some Slovak Catholics who refused to accept the bishop's failure to use his authority to uphold parishioners' rights.[44] Finally, after over a year of inaction by Canevin, some of Saint Elizabeth's members informed him they were no longer attending any church. The dissidents did not threaten to form an independent parish, but they had disassociated themselves from Saint Elizabeth's. Given this volatile situation and faced with aggressive lay demands, Canevin finally investigated the matter. After hearing testimony from parishioners, Canevin agreed that the lay complaints were justified and ordered Gasparik to hold elections.[45] Thus Father Gasparik learned that the bishop might not support a pastor's decision if it challenged sanctioned lay rights, jeopardized peace within the parish, and caused some parishioners to quit the church. When elections were finally held, seven of the eight men elected had been members of the contested committee.[46] Their reelection suggests that the parish was not dissatisfied with the committee. Rather, parishioners resented Gasparik's arbitrary disregard of lay rights. In this instance, the laity, with the bishop's help, triumphed over a pastor who had attempted to modify lay participation in the parish.

Some Pittsburgh Slovaks did not limit their involvement in church affairs to their parish in the "Steel City." In 1906, Pittsburgh Slovaks from the village of Teplá asked fellow citizens from Teplá and neighboring villages who were living in the United States to donate money so that a church could be built in a village near Teplá.[47] Sometimes, Slovaks in Hungary appealed directly to Slovaks in America for help to build churches in a village where no church existed.[48] These appeals suggest that, perhaps, lay initiative in the United States inspired some Slovaks in old world villages which lacked churches to follow the example of immigrants in America. The fact that

313

---

43. Petition from Saint Elizabeth's Parishioners to Bishop Regis Canevin, 21 January 1915, Saint Elizabeth Church, Church Committee File, OVGC.
44. The evidence suggests that only ten male members actively persisted in the effort to have elections held. Petition to the Right Reverend Regis Canevin (1916 (?)), Saint Elizabeth Church, Church Committee File, OVGC.
45. Testimony, (October) 1916; Bishop Regis Canevin to Rev. Coloman Gasparik, 4 December 1916, both documents contained in Saint Elizabeth Church, Church Committee File, OVGC.
46. Saint Elizabeth Church, Church Committee File, OVGC.
47. *Jednota*, 5 December 1906.
48. Ibid., 9 January 1907, 19 January 1914.

Pittsburgh Slovaks tried to help their countrypeople raises the possibility that the emergence of lay initiative in America had a far-reaching impact that went beyond Slovak national parishes in the United States. Indeed, lay initiative by immigrants in America may well have had some influence on the administrative structure of local churches in Hungary. Certainly, as the Pittsburgh case reveals, the involvement by Slovak Catholics in their churches cannot be attributed to an allegedly expanding lay participation in premigration churches. In Pittsburgh, Slovak lay initiative and parish participation resulted from an adjustment to different conditions in their new country.

A study of relations between Pittsburgh's Slovak Catholics and their bishops in the pre-World War I era reveals that lay initiative and lay involvement in parish affairs did not create necessarily tensions between immigrants and their bishops. The potential for conflict between Slovaks and the bishops did exist in Pittsburgh, especially as aggressive laypersons pressured church officials. However, the relations between Slovak Catholics and Pittsburgh's diocesan hierarchy were more typically characterized by mutual, although sometimes grudging, accommodation.

A combination of several factors worked to keep relations peaceful between church officials and Slovaks. In their efforts to found churches, Slovaks displayed a deference and respect for the bishop's authority in the diocese. Unlike some Polish Catholics in the United States, ethnic nationalism had not gained enough strength among Slovaks in the prewar era to cause them to challenge the bishop's control over church properties.[49] Furthermore, the diocese's system of permitting the election of church trustees by congregations sanctioned lay involvement in church affairs. This system gave parishioners a semblance of control in the churches they had founded and were supporting. Because the Pittsburgh diocese required lay participation, Slovak Catholics came to view the bishops as guardians of their new lay rights. Thus in some Slovak parishes lay initiative worked to defend legitimate lay rights rather than to foment conflict.

Part of the reason Pittsburgh's Slovaks avoided conflict was also due to premigration attitudes of respect for a bishop's authority. Contrary to many Italians, most Slovak Catholics who came to the United States toward the end of the nineteenth century were pious Catholics who did not bear anticlerical sentiments.[50] Thus Slovaks in general did not display the animosity toward

49. On Polish nationalism, see Greene, *For God and Country.*

50. Vecoli, "Prelates and Peasants." Relations between Pittsburgh's diocesan officials and some other immigrant groups, especially Italians, were different. These relations were different, in part, because Italian Catholics were not generally as aggressive in undertaking to found churches. Therefore, diocesan officials were concerned about the loss of Italians to the church and, hence, established organizations to work among Italian Catholics and among other immigrants who lived in remote sections of the diocese where there were no, or few, churches. For the response of Pittsburgh's Catholic church to some other immigrant groups,

the Catholic hierarchy that some other immigrant groups did. Nevertheless, Slovak deference toward Pittsburgh's Catholic church officials was accompanied by the belief that the prelates would: (1) be responsive and acquiesce in lay demands to organize churches; and, (2) serve as protectors of recognized lay rights. There were Slovak immigrants who were not reluctant to pressure Pittsburgh bishops into submitting to lay demands.

The assertive deference Slovak Catholics gave their bishops was strengthened by the church officials' perceptions of the role of immigrant laities in advancing Catholicism and by the officials' fear of aggressive lay actions. Pittsburgh's bishops welcomed the religious enthusiasm of Slovaks that caused them to support national churches. However, this aggressive laity also was perceived at times by church officials as a threat—dissatisfied lay Catholics might abandon their religion or, perhaps worse, form an independent Catholic parish. Pittsburgh's Catholic hierarchy tried to avoid conflicts that might spur Slovaks to take independent, defiant actions.

315

The potential for conflict between Slovaks and bishops was further muted because these bishops did not work to "Americanize" Slovak Catholics. Both Bishops Phelan and Canevin accepted national churches as necessary. Indeed, as late as 1914, while praising their efforts to build a church, Canevin urged Frankstown Slovaks to be proud of their religion *and* language.[51] Moreover, unlike Italian Catholics, Slovaks had not developed a system of religious folk customs which the American hierarchy found repugnant and wanted to change.[52] Hence, there was little basis for conflict between Slovak Catholics and Pittsburgh bishops over ethnic issues or religious practices.

Conflict, then, was not characteristic of relations between Pittsburgh's hierarchy and the city's Slovak Catholics even though these Catholics were not always subservient in dealing with diocesan officials. A history of Pittsburgh's Slovaks suggests that scholars cannot easily generalize about conflicts between immigrant laities and the American Catholic church. Such generalizations risk overlooking the fundamental differences among ethnic groups that influenced church-immigrant relations. Equally important, care must be taken to study the immigrant experience in individual dioceses. Additional studies may show that relations between Slovak Roman Catholics

---

and especially those whose laities were less aggressive in building churches, see *Pittsburgh Catholic*, 3 March and 31 March 1904, 25 May 1905, 21 June 1906, 2 July 1909, 19 January 1911. See also Rt. Rev. Regis Canevin, *An Examination Historical and Statistical into Losses and Gains of the Catholic Church* (n.p., 1912).

51. *Jednota*, 2 September 1914.

52. Vecoli, "Prelates and Peasants," pp. 227–225; idem, "Cult and Occult in Italian-American Culture." Slovak immigrants maintained many premigration religious folk traditions, but these traditions typically did not include elaborate public rituals similar to those followed by Italian immigrants and viewed by the American Catholic church hierarchy as unacceptable.

and the church hierarchy were different in other dioceses, but in early twentieth-century Pittsburgh, conflict often was avoided because bishops yielded, under pressure, to lay demands. Thus, perceptions of the laity's role, fear, and assertive deference combined to force both Pittsburgh's Catholic church officials and the Slovak laity to remain determined yet flexible as each adjusted to the other.

The American Hierarchy and Oriental Rite Catholics, 1890-1907

By Gerald P. Fogarty, S.J.

IN the midst of the liberal-conservative dispute which divided the American hierarchy in the last decade of the nineteenth century, one important controversy has gone virtually unnoticed in the literature on the period—the problem of oriental rite Catholics coming to the United States. On this issue liberals and conservatives united. John Ireland, who led the fight for liberal causes, led the fight against allowing the new immigrants to retain their married clergy. The hierarchy won, but it was a pyrrhic victory—thousands of Uniate Catholics joined the Orthodox Church. What is of concern here is the role of the American archbishops who in almost all of their annual meetings from 1890 to 1905 discussed the problem and succeeded in having the Congregation of Propaganda promulgate restrictive legislation for Uniates coming to America.

In the late 1880's and 1890's a relatively small but significant number of Carpatho-Russian and Galician Uniates immigrated to America[1] and settled in the coal mining regions of Pennsylvania and in Minneapolis.[2] It was a new phenomenon for American culture and the American Catholic Church: unlike the waves of immigrants from Ireland and Germany, these did not speak a western European language and they introduced the first departure from the Latin rite uniformly practiced throughout the United States up to that time. Moreover, they wished to remain separate and not be either Americanized or Latinized.[3] In Minneapolis, part of the Archdiocese of St. Paul, Ruthenian Uniates established their own parish in 1889 and brought over Father Alexis Toth of the Diocese of Eperjes, who came with the recommendation of his bishop. Ireland, the Archbishop of St. Paul, refused to recognize Toth as a validly ordained priest because the latter had been married even though then a widower.[4]

Ireland, who was already leading the opposition of the English-speaking bishops against the German demands to have their own parishes, preserve their language in their schools, and receive a greater voice in the American Church, brought the matter of oriental rite Catholics before the annual meeting of the archbishops on July

23, 1890. Priests of the "Greek Rite," he said, "claimed to have full jurisdiction over Greek Catholics in America, derived from Bishops of the Greek Rite in Europe. . . ." But the problem was not only one of jurisdiction as it was in regard to the Germans; it was also one of clerical celibacy. The archbishops treated both these problems and "unanimously agreed, that the President [James Cardinal Gibbons] should write to Propaganda in the name of all the Archbishops, an urgent letter praying that all Priests of the Greek Rite in America derive their jurisdiction entirely and exclusively from the Ordinaries in this country; and that none others but celibate Priests be allowed to come hither."[5] The archbishops were legitimately concerned with preserving ecclesiastical jurisdiction in the United States. But their refusal to recognize in this country the right granted to Uniate priests in Europe to be married had dire results for the Church.

In May, 1890, Propaganda had already issued a decree to the Archbishop of Paris stating that in regard to jurisdiction oriental rite priests and people outside their proper patriarchates were to be subject to the Latin rite ordinary.[6] But the congregation did not formally reply to the petition of the American archbishops. Instead it issued a letter in October, 1890, to John Ireland and Bishop Tobias Mullen of Erie supporting them in their actions toward oriental rite Catholics and decreeing that "priests of the Greco-Ruthenian rite, who desire to go to and remain in the United States of North America, ought to be celibate."[7]

Ireland and the other bishops had won, but their victory claimed the first in a series of victims. On March 25, 1891, Father Toth together with his congregation of about 365 immigrants were received into the Orthodox Church by Bishop Vladimir Sokolovsky of San Francisco. During the next few years Toth became a zealous missionary for the Orthodox Church among the Uniate Catholics especially in Wilkes-Barre.[8] The work of Toth and men like him, aided by the intolerant stance of the American hierachy, was eminently successful, for during the next few decades over 225,000 Carpatho-Russian and Galician Uniates entered the Orthodox Church.[9]

When the archbishops assembled for their annual meeting on November 29, 1891, they were preoccupied with the issues raised by the derogatory reports on the American Church submitted to Propaganda by the St. Raphaels-Verein and Peter Paul Cahensly, but they did discuss the oriental rite question. Since Propaganda had made no formal reply to the petition of the previous year, several bishops, it was reported, found that Greek priests claimed that the letters sent to Ireland and Mullen had no application outside the archdiocese of St. Paul and the diocese of Erie. The archbishops therefore requested that Cardinal Gibbons, Archbishop of Baltimore, should make a formal announcement of these Roman decisions to the whole hierarchy.[10]

During the year between the second and third meetings of the archbishops, one bishop at least attempted to mediate the problem. When the archbishops met in New York from November 16 to 19, 1892, they were most concerned with the discussion of Propaganda's ruling in favor of Ireland's controversial school plan and with the presence of Archbishop Francesco Satolli, who had come ostensibly as a special legate to represent the Holy See at the Columbian Exposition, but who, Ireland knew, was to be appointed permanent apostolic delegate. Nevertheless, Bishop John Lancaster Spalding was allowed to present Father Nicephorus Chenith, pastor of St. Michael's Greek Catholic Church in Passaic, New Jersey. Chenith and two other oriental rite priests composed the Priests' Committee which sought to provide priests for oriental rite congregations and guarantee them a proper salary. In the eyes of its members the committee was necessary because of Rome's indifference toward the immigrants and the bishops' refusal to grant faculties to married priests. As more oriental priests came to the country, the committee increased in importance and played a large role in preventing further Uniate losses to the Orthodox Church.[11]

Addressing the archbishops in Latin, Chenith asserted that Greek Catholics numbered about 10,000 and their spiritual care was committed to only three widowed priests because eleven others had been prohibited from exercising the ministry on account of their married status. Moreover, he said, the Orthodox Bishop of San Francisco was sending out missionaries to induce Greek Catholics to convert to the Orthodox Church. He therefore urged that married priests be allowed to minister to Greek Catholics, that a Greek priest, under the jurisdiction of the Latin ordinaries, be appointed superior of Greek Catholics, and that the legal customs of the Greeks be preserved.[12] He thus raised the dual issue the archbishops had foreseen: jurisdiction and clerical celibacy. The archbishops did not heed Chenith's plea, but instead "after mature deliberation it was agreed, that the rule laid down by the Propaganda should be insisted on, and that every effort should be made to in-

319

duce the Basilian monks to take the spiritual charge of the united
Greeks in this country." Finally the prelates voted that Michael
Corrigan, Archbishop of New York, present their opinions to Prop-
aganda.[13]

When the archbishops assembled in September, 1893, they
learned that Cardinal Miecislaus Ledochowski, in reply to Corrigan's letter, stated that married priests "might be retained *pro
tempore*, but that as far as possible Greek monks should be pro-
cured." This of course was not in accord with their sentiments expressed the previous year and they were ready to risk schism rather
than compromise on the issue of celibacy. They therefore resolved:

> that the presence of married priests of the Greek rite in
> our midst is a constant menace to the chastity of our un-
> married clergy, a source of scandal to the laity and there-
> fore the sooner this point of discipline is abolished before
> these evils obtain large proportions, the better for religion,
> because the possible loss of a few souls of the Greek rite,
> bears no proportion to the blessings resulting from uni-
> formity of discipline.[14]

It is clear that the archbishops were fearful of inroads being made
into Latin rite celibacy by the presence of a legitimate married
clergy. At a time when the American Church was struggling for
American acceptance of all its traditions, such an inroad would
endanger the internal union of the Church.

On April 12, 1894, Propaganda sent a letter to all Latin rite
bishops, but it had the American hierarchy especially in mind. According to reports, said the congregation, many priests of the Oriental rite had gone to America to tend to the spiritual needs of the
faithful of their rite, but many were either unemployed or collected alms without the proper canonical faculties, or engaged in
the practice of medicine or in business, thus giving scandal to the
faithful. It therefore warned the bishops that

> It is to be deplored that frequently these [priests] show
> to the Curias testimonial letters of their own prelate writ-
> ten in an oriental tongue, absolutely unknown in the
> aforesaid regions: therefore it is impossible for the Ordi-
> naries of the place to distinguish whether the one bearing
> them is a Catholic priest immune from every ecclesiastical
> censure, or whether he is burdened with one; whether he
> is a schismatic; or whether he is even a simple layman
> showing false documents. Wishing to provide a proper
> remedy for this evil this Sacred Congregation, with the
> approval of our holy Lord, recently sent letters to the Ori-

ental Prelates, in which it prescribed for them that, without the previous permission of the ordinary of the place *to which* [they were going], priests were not to be assigned to the aforesaid territory *(and these ought to be celibate or widowers);* that, without previously declaring it in writing to this Sacred Congregation and receiving permission from the same Congregation, they not depart for any diocese to which they might wish to go to establish a place of residence; that with this obtained, they present themselves before the Ordinary, under whose jurisdiction they ought to be, and petition and obtain from him the necessary faculties for performing the sacred rites by showing him, together with the permission mentioned before, discessorial letters of their proper Bishop approved by the Nuncio or Apostolic Delegate: nevertheless the prohibition against collecting alms without the proper faculty remains firm; but if it is done otherwise the same priests may not be admitted to the exercise of the sacred ministry.[13]

The American hierarchy had won its point with Propaganda. It assured that oriental rite priests would be subject to it and that none but celibate priests would come. However, the involved procedures set down by Propaganda for an oriental rite priest to come to America could not help but result in delays and it would be no wonder if pastorally-minded priests wishing to remain with their people emigrating to America would choose to ignore the norms even if they knew of them.

In the meantime, Father Chenith was still busy trying to bring the American bishops to accept a compromise on a married clergy. He appeared again before the archbishops at their meeting in Philadelphia on October 10, 1894, and his plea was similar to his earlier one of 1892. He asked for the appointment of a Greek Vicar General and for the temporary granting of faculties to married priests. Both these proposals met with the strong opposition of Archbishop Ireland, this time joined by Patrick Feehan, Archbishop of Chicago. These two prelates together with Corrigan and Patrick Ryan, Archbishop of Philadelphia, were appointed a committee "to examine what can be done to best provide for the spiritual interests of the Greek Catholics in this country, and to report to Cardinal Gibbons, if possible before His Eminence goes to Rome—otherwise to the next meeting of the Archbishops."[14]

On the day following the archbishops' meeting, the committee met and approved a plan submitted by Archbishop John Williams of Boston at the general meeting the day before. This plan (not noted in the official minutes) suggested that a Greek priest "en-joying the confidence of his Ecclesiastical Superior, should be rec-ommended to other Bishops in whose Dioceses the Greek faithful are found," so that he could provide information on Greek Cath-olic laity and priests. He was to have neither jurisdiction nor gen-eral faculties, but "he should receive in each Diocese such powers, only, as the Ordinary might see proper to confer." All the members of the committee "opposed the project of the appointment of a Vicar Apostolic for the Greek faithful, or even of a Vicar General, whose powers over the Greeks should extend throughout various Dioces [sic], or even over the whole country." This was the first time that the suggestion of the appointment of a vicar apostolic appears in the minutes of the archbishops' meetings, but the com mittee's rejection of it and of the appointment of a vicar general indicates the archbishops' desire to preserve territorial uniformity of jurisdiction, i.e. they did not want any independent ecclesiastical jurisdiction within the limits of any diocese. This point was strengthened by the committee's recommendation "that His Emi-nence, Cardinal Gibbons, be requested to inquire in Rome, if the Latin rite exclusively could be observed in the United States." The committee reaffirmed the archbishops' stance that only celibate priests should be admitted to the ministry in the United States and that the Holy See should be again petitioned in this regard. Finally, it suggested that Archbishop John Kain of St. Louis, the secretary of the archbishops' meetings, write to the other metropol-itans "to ascertain the number of Catholics of the Greek, Syrian, and other Oriental Rites in their Provinces, so that it may be prac-ticable in [the] future, to deal more intelligently with the various problems that may arise regarding these members of the Church."[17]

During the following year the hierarchy seems not to have been too concerned about the problem of oriental Catholics. There is no evidence that Archbishop Kain ever wrote to the other metro-politans. In fact, the committee's report, including this recommen-dation, was given verbatim and adopted unanimously at the arch-bishops' meeting held at the Catholic University on October 2, 1895, almost a full year after the committee met.[18] At the meeting the next year, the archbishops requested that Kain write to Father Chenith and Father Joseph Yasbek, a Maronite priest then in New York and later in Boston, to learn the number of oriental rite Catholics in the United States, "all possible details regarding the rites of these orientals," and "such suggestions as these Rev. Fathers may offer as to the most practicable and efficient manner of dealing with these different oriental Catholics."[19]

The paucity of references to the oriental rite problem during this period is understandable. By this time, the American hierarchy was virtually divided into two camps—those who followed John Ireland on his aggressive Americanization program and those who opposed him such as Corrigan and the German bishops — and the problem of Americanism was beginning to take focus. Nevertheless on May 1, 1897, Propaganda decreed that

> The Roman Church has diligently and watchfully exercised its office with apostolic charity and its supreme authority continuously to the end, that it exerts itself to strengthen and confirm the rights of Pastors and the faithful. Wherefore it has recognized the power of oriental people living in North America of exercising their own rite, but at the same time has zealously commended to them the submission owed to the Latin Ordinaries. Since these two conditions have been fulfilled, in recent years it has issued many useful norms by which it looks to the good of the same faithful and fosters their piety. Nevertheless it is a shame that not a few orientals because of the lack of a priest of their own rite remain almost destitute of spiritual aid. Therefore that this S. Congregation, moved by the petitions of many bishops, can meet their needs (while the prescriptions remain otherwise in force which were contained in circular letters issued on October 1, 1890 and April 12, 1894, especially in regard to sending to America worthy celibate priests, and in regard to preserving submission to Latin Ordinaries) with the approval of our Holy Father Leo: it made the following three decrees:
>
> I. Let the Oriental Faithful going to North America have the faculty, if it should be agreeable, of conforming themselves to the Latin rite; nevertheless they must go back to their own rite once they have returned to their country.
>
> II. It is not permitted for Orientals, who have established a true and permanent place of residence in North America, to transfer to the Latin rite, unless the permission of the Apostolic See is obtained in every case.
>
> III. In the Ecclesiastical provinces of North America, in which there are many Faithful of the Ruthenian rite, the Archbishop of each Province, after taking counsel with his suffragans, is to depute a Ruthenian priest commendable for his celibacy and capability, and if such a one is lacking a Priest of the Latin rite acceptable to the Ruthenians, who should exercise vigilance and direction over the people and clergy of the aforesaid rite, with, however,

entire dependence on the Ordinary of the place, who in accordance with his judgement should give him the faculties which he judges in the Lord to be necessary.[20]

Propaganda's decree contains several important points. First, it recognized the power of the oriental Catholics to preserve their own rite and therefore rejected the request of the archbishops' committee (if it was ever presented) to have the Latin rite alone observed in the United States. Second, it did seem to denigrate the oriental rite by allowing oriental Catholics temporarily in the United States to conform to the Latin rite, but this must be placed in the context· that there were still very few oriental rite priests available and the congregation was concerned with the spiritual welfare of the faithful. Third, the appointment of an oriental rite "deputy," was essentially the recommendation of Archbishop Williams adopted by the archbishops' committee. Nevertheless, while it was a halfway measure, it was a step toward the establishment of a separate oriental rite jurisdiction; the archbishops and Propaganda were beginning to take oriental rite Catholicism in America as a permanent phenomenon. At their meeting in 1897, the archbishops "expressed the hope that the instructions of the Holy See would be faithfully carried out" especially in regard to the appointment of a deputy. They made no comment on other aspects of the decree.[21]

During the remainder of the decade, Americanism divided the archbishops and distracted them from further consideration of the problem of oriental rite Catholics. But the condemnation of Americanism might have led John Ireland (and perhaps others) to soften his position against the immigrants or at least to remain neutral. Friedrich Graf Revertera, Austro-Hungarian Ambassador to the Holy See, was kept informed of the plight of Ruthenian immigrants in America through his government's consulates in New York and Philadelphia and he had discussed the matter with his own superiors and with Propaganda. The government in Vienna learned from its embassy in Washington that Ireland was coming to Rome early in 1899; it requested that Revertera treat the situation with the archbishop. Revertera found ample opportunity for his assignment in the aftermath of *Testem Benevolentiae*. Ireland, he said, wished "to wash himself clean of the reproach of Americanism" and in "repeated conversations" he proposed the recognition, at the next archbishops' meeting, of a common vicar general for the Ruthenians.[22] At that meeting, however, held at the Cath-

324

olic University on October 12, 1899, neither Ireland nor anyone else, according to the minutes, spoke on the question.[23]

The archbishops next broached the question in 1900 when Corrigan presented a report of the condition of Greek Rite Catholics, not included in the minutes of the meeting, but "seeming to indicate that some central authority, such as a Vicar Apostolic or Vicar General, had better be established, as a recognized medium between them and the Ordinaries of the country." The matter was referred to Corrigan and Ryan in whose provinces most of the oriental rite Catholics had settled.[24] The archbishops' resolution was an advance over their previous position and over Propaganda's decree of 1897. They were finally giving Father Chenith's proposal a benevolent hearing and were moving toward granting a separate oriental rite jurisdiction. Yet it would be some years before this would be carried into effect.

At the meeting in 1901, Corrigan and Ryan gave their reports. Corrigan noted that the regulations of the Holy See had been sufficiently promulgated among both the Greeks in the United States and their bishops in Europe as to solve the problem of ignorance of the law. Ryan mentioned the continued difficulty of proselytism by the Orthodox, but thought the problem of providing unmarried priests was being met by an increase in the number of Uniate students in Latin rite seminaries.[25] Four years later, however the archbishops rejected as inopportune Propaganda's suggestion that an oriental rite see be erected for the United States.[26] This resolution is not necessarily a retreat from their position of 1900 when they recommended that a vicar apostolic or vicar general and not an ordinary should be appointed.

Nevertheless, in 1907 the Holy See named Soter Stephan Ortynsky, a Basilian monk, the first oriental rite bishop in the United States. He was to be immediately subject to the Holy See and under the direction of the apostolic delegate. He had however no ordinary jurisdiction but was to receive delegated jurisdiction from the local ordinaries of the dioceses in which oriental rite Catholics resided.[27] Essentially, Ortynsky was a national vicar general, such as Chenith had suggested, but with episcopal dignity. His appointment by no means ended the problems of eastern Catholics and may very well have indicated Rome's ignorance of the complex situation which immigrants from various European nations, eastern and otherwise, faced in a new country. A Galician with strong Ukrainian patriotic leanings, Ortynsky antagonized Transcarpathians from

Hungary for his supposed nationalism and for imposing clerical celibacy in accordance with the papal letter *Ea Semper* (June 14, 1907), outlining his authority and prerogatives.[28] In 1913, the Holy See gave him full and ordinary jurisdiction over all Ruthenians and the jurisdiction of Latin rite bishops over these Catholics ceased from that date.[29] Nevertheless, the dissension among oriental rite Catholics continued and postponed the appointment of a successor to Ortynsky from his death in 1916 until 1924 when the Holy See erected the eparchies of Philadelphia and Pittsburgh and named two Byzantine Rite bishops, Constantine Bohachevsky, exarch of Philadelphia with jurisdiction over the Ukrainian Catholics, and Basil Takach, exarch of Pittsburgh with jurisdiction over the Podocarpathians.[30]

The attitude of the Latin rite archbishops toward the oriental rite Catholics coming to the United States is a tragic episode in the history of the American Church. A more understanding attitude on the part of men like John Ireland might have prevented the loss to the Uniate Church of 225,000 people. But the bishops of the time had a strong sense of their own prerogatives both in regard to Rome and in regard to the lower clergy. On the jurisdictional question, Ireland and other English-speaking bishops, including Corrigan, took the same approach toward the Germans. It was a matter not only of preserving episcopal rights but also of assimilating the Catholic Church to America. The disciplinary question of clerical celibacy endangered precisely this program of assimilation and, by the way, received a more than ready hearing in Rome which was itself somewhat ambivalent about permitting the oriental rites to retain a married clergy.

A generation after Ireland, the question was ceasing to be as crucial. In 1931, there was again agitation about the Roman regulation on celibacy among oriental rite Catholics. Archbishop Peter Fumasoni-Biondi, the apostolic delegate, asked the opinion of the American bishops about the matter. The answers were not univocal. Archbishop Michael Curley of Baltimore may have typified the pragmatic stance of some American bishops. Replying to the delegate, he noted that there had been no agitation in Baltimore. But he as much as admitted that he was not really concerned about it when he remarked: "I do not know the attitude of the Priest who is stationed in Baltimore on the matter. I understand that he is a married man." He therefore suggested that "whilst the continued attitude of the Holy See on the matter of Celibacy amongst the Ruthenian Clergy is of course the proper attitude, yet I doubt if now is the opportune time to enforce the law strictly."[31] Cardinal Patrick Hayes of New York, on the other hand, reflecting the fears of the 1890's, felt "that the over-emphasized sex age we are living in, would feel that the Church showed signs of weakening by modifying her legislation." The presence of married priests, he said, "does not contribute to our idea of unity, discipline and the holiness of the priestly office" and a change in legislation "might easily by degrees lessen the high ideal of our own priests with regard to celibacy and the obligations it imposes."[32] Two years later, however, Hayes was more moderate. While he still opposed the abolition of celibacy for the Ruthenians, "at the same time I believe that a dispensation should be granted in particular cases. . . ." He acknowledged that the Ruthenian people in general preferred a married clergy and that, with few exceptions, the wives were useful assistants in their husbands' ministry. Hayes concluded that the problem of allowing a married clergy to the oriental rite would increase with the conversion of Russian Orthodox priests, a project in which he was then engaged.[33]

Several factors contributed to the change in attitude of at least some members of the American Latin rite hierarchy toward the oriental rite. First, eastern European immigration never equaled that from western Europe and therefore the oriental rite Catholics did not really constitute a threat to the Latin rite. Second, American Catholics were sympathetic with those who had to flee the Bolshevik Revolution and were therefore more benevolent toward Russian Catholics and their married clergy. Finally, the American Catholic Church in the 1930's was more stable than it had been in the 1890's—it could afford to tolerate some pluralism, especially when it became apparent to some that the married clergy of the oriental rite could not undermine the western discipline of celibacy.

NOTES

1 Gerald Shaughnessy, S.M., *Has the Immigrant Kept the Faith?* (New York, 1925), pp. 163-169. Unfortunately Shaughnessy treats only the nationality and not the rite of Catholic immigrants. Hence he lists the net Catholic immigration from Austria-Hungary from 1881 to 1890 as 134,000 and from 1891 to 1900 as 232,000. Most of these were obviously Latin rite Catholics. From Greece he lists the net Catholic immigration from 1881 to 1890 as 10 and from 1891 to 1900 as 25; from Russia from 1881 to 1890 as 11,000 and from 1891 to 1900 as 12,000.
2 Dmitry Grigorieff, "The Orthodox Church in America from the Alaska Mission to Autocephaly," *St. Vladimir's Theological Quarterly,* XIV (1970), 202.

3 Keith S. Russin, "Father Alexis G. Toth and the Wilkes-Barre Litigations," St. Vladimir's Theological Quarterly, XVI (1972), 129-131.

4 Russin, p. 132; Grigorieff, p. 202.

5 Achives of the Archdiocese of Baltimore, hereafter abbreviated as AAB, 87 R 4, Meeting of the Archbishops, Boston, July 23-24, 1890.

6 Acta Sanctae Sedis, XXIV (1891-1892), 390-391.

7 Circular letter of Propaganda, Oct. 1, 1890, reprinted as enclosure with letter in AAB, Fumasoni-Biondi to Curley, Nov. 19, 1931. This document was not published in Acta Sanctae Sedis, but it is presumably the one sent to Ireland and Mullen.

8 Russin, pp. 134-135; Toth died in 1909.

9 Grigorieff, p. 202.

10 AAB 89 D 5, Meeting of the Archbishops, St. Louis, Nov. 27, 1891.

11 On the Priests' Committee, see Russin, pp. 139, 143. Chenith's name appears in the documents as Chanatti or Chanath.

12 AAB 91 B 8, Corrigan to Cardinal Ledochowski, Jan. 18, 1893, copy.

13 AAB 90 Q 3, Meeting of the Archbishops, New York, Nov. 16-19, 1892.

14 AAB 91 V 1/1, Meeting of the Archbishops, Chicago, Sept. 12-13, 1893.

15 Circular letter of Propaganda, April 12, 1894, included in AAB, Fumasoni-Biondi to Curley, Nov. 19, 1931; the document was not published in the Acta Sanctae Sedis.

16 AAB 93 L 4/1, Meeting of the Archbishops, Philadelphia, Oct. 10, 1894.

17 AAB 93 L 5, Meeting of the committee of Archbishops, Philadelphia, Oct. 11, 1894.

18 AAB, Meeting of the Archbishops, Washington, Oct. 2, 1895.

19 AAB 94 S 3, Meeting of the Archbishops, Washington, Oct. 22, 1896.

20 Acta Sanctae Sedis, XXX (1897-1898), 635-636.

21 AAB 95 U 6, Meeting of the Archbishops, Washington, Oct. 21, 1897.

22 Gabriel Andriányi, "Friedrich Graf Revertera, Erinnerungen," Archivum Historiae Pontificiae, X (1972), 268.

23 AAB 97 M 5, Minutes of the Annual Meeting of the Most Rev. Archbishops, 1899.

24 AAB 98 J 2, Meeting of the Archbishops, Washington, Oct. 11, 1900.

25 AAB 99 F 8, Meeting of the Archbishops, Washington, Nov. 21-22, 1901.

26 John Tracy Ellis, The Life of James Cardinal Gibbons, 1834-1921 (2 vols.: Milwaukee, 1952), I, 385.

27 Acta Sanctae Sedis, XLI (1908), 3-4.

28 Archives of the Archdiocese of New York, hereafter abbreviated as AANY, John Uhrin and Michail Maczko to Farley, Jan. 28, 1909. For the appointment of Ortynsky and the disputes which followed, see Bohdan P. Procko, "Soter Ortynsky: First Ruthenian Bishop in the United States, 1907-1916," The Catholic Historical Review, LVIII (Jan., 1973), 513-533; see especially pp. 518-519.

29 AANY, Giovanni Bonzano to Farley, Washington, Aug. 25, 1913. In his reply, Farley said that he had always favored the appointment of an ordinary for oriental rite Catholics; AANY, Farley to Bonzano, New York, Aug. 30, 1913.

30 AAB, Fumasoni-Biondi to Curley, Washington, Nov. 19, 1931; Procko, p. 533. Just before the appointment of the two bishops, the American hierarchy at its annual meeting discussed making oriental rite Catholics again directly subject to the local Latin rite bishop. Archbishop Edward J. Hanna, chairman of the administrative board of the Natholic Catholic Welfare Conference, presented the case to Fumasoni-Biondi, the apostolic delegate, who seems to have been receptive to the position; Archives of the United States Catholic Conference, circular letter of Edward J. Hanna to selected American bishops, Oct. 6, 1923. In 1958 Philadelphia was elevated to metropolitan status as an archeparchy. In 1969 Pittsburgh was elevated to metropolitan status and the archeparchy was transferred to Munhall.

31 AAB, Curley to Fumasoni-Biondi, Dec. 3, 1931.

32 AANY, Hayes to Fumasoni-Biondi, New York, Dec. 31, 1931.

33 AANY, Hayes to Cicognani, New York, Nov. 11, 1933; the letter to which this was a reply was returned to the apostolic delegation.

The *survivance* of French Canadians in New England (1865–1930): history, geography and demography as destiny*

Richard S. Sorrell
Brookdale College and
University of California, Santa Barbara

'Qui perd sa langue, perd sa foi. Loyauz, oui, mais Français toujours.' 'Améri-canisation? Oui! Irlandaisation? Jamais!' These pithy phrases express different aspects of a remarkable exercise in ethnic maintenance, achieved by a nation-ality which is little-known outside of its geographical base east of the Hudson River and Lake Champlain.   329

  Le fait français en Amérique is not confined to the province of Quebec. Those French Canadians who left their homeland and immigrated to New England are known, together with their descendants, as Franco-Americans.** This essay will emphasize the three major factors which promoted strong national survival among Francos, during the period from the Civil War to the Great Depression. *Survivance,* the French Canadian term for such survival, refers to their long-held belief that they have a divine mission to preserve their national 'race' and religion against Anglo-Saxon inroads, by insuring the continuation and transmission of their native *foi* (Roman Catholicism), *langue,* and *moeurs* (French Canadian customs).

  Many Americans think of French and French Canadian as one and the same, an error which does not endear them to either nationality. French Canadians are descendants of the few thousand French who settled in New France during the seventeenth century. However, there has been little popu-lation flow between the two areas since that time. French people have always felt their language and culture to be superior to those of the French Canadians, the isolated 'colonials'. French Canadians in turn are proud of their two centuries of survival as a nationality distinct from the French, whom they regard with distrust because of the willingness with which the mother country ceded Canada to England in 1763, and because of conservative French Canadian dislike of the French Revolution (Nish, 1966; Wade, 1968).

  The term 'Franco-American' includes both French and French Canadian immigrants to the United States, but emigration from French Canada has been much greater than from France. Since colonial times more than 700,000 people have emigrated from France to the States. Many of these were Protest-ant Huguenots who arrived before 1790, and almost all have assimilated into American society to a greater degree than have French Canadians. Canada has

Ethnic and Racial Studies Volume 4 Number 1 January 1981
© R.K.P. 1981 01401–9870/81/0401–0091 $1.50/1

sent more than four million people, one-third of whom have been French Canadian. Therefore, about two out of three Franco-Americans are of French Canadian ancestry (LaGumina and Cavaioli, 1974: 27, 217; Dinnerstein and Reimers, 1975: 168–69; Handlin, 1959: 16; Wade, 1966). However, almost all of the French Canadians came after the Civil War, and most settled in New England mill towns, where the ratio of French Canadian to French is much higher. For instance, in Woonsocket, Rhode Island, which had more French and Belgian French than other such cities due to ownership of woollen textile mills by Franco-Belgian industrialists, first and second generation French Canadian immigrants constituted 51 per cent of the population in 1920, while Franco-Belgians numbered only 3.4 per cent (Wessel, 1931: 227).

Migration to and fro across the Canadian-American border has been one of the greatest such movements in world history, involving more than six million people (Hansen, 1940). Most of the French Canadians who were part of this population flow left Quebec between 1865–90 and 1905–29. By the latter date, French Canadian stock in the United States numbered 1,106,000, one-third of them immigrants and two-thirds children of immigrants. Today it is estimated that if all generations are included, the total number of Franco-Americans with Canadian ancestry is around two million. This figure becomes more impressive when one realizes that it represents over a quarter of all North Americans of French Canadian stock. In 1900, after the first peak of immigration, almost as many 'ethnic French Canadians' lived in the United States as there were French Canadians remaining in the Quebec homeland (Hanham, 1977: 6; Truesdell, 1943: 60; Wade, 1968: xv; Vicero, 1968; Faucher, 1964; Paquet, 1964; Lavoie, 1972; Samuel, 1969).

When an American thinks about French influences in his country, the first image which comes to mind is that of New Orleans and Louisiana. French language and culture are still evident there, the result of Creoles and Cajuns who have been a presence in Louisiana since colonial times. However, few Franco-Americans of Quebec origin have settled there. Certain parts of the Midwest, particularly Michigan, have fairly large numbers of Francos, remnants of the New France fur trade, and later lumbering and mining. In 1930 New York ranked fourth among states in total number of those of French Canadian stock, primarily concentrated along the northern border where New York meets Quebec.

For the real center of Franco-Americana, one must look to New England, where approximately three-quarters of all those of French Canadian descent lived in 1930 (henceforth 'Franco-American' shall refer only to those of Quebec origin). Although less than 1 per cent of the total population of the United States in 1930 was of French Canadian stock (immigrants and children of immigrants), in New England the figure was 7 per cent. Massachusetts had the greatest number of Francos, but New Hampshire had the highest percentage of the total population which was Franco, 21, followed by Maine, Rhode Island, and Vermont, where the percentages were *circa* 13. Today, if all generations are included, these percentages have changed little, except that Maine's has increased slightly, while those of the other New England states have declined (Truesdell, 1943: 72–73, 86–89; Rumilly, 1958: 462; *Le Farog-forum*, 1978: 7).

Thus Francos have long been one of the most regionally concentrated immigrant-ethnic groups in the United States. However, the casual tourist in New England may not be aware of this. Unlike many other nationalities, French Canadians did not gravitate *en masse* to the largest cities of the area. Relatively few will be found in Boston, Providence, or Hartford. One must travel to the series of small and medium-sized cities (between 25,000–100,000 population) which form a large semicircle around Boston, and which were dependent upon textiles for their industrial livelihood in the decades after the Civil War, to find the 'Little Canadas' of New England. This semicircle, which includes southeastern Maine, the Merrimack Valley, the Blackstone River region, central and southeastern Massachusetts, and the Quinebaug region of Connecticut, contained 70 per cent of the Franco-Americans living in New England in 1900 (Vicero, 1968: 291, 294; Hansen, 1940: 214). This concentration has remained basically unchanged in the years since (Truesdell, 1943: 55; Arnell, 1949; Rimbert, 1954; Allen, 1972, 1974; *Le Farog-forum*, 1978: 7).

In the five major Franco urban centers (see map), ignored until recent years by immigrant historians who preferred to concentrate on the more glamorous metropolises, Franco-Americans have since 1900 made up a proportion of the total population far higher than their 7 per cent for all of New England. Indeed, their ratio can be rivaled by few other immigrant groups anywhere else in urban America. In Woonsocket and Lewiston, Maine, they have constituted nearly 60 per cent of each city's residents, while in Manchester, New Hampshire, and in Fall River and Lowell, Massachusetts, the percentage has been in the 20–35 per cent range. There are other cities of equal size with lesser but still significant percentages of Francos, as well as numerous smaller cities, towns and villages, in which from a quarter to over one-half of the twentieth century residents have been Franco; but the five above-named cities, combining size and percentage, are the historical centers of Franco-American life in New England (Vicero, 1968: 289, 294, 343; Truesdell, 1943: 86–91; Rumilly, 1958: 462; *Le Farog-forum*, 1978: 7).

How did this demographic concentration in small and medium-sized cities aid *survivance?* I feel that such environments were the best breeding ground for ethnic identity. Neither as dispersed as immigrant groups often found themselves in rural areas, nor as dwarfed as other nationalities were in great metropolises like New York or Chicago, the Little Canadas formed a large population bulk in their New England cities. Francos could dominate not only their ethnic neighborhood, but also the whole municipality, at least in a demographic sense.

In a city like Woonsocket, where I have done most of my primary research on Francos (Sorrell, 1975), such majoritarian status and demographic preponderance necessarily led to the development of a strong community life among Franco-Americans, which fostered *survivance.* French was literally the dominant laguage in *la ville la plus française d'Amérique* (the sobriquet

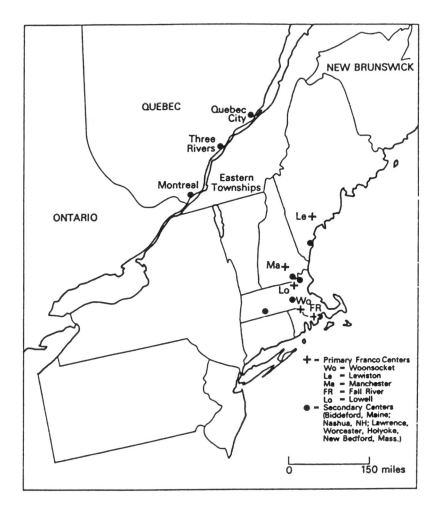

applied to Woonsocket) in the decades before the Depression. In industry, Franco workers made up the bulk of the textile work force and could converse among themselves in French, as well as with their Franco-Belgian managers and owners. In commerce, many of the retail stores were run by Franco-Americans, and even non-Franco business men realized the necessity of having a French-speaking clerk. In the national parishes, both in church and school, little English need intrude. On the street, a Franco-American could rest secure in the knowledge that two out of every three people he might meet would speak his language. Even in politics and city government, French was holding its own; one visitor to Woonsocket's City Hall in 1924 was there for an hour and heard no English spoken by anyone, even officials, except to him. This is not to deny that English was also often heard, and that most

Francos, except for elderly immigrants, were bilingual. Still, as the Federal Writers' Project put it in 1937, the 'most striking aspect of modern Woonsocket is the French character of the city. ...' The ethnic group's political, economic, and social position was nowhere as secure as their demographic situation. However, their unqualified demographic domination, and concomitant insularity, produced a feeling of security within the confines of the city (Federal Writers' Project, 1937: 311—12; Dexter, 1924; Sorrell, 1975: 102—26, 391—92).

Such dominance was aided by a process of 'chain' migration. Over a number of years a chain of people from the same region of Quebec would migrate in waves to the same neighborhood of a New England textile city. Many of these Francos were friends and relatives. Thus family, village, and regional solidarities, in addition to a national French Canadian identity, were transplanted to the new land. Every few years the Little Canada would be replenished by new immigrants fresh from their native land. Demographic dominance and chain migration were therefore instrumental in creating an atmosphere which nurtured *survivance* in New England (Theriault, 1960: 396—99).

333

The most obvious factor which promoted resistance to assimilation is, none the less, an important one: the closeness of the Quebec homeland. French Canadians whose families had spent generations on the same homestead would travel only as far as was necessary to find employment. Nevertheless, some felt that it would be better to follow the path of the *voyageurs*, and go to the American Midwest, where one could ply the traditional French Canadian trades of fur trapping and lumberjacking. At least this environment would be closer to that of Quebec than would the cities and factories of 'Puritan' New England. (Remember that New France and New England had been imperial, religious, and ethnic enemies throughout the years of colonial warfare.) But the pull of New England was greater than that of the Midwest. In this economics played as great a role as geography. New England's industries, particularly textiles, were booming during the Civil War and the decades which followed. The displaced youth of French Canada, both male and female, found steady work. Wages were low, but more than one could make in either rural or urban Quebec. The first emigrants were single males who sought seasonal labor during the winter in brickyards or on construction jobs. In the spring they returned to their father's farm in Quebec to help with agricultural work. Soon after the Civil War whole families were emigrating together, seeking year-round work in the textile mills where father, mother, and children could find employment. Many may have thought that they were doing this to save money so that they could eventually return to Quebec and buy a farm. Yet few did; the era of 'birds of passage' was quickly over (Hansen, 1940: 117—33, 159—81, 203—15, Podea, 1950: 174—75; Foley, 1939: 72—154).

Most French Canadian immigrants came from the Eastern Townships, the triangular section of Quebec south of the St. Lawrence and bordering on New York, Vermont, New Hampshire, and Maine. In New England's textile cities they were a few hundred land miles from the homeland, easily accessible after the Civil War by train. This differentiated Franco-Americans from European and Asian immigrants who were thousands of sea miles distant from their mother countries. This almost unique situation of Francos gave them the status of 'commuting immigrants', which they shared in the United States only with Mexicans and Puerto Ricans (Barkan, 1974, 1977).

Quebec was not some distant 'old world', a memory which might be returned to physically once or twice in your lifetime, if you were lucky. Even if a French Canadian family decided to settle permanently in New England, the ease of trips back and forth meant that those who wished could visit friends and relatives frequently. Such visits helped Franco-Americans renew ties to the homeland. They could fortify their desire to resist assimilation, as well as lessen any sense of alienation from the old world, a problem which plagued European immigrants. If one did not travel to Quebec, the province's newspapers were easy to obtain. As the twentieth century progressed it was possible to receive radio broadcasts, and later television transmissions, from Quebec stations. This strengthened linguistic and cultural ties (Association Canado-Americaine, 1936: 15–33, 87–94, 151–57).

The Catholicism of Francos, particularly their national parishes and accompanying parochial schools, played a dominant role in maintaining *survivance.* To belong to a Franco national parish, one had to be French Canadian by birth, descent, or marriage. Such parishes became the foci of Franco-American community life and the basic units of *survivance,* in those areas where Francos were sufficiently numerous and insistent in demanding that the hierarchy of the American Catholic Church establish them. If a community had a Franco national parish, it was possible to maintain *survivance.* If there were no such parish, the Francos in the town were quickly assimilated.

In these national parishes, the curé, vicars, and nuns came from Quebec. In later years they were recruited from the Franco community itself, and were then trained in Quebec. Except for the Mass, which was in Latin, all church activities were conducted in French. Church-related organizations and societies transformed the parish into a week-long social center. The parochial school was run by parish priests and nuns. English was taught, since even the most militant Franco-American admitted the necessity of learning it to get along in the work world. But French always occupied at least an equal footing. In some schools English had the status of a foreign language, and was taught for only an hour a day. Instruction was given in the history and traditions of Quebec, and an aura of religious conservatism pervaded the whole day. Public school was an anathema in the eyes of the Franco *survivance*-minded elite. No after-school catechism training could make up for the Americanizing influences of materialism and Protestantism which would be learned there. Only in a parochial school would there be emphasis on moral as well as intellectual training, and only in a Franco-American parochial school would French be given sufficient emphasis.

Many Franco children went to public schools, particularly in areas where there were no national parochial schools or where they were overcrowded.

334

However, in cities containing many Franco-American parishes, such as Manchester (eight parishes), Woonsocket (six), Fall River (six), Lowell (five), Lewiston (four), and New Bedford, Massachusetts (seven), the great majority of the ethnic group's children attended these parishes' parochial schools (Wessel, 1931: 12; L'Annuaire des Paroisses, 1948). Among Catholic immigrant groups, Francos were by far the most successful in creating national parishes and schools. By the 1940s there were almost 200 such parishes in New England, as well as another 100 mixed Franco-American parishes, where the clergy and the majority of parishioners were Franco, but in which some English language was used for the benefit of non-Francos. Nearly all of these parishes, national and mixed, had accompanying parochial schools (Theriault, 1960: 397; L'Annuaire des Paroisses, 1948; Hamon, 1891; Association Canado-Américaine, 1936: 75–84, 95–110, 167–77; Plante, 1940; Benoit, 1935: 93–129; Wade, 1950; Ciesluk, 1944).

335

The closeness of Quebec was largely responsible for the success which Francos had in establishing national parishes and schools. European immigrant groups always had difficulty getting clergy from the homeland to staff their national parishes. It was almost impossible for their children to acquire a higher education which would preserve feelings of nationality. Franco-Americans found it far easier to get national clergy from Quebec, and to send their sons and daughters there to obtain the *collège classique* education which would allow them to make their way in the world and become leaders of their own ethnic group.

Most second and third generation Franco children did not get such an education. Their parents held working class jobs in textile mills, and lived frugally in drab tenement districts. These children left school at an early age, and began working in the mills alongside their parents. Their limited horizons were due in part to their lack of education. For most, schooling was not a tool to enhance social mobility. It was rather a grounding in the essentials of conservative religion and *survivance*, to help one get through a life in the mills (Bouvier, 1964; Rosen, 1959).

After 1900 a small Franco-American elite, born in the United States and educated in Quebec, began to take the place of the previous generation of Franco leaders, who had been born in Quebec. This elite was made up primarily of people who entered the professions (clergy, doctor, lawyer) which had been the traditional enclave of the middle class in Quebec. These professionals became the recognized leaders of the Franco-American community, and began the task of convincing the mass of Francos of the need for *survivance* in this strange, new world. The second generation therefore carried on the Quebec tradition of maintaining national survival. Much of the Franco success in preserving *survivance* was due to the establishment of a New England-born elite which, contrary to the generational theory of Marcus Hansen (1938: 260), was not running away from or 'wish[ing] to forget' its heritage.

Quebec was not only close geographically to Franco-Americans; the *survivance* struggle there, with its nationalistic and religious ramifications, was the core of a living experience central in the existence of the Franco elite.

The fate and identity of both French Canadians and Franco-Americans were immediate, live, and unsettled issues, so neither culture was some long-resolved ancient heritage. The Franco elite inherited the French Canadian sense of history as destiny, epitomized by two of Quebec's mottos: *Je me souviens* ('I remember') and *Notre Maître, le passé* ('Our Master, the past'). Although the first appears as a slogan on provincial license plates, these are not empty phrases for a people who have had to struggle for two centuries to preserve *la survivance* in a nation dominated by *les Anglais*. The French Canadian elite preached incessantly about the close interrelationship of past and present. The result was a virtual cult of the past among *Québécois*, who were forever looking backwards.

336

The English Conquest of 1760 is the single most important event in French Canadian history. It became the central reference point of French Canadians and their *raison d'être*. Although the English conquered Canada, they did not eradicate the French Canadians' Roman Catholicism, French language, or customs, and did not disperse them as had been done to the Acadians ten years earlier. In fact, the English guaranteed *Canadiens* free exercise of their religion, language, French civil law, and seigneurial land system, partially as an inducement to keep them from joining the American colonials in the then-brewing Revolution.

But the Conquest and subsequent British rule had long-term effects upon the French Canadian mentality. Even if French Canadian rights were maintained, they were conquered and thus at the mercy of their conquerors. In the two centuries which have followed, the English and English Canadians have periodically threatened the national identity and special status of French Canadians in Canada, without ever carrying such threats to an assimilationist conclusion. *Canadiens* were kept in a subservient economic position in Quebec, where they were eliminated from active participation in commerce and industry. Doomed to a second rate status in their own land, they turned to the soil and retreated within a 'folk' society. The psychological effects of this 'form of slavery' made French Canadians a people obsessed with inferiority and persecution, to the extent that Pierre Vallières (1971), a Marxist *séparatiste*, has called them the 'white niggers of America'.

From this time on, French Canadians in Quebec were a nationality with a homeland (even today 80 per cent of the people living in the province are of French Canadian descent), but they did not have an independent, sovereign nation. The Conquest was the event which inaugurated their separate identity, distinct from that of England, English Canada, and France, and which began their long struggle to maintain this national identity within the larger framework dominated by *les Anglais* (the preceding four paragraphs are based on Neatby, 1966; Wade, 1968; Cook, 1966; Brunet, 1959; Bonenfant and Falardeau, 1946; Nish, 1966; Manning, 1962).

This long tradition of battling for national survival in Quebec aided those French Canadians who continued the struggle when they crossed the border in the years after 1865. By this time, their national identity in Quebec was fully developed. Such nationalism was stimulated by common descent, language, religion, and culture, and a shared territory. As a minority group in a country which they no longer controlled, Quebec's French Canadians had developed a sense of aloneness, an introspective consciousness of group solidarity, an obsession with national survival *(la survivance)*, a close intertwining of past and present *(je me souviens)*, the concept of a racial and religious divine mission, and a hundred years of survival techniques. In other words, Franco-Americans had a sense of being a minority, of being an ethnic group, before they arrived in the United States. In addition, because their combat was contemporaneous with the one still going on in the homeland, the question of national survival became a living issue for Francos in New England. The uncertainty of their motherland's position made the specter of assimilation in America more frightening and challenging.

The French Canadian Church elite directed this fierce, often fanatical, struggle to maintain *foi, langue,* and *moeurs,* both in Quebec and in New England. The Catholic Church in French Canada was neither monolithic nor omnipotent. But in the latter half of the nineteenth century the dominion of the Church hierarchy over the populace was solidified. The Church, rather than the provincial government, became the true leader of Quebec and self-proclaimed protector of the French Canadian heritage. This was not the nominal Catholicism of Italy or France. Church leaders directed the province's charitable and cultural activities. They indoctrinated the faithful in the importance of family, parish, school, and rural life, and in the dominance of spiritual over material. Control of education became the keynote of the Quebec Church, as fusing of language and religion was solidified within the schools (Wade, 1968, Chaps. 3–7, 12; Cook, 1967, 1969; Rioux and Martin, 1964; Brunet, 1958; Monet, 1965; Theriault, 1951: 229–83).

The Catholic Church in Quebec fashioned conservative nationalism into a potent force. Nationalism is seldom a spontaneous mass movement. In both Quebec and New England, it was the result of a conscious policy directed by an elite made up primarily of French Canadian and Franco-American religious figures. They led and the people followed. Without such leaders there would have been no *survivance.* Consequently the Franco elite was fortunate to have the direct and immediate example provided them by their Quebec counterparts. They repeated the admonitions to preserve religion, language, and customs, and the idea of the divine mission. Franco-Americans were told again and again to avoid intermarriage outside their religion or nationality. Until the post-World War II era, such advice was usually heeded, as Franco intermarriage rates were low in comparison to other white ethnic groups, apart from Jews (Wessel, 1931: 110–15; Forget, 1949: 6–16; Dexter, 1923: 208–19; Lemaire, 1964: 74). Maintenance of the native language was deemed especially important, since its loss was associated with the lapsing of ethnicity, which would lead to loss of religion. (Of course, when a French Canadian or Franco-American spoke of losing religion, he meant Catholicism. Protestantism was seen as only slightly preferable to heathenism or paganism.)

Home and family were deemed most important in the *survivance* struggle. There was a strongly conservative, religious flavor to this emphasis. Home and family constituted a holy environment in which one acquired the character necessary to avoid the melting pot of the United States, and its supposedly attendant values of materialism, individualism, and egotism. The French Canadian and Franco elites invariably identified these qualities with Protestantism. In their place the elite glorified *survivance* and group values, even to the point of advocating poverty, suffering, and martyrdom as the natural lot of their people. The role of the mother was central in all this. She would bear and raise a large family, since numbers meant strength in the *survivance* battle (French Canadians called this 'the revenge of the cradle': the way to fight *les Anglais* was to out-reproduce them!), and having many children meant putting them above self and money. Mother would be their first and most important teacher of the French language, and would implant within them a respect for the traditional Catholic virtues of duty and obedience (Benoit, 1935: 57–91; Association Canado-Américaine, 1936: 111–19; French, 1976).

A conflict theory of ethnicity is implicit in this view of the history of French Canada as destiny. One reason why French Canadians maintained *survivance* in Quebec was their lack of an independent homeland in which they could feel secure. It was conflict versus *les Anglais* which required them to remain vigilant and which sharpened their sense of group identity and awareness.

One might imagine that in New England the established 'Yankee' population would take the place of *les Anglais* in Quebec. This was not the case. It is ironic that, from the 1870s until the 1920s, nativistic conflict with a fellow Catholic immigrant group, the Irish, was more of a problem for Franco-Americans than was Yankee nativism. This antagonism was primarily due to religion.

The earlier-immigrating Irish had suffered through the first great era of American nativism, the Know-Nothing movement. They emerged from this bruised but in control of the hierarchy of the American Catholic Church, and convinced that they had won for themselves a place in American life. Masses of other Catholic immigrants arrived later in the nineteenth century, first Germans, then French Canadians, and finally southern and eastern Europeans. The Irish felt superior to these groups and were wary of them. They spoke a foreign language and no English, unlike most Irish, and were regarded by Protestant natives as racially inferior and unassimilable. Would their influx create a new age of anti-Catholic nativism which would treaten the tenuous niche that the Irish had carved out for themselves?

Consequently, the Irish hierarchy of the Church took an assimilationist position. In theory the Catholic Church in America guaranteed the right of immigrant groups to form their own national parishes. Hundreds of such parishes were created by non-English-speaking Catholics (we have seen that the Francos alone formed nearly 200). However, in reality Church administrators preferred territorial parishes which encompassed a specific geographical area (i.e., any Catholic within the boundaries could join), and viewed national parishes as temporary expedients. The Church hierarchy felt that in territorials all nationalities would mix and English would be the common language. This would help non-English-speaking nationalities adjust to American life and would lessen Protestant fears that Catholicism was a foreign threat. The Irish hierarchy also saw national parishes as signs of ethnic fragmentation within the Church, which they feared would break down the solidarity necessary if Catholics were to resist the Protestant atmosphere of America.

Such feelings on the part of the Irish are understandable and justifiable, from the hindsight of the historian, but they conflicted with the French Canadian heritage of resisting assimilation by intermeshing *foi, langue,* and *moeurs.* Church leaders outwardly stated that national parishes could be tolerated, since the passage of years and the passing away of the immigrant generations would bring about residential mobility and the extinguishing of native languages, thus dooming the old parishes. Nevertheless, Francos thought that the hierarchy tried to speed up the process by discriminating against their national parishes in a variety of ways. In addition, Franco-Americans resented Irish domination of the Church hierarchy, and disliked the tight administrative control which the diocese had over parishes, particularly concerning finances. French Canadians were not used to such control in Quebec, where the parish functioned almost independently and where there was lay participation in parish administration. Consequently, Francos in New England considered the Church hierarchy to be greedy, authoritarian, dictatorial, remote, and secretive. The Franco elite reserved its harshest criticisms for the Irish, as a people who had given up their Gaelic language in the homeland, who had fallen into a morass of *égoisme* and *matérialisme* in America, and who would soon drift away from their religion. (Francos conveniently overlooked the fact that the English conquerors had systematically stamped out the use of Gaelic, something they had not done to the French language in Quebec.) (Sources for the preceding four paragraphs: Rumilly, 1958: 50, 116, 129, 168, 174, 199; Foley, 1939: 490–91; Theriault, 1951: 364–68; Verrette, 1947–48; Benoit, 1935: 93–114; Ellis, 1969: Chaps. 3–4; Greeley, 1967: Chap. 6; Gleason, 1970: 65–80, 133–53; Linkh, 1975; Miller and Marzik, 1977; Gleason, 1968; Dolan, 1975; Tomasi, 1975; Greene, 1975; Buczek, 1974; Sanders, 1977.)

Franco-Americans were most angered by what they considered attempts on the part of various New England bishops to deny their people national parishes and priests, or to restrict existing national parishes in terms of their administrative and financial control. Major disputes occurred in Fall River (1886), Danielson, Connecticut (1895–97), and North Brookfield, Massachusetts (1899–1904), and culminated with the Corporation Sole controversy in Maine (1906–14), and the Sentinelle affair in Rhode Island (1924–29). These vitriolic battles featured vehement resistance by Francos against what they felt was persecution by the Church hierarchy. Militant Francos boycotted the Church (both in terms of contribution of money and attendance at Mass), held public protest meetings, formed their own schismatic parishes, sued Church officials in the civil courts, and appealed to Rome. Such activities often ended in excommunication for the rebels,

339

which usually brought about a grudging and half-hearted acquiescence to the authority of the Church hierarchy (Rumilly, 1958: 105–14, 130, 222, 238–39, 253–69, 277; Wade 1950; Foley, 1939: 215, 223, 440, 482; Theriault, 1951: 347–79; Verrette, 1947–48; Chevalier, 1972; Woodbury, 1967; Guignard, 1973; Sorrell, 1975, 1977).

My purpose here is neither to examine this religious conflict in depth, nor to cast blame on either side. If anything, in the course of my ongoing research on this topic (Sorrell, 1977–present, 1978), I am coming to have more sympathy for the viewpoint and policies of the Church hierarchy *vis-à-vis* Franco militants. This sympathy is based on a realization that the administrative and bureaucratic facets of such disputes were often as important as Franco-Irish ethnic and religious conflict, and an awareness that the majority of Francos usually did not support their militant ethnic brethren. My point

340

is that such conflict (both within the ethnic group, and between it and the Irish) served to stimulate Franco group awareness and *survivance.* Insecurity and combativeness bred identity in New England, just as they had in Quebec. It seems no mere coincidence that the two Catholic immigrant groups which had the most militant conflict with the Church hierarchy, Francos and Poles, were also the groups which clung the most tenaciously to their heritage (for Polish struggles, see Greene, 1966, 1978; Buczek, 1974, 1976a, 1976b; Miller and Marzik, 1977: 84–102; Galush, 1972; Monzell, 1969; Madaj, 1969; Platt, 1977). It also seems no accident that Franco *survivance* began to decline after the 1920s, when the last great battle with the Irish (the Sentinelle affair) was over.

The perceptive reader may be bothered by what seems to be a contradiction in my presentation to this point: if French Canadians had such an intense devotion to their homeland, where a panoply of *survivance* institutions existed to help them carry out the providential mission of racial and religious survival, why then did over a million emigrate to a country where the Anglo-Saxon, the Protestant, and the materialistic dominated?

The explanation is economics. The great majority of emigrants were simple *habitants,* rural farmers who faced a decline in the opportunities for making a living in the motherland, and therefore searched for better material conditions in America. French Canadian *habitants,* like many other immigrants, were products of a stable and deep-rooted traditional culture. They had limited horizons and were reluctant to emigrate unless conditions became virtually unbearable. The economic 'push' from Quebec had to be strong before they would leave. Since the Conquest the seigneurial system of landholding had undergone great strains. Rents were high and restrictions were many, rendering this system inferior to that of freehold land ownership during a period of expanding commercial and industrial demands upon farmers. Seigneurial tenure was abolished in the 1850s, but this did not end the province's economic troubles. French Canadians were backward farmers (mythology to the contrary) and had worn out the soil around the St. Lawrence by the 1830s. There was little other arable land in Quebec, and much of that was inaccessible or owned by speculators.

Population pressure, induced by the phenomenally high birth rate among French Canadians in the years after the Conquest (the revenge of the cradle), in combination with a declining mortality rate, posed a dilemma for the *habitant* family. The father could further divide his already overly sectioned plot of land. If this proved impractical, most of the children had to search for their living elsewhere. Since the cities of the province were not expanding fast enough to provide sufficient urban-industrial job opportunities, most of the rural overflow had to leave the sanctuary of Quebec. Thus the central irony in the French Canadian elite's program for *survivance:* devotion to family and land meant that most of the children would eventually have to leave both, and the homeland as well (Ouellet, 1966; Wade, 1968: Chaps. 3–8; Hansen, 1940: Chaps. 6–9; Creighton, 1937; Manning, 1962; Rioux and Martin, 1964; Careless, 1967; Jones, 1946; Parker, 1959; Roby, 1976).

The *habitant* who left Quebec probably didn't think about the larger meaning of his emigration, other than feeling a natural longing for his lost native land. However, many of the French Canadian elite who also made the journey must have had mixed feelings and a certain sense of guilt over the implication that their emigration meant they valued economic success and a new life more than *survivance* in Quebec. In other words, their leaving somehow signified a rejection of the French Canadian tradition which placed the divine mission above materialism and individualism. The vehemence that this now-Franco-American elite displayed in attempting to transfer *survivance* to New England, may have been an attempt to assuage feelings of guilt and redeem themselves in the eyes of those who remained at home. Perhaps they were saying: We may have left Quebec but we're taking our Quebec values with us.

If this was the cry of the emigrant, it ultimately did not fall on deaf ears. The initial reaction of Quebec's Church and provincial government leaders to emigration was unfavorable. They saw those departing as totally lost to *survivance,* since they would soon be dissolved within the Anglo-Protestant melting pot of the United States. Some *Québécois* simply dismissed the emigrants as 'rabble' of whom they were well rid.

By the 1870s provincial leaders, as well as the national government, realized the direness of the situation. Whole regions of Quebec were depopulated by *la fièvre aux Etats-Unis.* They began attempts at *repatriement,* trying to attract Franco-Americans to newly opened agricultural land on the Canadian prairies and in northern Quebec. Some did return during hard times in the States, when cyclical depressions threw them temporarily out of work. But repatriation produced few permanent results. Much of the land offered in Quebec proved unsuitable, and New England's industry continued to be too powerful a magnet. Finally, Church leaders in Quebec accepted the situation. Rather than moralizing over the loss or advocating return, they began in the 1880s to send French Canadian priests and nuns to New England, to establish parishes and promote *survivance* (Chaput, 1968; Wade, 1968: 260–61, 432–35; Rumilly, 1958: 41, 62–88).

French Canadian leaders initially were too pessimistic about the chances

341

for ethnic survival in New England. Yet, in the long run, their pessimism was probably justified. Although the years after 1930 are not my major concern, I must close with a brief survey of the ultimate failure of the dream of a 'Quebec in New England', or a 'Quebec-down-there', labels applied to Franco-Americana by the most optimistic of the *survivance*-minded elite.

My description of *survivance* has focused on the viewpoint of the elite. Obviously all Francos did not abide by its wishes; the reality of daily life could be far removed from espoused ideals. But many did listen to their leaders, and paid far more than lip service to such a program. As a result, the institutions used by Franco-Americans to resist assimilation and maintain national identity remained viable and vigorous for many years. Such institutions became even more vital in America than they had in the mother country. In New England the position of Francos was far more precarious than had been the case in Quebec, so it was important to instill active reliance upon *survivance* props in order to combat the new American environment. Many needed little coaxing, since they clung willingly to what was traditional in the face of an urban-industrial environment which was difficult to comprehend and which fostered insecurity.

The irony is that the Franco-American elite believed it was clinging to traditions developed in the homeland. Yet, even when *survivance* was strong, all of the traditions and institutions were being altered by the powerful American environment, and by differences between the situation of French Canadians in Quebec and that of Francos in New England. Parishes and schools became more of a focal point in New England, since the outside environment was more immediately threatening south of the border. The battle with the Irish within the Church was more intense in New England. National societies and the French language press fulfilled more of a need, since they were reference points by which a Franco-American could assure himself and others of his identity. This had been unnecessary within the largely rural and homogeneous sanctuary of Quebec. Even the closeness of Quebec, which I have put forth as a major factor in the maintenance of *survivance*, was somewhat illusory. For the generations of Francos born and raised in the United States, Quebec was a foreign land. More accessible than most, full of kith and kin who spoke your mother tongue and had similar customs, but nevertheless a foreign land with a different pace of life. Quebec could truly be a homeland only for those who were born there and lived there through adolescence.

Could *survivance* ever be as successful in New England as it was in Quebec? The answer is no, since New England was not Quebec, and therefore *survivance* à *la* motherland was not transferable. In America there was a tradition of separation of Church and state, and of no established religions, which meant that Catholicism could never play as dominant a role in Franco-American life as it did in Quebec. In any case, Francos did not control the hierarchy of the Catholic Church in America as did their brethren in French Canada. The guarantees French Canadians had won from their British rulers and English Canadian co-citizens, which protected their religion, language, laws, and customs in Quebec, could never be gained anew in the States. There,

Francos were merely one of many nationalities in a polyglot country, while in Canada some recognized them as one of two founding nationalities. This 'two nations' theory made French Canadians co-equal with English Canadians, the two having entered into a compact in 1867, when Canada became a confederated nation. Even most of those Canadians who did not acknowledge the above had to admit that French Canadians were at least a special minority, entitled to distinctive rights and privileges (Cook, 1967; Wade, 1968, particularly Chaps. 6–7). Finally, Franco-Americans could never numerically dominate New England, not even its mill towns, to the degree that French Canadians dominated Quebec. Without this demographic solidarity, assimilationist inroads were inevitable.

These inroads became increasingly evident in the years after 1930. Emigration from Quebec fell off drastically. During the Depression class concerns loomed larger than ethnicity. World War II gave most Americans a common purpose, and members of all nationalities who served in the war gained new horizons beyond their ethnic neighborhoods. An upsurge in prosperity and suburban living followed the war. The new accessibility of the American ideal of the middle class, coupled with occupational and residential mobility, meant a further breaking down of old ethnic identities. Specific difficulties which Franco-American *survivance* faced were the mounting financial problems of Catholic schools, and the apathy which Franco youths showed towards aspects of their heritage, such as the French language and conservative Catholic values (Rumilly, 1958: 504–46; Perreault, 1976: 38–46; Theriault, 1951: 341–550, 1960: 406–11; Lemaire, 1964: 40–65; Orban, 1976; Witt, 1979).

Some of these trends have been reversed in the 1970s, as a new generation of Francos, caught up in the neo-ethnic revival, is taking a greater interest in its ethnic past. Franco linguistic centers have recently emerged in New England as part of this ethnic renaissance, and these centers are trying to promote bilingualism among young Francos (Guy, 1976). Nevertheless, this new generation is far more distant from its heritage as a result of 50 years of inexorable acculturation. To young Francos of today, their history is just an interesting subject of study, rather than destiny. *Survivance* lives in Quebec, but is dead or moribund in New England. I am reminded of a friend, who was doing research for his doctoral dissertation on the Franco-Americans of Biddeford, Maine. Another Franco of the same age (early 30s) found him going through old issues of the now-defunct French language newspaper in Biddeford, and warned him — 'Don't you know there's a law in Maine against exhuming the dead?'

Notes

*This is a revised and expanded version of a presentation made at the annual meeting of the Southwestern Anthropological Association, 29 March 1979, Santa Barbara, California. "Both the presentation and this article were made possible by the National Endowment for the Humanities program of Fellowships-in-Residence, 1978–79; mine was a 'Dual Cultural Heritages in the United States' seminar, directed by Professor Paul J. Bohannan of the University of California, Santa Barbara."

**Unless otherwise designated, 'Franco-American' and 'Franco' will refer to the immigrants to New England and their descendants, while 'French Canadian' will refer to those who remained in the Quebec homeland.

References

ALLEN, J. 1972 'Migration Fields of French Canadian Immigrants to Southern Maine.' *Geographical Review* 62: 366–83 (July).

ALLEN, Y. 1974 'Franco-Americans in Maine: A Geographical Perspective.' *Acadiensis* 4: 32–66 (Autumn).

'L'Annuaire des Paroisses Franco-Américaines de la Nouvelle Angleterre, 1948.' Manuscript survey, Union St.-Jean-Baptiste d'Amérique, Woonsocket, Rhode Island.

ARNELL, W. 1949 'The French Population of New England.' *Geography* 34: 97–101, Pt. 2.

Association Canado-Américaine (eds) 1936 *Les Franco-Américains Peints par eux-mêmes.* Montreal.

BARKAN, E. 1974 'Commuting "Immigrants": Puerto Ricans, Mexicans, Amerindians, and French Canadians During the Past Century.' Presentation at the National Convention of the Organization of American Historians, Denver, Colorado, April.

BARKAN, E. 1977 'Proximity and Commuting Immigration: An Hypothesis explored via the Bi-polar Ethnic Communities of French Canadian and Mexican-Americans' in Jack Kinton (ed.), *American Ethnic Revival.* Aurora, Illinois, 163–83.

BENOIT, J. 1935 *L'âme Franco-Américaine.* Montreal.

BONENFANT, J. C. and FALARDEAU, J. C. 1946 'Cultural and Political Implications of French Canadian Nationalism.' Canadian Historical Association Report, 56–73.

BOUVIER, L. F. 1964 'La Stratification Sociale du Groupe Ethnique Canadien-Francais aux Etats-Unis.' Recherches Sociographiques 5: 371–79 (September–December).

BRUNET, M. 1958 La Présence Anglaise et les Canadiens. Montreal.

BRUNET, M. 1959 'The British Conquest: Canadian Social Scientists and the Fate of the *Canadiens.'* Canadian Historical Review 40: 93–107 (June).

BUCZEK, D. 1974 Immigrant Pastor: *the life of the Right Reverend Monsignor Lucyan Bójnowski of New Britain, Connecticut.* Waterbury, Conn.

BUCZEK, D. 1976a 'Polish American Priests and the American Catholic Hierarchy: A View From the Twenties.' Polish American Studies 33, 1: 34–43.

BUCZEK, D. 1976b 'Polish Americans and the Roman Catholic Church.' The Polish Review 21, 3: 39–61.

CARELESS, J. M. S. 1967 *The union of the Canadas: growth of Canadian Institutions, 1841–1857.* Toronto.

CHAPUT, D. 1968 'Some *Repatriement* Dilemmas.' *Canadian Historical Review* 49: 400–12 (December).

CHEVALIER, SISTER F. 1972 'The Role of French National Societies in the Sociocultural Evolution of the Franco-Americans of New England from 1860 to the Present.' Unpublished Ph.D. dissertation, Catholic University of America.

CIESLUK, J. 1944 *National Parishes in the United States.* Washington, D.C.

COOK, R. 1966 'Some French Canadian Interpretations of the British Conquest: une quatrième dominate de la pensée Canadienne-Française.' *Canadian Historical Association Papers,* 70–83.

COOK, R. 1967 *Canada and the French Canadian Question.* Toronto.

COOK, R. (ed.) 1969 *French Canadian Nationalism: an Anthology.* Toronto.

CREIGHTON, D. G. 1937 *The Commercial Empire of the St. Lawrence.* Toronto.

DEXTER, R. C. 1923 'The Habitant Transplanted: A Study of the French Candian in New England.' Unpublished Ph.D. dissertation, Clark University.

DEXTER, R. 1924 'Rhode Island: A Lively Experiment.' *The Nation* 118: 226–28 (27 February).

DINNERSTEIN, L. and REIMERS, D. M. 1975 *Ethnic Americans: a History of Immigration and Assimilation.* New York.

DOLAN, J. 1975 *The Immigrant Church: New York's Irish and German Catholics, 1815–1865.* Baltimore.

ELLIS, J. T. 1969 *American Catholicism.* New York.

Le *Farog-Forum*, 1978 'Du Nord au Sud: Les Franco-Américains' (janvier), 7.

FAUCHER, A. 1964 'L'émigration des Canadiens-français au XIXe siècle: position du problème et prespectives.' *Recherches Sociographiques* 5: 277–317 (September–December).

FEDERAL WRITERS' PROJECT 1937 *Rhode Island: a Guide to the Smallest State.* Boston.

FOLEY, A. R. 1939 'From French Canadian to Franco-American: A Study of the Immigration of the French Canadian into New England, 1650–1935.' Unpublished Ph.D. dissertation, Harvard University.

FORGET, U. 1949 *Les Franco-Américains et le 'Melting Pot'.* Fall River, Massachusetts.

FRENCH, L. 1976 'The Franco American Working Class Family' in Charles H. Mindel and Robert W. Habenstein (eds), *Ethnic Families in America.* New York, 323–46.

GALUSH, W. 1972 'The Polish National Catholic Church: A Survey of Its Origins, Development and Missions.' *Records of the American Catholic Historical Society of Philadelphia* 83: 131–49 (September–December).

GLEASON, P. 1968 *The Conservative Reformers: German-American Catholics and the social order.* Notre Dame, Indiana.

GLEASON, P. (ed.) 1970 *Catholicism in America.* New York.

GREELEY, A. 1967 *The Catholic Experience.* New York.

GREENE, V. 1966 'For God and Country: The Origins of Slavic Self-Consciousness in America.' *Church History* 35: 446–60 (December).

GREENE, V. 1975 *For God and Country: the rise of Polish and Lithuanian Ethnic Consciousness in America, 1860–1910.* Madison, Wisconsin.

GUIGNARD, M. 1973 'Maine's Corporation Sole Controversy.' *Maine Historical Society Newsletter* 12: 111–30 (Winter).

GUY, D. 1976 'New England's Franco-Americans: Vive la Difference? *Yankee* (July), 68–73ff.

HAMON, FATHER E. 1891 *Les Canadiens-Français de la Nouvelle Angleterre.* Quebec City.

HANDLIN, O. (ed.) 1959 *Immigration as a Factor in American History.* Englewood Cliffs, New Jersey.

HANHAM, H. J. 1977 'Canadian History in the 1970s.' *Canadian Historical Review* 58: 2–22 (March).

HANSEN, M. L. 1966 'The Problem of the Third Generation Immigrant' (1938), in Oscar Handlin (ed.), *Children of the uprooted.* New York, Chap. 18.

HANSEN, M. L. 1940 *The mingling of the Canadian and American Peoples.* New Haven, Connecticut.

JONES, R. L. 1946 'Agriculture in Lower Canada, 1792–1815.' *Canadian Historical Review* 27: 33–51.

LaGUMINA, S. J. and CAVAIOLI, F. J. 1974 *The ethnic dimension in American Society.* Boston.

LAVOIE, Y. 1972 *L'émigration des Canadiens aux Etats-Unis avant 1930: mesure du phénomène.* Montreal.

LEMAIRE, H. B. 1964 'Franco-American Efforts on Behalf of the French Language in New England.' Unpublished MS, Yeshiva University Language Resources Project.

LINKH, R. 1975 *American Catholicism and European Immigrants (1900–1924).* New York.

MADAJ, REVEREND M. J. 1969 'The Polish Immigrant, The American Catholic Hierarchy, and Father Wenceslaus Kruszka.' *Polish American Studies* 26: 16–29 (January–June).

MANNING, H. T. 1962 *The Revolt of French Canada: 1800–1835.* Toronto.
MILLER, R. M. and MARZIK T. D. (eds) 1977 *Immigrants and Religion in urban America.* Philadelphia.
MONET, J. 1965 'The Foundations of French Canadian Nationality, 1608–1867.' *Culture* (December), 456–66.
MONZELL, T. I. 1969 'The Catholic Church and the Americanization of the Polish Immigrant.' *Polish American Studies 26:* 1–15 (January–June).
NEATBY, H. 1966 *Quebec: The Revolutionary Age, 1760–1791.* Toronto.
NISH, C. (ed.) 1966 *The French Canadians, 1759–1766; Conquered? Half-conquered? Liberated?* Toronto.
ORBAN, E. 1976 'Facteurs politico-religieux et anglicisation des Franco américains au Vermont: indicateurs recents.' *Canadian Ethnic Studies* 8, 2: 34–49.
OUELLET, F. 1966 *Histoire Économique et Sociale du Québec, 1760–1850.* Montreal.
PAQUET, G. 1964 'L'émigration des Canadiens-français vers la Nouvelle-Angleterre, 1870–1910: prises de vue quantitatives. *Recherches Sociographiques* 5: 319–70 (September–December).
PARKER, W. H. 1959 'A New Look at Unrest in Lower Canada in the 1830s.' *Canadian Historical Review* 40: 209–17 (September).
PERREAULT, R. B. 1976 'One Piece in the Great American Mosaic.' *Le Canado-Américain* 2: 5–51 (avril–mai–juin).
PLANTE, BROTHER G. R. 1940 'The Franco-American Parish in New England.' Unpublished MA thesis, Fordham University.
PLATT, W. C. 1977 'The Polish National Catholic Church: An Inquiry Into Its Origins.' *Church History* 46: 474–89 (December).
PODEA, I. S. 1950 'Quebec to "Little Canada": The Coming of the French Canadians to New England in the Nineteenth Century.' *New England Quarterly* 23: 365–80 (September).
RIMBERT, S. 1954 'L'immigration Franco-Canadienne au Massachusetts.' *Revue Canadienne de Géographie* 8: 75–85 (juillet–oct.).
RIOUX, M. and MARTIN Y. (eds) 1964 *French Canadian Society.* Toronto.
ROBY, Y. 1976 *Les Québécois et les Investissements Américains (1918–1929).* Quebec City.
ROSEN, B. C. 1959 'Race, Ethnicity, and the Achievement Syndrome.' *American Sociological Review* 24: 46–60 (February).
RUMILLY, R. 1958 *Histoire des Franco-Américains.* Montreal.
SAMUEL, T. J. 1969 *The Migration of Canadian-born between Canada and the United States of America.* Ottawa.
SANDERS, J. W. 1977 *The Education of an urban minority: Catholics in Chicago, 1833–1965.* New York.
SORRELL, R. S. 1975 'The Sentinelle Affair (1924–1929) and Militant *Survivance:* The Franco-American Experience in Woonsocket, Rhode Island.' Unpublished Ph.D. dissertation, State University of New York at Buffalo.
SORRELL, R. S. 1977 'Sentinelle Affair (1924–1929) – Religion and Militant *Survivance* in Woonsocket, Rhode Island.' *Rhode Island History* 36: 67–79 (August).
SORRELL, R. S. 1978 'French Canadians in New England: Religion and Militant *Survivance*, 1870–1930.' Presentation at the Spring meeting of the American Catholic Historical Association, 7 April, Seton Hall University.
SORRELL, R. S. 1977–79 'French Canadians in New England: Religion and Militant *Survivance*, 1870–1930.' Ongoing research project suported by National Endowment for the Humanities.
THERIAULT, G. F. 1951 'The Franco-Americans in a New England Community: An Experiment in Survival.' Unpublished Ph.D. dissertation, Harvard University.
THERIAULT, G. F. 1960 'The Franco-Americans of New England' in Mason Wade (ed.), *Canadian Dualism.* Toronto, 392–411.

346

TOMASI, S. 1975 *Piety and Power: The Role of Italian Parishes in the New York Metropolitan Area, 1880–1930.* New York.

TRUESDELL, L. E. 1943 *The Canadian born in the United States: An Analysis of the statistics of the Canadian element in the population of the United States, 1850–1930.* New Haven, Connecticut.

VALLIÈRES, P. 1971 *White Niggers of America.* Toronto.

VERRETTE, ABBÉ A. 1947–48 'La Paroisse Franco-Américaine.' *Canadian Catholic Historical Association Report,* 125–39.

VICERO, R. D. 1968 'Immigration of French Canadians to New England, 1840–1900: A Geographical Analysis.' Unpublished Ph.D. dissertation, University of Wisconsin.

WADE, M. 1950 'The French Parish and *Survivance* in Nineteenth-Century New England.' *Catholic Historical Review* 36: 163–89 (July).

WADE, M. 1966 'French Canadians in the United States' *in Writings on Canadian-American Studies.* East Lansing, Michigan.

WADE, M. 1968 *The French Canadians, 1760–1967.* Toronto.

WESSEL, B. B. 1931 *An ethnic survey of Woonsocket, Rhode Island.* Chicago.

WITT, L. 1979 'Slip of the mother tongue for New England French.' *Christian Science Monitor:* B10–11 (7 March).

WOODBURY, K. B. JR. 1967 'An Incident Between the French Canadians and the Irish in the Diocese of Maine in 1906.' *New England Quarterly* 40: 260–69 (June).

347

"FATHER OF NEW ENGLAND LITHUANIANS"

Ethnicity and Catholicity must be inseparable,"[1] wrote Father Žebris a month before his death, as if penning a summary of his philosophy of life. From this vantage point alone, one can begin to assess him and his accomplishments, and his failures too. These intermingled facets are the key to his pioneer mentality. It is no exaggeration to judge that Žebris, from his beginning in the United States, was thinking and acting almost as if he were a papal legate exercising authority and responsibility over all Lithuanian immigrants. No other priest gave thought to visit nearly every known Balt colony as did Žebris in the fall and winter of 1893. He was a dynamic man whose temperament pushed him to break new ground. Indeed, he was first in many ways. As will be seen in later chapters, he was founder of the cooperative movement among Lithuanians in America, authored the first geography manual[*] ever published in the Lithuanian language, originated a vocabulary of terms for military drill, edited the first Balt newspaper in New England, and became the first resident Lithuanian priest in New England.

The 64-page primer on geography is a clue to the priest's vision. In his foreword, he explains that as a student in 1881 at the Kaunas seminary, he compiled ten pages of notes in question-answer style at the recommendation of a priest-mentor. The unidentified professor then borrowed the outline for teaching geography to children. Mindful of the press ban in Lithuania (1864-1904), Žebris happily told the reader: "Now that I am in America there is no danger whatever in having this little booklet put into print."[3]

Most significant in the geography text is Supplement No. III with its revealing inscription: "Places where there are Lithuanian churches in North America, or where there ought to be such churches". Žebris lists by location nineteen parishes, thirteen of which were in Pennsylvania. His thorough awareness of the condition of these congregations is clear from his explanatory notes: "Boston — priest, no church", and "Brooklyn — church, no priest". Under colonies in need of a parish or at least a chapel as a mission station, the writer compiled a list of thirty-two cities and towns, mostly in the northeast, but including Spring Valley, Illinois and St. Louis, Missouri. An additional three places were: Brazil, Tasmania, and Johannesburg. Žebris could have composed such a thorough tally only by regularly monitoring a wide variety of Lithuanian newspapers, recording every scrap of information from conversations with travelers, and practicing constant vigil for any detail of Lithuanians wherever they had settled. The priest's ecclesiastical status was simply that of pastor to the Balts of the Waterbury area. He had no other canonical assignment. But, his self-appointed field of endeavor and his relentless ambition were quite otherwise.

From his post at St. Joseph Parish, and later at St. Andrew, New Britain, this pioneer was constantly on the move, hearing confessions and preaching in Lithuanian (and Polish when needed); fostering mutual aid societies; propagating consumer efforts such as cooperative bakeries and grocery stores; explaining real estate procedures, bank loans and investments; and above all, giving impetus to hesitant brethren to act with firm hope of achieving their goals. Since more than half of the Balts came to the New World with no formal schooling, and some with only home instruction at best, Žebris spurred them on to learn reading and writing in both English and Lithuanian. To these immigrants, the priest played the role of father, leader, counsellor and advocate.

His roving apostolate was a large-scale repetition of his nine-month tour of Pennsylvania days. Depending on proximity of a given community, he made daytime visits, overnight stays, or extended stops of several days or more. For local trips, Žebris used horse-drawn wagons and for longer journeys he took a carriage or train, or combination of both. There is no evidence that he ever owned any personal mode of transportation, a fact suggesting the spartan lifestyle he followed.

He was instrumental in the founding of at least fifteen

parishes. Sometimes he was the first on the scene, at other times he built on the groundwork of an earlier itinerant priest. His practical instructions and persuasive rhetoric goaded newly-formed colonies to keep alive and implement their desire for a separate parish. He was partly responsible, and sometimes the exclusive force, for Lithuanian parishes at St. Joseph, Waterbury; St. Andrew, New Britain; Holy Trinity, Hartford; St. Anthony, Ansonia; St. George, Bridgeport; St. Casimir, New Haven. Outside Connecticut, he was linked to St. Rocco (later St. Casimir), Brockton; St. Joseph (later St. Peter), South Boston; St. Francis, Athol; Immaculate Conception, Cambridge — all in Massachusetts. Beyond New England, Žebris left his mark on Queen of Angels, Brooklyn and St. Casimir, Amsterdam — in New York state; and the two New Jersey parishes of Holy Trinity, Newark and Sts. Peter & Paul, Elizabeth. Parish histories and the ethnic press attest to this pioneer's role in organizing these religious units.

In Connecticut, the peripatetic cleric literally strove to reach every possible outpost. It is certain that he made one, and probably more trips to Branford, Broad Brook, East Hartford, East Windsor (Windsor Hill), Hazardville, Meriden, New Cannan, North Granby, Torrington, Wallingford. Notices ran continuously in *Rytas* announcing time, place and date of Žebris' appearances. Lithuanians from nearby towns were invited to a central location. Arrangements as to time and church were often indicated tentatively, hinging on the willingness of the pastor of a territorial or foreign-language parish to offer hospitality. For example, in one case he informed readers that he would be in either South Glastonbury or East Hartford on a particular day, depending on the place designated by the local pastor whose jurisdiction encompassed these two communities. A scheduling problem centered on the priest's inability to absent himself weekends from his resident church, since he was generally in charge of two churches simultaneously. While at Waterbury he was servicing New Britain, and later at New Britain he was catering to the Hartford mission, Exasperated with unreasonable demands ho told readers:

Let it be known to these fellow-nationals writing letters of request for Father Žebris to come on a Sunday or a Saturday evening — that in no way is it possible to leave his own parish to travel to a distant city. It would be better therefore not to make requests for those days.[4]

Immigrants came in waves preceding their clergy. Isolated Balts sometimes went a year or more without ever seeing one of their own spiritual guides. Their appreciation for a first "visitation" shines in a touching letter from a North Granby resident in the summertime of 1897. Reflecting on Žebris' presence in nearby Tarrifville, the correspondent poured out his emotions:

> ... my heart overflowed with the greatest joy such as people are capable of having. It was a June morning, but so beautiful and sweet-smelling, such as rarely occurs even in our most tranquil Farmington Valley. Since the Lithuanians live some distance from the Tarrifville church, we arose at four o'clock that morning. It was already bright and lovely. Birds were singing with all their might. Sunday the local priest had announced the coming of a Lithuanian priest . . . From the earliest morning a work of brotherly love began. Enployers excused some from work for such a noble purpose at church, whereas the employers of some others were so humane and thoughtful that out of affection for their Lithuanian hired hands they harnessed their horses and provided a ride to church. The beauty of the mornin. magnified with the making of Holy Confession. The heart danced with joy that we approached the table of the Eucharistic Lord. . . . We wept over this grand happiness.[5]

351

Another instance of a warm and successful welcome was a visit to the southwestern corner of the state in the late spring of 1898. Three Greenwich Balts met Žebris the day prior to the scheduled ministrations, and took him to the pastor of the local territorial church, in order to request the use of the mission in East Port Chester. So numerous were the penitents who flocked to the travelling priest that he heard confessions from mid-afternoon until eleven at night. The next day he offered Mass at 5 a.m., the typically early hour suitable for factory workers. As a farewell sign of respect, a troupe of men accompanied Žebris to the railroad depot to catch the 7 a.m. train. A beneficiary of the priest's coming remarked: ". . . there arose a joy that this season we were to partake of the Easter Lamb (receive Holy Communion), to hear the words of consolation and encouragement in our native tongue."[6] Deference to the priest was characteristic of devout Balts.

Žebris' linguistic gifts proved invaluable pastoral tools,

as for instance, when he toured the New Haven area. On that occasion, he advertised his accessibility in "every Slavonic tongue",[7] meaning Bohemian, Ukrainian and related dialects. The demand for unskilled labor in urban industrial areas drew Balts, Poles and other slavs to the same job markets. In ministering to Lithuanians, Žebris did not miss the opportunity to reach other ethnic neighborhoods. Possibly, some parishioners resented their pastor providing services for other ethnic groups, since a later complaint against him would be his frequent absences, even though the greatest part of his time was allotted to Lithuanians themselves.

The impediment of the Balts' widespread illiteracy in English is illustrated in Žebris' precise travel information in his newspaper. For example, he advised Branford Lithuanians to be sure to take the first streetcar on a particular Tuesday morning to reach St. Boniface Church, New Haven where he would be hearing confessions. Outlying rural areas received fewer visits. A correspondent from Broad Brook lamented the lack of clergy, adding that for some immigrants ". . . it has already been three years since even seeing a priest."[8] Žebris finally managed to make the rounds in that farm community the week prior to Palm Sunday in 1898. With satisfaction he observed the farmers coming to receive the Sacraments, noting that the majority of them were from Vilnius and its environs, and were now in the employ of old, established residents. Again, the priest alerted readers to the importance of liturgical singing as he took pains to identify the Lenten hymns — "Jėzau Kristau Maloniausis" and "Jėzų Kristų Judošius" sung by Broad Brook Lithuanians.

Lithuanians were scattered around Connecticut in over 30 cities and towns. For some settlements, Žebris could provide only transient attention. Meanwhile he was eyeing the more densely populated colonies as sites for new Balt churches. The zealot hoped to found a congregation in places such as Meriden, Union City (Naugatuck), and "at one time he considered the advisability of erecting a Lithuanian church so far away from New Britain as East Windsor Hill."[9] Indeed, Žebris did find it possible to establish separate congregations eventually at Hartford, Bridgeport, New Haven and Ansonia. The pioneer's role in these beginnings is detailed in this writer's study, "Lithuanian Immigrants and Their Irish Bishops in the Catholic Chuch of Connecticut" in the Arno Press anthology *The Other Catholics* (New York, 1978). But the priest's pastoral concern reached beyond his own state.

In the days of the 1893 depression and its aftermath, new foreigners were forced to take to the road in search of jobs. It is not surprising therefore to find Lithuanians drifting northward to Maine, New Hampshire and Vermont. Immigration records for 1899-1905 show a scattering of Balts as follows: Maine — 2,234; Vermont — 530; with the unsuspected number of 12,656 for New Hampshire. (Massachusetts led easily with over 37,000, while Connecticut trailed with nearly 16,000). While some Lithuanians migrated to the north from within America, others traveled directly to places such as Lewiston, Maine, noted for its shoe industry; others pushed farther north to the paper mills of Millinocket; some settled in New Hampshire, finding work in textile shops of Manchester, Nashua, and Exeter; the smallest contingent made their way to the marble quarries of the Rutland area in Vermont.

On one occasion at least, Žebris set out on an extended tour of two of the upper states. On May 11, 1898 he heard confessions at Rumford, Maine, and offered Mass at an early hour the next morning. Despite his brief stop of just a day and a half, the meticulous priest took time to gather statistics. He found in the Rumford area four Lithuanian families, 24 adults and a few children, but no single women. Next he went to Portland where he ministered to an isolated colony of eight families and 50 unmarried adults. Learning that the Portlanders a few years earlier had started a society now defunct, he urged them to revive it immediately.

From Maine, the missionary moved on by rail westward across the mountains to the tiny town of Lincoln, New Hampshire. The Catholic community there constituted a "station" of the mother church — St. Joseph in Woodsville under Father Patrick Cahill. In advance, Žebris instructed the Balts to be sure to obtain the pastor's consent in writing for the Lithuanian cleric's visit. Žebris was being scrupulous about church protocol and cautious toward Irish pastors. Here too, he made note of the immigrants, finding only one Balt family, 20 male adults, one unmarried woman, plus two Latvian families.[10] One cannot refrain from contrasting traveling conditions under which Žebris journeyed with modern highways and automobile convenience. The comparison came to mind as this writer returned to the Boston area after a research trip to the village in the White Mountains. Žebris evidently had an impulsive brand of zeal which sent him off in every direction, driven by his deep ethnic commitment.

Hearing of brethren in nearby New York, the mobile Žebris swung westward several times to Tuckahoe and Yonkers. Laboring under a penchant for data, he noticed a change of statistics at Tuckahoe between his visits of 1895 and 1897. Originally he had discovered twelve families and 30 laborers, whereas two years later in May he found only three families and three working people. The Yonkers settlement was a bit larger with fifteen families and 60 single adults, including a St. Vincent Society.[11]

Besides these jaunts to the suburbs, Žebris also went to Brooklyn, New York. In February, 1895 he greeted Balts at St. George Parish (soon renamed St. Mary of the Angels). This was the scene of his brief stay two years earlier on arrival in America, July, 1893. In his talk to the Brooklyn people he commended them for their persevering organizational strides, promising to return for confessions in the coming Easter season. The Lithuanians needed encouragement at this time. They were in a disturbed state after the sudden departure of the ill-fated Father Juodyšius (see Chapter Two), and were suffering intramural discord. In a letter of March 19, 1894 from Waterbury to an unidentified recipient, Žebris alluded to the uncertainties of the infant parish, commenting that he knew well that "the devil would like to devour the Lithuanians of Brooklyn, but the expectations of prayer and hope of good petitioners will be heard in the presence of God."[12] The historian of the Brooklyn diocese recognizes that Žebris aided Bishop John Loughlin and Father George Mundelein (future Chicago cardinal) in giving shape to the Lithuanian community.

In Massachusetts, the apostolic Žebris touched the lives of Balts in at least six colonies. For instance, he inspired the creation of a St. Lawrence Benefit Society December 19, 1894 in the city of the same name. After his change to New Britain in 1898, he traveled frequently to Lawrence, especially to assist in raising money for the proposed new church. When it was complete, Žebris was present among the immigrants May 30, 1903. He filled the role of deacon at the dedication Mass and preached the sermon. Afterwards, he continued intermittent appearances and very likely kept up mail contacts. Earlier, the *Rytas* print shop prepared the By-Laws for the St. Lawrence benefit group.[13]

In his junket around Balt colonies in his pre-Waterbury days, Žebris had included stopovers in New Jersey. There, at Elizabeth, September 4, 1893, he gathered fellow country-men to promote interest in a separate parish, and even went door-to-door recruiting a permanent committee to build a church. Again, he returned Seprem8er 17 for another rally which resulted in the clearcut decision to proceed. A $20 membership fee was asked of each potential parish-ioner. Several more Žebris visits took place in 1895 during which he counselled his listeners on church furnishings and church protocol. In a letter to Bishop Winald Wigger of the Newark diocese, Žebris reported about his visit of June 25, 1895 at the home of a Degutis family. The priest assured the prelate of the Lithuanians' willingness and ability to support a resident pastoi; and asserted that between the Elizabeth and Newark Balts, there was suf-ficient funding for a church.[14] Thanks greatly to Žebris, the parish of Sts. Peter & Paul was founded August 5, 1895. Holy Trinity, as an offshoot in nearby Newark, was also erected under Žebris' stimulus. The Connecticut pastor kept a sentimental tie with New Jersey, as for instance, when he returned to Elizabeth to witness a wedding in May, 1914, as well as annually helping at Forty Hours Devotions.[15]

One might wonder rightly if this immigrant priest were not capricious in his apostolate. Why did he travel so far from home when, for instance, there were several other clerics in Massachusetts soon after Žebris' arrival in Water-bury? The answer lies in a combination of two major factors. First, there was a pastoral vacuum. True, Archbish-op John Williams did assign Father Joseph Gricius to the Lithuanians of the Boston area in 1895. But, as Antanas Kučas notes in his history of the Boston parish, Gricius' peculiar accent alienated some parishioners, while his book-ish retiring ways kept him from circulating among the people to create strong bonds with the congregation. Soon the archbishop was pressured into appointing another Lithua-nian priest to a second church, leaving for a decade the strange and apparently unique condition of these competing ethnic parishes side by side. Gricius was ill-suited to move about, as did Žebris, to serve scattered Balts in eastern Massachusetts. Worcester too had a resident clergyman at this time, but one can discount him. He was morally inept, creating havoc in that central Massachusetts industrial center, and was eventually forced by his bishop to resign or face canonical trial. From 1898, the Balts of Brockton saw a rapid succession of pastors, none of whom could endure belligerent parish committee members at stormy St. Rocco Church. These original troubled priests seldom missionized outside their immediate pastoral sphere. So, one finds Žebris in Athol, Lawrence, Cambridge, Brockton, reaching out to otherwise neglected Balts. As to New York and New Jersey, it was the same problem — either a few unsuited or unavailable transients, or simply no priests at all. Secondly, besides the shortage of priests or lack of competent ones, one is again reminded of Žebris' temperament and ambitious character. His actions constantly and increasingly showed his frame of mind as a self-appointed supervisor of all Lithuanian immigrants. It is difficult to refrain from describing Žebris as a physical and pastoral dynamo, so much energy did he expend in all directions.

As noted above, in his geography Žebris' thoughts reached out as far as Brazil, Tasmania and South Africa. He probably engaged in correspondence with Lithuanians in those distant lands, certainly with Johannesburg, since his newspaper *Rytas* carried occasional news from there. Striking evidence of Žebris' international perspectives emerges in his attention to Balts of the United Kingdom. In the case of Leeds, England, he supplied detailed counsel in a lengthy article in *Rytas*. The directive is worth quoting in its entirety, not merely because of its recipients, but for the insights it furnishes about Žebris' vievs:

> I have before me a letter about conditions of our brethren in England. In the city of Leeds are found Lithuanians from all sectors of Lithuania. There is a colony of Lithuanians from the districts of Kaunas, Suvalkai and Gardinas. Lithuanians have multiplied here coming in the footsteps of Lithuanian Jews. The Lithuanians' occupations are sewing and tailoring. Wages are meager. Perhaps nowhere else do the Lithuanians live in such dependence on the Jews. Drunkeness is the entire "enlightment" and sole visible activity. Lithuanians of Leeds, under the influence of Jews, have lapsed morally to

the lowest degree. Sexual promiscuity accompanies drunkenness, blackening the reputation of Lithuanians. What is worse, to their destruction Lithuanians are mingling with Jewesses and English women; as is well known, a sexually loose life style presses down its victims into the worst calamities; as a result of which Lithuanians appear sickly, beaten down, tattered, unkempt. Lithuanians of the Suvalkai region have a spark of nationalistic feeling, but it is not visible. The people of Gardinas are the lowliest of all, but they are accounted as Masovians rather than Lithuanians. They read no newspapers. But once *Rytas* has been able to accomodate itself to them, it will not give up. To uplift our brethren's fallen spiritual condition it is imperative to observe the following:

1) the more generous-minded should distribute *Rytas* gratis;

2) Lithuanian Jews and Jewesses aside there should be called a mass meeting of all Lithuanians who speak Lithuanian — a coming together of all Lithuanians whether good or bad; but there should be forbidden any drunken person, and drinking should be excluded from the meeting;

3) there should be formed a fraternal mutual-aid society under the patronage of some saint whose life the Lithuanians may emulate, and there should be chosen leaders to attend to the affairs of the society: a president, his assistant, a treasurer, and secretary. If a society is quickly formed, the eyes of Lithuanians will be enlightened.[16]

Žebris' devotion to ethnicity and even ethnic exclusivity roars through this issue of *Rytas*. Nor does he conceal his strong desire to make his newspaper a voice for fellow Lithuanians everywhere. By means of this publication he strove to instruct, admonish and direct the lives of his blood brothers wherever they happened to settle. If there was any such thing as a world leader among Balt immigrants, Žebris, to some degree, approached this position.

In 1911 Father Milukas dubbed Žebris as "Father of Lithuanian Catholics of New England".[17] He was indeed all of that and more. His aims though were hardly limited to the spiritual requirements of fellow immigrants. He was ever alert to the total needs of his people, concerned about the jobless, the poor, the hungry. While at Waterbury, the multi-faceted priest was about to launch social welfare projects scarcely paralleled by any other Connecticut Catholic clergy of native or foreign stock. Perhaps few if any clergy anywhere in the United States undertook such a combination of endeavors. The next chapter unfolds the creative blueprints of this Lithuanian trailblazer.

NOTES FOR CHAPTER 4

1) *Katalikas,* Jan. 2, 1915.

2) *Trumpas Apraszymas Žemės, arba Žemerasztys* (A Short Description of the Earth, or a Geography) was printed by L.M.D. Demerckas at Tilsit, E. Prussia early in 1896, in a run of 4,000 copies. *Rytas* first advertised the primer in its issue of Apr. 23, 1896: ". . . Long hoped for and useful for many readers. Cost 15 ¢. In quantities of 100 or more, liberal discount. Let every Lithuanian hurry to procure it. 4,000 copies will rapidly be exhausted."

3) *ibid.*: "Dabar . . . nebėra jokios pariškados tą mažą knygutę išleisti atspausdinimui."

4) *Rytas,* Apr. 1, 1897.

5) *Rytas,* June 10, 1897.

6) *Rytas,* Mar. 24, 1898.

7) *Rytas,* Apr. 23, 1896. Žebris was scheduled for the German church. See also, *e.g.,* Apr. 29, 1897 wherein notice appears that he will be at the Polish church in New Britain for confessions in both Polish and Lithuanian. The very next day the multi-lingual cleric was slated for St. Peter Church, Hartford.

8) *Vienybė Lietuvninkų,* No. 6, p. 72, 1893.

9) Thomas S. Duggan. *The Catholic Church in Connecticut,* (Hartford, 1930), p. 277.

10) *Rytas,* May 5, 19, 1898. Lincoln is a good example of an isolated alien colony. Along with a handful of Russians, Ukrainians and French-Canadians, the Lithuanians were drawn here by the many sawmills such as Johnson Lumber Company seeking immigrant brawn for the physically demanding chores of the raw wood industry. See Dorothy M. Hanson, *Bicentennial Commemorative Book of the Town of Lincoln, New Hampshire, 1764-1964,* p. 48.

11) *Rytas,* May 20, 1897.

12) On Žebris' tie with the Brooklyn Lithuanians, see *Rytas,* June 11, 1896; Antanas Milukas, *Mūsų Spaudos Darbininkų*

Vargai (n.p.p., 1941), pp. 29-30; *Amerikos Lietuvių Katalikų Darbai* (1943), p. 6; John K. Sharp, History of the *Diocese of Brooklyn, 1853-1953*, 2 vols. (New York, 1954), Vol. II, p. 83. The Žebris letter is found in the Lithuanian archives of the University of Pennsylvania, among the papers of Vincas Ambrozevičius, activist in the area of Elizabeth, New Jersey. I am indebted to Vincas Maciūnas for a photocopy.

13) *Rytas* also printed By-Laws for the St. Rocco Society, Brockton, at the cost of $14 for 100 copies. On Žebris' Massachusetts activities, see *e.g. Rytas*, June 18, July 9, Oct. 22, Dec. 10, 1896. *Keleivis*, Oct. 9, 1905 mentions a Cambridge visit to a private home for a discussion on revelation. Though Father Gricius was available in nearby Boston, he was struggling with a dissident faction in his parish, and was not a likely candidate for a request from Cambridge Balts looking for guidance.

14) Archives Archdiocese of Newark, Letter File, Zebris to Wigger, June 27, 1895.

15) On Lithuanians in the Catholic Church of New Jersey, see Carl D. Hindrichsen, "The History of the Diocese of Newark" (unpubl. doct. diss., Catholic University, 1962).

16) *Rytas*, Dec. 24, 1896. On Žebris' promotion of cooperatives in America, see in addition to Chapter Five, *e.g. Rytas*, July 23, 1896; *Žvaigždė*, May 14, 1903; *Amerikos Lietuvių Katalikų Darbai*, p. 20, 45.

17) *Žvaigždė*, Apr. 14, 1911; *Žinynas, 1918*, p. 126 repeats the title.

359

Black Catholics in Nineteenth Century America

Cyprian Davis, O.S.B.

On July 11, 1793, *The Maryland Gazette,* published in Annapolis, printed the following announcement under the heading: "Baltimore. July 10."

Yesterday at three o'clock, arrived at Fells' Point, six ships [one a Guineaman, with negroes] four brigs, and four schooners, being part of the fleet which sailed from Cape Francois on the 23d ultimo. The passengers and crews amount to 619 persons. . .[1]

This fleet comprised refugees from the revolution then in progress on the island of Santo Domingo, now known as Haiti and the Dominican Republic. The Blacks on board the Guineaman would become the nucleus of the Black worshipping community that was established in the *chapelle basse* of St. Mary's Seminary on Paca Street. It was this Black Catholic community which would later become the first Black Catholic parish in the United States when St. Francis Xavier Church was established by the Jesuits, in 1864, as the parish for all Black Catholics in Baltimore.[2] Some eight years before the Fells' Point landing, in a letter to the acting secretary of state, Cardinal Antonelli, dated March 1, 1785, John Carroll, head of the Catholic missions in the newly formed United States, indicated that there were three thousand Catholic slaves in Maryland.[3]

The story of Black Catholicism in nineteenth century America begins in the last decades of the eighteenth. It begins with the story of American

---

1. *The Maryland Gazette.* July 10, 1793. (microfilm in the Library of Congress.)
2. Grace Sherwood, *The Oblates' Hundred and One Years* (New York, 1931), 131ff. and 149ff.
3. Thomas Hanley, S.J., *ed, The John Carroll Papers.* vol. I. 1755–1791 (Notre Dame, IN 1976), 179.

1

Catholicism itself, with the first implantation of the Church in America by the Spaniards, the French, and the English.[4] Moreover, the first wave of Catholic immigration to these shores, with the arrival of Haitian refugees at the end of the eighteenth and the beginning of the nineteenth centuries, was in large measure an immigration of Black Catholics. The history of nineteenth century Black Catholicism is divided by the Civil War, with the prior period divided into periods of implantation and development. The period after the Civil War, moreover, is one of solidarity and self-awareness. The outline, however, is much clearer than the details. Black Catholics like Black Americans in general have still to rediscover the details of their history. Names and dates are known, but details regarding piety, practice, and parochial structures in the Black Catholic community particularly prior to the Civil War is less well known. Only at the end of the nineteenth century will the Black Catholic community find a voice to address their fellow communicants and words to profess their understanding of a Faith which they so tenaciously held.

361

The Church in Bondage

Slavery stains the history of American Catholicism in the same way it stains the history of the rest of America. If the Church is where the people of God are, it will be agreed that prior to the Civil War part of the Catholic Church was enslaved. The remarkable fact is that Black Catholics themselves, though enslaved, contributed to the building up of the Church from their own resources.

By the year 1800 there were sizeable communities of Black Catholics in southern Maryland, southern Louisiana, southern Missouri, and western Kentucky. The city of Los Angeles had been established in 1781 with eleven families, all of whom were either Indjans or Africans or mixtures thereof.[5] It was Jean-Baptiste Pointe du Sable, a Black Catholic, French-speaking, trapper and woodsman, married to a woman of the Potawatomi tribe, who established the first settlement on the site of the future city of Chicago. In 1779, he was imprisoned by the British who mistrusted his influence on the Indians. By 1800 he had left the Chicago region, and in 1818 died in St. Charles, Missouri, where he was buried in the Catholic cemetery.[6]

4. The Black Catholic presence in Louisiana and Maryland is well known. Another example of this presence is St. Louis where the oldest Baptismal Registers attest to the baptism of many Blacks, see William Faherty, S.J., *Dream By the River* (St. Louis, 1973), 3-4.

5. David J. Weber, *Foreigners in Their Native Land: Historical Roots of the Mexican Americans* (Albuquerque, 1973), 33-35.

6. Sidney Kaplan, *The Black Presence in the Era of the American Revolution, 1770-1800* (Washington, D.C., 1973), 144-146.

362

In the first quarter of the nineteenth century certain of the slave holders were priests and religious. Recent research has begun to show the impact that slavery made on the consciences and mentality of both priests and religious.[7] The Jesuits owned about 300 slaves on their farm lands in Maryland in the 1830s. The Sisters of Charity of Nazareth in Kentucky owned thirty slaves at the time of the Emancipation Proclamation. Novices received into the Carmelites at the convent of Port Tobacco in southern Maryland came with their slaves. Other convents of religious women likewise had slaves[8] as well as individual churchmen like Archbishop Carroll and Bishop Flaget.[9] The problem was not so much whether the slaves were treated kindly, but rather the peculiar inability of American Catholics, even the clergy, to empathize with the plight of the Black population. The American bishops not only did not produce a Bartolomé de Las Casas, they resented the opinions of Catholics in the other parts of the world who saw the evils of slavery and denounced the cruelties that Blacks suffered.[10] Not only did the Maryland Jesuits own slaves, but eventually they sold them off as much for economic reasons as for moral reasons, especially since the slaves who were sold into the South were not sold to Catholics. The anti-Catholic attitudes of most of the leading Abolitionists certainly helped turn pre-Civil War white Catholics against the Abolitionists and against their program for the freeing of the slaves. It was a tragic reaction and a moral blindness that would enable, for example, even a great bishop like John England of Charleston to use his considerable powers of erudition to defend the institution of slavery in the southern states and assure the secretary of state, John Forsyth, that the condemnation of the slave trade by Pope Gregory XVI in 1839 did not really mean the condemnation of the "peculiar institution." In fact, it did not even prevent him from giving the impression that the Church historically gave unwavering support for slavery.[11] The Catholic Church in pre-Civil

---

7. See the essay of Sister Frances Jerome Woods. C.D.P., "Congregations of Religious Women in the Old South," in Randall M. Miller and Jon L. Wakelyn, *Catholics in the Old South: Essays on Church and Culture* (Macon, GA 1983), 99–123 and especially pp. 112–115. See also R. Emmett Curran, S.J., " 'Splendid Poverty': Jesuit Slaveholding in Maryland, 1805–1838," in *Ibid.,* 126–146. particularly p. 142 for the number of slaves in 1856.

8. Anna Blanche McGill, *The Sisters of Charity of Nazareth, Kentucky* (New York, 1917), and Nathaniel Green, *The Silent Believers (Louisville, 1972), 23ff.* See also Madeleine Hooke Rice, *American Catholic Opinion in the Slavery Controversy* (New York, 1944), 46 ff.

9. Rice, *American Catholic Opinion,* 80ff.

10. *Ibid.* 107ff.

11. John England, "Letters to the Hon. John Forsyth, On the Subject of Domestic Slavery," *The Works of the Right Rev. John England, First Bishop of Charleston* (Baltimore, 1849), III: 106–191. For an assessment of England's attitude, see Peter Clarke, *A Free Church in a Free Society: The Ecclesiology of John England, Bishop of Charleston, 1820–1842* (Greenwood, S.C., 1983) 390–413 and 476–478.

War days was bound not only in the slave members of that Church, but bound also by the intellectual and social strictures of her clergy and people who felt constrained to justify what many Catholics elsewhere had come to find unjustifiable.

Elements of Sanctity in a Society of Slaves

Despite the harshness of a slave society and despite the seeming indifference of many Church members to the devastating moral effects of slavery, the second half of the pre-Civil War period witnessed outstanding examples of piety and ministry among Black Catholics themselves. In 1829 the Haitian community, which met in the lower chapel of St. Mary's Seminary in Baltimore, produced the first Black American religious community. Elizabeth Lange (ca. 1800–1889), born in Cuba of Haitian parents, arrived in the Baltimore area sometime after 1817. She enlisted the aid of three other women, all Black, and began teaching the Black children of the *chapelle basse* community. Early on, the French Sulpician, Jacques Joubert de la Muraille, French aristocrat and former inhabitant of Haiti, supported the work of Elizabeth Lange and encouraged the formation of a religious community.

In 1831 the Oblate Sisters of Providence were approved by Pope Gregory XVI. A few years later these sisters faced an uncertain future following the death of Joubert. Maryland was a slave state, and Baltimore a southern city. The sisters were openly insulted. Black sisters were considered superfluous. Through the aid of St. John Neumann, the future bishop of Philadelphia and at the time Redemptorist superior, a young Bavarian Redemptorist, Thaddeus Anwander, became their chaplain. The sisters operated schools for Black children and a home for Black orphans. Even before the Civil War, despite hardships and poverty, the sisters had established schools for Black children outside of the city of Baltimore.[12]

363

---

12. Maria Lannon, *Mother Mary Elizabeth Lange* (Washington, D.C., 1976). See also Sherwood, *The Oblates' Hundred and One Years,* and Michael J. McNally, "A Minority of a Minority: The Witness of Black Women Religious in the Antebellum South," *Review for Religious* 40(1981): 260–269. One of the original Oblates, Therese Maxis Duchemin, left the community and journeyed to Monroe, Michigan, where in 1845 she became the foundress along with a Belgian priest, Louis Gillet, C.SS.R., of the Immaculate Heart of Mary Sisters. This community was not Black. Her story is a tragic one, see Sister Diane Edward Shea, IHM, and Sister Marita Constance Supan, IHM, "Apostolate of the Archives—God's Mystery Through History," *The Josephite Harvest* 85(1983):10–13. Charles Nerinckx, founder of the Sisters of Loretto and pioneer priest in Kentucky, began a small community of Black sisters in 1824. Nerinckx was forced to leave Kentucky that same year and his community of Black sisters was disbanded. See Camillus Maes, *The Life of Rev. Charles Nerinckx* (Cincinnati, 1880), 510.

Lower chapel at St. Mary's Seminary, Baltimore.
(Courtesy: Sulpician Archives)

364

Even more moving is the story of the Holy Family Sisters in New Orleans. For a long time the "Free People of Color" occupied a mid-point between Black slaves and the white population. French in language and in culture, often well educated, light compexioned, and tightly knit as a community, the "Free People of Color" in New Orleans typified the way certain Black communities were able to move from the degradation of slavery to positions on the fringe of both worlds. In the case of New Orleans, the women from this milieu were often chosen as concubines for the well-to-do. New Orleans in the period before the Civil War was a city with a façade of Catholic respectability and public and private vice.

Into this world was born in 1813, Henriette Delille, a free woman of color. As a young girl whe was permitted by her family to engage in charitable work for the slaves and the Black poor in New Orleans at the side of a French sister, Soeur Ste-Marthe, and a lay woman from France, Marie Jeanne Aliquot. When eventually Henriette became old enough, this strikingly beautiful woman was expected to establish a liaison with a man of means, but she refused. Instead she had the desire to become a nun.

Two attempts were made to found a religious community of Black women and white women. The laws prevented it. Eventually, Henriette Delille and another free woman of color, Juliette Gaudin, formed a re-

365

*Mother Mary Elizabeth Lange,
foundress of the Oblate Sisters of
Providence, 1829*

ligious community in 1842. In the beginning it was necessary to form an association with certain Creole laypersons to be incorporated. It was known as the Association of the Holy Family. The sisters ministered to the slaves and the poor Blacks of the city. They taught slave children. established a hospice for the sick poor, nursed the sick in their homes. established an orphanage, and eventually founded a school for girls from free Black families. Only in 1852 could the sisters make public vows. Not until 1872 could the sisters wear a religious habit in public. By that time. the foundress, Henriette Delille, was dead. She died in 1862 at the age of fifty.[13]

Despite hardships and opposition, Black religious women were able to establish two religious orders in the United States that still exist today with numerous convents and schools. These women are witnesses to the courage, devotion, and faith of the Black Catholic community as a whole prior to the Civil War. This Black Catholic community not only gave support to these sisters, it also provided the vocations. Such vocations are an indication of the faith this community possessed. More research into the records of these two Black religious communities might permit historians to identify Black Catholic families, to situate the geographical locations of the families, and eventually to analyze the relationships between the various communities even during the dark period of slavery. With modern tools of research it is to be hoped that a prosopographical

---

13. Sister Audrey Marie Detiege, *Henriette Delille, Free Woman of Color* (New Orleans. 1976).

366

*Father James Hector Joubert, S.S.,
founder of the Oblates (1777-1843)*
(Courtesy: Sulpician Archives)

index of nineteenth-century Black Catholics might be begun. Such an index might serve as a means of finding out more about the social and economic status of individuals and families in the Black Catholic Community.

New York City was the scene for the work of a saintly Black Catholic, Pierre Toussaint (1766-1853). Pierre Toussaint is another example of the impact that Haitians made on the early nineteenth-century Black Catholic community in the United States. Toussaint was born a slave on the Bérard Plantation in Haiti at the end of the eighteenth century. He came to New York in 1787 with the young heir of the property and his wife along with some relatives. The young Bérard returned to Haiti just at the outbreak of the rebellion and there he died. The young Haitian slave was left the task of supporting the Widow Bérard, who was frail in body and mind, and his other relatives. As a hairdresser, he became the confidant and adviser of the many great ladies whose houses he visited to style their hair. He also became a one-man charity agency. Collecting money for charity, nursing the victims of the Yellow Fever epidemic, giving shelter and training to homeless Black youths, buying the freedom of his sister and his future wife, and only receiving his own freedom from his mistress on her deathbed in 1807, Pierre Toussaint's self-effacing and laborious life was filled with works of piety and Christian service. It was made heavy by personal sorrow and the weight of other people's problems assumed as his own. When Pierre Toussaint died June 30, 1853, at the age of eighty-six, people from all ranks of society flocked to his funeral.

Juliet Gaudin (1808–1887) and Henrietta Delille (1813–1862), foundresses of the Sisters of the Holy Family of Black Sisters in the United States (New Orleans, 1842)

(Courtesy: Elio Gasperet:)

This man, whose cause for beatification has been introduced, was at his death probably the best known Black man and most revered Catholic in the city of New York.[14]

Pierre Toussaint died in New York on the eve of the Civil War. His life was the story of grace under pressure. His life of deprivation even in the relatively free atmosphere of pre-Civil War New York was typical for Northern Blacks at the time. His response was to turn humiliation and hostility into so many building blocks to sanctity. Yet sanctity is an intensely personal response. It tells us little of the Black Catholic Community at the mid-point of the nineteenth century. Only further research can help uncover the day-to-day existence of Black Catholics, North and South, before the Civil War.[15] How did they worship? How did they sing? Who preached to them? How many received the sacraments regularly? Who blessed their marriages? How did the Church extend her protection in the face of concubinage, rape, floggings, and more, in the Catholic

14. Ellen Tarry, *The Other Toussaint: A Modern Biography of Pierre Toussaint, Post-Revolutionary Black* (Boston, 1981).

15. As pointed out by Peter Hogan, S.S.J. in this issue, recent methods for studying Black history and fresh questions posed to the sources, new and old, should yield more information about Black Catholics in the antebellum period. See also Albert Raboteau. *Slave Religion: The 'Invisible Institution' in the Antebellum South* (New York, 1978), 112–114; 271–275.

368

*Peter Toussaint (1766–1853),
Haitian-born philanthropist of Old
New York*
(Courtesy: Elio Gasperetti)

community of the South? How did they fit into a Church whose chief ministers and the majority of their flock showed little enthusiasm for the eventual emancipation of Blacks and even for any recognition of their basic human rights?

For the majority of the bishops, slavery was a political issue.[16] For the majority of the Catholic laity in the North, Blacks were a threat to economic well-being.[17] For a Catholic intellectual like Orestes Brownson, Blacks were an essentially inferior breed doomed to eventual extinction.[18] For a relatively enlightened bishop like William Henry Elder of Natchez (later Cincinnati), they were a painful pastoral problem.[19] With the exception of a few, like Archbishop John Purcell of Cincinnati, practically no Catholic voices were raised in prophetic words to address the moral or the humanitarian issues of the slave system.[20] In the end, the saintly life of a quiet, gentle Black man who spoke English with a French accent was the

---

16. Peter Guilday, *A History of the Councils of Baltimore (1791–1884)* (New York, 1932), 169–182.

17. Rice, *American Catholic Opinion*, 125ff.

18. Orestes Brownson, "Abolition and Negro Equality" (April, 1864) in Henry F. Brownson, ed. *The Works of Orestes A. Brownson* ([Detroit, 1882–1887]) XVII: 537–560, and 557ff.

19. "Bishop Elder on the Apostolate to the Negro Slaves in Mississippi, 1858, in John Tracy Ellis, ed. *Documents of American Catholic History*, 2nd ed. (Milwaukee, 1962) 325–329.

20. *The Catholic Telegraph*, edited by Fr. Edward Purcell (1808–1881), brother to the archbishop, was decidedly anti-slavery. See "Father Purcell's Stand in Behalf of Emancipation of the Slaves, April 8, 1863" in *Ibid.*, 378–383. Archbishop Purcell came out for emancipation on the eve of the Civil War. *Ibid.*, 379.

best authentic redemptive sign the Church could muster in that desperate time. Perhaps in this way too, Pierre Toussaint was a sign of the collective destiny of Black Catholics during that period.

The Promise of a Golden Harvest

Martin J. Spalding (1810–1872), archbishop of Baltimore, called the Second Plenary Council of Baltimore to regulate the affairs of the American Church on the morrow of the Civil War. Many questions needed solving, not the least of which was the responsibility of the Church to the four million newly emancipated slaves. Spalding with the concurrence of the Holy See had a plan he wished to have implemented by the national synod. He expressed this to the American bishops when he stated that:

> . . . it is . . . the most urgent duty of all to discuss the future status of the negro. Four million of these unfortunates are thrown on our Charity, and they silently but eloquently appeal . . . for help. It is a golden opportunity for reaping a harvest of souls, which neglected may not return. . . .[21]

Spalding's plan as outlined by the Congregation of the Propaganda for the assembled bishops was to establish a national ordinariate with nationwide jurisdiction to co-ordinate the efforts and the program for the evangelization and the pastoral care of the nation's 150,000 Black Catholics. The assembled bishops rejected the proposal almost to a man in a session that was more or less extraordinary according to time (it was held after the close of the regular session, that is October 22, 1866) and in manner—it was filled with bitterness and rancor. The principal result was the "golden opportunity for a harvest of souls" was lost.[22]

At the close of the synod, the assembled bishops issued a pastoral letter in which they addressed the various issues facing the American Church. They had a rather less than enthusiastic comment on the emancipation of the slaves . . .

> We must all feel, beloved Brethren, that in some manner a new and most extensive field of charity and devotedness has been opened to us, by the emancipation of the immense slave

369

---

21. The quotation is in Edward Misch, "The American Bishops and the Negro From the Civil War to the Third Plenary Council of Baltimore, 1865–1884 (Ph.D. diss., Pontifical Gregorian University, 1968), 20.

22. *Ibid.* The minutes for this extraordinary session are in the Baltimore Cathedral Archives, 39A–D5, 3–10.

population of the South. We could have wished, that in accordance with the action of the Catholic Church in past ages, in regard to the serfs of Europe, a more gradual system of emancipation could have been adopted, so that they might have been in some measure prepared to make better use of their freedom, than they are likely to do now. . . .[23]

In the end the bishops urged religious to come from Europe to take over the evangelization of the Black population. In 1871 the Mill Hill Fathers, founded in England by Cardinal Vaughan in 1866, began apostolic work among the Black populations in America.

370   Although Black religious women were the first examples of vocations among the Black Catholic community, by the time of the Second Plenary Council of Baltimore in 1866, there were three Black Catholic priests in the country. These were the three sons of Michael Morris Healy, slave holder and farmer in Georgia, who had ten children by one of his slaves, Mary Eliza. He sent some of his sons north to be educated. Three of them eventually became priests. James Augustine Healy (1830–1900), ordained in Paris in 1854, was a priest of the diocese of Boston and would later be named in 1875 Bishop of Portland in Maine. His brother, Sherwood Alexander (1836–1875) became a priest in Rome in 1858. He too belonged to the diocese of Boston. His brilliant career was cut short by an untimely death in 1875. A third brother, Patrick Francis Healy (1834–1919) who joined the Jesuits, was educated at Louvain, and there was ordained priest in 1865. He would return to the United States and become the "second founder" of Georgetown University; first as rector then as president. The brothers were known to be Black. Before the Civil War, they were legally slaves. Patrick Healy was understandably forced to keep his racial origins secret. Blacks were not welcomed at the University. Disclosure certainly weighed upon him and perhaps contributed along with ill health to his long retirement after 1882, dying only in 1910. Bishop Healy never really hid his identity, but he also never really identified with the Black Catholic community. Nothing in his actions nor in his relations gave any indication of solidarity or support.[24]

------

23. *Sermons Delivered During the Second Plenary Council of Baltimore October, 1866, and Pastoral Letter of the Hierarchy of the United States* (Baltimore, 1866). See "Pastoral Letter," section XII. "The Emancipated Slaves," 237.

24. For the life of James Augustine Healy, see Albert S. Foley, S.J., *Bishop Healy: Beloved Outcaste* (New York, 1954). For an attempt to understand the psychological foundations of the three brothers, see Joseph Taylor Skerrett, Jr., " 'Is There Anything Wrong With Being a Nigger?' Racial Identity and Three Nineteenth Century Priests," *Freeing the Spirit* 5(1977): 30–37. For further information on all three brothers, see Albert S. Foley, S.J., *God's Men of Color: The Colored Catholic Priests of the United States, 1854–1954* (New York, 1955), 1–31.

The First Recognized Black Priest

Augustine Tolton was the first Black priest in the United States, universally recognized as Black, and enthusiastically hailed by the Black Catholic community. He was born in Ralls County, Missouri in 1854, the second of three children of Peter Paul Tolton and Martha Tolton, both slaves. Martha Tolton came originally from Kentucky, as part of a wedding dowry. Her husband escaped and joined the Union Army during the Civil War, and later died of an illness in St. Louis. Martha escaped with her three children by crossing the Mississippi. She settled with her children in Quincy, Illinois. There she found freedom, but she also found a great deal of hostility. She insisted on a Catholic education for her children in face of the overt opposition of the parishioners to the Black children. Despite this opposition, Martha Tolton reared her children as Catholics and made a living. Her son showed the same kind of determination and persistence when he announced that he wanted to become a priest. No American seminary would receive him. Eventually through the efforts of the Franciscan Minister General, he was accepted as a student in the seminary of the congregation of the Propaganda in Rome in 1880. Six years later in 1886, this former slave was ordained priest in the Lateran Basilica. Originally intended for the missions in Africa, because of the persistence of Cardinal Simeoni,[25] prefect of the Propaganda, Tolton was ordained for the diocese of Alton in Illinois.

371

Chicago was the scene of most of Tolton's labors. He transferred to the Chicago archdiocese because of the racist antipathy of some in Quincy. He began work there in 1889. Still, Tolton was not confined to one area. He spent himself tirelessly for the Black Catholic community, preaching, teaching, speaking, writing, lending his presence. He was for the Black Catholic people a sign of what the Church could be. Tolton identified completely with the Black Catholic community. His untimely death in 1897 at the age of forty-three was a loss most keenly felt by the Black Catholic community of the United States.[26]

The Voice of Black Catholics

Black Americans began meeting in conventions and congresses early in the nineteenth century. The first annual Black Convention was organized

---

25. Giovanni Simeoni (1816–1892), made a cardinal in 1875, served as secretary of state from 1876–1878, and then prefect of the Congregation for the Propagation of the Faith from 1878–1892. See notice by A. Randall, *The New Catholic Encyclopedia* (Washington, D.C., 1967) 13:219.

26. Sister Caroline Hemesath, O.S.F., *From Slave to Priest: Biography of the Rev. Augustine Tolton (1854–1897)* (Chicago, 1973).

372

*Father Augustine Tolton (1854–1897),
the first Black priest whose parents
were slaves*

(Courtesy: Josephite Archives)

in Philadelphia in 1830 by Richard Allen, the founder of the African Methodist Episcopal Church. All during the pre-Civil War period, when Blacks met in convention, prominent Black clergymen took a leading part. It was only in the last decade of the nineteenth century, however, that the Black Catholic community found its voice and proclaimed its presence and detailed its concerns so that all could hear.

It was the work of one man that made it possible. His name was Daniel Rudd, who was born a slave in 1854 in Bardstown, Kentucky, where he was reared a Catholic. Following the Civil War, he was educated in Springfield, Ohio where his brother had gone to establish himself. About 1886, Rudd began a weekly newspaper, which eventually took as its name the *American Catholic Tribune* and it became avowedly a Black, Catholic, weekly newspaper. Rudd stated that he wanted to make the Catholic Church better known in the Black community.[27] He was personally convinced that the Catholic Church was the one great hope for Black people in America. In his editorials he constantly developed this theme. "The Catholic Church alone can break the color line. Our people should help

---

27. This statement by Rudd was reprinted in the *Washington Bee* for September 11, 1886 on page 1. (microfilm in The Library of Congress.) The *Washington Bee* was an important Black newspaper in the District of Columbia.

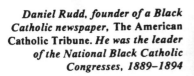

*Daniel Rudd, founder of a Black
Catholic newspaper,* The American
Catholic Tribune. *He was the leader
of the National Black Catholic
Congresses, 1889–1894*

373

Her to do it."[28] Rudd lectured on this topic in all parts of the United
States. Finally, in 1888 he had the idea to call a Black Catholic Congress.

This first Black Catholic Congress was held in Washington, D.C. at St.
Augustine's Parish, one of the oldest Black parishes in the country, from
January 1–4, 1889. The delegates numbered about one hundred Black
men from all parts of the United States. Augustus Tolton opened it with
Mass. Members of the Catholic hierarchy and Black Protestant ministers
were present. The delegates were received at the White House by President Grover Cleveland, and Pope Leo XIII sent a cablegram with his
blessing. It was a tremendous success. At the end of the congress, the
delegates issued an address to their fellow Catholics in the country. Filled
with enthusiasm the delegates called for the establishment of Catholic
schools, including industrial schools especially for Black children; for the
admittance of Blacks to labor unions; for an end to poor housing; and for
other social needs.

There were four other Black Catholic Congresses in the next five years.
In 1890 they met in Cincinnati, in 1892 in Philadelphia, in 1893 in
Chicago, and in Baltimore in 1894. The delegates became more and more
specific in their demands. In Philadelphia they formed themselves into the

---

28. *American Catholic Tribune* (later referred to as ACT), January 3, 1891. All extant copies of
the ACT are in the archives of the American Catholic Historical Society in St. Charles Borromeo
Seminary, Overbrook, Philadelphia, PA. It is now available on microfilm from the American Theological Library Association, Board of Microtext.

St. Peter Claver Union. That same year they instituted a committee of grievances to investigate by means of a questionnaire addressed to all the United States bishops the forms of discrimination against Black Catholics in the churches throughout the country. Despite the militant tone that entered into their discussions and resolutions, they vividly proclaimed their joy and pride in their Catholic faith.

At the fourth congress held in Chicago as part of the Columbian Exposition and at the same time as the second lay Catholic Congress held there, they wrote:

374

> With thorough confidence in the rectitude of our course, in the enduring love of Mother Church, and the consciousness of our priesthood, we show our devotion to the church, our jealousy of her glory and our love for her history. . . .
>
> . . .above all things, we rejoice that our church, the church of our love, the church of our faith, has not failed to stand by her historic record. For did not Holy Church canonize Augustine and Monica, Benedict the Moor and Cyprian. . . .[29]

The fifth congress was the last. Despite the lack of documentation, it seems fairly certain that one of the reasons why the congresses ceased was in part because of the more militant tone of its members.

What is significant is that Black Catholics were the first to hold a lay Catholic congress in this country. The general lay Catholic Congress held in November, 1889 in Baltimore, to commemorate the centenary of the establishment of the American hierarchy, was the first of two, and Daniel Rudd was also on the steering committee for this first congress.[30]

These congresses brought together Black Catholic laymen from all over the country. These men were leaders in their communities. They numbered such men as Frederick McGhee (1861–1912), a prominent Black lawyer from St. Paul, friend to W.E.B. DuBois, and one of the founding members of the NAACP and founder also of the legal arm of the NAACP

---

29. The original draft of this resolution is found in the University of Notre Dame Archives. IX-1-0. William J. Onahan, *Columbian Catholic Congress: Speeches, Resolutions, and Miscellaneous Addresses.* It is entitled "Address of the 4th Congress of Colored Catholics to the Rev. Clergy of the Catholic Church of America." The fourth Black Lay Catholic Congress was independent of the Columbian Catholic Congress, but they held one joint session. For further information on the five Black Lay Catholic Congresses, see David Spalding, C.F.X., "The Negro Catholic Congresses, 1889–1894," *The Catholic Historical Review* 52 (1966–1967):66–87. The proceedings of the first three congresses were published by Daniel Rudd at his press in Cincinnati, *Three Catholic Afro-American Congresses* (Cincinnati, 1893), reprinted in *The American Catholic Tradition* (Jay P. Dolan, ed., (New York, 1978).

30. *Souvenir Volume of the Centennial Celebration and Catholic Congress. 1789–1889.* (Detroit, 1889). Note photograph of Rudd on p. 21. Information on Rudd's involvement in the first lay Catholic Congress in 1889 is contained in the Henry Brownson Letters in the University of Notre Dame archives. Further information on Rudd is also to be found in the Josephite Archives in Baltimore, MD and the Cincinnati Archdiocesan Archives.

that exists today[31]; and William Henry Smith (1840–1903) librarian of the House of Representatives library for two terms, 1881–83 and 1889–92, one of the highest ranking Black officials in the Federal government at the time.[32] James Spencer (1849–1911) was a member of the South Carolina Legislature for 1874–1876 and was secretary of the trustees of St. Peter's Catholic Church, the Black Catholic Church in the city of Charleston.[33] Spencer was one of the leading figures during the five Black Lay Catholic congresses. John Edward West Thompson (1860–1918), a graduate of the Yale Medical School and a former student at the Sorbonne, served as minister to Haiti from 1885–1889. He participated in the third congress.[34]

Several of the congress members were active in local politics. Washington Parker (1848–1915) was very active in local Republican politics in New York City; while Robert N. Wood (1864–1915) was very active in Democratic politics and was the printer of the *Crisis Magazine*, the publication of the NAACP.[35]

Lincoln Vallé, who was born in 1854 and who died sometime after 1923, was a newspaperman from St. Louis who collaborated very closely with Rudd on the *American Catholic Tribune*. He lived for a while in Chicago and was also active in all of the congresses. He is most remarkable for the apostolic work he carried on in the Black community in Milwaukee from about 1908–1912. It was through his efforts that St. Benedict the Moor Parish in Milwaukee was established under the care of the Capuchins as a Black Catholic parish.[36] In a sense the apostolic activity of Lincoln Vallé was a statement of the faith and zeal of the Black lay congresses and their concern for the Church and its work of evangeliza-

---

31. For general information on McGhee, see "Biographies of Black Pioneers," *Gopher Historian* (1968–1969), 18. Correspondence between McGhee and Booker T. Washington is found in The Booker T. Washington Papers in the Manuscript Division of the Library of Congress. Correspondence with DuBois is in the W.E.B. DuBois Papers at the University of Massachusetts, Amherst.

32. See E. Raymond Lewis, "The House Library" *Capitol Studies* (Fall, 1975): 127 and "The Colored One-Third of the National Capital," an unsigned article in the *St. Joseph's Advocate* 12(1894): 601–602.

33. Thomas Holt, *Black Over White: Negro Political Leadership in South Carolina During Reconstruction.* (Urbana, 1977), 189 and Appendix A. Table 5. As trustee for St. Peter's see letters in the Josephite Archives, Letter to Bishop Northrop and reply, 2–R–li and 2–R–lk.

34. See Thompson's obituary notice in Yale University, *Obituary Record of Graduates deceased during the Year Ending July 1, 1920* (New Haven, 1921), 1606.

35. See obituary notice for Washington Parker in the *New York Age*, the prestigious Black newspaper in New York City, for Thursday, September 23, 1915. In the same newspaper is the obituary notice for Robert Wood for Thursday, October 7, 1915. Information regarding Wood's printing of *The Crisis* is found in the W.E.B. DuBois Papers. Wood was a controversial figure because of his political activities and was frequently mentioned in the Black press.

36. Valle's activity in Milwaukee is found in the following brochure on St. Benedict the Moor Parish in the Josephite Archives: *History of St. Benedict the Moor, Catholic Colored Mission.*

376

*Dr. Thomas Wyatt Turner, botanist,
educator, civil rights activist, and
prominent Catholic layman*
(Courtesy: Elio Gasperetti)

tion. It was also a bridge between nineteenth century Black Catholic endeavors and the more vigorous Black Catholicism soon to emerge.

By 1899 the *American Catholic Tribune* had ceased publication.[37] Rudd later moved to Arkansas where he went into business.[38] By 1900. moreover, a Black Catholic lay leader of the next century, Thomas Wyatt Turner (1877–1978), was an undergraduate at Howard University in the nation's capital. In about a dozen years he would launch a new Black Catholic lay movement.

Although at first the five lay congresses might seem a failure or perhaps at best an unfinished experiment, they should be considered a success. For the first time in United States Catholic history, Black Catholics expressed to a national audience their sense of identity, their pride, and their confidence as Catholics and as Blacks. They articulated their beliefs in a language that was original and eloquent. Without a body of ordained priests who shared their history and their racial identity and without a cohesive tradition, the Black Catholic laity at the end of the nineteenth century emerged as a people conscious of its responsibility and devoted to a common ideal. In the next century this unique corner of the vineyard would yield a richer wine.

---

37. In 1894 Rudd moved the printing offices of the ACT from Cincinnati to Detroit. The *Detroit City Directory* gives Rudd's address as 37 Mullett Street from 1894–1895 and as 469 Monroe Avenue in 1897. See ACT for February 8, 1894.

38. See Theophilus Bond and Dan A. Rudd, *From Slavery to Wealth: The Life of Scott Bond.* (Madison, AR, 1917). See also the Bishop Morris Letters in the Little Rock Diocesan Archives for the years 1919–1920.

9

The Hispanic Catholics

For decades the church had struggled with the nationality issue, moving back and forth between Americanization and pluralism, trying first mixed parishes, then ethnic parishes, and eventually moving back to mixed parishes. By the mid-1920s, with immigration restriction laws in place and anti-Catholicism rampant, a new generation of church leaders like George Cardinal Mundelein in Chicago and Francis Cardinal Spellman in New York began de-emphasizing the nationality issue, portraying Roman Catholicism as an institution capable of absorbing the "new immigrants" and acculturating them to American society. But after 1924, just as European immigration declined dramatically, immigration from Mexico, Puerto Rico, and later Cuba began rising. From 78,000 people in 1838, the Hispanic-American community would grow to more than 20 million people by 1984. Including undocumented workers, there would be 15 million Mexicans living in the United States. Because Puerto Rico, as a commonwealth partner of the United States, was exempt from immigration laws, as many as 2.5 million Puerto Ricans would be occupying northeastern ghettoes by the early 1980s. Between the Castro revolution of 1959 and the exodus of 1980, more than 1 million Cubans settled in the United States, most in Miami and the Southeast. The vast majority of the Hispanic immigrants were Roman Catholics, and once again church leaders faced the task of absorbing a large, alien population. By the time the Hispanics began arriving in large numbers, the golden age of the nationality parishes was over, at least in terms of the establishment of new ones. Church leaders returned once again to the idea of the mixed parish as the best way of incorporating the newest wave of immigrants.[1]

Like the Catholicism of the eastern and southern Europeans,

147

Hispanic Catholicism differed substantially from the religious traditions of the Irish. Hispanic Catholicism emerged from the Spanish conquest of New World indigenous societies. Despite major differences in customs, history, and racial background, the Cubans, Puerto Ricans, and Mexicans all mixed Spanish and American Indian values. Since the voyages of Columbus until the Spanish American War of 1898, Puerto Rico and Cuba were colonies of Spain, as was Mexico between the arrival of Cortés in 1519 and the end of the revolution in 1821. Hispanics inherited from Spain a spiritual individualism which viewed the soul as the most important ingredient of character. It was a romantic individualism in the tradition of Don Quixote, emphasizing honor, self-respect, integrity, individual courage, and personal self-expression. From American Indians Hispanics learned to trust one another, live in a kind of spiritual communalism, and feel comfortable with the rhythms of nature. A fourth group of Hispanic Catholics, the Filipinos, did not come from Spanish and American ancestry, but they too shared a religious culture fusing native values with Spanish Catholicism.[2]

When the Spanish empire first began expanding into Latin America and the Philippines in the sixteenth century, the *conquistadores* had an overpowering conviction that Roman Catholicism was the one true faith and that it was their solemn moral duty to teach and then impose it on the native peoples they encountered. Spaniards made no distinctions between church and state or religion and community; indeed, they built New World communities, or *pueblos*, where the Catholic faith and Spanish language were rigidly communicated to indigenous people. In the pueblos, Spaniards organized towns around the concept of peoplehood. The true meaning of life could be realized only within the context of those communities. The Spanish colonies in Mexico, Puerto Rico, Cuba, and the Philippines were all organized around that principle. At the center of community life, structurally as well as spiritually, were the town plaza and its church where people met, celebrated, and worshiped. The church building dominated the plaza, signifying that God was a member of the community along with everyone else. Richard Rodríguez, recalling his parents' descriptions of those Mexican communities in the 1930s, said:

> The steps of the church defined the eternal square where children
> played and adults talked after dinner. He remembers the way the

Hispanic Catholics
church building was at the center of town life. She remembers the
way one could hear the bell throughout the day, telling time. And
the way the town completely closed down for certain feastdays.
He remembers that the church spire was the first thing he'd see
walking back to town. Both my parents have tried to describe
something of what it was like for them to have grown up Catholic
in small Mexican towns. They remember towns where everyone
was Catholic.[4]

379

Since virtually everyone was Catholic, community identity was synonymous with church identity. Being a Roman Catholic really
meant being part of that Roman Catholic *pueblo*, a birthright rather
than the fruits of any individual spiritual or emotional experience.
Again, Richard Rodríguez remembers that

> I was *un católico* before I was a Catholic. That is, I acquired my
> earliest sense of the Church—and my membership in it—through
> my parents' Mexican Catholicism. It was in Spanish that I first
> learned to pray. I recited family prayers—not from any book. And
> in those years when we felt alienated from *los gringos*, my family
> went across town every week to the wooden church of Our Lady
> of Guadalupe, which was decorated with yellow Christmas lights
> all year long.[1]

But a Roman Catholic identity did not imply devotion to the
institutional church. Unlike the church of Ireland or French Canada,
which had struggled for survival in a hostile environment and inspired intense loyalty among parishioners, the Latin American
church had no political competition for years. Roman Catholic authority was at the very center of political life. There was no rivalry
with foreign cultures, religions, or politics to sharpen Catholic identity or attract people to the institutional church as the vehicle for
their survival. In Latin America, Catholic identity was not an intense
fidelity to the church, its clerics, and its sacraments, but an individual sense of belonging to a larger community of Catholic people.
Religiosity and devotion to the church were not necessarily synonymous for most Hispanic Catholics.
  True piety did not depend on regular attendance at Mass and
confession, reception of the sacraments, donations of money, obedience to church teachings in politics and family life, or support of the

clergy. Indeed, a Hispanic Catholic could be quite indifferent toward the sacraments, even quite hostile to formal church teachings and alienated from church clerics, and yet still see himself as a good Catholic, a valuable, functioning member of the Catholic *pueblo*. In their communities, Hispanic Catholics attached a spiritual dimension to "La Raza," or the people, valuing the quality of *personalismo* in which intimate, personal relationships and internal stability transcended all impersonal, bureaucratic relationships. *Personalismo* on a spiritual plane left Hispanic Catholics with a profound sense of faith in *los santos*—the Catholic saints, who, in return for prayers, lighted candles, devotional promises, and roadside and fireside shrines, would provide assistance, protection, and direction. The church sometimes seemed bureaucratic to the Hispanic Catholic, and as such contradicted the cult of *personalismo*. Instead, Hispanics approached divinity through the medium of *los santos*, not through the sacraments or the priesthood.[5]

In Mexico, peasants were profoundly religious people in the nineteenth century, and like many eastern and southern Europeans, they did not separate the natural and supernatural worlds. Throughout the entire range of life, the Mexican peasant interpreted the world as a balance of opposites—a teetering scale of pleasure and pain, creation and destruction, health and sickness, acceptance and rejection, hope and despair, and life and death. At the top of this world, making sure that all suffering was eventually relieved and all prosperity eventually humbled, was God. In everyone's life, achieving a harmony between extremes was the only way of surviving. Lack of balance, disharmony, or a life of emotional extremes was certain to precipitate illness, misfortune, and pain. Mexican religion, both formal Catholicism and older folk traditions, was geared to achieving that cosmic balance, making sure that the natural world and the supernatural were always functioning on the same plane.[6] In dealing with the challenges of life, the Mexican peasants worked hard at controlling their environment, but true courage, or *machismo*, was not so much a matter of control as it was a question of understanding and accepting reality and of using the medium of *los santos* for necessary assistance.[7]

Like the *contadini* of southern Italy, the Mexican peasants were Roman Catholics without much formal loyalty to the institutional church. As a *mestizo* people racially despised for generations in Mexico by *peninsulares* (Spaniards born in Spain) and *criollos*

Hispanic Catholics

(Spaniards born in Mexico), Mexican peasants had a strong resentment of Europeans. Throughout the history of New Spain, most ranking clerics of the church were *peninsulares* and *criollos*; peasants often felt little affection for them. Usually allied with the Spanish elite controlling politics and economic power, the church was a conservative, propertied force in Mexico, controlling vast amounts of land while peasants often starved.[8] Many peasants saw the church as an adversary, and periodically throughout the nineteenth and twentieth centuries they attacked church property and expelled priests from the countryside. In the American borderlands of Texas, New Mexico, Arizona, and California during the nineteenth century, most Catholic clergymen were French, German, or Irish missionaries who spoke little Spanish and disdained Hispanic culture. One Mexican parishioner, when asked about the church, replied:

> These priests are good and educated men and we must respect them. But they do not understand everything. Their learning is from books. Any man can become a priest. It is not the best life and some undertake it as a form of penance. . . . When one wants help from God, one should go to someone who knows him. The priest's duty is to say mass. He runs the machinery of the church. He does not see into the trouble of one's soul.[9]

Many peasant immigrants to the United States also came from areas in Mexico where priests and parochial schools were few. Whether from open hostility or indifference, the Mexican peasants pouring into the Southwest after 1911 had a substantial distance from the church.

But while maintaining an emotional distance from the clergy and comfortably avoiding many authoritarian prohibitions of Roman Catholicism, Mexicans nevertheless considered themselves spiritual Catholics. Usually uninformed about theology and often unwilling to accept pastoral admonitions to donate money and render obedience, the peasants still functioned within a Catholic emotional world. Most made sure their children received the sacraments of baptism and confirmation and were faithful in praying the rosary. When visiting priests reached rural ranching communities, Mexican peasants received them with open arms, readying infants for baptism, youths for instruction in the catechism, and unwed couples for marriage. Temporary altars, crucifixes, *santitos* (images of saints), and confessionals appeared. In their homes, however humble, the peasants maintained elaborately decorated altars, replete with *santitos*, statues of the Virgin Mother, flowers, candles, drawings of deceased relatives, and votive figures. In the presence of that home altar, peasant families confronted the vicissitudes of life.[10]

Like the peasant villagers of southern and eastern Europe, Mexicans and Mexican Americans built their social life around the Catholic calendar, with *fiestas* and celebrations intermittently relieving the drudgery of daily existence. Beginning January 17 with the feast of St. Anthony the Abbot, when peasants decorated and paraded pets and farm animals past the church, the peasants went on to celebrate religious events like *Candelaria* (Purification) in February, Holy Week in April, All Saints' Day in November, Our Lady of Guadalupe on December 12 (Mexico's patron saint day), and *Posadas* during Christmas. They closed the year with the Day of Innocents on December 28, a memorial celebration of King Herod's massacre of children during his search for the infant Jesus. In between these religious *fiestas,* Mexican peasants also celebrated the days of St. Anthony, St. John, St. James, Santa Anna, St. Peter, and Santa Cruz.[11]

The frequent observance of saints' days reflected the universal appeal Catholic saints had for Mexican peasants. The peasants' devotion was similar in intensity to the *clientismo* of the southern Italians. Although their belief in *La Raza* convinced them of God's divine approbation, they too felt the need for intermediaries between people and heaven. Their unwillingness to rely always on priests to direct their relationship with God reinforced the need for saints. The Virgin of Guadalupe was their favorite, with a pilgrimage to her basilica in Mexico City the devotional peak of one's life. The Virgin Mother intervened with God, averted danger, cured illnesses, ended drought, and helped maintain the precarious balance of life. Mexican peasants also turned to particular saints to work out particular problems. The Virgin of San Juan helped people with family difficulties; St. Christopher, the patron saint of travelers, helped migrant workers; St. Anthony the Abbot protected farm animals; and St. Martin the Horseman helped bring prosperity.

Mexican peasants also had a folk Catholicism that blended European and Indian traditions. Even their most sacred religious devotion, that to the Virgin of Guadalupe, was inseparably connected to the indigenous past; for centuries before the appearance of the Virgin in 1531, a female goddess had appeared at the same site to Aztec worshipers. The Aztec emphasis on collective security (once sought through human sacrifice) survived in the commitment to *La Raza*, which guaranteed community life in the present while formal Catholicism sought to guarantee individual life in the future. Folk Catholicism intimately linked peasants to the continuum between the natural and supernatural worlds, giving them some sense of control over their environment. While formal Catholicism often preached passivity and resignation to the forces of the universe, folk religion gave peasants power, relieving their guilt about any personal failures to fulfill church expectations while leaving them in direct contact with divine power. The religion of *La Raza*, though hundreds of years removed from its Aztec beginnings, was essentially a *mestizo* faith emphasizing communalism in the present and individual salvation in the next world, without any heavy theological overtones about exactly what merited eternal life.

Older religious rituals, much to the dismay of many Catholic priests, had merged with formal ceremonial occasions. Even though succeeding generations of foreign priests urged peasants to abandon their "superstitions," the peasants held fast to them as the only way of surviving tragedy and externally imposed authority. On St. John's Day in June, for example, which peasants called *El Dia de Bañar* (Day of Bathing), the celebrants ritually immersed themselves in a pond, river, lake, or tub as an atoning purification. On the same day women dampened their hair, then kneeled and spread their hair over the doorsill while members of a religious procession cut it off with hatchets. Festival parades with bands of violinists, fireworks, gunfire, and people walking barefoot or on their knees were common. On All Souls' Day, when the family gathered at the cemetery to commemorate the dead, peasants decorated the graves with flowers, images and pictures of saints and of the dead, bottles and oyster shells, and old personal mementos. A whole range of folktales mixed with Catholic theology to explain the peasant world. Mexican *tejanos*, for example, annually rejoiced at the story of San Miguel, the patron saint of El Paso valley, who appeared with a flaming sword at the tower of the parish church to ward off an attacking band of Civil War marauders.

Faith in divine intervention was the core of peasant folk religion. Peasants had enormous faith in miracles—the willingness of

383

God to intervene in individual affairs, usually for the good of an
entire community, at the request of pleading patron saints and often
through the medium of particularly gifted men and women. Among
Mexican peasants, the most gifted people functioning outside institutional Catholicism were the *curanderos,* or healers. Since illness
and misfortune were rooted in an imbalance between man and
nature, usually through sin and disobedience, which witches *(bru-
jas)* could exploit, the powers of the *curanderos* had spiritual and
supernatural overtones. An old *tejano* peasant once remarked:

384

> Witches cannot harm the good. A pure person who has followed
> God's way is safe from them. A witch cannot affect flesh that is
> pure. But each sin puts a bit of evil in a man. It is through this evil
> that the witches work. If you have no sin in you, then you are safe.
> But where can you find a member of *La Raza* who has not at some
> time sinned? It is our fate.[12]

Curanderos mixed the popular beliefs and empirical remedies
of both Spanish and Indian culture, using natural herbs and plants as
well as chants, hexes, and blessings to restore balance and heal
sickness. Some *curanderos* whose powers were particularly strong
achieved the status of sainthood among Mexican peasants. An elderly man referred to as the "God of Hosts" reportedly healed the sick,
cured the blind, mobilized paraplegics, and fed thousands of people
with a few tortillas in northern Mexico in 1861. Teresa Urrea apparently healed thousands of people in El Paso in 1896 after spiritual
voices called her to spend her life administering to the sick. The
curandero Don Pedrito Jaramillo wandered for years throughout
south Texas curing thousands of people in the 1880s and 1890s.
After his death Mexican and Mexican-American peasants placed his
picture among the pantheon of saints adorning family altars and
frequently prayed to him for health and well-being. These, of
course, were some of the "superstitions" church leaders wanted the
peasants to abandon.[13]

Religious life among Cuban immigrants was even more complex. Like Mexico, Cuba was overwhelmingly Catholic, enjoyed a
strong *pueblo* identity, and lacked strong commitments to the institutional church. There was also a class dimension to Cuban Catholicism in which different levels of piety and devotional observances
separated peasants from elites, a distinction not as clear among

Mexican Catholics, at least among those coming to the United States. The Cuban immigrants came to America in two waves: an upper-class migration beginning in 1959 when Castro came to power and a peasant migration in the late 1970s and early 1980s. Their religious backgrounds contributed even more variety to American Catholicism.

In the Spanish colonial empire, the church was responsible for the moral and spiritual guidance of the people, but the Catholic clergy was under imperial direction. Church and state in Cuba did not really separate until after 1898, when the independence movement triumphed during the Spanish-American War. Spain had enjoyed a papal grant of power allowing the king to appoint, assign, and dismiss priests and collect tithes. Highly dependent on the governing classes, the church became a conservative force identified closely with the interests of the elite. Because of its upper-class bias, links to the conservative forces of the Spanish Crown, and intense opposition to the independence movement, the church alienated large numbers of Cubans, who equated it with corruption, conservatism, and authoritarian control. When Fidel Castro came to power in 1959, there were only two hundred parishes serving 6 million people on the island. Only seven hundred priests worked in those parishes. While Ireland had one parish for every 3,000 people and one priest for every 450 people, Cuba had only one parish for every 30,000 people and one priest for every 8,500 people. Even Mexico had one parish for every 14,500 people and one priest for every 3,700 people.[14]

The Cuban church for the most part served the needs of the urban middle and upper classes. Cuban priests almost always came from the upper classes. Traditionally, well-to-do Cubans had been more committed to the church, more likely to attend Mass as a family, to contribute financially, and to obey pastoral teachings. During the nineteenth century, the church had come under the influence of Jansenist morality and had accepted the importance of internal faith as well as external observances of piety. Those values persisted into the twentieth century, giving a small number of Cuban Catholics a kind of piety not unlike that of the Irish, Basques, or French Canadians. When Fidel Castro came to power and expropriated large amounts of property while converting the economy to socialism, large numbers of upper-class Cubans headed for the United States. Unlike immigrants from Mexico, Puerto Rico, and Central

385

America, they were more than nominal Catholics, more likely to identify with the institutional church.[15]

But the Cuban migration of the 1970s and early 1980s was quite different—a movement of peasants and workers rather than of the well-to-do. Not only were these peasants usually nominal Catholics enjoying a *pueblo* identity without feeling much loyalty to the church itself, they were also more likely to have a syncretic faith mixing formal Catholicism with traditional African folk beliefs. Unlike Mexico, where few Africans settled, Cuba had large plantations and large numbers of slaves. Blacks were a significant part of the population, totaling perhaps 17 percent by 1960 and outnumbering whites in several regions. Among large numbers of Cuban blacks as well as lower-class whites and those of mixed blood, religious beliefs revolved around syncretic Afro-Catholic rituals. Although the educated Cuban upper classes believed that the cults were based on barbaric superstitions, the lower classes, especially Africans, were drawn to them. It was often difficult to distinguish Roman Catholicism from such cults as Santería, Abakua, Mayombería, Regla de Palo, and Regla Conga.[16]

The largest of the Afro-Cuban religions was Santería, several closely related faiths distinguished by the ethnic backgrounds of their devotees. The most influential of the Santería cults was Lucumi, a group fusing the Yoruba language of West Africa with Spanish. Others included the Arara from Dahomey and *vodún* spiritualism from Haiti, a combination of French and Fon cultures. All of the Santería cults mixed selected Catholic rituals with African mythology, identifying themselves nominally as Catholics, equating Catholic saints with various African deities, and interpreting Catholicism as the Spanish-community version of Santería. Among the Lucumi, Yoruba gods and Catholic saints were treated as replicas of one another, known as *santos* in Spanish and *orishas* in Yoruba. St. Barbara was the same person as Shango, the god of war, while St. Francis of Assisi was equated with Orunmila, the god of destiny. Elegua guarded the gates of Heaven for Yorubans and was the same as St. Peter in Cuban Santería. The most important of the *orishas* was Odudua, identified with the Virgin of Carmen, to whom the Lucumi sacrificed white chickens every month. Each believer also had a patron saint to bring protection and prosperity—Yemaya, the goddess of the sea, for sailors; Ogun, the equivalent of John the Baptist, for blacksmiths and soldiers; or Oshun, the patroness of

386

lovers. Santería rituals combined such Catholic practices as lighting candles and reciting the Lord's prayer and the rosary with chants, drumming, animal sacrifices, secret oaths, visionary trances, and spiritual possessions. The Afro-Cuban cults accompanied many peasant immigrants to America.[17]

Although not Hispanic Catholics, Haitian immigrants often accompanied the second wave of Cubans to the United States in the late 1970s and 1980s. Like lower-class Cuban Catholicism, Haitian religion retained powerful African roots and a strong voodoo connection. From the mid-1600s, when they were first transported as slaves from Africa to Haiti, they were forbidden to practice tribal religions. Forced converts to Roman Catholicism, the Haitians refused to abandon African voodoo, instead fusing the two into a single religion. Afro-Haitian Catholicism acknowledges God as the creator of heaven and earth, the *Gran Met,* a deity powerful but remote who delegated the mundane management of human affairs to intermediary spirits called *loa.* Haitians saw those spirits everywhere, in trees, ponds, rivers, waterfalls, caves, springs, lakes, valleys, or groves. Competition between good and evil spirits is the essence of life, and voodoo Catholicism maintains harmony in the world. Every July 16, Haitians celebrate the Vyej Marik, or the apparition of the Virgin of Miracles, Our Lady of Mount Carmel, on top of a palm tree at Ville Bonheur. The annual pilgrimage brings tens of thousands of people to the village—priests and nuns, rich and poor, voodoo practitioners, and wealthy businessmen—all to propitiate the *loa* Legba (St. Peter), known as the master of roads and pathways, make ritual stops at sacred trees, and to wash themselves in the sacred Saut d'Eau waterfalls of the Tombe River. Such voodoo spirits as Danbala Wedo, the snake symbol, or Aida Wedo or Ezili Freda possess the bodies of the worshipers. On the next morning, the pilgrims return to the village square to hear the standard Catholic Mass delivered from the church balcony.

Ever since their first attempts to convert the African slaves, Roman Catholic authorities in Haiti have attempted to suppress the Old World religion. Periodically over the centuries, the church has waged a political campaign against African-Catholic syncretic beliefs, the most recent one in 1941 when the Haitian government spearheaded an "antisuperstition" crusade involving destruction of temples and sacred natural settings. To the French and Irish priests serving in Haiti during the seventeenth, eighteenth, nineteenth, and twentieth centuries, the mixture of formal religion and voodoo was the epitome of sacrilege. The drinking of bull and chicken blood at religious ceremonies, the identification of St. Jacques with the African god of war Ougou Feray, the mud baths, and the hexes and charms all alienated the priests, but the traditions survived and came into the dioceses of the American church, especially in Florida, with the wave of Haitian immigrants in the early 1980s.[18]

388

A similar mix occurred in the Philippines. In order to secure part of the Asian spice trade, gain economic access to China and Japan, and convert the Filipinos to Christianity, Spain expanded into the Philippines in 1565. Unlike the conquest of Mexico, that of the Philippines was bloodless. The Philippines was a geographical quagmire of seven thousand separate islands, only eleven larger than one thousand square miles, and even those were marked by rugged mountains and jungles. Geographical particularism, political decentralization, and complex linguistic diversity characterized Filipino society and made for little organized resistance to Spanish colonization. But that regional diversity also made imposition of a single culture throughout the archipelago almost impossible. Although Spanish political control of the islands lasted from 1565 to 1898, cultural domination was never so complete; indeed, the natives managed to "Philippinize" Spanish culture and convert it to their own uses. Filipino Catholicism was a prime example.[19]

In preconquest Filipino society, a variety of gods, goddesses, and rituals governed the cycle of religious life. Although most Filipino ethnic groups had some notion of a supreme being—Bathala in the Tagalog language or Laon in Baseyan—responsible for creating the earth, it was not a deity playing a direct role in everyday affairs. As in most peasant societies, Filipino religious beliefs combined the world of natural objects and living things with spirits and with formal, institutional devotions. Filipinos worshiped nature, offering devotion to mountains, caves, rivers, the sun, the moon, and the stars as well as to such animals as crows, sharks, and crocodiles. They also worshiped a world of spirits. A large pantheon of deities and spirits ready to interfere in people's lives animated Filipino religion. The good spirits were known as *anitos* and the bad spirits as *diwatas.* Only a complicated series of ritual prayers, promises, and sacrifices could placate the wrath of *diwatas* or stimulate the generosity of *anitos.*[20]

Spain then imposed Roman Catholicism on this world of spirits.

The church tried to convert the entire Filipino society and to make Christianity an integral part of daily life. Spanish clerical and political officials required a whole range of daily devotions from parishioners in the *cabecera* villages where churches stood and priests resided. In most of those villages, women and children met each day at the large cross in the main plaza and recited the rosary, and at sunset children often chanted the rosary while walking through the streets. Most Filipinos, however, lived far away from those central villages, in rural areas where priests and churches were few and far between. The natives proved highly selective in their approach to Catholicism, adapting it to local circumstances and endowing it with a unique devotional content. Filipinos combined an external devotion to formalized ritual with a general indifference to theological and institutional subtleties; accepted magic and continued to be devoted to the spirits of ancestors and to the world of nature; had a powerful belief in miraculous cures; maintained a conspiracy of silence in which they refused to pass on to Spanish priests any news or evidence of "paganism" or religious unorthodoxy; and received infrequently the sacraments of the church.

But while seldom participating in conventional observances of the Catholic faith, rural Filipinos readily accepted the *fiesta* system to celebrate Holy Week, Corpus Christi, and local patron saints' days. Although most Filipinos rejected the seventeenth- and eighteenth-century attempts of Jesuit priests to introduce flagellation rituals as forms of penance, the practice did take root among a minority and persisted into the twentieth century. Forms of such penance ranged from walking on one's knees the length of a rough marble church floor to marching long distances with paid assistants whipping bare backs with rope-bamboo lashes. Most Filipinos readily accepted sensuous observances like candlelight parades, processional floats, the smell of incense, loud music, Gregorian chants, and elaborate pageantry. Because Filipino society had long been kin-oriented, Filipinos also quickly adopted the principle of coparenthood *(compadrazgo)* or godparenthood. During the eighteenth and nineteenth centuries, the elaborate ceremonies of Spanish Catholicism overpowered pagan rituals, eliminating, for example, the pre-Hispanic pattern of ritual drinking of alcoholic beverages. But in the process of absorbing Spanish Catholicism, Filipinos created a folk Catholicism of their own. In the past they had appealed to *anitos* and *diwatas,* but now they performed the same rituals for

389

Catholic saints. No single cult of mass appeal such as that of the Virgin of Guadalupe or of the Black Madonna of Czestochowa appeared, but Filipinos did have locally or regionally powerful saints capable of protecting and nourishing them, such as the Black Nazarene of Quiapo, Manila. In Filipino Catholicism, the miraculous powers of the supernatural permeated folk religion, providing a cultural unity previously unknown in the archipelago.[21]

A major schism, similar to the independent church movements in the United States, divided Filipino Catholicism after the Spanish American War of 1898. As the drive for Filipino independence gained momentum in the 1890s, resentment of the church's close relationship with Spanish authorities grew more intense. When armed rebellion erupted in 1896, Emilio Aguinaldo, the leader of the independence movement, appointed Gregoria Aglipay, a Filipino priest, to head the Philippine Independent church. By 1898 the church claimed more than 1 million members. Aguinaldo told the Catholic clergy to pledge allegiance to Aglipay or be labeled traitors to the Philippines. The Filipino independence movement had long looked to the day when Spanish power would be eliminated, but after 1898 the United States became the imperial enemy. When American officials and military personnel began arriving in the archipelago, Aguinaldo turned his wrath on them, enveloping the islands in a bitter guerrilla war between 1899 and 1902. At the same time, when Vatican officials accepted U.S. demands to appoint American rather than Filipino clerics to the church bishoprics, Aglipay's Philippine Independent church gained even more momentum. Dennis Dougherty, later the Cardinal Archbishop of Philadelphia, became bishop of the diocese of Nueva Segovia in the Philippines in 1903 and had to deal with the Aglipay schism, which by 1904 claimed more than one-quarter of the population and half the property of the Roman Catholic church in the Philippines. Although membership in the Philippine Independent church peaked and then declined after 1905, many Filipino immigrants brought its teachings with them to the United States.[22]

Finally, like the other Hispanic Catholics, the Filipinos too had a rich, syncretic folk religion, but it was complicated by the ethnic and linguistic background of the islands. When the Spaniards first arrived in the sixteenth century, they encountered hundreds of separate ethnic and linguistic groups but succeeded in superimposing Roman Catholicism on 90 percent of them. Naturally, folk reli-

390

gions emerged that fused the secular and spiritual worlds as well as ancient tribal religions and Christianity. Perhaps the best known of them was the *Guardia de Honor.* Originally founded in Central Luzon by the Dominicans as a confraternity devoted to the Virgin Mary, the Guardia slowly changed into a millennial cult led by "Baltazar," a charismatic figure who succeeded by 1900 in getting perhaps twenty-five thousand Filipinos to worship him along with the Virgin, Jesus, the Holy Ghost, and the Twelve Apostles. There were literally dozens of other folk religions throughout the islands, and many of them came to America with the formal Catholicism of the Filipino immigrants.[23]

391

In Puerto Rico, Spanish Catholicism went through similar stages: formal imposition on the native people, syncretic development of a folk religion, indifference to complicated theological questions and affairs of the institutional church, and the evolution of an overwhelming *pueblo* identity. The first Roman Catholic diocese in the New World was established at San Juan, Puerto Rico, in 1511, and until 1898, when Puerto Rico became an American territory, the diocese of San Juan was administered by a series of Spanish-born bishops. The only exception was Bishop Juan Alejo Arizmundi, a Puerto Rican native who presided over the diocese between 1803 and 1814. The lack of a native Puerto Rican clergy, the consecutive tenure of Spanish bishops, the close relationship between the church and the upper classes, and the opposition of the church to the nineteenth-century Puerto Rican independence movement all contributed to a sense of alienation among peasants. Although nominally Roman Catholic, they had little affection for or attraction to the institutional church.[24]

After 1898 church administration in Puerto Rico resembled that in the Philippines, with American priests and bishops replacing Spaniards. A clash of cultures occurred as Irish Catholicism confronted Hispanic values. The American church's emphasis on strict morality and obedience, the sacraments, the importance of parochial schools, the necessity of daily devotions, and the transcendence of religious asceticism contrasted sharply with the folk liberalism of Puerto Rican Catholicism. Irish-American administration did stimulate improvements in religious instruction, ritual devotion, church attendance, and the number of Puerto Ricans taking up vocations, but the church still failed to overcome the alienation of the masses.[25]

Catholic Immigrants in America

In several ways the alienation even increased. Irish-American priests staffed the parishes and parochial schools, and American-born bishops controlled the dioceses, creating a great distance between parishioners and church officials. It was not until 1961 that a Puerto Rican native, Luís Aponte Martínez, was ordained as bishop and assigned to an island diocese. Few American priests, nuns, or lay personnel spoke Spanish, and the parochial schools followed an American model, with little time given to Hispanic culture and history. Because the church insisted on rigorous administrative standards and on charging tuition, the parochial schools became elite institutions serving the upper class. During the 1940s and 1950s, as liberal and radical political movements appeared in Puerto Rico, American church leaders became identified with the forces of tradition and conservatism, opposing birth control and land reform. In 1960 the church endorsed the *Partido Acción Cristiana*, a conservative party opposed to the more liberal *Partido Popular*. The Catholic party received less than 10 percent of the vote, an indication of how large numbers of Puerto Ricans felt about the church. Americans had managed to assume completely the conservative role in church government, which the Spanish had vacated in 1898.[26]

But despite their nominal Catholicism, at least in a formal sense, which was a "womb to tomb" faith with little in between, the Puerto Ricans were highly religious, and most of them identified themselves as Roman Catholics. Most homes displayed a variety of holy pictures, crucifixes, and religious statues; children feared *el diablo* (the devil) and loved *Papá Dios* (Father God); people crossed themselves frequently and prayed regularly, usually to a favorite saint; participated in *fiestas* and processions of Holy Week, Christmas, Epiphany, and patron saint days; and frequently called on priests to bless homes, businesses, cars, and animals. And yet, attendance at Mass, communion, and confession remained infrequent; entering religious orders was rare; and financial support of the church was rather miserly. Such was the pattern of Hispanic Catholicism.[27]

Unlike the other Roman Catholic immigrants, the Mexicans, Puerto Ricans, Cubans, and Filipinos came after the zenith of the nationality parishes in the early 1900s. Bishops like Mundelein, O'Connell, Dougherty, and Spellman had turned to mixed, territorial parishes to assimilate the Hispanic immigrants into the church and larger society. Even without the "Americanization" commitments of the new generation of bishops, the Hispanic Catholics hardly produced enough ethnic priests to staff nationality parishes; nor were parishioner activity, financial resources, or financial commitments sufficient to support nationality churches. In Corpus Christi, Texas, in 1940, there were 147,000 Mexicans and only 14,000 Anglos in the diocese, but English-speaking priests outnumbered Spanish-speaking priests by 115 to 22. New nationality parishes were quite rare. The diocese of Miami, Florida, had been created in 1958, with Coleman F. Carroll as its first bishop. By 1960 there were 65 parishes and 308,000 Roman Catholics in the diocese, with the vast majority of the priests Irish American. In 1982, after more than twenty years of Cuban immigration, the Catholic population of the Archdiocese of Miami had reached nearly 900,000 people in 134 parishes. There were sixty-seven Spanish-surnamed priests in the diocese, with thirteen of them Cuban-born, and Augustin A. Roman, a Cuban native, serving as an auxiliary bishop for Archbishop Edward A. McCarthy. Bishop Roman was "Episcopal Vicar for the Spanish-speaking People" and supervised a number of diocesan societies for Cubans. But neither Bishop Carroll nor Archbishop McCarthy had turned to the separate nationality-parish model to handle the influx of Cuban immigrants. Puerto Ricans were not too different from Mexicans or Cubans. In the early 1960s, there were only 15,000 Puerto Rican children in New York parochial schools, less than 10 percent of those of school age, and only one native Puerto Rican priest in the archdiocese.[28]

The church's approach to the Puerto Ricans illustrated the demise of the nationality parish. During his tenure as Archbishop of Philadelphia between 1918 and 1951, Denis Cardinal Dougherty established 112 new parishes and 145 parochial schools, but he was like Mundelein in his opposition to nationality parishes. Ninety miles north, in New York, Francis Cardinal Spellman took the same position. In the 1920s a few Puerto Rican nationality parishes appeared—La Milagrosa parish in 1926 on 114th Street and Seventh Avenue and Holy Agony parish in 1930 at Third Avenue and 103d Street. But in 1939 Cardinal Spellman ended the practice, placing Puerto Rican immigrants in mixed parishes. He was not insensitive to their needs. He took St. Cecilia parish in East Harlem, for example, and turned it over to Spanish-speaking American priests who had worked in Puerto Rico, while leaving intact its designation as a

393

territorial parish also serving remaining German and Irish parishioners. But Spellman generally worried about the wisdom of retaining nationality parishes, not only because they seemed to retard
assimilation and to perpetuate the image of the church as a foreign
institution, but also because they were so temporary. By the third
generation, the English-speaking grandchildren of German, Slavic,
and Italian immigrants were heading for the suburbs, leaving behind
huge nationality churches with a few dozen elderly members. For
Spellman, the inexorable forces of assimilation always destroyed the
nationality churches; so why not move instead to integrated, mixed
parishes serving elderly immigrants of an earlier generation as well
as the young immigrants of the latest group? In a few generations,
when earlier immigrants had left behind their elderly in the move to
the suburbs and new immigrants filled the ghettoes, the church
buildings, activity centers, and parochial schools would still be
useful and available.[29]

A similar situation prevailed among Mexican Catholics in Los
Angeles, where the American church hierarchy looked upon the
immigrants with a mixture of concern, disdain, and fear. They very
much wanted Mexicans to move into the institutional church, but
they were concerned about the lack of Mexican priests, the detachment of the peasants from church ceremonies, and some of their
devotional practices, and they were afraid that the immigrants
would be vulnerable to evangelization by Protestants or Commu-
nists. German and Irish church leaders, conditioned to centralization in diocesan authority and devotion to the local parish, were
disturbed that Mexican piety was so frequently divorced from the
institutional church.[30]

Mexican Catholics were not, of course, totally indifferent or
hostile to the church. They were members of the Catholic *pueblo,*
and priests were necessary for the major spiritual rites of passage—
baptism, confirmation, communion, confession, marriage, and extreme unction. Mexican immigrants settling in areas where there
were no churches often exhibited the same lay initiative as other
immigrants. At San José Parish in Nueces County, Texas, for example, they established three saints' societies in 1898 while another
group from Tamualipas in Mexico formed a confraternity in 1904.
Sixty families at La Cejita established six sodalities and confraternities between 1907 and 1916, and the next year asked the bishop to
establish a parish for them. But while the Irish or Poles or French

Canadians placed great trust in the priest as a representative of God in everyday life and in the necessity of daily and weekly religious devotions and sacramentals, the Mexicans expressed much of their spirituality outside the network of priest and chapel.[31]

Because of divergent attitudes of clerics and immigrants, as well as the racial hostility of many Yankee and Irish Catholics, the church played no major role in mediating the collision between Anglo and Hispanic cultures or in assimilating the immigrants. Like the Irish and other immigrant priests in the late nineteenth century, clerical leaders in the Mexican communities did not want to trigger any twentieth-century reaction against the church; so they remained politically quite conservative on social issues. Still concerned about its image, the church was not about to do much to improve the social situation of the immigrants, at least beyond supporting the charitable institutions established in other dioceses. Consequently, the institutional church, so central to the lives of many European immigrant groups, was underdeveloped among the Mexicans. In 1930, for example, while there were 179 parochial schools, twelve orphanages, nine reform schools, seven homes for the aged, two rest homes, and nine hospitals for the 305,000 Catholics of the archdiocese of Baltimore, there were only twenty-seven schools, one orphanage, and three hospitals serving the nearly 170,000 Catholics in the diocese of Corpus Christi, Texas.[32]

Not until after World War II did church leaders, especially in Los Angeles, become particularly concerned about the Mexican immigrants and the need to Americanize them. Archbishop J. Francis McIntyre took his cue from Francis Cardinal Spellman in New York in attempting to absorb the Hispanic immigrants into the institutional church. McIntyre inaugurated a vigorous campaign to build parochial schools in the archdiocese of Los Angeles. In 1940, there were 98 parochial schools with an enrollment of 29,151 students serving a Catholic population of 317,000; by 1960 that had grown to 327 schools with 159,000 students serving 1,297,000 Catholics.[33] Many of those schools no doubt served the waves of eastern and midwestern Catholics settling in California after World War II, but by 1960 practically every parish in the barrios of East Los Angeles had a parochial school.

In the 1960s and 1970s, church leaders also began taking a closer look at Mexican-American economic problems. The National Catholic Welfare Conference had formed the Bishops' Committee for the Spanish-Speaking in 1943, but when César Chávez and the Farm Workers Organizing Committee began boycotting the growers of California and south Texas in the 1960s and 1970s, a number of church leaders became actively involved. Archbishop Robert Lucey of San Antonio had long expressed concern about immigrant poverty. Still, most church leaders took the high road, urging conciliation and compromise and a general spirit of equity and fairness for the workers. Because some parish priests did join the picketing and demonstrations, growers criticized the church, but since the church did not formally endorse the strikes, Mexican workers grew more alienated. It was all César Chávez could do to keep many of the immigrants from picketing diocesan headquarters in Los Angeles, San Francisco, and south Texas.[34] The church and Mexican Catholics had still not reached across that centuries-old institutional barrier.

The decline of the nationality parish coincided with the Hispanic influx and reinforced Hispanics' alienation from the church. In the nineteenth and twentieth centuries, the nationality parishes had helped maintain close communication between the immigrants and the church, providing immigrants with a strong institutional setting within which they could adjust to American society. Immigrants were able for a time to continue Old World rituals and holidays and meet with people familiar with Old World values. The buildings of the parish, along with the immigrants' identity as parishioners, left them with a sense of belonging in the community. Hispanic immigrants, because they had few native priests and settled in areas where active Catholic parishes were already functioning, did not enjoy those advantages, especially since they had no opportunities to establish their own parishes. Not until 1970, when Father Patricio Flores was ordained auxiliary bishop of San Antonio, was there a Hispanic bishop in the United States; by that time as well there were only fourteen hundred Hispanic priests in the United States, and only a third of them were American born.[35] The church hardly played the critical role in the lives of Hispanic immigrants that it had played in the lives of so many eastern and southern Europeans.

Hispanic apathy about the institutional church became a source of real concern to the American Catholic hierarchy, just as earlier Irish and German prelates had worried about the Italians and East Europeans. In the summer of 1985, Hispanic Catholics from 130 dioceses in the United States met in Washington, D.C., to discuss the problem. Termed III Encuentro, the meeting underscored the distance many Hispanics felt from the church. Archbishop Patricio Flores claimed there that Spanish-speaking Protestant evangelists were making real headway in the Hispanic community; that only 185 of the 1,500 Hispanic priests in the United States were American-born; that nearly 40 percent of Hispanic Catholics never attend Mass; and that only 1 percent of Hispanic youths were at all active in the church. In its 1983 Pastoral Letter on Hispanic Ministry, the National Conference of Catholic Bishops had expressed similar concerns, fearing that serious "leakage" was undermining the reality of the Catholic *pueblo* in the United States.[36]

PASTORAL CARE OF VIETNAMESE CATHOLICS IN THE UNITED STATES

A Preliminary Report

The purposes of this report[1] are to present an overview of the pastoral care of the Vietnamese Catholics throughout the United States, evaluate the present situation and its problems and successes, and finally, to outline some future directions for special ministry to this new group of immigrants from a different ethnic and cultural tradition.

1. Vietnamese in the United States

As of July 1985, the Southeast Asian refugee population in the United States (from Laos, Cambodia and Vietnam) reached 755,731. Vietnamese account for about two-thirds of this number. Among the one-half million Vietnamese, it is estimated that over 150,000 are Catholics with large concentrations in Louisiana, Texas, California (Orange County, San Jose), Washington (Seattle), Northern Virginia and generally in the South and West. Since 1975, resettlement efforts undertaken by Migration and Refugee Services of the United States Catholic Conference of Bishops in conjunction with local diocesan offices have been very successful. In fact, the Catholic Church has been in the forefront of the refugees resettlement from Indochina, providing sponsorship for about 45% of all refugees coming into the United States without distinction as regards religious faith.

---

[1]. This report has been prepared by the office of Pastoral Care of Migrants and Refugees, staff service of the National Conference of Catholic Bishops' Committee on Migration and Tourism, with the assistance of Rev. Joseph Thuy. A survey of the needs, achievements and resources of the Vietnamese Catholics in the United States in the ten year period following their immigration to this country is presently underway and is expected to be completed in the Spring of 1986.

2. Pastoral Care: The Beginnings

From the very beginning of the refugee exodus from Southeast Asia, many ordinaries and diocesan migration offices have been involved in the resettlement process of Vietnamese refugees.

This massive task of resettlement was accomplished under the auspices of the United States Catholic Conference through the Office of Migration and Refugee Services. This Conference office solicited the support of the local dioceses, and almost all of them were active in the resettlement program by the time the inflow of refugees peaked. Over 256,000 Vietnamese refugees, 45% of the total refugee population, were resettled by the Conference through the dioceses. Not only Catholic refugees were resettled but many Buddhist and refugees of other faiths as well. Many Catholics, on the other hand, were also resettled by other denominations and non–denominational agencies, because religious preference could not be weighed as the only consideration for resettlement by denominational agencies. This fact has complicated the pastoral care of the Vietnamese Catholics who became scattered in many areas and who are provided resettlement assistance by other religious organizations. However, this situation has proved to be a danger to the loss of faith only in some instances due to the special efforts of the Church to minister to all refugees, not just those resettled through the diocesan migration offices.

In sponsoring the refugees in their dioceses, local church officials also requested Vietnamese–speaking priests to administer the Sacraments and to offer pastoral care. In many cases, Vietnamese priests were recruited from the refugee camps of Fort Chaffee, Arkansas, Camp Pendleton, California and Fort Indiantown Gap, Pennsylvania. In the first wave of refugee arrivals, there were more than 40 priests who escaped from Vietnam. In addition, about 20 other priests were studying in the United States when the Saigon government fell in 1975. These priests were scattered in different dioceses and served the spiritual needs of the people.

At the beginning of 1976, the Congregation for the Evangelization of Peoples issued guidelines that encouraged the Vietnamese priests to incardinate into United States dioceses. The largest group of religious priests and seminarians who left Vietnam under the explicit order of their Founder were members of the Congregation of the Mother Co-Redemptrix (CMC). Many of them went to the refugee processing center in Fort Chaffee. On June 5, 1975, the Most Reverend Bernard Law, then Bishop of Springfield-Cape Girardeau, came to Fort Chaffee with his staff to meet the CMC religious and officially sponsored them for his diocese. The first group of 48 persons were welcomed to Our Lady of the Ozarks camp in Carthage, Missouri, owned by the Oblate Fathers (OMI). Today, this Vietnamese congregation plays an important role in the pastoral care of the Vietnamese Catholics.

400

Toward the end of 1977, 103 Vietnamese diocesan priests already had an agreement for residence and ministry with a diocesan bishop in the United States. At the same time, 50 Vietnamese religious priests were also canonically settled through their superiors who had worked out appropriate arrangements for their community life and pastoral activity. In this way, 95% of all the Vietnamese priests present in the United States at the time were becoming part of the normal life of the Church. In a parallel way, Catholic refugees were beginning their process of integration inth the Church through a variety of pastoral structures, the welcome of local bishops and the active support of their priests.

3. Vietnamese Parishes and Missions

Over 130 Vietnamese Catholic communities and Catholic Vietnamese Unions are actively functioning in 28 dioceses throughout the United States. Among these, ten ethnic and personal parishes have been decreed and established by the bishops in various states from Virginia to Nebraska. These personal parishes enjoy the canonical status of a diocesan parish and the Vietnamese pastor is appointed by the local bishop. Their names reflect the Vietnamese special devotion to Mary and their Blessed Martyrs. They are:

1. The Vietnamese Blessed Martyrs Church - Arlington, Virginia

2. The Vietnamese Blessed Martyrs Church - Richmond, Virginia

3. The Vietnamese Blessed Martyrs Church - Sacramento, California

4. Queen of Vietnamese Martyrs Church - Port Arthur, Beaumont, Texas

5. Mary, Queen of Vietnam Church - New Orleans, Louisiana

6. Holy Family Church - Thibaudeaux, Louisiana

7. Our Lady of the Assumption - Amarillo, Texas

8. Immaculate Heart of Mary Church - Lincoln, Nebraska

9. Sts. Peter and Paul Church - Panama City, Florida

10. Our Lady of Vietnam - Washington, DC

401

Among these parishes, the one in New Orleans has the second largest Catholic population (10,000). The Vietnamese Catholic Center of the Diocese of Orange, California, cares for more than 15,000 Catholics. The Archdiocese of Los Angeles ranks third, together with San Jose, Houston, and Portland, in the number of Vietnamese Catholics ranging between 4,000 to 5,000 in each. Seattle, San Francisco, Oakland, Fresno, Denver and Biloxi each have a population of approximately 2,000 to 3,000.

These parishes and communities are mostly autonomous and fulfill their own needs according to their local situation. They depend on the leadership of the individual chaplain or pastor and on the degree of involvement and know-how of the elected representatives of the Vietnamese community. Their activities are limited to Sunday liturgy, some catechism, and a few special cultural events during the course of the year; for example, Christmas, Vietnamese Tet or feasts of the Vietnamese Blessed Martyrs.

4. Diocesan Pastoral Programs for Vietnamese

In areas of Vietnamese concentration, diocesan programs for Vietnamese have been encouraged. Diocesan coordination offices or programs for Vietnamese language ministry have been established in many dioceses. In the Archdiocese of New Orleans with its large concentration of Catholic refugees, the Vietnamese Apostolate was established in 1975, and has a team of five priests to provide for pastoral care. The team developed a comprehensive program for ministry with the assistance of three religious congregations: the Incarnational Consecration (IC), a pious institute of men and women founded by Reverend Viet Anh in 1969 in Vietnam, the Holy Rosary Sisters who had been on the staff of St. Charles Borromeo Seminary in Philadelphia, and the Lovers of the Cross, Sisters of Phat Diem.

The Vietamese Apostolate in New Orleans also publishes the monthly news magazine Dan Chua (circulation: 5,000) as a media instrument of evangelization to Vietnamese refugees. In 1984, the New Orleans Vietnamese Apostolate included the largest Vietnamese parish with 10,000 members — Mary, Queen of Vietnam.

Another diocesan coordination program was initiated by the Diocese of Orange, California. The Vietnamese Catholic Center with a team of 6 priests and a community of the Lovers of the Holy Cross of Phat Diem Sisters take care, respectively, of the ministry of Sacraments and of religious education of 15,000 people resettled in Orange County.

The Diocese of Portland, Oregon established a multicultural center, the Southeast Asian Vicariate, to serve pastoral needs of about 4,000 Catholic Indochinese refugees. The diocese purchased a convent for the Southeast Asian Pastoral Center.

The Diocese of San Jose has a pastoral Center with a team of 4 priests to coordinate the Vietnamese ministry and to direct an Electronic Vocational Program for the training of newly-arrived refugees resettled in the Bayside area of California.

There are other programs for the pastoral care of Vietnamese coordinated on the diocesan level in Philadelphia, Harrisburg, San Diego, Seattle, and Denver, to name a few. These communities are privileged to have a full-time Vietnamese priest assigned by the ordinary to this area of service, and they call themselves Community of Vietnamese Catholics of the specific Diocese where they reside. This community is a single Catholic organization with pastoral programs accountable to the local bishop.

5. Other Pastoral Resources and Programs

(1) In the Midwest, the Congregation of the Mother Co-Redemptrix (CMC) has opened its Provincial House in Carthage, Missouri to thousands of pilgrims who come to celebrate Marian Day, a weekend festival of religious and cultural activities that include a Pontifical Mass, liturgy for various groups, processions in honor of Mary and the Vietnamese Blessed Martyrs, prayer group meetings, adoration of the Blessed Sacrament, reconciliation services and cultural performances. This Marian Day has become an annual pilgrimage for the Vietnamese since 1978. The number of participants has increased every year from over one thousand in the first year to 22,000 in August 1985. Commenting on the Marian Day, Cardinal Bernard Law of Boston said, "It's a faith experience, they come to pray."

403

(2) In the East, the Vietnamese Catholics are scattered in small numbers and tend to be assimilated into local English-speaking parishes. No Vietnamese pastoral center has been established, except the two personal parishes in the Arlington and Richmond dioceses of Virginia.

(3) The Retreat Movement. Vietnamese youth are a special concern for pastoral care. From the beginning, priests and community leaders, who were well aware of the many urgent problems and serious crises encountered by young refugees, made many attempts to bring together the youth in retreats to instruct, to guide, to share problems

and convictions in order to help them cope with the new culture and a very different environment. These movements, however, lacked continuity and could not meet the overwhelming need for change and adjustment to a new life.

In 1982, Father Julien Elizalde Thanh, S.J., was assigned by his superior to come to the United States from Manila to devote himself full-time to preaching retreats to large groups of Vietnamese youth. He and his team spent six months going across the United States and Canada, using the Spiritual Exercises of the Jesuits to help Vietnamese young people rediscover the meaning and purpose of life. The impact was overwhelming. Because there are so many requests from various Vietnamese communities throughout the country, Father Elizalde and his team have to schedule retreats all year long to meet the demands of the youth. The Retreat Movement with the Ignatian approach, led by the Vietnamese-speaking Jesuit, has proved a great success among the Vietnamese communities.

The initial impact of the retreat, the desire for conversion, the understanding of Christ's message are likely to fade away unless there is a follow-up program. Thus, Christian Life Communities (CLC) have been started in many locations to sustain the spiritual commitments of young Vietnamese.

(4) The Renew Program has also been introduced to a number of Vietnamese communities in New Orleans, Houston, Seattle, and San Jose by Father Joachim Le Quang Hien of Spokane. This program facilitates the communications process and understanding among community members. It is enthusiastically received by priests and laity alike.

In less than a year since the second convention of Vietnamese Catholics in New Orleans, the Renew Program has been requested and, accordingly, organized in dozens of Vietnamese communities across the United States.

(5)   Along with the Cursillo Movement which holds annual retreats in Orange County and New Orleans, many pious groups such as the Legion of Mary, the Third Order of Saint Francis, the devotion to Our Lady of Fatima and the Rosary are active on the West Coast and in the southern part of the United States.

6.   Vietnamese Catholic Associations

(1)   The Vietnamese Catholic Student Association is probably the oldest Indochinese organization in North America. The association was established in 1951 by a group of Vietnamese Catholic students and their chaplain, Father Jacques Houssa. Its purpose was to strengthen the brotherly ties among all Vietnamese nationals living in the United States and Canada — regardless of political or religious affiliation, to exchange ideas and experiences, and to promote mutual understanding and solidarity among the Vietnamese.

405

Each year the association organizes two conventions, one in the summer and one at Christmas-time for all Vietnamese living in the United States and Canada. Its activities include fund-raising for war victims, natural disasters, and orphanages; chartered flights for home visits; and the compilation of a national directory to help Vietnamese locate their relatives and friends.

The collapse of Indochina in April 1975 brought more than 130,000 Vietnamese refugees to four camps in the United States. Members of the association have visited and organized orientation programs for refugees in the camps, assisted young adults in their college orientation, and published the CHUONG VIET magazine which provides information on events and activities of various resettlement programs.

The 29th annual convention held at Mercy Center in the Washington, D.C. area on August 23-26, 1979, became a turning point for the association. The special convention drew more than 300 representatives from 21 states. The convention also decided to change its objectives, structure and name to adjust to the new situation, yet preserve its initial goals to promote Vietnamese cultural heritage and to enhance academic research and higher education according to Christian principles. Thus, the Vietnamese Catholic Student Association in America became "The Vietnamese Catholic Student and Professionals in the United States."

Since 1979, the association has restricted its activities to the fields of culture, education and scientific research, since other organizations could address a broader representation of a very large Catholic population resettled in the United States. The national organization of Catholic communities was also under way at this time to become the Federation of Vietnamese Catholics in the following year, 1980.

(2)   The Federation of Vietnamese Catholics in the United States

The first convention of Vietnamese Catholics was held in July of 1980 at St. Patrick's College in Mountain View, California. It attracted 8,000 Vietnamese Catholics from across the United States with more than 300 representatives of local communities, 100 priests and 200 seminarians and women religious. This was a highlight for the refugee community as a whole. The response was enthusiastic and favorable. It was the largest gathering of an organization of Vietnamese Catholics since the 1975 Exodus.

After three days of conferences, meetings, discussions, prayer, and liturgical celebrations, a communique was issued, plans of action were adopted, and the Federation of Vietnamese Catholics was formed to coordinate programs for pastoral outreach to the more than 85,000 Catholics in the 70 communities throughout the United States at that time. Father Joseph Van Tinh, liaison to the NCCB Committee on Migration and Tourism and then president of the community of Vietnamese clergy, religious and seminarians was nominated president of the Federation.

In the summer of 1982, at the bi-annual meeting of the Vietnamese clergy and religious, Father Dominic Mai Thanh Luong was elected to lead the Federation as its second president.

During the period 1982-84, new communities were formed, priests who escaped from Vietnam were sponsored, newly ordained priests from different dioceses have increased, important pastoral needs have been identified, and the cooperation of the Vietnamese religious sisters in catechism programs for children has been secured.

Following the secondary migration movements, many women's religious congregations were relocated in areas more highly populated by refugees such as New Orleans, Orange County, Portland, Houston, and Biloxi, Mississippi.

In July 1984, the second convention of the Federation was held in New Orleans. It was an impressive demonstration of faith: 15,000 people came to New Orleans to celebrate, pray, discuss, and share their faith experiences with fellow Vietnamese. They represented 135,000 Catholics in more than 130 parishes and communities. At the end of the convention, a plan of action was adopted in line with of the Convention's motto, "Faith in the New Land." These pastoral recommendations are significant:

1. to promote Bible study within the Vietnamese families and communities

2. to organize and expand the Vietnamese Catholic youth movement into all communities

3. to implement family and community renewal programs

4. to invite more lay participation into apostolic and pastoral activities in parishes and communities

5. to support possible candidates for vocation to the priesthood and religious life, especially those without families.

7. The Community of Vietnamese Clergy, and Religious

This organization of priests and religious came into existence in 1971 in the United States to provide pastoral care and guidance to the Vietnamese Catholic Student Association. The priests and religious were students and themselves members of the association. They numbered about 25 and resided mostly on the East Coast.

In 1975, many of them interrupted their studies to go to Fort Chaffee and Fort Indiantown Gap to act as chaplains and assist their fellow priests and religious fleeing from Vietnam. From that migration, the number of priests, religious and seminarians increased dramatically, and the community needed some restructuring to meet the new situation.

At the annual meeting in Philadelphia during the International Eucharistic Congress, the priests, seminarians and sisters elected Rev. Nguyen van Tinh, a refugee priest living in Mountain View, California, as the new president. The community is only a mutual assistance group to help with adjustment to a difficult new environment.

408

Priests, seminarians, and sisters were located and sponsored in various dioceses around the country.

Today there are about 230 Vietnamese priests, 320 Vietnamese women in religious communities and about 170 minor seminarians, 56 of them in 2 minor seminaries in Wisconsin and Boston, and over seventy seminarians in college and theology.

(1)   Priests

A total of 237 priests, including 14 newly ordained in 1985, are living in about 28 dioceses of the United States. Of these, 175 are diocesan priests and 55 (or 22%) are from various religious orders — the largest number being the CMC religious priests (29 priests serving in 10 missions from Boston to Denver and at the provincial House in Carthage, Missouri).

Seven Redemptorists are in Los Angeles and Portland, eight Dominicans are in Houston, four Jesuits are in special ministry, three Dormus Dei priests are in Thibaudeaux, Lousiana, and the three IC priests are in Baton Rouge, Louisiana.

The diocesan priests are mostly incardinated in various dioceses and serve as assistants and associates in American parishes. There are five Vietnamese priests assigned as pastors to small, English-speaking parishes. There are also a dozen or so priests who escaped from Vietnam and are presently unable to work because of the English language barrier, sickness, or old age. They live with relatives and are on welfare. Many of the Vietnamese priests are living in the most populated refugee areas such as California, Texas, Lousiana, and Metropolitan Washington, D.C.

There are a number of isolated places in the South and the Midwest with no priests available to administer the Sacraments.

(2) Women Religious

As of June 1985, there were 320 Vietnamese women in religious communities in the United States. This figure includes significant numbers of aspirants, postulants and novices. The median age of professed sisters is in the range of 30-40 years. There is a wide geographical distribution across the United States with greater concentration in Texas, Louisiana and California. Many of the sisters have a poor self-image due to their status as refugees. Some lack educational opportunities and frequently have to undertake arduous work to meet basic physical needs. The language barrier is still a major problem, but there is a steady growth and involvement of the Vietnamese sisters in the apostolate and in the Church in the United States. Many bishops have helped the sisters.

8. Vietnamese Seminarians

Seminarians receive special attention from the office of Migration and Refugee Services (MRS) and from Pastoral Care of Migrants and Refugees (PMCR) of the National Conference of Catholic Bishops/United States Catholic Conference. This attention focuses on three areas of concern — the refugee camps, the resettlement process and placement in seminaries. The number of seminarians currently placed is also reported here.

409

(1) Refugee Camps

American and other priests and religious who are engaged in pastoral assistance in the refugee camps are alert to the presence of seminarians and have made special efforts to identify, counsel and support seminarians who escaped from Vietnam.

The 1983 pastoral visit to refugee camps in Southeast Asi of the NCCB Committee on Migration and Tourism sought to assess the situation of seminarians for the purpose of facilitating the continuity and pursuit of their vocation. PCMR maintains contact with the pastoral agents in the camps and receives, accordingly, pertinent information on seminarians.

A survey is in progress to count the number of seminarians in the camps, whether or not these young men are considered for admission to the United States. MRS/New York has solicited the cooperation of the Joint Voluntary Agencies in the camps on this matter.

Vietnamese—language catechetical and liturgical materials are forwarded to the camps. In the past, special arrangements were made with American Government representatives for the acceptance of particular seminarians who otherwise could not exit from closed camps, i.e., refugee camps from where resettlement was not possible.

(2) Resettlement Process

To facilitate the process of welcome of refugee seminarians, a special mechanism for their resettlement has been worked out by Migration and Refugee Services and Pastoral Care of Migrants and Refugees.

The following steps are used in the resettlement process of the Vietnamese refugee seminarians coming to the United States from Southeast Asia:

1. On receiving biographical data which indicate the presence of relatives in the United States, Migration and Refugee Services-USCC (MRS/NY) telexes the Joint Voluntary Agencies (JVA) in Southeast Asia to request a re-interview with the refugee seminarians and ask whether they wish to be placed with their relatives or proceed directly to a seminary to pursue their vocation.

2. For those seminarians wishing resettlement with their relatives:

    a. MRS/NY contacts the diocesan resettlement office and advises that the refugee was a seminarian and requests verification.

    b. MRS/NY sends a copy of USCC assurance to Pastoral Care of Migrants and Refugees (PCMR) for its records.

    c. After arrival, PCMR writes to the local parish priest to request a post arrival visit to the newly arrived seminarian to ascertain whether or not he wishes to pursue his studies.

3. For those seminarians who have no friends or relatives and those that wish to bypass their relatives and proceed directly on arrival to a seminary:

    a. MRS/NY alerts PCMR, sends a copy of the bio data and awaits name and addresses of seminary or diocese which agreed to accept the seminarian on arrival.

411

    b. Upon receipt of placement information MRS/NY issues sponsorship assurance to overseas JVA and copy to PCMR.

Vietnamese seminarians coming directly from the refugee camps in Southeast Asia present a particular challenge. First, on their arrival they tend to disperse across the country in the effort to meet with friends and relatives—often in places different from those listed in their sponsorship papers. Given this situation, it is very difficult to keep in touch with these seminarians during their first months in the United States. Second, an immediate concern that prevents these seminarians from pursuing their vocation upon their arrival in this country is the desire to earn some money to send to Vietnam to pay for their escape or to help their families. Third, confronted with a freer environment, some young people who were in seminaries in Vietnam opt for a different vocation in life.

Notwithstanding these difficulties, a concerted effort is made to encourage the immediate entrance of these seminarians into a seminary program.

(3) Placement in seminaries

Bishops, vocation directors or Vietnamese-speaking priests of the area where the seminarians resettle are notified of their arrival by PCMR. At present, seminarians resume their regular studies by 1) entering seminaries with special programs, 2) preparing

-14-

to enter regular courses on their own with the help of Vietnamese and American priests and 3) joining one of two transition houses which have been established for the purpose of offering orientation toward vocational decision and the study of English. Data is being collected to clarify these different approaches to the pursuit of seminary studies in order to improve communication and assistance on the part of all concerned.

The 'transition house' in Houston now has 10 seminarians, and it is directed by Rev. Joseph Bang, O.P. The New Orleans 'transition house', established in 1982, has five seminarians in residence and is directed by Rev. Dominic Luong.

412

As previously stated, newly-arrived seminarians face financial difficulties. Some bishops and religious communities have provided Vietnamese seminarians with full scholarships.

The Vietnamese Vocation Guild mobilizes the Vietnamese community to pray and contribute for the increase of Vietnamese vocations. The Vocation Guild has the full support and cooperation of the Vietnamese Catholic Federation. Chapters of the Vocation Guild are already active in Houston, New Orleans, Portland and Orange, California. A nationwide drive for vocations to the priesthood among young Vietnamese needs financial support and coordinated planning. The Guild is pursuing this objective and is contacting funding sources particularly interested in helping seminarians.

(4) Number of Vietnamese Seminarians in the United States

The actual number of Vietnamese seminarians given by the Vietnamese Catholic Federation is as follows: college level and theological studies total 72: a) 24 in the Divine Word Congregation seminaries; b) 16 at St. Joseph Seminary in Mountain View, California; c) 18 at Notre Dame and St. Benedict seminaries in New Orleans, Louisiana; d) 6 in Los Angeles; e) 4 in Houston; and f) a few others in the various seminaries of the country. Young men in the Minor Seminary number about 170 in dioceses and religious seminaries. For example, there are 46 in East Troy, Wisconsin, with the Divine Word Fathers, and ten in Boston. The two 'transition houses' in Houston and New Orleans shelter 10 and 5 students, respectively. Finally, there are also some 16 seminarians, residing in California, who have regular contacts with Vietnamese priests and Catholic communities and who are struggling to reach a final decision on their vocation.

As the total number of Vietnamese seminarians indicate, a variety of programs has been developed — scholarships, special English classes, and transition houses by diocesan bishops and religious communities — for those Vietnamese who are interested in pursuing a priestly or religious vocation. Unfortunately, there are seminarians, who by force of circumstances or personal choice, remain unassisted. Efforts are underway to locate and assist these young men in their journey toward priesthood.

9. National Coordination of the Vietnamese Apostolate

At the national level, the coordination of the Vietnamese Apostolate is carried out by the National Conference of Catholic Bishops through the office of Pastoral Care of Migrants and Refugees. The exodus from Vietnam and from the refugee camps in Southeast Asia continues. The United States remains the country that takes in most of the Vietnamese refugees. Through Migration and Refugee Services and the diocesan offices, the Church is the main vehicle for refugee resettlement. From the pastoral point of view, several areas of concern continue to require special care:

1. The resettlement of priests, women religious, and seminarians from the camps in Southeast Asia. PMCR finds diocesan bishops, religious communities and seminary programs to meet the particular needs of Vietnamese religious personnel.

2. Under consideration by the NCCB Committee on Migration and Tourism is the situation of elderly and sick Vietnamese priests.

3. The continued formation of Vietnamese priests and women religious, who because of language and cultural background, need particular programs, is provided through workshops and meetings coordinated and supported by the Bishops through PCMR.

4. To facilitate interaction and fellowship among Vietnamese women religious, PCMR

413

has developed a comprehensive directory of Vietnamese religious women and their communities. A similar directory is available for the Vietnamese priests.

The NCCB Committee on Migration regularly reviews the pastoral needs of the Vietnamese community and offers its services to diocesan bishops with special requests.

414

The Heritage of
American Catholicisim